# IN THE FOOTSTEPS OF OUR ANCESTORS

*In the Footsteps of Our Ancestors* details, through archaeological analysis, the dispersal of our species, *Homo sapiens*, providing a broad examination of evidence for early human migration into Asia and Oceania. Those migrations are crucial to our understanding of the global story of human evolution and cultural diversification. Chapters from an international team of experts provide the new geographical and temporal coverage. Controversies around timing, pathways, and competing models of migrations are explored in regions where archaeological data can be scarce. Genetic and archaeological data often seem inconsistent, but this book uses syntheses of archaeological evidence to give an updated view of our current knowledge of when and how these regions were first settled. These analyses help us understand the pattern of human movement and adaptation that led to the contemporary distribution of our species. This book provides the latest coverage of this important topic and contributes to thinking about the history of our species.

*In the Footsteps of Our Ancestors* is an essential text for researchers and students of archaeology, anthropology, and human evolution.

**Takeshi Ueki** is a Professor Emeritus at Kyoritsu Women's University System. He specializes in the Upper Palaeolithic Period of the Japanese Archipelago and is Chairperson of the Japan Association for Archaeoinformatics.

**Glenn R. Summerhayes** has worked on the archaeology of Papua New Guinea for the past 40 years. Since 2005 he has been Professor of Anthropology at Otago University.

**Peter Hiscock** researches evolutionary processes operating in human social and economic life.

# IN THE FOOTSTEPS OF OUR ANCESTORS

Following *Homo sapiens* into Asia and Oceania

Edited by Takeshi Ueki, Glenn R. Summerhayes, and Peter Hiscock

LONDON AND NEW YORK

Designed cover image: An Outline map of Asia. Created by The Teikoku Shoin Company. Additional work done by Artist Hiroyuki Watanabe.

First published 2025
by Routledge
4 Park Square, Milton Park, Abingdon, Oxon OX14 4RN

and by Routledge
605 Third Avenue, New York, NY 10158

*Routledge is an imprint of the Taylor & Francis Group, an informa business*

© 2025 selection and editorial matter, Takeshi Ueki, Glenn R. Summerhayes, and Peter Hiscock; individual chapters, the contributors

The right of Takeshi Ueki, Glenn R. Summerhayes, and Peter Hiscock to be identified as the authors of the editorial material, and of the authors for their individual chapters, has been asserted in accordance with sections 77 and 78 of the Copyright, Designs and Patents Act 1988.

All rights reserved. No part of this book may be reprinted or reproduced or utilised in any form or by any electronic, mechanical, or other means, now known or hereafter invented, including photocopying and recording, or in any information storage or retrieval system, without permission in writing from the publishers.

*Trademark notice:* Product or corporate names may be trademarks or registered trademarks, and are used only for identification and explanation without intent to infringe.

*British Library Cataloguing-in-Publication Data*
A catalogue record for this book is available from the British Library

*Library of Congress Cataloging-in-Publication Data*
Names: Hiscock, Peter, 1957- editor. | Summerhayes, Glenn R., 1954- editor. | Ueki, Takeshi, 1946- editor.
Title: In the footsteps of our ancestors : following homo sapiens into Asia and Oceania / edited by Peter Hiscock, Glenn R. Summerhayes, and Takeshi Ueki.
Description: Abingdon, Oxon ; New York, NY : Routledge, 2024. | Includes bibliographical references and index.
Identifiers: LCCN 2024026708 (print) | LCCN 2024026709 (ebook) | ISBN 9781032547824 (hardback) | ISBN 9781032547800 (paperback) | ISBN 9781003427483 (ebook)
Subjects: LCSH: Prehistoric peoples--Asia. | Prehistoric peoples--Oceania. | Paleolithic period--Asia. | Paleolithic period--Oceania. | Human beings--Migrations.
Classification: LCC GN851 .I5 2024 (print) | LCC GN851 (ebook) | DDC 950/.1--dc23/eng/20240710
LC record available at https://lccn.loc.gov/2024026708
LC ebook record available at https://lccn.loc.gov/2024026709

ISBN: 978-1-032-54782-4 (hbk)
ISBN: 978-1-032-54780-0 (pbk)
ISBN: 978-1-003-42748-3 (ebk)

DOI: 10.4324/9781003427483

Typeset in Times New Roman
by KnowledgeWorks Global Ltd.

# CONTENTS

*List of Figures*          *vii*
*List of Tables*          *xv*
*List of Contributors*          *xvi*
*Preface*          *xix*

1 Beginnings: Africa and Beyond          1
   *Peter Hiscock and Kim Sterelny*

2 The Colonisation of South Asia by *Homo sapiens*: Assessing
   Alternative Hypotheses through Cladistic Analyses of Lithic Assemblages          22
   *Chris Clarkson, Ravi Korisettar, Ceri Shipton, Mark Collard,
   and Briggs Buchannan*

3 The Settlement of Mainland Southeast Asia by Anatomically
   Modern Humans          38
   *Charles Higham*

4 A Middle to Late Upper Pleistocene Lithic Industry from North Vietnam          69
   *Anatoly P. Derevianko and Alexander V. Kandyba*

5 Early Modern Humans in Island Southeast Asia          87
   *Daud Tanudirjo*

6 Northern Sahul and the Bismarck Archipelago          111
   *Glenn R. Summerhayes*

7 Human Dispersal Across Southern and Central Sahul          125
   *Peter Hiscock and Kim Sterelny*

| | | |
|---|---|---|
| 8 | The Peopling of East Asia: Perspectives from the Russian Far East<br>*Andrey V. Tabarev* | 138 |
| 9 | Early Peopling in and Around Taiwan: Pleistocene through Middle Holocene Groups before the Austronesian Era<br>*Hsiao-chun Hung, Chin-yung Chao, Hirofumi Matsumura, and Mike T. Carson* | 150 |
| 10 | The Arrival of Modern Humans in North China during the Late Palaeolithic<br>*Xing Gao and Feng Li* | 178 |
| 11 | The Philippines: Origins to the End of the Pleistocene<br>*Alfred Pawlik and Philip Piper* | 201 |
| 12 | Emergence of Pleistocene Modernity and Its Background in the Korean Peninsula<br>*Yongwook Yoo* | 226 |
| 13 | Analyzing Japanese Sites Belonging to the Initial Period of the Upper Palaeolithic: Creating Macro-Models<br>*Takeshi Ueki* | 245 |
| 14 | Archaeological Materials from the Japanese Early Upper Palaeolithic and Their Implications<br>*Takuya Yamaoka* | 284 |
| 15 | Pleistocene Okinawa: Unique Culture and Lifeway in the Oceanic Islands of the Western Pacific<br>*Masaki Fujita* | 312 |

*Appendix A: Comparison of Radiocarbon and Calibrated Dates* — *326*
*Yuichiro Kudo*

*Appendix B: Analysing the Age and Heating History of Archaeological Materials Using Remanent Magnetization* — *351*
*Hideo Sakai*

*Index* — *357*

# FIGURES

1.1  Global genetic patterns beyond Africa. (A) Heterozygosity relative to the distance from East Africa (redrawn from Ramachandran et al. 2005, following DeGiorgio et al. 2009). (B) Linkage disequilibrium at 10 kb relative to the distance from East Africa (redrawn from DeGiorgio et al. 2009, data analysis from Jakobsson et al. 2008). (C) Slope of the ancestral allele frequency spectrum (redrawn from DeGiorgio et al. 2009, based on analysis in Li et al. 2008)   4
2.1  Map showing key sites mentioned in the text and modelled routes of colonisation across South Asia after Field et al. (2007). Topographic and bathymetric data was obtained from GEBCO 2014 Grid, version 20150318, http://www.gebco.net   25
2.2  Hypothetical cladograms representing modern human dispersal of out of Africa   28
2.3  The 50% majority-rule consensus of the most parsimonious cladograms ($n = 26$)   31
3.1  Variations in the world temperature during MIS 1-6 derived from the Vostok Antarctic ice core   39
3.2  Changes in the sea level during MIS 1-6   40
3.3  The pollen spectrum from Nong Pa Kho lake in Northeast Thailand showing the dramatic change in the vegetation at the onset of MIS 1   41
3.4  Map showing vegetation reconstructed for a glacial period and the location of sites mentioned in the text beyond mainland Southeast Asia. The dotted lines show the coastal route that has been suggested as a possible expansionary corridor from Africa to Australia. (1) Jebel Irhoud, (2) Herto, (3) Jawalapuram, (4) Jebel Faya, (5) Mt. Toba, (6) Batatomba-lena, Fahien-lena, (7) Madjedbebe   43

| | | |
|---|---|---|
| 3.5 | The location of the sites mentioned in the text. (1) Zhiren Cave, (2) Longtanshan, (3) Tham Pa Ling, (4) Callao Cave, (5) Niah, (6). Lang Rongrien, Moh Khiew, (7) Bukit Bunuh, (8). Xiaodong, Dedan, (9) Nguom, (10) Hang Cho, Son Vi, Xom Trai, (11) Hang Boi, (12) Tham Lod, Ban Rai, (13) Banyan Valley Cave, (14) Steep Cliff Cave, (15) Spirit Cave, (16) Lang Kamnan, (17) Khao Toh Chong, Sakai Cave, (18) Gua Cha, (19) Gua Gunung Runtuh, (20) Gexinqiao, Baida, Kantun, (21) Beidaling, (22) Datangcheng, (23) Dingsishan, (24) Con Co Ngua, Da But, (25) Nong Nor, (26) Doi Pha Kan, (27) Huai Hin, (28) Lida Ajer, (29) Quynh Van, Thach Lac, (30) Ru Diep, (31) Bau Du, (32) Chongtang, (33) Tham Khuong | 47 |
| 3.6 | The great cave of Niah on the northern coast of Borneo, where an early Anatomically Modern Human skull has been found | 49 |
| 3.7 | Excavations at the cave of Lang Rongrien have revealed a long occupation sequence against a backdrop of environmental change | 51 |
| 3.8 | Sumatraliths, or unifacial discoids are the most widespread of Hoabinhian stone tools | 52 |
| 3.9 | The cave of Tham Lod in Northern Thailand, where early hunter-gatherer occupation has been dated to 35,700 years ago | 54 |
| 3.10 | Most Hoabinhian burials were found in a flexed position with few mortuary offerings. This example comes from Ban Rai in Northern Thailand and dates to about 10,000 years ago | 55 |
| 3.11 | Distribution map of the Vietnamese sites mentioned in the text. (1) Lang Vanh, (2) Du Sang, (3) Hang Chu, (4) Hang Dang, (5) Hang Dong Truong, (6) Hang Lang Gao, (7) Mai Da Nuoc, (8) Hang Cho, (9) Xom Trai, (10) Nguom, (11) Dieu, (12) Con Co Ngua, (13) Tham Khuong | 59 |
| 3.12 | The site of Beidaling, along the Honshui River in Central Guangxi | 60 |
| 4.1 | Distribution of the Palaeolithic sites in Vietnam. Nguomian sites: (1) Nuong, (2) Nguom, (3) Mieng Ho; Sonvian sites, (4) Nam Tun, (5) Tham Khuong, (6) Ben Den, (7) Hang Pong I, Hang Pong II, (8) Ban Cai, (9) Pa Mang, Hang Co, (10) Ban Pho, (11) 98 sites in Vinh Phuc Province, (12) Van Thang, (13) Minh Khai, Khe Tau, (14) Phung Nguyen, (15) Con Moong, (16) Nui Mot; Hoabinhian sites, (15) Con Moong, (17) Anh Ro, Ma Xa, (18) Xom Sat, Thac Son, (19) Lang Bon, (20) Hang Diem, (21) Da Bac, (22) Thac Long, Loc Tinh, (23) Gia Bac, (24) Tham Hoi, (25) Yen Lac, (26) Kim Bang, (27) Xom Thon, (28) Xom Tham | 71 |
| 4.2 | Nguomian industry: (1) – single platform core, (2 and 7) choppers, (3) single scraper, (4) ventral scraper, (5) single scraper made on cobble, (6) single scraper made on blade flake | 72 |
| 4.3 | Sonvian industry: (1) chopping, (2, 4, 5, 8) chopper, (3, 6, 7) transverse scraper made on cobble, (9, 10, 11, 12) convergent convex scrapers | 77 |
| 4.4 | Hoabinhian industry: (1, 2, 4) Hoabinhian-type axes, (3, 5, 6) sumatraliths, (7, 8, 9) convex scrapers | 81 |
| 4.5 | Four areas for the origins of the Upper Palaeolithic culture and anatomically modern humans | 84 |
| 5.1 | Locations of important archaeological sites mentioned in the text and reconstructed migration routes followed by archaic hominins and early modern humans in Southeast Asia | 88 |

| | | |
|---|---|---|
| 5.2 | Palaeoenvironment of Island Southeast Asia during the low sea levels, showing the estimated savanna corridor and possible heath forest area and ancient river system | 91 |
| 5.3 | One of the red-colour Cave paintings of possibly warty pig in Maros Cave | 99 |
| 5.4 | Stone flakes recovered from Liang Bua resembles to flakes from Timorese Caves produced by early modern human | 101 |
| 5.5 | Fossils of *Homo floresiensis* excavated in Liang Bua, Flores | 104 |
| 6.1 | Migrations of people to Sahul | 112 |
| 6.2 | Pleistocene sites of Papua New Guinea mentioned in text | 113 |
| 6.3 | Archaeological sites in the Ivane Valley | 115 |
| 6.4 | Late Pleistocene stone tools, Ivane Valley | 116 |
| 6.5 | Late Pleistocene stone tools, Ivane Valley | 117 |
| 6.6 | Waisted tools from Highland New Guinea. Top: Pleistocene contexts from Kosipe, Ivane valley; bottom: Holocene contexts from site of Yuk | 118 |
| 7.1 | Location of Central and Southern Sahul, and of sites mentioned in the chapter | 126 |
| 8.1 | Territories of the maritime region and Sakhalin Islands, Russian Far East with the group of sites mentioned in the text. (1) Osinovka and Geographical Society Cave; (2) Final Palaeolithic sites in the coastal zone (Ustinovka and Suvorovo groups); (3) Final Palaeolithic sites in the inland zone (Gorbatka 3 and Ilistaya 1); (4) Astrakhanka site; (5) Palaeolithic sites on Sakhalin (Sennaya 1, Ogon'ki 5) | 139 |
| 8.2 | Coastal zone. Ustinovka 1 site. Blade industry | 141 |
| 8.3 | Coastal zone. (1–8) Microblade industry; (9) Reconstruction of microblade production in a hand device; (10–18) burins | 143 |
| 8.4 | Inland zone. Obsidian industry. (1–4, 9) microblade cores; (5, 6) bifacial preforms for microblade cores; (7) fragment of bifacial point; (8) end scraper | 145 |
| 9.1 | Evolution of the Taiwan coastline since the Last Glacial Maximum (LGM) | 151 |
| 9.2 | Major Palaeolithic and Holocene Preceramic sites on the island of Taiwan, noting the location of the Kuroshio Current | 152 |
| 9.3 | The Penghu 1 mandible, right half (Photograph by Hsiao-chun Hung, courtesy Kun-yu Tsai and Chun-hsiang Chang) | 152 |
| 9.4 | The chronology of human remains (in italics) and archaeological sites with Palaeolithic and Preceramic associations discussed in this chapter. Note: a possible pottery association is unclear in the cultural layer of Liangdao 2 on Liang Island | 153 |
| 9.5 | The humerus of "Haixia Man (Strait Man)" (Collection of the Shishi Museum in Fujian, courtesy Xuechun Fan) | 154 |
| 9.6 | An antler of Père David's deer (*Elaphurus davidianus*) with intentional cut marks (after Ho (2011: 36), courtesy Chuan-kun Ho) | 155 |
| 9.7 | The two individuals excavated from the Daowei I shell midden on Liang Island In Taiwan Strait. Liangdao 2 (top) is dated to 7300 cal. BP, and Liangdao 1 (bottom) to 8300 cal. BP. Credits: 1 and 2 after Chen and Chiu (2013); 3: Photography by Hsiao-chun Hung, courtesy Chung-yu Chen) | 159 |
| 9.8 | An undated human skull fragment, shown in two views, collected from the Cailiao Stream in Zuozhen, Tainan, southwest Taiwan (photography by Hsiao-chun Hung, courtesy Kun-yu Tsai) | 160 |

9.9 The distribution of caves and rock shelters sites on the Loham Cliff (abbreviation: LH) in the Baxian Cave Complex, eastern Taiwan. Site codes have a number following "LH", for example, "1" in the figure means site LH-1. Three of the excavated sites (LH-2, 27, and 34; 40–72 m asl) have Holocene Preceramic occupations, ca. 6.7–4.8 kya, whereas nine sites (LH-4, 5, 6, 7, 24, 27, 29, 30, and open terrace B; 72–197 m asl) have Late Pleistocene occupations, ca. 30–15 kya (revised after Tsang (2017: XIII)) 161

9.10 Chaoyin Cave (LH-2, 40 m asl), with abundant Preceramic cultural remains dated to 6700–4800 cal. BP (photography by Hsiao-chun Hung) 162

9.11 Preceramic (Holocene) lithics from Chaoyin Cave (LH-2; See location 2 in figure 9.9), ca. 6700–4800 cal. BP, including pebble choppers (1), large flakes (2 and 3), and small quartz flake implements (4–11) (1–3 after Tsang et al. (2015: 407), and 4–11 after Sung (1969); courtesy Wen-hsun Sung and Cheng-hwa Tsang) 163

9.12 Palaeolithic (Pleistocene) lithics from Anonymous Cave 11 (LH-30; See location 30 in figure 9.9), ca. 30,000–21,000 cal. BP, including choppers (1), flakes (2–4, 6–11) and a pebble hammer (5) (after Tsang et al. (2015: 86–92); courtesy Cheng-hwa Tsang) 164

9.13 Cheng-hwa Tsang and Peter Bellwood standing at the base of Anonymous Cave 10 (LH-29), 142 m asl (see location 29 in figure 9.9), with deposits dated to 29,000–22,000 cal. BP. The Palaeolithic remains first appear 7.5 m below the surface (photography by Hsiao-chun Hung) 165

9.14 The Pacific Ocean from Anonymous Cave 10, 142 m asl (LH-29, see location 29 in figure 9.9) during excavation in 2014 (photography by Hsiao-chun Hung) 166

9.15 The Xiaoma Cave complex along the base of a former sea-cliff, eastern Taiwan (photography by Mike T. Carson) 167

9.16 Preceramic stone tools from the Xiaoma Caves, ca. 6200 to 5700 cal. BP, including cobble chopping tools (1) and flakes (2–4) (after Lee (2004), courtesy Tsuo-ting Lee) 168

9.17 The squatting burial of the Xiaoma Woman in Xiaoma C5 (after Huang and Chen (1990), courtesy Shih-chiang Huang) 168

9.18 A neighbour joining (NJ) tree generated from Q-mode correlation coefficients based on 13 cranial morphometric measurements from Australia and Melanesia (MEL), Northeast Asia (NEA), Southwest Asia (SWA), Europe (EU), and Africa (AF). This tree has four major clusters, with Australo-Melanesian and African groups clustered together at the bottom. A sub-cluster formed by Xiaoma, Philippine Negritos, and Andaman Islanders lies at the base of the diagram (see Matsumura et al. (2021) for the data sources and analytical methods) 169

9.19 A rock shelter in Eluanbi II, southern Taiwan (photography by Hsiao-chun Hung) 170

9.20 A cobble tool (1) flake tool (2) shell scraper (3) and bone chisel (4) from Eluanbi II (after Li (1983), courtesy Kuang-chou Li) 171

9.21 A pointed cobble chopping tool ("oyster pick", shown from both sides) from Longxia Cave (photography by Chin-yung Chao) 171

| | | |
|---|---|---|
| 10.1 | Geographic locations of sites mentioned in this paper. AMH: anatomical modern human, Archaic: archaic *Homo sapiens*. (1) Denisova cave, (2) Xiahe Baishiya cave, (3) Tongtian cave, (4) Jinsitai cave, (5) Jinniushan, (6) ZKD Upper Cave, (7) Tianyuan Cave, (8) Banjingzi, (9) Xujiayao-Houjiayao, (10) Wulanmulun, (11) Shuidonggou locality 1, (12) Shuidonggou locality 2, (13) Nwya Devu, (14) Xujiacheng, (15) Dali, (16) Lingjing, (17) Hualong cave, (18) Huanglong cave, (19) Fuyan cave, (20) Zhiren cave, (21) Luna cave, (22) Maba, (23) Panxiandadong | 180 |
| 10.2 | Chronology of key sites mentioned in this paper and palaeoenvironmental records. (a) Temperature anomaly record derived from the EPICA Dome C (EDC) ice-core deuterium record (Lowe and Walker, 2015). (b) $x_{fd}$ ($10^{-8}$ m$^3$ kg$^{-1}$) data in the Luochuan loess section in northern China (Hao, 2012). AMH: anatomical modern human | 191 |
| 11.1 | Geographical location of the Philippines with potential migration routes and relevant sites | 203 |
| 11.2 | Lithic artefacts from Arubo, Nueva Ecjia. (A) handaxe; (B) large flake with pointed retouch; (C) 'horse-hoof' core; (D) core on a larger flake with striking platform on ventral; (E) unifacially modified flake tool with distal reduction on ventral (after Pawlik 2004; Teodosio 2005) | 205 |
| 11.3 | Pebbles used as hammerstones (A–C) and fragments thereof with use traces (D–F); (G, H) Hammerstones with waisted modification re-used as Netsinkers. Bubog I and II, Ilin Island (Photos: A. Pawlik) | 211 |
| 11.4 | Bone and shell tools. (A, B) Flaked and modified Geloina shells from Bubog I; (C) bone fishing gorge from Bubog I (Photos: A. Pawlik) | 212 |
| 12.1 | Geological zones of the Korean Peninsula (From Yi 1989) | 229 |
| 12.2 | Mountain ranges and major river channel systems of the Korean Peninsula | 230 |
| 12.3 | Microcores and presumed bone tools discovered at *Mandalri* site | 233 |
| 12.4 | Major Palaeolithic localities mentioned in this chapter | 235 |
| 12.5 | Handaxes and cleavers from the *Imjin-Hantan* River Area (IHRA), Korea | 236 |
| 12.6 | Lithic specimens from the *Seokjangri* site (No scales) | 238 |
| 12.7 | Late palaeolithic specimens from the *Hopeongdong* site | 239 |
| 12.8 | Stemmed points discovered from the *Yongsandong* site | 240 |
| 12.9 | Lithic types discovered from the *Jingeuneul* site | 240 |
| 13.1 | (A) Shoreline 24,000 years BP, 120 m lower (Machida 2007, 27). (B) Present day shoreline and sea currents | 246 |
| 13.2 | Late Quaternary regional Tephra distributions over Japan and surrounding countries (Machida and Arai 2003, 54, partially revised) | 248 |
| 13.3 | (A) Vegetation zones in East Asia during the Last Glacial Maximum (from Sugiyama 2010, 168) and (B) potential vegetation zones in present day Japan (from Numata and Iwase 2002, 20) | 249 |
| 13.4 | Palaeo-vegetation in Japan during the Last Glacial Maximum (Okamura et al. 1998, 167) | 250 |
| 13.5 | Late Pleistocene mammals of Honshu, Shikoku, and Kyushu, Japan (Kawamura 2005, 53) | 251 |
| 13.6 | Initial Period Upper Palaeolithic excavation sites fulfilling four conditions | 254 |

xii  Figures

13.7  All types of features. **Fist-sized pebble cluster** (1): Only the shaded stone 623 was clearly burned; **Flake Clusters** (2): Small ring of flake clusters; **Areas of carbon concentration** (3): In a 50 × 100 m area, 15 carbon clusters were scattered; **Burned soil** (hearth) (4): In a 1.5 m area, burned soil is surrounded by bits of carbon; **Pit trap** (5): Bag-shaped pit type; **Small pit** (6): For storage? Tree hole?; **Shallow hole** (7): Use unknown. No carbon or burned soil                                                                                                       257

13.8  Stone Implement Group. **Grindstone** (8): Polishing traces and/or abrasion marks evident. Surface is smooth; **Pounding stones** (9, 10): Marks of chipping (9) and micro-chipping (10) can be seen; **Stone plate** (11): Upper surface very slightly depressed with polishing/abrasion marks; **Whetstone** (12): Polishing/abrasion marks evident. One side is smooth; **Anvil stone** (13): Working surface is pockmarked; **Stone choppers** (14, 15)                         261

13.9  Flaked Stone Tool Group. **Backed points** (16, 17): Backs and bases are blunted; **Trapezoids** (18–21): Shorter backed points with sharp top and both sides of the bottom blunted; **Blades** (22, 23): Systematically flaked off a stone core; **Drills** (24, 25): Sectioned horizontally, the points are triangular or pyramidal. Used to make holes in animal skins; **Edge-ground adzes** (26, 27): First appeared in the Initial Period, then disappeared until the Jomon Age. Used in scraping and hoeing; **Chipped adzes** (28, 29): Same use as the polished type. In continuous use. 28, very rare, appears to have a hilt (for attachment?)                                                                                                       263

13.10 Flaked Stone Tools and Refuse Group. **Scrapers** (30–32): Ends and/or sides sharpened. Used in cleaning hides; **Wedge-shaped stones** (33–35): Possibly wedges or cores; **Flakes and chips** (36–42): Pieces struck off stone cores (flakes) or small stone bits (chips); **Core** (43): Stone in use for striking off tools or the leftover center; **Natural stones** (44, 45): Unworked stones for tool-making; **Reassembled core and its struck-off parts** (46): Carefully put together by a specialist over one month                                                          264

13.11 Dendrogram of total data values                                                                                          270

13.12 Dendrogram of data values for 20 variables in Table 13.4, excluding stone refuse and raw ore (Ward's Method)                                                                             270

13.13 Dendrogram of standardized values for 23 variables in Table 13.4 (Ward's Method)                                                                                                                    271

13.14 Dendrogram of standardized values for 20 variables in Table 13.4, excluding stone. Refuse and raw ore (Ward's Method)                                                                 271

13.15 Model 1. Frequency of occurrence of features and artifacts from the Initial Period of the Upper Paleolithic in Japan                                                                          279

14.1  Map of Japan                                                                                                                            285

14.2  Topographic and biome-level vegetation map of MIS 3 in East Asia (Takahara and Hayashi (2015, fig. 22.2)                                                                              286

14.3  Distribution of archaeological sites during the Palaeolithic and the Incipient Jomon Period in the Japanese Islands (Japanese Palaeolithic Research Association 2010)                                                                                                       289

14.4  Map, showing obsidian sources (modified from Ikeya (2015, fig. 25.1)                                    291

| | | |
|---|---|---|
| 14.5 | Stratigraphic sequences and Palaeolithic chronology of the UP in the Mt. Ashitaka area (modified from Ikeya et al. (2011, fig. 14.10) | 292 |
| 14.6 | Representative formal stone tools during the EUP in the Mt. Ashitaka area, drawn from excavation reports of sites (Takao 1989; Numazu City Board of Education 1990; Ikeya 1998, 2004; Sasahara 1999; Mibu and Sugiyama 2009; Takao and Harada 2011) | 294 |
| 14.7 | Definitions of formal flaked tools (modified from Yamaoka (2011, fig. 14.4) | 295 |
| 14.8 | Changes of lithic assemblages during the EUP in the Musashino Uplands (Yamaoka et al. 2023, fig. 5) | 295 |
| 14.9 | Circular aggregation from the Kamibayashi site (modified from Idei et al. (2004, fig. 640) | 300 |
| 14.10 | Pitfalls from the Hatsunegahara site (modified from Suzuki et al. (1999, figs. 175 and 245) | 301 |
| 15.1 | Palaeolithic sites and the ages of the oldest layer in the Ryukyu archipelago. The light gray area shows the estimated coastline at the Last Glacial Maximum (LGM) period | 313 |
| 15.2 | The location (upper left) and the cross section (lower) of Sakitari cave site. The section and the major remains of Trench I and Pit I (upper right) | 318 |
| A.1 | The Principles of Radiocarbon Dating. Once an organism has died and ceased its carbon exchange with the environment, the $^{14}C$ in the organism will have been reduced to half its original amount in 5,730 years, a quarter of its original amount in 11,460 years, and an eighth of its original amount in 17,190 years | 327 |
| A.2 | The Relationship between $^{14}C$ Reduction and Chronology (Kudo 2012). In regular accelerator-based dating, the accelerator and vacuum-refining equipment yield a background of around 40,000–45,000 $^{14}C$ BP. Accordingly, the routine measurements typically go back no further than 45,000 $^{14}C$ BP | 328 |
| A.3 | IntCal20 Calibration Curve. The IntCal20 calibration curve presents a theoretical straight line that assumes a one-to-one relationship between radiocarbon dates and calibrated dates. Divergence from this line indicates a gap between calendar years and radiocarbon years. For example, if something is radiocarbon dated to around 30,000 years in the past (30,000 $^{14}C$ BP), the calibrated date will be around 34,440 cal BP, a gap of around 4,400 years | 329 |
| A.4 | Example of Calibration of a radiocarbon date by OxCal (Ramsey 2009) | 330 |
| A.5 | Musashino Plateau and Sagami Plateau Stratotypes and the Radiocarbon Ages of Key Stone tools (Kudo 2012) | 334 |
| A.6 | Stratigraphy of the Fujiishi site and radiocarbon dates to Each Cultural Stratum excavated under the AT Tephra (ca. 30,009 varve BP) (modified after Shizuoka Archaeological Research Institute, 2010) | 335 |
| A.7 | The distribution of Early Upper Palaeolithic sites dated to as far back as 34,000 cal BP | 340 |
| B.1 | Result of Thelliers' method | 352 |
| B.2 | The heated temperature distribution obtained by magnetic study of the hearth in the Neanderthal Douara Cave | 352 |

B.3 Changes in the geomagnetic field during the past 2000 years (Hirooka 1971; Sakai and Hirooka 1986) 353
B.4 Timetable of the polarity events of the geomagnetic field during the last few tens of thousands of years (referred from Channell 2006) 354
B.5 Geomagnetic field intensity during the last 80,000 years. Data (0–50,000 years) is from the summary by Barbetti and Flude (1979); Data (1–10,000 years) is from the summary by McElhinny and Senanayake (1985) 355
B.6 Directional distribution of the remanent magnetization 355
B.7 The site of the Palaeolithic ruin 356

# TABLES

| | | |
|---|---|---|
| 2.1 | List of technological traits used in the cladistics analysis by region and period | 29 |
| 2.2 | Results of the Kishino-Hasegawa test comparing the observed cladogram with the three hypothetical cladograms | 32 |
| 6.1 | The earliest Late Pleistocene sites | 114 |
| 9.1 | C14 dates from Palaeolithic and Preceramic sites in Taiwan | 157 |
| 10.1 | Location and age of key sites mentioned in this chapter | 181 |
| 12.1 | Hominin fossils discovered in the peninsula | 232 |
| 13.1 | Twelve oldest sites with cal $^{14}$c dates from the Initial Period of the Upper Palaeolithic Age in Japan | 252 |
| 13.2 | Investigation groups and excavation reasons | 255 |
| 13.3 | Elevation and distance to fresh water by site | 255 |
| 13.4 | Number of features and artifacts excavated from the Initial Period (39,000–34,000 cal BP) of the Upper Palaeolithic Age (39,000–16,000 cal BP) in Japan | 259 |
| 13.5 | Identifying types of stone used by site in features and artifacts from the Initial Period of the Upper Palaeolithic Age in Japan | 266 |
| 13.6 | Archeological investigation of Initial Period Upper Palaeolithic sites in Japan by investigating institute location, and vegetation | 273 |
| 13.7 | Types and raw materials of features and artifacts from 12 oldest sites | 275 |
| 13.8 | Model 2. Synthesized model of 12 sites from the Initial Period of the Upper Palaeolithic of the Japanese Archipelago | 277 |
| A.1 | Radiocarbon dates related to the early evidence of *Homo sapiens* in the East and South East Asia: example of the Tianyuan Cave and Niah Cave (Shang et al. 2007; Barker et al. 2007) | 331 |
| A.2 | Examples of date notation | 333 |
| A.3 | List of radiocarbon dates of the representative Early Upper Palaeolithic sites dated to as far back as 34,000 cal BP | 336 |
| A.4 | Correspondence table of radiocarbon dates and calibrated dates using IntCal20 | 341 |

# CONTRIBUTORS

**Briggs Buchannan** is professor of Anthropology at the University of Tulsa. His research interests include quantitative methods, lithic analysis and Ice Age America.

**Mike T. Carson** is a specialist in Pacific archaeology and has worked extensively in Micronesia, and Polynesian. He lectures at the University of Guam.

**Chin-Yung Chao** specializes in Taiwan archaeology. He is the Director of the Archaeology Institute at National Cheng Kung University in Tainan City.

**Chris Clarkson** is professor in archaeology in the School of Social Science, University of Queensland, specializing in lithics, Indigenous Australian archaeology, and modern human origins and dispersals.

**Mark Collard** is an evolutionary anthropologist with a wide interest in hominin fossil record. He is a Professor in archaeology at Simon Fraser University, Canada.

**Anatoly P. Derevianko** is Scientific Director at the Russian Institute of Archaeology and Ethnography. One of his research interests is the initial human settlement of North, Central, and East Asia.

**Masaki Fujita** is a researcher at the National Museum of Nature and Science at Tsukuba, and an expert in physical anthropology of the Japanese Archipelago, specializing in the Ryukyu Islands' Palaeolithic Period.

**Xing Gao** is a member of the Institute of Vertebrate Paleontology and Paleoanthropology, Chinese Academy of Sciences, where he studies human evolution, adaptation and behaviour, and technology.

**Charles Higham** is one of the world's leading archaeologists working in southeast Asia's past. He is emeritus professor in archaeology at Otago University. He held the Foundation Chair in Anthropology for over 35 years.

**Peter Hiscock** researches evolutionary processes operating in human social and economic life.

**Hsiao-chun Hung** is a world-leading archaeologist working in East and Southeast Asia being a prodigious researcher and publishes. She is a Senior Fellow in the School of Culture, History and Languages at the Australian National University, Canberra.

**Alexander V. Kandyba** is a senior researcher at the Russian Institute of Archaeology and Ethnography. His research focus is the Palaeolithic of Vietnam.

**Ravi Korisettar** works at Karnatak University, India, and has a research focus on the Palaeolithic of South Asia.

**Yuichiro Kudo** works at Gakushuin Women's College, and is a specialist in chronology, archaeology and palaeoenvironment of Japan.

**Feng Li** is a specialist in the rise and collapse of Bronze Age culture in China and the early Chinese state. He is professor of Early Chinese History and Archaeology at Columbia University.

**Hirofumi Matsumura** is a world-leading palaeoanthropologist looking at human origins and adaptations. He is professor in the Sapporo Medical University, Sapporo, Hokkaido, Japan.

**Alfred Pawlik** is a Palaeolithic archaeologist research Philippine's past. He is professor in the Department of Sociology and Anthropology, Ateneo de Manila University, Quezon City, Philippines.

**Philip Piper** is a archaeozoologist specializing in East and Southeast Asian archaeology. He is Professor of Archaeology at the Australian National University, Canberra.

**Hideo Sakai** is Professor emeritus at Fukui University. He specialties are analysis of stone tools found at archaeological sites as well as pollen analysis and remanent magnetization detection.

**Ceri Shipton** works on the Stone Age of the Indian Ocean rim: featuring the prehistories of East Africa, Arabia, India, Wallacea, and northern Sahul. He is a Lecturer in Palaeolithic Archaeology, at University College London.

**Kim Sterelny** is a professor of philosophy at the ANU. His core interests lie at the intersection of philosophy and the sciences. In recent years his particular focus has been on the evolution of human social life.

**Glenn R. Summerhayes** has worked on the archaeology of Papua New Guinea for the past 40 years. Since 2005 he has been Professor of Anthropology at Otago University.

**Andrey V. Tabarev** investigates the archaeology of eastern Asia. He is a researcher at the Russian Institute of Archaeology and Ethnography, Novosibirsk, Russia.

**Daud Tanudirjo** is a leading Indonesian prehistoric archaeologist working on Austronesian studies and early Indonesian's past. He is Professor in the Department Arkeologi, Fakultas Ilmu Budaya, Universitas Gadjah Mada, Yogyakarta, Indonesia.

**Takeshi Ueki** is Professor Emeritus at Kyoritsu Women's University System. He specializes in the Upper Palaeolithic Period of the Japanese Archipelago, and is Chairperson of the Japan Association for Archaeoinformatics.

**Takuya Yamaoka** is Professor at Shizuoka University, Japan. He specializes in the prehistory of the Palaeolithic and Jomon Periods in the Japanese Archipelago.

**Yongwook Yoo** is a lithic specialist working on Korea's past. He is Professor of Archaeology at Chungnam National University, Daejeon, South Korea.

# PREFACE

A number of years have passed since we archaeologists decided to edit a book on the topic of *Homo sapiens sapiens*' (Modern Humans') migration into Asia and Oceania. To that end we contacted leading researchers in countries all over Asia and Oceania to consider basic questions. Where and when did these Upper Palaeolithic Modern Humans travel, what implements did they leave behind, and what sort of lifestyle did they follow? There is a great deal of evidence that members of other *Homo* species set out even earlier in the Lower Palaeolithic period, but we decided to focus on these Upper Palaeolithic migrants who, as *Homo sapiens sapiens* (commonly abbreviated to just Homo sapiens), are our direct ancestors.

Though we the editors are archaeologists ourselves, yet we cannot ignore advances made in other fields. For example, palaeo-anthropologists have been the leading researchers in the investigation of human evolution from the time proto-humans separated from other primates up to the emergence of Modern Humans. Researchers in DNA analysis, on the other hand, deal with completely different data. While broadly speaking, this field is concerned with polymorphic analysis in molecular haematology and advances in medical treatment, subfields within this genre are directly applicable to our goal of clarifying the origins and migrations of Modern Humans. In the end palaeo-anthropologists, molecular anthropologists (palaeo-geneticists), and archaeologists share many of the same goals: clarifying where we came from, how we developed, and how we spread around the earth.

In every field of study, however, problems arise. Palaeo-anthropologists, who have made the best contributions toward showing human development from Sahelanthropus up to Modern Humans, are nevertheless still striving to connect those palaeo-humans into one big evolutionary tree. Since their main conclusions are based on the evolution of human bones, little can be said about the actual people involved, their minds, family structures, subsistence practices, or lifestyles in general.

For molecular anthropologists, the study of DNA means investigating the known haplogroups to show where they first appeared and where and when they split and dispersed. Despite being such a new field of research with a history of less than half a century, they have already reached many significant conclusions. However, within the more than 20 known haplogroups, each bone contains several of them so that conclusions are given in percentages and interpretation is immensely complicated.

This is where archaeology can help both palaeo-anthropology and molecular anthropology. Archaeology has benefited from internal developments in dating methods, stratigraphy, petrology, pollen analysis, botany, zoology, chemistry, etc., becoming, in effect, an interdisciplinary field. Since conclusions in archaeology are backed up by pertinent research in these other fields, these are particularly well placed to, in turn, back up conclusions drawn by palaeo- and molecular anthropologists. We can anticipate future academic conferences in which archaeologists, palaeo-osteologists, and molecular anthropologists report their theories and conclusions together, allowing these to be supported or not and suggesting the direction of future studies where they don't agree. This might be called interdisciplinary research comparison, which will benefit every field. In the absence of a time machine, attempting the reconstruction of past societies and cultures by making inferences from isolated fields must give way to corroboration using the data of many other areas of research. Only then can we confidently propose general theories about the lives of past peoples.

To trace the paths of Modern Humans (*Homo sapiens sapiens*) into Asia and Oceania, we asked leading researchers in relevant regions to present their current data on the arrival and dispersal of our ancestors and, to the extent possible, illuminate their lifestyles. Many questions still remain. Did they encounter earlier migrants, absorbing aspects of their culture and indeed the people themselves, or did they wipe out these earlier cultures in their advance? And to what extent did they themselves benefit or suffer from the later arrival of Neolithic peoples? We cannot yet confidently argue such processes of cultural change. However, over the next ten or twenty years it is our hope that interdisciplinary research comparison will allow us to better understand different aspects of ancient cultures and how they changed over time.

Takeshi Ueki, Ph.D.
*Professor Emeritus, Kyoritsu Women's University System*
*Chairperson, Japan Association for Archaeoinformatics*
*August 2023 (during the time of COVID-19)*

# 1
# BEGINNINGS

Africa and Beyond

*Peter Hiscock and Kim Sterelny*

### Out of Africa

In the late nineteenth century, it was clear that the biological origin of *Homo sapiens* was located in Africa. Darwin (1871, 199) reasoned on the biogeographical evidence for that, writing:

> In each great region of the world the living mammals are closely related to the extinct species of the same region. It is therefore probable that Africa was formerly inhabited by extinct apes closely allied to the gorilla and chimpanzee; and as these two species are now man's nearest allies, it is somewhat more probable that our early progenitors lived on the African continent than elsewhere.

With new fossil and genetic evidence, Darwin's conclusion is sustained and forms the starting point for a story of human dispersion beyond Africa. While hominins evolved in Africa, manifestly they did not stay there. Hominin dispersals out of Africa raise important questions about (i) the timings and pathways out of Africa and beyond; (ii) the taxa – which hominins left; and (iii) the conditions that made movement out of Africa possible. One question in particular has tantalised researchers: to what extent did these movements depend on extrinsic factors, with climate change removing or ameliorating barriers otherwise limiting hominins to their African homelands, and to what extent did movement depend on novel biological and/or cultural capacities of the migrants. For example, as we shall shortly note, the first out of African migrants were probably habilines, hominins similar to *Homo habilis*. Australopiths, their presumptive ancestor, has never been found out of Africa. Is this because they lacked capacities to reach and establish in Eurasian habitats; capacities their habiline descendants had? Alternatively, perhaps hominin-compatible pathways through the Arabian Peninsula, the Nile Valley, or Sinai only opened after the habilines disappeared. Do those factors constrain and explain the timing and frequency of hominid movements beyond Africa? And are migrations of *H. sapiens* beyond Africa an exception to the patterns shown by earlier hominids, perhaps being a late pulse that spread directionally and rapidly across the globe as some have hypothesised. This chapter takes up some of these questions, and focusses on the number, timing, and complexity of movements from Africa. We begin with the earliest migrations out of Africa in the early Pleistocene.

## Fossil Evidence for Early Movements Out of Africa

A long sequence of fossils provides evidence of Hominid evolution within Africa. Within and without Africa, these fossils are often given distinct species names: *H. habilis*, *Homo erectus*, *Homo Heidelbergensis*, and the like. The biological status of these supposed species is far from clear, as fossils are fragmentary, and we have very limited evidence of the extent of species-level variation in hominid populations. It is useful to conceptualise these fossils as representing grades, identified by their size and their degree of encephalisation. Both seem to increase over time, with this trend increasingly well documented in Africa. The general sequence from Australopithecines to Habilines (*H. habilis*/*H. rudolfensis*) and then to *H. erectus*/*Homo ergaster*, *H. heidelbergensis*, and then to *H. sapiens*, is clear. Fossils of some of these taxa have been found outside Africa, in equatorial or temperate parts of the Old World, but the critical feature for our discussion is that the oldest examples of each taxa/grade are found in Africa. Greater antiquity of African examples, relative to Eurasian ones, is consistent with African origins followed by dispersion to the rest of the Old World.

Out-of-Africa dispersions have happened multiple times with multiple hominid species. It has been common to define two 'Out of Africa' events, but as we discuss below there were likely to have been multiple dispersions and they may be better thought of as phases of migration rather than singular events. Additionally, the dispersions we know of were those successful enough to leave large-scale archaeological or genomic signatures, and there may have been many more, smaller, and less visible events.

What is widely recognised as the first Out of Africa (OOA) dispersion, the first dispersion phase, appears to have occurred prior to 2 mya, as *H. habilis* or a related form (*H. ergaster*) spread beyond Africa and became established in South and East Asia and in at least parts of broader Europe. Even the tiny *Homo floresiensis* found in distant Southeast Asia seems likely to have derived from *H. habilis* or similar species (Argue et al. 2017). The earliest fossil evidence of this expansion comes from the site of Dmanisi in Georgia, which is dated to c.1.85–1.77 by potassium-argon and argon-argon techniques as well as a distinct palaeomagnetic reversal (Lordkipanidze et al. 2013). Fossils from a number of individuals have been recovered from the site, and although they display considerable variability, they are now considered to represent a population descended from *H. habilis*, and which had already differentiated from that species (Rightmire et al. 2017).

There have been several mechanisms proposed for the successful spread of hominids from Africa to the high latitudes at this early time. One was that many African animal species, perhaps even the savannah niche in which they lived, had expanded beyond Africa, and hominids had expanded with them (e.g. Klein 1999). This notion has now been refuted by studies that show only some taxa had expanded from Africa, that these were generally limited to nearby regions and were not found in distant regions such as the Caucasus where Dmanisi is located (Tappen 2009; Belmaker 2010). Belmaker points out that the savannah-like environments of the Sinai (a relatively early OOA region) are in fact ecologically quite different from African savannahs, with a long hot dry season, selecting against specialist grazers, requiring more generalist grazing/browsing strategies, so it is no anomaly that the fauna is predominantly Eurasian. The same is true of the highly seasonal Dmanisi, which likewise had a Eurasian fauna (e.g. with bears rather than pigs).

Another proposal was that hominids had expanded beyond Africa as scavengers of the prey of dispersing carnivores (Arribas and Palmqvist 1999), but this is not at all a likely explanation. Even within Africa, there is no demonstration that scavenged meat was a critical hominin resource, defining the locations hominins could live. Moreover, later reviews have shown that African fauna was generally restricted to the southern Levant, that the association of early hominids and carnivore guilds is not well documented and that the key carnivore discussed (*Megantereon* sp.) was present in Eurasia from c.3 mya (Belmaker 2010). Additionally, the evidence of cut-marks on the long bones of cervids and bovids show defleshing of meat not typically left behind by large cats, suggesting that hominids had first access to carcases at Dmanisi (Tappen 2009, 40). It seems more likely that early hominids dispersed to quite non-African niches by being foragers capable to adjusting to varied circumstances (Belmaker 2010), perhaps with other characteristics such as increased life span providing functional advantage for the groups (Tappen 2009). It is clear then that the first OOA expansions depended on distinctively hominid capacities, but it might also have required climate change to open pathways that were previously closed.

Dmanisi is not an isolated example of early excursions of hominids beyond Africa. While there are no other substantial fossil remains known from Eurasia earlier than approximately 1.7 mya, there are abundant and unambiguous stone artefacts found in South and East Asia at about the same time as occupation at Dmanisi. Perhaps the most stunning are the assemblages of simple cores and flakes in stratified open deposits in the Chinese Loess Plateau, at approximately 2.1 mya (Zhu et al. 2018). Those assemblages indicate that hominids spread far beyond Africa, occupying tropical, sub-tropical, temperate, even some sub-arctic environments. The key point about the earliest hominid expansion from Africa, as represented by Dmanisi or China's Loess Plateau, is that in the right conditions early hominids successfully dispersed across much of Eurasia without any of what are considered the more sophisticated technologies, social lives or communication capacities that are found in later hominids. This point is germane to consideration of later hominid dispersions.

Subsequent physical and cultural evolution across Eurasia may not have always been independent from developments in Africa. For example, later sites near Africa, such as Ubeidiya in the Levant, which dates to c.1.4–1.6 mya, display innovations that probably arose in Africa. At Ubeidiya there are sparse hominid fossils indicating creatures that may have been *H. ergaster*, and handaxes, which were not present at Dmanisi or early OOA sites (Belmaker et al. 2002). It is of course possible that these are independent inventions. However, given the relative proximity of this site to pathways out of Africa, these patterns most likely reveal ongoing contact between the southern Levant and Africa (where handaxes had been present for at least 2–300,000 years previously). They may even represent yet another migration from Africa that has not been adequately distinguished from the initial migration. Indeed, since there is no fossil evidence of Denisovans or Neanderthals in Africa, and since nuclear DNA evidence suggests that the lineage leading to sapiens diverged from that leading to the Denisovan-Neanderthal sister taxa somewhere between 550 and 765 kya, the common ancestor of Neanderthals, Denisovans, and Sapiens presumably spread out of Africa around 750 kya.

These earlier hominins seem to have been replaced by the migrations of *H. sapiens* OOA, though with some genetic traces of these earlier-evolving hominins in the DNA of these later migrations. We now turn to the pattern and timing of those events. Understanding these histories of sapiens movement is particularly challenging, because genetic and archaeological data often seem inconsistent, and because purely archaeological traces of hominin presence rarely specify the taxon responsible for the material debris left behind.

## Modern Biological Diversity as Signals of OOA Dispersion

Genetic data make clear patterns of migration or migrations that lead to the contemporary cosmopolitan distribution of our species. Expansion of human populations OOA has left distinct structures in the genetic differences between populations (see Figure 1.1). The level of genetic variation, its heterozygosity, declines with distance from the northeast margin of Africa (Ramachandran et al. 2005 – see Figure 1.1A). This is an extremely strong trend, explaining almost 80% of the geographical variation outside Africa. At the same time what is termed linkage disequilibrium increases with distance from Africa (Jakobsson et al. 2008 – Figure 1.1B). Linkage disequilibrium is the non-random association of alleles of different loci, and increased values typically indicates alleles have recently increased to high frequencies under strong selection (Slatkin 2008). A third trend has been noted in what are termed ancestral allele frequencies (AAFs), which progressively reduce in populations that are progressively further from Africa (Li et al. 2008). Modelling has shown that all of these are explicable if the dispersion of *H. sapiens* beyond Africa occurred through a serial founder effect, in which there have been successive migration of only a small fraction of individuals from the previous location to the new one, usually carrying only a fraction of the genetic diversity in the founding population. Increased linkage disequilibrium and heightened AAFs would follow from local selection on small founding groups. Moreover, those patterns suggest that (by evolutionary standards) this series of founding events is fairly recent, as not much novel variation has been generated in these populations.

Modelling of dispersal mechanisms, particularly by DeGiorgio and colleagues, found that the empirical evidence conforms strongly with the simplest model of serial founder effects with no migration between neighbours and no archaic admixture (DeGiorgio et al. 2009), though more recent findings identify admixtures of Denisovans and Neanderthals, and extended gene flow between regions (see below). Adding symmetrical migration between neighbouring groups in their models changed the patterns little, and so DeGiorgio and colleagues reasoned that interactions

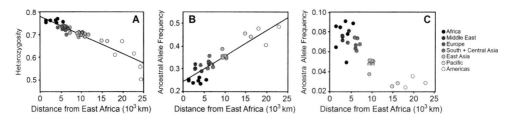

FIGURE 1.1  Global genetic patterns beyond Africa. (A) Heterozygosity relative to the distance from East Africa (redrawn from Ramachandran et al. 2005, following DeGiorgio et al. 2009). (B) Linkage disequilibrium at 10 kb relative to the distance from East Africa (redrawn from DeGiorgio et al. 2009, data analysis from Jakobsson et al. 2008). (C) Slope of the ancestral allele frequency spectrum (redrawn from DeGiorgio et al. 2009, based on analysis in Li et al. 2008).

between groups of *H. sapiens* were not a major contributor to the global patterns. However, that conclusion presumed linear and unidirectional population dispersals across Eurasia, and the situation is likely to have been more complex given other processes recently discovered.

One process was archaic admixture, meaning hybridisation of *H. sapiens* with other hominids descended from earlier migrations out of Africa (see below). Hybridisation can have powerful effects on all three characteristics, because it adds genetic variation to the *H. sapiens* genome outside Africa. Persistent, repeated, archaic admixture across Eurasia would have produced a pattern quite different to the one we see today, with increased heterozygosity and decreased linkage disequilibrium visible as distance from Africa increases. We do not see that in Figure 1.1, inconsistent with substantial admixture in multiple regions as the ancestors of modern *H. sapiens* dispersed out of Africa. However, adding a small amount of archaic admixture at a number of points beyond Africa does not alter the general trends modelled in regional genomics, instead it resets the heterozygosity (see DeGiorgio et al. 2009, 16060). For these reasons we might think that the dispersion process by which the ancestors of modern *H. sapiens* spread across the globe most likely occurred through the fissioning of regional populations, with relatively small groups moving into adjacent regions creating the serial founder process, along with some cases of gene exchange with other hominins already present.

Notwithstanding those broad patterns, genomes are complex, and it has long been known that different components can have distinct histories, with some histories contradicting the idea of a single, unidirectional spread of *H. sapiens* from the edge of Africa. For example, global patterning in the Y chromosome has been interpreted as evidence for early gene flow in the opposite direction – towards Africa (e.g. Hallast et al. 2021a, 2021b). Phylogenetic differences in Y chromosomes are often defined by Y haplogroups labelled with letters of the alphabet. These haplogroups represent major branches of the phylogenetic tree, with many hundred mutations unique to each haplogroup. For example, 'CF' is a lineage that gives rise to 'C' and 'FT' lineages, and in turn 'FT' is ancestral to newer lineages such as 'F', 'G', and others. While Y chromosomes found in non-African populations (e.g. C, D, and FT) are generally distinct from those dominant in Africa (e.g. A, B, and E), supporting out-of-African processes, the phylogeography of Y lineages greatly complicates simple dispersal models. Non-African lineages (C, D, and FT) diversified rapidly in the period 44.4–64.1 kya, and in recent humans the sub-lineages have clear geographical patterning. Lineage C split into C1 and C2; C1 now found in East, Southeast, South Asia, and Oceania; C2 in East and Southeast Asia, and North/Central/West Asia (Hallast et al. 2021a). D is found only in East and Southeast Asia. The FT lineages initially split into F and others (GHIJK); F is found only in East and Southeast Asia, whereas GHIJK and their sub-lineages are found across almost all the non-African lands.

The significance of this Y-phylogeny and its modern distributions is threefold. First, ancestral non-African lineages C, D, and FT (all other non-African Y-lineages) split early, estimated at 70–80 kya with a substantial further diversification of all non-African Y-lineages around 55 kya (Hallast et al. 2021a). Multiple discrete phases of early diversification in a single region beyond Africa is not the pattern predicted by simple models of serial founder effects gradually reducing diversity as migrations move away from Africa.

That brings us to the second implication of the Y chromosome history. Early diverging non-African Y-lineages are today located in Central and Eastern Asia, not in Western Asia, near Africa, as would be predicted in any simple model of unidirectional expansion of *H. sapiens* from Africa into Western Asia and finally to Eastern Asia – those early lineages are instead found in the furthest parts of Eurasia from the margins of Africa. If the current distribution of

C and D lineages in Central and Eastern Asia is an indication that they developed there, this would be evidence of a node of early Y chromosome lineage generation in eastern Eurasia. This seems a likely conclusion because while local extinction of C and D lineages in Western Asia, or positive selection for different variants of FT lineages, in different regions, could in theory produce such a pattern, those proposals are difficult to sustain. Y chromosomes are small, with relatively few functional genes, making them a less likely target of selection. There is doubt that positive selection has been operating on the human Y chromosome over this period (Jobling and Tyler-Smith 2017), and the complete elimination of early lineages in Western Asia points to more complex processes.

The third implication of the Y-chromosome pattern is that Y chromosome diversification occurred in the east of Eurasia, where lower genetic effective population sizes may have resulted in more genetic drift, likely indicates massive multi-directional spread of Y lineages. Production of the recent Y chromosome patterns resulted from the early divergence of C, D, and FT lineages in the East *and* the subsequent replacement of earlier variants in the west by the later spread of G, H, I, J, and K lineages from their origin points in East and Southeast Asia (see Hallast et al. 2021a, 2021b). That secondary zone of diversification, not only outside Africa but also in Eastern Eurasia, fed intercontinental genetic movements westward, back towards Africa. Such a genetic flow is more complex than simple OOA models predict, but is consistent with large-scale and well-documented intercontinental movements earlier (OOA) and also later in time, when there is abundant genetic evidence for multiple movements in the last 30 kya (e.g. Seguin-Orlando et al. 2014; Fu et al. 2016; Yang et al. 2017; Sikora et al. 2019). Multi-directional migration and gene flow in central and eastern Eurasia are also supported by other genomic analyses, such as the evidence that South Asia was colonised by groups coming from the east (Marrero et al. 2016). Complex population histories, involving persistent sub-populations and networks of gene flow between them, are also identified in emerging *H. sapiens* within Africa (Fan et al. 2023). This is consistent with known environmental changes opening and reinstating barriers to movement within Africa, not just between Africa and Eurasia. It seems that complex evolutionary patterns involving multiple geographic nodes of interbreeding and diversification articulated by multi-directional dispersion of emerging lineages are common among hominids within and beyond Africa. More elaborate models of early movements of sapiens beyond Africa increase our ability to understand the disparate genetic and archaeological patterns that have been identified.

**Early Exit of *Homo sapiens* from Africa: Genetic Evidence**

The reality of *H. sapiens* originating in Africa is clear, but there is considerable uncertainty about both the number and timing of migrations beyond Africa. More significantly, there is now the question of what genomes were carried by each 'wave' of *H. sapiens* moving into Eurasia.

A once common reading of the genetic evidence suggests that living non-African sapiens populations derive from a single, and quite recent exit from Africa, at a late time c.50–70 kya. On this view, sapiens dispersed rapidly both to the east (Asia, South East Asia, Sahul, and eventually Oceania) and to the north and west, into and through Europe. This 'Late Exit' (LE) model argues that migrating sapiens displaced other hominid populations (with some gene exchange) by virtue of cultural (and perhaps cognitive) advances that allowed them to out-compete those already present in each region. This view often predicts that fossil signals of sapiens' arrival in Europe, Asia, and South East Asia will coincide with a sharp change in material culture (see

O'Connell et al. 2018 for a defence of this position). We return to that claim later in this chapter, but first we examine the growing evidence for earlier and more complex dispersion events.

Genetic and archaeological evidence can be read as evidence of an 'Early Exit' (EE) from Africa, with *H. sapiens* evolving in Eurasia and hybridising periodically with other hominid species over a long period. These OOA population movements were likely complex, occurred multiple times, and involved backwards migration of populations towards and into Africa. Here we discuss the biological evidence for, and likely configuration of, the early exit of humans from Africa.

On strand of genetic evidence for OOA dispersion comes from interactions of other hominid species with *H. sapiens* in Eurasia. The nuclear genome (nDNA) of Neanderthals and Denisovans shows they are more closely related to each other than to humans, a pattern consistent with them diverging only after their common ancestor had diverged from *H. sapiens* (Prüfer et al. 2014). Mitochondrial (mtDNA) shows a different story in which Neanderthals and Denisovans have different lineages and Neanderthals were closer to the mtDNA of *H. sapiens* than to Denisovans. This pattern can be explained if Neanderthal mtDNA differentiated after their split with Denisovans because of gene flow from *H. sapiens* into Neanderthals. Evidence in favour of that hypothesis comes from the genome of earlier pre-Neanderthal hominids in western Europe, at Sima de los Huesos, dated to more than 300 kya. These bone samples were found to have mtDNA deriving from a common ancestor with Denisovans, something not found in any Neanderthals from the western Europe (Meyer et al. 2014). This suggests introgression of mtDNA from a different hominid into the Neanderthal population. Specific investigations of such admixture events have helped define their antiquity.

A Neanderthal from the Altai region was estimated to have had 1.0–7.1% gene flow from *H. sapiens* into its ancestors (Kuhlwilm et al. 2016). That Altai Neanderthal had more of those 'African' haplotypes than the Denisovan genomes, indicating regional variation in the interaction with *H. sapiens*. Introgression of presumed African haplotypes into the Altai Neanderthal population was estimated to have occurred 100–230 kya. This hypothesis was explicitly tested by analysis of a Neanderthal femur from Hohlenstein–Stadel Cave in southwestern Germany, where an inflow of mtDNA into Neanderthals was estimated to date between 460 and 219 kya (Posth et al. 2017). The mtDNA of the Hohlenstein–Stadel individual was deeply divergent from the Altai Neanderthal, though more similar to it than to the Denisovan-like mtDNA of the Sima de los Huesos hominin. Posth and colleagues suggest that an expansion of the population represented by the Altai Neanderthal led to a species-wide footprint of mtDNA shaped by gene flow from *H. sapiens*. This must have been both outside Africa and significantly earlier than the 'late exit' dates of 50–70 kya.

Another calculation estimates the time to most recent common ancestor (TMRCA) for all Neanderthal mtDNAs as approximately 160 kya. Since the introgressed mtDNA from *H. sapiens* is included in that calculation the admixture happened before that date. Consequently, the minimum age for this particular hybridisation between Neanderthals and *H. sapiens* is 160 kya, and the estimate by Posth et al. (2017) is that more likely it occurred before 219 kya. Since Neanderthals have not been found within Africa archaic *H. sapiens* moved out of Africa into west Asia where hybridisation occurred. Those specific age estimates all depend on small sample sizes and it is difficult to test estimates of the rate of various population genetic processes. However, discordance between mtDNA and nDNA is robust, with nDNA grouping Neanderthals with Denisovans, and mtDNA grouping Neanderthals with *H. sapiens*. Sapiens-Neanderthal genetic exchange is the only parsimonious explanation of this discordance. As there is vastly more nDNA than mtDNA, nuclear gene flow of Denisovans into Neanderthals is not a credible alternative. This mtDNA gene flow from sapiens had to happen ex-Africa and anciently enough for the reshaped Neanderthal mtDNA across their entire population. This chronology, with dispersion significantly before about 100 kya, represents part of the 'early' OOA dispersion of sapiens dispersion.

Genomic data supports at least one long-lived and demographically substantial expansion out of Africa prior to 200 kya, although multiple expansions are likely as we will explain. The genetic composition of pre-200 kya migrating populations is unclear, but they were successful enough to persist over a considerable period and numerous enough to greatly impact Neanderthal DNA. Introgression with these *sapiens* migrants resulted in complete mtDNA turnover.

Those early migrations have often been dismissed, with archaeologists and geneticists treating them as uninteresting and unsuccessful and short-term because they were thought to have been replaced by later migrations from Africa. For example, one view is that those early migrations out of Africa were 'ephemeral', short-lived and ultimately unsuccessful (e.g. Haslam et al. 2018). It is premature to draw that conclusion. While existing genetic and archaeological data do not indicate that early migrations of *H. sapiens* from Africa permanently replaced other hominids within the greater Levant region or beyond, neither do they convincingly show short-lived or unsuccessful occupation.

Moreover, there is genetic evidence of a sapiens migration later that the one which allowed the reorganisation of Neanderthal mtDNA, but earlier than the estimates of 50–70 kya. Cabrera (2023) argues there was a very successful migration of *H. sapiens* from Africa about 130 kya, populating Southwest Asia. Variation in the geographical frequency of mtDNA haplogroups derived from the ancestral L3′4′6 clade, is consistent with splitting of that clade into L6, L3, and L4 branches in Southwest Asia, not within Africa (see also Lazaridis et al. 2016; Bergström et al. 2021). Sub-branches of L6 and L4 are well-represented in Western Asia today, from all phases of sub-lineage splitting, consistent with haploid evolution taking place in that region. The timing of those splits, calculated by Cabrera (2023) as coalescent ages, is 105–264 kya (95% CI) for L3′4′6, and 87–184 kya (also 95% CI) for L3′4. If the lineages did indeed separate in Western Asia then the *H. sapiens* ancestral to living non-African humans were likely present beyond Africa well before 100 kya. In that scenario the L3 basal lineages migrated back into Africa at a later date, also introducing Neanderthal material into African genomes (Cabrera et al. 2018). Independent genomic evidence for a prolonged residence in Western Asia prior to later dispersions of *H. sapiens* has been inferred from patterns of hard selective sweeps calculated to date to 74–91 kya (95% CI) (Tobler et al. 2023). The basal Eurasian lineage formed in Western Asia before again hybridising with Neanderthals ~74 kya and then splitting into European and Asian pools (Lazardis et al. 2016; Schaefer et al. 2021). Multiple serial dispersals into broader Eurasia from a 'hub' somewhere in Western Asia is a mechanism increasingly employed to explain genomic and archaeological patterns found in western and northern Eurasia (e.g. Vallini et al. 2022).

Neanderthal genes are more pronounced in people from Central and East Asia than in those from western Eurasia, an unanticipated pattern sometimes explained as a result of selection and/or lower population size in the east (e.g. Schaefer et al. 2021). Those mechanisms are not adequate, however, since neither selection nor smaller population size can explain Eurasian variation in the abundance of Neanderthal genes (e.g. Kim and Lohmueller 2015; Petr et al. 2019). Other mechanisms are likely to be involved, including the chronology of groups leaving western Eurasia and the patterns and intensity of gene flow between regions, creating a complex history of admixture across Eurasia.

The implication of this finding is that the global dispersion of modern humans did not begin with the migration of *H. sapiens* out of Africa in the 50–70 kya period as discussions of Late Exit models sometimes imply (see below). Instead, the global dispersal was likely begun by populations long-established in Western Asia and adjoining areas, who commenced large-scale expansion into new regions around 70 kya and later. Archaeological evidence is broadly consistent with that process.

## Early Exit of *Homo sapiens* from Africa: Archaeological Evidence

*H. sapiens* descended from a lineage that split from the ancestors of Neanderthals and Denisovans perhaps 7–800 kya (Rogers et al. 2017). It has been estimated that recognisable though 'archaic' versions of *H. sapiens* probably developed something like 350 kya (e.g. Mounier and Lahr 2019). That estimate is an extrapolation backwards from the earliest recovered fossils that resemble later sapiens. The oldest is arguably from Jebel Irhoud in Morocco, dated to about 280 kya (Richter et al. 2017), although there has been discussion of its taxonomic assignment. Another skull from Florisbad in South Africa, is now thought to be an archaic *H. sapiens* dated to 224–294 kya (Grün et al. 1996). A third set of fossils commonly considered to represent early *H. sapiens* come from Omo-Kibish I in Ethiopia, and is dated to almost 200 kya (Mcdougall et al. 2005).

Beyond Africa the oldest distinctly *H. sapiens* fossil is the cranial fragment of Apidima 1, found in a cave in southern Greece. The specimen falls within the morphological range of fossil *H. sapiens*, being close to Skhul 5 in metrical shape indices, and although the specimen was redeposited and the dating is controversial it is thought to be c.210 kya (Harvati et al. 2019). Another early fossil is the jaw from Misliya cave in the Levant, dated to 177–194 kya (Hershkovitz et al. 2018). These fossil finds correspond impressively with inferences from genomic patterns for movements of *H. sapiens* out of Africa before 150–200 kya.

Later in time we have the multiple burials at Es-Skhul Cave in Israel. Fossils of seven adults and three children have been recovered from this site, dated to about 119 kya via thermoluminescence dating methods, and to a slightly younger antiquity of 81–101 kya by electron spin resonance (Bar-Yosef 1998). While the older date using thermoluminescence is usually preferred, either set of dates indicates the presence of *H. sapiens* in the range of 80–130 kya. Significantly, several of these individuals were represented by articulated skeletons, probably buried, and in the case of the Skhul 5 individual grave goods in the form of a boar mandible had been placed on his chest. Additionally, *Nassarius* shells were found and are best interpreted as decorative/signalling objects, perhaps used as beads (Vanhaeran et al. 2006). While there are reasons for a good deal of caution about the distinction between behaviourally modern hominids and those with more archaic lifeways, the use of decoration and material symbols is supposedly one key characteristic of 'behaviourally modern' humans. The Skhul finds suggest deeper origins of those behaviours beyond Africa. Archaeological evidence from the Levant therefore indicates the presence of *H. sapiens* outside Africa at least 180 kya, and that at 100 kya or before, those humans displayed a range of 'modern' behaviours.

Where diagnostic human skeletal fragments can be found they provide unambiguous markers, but such remains are infrequent and their dating must be carefully considered. More commonly the presence of *H. sapiens* in regional archaeological sequences has been diagnosed by observations of changes to artefacts, and the technologies that produced them. The inference from technology to taxon risks both false positives and false negatives. In general, we lack clear evidence that techniques used by sapiens were never used by contemporaneous Neanderthals (or Denisovans). Moreover, sapiens populations sometimes used only techniques that originated deeper in time.

Recently discussed presumptive markers for the arrival of *H. sapiens* include lithic cores or retouched flakes and the systems of flaking they represent. For instance, there have been claims that some kinds of cores are distinctive of *H. sapiens*, particularly 'nubian cores' in western Asia (see Will et al. 2015), and/or that microblades and microliths found in Africa, Western, and Southern Asia are indicative of sapiens (Mellars et al. 2013). However, no exclusive association with *H. sapiens* fossils has been demonstrated, and we have evidence from the Levant of Neanderthals and *H. sapiens* having quite similar technologies (see Groucutt et al. 2019). Similar difficulties currently exist for other classes of material culture, such as bone instruments and rock art and burials. These technologies may not have been unique to sapiens. Moreover, even if some groups of *H. sapiens* did have distinctive tools or practices the absence of those objects and behaviours are not sufficient to conclude that the hominid present was not *H. sapiens*. Archaeological evidence of uniquely sapiens practices at most indicates the minimum antiquity of their presence. It follows that the population histories of our species' movements out of Africa are hard to reconstruct from common archaeological evidence, making a variety of population and dispersal models untestable.

For example, Mishra and her colleagues suggested that *H. sapiens* exited Africa around 130 kya, spreading across tropical and subtropical environments of central and eastern Eurasia during warm conditions of Marine Isotope Stage 5, and colonising China and Southeast Asia before 100 kya (Mishra et al. 2013). At the time their paper was published a number of sites appeared to contain early *H. sapiens* fossils in China, such as Huanglong, Fuyan, and Sanyou Caves, suggesting to Mishra that expanding populations had reached China well before 100 kya but had bypassed South Asia. She considered that in much of South Asia technological evolution was continuous, in turn indicating continuity in the pre-sapiens hominid taxa making those artefacts (see also Anil et al. 2022). Combining that proposition and the observation that microblades appearing in India around 70 kya were rather like those in South and East Africa, they argued that *H. sapiens* did not move into that region until much later than the exit from Africa. Similar timing for the arrival of *H. sapiens* in Southern Asia has been advocated by others based on the age of technological changes, although without arguing that the exit from Africa was substantially earlier (e.g. Clarkson et al. 2020). Genetic evidence now supports a later colonisation of South Asia, though not with a chronology that matches archaeological ones such as proposed by Mishra (see Marrero et al. 2016).

This archaeological case for early migration into Eastern Eurasia by *H. sapiens* has been based mainly on fossil material. For instance, in China, during the last decade, a series of teeth and jaws have been recovered and dated at sites such as at Zhirendong (Liu et al. 2010), Huanglong (Shen et al. 2013), Luna (Bae et al. 2014), and Fuyan (Liu et al. 2015). *H. sapiens* was inferred to have been present before 80 kya and probably between 120 and 150 kya. If correct, it would follow that *H. sapiens* reaching eastern Eurasia had most likely descended from the populations that had emerged from Africa in the period 160–250 kya and left their imprint on Neanderthal genomes.

Dating creates difficulties for archaeological claims of human occupation in East Asia before 100 kya, or before 50 kya for that matter! Many of the previously old fossils in Southern China have been redated and the human occupation of many has been revised to less than 50 kya (Sun et al. 2021). However, it remains possible that earlier dispersions may be evidenced by fossils such as the Zhirendong mandible, which has a series of archaic features and is dated to

>130 kya (Ge et al. 2020), although further assessment of their taxonomic status may be necessary. If archaic sapiens fossils are identified in some regions of East Asia well before pre-75 kya, we will probably be observing distinct regional variation in early occupation, perhaps tracking early movements of *H. sapiens*.

However, regional variation may also partly reflect sample size and preservational effects, making it hard to find earlier dateable sites with human remains. The difficulty of discovering evidence is reflected in the rarity of sites. Those older than 40–45 kya with clear evidence of *H. sapiens* have been hard to find in East and Southeast Asia. As always, when sites are rare, those found will almost certainly not be the oldest. However, those few sites from which fossils have been recovered and intensively dated provide strong evidence for the minimum age of a dispersion by *H. sapiens* in eastern Eurasia and peninsula and island Southeast Asia. A number of regions have yielded apparently well-dated specimens of *H. sapiens* at somewhat early dates (c.65–90 kya), consistent with movements out of western Asia before 70 kya. For example, at Tam Pà Ling Cave in northern Laos a *H. sapiens* frontal bone (TPL 6) and tibial fragment (TPL 7) have been dated. Using multiple dating methods TPL7, the lowest sapiens fossil, is stratigraphically below rock-fall-capped sediments modelled as 68–86 kya (at 1σ). Although a very imprecise age estimate the average minimum date for this fossil is c.63.8–65.5 kya, pointing towards *H. sapiens* being present at least 65,000 years ago, but probably much earlier (see Freidline et al. 2023). A second example is from Lida Ajer Cave in western Sumatra, which has teeth below a flowstone likely 58–78 kya (at 2σ). Those teeth have been identified as *H. sapiens* in size and enamel thickness (Westaway et al. 2017. These sites have been difficult to find and to date, and mapping fossils onto a specific taxon can be difficult. However, they currently indicate that *H. sapiens* were likely present in the far southeast of Eurasia before 60–65 kya, and perhaps long before that time. Those dates are comparable with the oldest ages plausibly claimed from Sahul (Australia and New Guinea), at Madjedbebe where the lowest artefacts are recovered from sediments dated to about 60–70 kya (Clarkson et al. 2017). All of these sites have complex formational histories and low precision chronologies, but taken together they seem to indicate the presence of *H. sapiens* in these regions by 60–70 kya – broadly consistent with the genetic evidence supporting an early OOA dispersal, and within the range estimated for the genetic divergence of Australian/Papuan and Eurasians in some analyses (e.g. Malaspinas et al. 2016).

**Late Out of Africa Claims: Genetics**

As we have discussed, the interpretation of genetic, fossil, and archaeological data is complicated by multiple and ramified dispersals of *H. sapiens*, first from Africa and subsequently from western Asia and other nodes. Contrary to evidence described above for early models of our ancestors, a different reading of genetic evidence suggests that all but the last dispersion failed, and that ancestors of all current non-African humans left Africa only very recently, rapidly expanding across most tropical, sub-tropical and temperate environments. This is what is often termed a 'late exit' model.

This model has been framed in a variety of ways, but the logic is that dispersion cannot have begun earlier than the antiquity of the most recent common ancestor (MRCA) of non-Africans. Age of a non-African MRCA has typically been calculated as the antiquity of the L3 mtDNA lineage, as it is from that haplogroup that all non-African mtDNA descends. Several analyses hypothesised the L3 lineage emerged in Africa, and relatively recently. These estimates were criticised, particularly by Scally and Durbin (2012) who used multiple lines of evidence to claim other studies had over-estimated the rate of genomic change and hence had under-estimated the time depth represented by the evolution of the L3 lineage. There is also a proposal that mutation rates have been different for African and non-African populations (Mallick et al. 2016). In response, researchers have used mtDNA extracted from independently dated Pleistocene skeletons, and from the genomic differences they calculate substitution rates over the last 40 kya. Employing those rates, estimates of time to MRCA are inferred. As an example, the research group led by Fu estimated a MRCA for all modern humans as 120–197 kya (95% HPD) and an MRCA for L3 as 62.4–94.9 kya (95% HPD). If accurate this age range would indicate the likely maximum antiquity for the movement of *H. sapiens* into Eurasia (Fu et al. 2013a, 2013b). The same analysis also estimated a MRCA of the Q haplogroup, often taken to indicate the maximum possible age for the settlement of Sahul, as 30–54.9 kya.

While the reasoning behind these estimates is strong, we note that the use of these estimates can be complex. Sometimes discussions cite mid-point values rather than the 95% window given by the Bayesian analysis. This would involve citing 78.3 kya as the MRCA for L3, rather than the calculated highest posterior density (HPD) interval of 62.4–94.9 kya. Although HPD is not strictly equivalent to frequentist expressions of dispersion (such as quartile intervals or variance), the obvious analogue is the imprecision of citing mean rather than a two-standard deviation window. Focussing on the 95% window estimate gives a sense of the low resolution of all estimates of lineage splits. Taking, as an example, the estimate of L3 MRCA provided by Fu et al. (2013b), of 62.4–94.9 kya, we see a window more than 30,000 years long, which is big in both absolute and relative terms. Large uncertainties about lineage splits are relevant to any consideration of the details of late OOA claims.

More noteworthy is variation in published estimates of divergence times, for the earliest population divergence among humans, and the divergence of L3 and appearance of other haplogroups (e.g. Henn et al. 2018). Estimates are affected by a number of factors, including sample, mutation rate employed, computational methods and model assumption (see Ho et al. 2011; Bromham et al. 2017; Bromham 2019), and it is unsurprising that different values are calculated by different research projects and over time as disciplines progress. However, disparate estimates offer little guidance on the critical issue of when the hypothesised late/single migration beyond Africa took place. Estimates over the last decade or so would allow a single/late migration as early as 85–90 kya or as late as 40 kya (e.g. Fu et al. 2013b; Henn et al. 2012; Soares et al. 2012; Schiffels and Durbin 2014; Mallick et al. 2016; Haber et al. 2019; Lipson et al. 2020; Montinaro et al. 2021).

**Mixed Migration Models: Genetics**

Some analyses report small components (typically <10%) of modern genomes that likely date to more than 100 kya, as indicating modern human populations outside Africa are probably the result of admixtures between earlier (>100 kya) and later (<70 kya) OOA migrating sapiens populations (e.g. Schiffels and Durbin 2014; Pagani et al. 2016). Other analyses have found that if time since common ancestors is calculated separately for each geographic region (sometimes using a newer statistic called MSMC: multiple sequential Markovian coalescent), the antiquity of lineage splits is significantly different between populations, consistent with varied admixture between populations that dispersed both earlier and later (e.g. Pagani et al. 2016). One study calculated early divergence times from East Africa for Australian and New Guinean people, and concluded those do not overlap with far later divergence estimates for other regions such as Europe or Central Asia, a pattern consistent with multiple exits (Tassi et al. 2015). These observations are hard to explain in models of a single exit but are congruent with later migrations from Africa having extended genetic exchanges with human groups already resident in Western Asia before their descendants began to expand to more distant regions. Even geneticists advocating only late migrations across Eurasia now consider it necessary to hypothesise multiple migrations originating from a source already outside Africa, in Western Asia (e.g. Vallini et al. 2022). We consider it plausible, and consistent with evidence for admixtures, that a multicomponent and ramified process of migration and genetic admixture in several *H. sapiens* populations colonising new landscapes across Eurasia in the Pleistocene. That is especially true as it is difficult to construct a plausible ecological-economic model of a single, late migration, rapid dispersal, and replacement, given that it is now clear that the package of traits jointly taken to indicate behavioural modernity was assembled piecemeal in the Middle stone Age, and that earlier sapiens dispersing from Africa would have many of these 'modern' capacities. Evidence for behavioural variability, even 'flexibility', developing in the African Middle Stone Age is consistent with many 'modern' behaviours being present in African human groups at the time earlier migrations occurred (see McBrearty and Brooks 2000; Kandel et al. 2016).

It is worth considering the implications of multiple OOA exits for arguments made about archaeological evidence. As we noted above, models of a multiple exit from Africa by populations that then exchanged genes before dispersing further fits better with skeletal evidence found by archaeologists in broader western Asia than a single late OOA model. They are also consistent with inferences of prolonged and multidirectional movements, accompanied by genetic exchanges, between *H. sapiens* populations across Eurasia.

Models of multiple exits, like some early exit models, do not preclude expansion(s) of *H. sapiens* beyond Western Asia prior to another more extensive expansion sometime since 90 kya. Over time this could represent several lineages of *H. sapiens*, likely distinguished at least by haplogroups, moving across parts of Eurasia and interbreeding with not only other hominid species but also with other human groups carrying different genetic brands. That process would explain the earlier genomic components in various human populations today, but creates significant difficulties for archaeological inferences from artefacts and the skeletal remains of *H. sapiens*, since these materials cannot be robustly assigned to specific lineages without associated palaeogenomics. It is increasingly difficult to show that sapiens had technical capacities beyond those of contemporaneous hominids. It is even less likely that sapiens from specific genomic lineages had distinctive archaeological footprints. As genetics do not unambiguously point to a single, fast and directional migration of *H. sapiens* spreading out from Africa, regional archaeological sequences cannot be constrained by any specific genetic OOA model.

**Reconciling Genetic and Archaeological Chronologies**

Both genomic and archaeological evidence are used to discuss the age of colonisation in different regions outside Africa. Some publications constrain archaeological and genomic interpretations against each other, creating stories largely from events that are congruent between the two data streams (e.g. Vallini et al., 2022; Tobler et al., 2023). This seems plausible in regions that currently have archaeological finds that are conformable with and taken as supporting specific genetically based dispersion models and chronologies. For example, a human skeleton excavated from Tianyuan Cave in northern China, and radiocarbon dated to c.40 kya, was identified as belonging to haplogroup B, and plausibly belonged to dispersing populations that were related to the ancestors of present-day peoples in both Asia and the Americas (Fu et al. 2013a). That individual was part of a lineage thought to have separated from European populations perhaps only a few thousand years earlier, giving a sense that colonisation of the region may not have been much earlier. Arrival of humans in East Asia at about 45 kya would be congruent with any of the models we have discussed, although those estimates are usually considered evidence of late-exit OOA dispersal of the ancestors of modern populations. Similar or even later ages are suggested for dispersal of *H. sapiens* into Southern China (e.g. Sun et al. 2021), and are also read as representing a single, late dispersion.

Other regions, distant from Africa, increasingly show evidence for occupation by *H. sapiens* prior to 60–70 kya, evidence that does not easily fit most late/single exit models of dispersion. We have already discussed skeletal fragments from Tam Pà Ling Cave in Laos likely to predate 65 kya and in Lida Ajer Cave in Sumatra that are likely older than 60 kya, as well as a number of sites in Australia and New Guinea that appear to predate 55 kya. If these sites indicate the presence of *H. sapiens* in these regions before 60–70 kya then they cannot be explained by the most extreme dates advocated for a single migration out of Africa in the period 40–65 kya.

This topic has been the focus of extended debates in Sahul. There, in the northern parts of the continent, basal levels of a number of sites have been inferred to have been occupied before than 50 kya, and in some cases before 55–60 kya (Clarkson et al. 2017; Norman et al. 2022). Researchers criticising those inferences have employed two arguments (e.g. O'Connell et al. 2018). The first is to hypothesise that all such sites within Sahul, as well as in Southeast Asia, are likely to have dating and identification errors. The second is to constrain possible dispersal chronology to the younger genomic dates proposed for a late event movement of *H. sapiens* OOA. The first concern must be addressed on a site-by-site basis, and remains an ongoing question. However, constraining acceptable archaeological dates for ancestral modern *H. sapiens* to 40–60 kya on the basis of current genomic estimates is not warranted, given the evidence and diversity of estimates we have discussed above. Genomic patterns as they are currently depicted have multiple plausible solutions. Given current imprecision in dating genomic and archaeological changes, in many instances, neither can be used to constrain the other.

It is also plausible that genomic and archaeological evidence are telling us about different aspects of human dispersions, and will not be necessarily congruent. Lineage splits do not date colonisation events and are often poorly located in space. More significantly lineage splits identified from modern genomes have sometimes traced the chronology of some ancestors and not others, as in the case of mtDNA. Moreover, they express only the history of extant lineages. Archaeological data on the other hand, has not been shown to be lineage sensitive for different dispersion events of *H. sapiens* from either Africa or Western Asia, and so archaeological phenomena are precisely located geographically but with uncertain taxonomic relationships. Importantly archaeological materials record extinct as well as extant lineages.

Those differences mean that some dispersing *H. sapiens* populations may have generated archaeological residues without leaving obvious, or even any (in the case of extinct lineages), signature in modern genomes. Archaeology may track dispersing groups whose genes have not yet been detected in Eurasian populations, and will leave a record of expansions that is not reflected in genomic analyses without large regional palaeogenomic data. That situation may make archaeological evidence for sapiens in any region appear older than genomic evidence indicates. Conversely, populations descended from lineages that dispersed from Africa/Western Asia relatively early might arrive relatively late in regions that were not previously occupied by *H. sapiens*, making regional archaeological records for a dispersion younger than genomic estimates for lineage splits. Disjunctions of this kind do not necessarily imply that one of the reconstructed chronologies must be in error. Disjunctions may instead contain information about migration histories.

## Conclusion

Both genomic and archaeological evidence record dispersions of *H. sapiens* eastward across Eurasia. Those records currently do not mirror each other, in part because they may be telling somewhat different stories. However, both indicate the dispersal was a complex process rather than a singular event.

Multiple species of the genus *Homo* evolved in Africa and left that continent to occupy Eurasia. This happened multiple times. Different species of hominids left Africa, each with different social lives and different technology. This indicates that those geographical expansions required only low thresholds for technology, social structure, and cognitive capacity.

Since *H. sapiens* evolved, in the last 300 kya, there have again been multiple migrations beyond Africa, establishing populations in Eurasia and in some times and places hybridising with other hominids, modifying the evolution of both species. Resident populations of sapiens existed outside Africa for much of that period, and perhaps persisted continuously in Western Asia.

Over that period the genome of *H. sapiens* evolved, with mutations creating new lineages, most often identified for mtDNA and Y chromosomes. Lineage differentiation and migration, together with hybridisation, helped generate both geographical and chronological variations in our species. The result was genomic differences between human populations within Africa and those outside, as well as between different regions across Eurasia. Genomic research reveals a complex story, in which populations carrying ancestral mtDNA spread from Africa or Western Asia one or more times in the period 45–100 kya, but those populations may have been descendants of, and had genetic contributions from, earlier populations of *H. sapiens* who were still living in Western Asia. Some populations may also have spread back from Western Asia into Africa. While global patterns of mtDNA reflect migrations spreading eastwards across Eurasia, genes flowed in other directions. Y chromosome lineages outside Africa descended from lineages that likely emerged in East Asia and then replaced forms across Eurasia, revealing a strong westward spread of people and/or genes. Genetic variation outside Africa was not created in a single, rapid process involving migrations in only one direction or in a single wave. Instead, the genetic evidence reveals sustained multi-directional interactions between population networks as well as population growth and migration. There were hubs of lineage differentiation in both Western and Eastern Eurasia, and perhaps in other localities.

Finally, we remind the reader of the limits on the data. In most cases, neither the speed of colonisation, nor the genetic identity of the colonisers, is well-understood, In many cases, in the critical 100–40 kya window, both archaeological and genetic data have low temporal resolution, making it impossible to precisely map one onto the other. Furthermore, while genetic data is taxon-specific, genetic events do not come with geographical tags. In contrast, archaeological data is geographically specific, but often taxon-ambiguous. There are apparent timing anomalies between different regions which, if real, are puzzling. For example, current evidence of *H. sapiens* is much later for portions of continental South and East Asia than in portions of island Southeast Asia and Sahul where geographical barriers to movement seem to have been more pronounced. Puzzles such as that remind us that we are exploring complex migration processes with sparse evidence gained from analytical approaches that are still being developed. The emerging picture is tantalising, but the evidence and inferences we currently have are preliminary and likely to change. Constraining genomic interpretations to select archaeological interpretations, or vice versa, is at this time a risky and potentially unprofitable procedure.

## References

Anil, Devara, Chauhan, Naveen, Ajithprasad, P, Devi, Monika, Mahesh, Vrushab, and Khan, Zakir. 2022 An early presence of modern human or convergent evolution? A 247 ka middle Palaeolithic Assemblage from Andhra Pradesh, India. *Journal of Archaeological Science, Reports* 45, 103565.

Argue, Debbie, Groves, Colin P., Lee, Michael S.Y., and Jungers, William L. 2017 The affinities of *Homo floresiensis* based on phylogenetic analyses of cranial, dental, and postcranial characters. *Journal of Human Evolution* 107, 107–33.

Arribas, Alfonso, and Palmqvist, Paul. 1999 On the ecological connection between Sabre-tooths and Hominids: Faunal dispersal events in the lower Pleistocene and a review of the evidence for the first human arrival in Europe. *Journal of Archaeological Science* 26, 571–85.

Bae, Christopher J, Wang, Wei, Zhao, Jianxin, Huang, Shengming, Tian, Feng, and Shen, Guanjun. 2014 Modern human teeth from late Pleistocene Luna cave (Guangxi, China). *Quaternary International* 354, 169–83.

Bar-Yosef, Ofer. 1998 The chronology of the Middle Paleolithic of the Levant, in *Neandertals and Modern Humans in Western Asia*, eds Akazawa, Takeru., Aoki, Kenichi, and Bar-Yosef, Ofer. New York: Plenum Press, 39–56.

Belmaker, Miriam. 2010 Early Pleistocene faunal connections between Africa and Eurasia: An ecological perspective, in *Out of Africa I. The First Hominin Colonization of Eurasia*, eds Fleagle, John, Shea, John, Grine, Frederick, Baden, Andrea, and Leakey, Richard. Dordrecht: Springer, 183–205.

Belmaker, Miriam, Tchernov, Eitan, Condemi, Silvana, and Bar-Yosef, Ofer. 2002 New evidence for hominid presence in the Lower Pleistocene of the Southern Levant. *Journal of Human Evolution* 43, 43–56.

Bergström, Anders, Stringer, Chris, Hajdinjak, Mateja, Scerri, Eleanor, and Skoglund, Pontus. 2021 Origins of modern human ancestry. *Nature* 590, 229–37.

Bromham, Lindell, Duchêne, Sebastián, Hua, Xia, Ritchie, Andrew, Duchêne, David, and Ho, Simon. 2017 Bayesian molecular dating: Opening up the black box. *Biological Reviews* 93, 1165–91.

Bromham, Lindell. 2019 Six impossible things before breakfast: Assumptions, models, and belief in molecular dating. *Trends in Ecology and Evolution* 34, 474–86.

Cabrera, Vincente, Marrero, Patricia, Abu-Amero, Khaled, and Larruga, Jose. 2018 Carriers of mitochondrial DNA macrohaplogroup L3 basal lineages migrated back to Africa from Asia around 70,000 years ago. *BMC Evolutionary Biology* 18, 1–16.

Cabrera, Vincente. 2023 Following the evolution of *Homo sapiens* across Africa using a uniparental genetic guide. *Medical Research Archives* 11, 1–20.

Clarkson, Chris, Harris, Clair, Li, Bo, Neudorf, Christina, Roberts, Richard, Lane, Christine, Norman, Kasih, Pal, Jagannath, Jones, Sacha, Shipton, Ceri, Koshy, Jinu, Gupta, M., Mishra, D., Dubey, A., Boivin, Nicole, and Petraglia, Michael. 2020 Human occupation of northern India spans the Toba super-eruption ~74,000 years ago. *Nature Communications* 11, 961.

Clarkson, Chris, Jacobs, Zenobia, Marwick, Ben, Fullagar, Richard, Wallis, Lynley, Smith, Mike, Roberts, Richard, Hayes, Elspeth, Lowe, Kelsey, Carah, Xavier, Florin, Anna, McNeil, Jessica, Cox, Delyth, Arnold, Lee, Hua, Quan, Huntley, Jillian, Brand, Helen, Manne, Tiina, Fairbairn, Andrew, Shulmeister, James, Lyle, Lindsey, Salinas, Makiah, Page, Mara, Connell, Kate, Park, Gayoung, Norman, Kasih, Murphy, Tessa, and Pardoe, Colin. 2017 Human occupation of northern Australia by 65,000 years ago. *Nature* 547, 306–10.

Darwin, Charles. 1871 *The Descent of Man, and Selection in Relation to Sex*. London: John Murray.

DeGiorgio, Michael, Jakobsson, Mattias, and Rosenbergn, Noah. 2009 Explaining worldwide patterns of human genetic variation using a coalescent-based serial founder model of migration outward from Africa. *Proceedings of the National Academy of Science* 106, 16057–62.

Fan, Shaohua, Spence, Jeffrey, Feng, Yuanqing, Hansen, Matthew, Terhorst, Jonathan, Beltrame, Marcia, Ranciaro, Alessia, Hirbo, Jibril, Beggs, William, Thomas, Neil, Nyambo, Thomas, Mpoloka, Sununguko, Mokone, Gaonyadiwe, Njamnshi, Alfred, Fokunang, Charles, Meskel, Dawit, Belay, Gurja, and Song, Yun. 2023 Whole-genome sequencing reveals a complex African population demographic history and signatures of local adaptation. *Cell* 186, 923–39.

Freidline, Sarah, Westaway, Kira, Joannes-Boyau, Renaud, Duringer, Philippe, Ponche, Jean-Luc, Morley, Mike, Hernandez, Vito, McAllister-Hayward, Meghan, McColl, Hugh, Zanolli, Clement, Gunz, Philipp, Bergmann, Inga, Sichanthongtip, Phonephanh, Sihanam, Daovee, Boualaphane, Souliphane, Luangkhoth, Thonglith, Souksavatdy, Viengkeo, Dosseto, Anthony, Boesch, Quentin, Patole-Edoumba, Elise, Aubaile, Francoise, Crozier, Francois, Suzzoni, Eric, Frangeul, Sebastien, Bourgon, Nicolas,

Zachwieja, Alexandra, Dunn, Tyler, Bacon, Anne-Marie, Hublin, Jean-Jaques, Shackelford, Laura, and Demeter, Fabrice. 2023 Early presence of *Homo sapiens* in Southeast Asia by 86–68 kyr at Tam Pà Ling, Northern Laos. *Nature Communications* 14, 3193.

Fu, Qiaomei, Posth, Cosimo, Hajdinjak, Mateja, Petr, Martin, Mallick, Swapan, Fernandes, Daniel, Furtwängler, Anja, Haak, Wolfgang, Meyer, Matthias, Mittnik, Alissa, Nickel, Birgit, Peltzer, Alexander, Rohland, Nadin, Slon, Viviane, Talamo, Sahra, Lazaridis, Iosif, Lipson, Mark, Mathieson, Iain, Schiffels, Stephan, Skoglund, Pontus, Derevianko, Anatoly, Drozdov, Nikolai, Slavinsky, Vyacheslav, Tsybankov, Alexander, Cremonesi, Renata, Mallegni, Francesco, Gély, Bernard, Vacca, Eligio, Morales, Manuel, Straus, Lawrence, Neugebauer-Maresch, Christine, Teschler-Nicola, Maria, Constantin, Silviu, Moldovan, Oana, Benazzi, Stefano, Peresani, Marco, Coppola, Donato, Lari, Martina, Ricci, Stefano, Ronchitelli, Annamaria, Valentin, Frédérique, Thevenet, Corinne, Wehrberger, Kurt, Grigorescu, Dan, Rougier, Hélène, Crevecoeur, Isabelle, Flas, Damien, Semal, Patrick, Mannino, Marcello, Cupillard, Christophe, Bocherens, Hervé, Conard, Nicholas, Harvati, Katerina, Moiseyev, Vyacheslav, Drucker, Dorothée, Svoboda, Jiří, Richards, Michael, Caramelli, David, Pinhasi, Ron, Kelso, Janet, Patterson, Nick, Krause, Johannes, Pääbo, Svante, and Reich, David. 2016 The genetic history of Ice Age Europe. *Nature* 534, 200–05.

Fu, Qiaomei, Meyer, Matthias, Gao, Xing, Stenzel, Udo, Burbano, Harnan, Kelso, Janet, and Pääbo, Svante. 2013a DNA analysis of an early modern human from Tianyuan Cave, China. *Proceedings of the National Academy of Science* 110, 2223–7.

Fu, Qiaomei, Mittnik, Alissa, Johnson, Philip, Bos, Kirsten, Lari, Martina, Bollongino, Ruth, Sun, Chengkai, Giemsch, Liane, Schmitz, Ralf, Burger, Joachim, Ronchitelli, Anna, Martini, Fabio, Cremonesi, Renata, Svoboda, Jiri, Bauer, Peter, Caramelli, David, Castellano, Sergi, Reich, David, Pabo, Svante, and Krause, Johannes. 2013b A revised timescale for human evolution based on ancient mitochondrial genomes. *Current Biology* 23, 553–9.

Ge, Junyi, Deng, Chenglong, Wang, Yuan, Shao, Qingfeng, Zhou, Xinying, Xing, Song, Pang, Haijiao, and Jin, Changzhu. 2020 Climate-influenced cave deposition and human occupation during the Pleistocene in Zhiren Cave, Southwest China. *Quaternary International* 559, 14–23.

Groucutt, Huw, Scerri, Eleanor, Stringer, Chris, and Petraglia, Michael. 2019 Skhul Lithic technology and the dispersal of *Homo sapiens* into Southwest Asia. *Quaternary International* 515, 30–52.

Grün, Rainer, Brink, James, Spooner, Nigel, Taylor, Lois, Stringer, Chris, Franciscus, Robert, and Murray, Andrew. 1996 Direct dating of Florisbad hominid. *Nature* 382, 500–1.

Haber, Marc, Jones, Abigail, Connell, Bruce. Asan, Arciero, Elena, Yang, Huanming, Thomas, Mark, Xue, Yali, and Tyler-Smith, Chris. 2019 A rare deep-rooting D0 African Y-chromosomal haplogroup and its implications for the expansion of modern humans Out of Africa. *Genetics* 212, 1421–8.

Hallast, Pille, Agdzhoyan, Anastasia, Balanovsky, Oleg, Xue, Yali, Tyler, and Smith, Chris. 2021a A Southeast Asian origin for present-day non-African human Y chromosomes. *Human Genetics* 140, 299–307.

Hallast, Pille, Agdzhoyan, Anastasia, Balanovsky, Oleg, Xue, Yali, Tyler, and Smith, Chris. 2021b Early replacement of West Eurasian male Y chromosomes from the east. *BioRxiv*. https://doi.org/10.1101/867317

Harvati, Katerina, Röding, Carolin, Bosman, Abel, Karakostis, Fotios, Grün, Rainer, Stringer, Chris, Karkanas, Panagiotis, Thompson, Nicholas, Koutoulidis, Vassilis, Moulopoulos, Lia, Gorgoulis, Vassilis, and Kouloukoussa, Mirsini. 2019 Apidima Cave fossils provide earliest evidence of *Homo sapiens* in Eurasia. *Nature* 571, 500–4.

Haslam, Michael, Oppenheimer, Stephen, and Korisettar, Ravi. 2018 Out of Africa, into South Asia: A review of archaeological and genetic evidence for the dispersal of *Homo sapiens* into the Indian subcontinent, in *Beyond Stones and More Stones: Defining Indian Prehistoric Archaeology*, ed Korisettar, Ravi. Bangalore: Mythic Press.

Henn, Brenna, Cavalli-Sforza, Luigi, and Feldman, Marcus. 2012 The great human expansion. *Proceedings of the National Academy of Science* 109, 17758–64.

Henn, Brenna, Steele, Teresa, and Weaver, Timothy. 2018 Clarifying distinct models of modern human origins in Africa. *Current Opinions in Genetic Development* 53, 148–56.

Hershkovitz, Israel, Weber, Gerhard, Quam, Rolf, Duval, Mathieu, Grün, Rainer, Kinsley, Leslie, Ayalon, Avner, Bar-Matthews, Miriam, Valladas, Helene, Mercier, Norbert, Arsuaga, Juan, Martinón-Torres, Maria, Bermúdez de Castro, Jose, Fornai, Cinzia, Martín-Francés, Laura, Sarig, Rachel, May, Hila, Krenn, Viktoria, Slon, Viviane, Rodríguez, Laura, García, Rebecca, Lorenzo, Carlos, Carretero, Jose, Frumkin, Amos, Shahack-Gross, Ruth, Bar-Yosef Mayer, Daniella, Cui, Yaming, Wu, Xinzhi, Peled, Natan, Groman-Yaroslavski, Iris, Weissbrod, Lior, Yeshurun, Reuven, Tsatskin, Alexander, Zaidner,

Yossi, and Weinstein-Evron, Mina. 2018 The earliest modern humans outside Africa. *Science* 359, 456–9.

Ho, Simon, Lanfear, Robert, Bromham, Lindell, Phillips, Matthew, Soubrier, Julien, Rodrigo, Allen, and Cooper, Alan. 2011 Time-dependent rates of molecular evolution. *Molecular Ecology* 20, 3087–101.

Jakobsson, Mattias, Scholz, Sonja, Scheet, Paul, Gibbs, Raphael, VanLiere, Jenna, Fung, Hon-Chung, Szpiech, Zachary, Degnan, James, Wang, Kai, Guerreiro, Rita, Bras, Jose, Schymick, Jennifer, Hernandez, Dena, Traynor, Bryan, Simon-Sanchez, Javier, Matarin, Mar, Britton, Angela, van de Leemput, Joyce, Rafferty, Ian, Bucan, Maja, Cann, Howard, Hardy, John, Rosenberg, Noah, and Singleton, Andrew. 2008 Genotype, haplotype and copy-number variation in world-wide human populations. *Nature* 451, 998–1003.

Jobling, Mark, and Tyler-Smith, Chris. 2017 Human Y-chromosome variation in the genome-sequencing era. *Nature Reviews Genetics* 18, 485–97.

Kandel, Andrew, Bolus, Michael, Bretzke, Knut, Bruch, Angela, Haidle, Miriam, Hertler, Christine, and Michael, Märker. 2016 Increasing behavioral flexibility? An integrative macro-scale approach to understanding the middle Stone Age of Southern Africa. *Journal of Archaeological Method and Theory* 23, 623–68.

Kim, Bernard, and Lohmueller, Kirk. 2015 Selection and reduced population size cannot explain higher amounts of Neanderthal ancestry in East Asian than in European human populations. *American Journal of Human Genetics* 96, 454–461.

Klein, Richard. 1999 *The Human Career: Human Biological and Cultural Origins*. Chicago: University of Chicago Press.

Kuhlwilm, Martin, Gronau, Ilan, Hubisz, Melissa, de Filippo, Cesare, Prado-Martinez, Javier, Kircher, Martin, Fu, Qiaomei, Burbano, Hernán, Lalueza-Fox, Carles, de la Rasilla, Marco, Rosas, Antonio, Rudan, Pavao, Brajkovic, Dejana, Kucan, Željko, Gušic, Ivan, Marques-Bonet, Tomas, Andrés, Aida, Viola, Bence, Pääbo, Svante, Meyer, Matthias, Siepel, Adam, and Castellano, Sergi. 2016 Ancient gene flow from early modern humans into Eastern Neanderthals. *Nature* 530, 429–33.

Lazaridis, Iosif, Nadel, Dani, Rollefson, Gary, Merrett, Deborah, Rohland, Nadin, Mallick, Swapan, Fernandes, Daniel, Novak, Mario, Gamarra, Beatriz, Sirak, Kendra, Connell, Sarah, Stewardson, Kristin, Harney, Eadaoin, Fu, Qiaomei, Gonzalez-Fortes, Gloria, Jones, Eppie, Roodenberg, Songül, Lengyel, György, Bocquentin, Fanny, Gasparian, Boris, Monge, Janet, Gregg, Michael, Eshed, Vered, Mizrahi, Ahuva-Sivan, Meiklejohn, Christopher, Gerritsen, Fokke, Bejenaru, Luminita, Blüher, Matthias, Campbell, Archie, Cavalleri, Gianpiero, Comas, David, Froguel, Philippe, Gilbert, Edmund, Kerr, Shona, Kovacs, Peter, Krause, Johannes, McGettigan, Darren, Merrigan, Michael, Merriwether, Andrew, O'Reilly, Seamus, Richards, Martin, Semino, Ornella, Shamoon-Pour, Michel, Stefanescu, Gheorghe, Stumvoll, Michael, Tönjes, Anke, Torroni, Antonio, Wilson, James, Yengo, Loic, Hovhannisyan, Nelli, Patterson, Nick, Pinhasi, Ron, and Reich, David 2016. Genomic insights into the origin of farming in the ancient Near East. *Nature* 536: 419–24.

Li, Jun, Absher, Devin, Tang, Hua, Southwick, Audrey, Casto, Amanda, Ramachandran, Sohini, Cann, Howard, Barsh, Gregory, Feldman, Marcus, Cavalli-Sforza, Luigi, and Myers, Richard. 2008 Worldwide human relationships inferred from genome-wide patterns of variation. *Science* 319, 1100–4.

Lipson, Mark, Ribot, Isabelle, Mallick, Swapan, Rohland, Nadin, Olalde, Iñigo, Adamski, Nicole, Broomandkhoshbacht, Nasreen, Lawson, Ann, López, Saioa, Oppenheimer, Jonas, Stewardson, Kristin, Asombang, Raymond, Bocherens, Hervé, Bradman, Neil, Culleton, Brendan, Cornelissen, Els, Crevecoeur, Isabelle, de Maret, Pierre, Fomine, Forka, Lavachery, Philippe, Mindzie, Christophe, Orban, Rosine, Sawchuk, Elizabeth, Semal, Patrick, Thomas, Mark, Van Neer, Wim, Veeramah, Krishna, Kennett, Douglas, Patterson, Nick, Hellenthal, Garrett, Lalueza-Fox, Carles, MacEachern, Scott, Prendergast, Mary, and Reich, David. 2020 Ancient West African foragers in the context of African population history. *Nature* 577, 665–70.

Liu, Wu, Jin, Chang-Zhu, Zhang, Ying-Qi, Cai, Yan-Jun, Xing, Song, Wua, Xiu-Jie, Cheng, Hai, Edwards, Lawrence, Pan, Wen-Shi, Qin, Da-Gong, An, Zhi-Sheng, Trinkausg, Erik, and Wu, Xin-Zhi. 2010 Human remains from Zhirendong, South China, and modern human emergence in East Asia. *Proceedings of the National Academy of Science* 107, 19201–6.

Liu, Wu, Martinón-Torres, María, Cai, Yan-jun, Xing, Song, Tong, Hao-wen, Pei, Shu-wen, Jan Sier, Mark, Wu, Xiao-hong, Edwards, Lawrence, Cheng, Hai, Li, Yi-yuan, Yang, Xiong-xin, Bermúdez de Castro, José, and Wu, Xiu-jie. 2015 The earliest unequivocally modern humans in southern China. *Nature* 526, 696–9.

Lordkipanidze, David, Ponce de León, Marcia S., Margvelashvili, Ann, Rak, Yoel, Rightmire, G. Philip, Vekua, Abesalom, and Zollikofer, Christoph P. E. 2013 A complete skull from Dmanisi, Georgia, and the evolutionary biology of early homo. *Science* 342, 326–31.

Malaspinas, Anna-Sapfo, Westaway, Michael, Muller, Craig, Sousa, Vitor, Lao, Oscar, Alves, Isabel, Bergström, Anders, Athanasiadis, Georgios, Cheng, Jade, Crawford, Jacob, Heupink, Tim, Macholdt, Enrico, Peischl, Stephan, Rasmussen, Simon, Schiffels, Stephan, Subramanian, Sankar, Wright, Joanne, Albrechtsen, Anders, Barbieri, Chiara, Dupanloup, Isabelle, Eriksson, Anders, Margaryan, Ashot, Moltke, Ida, Pugach, Irina, Korneliussen, Thorfinn, Levkivskyi, Ivan, Moreno-Mayar, Víctor, Ni, Shengyu, Racimo, Fernando, Sikora, Martin, Xue, Yali, Aghakhanian, Farhang, Brucato, Nicolas, Brunak, Søren, Campos, Paula, Clark, Warren, Ellingvåg, Sturla, Fourmile, Gudjugudju, Gerbault, Pascale, Injie, Darren, Koki, George, Leavesley, Matthew, Logan, Betty, Lynch, Aubrey, Matisoo-Smith, Elizabeth, McAllister, Peter, Mentzer, Alexander, Metspalu, Mait, Migliano, Andrea, Murgha, Les, Phipps, Maude, Pomat, William, Reynolds, Doc, Ricaut, Francois-Xavier, Siba, Peter, Thomas, Mark, Wales, Thomas, Wall, Colleen, Oppenheimer, Stephen, Tyler-Smith, Chris, Durbin, Richard, Dortch, Joe, Manica, Andrea, Schierup, Mikkel, Foley, Robert, Lahr, Marta, Bowern, Claire, Wall, Jeffrey, Mailund, Thomas, Stoneking, Mark, Nielsen, Rasmus, Sandhu, Manjinder, Excoffier, Laurent, Lambert, David, and Willerslev, Eske. 2016 A genomic history of Aboriginal Australia. *Nature* 538, 207–14.

Mallick, Swapan, Li, Heng, Lipson, Mark, Mathieson, Iain, Gymrek, Melissa, Racimo, Fernando, Zhao, Mengyao, Chennagiri, Niru, Nordenfelt, Susanne, Tandon, Arti, Skoglund, Pontus, Lazaridis, Iosif, Sankararaman, Sriram, Fu, Qiaomei, Rohland, Nadin, Renaud, Gabriel, Erlich, Yaniv, Willems, Thomas, Gallo, Carla, Spence, Jeffrey, Song, Yun, Poletti, Giovanni, Balloux, Francois, van Driem, George, de Knijff, Peter, Romero, Irene, Jha, Aashish, Behar, Doron, Bravi, Claudio, Capelli, Cristian, Hervig, Tor, Moreno-Estrada, Andres, Posukh, Olga, Balanovska, Elena, Balanovsky, Oleg, Karachanak-Yankova, Sena, Sahakyan, Hovhannes, Toncheva, Draga, Yepiskoposyan, Levon, Tyler-Smith, Chris, Xue, Yali, Abdullah, Syafiq, Ruiz-Linares, Andres, Beall, Cynthia, Di Rienzo, Anna, Jeong, Choongwon, Starikovskaya, Elena, Metspalu, Ene, Parik, Jüri, Villems, Richard, Henn, Brenna, Hodoglugil, Ugur, Mahley, Robert, Sajantila, Antti, Stamatoyannopoulos, George, Wee, Joseph, Khusainova, Elza, Khusnutdinova, Rita, Litvinov, Sergey, Ayodo, George, Comas, David, Hammer, Michael, Kivisild, Toomas, Klitz, William, Winkler, Cheryl, Labuda, Damian, Bamshad, Michael, Jorde, Lynn, Tishkoff, Sarah, Watkins, Scott, Metspalu, Mait, Dryomov, Stanislav, Sukernik, Rem, Singh, Lalji, Thangaraj, Kumarasamy, Pääbo, Svante, Kelso, Janet, Patterson, Nick, and Reich, David. 2016 The Simons genome diversity project: 300 genomes from 142 diverse populations. *Nature* 538, 201–6.

Marrero, Patricia, Abu-Amero, Khaled, Larruga, Jose, and Cabrera, Vicente. 2016 Carriers of human mitochondrial DNA macrohaplogroup M colonized India from Southeastern Asia. *BMC Evolutionary Biology* 16, 246.

McBrearty, Sally, and Brooks, Alison. 2000 The revolution that wasn't: A new interpretation of the origin of modern human behavior. *Journal of Human Evolution* 39, 453–563.

McDougall, Ian, Brown, Francis, and Fleagle, John. 2005 Stratigraphic placement and age of modern humans from Kibish, Ethiopia. *Nature* 433, 733–6.

Mellars, Paul, Gori, Kevin, Carr, Martin, Soares, Pedro, and Richards, Martin. 2013 Genetic and archaeological perspectives on the initial modern human colonization of Southern Asia. *Proceedings of the National Academy of Science* 110, 10699–704.

Meyer, Matthias, Fu, Qiaomei, Aximu-Petri, Ayinuer, Glocke, Isabelle, Nickel, Birgit, Arsuaga, Juan-Luis, Martinez, Ignacio, Gracia, Ana, Bermudez de Castro, Jose, Carbonell, Eudald, and Paabo, Svante. 2014 A mitochondrial genome sequence of a hominin from Sima de los Huesos. *Nature* 505, 403–6.

Mishra, S, Chauhan, N., and Singhvi, A.K. 2013 Continuity of microblade technology in the Indian subcontinent since 45 ka: Implications for the dispersal of modern humans. *PLoS ONE* 8, e69280.

Montinaro, Francesco, Pankratov, Vasili, Yelmen, Burak, Pagani, Luca, and Mondal, Mayukh. 2021 Revisiting the out of Africa event with a deep learning approach. *The American Journal of Human Genetics* 108, 2037–51.

Mounier, Aurélien, and Lahr, Marta. 2019 Deciphering African late middle Pleistocene hominin diversity and the origin of our species. *Nature Communications* 10, 3406.

Norman, Kasih, Shipton, Ceri, O'Connor, Sue, Malanali, W., Collins, P., Wood, R., Saktura, W.M., Roberts, R.G., and Jacobs, Z. 2022 Human occupation of the Kimberley coast of northwest Australia by 50,000 years ago. *Quaternary Science Reviews* 288, 107577.

O'Connell, James, Allen, Jim, Williams, Martin, Williams, Alan, Turney, Chris, Spooner, Nigel, Kamminga, Johan, Brown, Graham, and Cooper, Alan. 2018 When did *Homo sapiens* first reach Southeast Asia and Sahul? *Proceedings of the National Academy of Science* 115, 8482–90.

Pagani, Luca, Lawson, Daniel John, Jagoda, Evelyn, Mörseburg, Alexander, Eriksson, Anders, Mitt, Mario, Clemente, Florian, Hudjashov, Georgi, DeGiorgio, Michael, Saag, Lauri, Wall, Jeffrey, Cardona, Alexia, Mägi, Reedik, Wilson Sayres, Melissa, Kaewert, Sarah, Inchley, Charlotte, Scheib, Christiana, Järve, Mari, Karmin, Monika, Jacobs, Guy, Antao, Tiago, Mircea, Florin, Iliescu, Kushniarevich, Alena, Ayub, Qasim, Tyler-Smith, Chris, Xue, Yali, Yunusbayev, Bayazit, Tambets, Kristiina, Mallick, Chandana, Saag, Lehti, Pocheshkhova, Elvira, Andriadze, George, Muller, Craig, Westaway, Michael, Lambert, David, Zoraqi, Grigor, Turdikulova, Shahlo, Dalimova, Dilbar, Sabitov, Zhaxylyk, Sultana, Gazi, Lachance, Joseph, Tishkoff, Sarah, Momynaliev, Kuvat, Isakova, Jainagul, Damba, Larisa, Gubina, Marina, Nymadawa, Pagbajabyn, Evseeva, Irina, Atramentova, Lubov, Utevska, Olga, Ricaut, François-Xavier, Brucato, Nicolas, Sudoyo, Herawati, Letellier, Thierry, Cox, Murray, Barashkov, Nikolay, Škaro, Vedrana, Mulahasanovic, Lejla, Primorac, Dragan, Sahakyan, Hovhannes, Mormina, Maru, Eichstaedt, Christina, Lichman, Daria, Abdullah, Syafiq, Chaubey, Gyaneshwer, Wee, Joseph, Mihailov, Evelin, Karunas, Alexandra, Litvinov, Sergei, Khusainova, Rita, Ekomasova, Natalya, Akhmetova, Vita, Khidiyatova, Irina, Marjanovi, Damir, Yepiskoposyan, Levon, Behar, Doron, Balanovska, Elena, Metspalu, Andres, Derenko, Miroslava, Malyarchuk, Boris, Voevoda, Mikhail, Fedorova, Sardana, Osipova, Ludmila, Lahr, Marta, Gerbault, Pascale, Leavesley, Matthew, Migliano, Andrea, Petraglia, Michael, Balanovsky, Oleg, Khusnutdinova, Elza, Metspalu, Ene, Thomas, Mark, Manica, Andrea, Nielsen, Rasmus, Villems, Richard, Willerslev, Eske, Kivisild, Toomas, and Metspalu1, Mait. 2016 Genomic analyses inform on migration events during the peopling of Eurasia. *Nature* 538, 238–42.

Petr, Martin, Pääbo, Svante, Kelso, Janet, and Vernot, Benjamin. 2019 Limits of long-term selection against Neandertal introgression. *Proceedings of the National Academy of Science* 116, 1639–44.

Posth, Cosimo, Wißing, Christoph, Kitagawa, Keiko, Pagani, Luca, van Holstein, Laura, Racimo, Fernando, Wehrberger, Kurt, Conard, Nicholas, Kind, Claus, Bocherens, Hervé, and Krause, Johannes. 2017 Deeply divergent archaic mitochondrial genome provides lower time boundary for African gene flow into Neanderthals. *Nature Communications* 8, 16046.

Prüfer, Kay, Racimo, Fernando, Patterson, Nick, Jay, Flora, Sankararaman, Sriram, Sawyer, Susanna, Heinze, Anja, Renaud, Gabriel, Sudmant, Peter, de Filippo, Cesare, Li, Heng, Mallick, Swapan, Dannemann, Michael, Fu, Qiaomei, Kircher, Martin, Kuhlwilm, Martin, Lachmann, Michael, Meyer, Matthias, Ongyerth, Matthias, Siebauer, Michael, Theunert, Christoph, Tandon, Arti, Moorjani, Priya, Pickrell, Joseph, and Pääbo, Svante. 2014 The complete genome sequence of a Neanderthal from the Altai Mountains. *Nature* 505, 43–49.

Ramachandran, Sohini, Deshpande, Omkar, Roseman, Charles, Rosenberg, Noah, Feldman, Marcus, and Cavalli-Sforza, Luca. 2005 Support from the relationship of genetic and geographic distance in human populations for a serial founder effect originating in Africa. *Proceedings of the National Academy of Science* 102, 15942–7.

Richter, Daaniel, Grün, Rainer, Joannes-Boyau, Renaud, Steele, Teresa, Amani, Fethi, Rué, Mathieu, Fernandes, Paul, Raynal, Jean-Paul, Geraads, Denis, Ben-Ncer, Abdelouahed, Hublin, Jean-Jacques, and McPherron, Shannon. 2017 The age of the hominin fossils from Jebel Irhoud, Morocco, and the origins of the Middle Stone Age. *Nature* 546, 293–6.

Rightmire, Philip, Ponce de León, Marcia S, Lordkipanidze, David, Margvelashvili, Ann, and Zollikofer, Christoph. E. 2017. Skull 5 from Dmanisi: Descriptive anatomy, comparative studies, and evolutionary significance. *Journal of Human Evolution* 104, 50–79. https://doi.org/10.1016/j.jhevol.2017.01.005 [Epub 2017].

Rogers, Alan, Bohlender, Ryan, and Huff, Chad. 2017 Early history of Neanderthals and Denisovans. *Proceedings of the National Academy of Sciences* 114, 9859–63.

Scally, Aylwyn, and Durbin, Richard. 2012 Revising the human mutation rate: Implications for understanding human evolution. *National Review of Genetics* 13, 745–53.

Schaefer, Nathan, Shapiro, Beth, and Green, Richard. 2021 An ancestral recombination graph of human, Neanderthal, and Denisovan genomes. *Science Advances* 7, 1–16.

Schiffels, Stephan, and Durbin, Richard. 2014 Inferring human population size and separation history from multiple genome sequences. *Nature Genetics* 46, 919–25.

Seguin-Orlando, Andaine, Korneliussen, Thorfinn, Sikora, Martin, Malaspinas, Anna-Sapfo, Manica, Andrea, Moltke, Ida, Albrechtsen, Anders, Ko, Amy, Margaryan, Ashot, Moiseyev, Vyacheslav, Goebel,

Ted, Westaway, Michael, Lambert, David, Khartanovich, Valeri, Wall, Jeffrey, Nigst, Philip, Foley, Robert, Lahr, Marta, Nielsen, Rasmus, Orlando, Ludovic, and Willerslev, Eske. 2014 Paleogenomics. Genomic structure in Europeans dating back at least 36,200 years. *Science* 346, 1113–8.

Shen, Guanjun, Wu, Xianzhu, Wang, Qian, Tu, Hua, Feng, Yue-xin, and Zhao, Jian-xin. 2013 Mass spectrometric U-series dating of Huanglong cave in Hubei Province, Central China: Evidence for early presence of modern humans in eastern Asia. *Journal of Human Evolution* 65, 162–7.

Sikora, Martin, Pitulko, Vladimir, Sousa, Vitor, Allentoft, Morten, Vinner, Lasse, Rasmussen, Simon, Margaryan, Ashot, de Barros Damgaard, Peter, de la Fuente, Constanza, Renaud, Gabriel, Yang, Melinda, Fu, Qiaomei, Dupanloup, Isabelle, Giampoudakis, Konstantinos, Nogués-Bravo, David, Rahbek, Carsten, Kroonen, Guus, Peyrot, Michaël, McColl, Hugh, Vasilyev, Sergey, Veselovskaya, Elizaveta, Gerasimova, Margarita, Pavlova, Elena, Chasnyk, Vyacheslav, and Willerslev, Eske. 2019 The population history of northeastern Siberia since the Pleistocene. *Nature* 570, 182–8.

Slatkin, Montgomery. 2008 Linkage disequilibrium—Understanding the evolutionary past and mapping the medical future. *Nature Reviews Genetics* 9, 477–85.

Soares, Pedro, Alshamali, Farida, Pereira, Joana, Fernandes, Verónica, Silva, Nuno, Afonso, Carla, Costa, Marta, Musilová, Eliska, Macaulay, Vincent, Richards, Martin, Černý, Viktor, and Pereira, Luísa. 2012 The expansion of mtDNA Haplogroup L3 within and out of Africa. *Molecular Biology and Evolution* 29, 915–27.

Sun, Xue-feng, Wen, Shao-qing, Lu, Cheng-qiu, Zhou, Bo-yan, Curnoe, Darren, Lu, Hua-yu, Hong-chun, Li, Wang, Wei, Cheng, Hai, Yi, Shuang-wen, Jia, Xin, Du, Pan-xin, Xu, Xing-hua, Lu, Yi-ming, Lu, Ying, Zheng, Hong-xiang, Zhang, Hong, Sun, Chang, Wei, Lan-hai, Han, Fei, Huang, Juan, Edwards, Lawrence, Jin, Li, and Li, Hui. 2021 Ancient DNA and multimethod dating confirm the late arrival of anatomically modern humans in southern China. *Proceedings of the National Academy of Science* 2021, e2019158118.

Tappen, Martha. 2009 The wisdom of the aged and Out of Africa 1, in *Transitions in Prehistory: Essays in Honor of Ofer Bar-Yosef*, eds. Shea, John, and Daniel, Lieberman. Oxford: Oxbow Books for the American Schools of Prehistoric Research.

Tassi, Francesca, Ghirotto, Silvia, Mezzavilla, Massimo, Vilaça, Sibelle, De Santi, Lisa, and Barbujani, Guido. 2015 Early modern human dispersal from Africa: Genomic evidence for multiple waves of migration. *Investigative Genetics* 6, 1–16.

Tobler, Raymond, Souilmi, Yassine, Huber, Christian, Bean, Nigel, Turney, Chris, Grey, Shane, and Cooper, Alan. 2023 The role of genetic selection and climatic factors in the dispersal of anatomically modern humans out of Africa. *Proceedings of the National Academy of Science* 120, e2213061120.

Vallini, Leonardo, Marciani, Giulia, Aneli, Serena, Bortolini, Eugenio, Benazzi, Stefano, Pievani, Telmo, and Pagani, Luca. 2022 Genetics and material culture support repeated expansions into Paleolithic Eurasia from a Population Hub Out of Africa. *Genome Biology and Evolution* 14. https://doi.org/10.1093/gbe/evac045

Vanhaeran, Mariah, d'Errico, Francesco, Stringer, Chris, James, Sarah, Todd, Jonathan, and Mienis, Henk. 2006 Middle Paleolithic Shell beads in Palestine and Algeria. *Science* 312, 1785–8.

Westaway, K. E., Louys, J., Due Awe, R., Morwood, M., Price, G., Zhao, J., Aubert, M., Joannes-Boyau, R., Smith, M., Skinner, M., Compton, T., Bailey, R., van den Bergh, G., de Vos, J., Pike, A., Stringer, C., Saptomo, E., Rizal, Y., Zaim, J., Santoso, W., Trihascaryo, A., Kinsley, L., and Sulistyanto, B. 2017 An early modern human presence in Sumatra 73,000–63,000 years ago. *Nature* 548, 322–5.

Will, Manuel, Mackay, Alex, and Phillips, Natasha. 2015 Implications of Nubian-like core reduction systems in southern Africa for the identification of early modern human dispersals. *PLoS ONE* 10: e0131824.

Yang, Melinda, Gao, Xing, Theunert, Christoph, Tong, Haowen, Aximu-Petri, Ayinuer, Nickel, Birgit, Slatkin, Montgomery, Meyer, Matthias, Pääbo, Svante, Kelso, Janet, and Fu, Qiaomei. 2017 40,000-year-old individual from Asia provides insight into early population structure in Eurasia. *Current Biology* 27, e3209.

Zhu, Zhaoyu, Dennell, Robin, Huang, Weiwen, Wu, Yi, Qiu, Shifan, Yang, Shixia, Rao, Zhiguo, Hou, Yamei, Xie, Jiubing, Han, Jiangwei, and Ouyang, Tingping. 2018 Hominin occupation of the Chinese Loess Plateau since about 2.1 million years ago. *Nature* 559, 608–12.

# 2

# THE COLONISATION OF SOUTH ASIA BY *HOMO SAPIENS*

Assessing Alternative Hypotheses through Cladistic Analyses of Lithic Assemblages

*Chris Clarkson, Ravi Korisettar, Ceri Shipton, Mark Collard, and Briggs Buchannan*

### Introduction

Some of the most important questions about the colonisation of South Asia by modern humans remain unanswered. For example, we are uncertain about which route or routes were used, nor the economy and technology in place at the time. The situation is made more difficult by a dearth of sites, and a total absence of fossils dated to the relevant time period, which is 100–40 ka before present (BP). The humid tropical environment of South Asia is not conducive to the preservation of organic materials like human bone and items of material culture that may be indicative of modern human artisanship. At present, a huge temporal gap exists between the archaic Hathnora skullcap (dated at around 400 ka) and the oldest known modern human remains from Fa Hien Lena Cave in Sri Lanka dated to around 35–46 ka (Wedage et al. 2019a, 2019b; Kennedy 2000). The genetic record from modern populations and more limited ancient DNA also indicates a disjunct between estimates for Out of Africa of c.50–72 ka (Malaspinas et al. 2016; Mallick et al. 2016), vestiges of an earlier Out of Africa dispersal preserved in Neanderthal and modern genomes (Kuhlwilm et al. 2016; Pagani et al. 2016; Posth et al. 2017), and the burgeoning modern human fossil record pointing to one or more exits from Africa between 200 and 100 ka (Schwarcz et al. 1988; Stringer et al. 1989; Grün et al. 2005; Demeter et al. 2012; Liu et al. 2015; Westaway et al. 2017; Groucutt et al. 2018; Hershkovitz et al. 2018; Shackelford et al. 2018; Harvati et al. 2019). Solving the problem of modern human arrival in South Asia has therefore fallen largely on archaeology, and comparative investigations of stone technology in particular. Work at numerous sites in India has centred on finding and dating sites in this crucial 100–40 ka temporal window and documenting the stone technologies present in those sites with a view to determining the identity of their hominin creators. However, stone tool technology is notoriously unreliable for determining hominin species (Foley and Lahr 2003). This is especially so given that there is much overlap in the technology and behavioural capabilities of Neanderthals and contemporaneous sub-Saharan modern humans, and that there are clear signs of convergence in stone technology throughout later human evolution (Clarkson et al. 2018). South Asia also offered a unique environment compared to what the colonists would have been familiar with farther west and hence adaptation likely transformed toolkits. All of these factors may confound a technological signal for a given hominin species. However, as Clarkson (2014) has argued, such a signal may nevertheless exist and is worth the search. It is still early days in the quest for definitive answers to the question of 'when, how and with what did *Homo sapiens* arrive in South Asia?'

In the present paper we review hypotheses about the colonisation of South Asia by modern humans, discuss key sites across the subcontinent that fall into the 100–40 ka temporal window for the possible arrival of modern humans, and examine the associated stone artefact industries. From this review, we attempt to draw some preliminary conclusions about when modern humans may first have arrived in South Asia, presenting finds from key sites and an analysis in which we used a suite of methods from evolutionary biology called cladistics to test between three key hypotheses: (1) that modern humans arrived after 60 ka with a Howeisons' Poort-like microlithic technology; (2) that modern humans arrived at least 100–200 ka with a Middle Stone Age (MSA) (also known as Middle Palaeolithic outside of Africa) toolkit featuring Levallois and handaxe technology; and (3) that modern humans arrived between 100 and 50 ka with an essentially sub-Saharan African MSA technology that included recurrent Levallois and point technology.

## Out of Africa and Entry into South Asia: Hypotheses

In the last few years, archaeologists have put forward three competing models of the process by which *H. sapiens* colonised the Middle East, Europe, Asia, and Australasia. Mellars (2006) and Mellars et al. (2013) have argued that *H. sapiens* left Africa sometime after 60 ka with a distinctive, Howeisons' Poort-like microlithic technology, arriving in South Asia by around 50 ka. Other cultural components, he suggests, included engraved cross-hatched designs, bone or antler projectile technology, and the manufacture of perforated disc-shaped beads. Mellars (2006) and Mellars et al. (2013) contend that this package was lost *en route* to Southeast Asia and Australia due to successive founder effect and changes in raw material availability, resulting in a much-simplified technology arriving in Australia without microlithic artefacts. For the purposes of this paper, we will call this the *Late out of Africa with microlithic technology* model.

Another possibility is that modern human lineages populated Eurasia, including India, at least 100–200 ka, consistent with the early modern human fossil evidence from Greece, China, and Israel (Schwarcz et al. 1988; Valladas et al. 1988; Stringer et al. 1989; Grün et al. 2005; Liu et al. 2015; Hershkovitz et al. 2018; Harvati et al. 2019). These studies point to one or more periods, perhaps climatically driven, in which *H. sapiens* moved out of Africa and either became extinct or interbred with later populations of anatomically modern humans. In Africa, assemblages of this age contain Levallois and handaxe technology (Garrod 1937; Groucutt 2018 Sahle et al. 2019). In India, contemporaneous assemblages include distinctive Late Acheulian assemblages that feature Levallois and/or handaxe technology, as seen at sites such as Patpara, Sihawal, and Bamburi 1, dated to c.140–104 ka in the Middle Son Valley of northern India (Haslam et al. 2011; Shipton et al. 2013). We term this the *Early out of Africa with hybrid MSA technology* model.

Lastly, several studies have proposed that the *H. sapiens* dispersal into South Asia took place significantly earlier than posited by Mellars (2006) and Mellars et al. (2013), but not as early as the fossil evidence from Greece, Israel, and China might suggest (Petraglia et al. 2007, 2010; Armitage et al. 2011; Rose et al. 2011; Blinkhorn et al. 2013; Clarkson 2014; Clarkson et al. 2020). Instead, according to this model, recent evidence from Southeast Asia and Australia implies that modern humans made their way across Arabia and into South Asia sometime before 65 ka (Demeter et al. 2012; Clarkson et al. 2017; Westaway et al. 2017; Groucutt et al. 2018). Petraglia et al. (2009) have argued that a reduced Thar Desert may have allowed *H. sapiens* to move into India prior to the Toba eruption at 75 ka. Recently, Blinkhorn et al. (2013) and Clarkson et al. (2020) have drawn attention to the similarity of certain elements of Indian lithic assemblages to MSA tools from East Africa, including discoidal, recurrent, and preferential Levallois and Nubian point core technology alongside point and scraper products. They suggest that this may indicate *H. sapiens'* colonisation of South Asia with Levallois technologies well before 50 ka, but probably not before 100 ka. Here we term this the *Late out of Africa with MSA technology* model.

The *Late out of Africa with microlithic technology* model is consistent with genetic estimates of 50–72 ka for the timing of modern human expansion across Eurasia and Australasia. However, microlithic industries do not appear in South Asia or Europe until after 45 ka (Clarkson et al. 2009; Perera et al. 2011; Mishra et al. 2013), between 5000 and 20,000 years after *H. sapiens* had likely colonised Australia (Clarkson et al. 2017). Furthermore, most lithic industries along the Indian Ocean Rim dating to the relevant timeframe exhibit centripetal and single/multiplatform core reduction strategies with or without bipolar technology and lack any evidence of microlithic production (Clarkson 2014).

We further examine these three hypotheses below, but first we review key sites in South Asia from which the evidence is derived.

## Key Sites in South Asia Dating 100–40 ka

Many sites in South Asia have seen detailed excavation and analysis, but few have undergone comprehensive and high-precision dating using modern techniques such as Accelerator Mass Spectrometry (AMS) radiocarbon and luminescence dating. Furthermore, it has long been noted that there is an absence of sites along the west coast as well as in the Tamil Nadu plains. The northern foothills of the Nilgiris to the rest of the rocky triangle between the Narmada River to the north is rich in sites, and there is much potential in that region for identifying more sites. Despite more than a 100 years of surveys, no Pleistocene sites are known along the western seaboard and south of the Kaveri in the southern peninsula (Korisettar 2007). This remains an ongoing bias in the archaeological record and makes testing the hypothesis of a coastal dispersal more difficult. Here we review 11 sites from widespread regions of South Asia and draw some conclusions about their technologies and place in the dispersal debates (Figure 2.1).

### Late Acheulian Sites

*Attirampakkam*

The earliest Levallois technology in South Asia occurs in an industry with Acheulean handaxes and cleavers at Attirampakkam in Tamil Nadu, which dates to over 300 ka (Akhilesh et al.

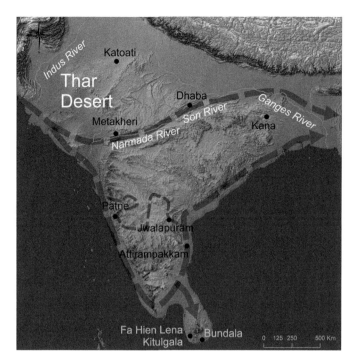

FIGURE 2.1   Map showing key sites mentioned in the text and modelled routes of colonisation across South Asia after Field et al. (2007). Topographic and bathymetric data was obtained from GEBCO 2014 Grid, version 20150318, http://www.gebco.net.

2018). However, in this early manifestation the Levallois technology does not appear to be recurrent, in the same way as the overlying layers. Levallois products were typically point forms. Bifaces continue in association with Levallois technology although at decreasing frequency until ~172 ka, after which there is a hiatus until 74 ka when bifaces are no longer present.

*Middle Son River Valley: Patpara, Sihawal, and Bamburi 1*

These three sites represent a transitional Acheulian to Middle Palaeolithic industry with handaxes and cleavers alongside Levallois technology dating to ~140–104 ka. Recurrent centripetal flaking dominates the Levallois core technology (Shipton et al. 2013).

## Middle Palaeolithic Sites

*Katoati, Thar Desert, Rajasthan*

Katoati is the earliest known definitive Middle Palaeolithic occupation, with Levallois technology and an absence of bifaces from ~96 ka (Blinkhorn et al. 2013). Levallois products are typically points and the use of distal preparation is reminiscent of the Nubian technology documented in the Nile Valley and Arabia. Middle Palaeolithic occupation at Katoati is still evident at 77 ka and later.

*Dhaba, Middle Son River Valley*

This site presents a long sequence of Middle Palaeolithic occupation stretching from 78 ka, through the Toba ash, to the transition to a microlithic industry ~48 ka (Clarkson et al. 2020). Recurrent centripetal is the dominant mode of Levallois flaking with a variety of products including Levallois flakes, blades, and points.

*Jwalapuram 3 and 22, Jwalapuram River Valley*

Jwalapuram 22 is a locality underlying the Toba ash while nearby Jwalapuram 3 has occupation below and above the ash (Haslam et al. 2010, 2012; Clarkson et al. 2012). From below the ash there are a variety of Levallois products with the cores and dorsal scar patterns on flakes indicating both recurrent centripetal and recurrent unidirectional preparation. These modes of Levallois technology continue above the ash but there are no points among the products.

*Patne, Maharashtra*

Patne was excavated some time ago and represents a composite of many sections from a large area (Sali 1985). As such, its dating may be problematic. However, the site is important in documenting a gradual transition from late Middle Palaeolithic to Microlithic assemblages. The site contains engraved ostrich eggshell from the microlith layers that are at least 25 ka and abundant backed microliths and blade technology.

*Site 70, Bundala, Sri Lanka*

This site has a long sequence of technological change in a red earth close to the ocean on the southern tip of Sri Lanka (Deraniyagala 1989). The sequence shows discoidal core and scraper technology with backed artefacts later in the sequence, spanning at least the last 70 ka according to Infrared Stimulated Luminescence dating from the 1980s. The assemblage is made almost entirely on quartz, and this may limit the technical finesse of artefacts to some degree.

**Microlithic Sites**

*Mehtakheri, Narmada River Valley*

From 45 ka microblade technology is known from this site in central India (Mishra et al. 2013), approximately coeval with its appearance at Dhaba. Backed microliths occur among the retouched tools at both sites.

*Jwalapuram 9*

A microblade technology begins >35 ka here, again featuring backed microliths (Clarkson et al. 2009).

*Kana, Bengal*

In eastern India, microblade technology and backed artefacts are documented from 42 ka at Kana (Basak and Srivastava 2017).

*Kitulgala Beli-lena and Fa Hien Lena Caves, Sri Lanka*

Microliths including backed artefacts are also known from Sri Lanka from 45 ka, but unlike mainland India there is no microblade technology here, with blanks produced largely using bipolar flaking (Wedage et al. 2019a, 2019b, 2020).

## Cladistic Analysis

Cladistics is a method of reconstructing evolutionary or 'phylogenetic' relationships. Within the cladistic framework, if two taxa exhibit a derived similarity that is not exhibited in a third taxon, this provides evidence that they are descended from a common ancestor of more recent origin than the last common ancestor shared with the third taxon, and therefore are more closely related to each other than either is to the third taxon. Ideally, the distribution of similarities among a group of taxa will be such that the characters support relationships that are congruent with one another. Normally, however, a number of characters will suggest relationships that are incompatible. This problem is overcome by finding the tree diagram or 'cladogram' that requires the least number of evolutionary changes to account for the distribution of character states among the taxa. This approach is based on the principle of parsimony, the methodological injunction that states that explanations should never be made more complicated than is necessary (Sober 1988). Similarities that are consistent with the most parsimonious cladogram are assumed to be the consequence of shared ancestry and are referred to as "homologies", while similarities that conflict with the most parsimonious cladogram are labelled "homoplasies". Homoplasies can arise through several processes, including convergence and horizontal transmission (Sanderson and Hufford 1996).

Cladistics was originally developed to reconstruct the phylogenetic relationships among species (Hennig 1966), and is still widely used for this purpose (e.g. Christiansen 2008; Smith and Grine 2008; Dohrmann et al. 2009; Rindal and Brower 2011; Goloboff et al. 2018), but in recent years it has been increasingly used to tackle problems in the social sciences and humanities as well (e.g. Robinson and O'Hara 1996; Holden 2002; Tehrani and Collard 2002, 2009; Jordan and Shennan 2003; Rexová et al. 2003; Ben Hamed et al. 2005; Eagleton and Spencer 2006; Larsen 2011; Lycett 2017). This cross-disciplinary borrowing of cladistics is premised on the idea that the transmission of language and culture share key features in common with the transmission of genes (e.g. Boyd et al. 1997; Collard and Shennan 2000). Crucially for present purposes, among the uses to which social scientists and humanists have put cladistics is the reconstruction of prehistoric colonisation events from linguistic and archaeological data (e.g. Gray and Jordan 2001; Holden 2002; Buchanan and Collard 2007; Jennings and Waters 2014; O'Brien et al. 2014; Smallwood et al. 2019). Languages and artefacts have long been used to reconstruct colonisation events in prehistory, but most of the relevant studies are narrative in nature, and therefore it is difficult to assess the merits of contradictory findings. Cladistics is advantageous in this regard because it allows competing hypotheses to be compared statistically (Gray and Jordan 2001; Buchanan and Collard 2007).

We analysed stone tool assemblages from sites dated >42 ka along the hypothesised eastward arc of dispersal from Africa to Australia (Lahr and Foley 1994; Field et al. 2007; Oppenheimer 2009; Clarkson 2014). We recorded assemblage composition from 57 sites in Sub-Saharan Africa, Arabia, the Levant, Europe, India, Southeast Asia, New Guinea/Melanesia, and Australia. We clustered the assemblages into 11 taxa (Figure 2.2). The taxa are defined

**28** Chris Clarkson, Ravi Korisettar, Ceri Shipton, et al.

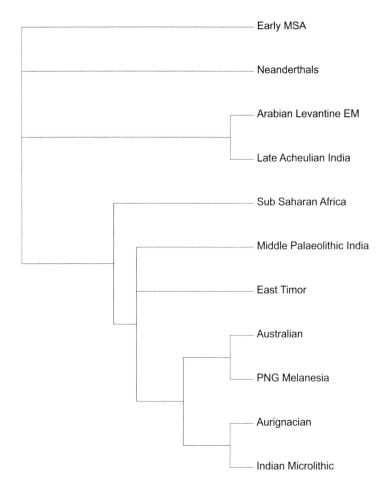

**FIGURE 2.2** Hypothetical cladograms representing modern human dispersal of out of Africa.

according to time, space, and putative species affiliation. The characters we examined are 19 commonly recognised artefact types and core reduction strategies (Table 2.1). We coded the presence of a particular artefact type or reduction strategy as 1 and its absence as a 0. Sites were coded for the 19 characters based on the archaeological literature and, in some cases, the analysis of the assemblages themselves (Table 2.1).

The character state data matrix was subjected to maximum parsimony analysis in PAUP* 4.0 (Swofford 1998) using the branch-and-bound search routine, which is guaranteed to find the shortest length cladogram. The characters were treated in such a way that a change from 0 to 1 cost the same in terms of number of steps as a change from 1 to 0. Because the analysis yielded multiple equally parsimonious cladograms, we generated a consensus cladogram, which showed the relationships among taxa that all the equally parsimonious cladograms have in common. We created a majority-rule consensus cladogram. A clade must appear in 50% of the cladograms in order to be retained in a consensus cladogram.

The goodness of fit between the dataset and the most parsimonious cladograms was assessed with the Retention Index (RI). The RI measures the number of similarities in a dataset that are

TABLE 2.1 List of technological traits used in the cladistics analysis by region and period.

| Site Clusters | Bifacial Radial Cores | Hierarchical Surfaces | Prepared Recurrent Removals | Preferential Removals | Shaping of Upper Surface | Bidirectional | Unifacial Radial | Formally Retouched Artefacts | Levallois Points (Including Nubian) | Handaxes | Blades > 4 cm (>10%) | Tanging | Points | Bipolar | Unidirectional Cores | Backed Microliths | Microblades <4cm (>10%) | Axes | Edge Ground Axes |
|---|---|---|---|---|---|---|---|---|---|---|---|---|---|---|---|---|---|---|---|
| Early MSA (Outgroup) | 1 | 1 | 1 | 1 | 1 | 1 | 1 | 0 | 0 | 1 | 1 | 0 | 0 | 0 | 0 | 0 | 0 | 0 | 0 |
| Neanderthals | 1 | 1 | 1 | 1 | 1 | 1 | 1 | 1 | 1 | 1 | 1 | 0 | 1 | 0 | 0 | 0 | 0 | 0 | 0 |
| Arabian/Levantine Early Moderns | 1 | 1 | 1 | 1 | 1 | 1 | 1 | 1 | 1 | 1 | 1 | 1 | 1 | 0 | 1 | 0 | 0 | 0 | 0 |
| Late Acheulian India (>100 ka) | 1 | 1 | 1 | 1 | 1 | 1 | 0 | 1 | 1 | 1 | 1 | 0 | 1 | 0 | 1 | 0 | 0 | 0 | 0 |
| Sub-Saharan Africa | 1 | 1 | 1 | 1 | 1 | 1 | 1 | 1 | 1 | 0 | 1 | 1 | 0 | 1 | 1 | 1 | 0 | 0 | 0 |
| Middle Palaeolithic (<100 ka) India | 1 | 0 | 0 | 0 | 0 | 0 | 0 | 1 | 0 | 0 | 1 | 0 | 1 | 1 | 1 | 0 | 0 | 0 | 0 |
| East Timor | 1 | 0 | 0 | 0 | 0 | 0 | 0 | 0 | 0 | 0 | 0 | 0 | 0 | 1 | 1 | 0 | 0 | 0 | 0 |
| Australian | 1 | 0 | 0 | 0 | 0 | 0 | 0 | 0 | 0 | 0 | 0 | 0 | 1 | 0 | 1 | 0 | 0 | 1 | 1 |
| PNG/Melanesia | 0 | 0 | 0 | 0 | 0 | 0 | 0 | 0 | 0 | 0 | 1 | 0 | 0 | 0 | 0 | 0 | 0 | 1 | 0 |
| Aurignacian | 0 | 0 | 0 | 0 | 0 | 0 | 0 | 1 | 0 | 0 | 1 | 0 | 1 | 1 | 1 | 1 | 1 | 0 | 0 |
| Indian Microlithic | 1 | 1 | 1 | 0 | 0 | 0 | 0 | 1 | 0 | 0 | 0 | 0 | 0 | 1 | 1 | 1 | 1 | 0 | 0 |

inferred to be homologies in relation to a given cladogram. The RI is insensitive to the presence of derived character states that are present in only a single taxon, or 'autapomorphies'. The RI is also insensitive to the number of characters and taxa employed, which means that RIs can be compared among studies (Sanderson and Donoghue 1989). RIs for the most parsimonious cladograms were calculated and compared to RIs for 21 biological and 21 cultural datasets reported by Collard et al. (2006).

Next, following Jordan and Shennan (2003) and Buchanan and Collard (2007), we used the Kishino-Hasegawa (K-H) test (Kishino and Hasegawa 1989) to evaluate the goodness-of-fit between the hypothetical dispersal models and the consensus of the most parsimonious cladograms. In the K-H test, cladogram length, the standard deviation of length values, and the t statistic are used to measure the significance of the difference in cladogram-to-dataset fit between the most parsimonious cladogram(s) and one or more hypothetical cladograms and, where relevant, the difference of fit among the hypothetical cladograms. If the difference in length between any two cladograms is more than 1.96 times the standard deviation, then they are deemed to be significantly different at $p < 0.05$.

We created hypothetical cladograms based on the three Out of Africa dispersal models. These are illustrated in Figure 2.3 and can be summarised as follows:

1 *Late out of Africa with microlithic technology*. This model is consistent with Mellars' (2006) and specifies a late African exit with backed microblade technology, entering India and Europe sometime after 60 ka. According to this model, SE Asian, New Guinean/Melanesian, and Australian technologies are descended from Arabian/Levantine technology but lack microliths because they were lost en route due to founder effect.
2 *Early out of Africa with hybrid MSA technology*. This model posits an early dispersal from Africa, at least 100–200 ka, and possession of an MSA toolkit that featured Levallois and handaxe technology. The Aurignacian is considered a separate offshoot to the Levallois technology that dispersed eastwards and arrived in India prior to the Toba eruption. SE Asian, New Guinean/Melanesian, and Australian technologies are hypothesised to be descended from late Acheulian Indian technologies, while the Indian Microlithic is posited to be indigenous to the subcontinent (Petraglia et al. 2009).
3 *Late out of Africa with MSA technology*. This model takes into account recent genetic evidence for an African exodus after the Toba eruption at 75 ka, and posits that the migrants had a late Levallois toolkit that lacked both handaxes and microliths. SE Asian, New Guinean/Melanesian, and Australian toolkits are seen as descended from Indian post-Toba technologies. The Aurignacian and Indian Microlithic share a common ancestor with Levallois post-Toba assemblages but it is implied that Australia was already colonised by the time this split took place.

The parsimony analysis returned 26 equally parsimonious cladograms with tree lengths of 34. The RIs for these cladograms (0.66) are comparable to those obtained from datasets used to reconstruct the relationships of species and higher-level biological taxa (Collard et al. 2006). This suggests that the dataset contains a reasonably strong signal of branching, which supports the idea of using it to track the dispersal of early *H. sapiens* from Africa to Eurasia and Australia.

Figure 2.3 presents the 50% majority-rule consensus of the most parsimonious cladograms. The topology of the consensus cladogram suggests that the 75–50 ka Sub-Saharan African technological tradition is ancestral to those found in South Asia, Southeast Asia, New Guinea/

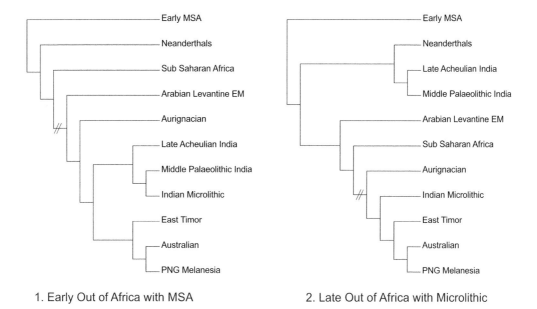

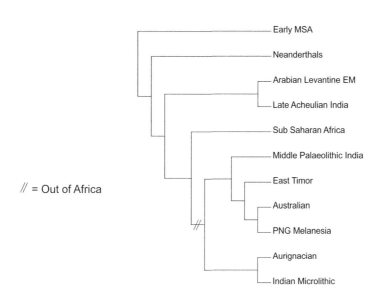

FIGURE 2.3   The 50% majority-rule consensus of the most parsimonious cladograms ($n = 26$).

Melanesia, and Australasia after the Toba eruption. Lithic assemblages found prior to the Toba eruption in Arabia and India appear similar to each other and likely pre-date the expansion of *H. sapiens* out of Africa that resulted in the colonisation of Australia, or represent an earlier expansion of *H. sapiens*. They are therefore likely to be associated either with archaic hominin species such as *Homo heidelbergensis* or an earlier dispersal of *H. sapiens* that has not contributed to extant populations. Lastly, the consensus cladogram suggests that the European

**TABLE 2.2** Results of the Kishino-Hasegawa test comparing the observed cladogram with the three hypothetical cladograms.

| Model | Length | diff | SD | t | P* |
|---|---|---|---|---|---|
| Observed cladogram | 34 | (best) | | | |
| 1. Early out of Africa with MSA | 44 | 10 | 3.67 | 2.73 | 0.0138* |
| 2. Late out of Africa with microlithic | 40 | 6 | 2.92 | 2.05 | 0.0551 |
| 3. Late out of Africa with MSA | 34 | 0 | 2.05 | 0 | 1.000 |

Aurignacian, Indian microlithic, New Guinea/Melanesian, and Australian technological traditions are offshoots of a technological tradition that developed subsequent to the post-Toba dispersal of *H. sapiens* into South Asia and Southeast Asia.

The K-H test in which we compared the consensus cladogram to the three hypothetical cladograms revealed that the *Late out of Africa with MSA technology* (Model 3) and *Late out of Africa with microlithic technology* (Model 2) models were not significantly different from the 50% majority-rule consensus cladogram (Table 2.2). Of these two models, the *Late out of Africa with MSA technology* is a better fit to the observed cladogram having the same tree length and structure, whereas the *Late out of Africa with microlithic technology* model was six steps longer than the observed cladogram. The *Early out of Africa with hybrid MSA technology* (Model 1) model was significantly different than the observed cladogram. Thus, the K-H test indicates that the late out of Africa scenario involving *H. sapiens* with an MSA technology lacking backed microliths is the model that best fits the currently available technological data.

## Conclusion

Phylogenetic methods offer a powerful means of testing models of human dispersal using cultural datasets. Using data from 57 Palaeolithic stone tool assemblages and a suite of phylogenetic methods called cladistics, we tested between the three main hypotheses concerning the colonisation of South Asia. The hypothesis that was best supported by the data was the one in which modern humans left Africa relatively late—but most likely before the Toba eruption at 75 ka—and did so with a late Levallois technological assemblage, which lacked both handaxes and microliths. Improved dating, larger sample sizes and better descriptions of lithic assemblages from many sites, as well as the discovery of new sites, would be beneficial for refining analyses like these, but current models must be tested against the available evidence. In this case, our phylogenetic analyses offer strong support for a non-microlithic technology accompanying *H. sapiens* eastward out of Africa. We suggest the possibility of a later spread of microlithic technology from the Middle East into the Indian Sub-continent after 45 ka, although the mechanisms and archaeological signature for such a demographic event await future investigation.

## Acknowledgements

We thank the editors for the invitation to contribute this chapter. We also thank Kasih Norman for generating the Digital Elevation Map (DEM) basemap for Figure 2.1. CC is supported by an Australian Research Council Future Fellowship. MC is supported by the Canada Research Chairs Program, the Canada Foundation for Innovation, the British Columbia Knowledge Development Fund, and Simon Fraser University.

# References

Akhilesh, Kumar, Pappu, Shanti, Rajapara, Haresh, Gunnell, Yanni, Shukla, Anil, and Singhvi, Ashok. 2018 Early Middle Palaeolithic culture in India around 385–172 ka reframes Out of Africa models. *Nature 554*, 97.
Armitage, Simon, Jasim, Sabah, Marks, Aanthony, Parker, Adrian, Usik, Vitaly, and Uerpmann, Hanspeter. 2011 The southern route "out of Africa": Evidence for an early expansion of modern humans into Arabia. *Science 331*, 453–456.
Basak, Bishnupriya, and Srivastava, Pradeep. 2017 Earliest dates of microlithic industries (42–25 ka) from West Bengal, Eastern India: New light on modern human occupation in the Indian subcontinent. *Asian Perspectives 56*, 237–259.
Ben Hamed, Mahe, Darlu, Pierre, and Vallée, Nathalie. 2005 On cladistic reconstruction of linguistic trees through vowel data. *Journal of Quantitative Linguistics 12*, 79–109.
Blinkhorn, James, Achyuthan, Hema, Petraglia, Michael, and Ditchfield, Peter. 2013 Middle Palaeolithic occupation in the Thar Desert during the Upper Pleistocene: The signature of a modern human exit out of Africa? *Quaternary Science Reviews 77*, 233–238.
Boyd, Robert, Borgerhoff-Mulder, Monique, Durham, William, and Richerson, Peter. 1997 Are cultural phylogenies possible? in *Human by Nature: Between Biology and the Social Sciences*, eds Weingart, Peter, Mitchell, Sandra., Richerson, Peter, and Maasen, Sabine. Hove: Psychology Press, 355–386.
Buchanan, Briggs, and Collard, Mark. 2007 Investigating the peopling of North America through cladistic analyses of Early Paleoindian projectile points. *Journal of Anthropological Archaeology 26*, 366–393.
Christiansen, Per. 2008 Evolutionary convergence of primitive Sabertooth craniomandibular morphology: The clouded leopard (*Neofelis nebulosa*) and *Paramachairodus ogygia* compared. *Journal of Mammalian Evolution 15*, 155–179.
Clarkson, Chris, Petraglia, Michael, Korisettar, Ravi, Haslam, Michael, Boivin, Nicole, Crowther, Alison, Ditchfield, Peter, Fuller, Dorian, Miracle, Preston, Harris, Clair, Connell, Kate, James, Hannah, and Koshy, Jinu. 2009 The oldest and longest enduring microlithic sequence in India: 35 000 years of modern human occupation and change at the Jwalapuram Locality 9 Rockshelter. *Antiquity 83*, 326–348.
Clarkson, Chris. 2014 East of Eden: Founder effects and the archaeological signature of modern human dispersal in *Southern Asia*, in *Australia and the Search for Human Origins*, eds Dennell, Robin, and Porr, Martin. Cambridge: Cambridge University Press, 76–89.
Clarkson, Chris, Jones, Sacha, and Harris, Clair. 2012 Continuity and change in the lithic industries of the Jurreru Valley, India, before and after the Toba eruption. *Quaternary International 258*, 165–179.
Clarkson, Chris, Jacobs, Zenobia, Marwick, Ben, Fullagar, Richard, Wallis, Lynley, Smith, Mike, Roberts, Richard, Hayes, Elspeth, Lowe, Kelsey, Carah, Xavier, Florin, Anna, McNeil, Jessica, Cox, Delyth, Arnold, Lee, Hua, Quan, Huntley, Jillian, Brand, Helen, Manne, Tiina, Fairbairn, Andrew, Shulmeister, James, Lyle, Lindsey, Salinas, Makiah, Page, Mara, Connell, Kate, Park, Gayoung, Norman, Kasih, Murphy, Tessa, and Pardoe, Colin. 2017 Human occupation of northern Australia by 65,000 years ago. *Nature 547*, 306–310.
Clarkson, Chris, Hiscock, Peter, Mackay, Alex, and Shipton, Ceri. 2018 Small, sharp, and standardized: Global convergence in backed-microlith technology, in *Convergent Evolution in Stone-Tool Technology*, eds O'Brien, Michael J., Buchanan, Briggs, and Eren, Metin I. Cambridge: MIT Press, 175–200.
Clarkson, Chris, Harris, Claire, Li, Bo, Neudorf, Christina, Roberts, Richard, Lane, Christine, Norman, Kasih, Pal, Jagannath, Jones, Sacha, Shipton, Ceri, Koshy, Jinu, Gupta, M. C., Mishra, D. P., Dubey, A. K., Boivin, Nicole, and Petraglia, Michael. 2020 Human occupation of northern India spans the Toba super-eruption ~74,000 years ago. *Nature Communications 11*, 1–10.
Collard, Mark, and Shennan, Stephen. 2000 Processes of culture change in prehistory: A case study from the European Neolithic, in *Archaeogenetics: DNA and the Population Prehistory of Europe*, eds Renfrew, C., and Boyle, K. Cambridge: McDonald Institute for Archaeological Research, 89–97.
Collard, Mark, Shennan, Stephen, and Tehrani, Jamshid. 2006 Branching, blending, and the evolution of cultural similarities and differences among human populations. *Evolution and Human Behavior 27*, 169–184.
Demeter, Fabrice, Shackelford, Laura, Westaway, Kira, Duringer, Philippe, Sayavongkhamdy, Thongsa, and Bacon, Anne-Marie. 2012 Reply to Pierret et al.: Stratigraphic and dating consistency reinforces the status of Tam Pa Ling fossil. *Proceedings of the National Academy of Sciences 109*, E3524–E3525.
Deraniyagala, Siran. 1989 *The Prehistory of Sri Lanka: An Ecological Perspective*. Harvard: Harvard University Press.

Dohrmann, M., Collins, A., and Wörheide, G. 2009 New insights into the phylogeny of glass sponges (Porifera, Hexactinellida): Monophyly of Lyssacinosida and Euplectellinae, and the phylogenetic position of Euretidae. *Molecular Phylogenetics and Evolution 52*, 257–262.

Eagleton, Catherine, and Spencer, Matthew. 2006 Copying and conflation in Geoffrey Chaucer's treatise on the astrolabe: A stemmatic analysis using phylogenetic software. *Studies in History and Philosophy of Science Part A 37*, 237–268.

Field, Julie, Petraglia, Michael, and Lahr, Marta. 2007 The southern dispersal hypothesis and the South Asian archaeological record: Examination of dispersal routes through GIS analysis. *Journal of Anthropological Archaeology 26*, 88–108.

Foley, Robert, and Lahr, Marta. 2003 On stony ground: Lithic technology, human evolution, and the emergence of culture. *Evolutionary Anthropology: Issues, News, and Reviews 12*, 109–122.

Garrod, Dorothy. 1937 The stone age of Mount Carmel I. *Excavations at the Wadyel-Mughara*. Oxford: Oxford University Press.

Goloboff, Pablo, Torres, Ambrosio, and Arias, Salvador. 2018 Weighted parsimony outperforms other methods of phylogenetic inference under models appropriate for morphology. *Cladistics 34*, 407–437.

Gray, Russel, and Jordan, Fiona. 2001 Erratum: Correction: Language trees support the express-train sequence of Austronesian expansion. *Nature 409*, 743–743.

Groucutt, Huw, Grün, Rainer, Zalmout, Iyad, Drake, Nick, Armitage, Simon, Candy, Ian, Clark-Wilson, Richard, Louys, Julien, Breeze, Paul, Duval, Mathieu, Buck, Laura, Kivell, Tracy, Pomeroy, Emma, Stephens, Nicholas, Stock, Jay, Stewart, Mathew, Price, Gilbert, Kinsley, Leslie, Sung, Wing, Alsharekh, Abdullah, Al-Omari, Abdulaziz, Zahir, Muhammad, Abdullah, Memesh, Abdulshakoor, Ammar, Bahameem, Ahmed, Al Murayyi, Khaled, Zahrani, Badr, Scerri, Eleanor, and Michael, D. Petraglia. 2018 *Homo sapiens* in Arabia by 85,000 years ago. *Nature Ecology & Evolution 2*, 800–809.

Grün, Rainer, Stringer, Chris, McDermott, Frank, Nathan, Roger, Porat, Naomi, Robertson, Steve, Taylor, Lois, Mortimer, Graham, Eggins, Stephen, and McCulloch, Malcolm. 2005 U-series and ESR analyses of bones and teeth relating to the human burials from Skhul. *Journal of Human Evolution 49*, 316–334.

Harvati, Katerina, Röding, Carolin, Bosman, Abel, Karakostis, Fotios, Grün, Rainer, Stringer, Chris, Karkanas, Panagiotis, Thompson, Nicholas, Koutoulidis, Vassilis, Moulopoulos, Lia, Gorgoulis, Vassilis, and Kouloukoussa, Mirsini. 2019 Apidima Cave fossils provide earliest evidence of *Homo sapiens* in Eurasia. *Nature 571*, 500–504.

Haslam, Michael, Clarkson, Chris, Petraglia, Michael, Korisettar, Ravi, Jones, Sasha, Shipton, Ceri, Ditchfield, Peter, and Ambrose, Stanley. 2010 The 74 ka Toba super-eruption and southern Indian hominins: Archaeology, lithic technology and environments at Jwalapuram Locality 3. *Journal of Archaeological Science 37*, 3370–3384.

Haslam, Michael, Roberts, Richard, Shipton, Ceri, Pal, J.N., Fenwick, Jacqueline, Ditchfield, Peter, Boivin, Nicole, Dubey, A., Gupta, M., and Petraglia, Michael. 2011 Late Acheulean hominins at the Marine Isotope Stage 6/5E transition in North-Central India. *Quaternary Research 75*, 670–682.

Haslam, Michael, Clarkson, Christopher, Roberts, Richard, Bora, Janardhana, Korisettar, Ravi, Ditchfield, Peter, Chivas, Allan, Harris, Clair, Smith, Victoria, Oh, Anna, Eksambekar, Sanjay, and Boivin, Nicole. 2012 A southern Indian Middle Palaeolithic occupation surface sealed by the 74 ka Toba eruption: Further evidence from Jwalapuram Locality 22. *Quaternary International 258*, 148–164.

Hennig, Will. 1966 *Phylogenetic Systematics*. Urbana, IL: University of Illinois Press.

Hershkovitz, Israel, Weber, Gerhard, Quam, Rolf, Duval, Mathieu, Grün, Rainer, Kinsley, Leslie, Ayalon, Avner, Bar-matthews, Miryam, Valladas, Helene, Mercier, Norbert, Arsuaga, Juan, Martinón-torres, María, de Castro, José, Fornai, Cinzia, Martín-Francés, Laura, Sarig, Rachel, May, Hila, Krenn, Viktoria, Slon, Viviane, Rodríguez, Laura, García, Rebeca, Lorenzo, Carlos, Carretero, Jose, Frumkin, Amos, Shahack-Gross, Ruth, Mayer, Daniella, Cui, Yaming, Wu, Xinzhi, Peled, Natan, Groman-Yaroslavski, Iris, Weissbrod, Lior, Yeshurun, Reuven, Tsatskin, Alexander, Zaidner, Yossi, and Weinstein-Evron, Mina. 2018 The earliest modern humans outside Africa. *Science 359*, 456–459.

Holden, Clare. 2002 Bantu language trees reflect the spread of farming across Sub-Saharan Africa: A maximum-parsimony analysis. *Proceedings of the Royal Society of London. Series B: Biological Sciences 269*, 793–799.

Jennings, Thomas, and Waters, Michael. 2014 Pre-Clovis lithic technology at the Debra L. Friedkin site, Texas: Comparisons to Clovis through site-level behavior, technological trait-list, and cladistic analyses. *American Antiquity 79*, 25–44.

Jordan, Peter, and Shennan, Stephen. 2003 Cultural transmission, language, and basketry traditions amongst the California Indians. *Journal of Anthropological Archaeology 22*, 42–74.

Kishino, Hirohisa, and Hasegawa, Masami. 1989 Evaluation of the maximum likelihood estimate of the evolutionary tree topologies from DNA sequence data, and the branching order in Hominoidea. *Journal of Molecular Evolution 29*, 170–179.

Kennedy, Kenneth. 2000 *God-Apes and Fossil Men: Paleoanthropology of South Asia*. Ann Arbor: University of Michigan Press.

Korisettar, Ravi. 2007 Toward developing a basin model for Paleolithic settlement of the Indian subcontinent: Geodynamics, monsoon dynamics, habitat diversity and dispersal routes, in *The Evolution and History of Human Populations in South Asia*, eds Petraglia, Michael D., and Allchin, Bridget. Dordrecht: Springer, 69–96.

Kuhlwilm, Martin, Gronau, Ilan, Hubisz, Melissa, de Filippo, Cesare, Prado-Martinez, Javier, Kircher, Martin, Fu, Qiaomei, Burbano, Hernán, Lalueza-Fox, Carles, de la Rasilla, Marco, Rosas, Antonio, Rudan, Pavao, Brajkovic, Dejana, Kucan, Željko, Gušic, Ivan, Marques-Bonet, Tomas, Andrés, Aida, Viola, Bence, Pääbo, Svante, Meyer, Matthias, Siepel, Adam, and Castellano, Sergi. 2016 Ancient gene flow from early modern humans into Eastern Neanderthals. *Nature 530*, 429–433.

Lahr, Marta, and Foley, Robert. 1994 Multiple dispersals and modern human origins. *Evolutionary Anthropology: Issues, News, and Reviews 3*, 48–60.

Larsen, Anna. 2011 Evolution of Polynesian bark cloth and factors influencing cultural change. *Journal of Anthropological Archaeology 30*, 116–134.

Liu, Wu, Martinón-Torres, Maria, Cai, Yan-jun, Xing, Song, Tong, Hao-wen, Pei, Shu-wen, Sier, Mark, Wu, Xiao-hong, Edwards, Lawrence, Cheng, Hai, Li, Yi-yuan, Yang, Xiong-xin, de Castro, José, and Wu, Xiu-jie. 2015 The earliest unequivocally modern humans in southern China. *Nature 526*, 696.

Lycett, Stephen. 2017 A multivariate and phylogenetic analysis of Blackfoot biographic art: Another look at the Deadmond robe. *Plains Anthropologist 62*, 201–218.

Malaspinas, Anna-Sapfo, Westaway, Michael, Muller, Craig, Sousa, Vitor, Lao, Oscar, Alves, Isabel, Bergström, Anders, Athanasiadis, Georgios, Cheng, Jade, Crawford, Jacob, Heupink, Tim, Macholdt, Enrico, Peischl, Stephan, Rasmussen, Simon, Schiffels, Stephan, Subramanian, Sankar, Wright, Joanne, Albrechtsen, Anders, Barbieri, Chiara, Dupanloup, Isabelle, Eriksson, Anders, Margaryan, Ashot, Moltke, Ida, Pugach, Irina, Korneliussen, Thorfinn, Levkivskyi, Ivan, Moreno-Mayar, Víctor, Ni, Shengyu, Racimo, Fernando, Sikora, Martin, Xue, Yali, Aghakhanian, Farhang, Brucato, Nicolas, Brunak, Søren, Campos, Paula, Clark, Warren, Ellingvåg, Sturla, Fourmile, Gudjugudju, Gerbault, Pascale, Injie, Darren, Koki, George, Leavesley, Matthew, Logan, Betty, Lynch, Aubrey, Matisoo-Smith, Elizabeth, McAllister, Peter, Mentzer, Alexander, Metspalu, Mait, Migliano, Andrea, Murgha, Les, Phipps, Maude, Pomat, William, Reynolds, Doc, Ricaut, Francois-Xavier, Siba, Peter, Thomas, Mark, Wales, Thomas, Wall, Colleen, Oppenheimer, Stephen, Tyler-Smith, Chris, Durbin, Richard, Dortch, Joe, Manica, Andrea, Schierup, Mikkel, Foley, Robert, Lahr, Marta, Bowern, Claire, Wall, Jeffrey, Mailund, Thomas, Stoneking, Mark, Nielsen, Rasmus, Sandhu, Manjinder, Excoffier, Laurent, Lambert, David, and Willerslev, Eske. 2016 A genomic history of Aboriginal Australia. *Nature 538*, 207–214.

Mallick, Swapan, Li, Heng, Lipson, Mark, Mathieson, Iain, Gymrek, Melissa, Racimo, Fernando, Zhao, Mengyao, Chennagiri, Niru, Nordenfelt, Susanne, Tandon, Arti, Skoglund, Pontus, Lazaridis, Iosif, Sankararaman, Sriram, Fu, Qiaomei, Rohland, Nadin, Renaud, Gabriel, Erlich, Yaniv, Willems, Thomas, Gallo, Carla, Spence, Jeffrey, Song, Yun, Poletti, Giovanni, Balloux, Francois, van Driem, George, de Knijff, Peter, Romero, Irene, Jha, Aashish, Behar, Doron, Bravi, Claudio, Capelli, Cristian, Hervig, Tor, Moreno-Estrada, Andres, Posukh, Olga, Balanovska, Elena, Balanovsky, Oleg, Karachanak-Yankova, Sena, Sahakyan, Hovhannes, Toncheva, Draga, Yepiskoposyan, Levon, Tyler-Smith, Chris, Xue, Yali, Abdullah, Syafiq, Ruiz-Linares, Andres, Beall, Cynthia, Di Rienzo, Anna, Jeong, Choongwon, Starikovskaya, Elena, Metspalu, Ene, Parik, Jüri, Villems, Richard, Henn, Brenna, Hodoglugil, Ugur, Mahley, Robert, Sajantila, Antti, Stamatoyannopoulos, George, Wee, Joseph, Khusainova, Elza, Khusnutdinova, Rita, Litvinov, Sergey, Ayodo, George, Comas, David, Hammer, Michael, Kivisild, Toomas, Klitz, William, Winkler, Cheryl, Labuda, Damian, Bamshad, Michael, Jorde, Lynn, Tishkoff, Sarah, Watkins, Scott, Metspalu, Mait, Dryomov, Stanislav, Sukernik, Rem, Singh, Lalji, Thangaraj, Kumarasamy, Pääbo, Svante, Kelso, Janet, Patterson, Nick, and Reich, David. 2016 The Simons genome diversity project: 300 genomes from 142 diverse populations. *Nature 538*, 201–206.

Mellars, Paul. 2006 Going East: New genetic and archaeological perspectives on the modern human colonization of Eurasia. *Science 313*, 796–800.

Mellars, Paul, Gori, Kevin, Carr, Martin, Soares, Pedro, and Richards, Martin. 2013 Genetic and archaeological perspectives on the initial modern human colonization of southern Asia. *Proceedings of the National Academy of Sciences 110*, 10699–10704.

Mishra, Sheila, Chauhan, N., and Singhvi, A. 2013 Continuity of microblade technology in the Indian Subcontinent since 45 ka: Implications for the dispersal of modern humans. *PLoS ONE 8*, e69280.

O'Brien, Michael, Boulanger, Matthew, Buchanan, Briggs, Collard, Mark, Lyman, Lee, and Darwent, John. 2014 Innovation and cultural transmission in the American Paleolithic: Phylogenetic analysis of eastern Paleoindian projectile-point classes. *Journal of Anthropological Archaeology 34*, 100–119.

Oppenheimer, Stephen. 2009 The great arc of dispersal of modern humans: Africa to Australia. *Quaternary International 202*, 2–13.

Pagani, Luca, Lawson, Daniel, Jagoda, Evelyn, Mörseburg, Alexander, Eriksson, Anders, Mitt, Mario, Clemente, Florian, Hudjashov, Georgi, DeGiorgio, Michael, Saag, Lauri, Wall, Jeffrey, Cardona, Alexia, Mägi, Reedik, Sayres, Melissa, Kaewert, Sarah, Inchley, Charlotte, Scheib, Christiana, Järve, Mari, Karmin, Monika, Jacobs, Guy, Antao, Tiago, Iliescu, Florin, Kushniarevich, Alena, Ayub, Qasim, Tyler-Smith, Chris., Xue, Yali, Yunusbayev, Bayazit, Tambets, Kristiina, Mallick, Chandana, Saag, Lehti, Pocheshkhova, Elvira, Andriadze, George, Muller, Craig, Westaway, Michael, Lambert, David, Zoraqi, Grigor, Turdikulova, Shahlo, Dalimova, Dilbar, Sabitov, Zhaxylyk, Sultana, Gazi, Lachance, Joseph, Tishkoff, Sarah, Momynaliev, Kuvat, Isakova, Jainagul, Damba, Larisa, Gubina, Marina, Nymadawa, Pagbajabyn, Evseeva, Irina, Atramentova, Lubov, Utevska, Olga, Ricaut, François-Xavier, Brucato, Nicolas, Sudoyo, Herawati, Letellier, Thierry, Cox, Murray, Barashkov, Nikolay, Škaro, Vedrana, Mulahasanović, Lejla, Primorac, Dragan, Sahakyan, Hovhannes, Mormina, Maru, Eichstaedt, Christina, Lichman, Daria, Abdullah, Syafiq, Chaubey, Gyaneshwer, Wee, Joseph, Mihailov, Evelin, Karunas, Alexandra, Litvinov, Sergei, Khusainova, Rita, Ekomasova, Natalya, Akhmetova, Vita, Khidiyatova, Irina, Marjanović, Damir, Yepiskoposyan, Levon, Behar, Doron, Balanovska, Elena, Metspalu, Andres, Derenko, Miroslava, Malyarchuk, Boris, Voevoda, Mikhail, Fedorova, Sardana, Osipova, Ludmila, Lahr, Marta, Gerbault, Pascale, Leavesley, Matthew, Migliano, Andrea, Petraglia, Michael, Balanovsky, Oleg, Khusnutdinova, Elza, Metspalu, Ene, Thomas, Mark, Manica, Andrea, Nielsen, Rasmus, Villems, Richard, Willerslev, Eske, Kivisild, Toomas, and Metspalu, Mait. 2016 Genomic analyses inform on migration events during the peopling of Eurasia. *Nature 538*, 238.

Perera, Nimal, Kourampas, Nikos, Simpson, Ian, Deraniyagala, Siran, Bulbeck, David, Kamminga, Johan, Perera, Jude, Fuller, Dorian, Szabo, Katherine, and Oliveria, Nuno. 2011 People of the ancient rainforest: Late Pleistocene foragers at the Batadomba-lena Rockshelter, Sri Lanka. *Journal of Human Evolution 61*, 254–269.

Petraglia, Michael, Clarkson, Christopher, Boivin, Nicole, Haslam, Michael, Korisettar, Ravi, Chaubey, Gyaneshwer, Ditchfield, Peter, Fuller, Dorian, James, Hannah, Jones, Sacha, Kivisild, Toomas, Kivisild, Toomas, Koshy, Jinu, Lahr, Marta, Metspalu, Mait, Roberts, Richard, and Arnold, Lee. 2009 Population increase and environmental deterioration correspond with microlithic innovations in South Asia ca.35,000 years ago. *Proceedings of the National Academy of Sciences 106*, 12261–12266.

Petraglia, Michael, Korisettar, Ravi, Boivin, Nicole, Clarkson, Chris, Ditchfield, Peter, Jones, Sacha, Koshy, Jinu, Lahr, Marta, Oppenheimer, Clive, Pyle, David, Roberts, Richard, Schwenninger, Jean-Luc, Arnold, Lee, and White, K. 2007 Middle Palaeolithic assemblages from the Indian sub-continent before and after the Toba super-eruption. *Science 317*, 114–116.

Petraglia, Michael, Haslam, Michael, Fuller, Dorian, Boivin, Nicole, and Clarkson, Chris. 2010 Out of Africa: New hypotheses and evidence for the dispersal of *Homo sapiens* along the Indian Ocean rim. *Annals of Human Biology 37*, 288–311.

Posth, Cosimo, Wißing, Christoph, Kitagawa, Keiko, Pagani, Luca, van Holstein, Laura, Racimo, Fernando, Wehrberger, Kurt, Conard, Nicholas, Kind, Claus, Bocherens, Herve, and Krause, Johannes. 2017 Deeply divergent archaic mitochondrial genome provides lower time boundary for African gene flow into Neanderthals. *Nature Communications 8*, 1–9.

Rexová, Katerina, Frynta, Daniel, and Zrzavý, Jan. 2003 Cladistic analysis of languages: Indo-European classification based on lexicostatistical data. *Cladistics 19*, 120–127.

Rindal, Eirik, and Brower, Andrew. 2011 Do model-based phylogenetic analyses perform better than parsimony? A test with empirical data. *Cladistics 27*, 331–334.

Robinson, Peter, and O'Hara, Robert. 1996 Cladistic analysis of an Old Norse manuscript tradition. *Research in Humanities Computing 4*, 115–137.

Rose, Jeffrey, Usik, Vitaly, Marks, Anethony, Hilbert, Yamandu, Galletti, Christopher, Parton, Ash, Geiling, Jean Marie, Černý, Viktor, Morley, Mike, and Roberts, Richard. 2011 The Nubian complex of Dhofar, Oman: An African middle stone age industry in southern Arabia. *PLoS ONE 6*, e28239.

Sahle, Yonatan, Beyene, Yonas, Defleaur, Aalban, Asfaw, Berhane, and Woldegabriel, Giday. 2019 Human emergence: Perspectives from Herto, Afar Rift, Ethiopia, in *Modern Human Origins and Dispersal*, eds Sahle, Y., Reyes-Centeno, H., and Bentz, C. Tübingen: Kerns Verlag, 105–136.

Sali, S. 1985 The Upper Palaeolithic culture at Patne, District Jalgaon, Maharashtra. *Recent Advances in Indo-Pacific Prehistory 1985*, 137–145.
Sanderson, Michael, and Donoghue, Michael. 1989 Patterns of variation in levels of homoplasy. *Evolution 43*, 1781–1795.
Sanderson, Michael, and Hufford, Larry eds. 1996 *Homoplasy: the Recurrence of Similarity in Evolution*. Academic Press, London.
Schwarcz, H.P., Grün, R., Vandermeersch, B., Bar-Yosef, O., Valladas, H., and Tchernov, E. 1988 ESR dates for the hominid burial site of Qafzeh in Israel. *Journal of Human Evolution 17*, 733–737.
Shackelford, Laura, Demeter, Fabrice, Westaway, Kira, Duringer, Philippe, Ponche, Jean-Luc, Sayavongkhamdy, Thongsa, Zhao, Jian-Xin, Barnes, Lani, Boyon, Marc, Sichanthongtip, Phonephanh, Sénégas, Frank, Patole-Edoumba, Elise, Coppens, Yves, Dumoncel, Jean, and Bacon, Anne-Marie. 2018 Additional evidence for early modern human morphological diversity in Southeast Asia at Tam Pa Ling, Laos. *Quaternary International 466*, 93–106.
Shipton, Ceri, Clarkson, Christopher, Pal, J., Jones, Sasha, Roberts, Richard, Harris, Claire, Gupta, M., Ditchfield, Peter, and Petraglia, Michael. 2013 Generativity, hierarchical action and recursion in the technology of the Acheulean to Middle Palaeolithic transition: A perspective from Patpara, the Son Valley, India. *Journal of Human Evolution 65*, 93–108.
Smallwood, Ashley, Jennings, Thomas, Pevny, Charlotte, and Anderson, David. 2019 Paleoindian Projectile-point diversity in the American Southeast: Evidence for the mosaic evolution of point design. *PaleoAmerica 5*, 218–230.
Smith, Heather, and Grine, Frederick. 2008 Cladistic analysis of early *homo* crania from Swartkrans and Sterkfontein, South Africa. *Journal of Human Evolution 54*, 684–704.
Sober, Elliot. 1988 The principle of the common cause, in *Probability and Causality*, ed. Fetter, J.H. Dordrecht: Springer, 211–228.
Stringer, Chris, Grün, Rainer, Schwarcz, H., and Goldberg, P. 1989 ESR dates for the hominid burial site of Es Skhul in Israel. *Nature 338*, 756–758.
Swofford, David. 1998 *Phylogenetic Analysis Using Parsimony*. Champaign, IL: Illinois Natural History Survey.
Tehrani, Jamshid, and Collard, Mark. 2002 Investigating cultural evolution through biological phylogenetic analyses of Turkmen textiles. *Journal of Anthropological Archaeology 21*, 443–463.
Tehrani, Jamshid, and Collard, Mark. 2009 On the relationship between interindividual cultural transmission and population-level cultural diversity: A case study of weaving in Iranian tribal populations. *Evolution and Human Behavior 30*, 286–300.
Valladas, H., Reyss, J.-L., Joron, J.-L., Valladas, G., Bar-Yosef, O., and Vandermeersch, B. 1988 Thermoluminescence dating of Mousterian 'Proto-Cro-Magnon' remains from Israel and the origin of modern man. *Nature 331*, 614–616.
Wedage, Oshan, Amano, Noel, Langley, Michelle, Douka, Katerina, Blinkhorn, James, Crowther, Alison, Deraniyagala, Siran, Kourampas, Nikos, Simpson, Ian, Perera, Nimal, Picin, Andrea, Boivin, Nicole, Petraglia, Michael, and Roberts, Patrick. 2019a Specialized rainforest hunting by *Homo sapiens* ~ 45,000 years ago. *Nature Communications 10*, 1–8.
Wedage, Oshan, Picin, Andrea, Blinkhorn, James, Douka, Katerina, Deraniyagala, Siran, Kourampas, Nikos, Perera, Nimal, Simpson, Ian, Boivin, Nicole, Petraglia, Michael, and Roberts, Patrick. 2019b Microliths in the South Asian rainforest ~45-4 ka: New insights from Fa-Hien Lena Cave, Sri Lanka. *PLoS ONE 14*, e0222606.
Wedage, Oshan, Roberts, Patrick, Faulkner, Patrick, Crowther, Alison, Douka, Katerina, Picin, Andrea, Blinkhorn, James, Deraniyagala, Siran, Boivin, Nicole, Petraglia, Michael, and Amano, Noel. 2020 Late Pleistocene to early-Holocene rainforest foraging in Sri Lanka: Multidisciplinary analysis at Kitulgala Beli-lena. *Quaternary Science Reviews 231*, 106200.
Westaway, K. E., Louys, J., Due Awe, R., Morwood, M., Price, G., Zhao, J., Aubert, M., Joannes-Boyau, R., Smith, M., Skinner, M., Compton, T., Bailey, R., van den Bergh, G., de Vos, J., Pike, A., Stringer, C., Saptomo, E., Rizal, Y., Zaim, J., Santoso, W., Trihascaryo, A., Kinsley, L., and Sulistyanto, B. 2017 An early modern human presence in Sumatra 73,000–63,000 years ago. *Nature 548*, 322–325.

# 3

# THE SETTLEMENT OF MAINLAND SOUTHEAST ASIA BY ANATOMICALLY MODERN HUMANS

*Charles Higham*

## Introduction

Anatomically modern humans (AMHs) evolved in Africa, the earliest being dated to about 300,000 years ago (ka). Tracing their expansion into the rest of the world was first followed on the basis of traditional archaeological evidence: the recovery of occupation sites that contained what they made, what they gathered and consumed, and rarely, their burials. For the archaeologist, one of the first responsibilities, having excavated and analysed these sites, is to secure a reliable chronology. This can be done for settlement up to about 50 ka by mean of radiocarbon dating. Beyond this point, radiocarbon ceases to be applicable, and other techniques are now available. For example, optically stimulated luminescence (OSL) dating, can be applied to material within a range of hundreds of thousands of years such as quartz or feldspar grains from an archaeological sediment, by measuring the amount of emitted light (Rhodes 2011).

Traditional research methods have more recently received new impetus and accuracy by the analysis of the DNA of prehistoric and modern humans. This vital approach can be used both to reveal the genetic links between different peoples both past and present, and to establish an approximate timescale using the presumed rate of mutations in DNA. It was the analysis of mtDNA that first pointed to African origins for AMHs worldwide. A third approach is to apply simulations to the expansion of AMHs, by accepting basic assumptions, that humans would take, for example, lines of least resistance or greatest opportunity. At its simplest, a human group is more likely to expand along a convenient river course or coast line, than attempt to cross an Alpine pass or an extensive desert (Ray et al. 2008).

When combined, these three techniques provide a consistent template for tracing the earliest expansionary pathway of AMHs from northeast Africa to the Near East, then India and Southeast Asia into greater Australia. The details to this general picture, however, have yet to be filled in.

Weighing the evidence for one or more expansionary movements by AMHs into Southeast Asia and beyond must now be undertaken in the context of what are known as Marine Isotope Stages (MIS) in the earth's history, that cover at least the last 80 ka, and possibly, as much as 130 ka. These stages have been constructed from the oscillating values of oxygen isotopes

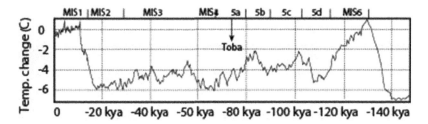

FIGURE 3.1  Variations in the world temperature during MIS 1-6 derived from the Vostok Antarctic ice core.

($\delta^{18}O = {}^{18}O/{}^{16}O$) in the marine organisms that accumulate in ocean beds. By taking cores from the seabed, or from Greenland and Antarctic ice sheets, it is possible to trace climatic changes, a high value for $\delta^{18}O$ reflecting cold conditions, and low values a period of relative warmth. The Vostok ice core in Antarctica, for example, has recorded temperature variations over the last 400,000 years (Barnola et al. 1987). The most recent Marine Isotope Stage, MIS 1 indicates relative warmth, and preceding that, MIS 2 (29–14 ka) represents the last glacial maximum. MIS 3 (29–60 ka) was markedly warmer than its successor, with periods of notably rapid increases in temperature, and fluctuations in the sea level (Figure 3.1) that were interspersed with phases of increased cold (Siddall et al. 2008; Van Meerbeeck et al. 2009). While not demonstrating the extremes of MIS 2, MIS 4 (80–60 ka) was a period of lowered sea levels and colder conditions.

It was during this stage that a major event took place that has direct implications on tracing the expansion of AMHs into Southeast Asia and beyond: the eruption of Mount Toba in Sumatra. This massive volcanic eruption deposited tephra over a wide area. Dated to approximately 71.6 ka, there is an ongoing controversy as to whether the material remains of AMH activity are stratified below Toba tephra, or only above it, which remains to be resolved.

MIS 5 is divided into five sub-phases, and becomes relevant to settlement by AMHs only if indeed, there remains predate Toba. The earliest sub-phase, MIS 5e, lasted from about 130 to 115 ka. It began with a period of global warmth, with sea levels rising about 6 m higher than at present, during which the mean temperature rapidly declined. After a period of increased warmth during MIS 5d (115–106 ka), the global temperature again fell sharply. There was a general trend of warmer conditions with MIS 5c until 100 ka, followed by a long decline until 90 ka, and a further period of higher temperatures at about 85 ka. The key point, is that the climate fluctuated, on occasion very rapidly indeed, throughout MIS 5, and this would have had a profound impact on the experiences of AMHs as they expanded eastward from their African homeland.

The seabed surrounding the islands of Southeast Asia is not far below the present ocean surface. Changes in global temperatures exert a major impact on the rise and fall of sea levels and consequent opportunities for the movement of AMH's or their absence (Figure 3.2).

During periods of intense cold, the expansion of the polar ice and advance of continental glaciers absorbed water from the world's oceans, and in the particular case of Southeast Asia, opened to human settlement a vast area, known as Sundaland. This in turn created favourable conditions for the expansion of human communities by eliminating or reducing marine barriers. The converse, inevitably was that global warming led to rapid rises in the sea level and the formation of islands on higher ground. Thus, during the height of the last glacial maximum

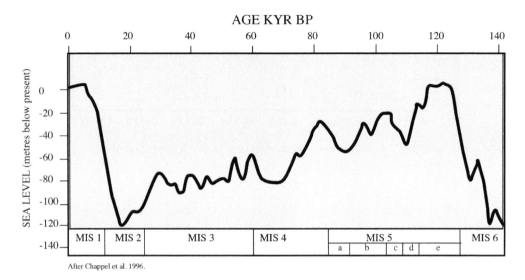

**FIGURE 3.2** Changes in the sea level during MIS 1-6.
*Source:* Chappel and Shackleton (1996).

during MIS 2, Sumatra, Java, and Borneo were part of the Asian mainland and further east, New Guinea, Australia, and Tasmania comprised one landmass. Nevertheless, at no stage was greater Australia visible from Asia. There was still a significant body of ocean to be traversed. With the end of the last glacial maximum, the sea level rose by about 130 m, drowning Sundaland and at the same time, doubtless inundating many key archaeological sites. The rapidity of this transition into MIS 1 is seen clearly in the pollen spectrum from the Nong Pa Kho lake sediments in Northeast Thailand, where a pine-oak forest was replaced by a tropical broadleaf forest from about 10 ka (Figure 3.3; Penny 2001).

The climate of mainland Southeast Asia is dominated today by the monsoon. During the northern winter, from October until April, the intense cold creates high atmospheric pressure over the Tibetan plateau and East Asia, which generates a cold, dry wind system with prevailing northeasterly winds in Southeast Asia, bringing a long dry season. Aridity varies with regional conditions, but in rain shadow areas like the Khorat Plateau of Northeast Thailand, months can go by with no significant rainfall. From May, the pattern reverses. High pressure over the Indian Ocean drives a southerly airflow bringing humid rains to the mainland. Changes in the earth's temperature affect the intensity of the monsoon. Glacial periods with low sea levels greatly increase aridity while warmer interglacial or interstadial periods raise sea levels, increase the extent of open water and bring much warmer and wetter conditions. Such climatic changes in prehistory must also be borne in mind when considering openings and barriers to human expansion out of Africa in the first place, for clearly, arid deserts in the Near East would have discouraged such movements, just as warm and moist conditions could have facilitated exploration.

These climatic oscillations have a direct impact on the natural vegetation. About 130 ka, at the end of MIS 6, there was a rapid period of warming and with it, a period of increased rainfall with a strengthening monsoon in Southeast Asia. The natural consequence was the spread of rainforest as then found on the island of Java, with a new suite of animals known as the Punung fauna (Westaway et al. 2007). Cooling at the end of MIS 5 saw the contraction of the rainforest,

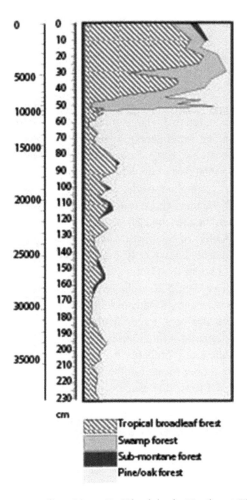

FIGURE 3.3   The pollen spectrum from Nong Pa Kho lake in Northeast Thailand showing the dramatic change in the vegetation at the onset of MIS 1.

Source: Dr D. Penny.

and a savannah corridor developed across Sundaland, leading to the demise of the orangutan and gibbon, and spread of herbivores. Thus, with each oscillation in the climate, and we now know that these could be experienced within a single lifetime, there were consequences in terms of the habitats experienced by AMHs if they progressively moved east during this stage.

These hunter gatherers would thus have encountered a range of environments each of which presented its own set of challenges. It might be thought reasonable from a modern perspective, to progress, generation by generation, by following the shoreline. Indeed, Oppenheimer (2014) has described the early AMHs as beachcombers. However, much of coastal Southeast Asia supports a deep belt of mangroves within which fish, shellfish, and crabs are the principal food resources, together with pigs and macaques. But the dense tangle of roots makes easy passage through mangroves virtually impossible. Occupying a mangrove estuary presents many opportunities for exploiting marine food sources, only if watercraft were available.

The canopied rainforests of Southeast Asia are one of the richest habitats known in terms of bioproductivity, but this concentrates well above ground level, and is manifested in a wide range of arboreal species that are not easy to exploit without the development of the blowpipe or bow and arrow. The contrast between the rainforest and more open terrain supporting savannah grassland that expanded under cooling conditions is significant. Primates, squirrels, civets, and other arboreal specialists, with more solitary rhinoceros and bears at ground level, dominate the former. The latter is better suited to the large grazers, of which there are many: three species of wild cattle, large medium, and small deer, pigs, elephants, and their predators the tiger and leopard.

Lakes and rivers are also a vital part of the Southeast Asian environment. To this day, fishing and shellfish are a ubiquitous component of the diet, and access to water was doubtless a major contributor to where early humans chose to live. There is also a further species that AMHs would have encountered when they reached SEA: other humans.

*Homo erectus* preceded AMHs in Southeast Asia by about 1.7 million years, while *Homo floresienses* and *Homo luzonensis*, known only from the islands of Flores and Luzon respectively, might once have had a wider distribution. There is also the enigma of the Denisovans. This species of human has been identified on the basis of DNA from bones and a tooth at least 200,000 years old, found at the cave of Denisova in Siberia (Reich et al. 2011; Douka et al. 2019). Denisovan genes have also been traced in Australian Aborigines, Philippine Negritos and Melanesians. Very recently and for the first time, a Denisovan has been identified in mainland Southeast Asia. A juvenile tooth, probably from a girl aged between 3.5 and 8 years, has been found at Tam Ngu Hao, a cave located in the Truong Son Range in Laos (Demeter et al. 2022). Dating in the region of 140 ka, the shape of the molar is distinct from equivalent teeth in *H. erectus*, the other possible source. At an altitude of 1116 m, the young Denisovan lived in a relatively open habitat populated by wild cattle, deer and rhinoceros to judge from the teeth found in the same layer. Precisely how the Denisovans relate to *H. erectus*, if at all, remains to be explored.

**Out of Africa: Crossing the Gate of Grief**

Our understanding of the origins of AMHs has been revolutionised by discoveries at Jebel Irhoud in Morocco (Figure 3.4). Here, excavations have uncovered a settlement that has provided the perfect triad of evidence: human remains, reliable dates and the tools and animal bones that reflect subsistence. The skull is one of the most crucial bones for any assessment of prehistoric people, and an exhaustive analysis of the shape of the crania and the jawbones place the Irhoud individuals squarely in the range of modern humans, even though the shape retained archaic features. New dating evidence places the occupation of Irhoud in the vicinity of 315 ka (Hublin et al. 2017; Richter et al. 2017). Between 330 and 300 ka, northwest Africa presented an open and relatively dry environment, green enough to support cattle and horses that humans preyed upon. Again, the stone tools at Irhoud include flakes and blades struck from the parent core, a characteristic of an advancing and more sophisticated industry than hitherto.

Irhoud is the earliest site yet to provide evidence for early AMHs, but a growing number of other settlements now indicate that their occupation covered much of Africa. Herto in Ethiopia is strategically located to give easier access than Irhoud to the crossing of the Bab el-Mandeb (Gate of Grief) at the southern end of the Red Sea, into Asia. Here, three skulls dated to about 160 ka have several features, such as a large brain and domed frontal bone that characterise

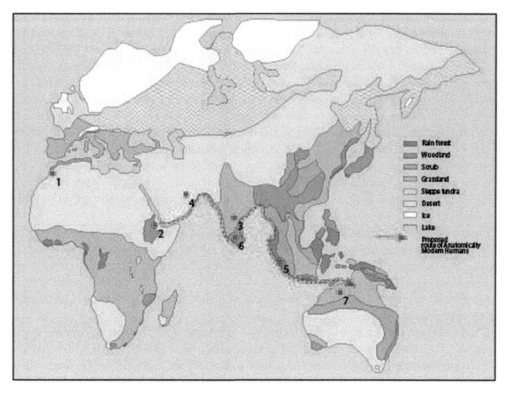

FIGURE 3.4  Map showing vegetation reconstructed for a glacial period and the location of sites mentioned in the text beyond mainland Southeast Asia. The dotted lines show the coastal route that has been suggested as a possible expansionary corridor from Africa to Australia. (1) Jebel Irhoud, (2) Herto, (3) Jawalapuram, (4) Jebel Faya, (5) Mt. Toba, (6) Batatomba-lena, Fahien-lena, (7) Madjedbebe.

AMHs. Intriguingly, the skulls bear cut marks that might reflect mortuary rituals. These early humans lived in an environment that harboured hippopotami and wild cattle (Stringer 2003). Wetter conditions also prevailed in the southern Ethiopian site of Omo, where AMH remains have been recovered in deeply stratified contexts dated to nearly 200 ka (McDougall et al. 2005). These sites provide evidence for hunting large herbivores, but at Abdur, on the Red Sea coast of Africa, Middle Stone Age artefacts are associated with recurrent evidence for the collection of shellfish at least 120 ka. This location is on the very doorstep of the most likely route out of Africa, and shows clear adaptation to a marine environment that might well have encouraged the exodus east.

## Going East

There are two likely routes out of Northeast Africa, the Sinai, and the Bab el-Mandeb crossing of the southern entrance to the Red Sea. During periods of glacial cold, the Arabian Peninsula would have been arid and inhospitable, but with interglacial periods, conditions would have favoured human settlement, with more vegetation, herbivorous animals, and watercourses. When AMHs left Africa on an exodus that was ultimately to reach Tasmania remains an open question, but resolving alternative dates and possible routes must take into account the impact of climatic change on the environments that had to be crossed. MIS 5 was a relatively warm phase. Although the northern parts of Africa and Arabia would have then been under desert, the region on either side of the Bab el-Mandab strait would have sustained a tropical woodland populated by large herbivores and food plants (Boivin et al. 2013). By following a coastal route towards the Arabian Gulf, expanding humans could have taken advantage of tropical savannah and woodland conditions. When our imaginary human groups reached western India during this period, the dry tropical woodland conditions lay behind the coastal tract, backed by a tropical savannah. Hence it is reasonable to imagine a scenario, which facilitated land-based expansion. Similar habitats stretched into Southeast Asia until the first tropical forest with its markedly thinner food resources were encountered in the Thai/Malay peninsula. Thus there was a clear inland pathway for expansion in contrast to the notion that the coast was the principal and most attractive route east (Boivin et al. 2013).

During the cold conditions of MIS 4, the situation changed dramatically. Desert expanded to cover extensive areas of North Africa and Arabia. In northwest India, the Thar Desert dominated. The sea level fell, exposing Sundaland, across which a grassland corridor opened from modern Myanmar to Java, and on into northern Australia. As a consequence, this period became less conducive to human expansionary moves out of Africa, but facilitated movement through mainland Southeast Asia.

There are thus two such phases of interglacial warmth that are relevant to any review of the expansion of AMHs out of Africa. One lasted at the transition of GIS 6-5e, that is between 135 and 120 ka. The other was later, from 82 to 78 ka during GIS 5a. There is clear evidence of human occupation of the FAY-NE1 rock shelter at Jebel Faya, in the United Arab Emirates, that is dated to about 125 ka, during a period of increased rainfall. This comprises a range of stone artefacts including small hand axes and scrapers that resemble Middle Stone Age assemblages in Africa. Occupation of this region continued at FAY-NE1 with two further contexts with dates of about 40 ka. Armitage et al. (2011) conclude that there could well have been an expansionary settlement by AMH from Northeast Africa as the Bab el-Mandeb strait was relatively narrow, but wetter conditions were developing at the onset of GIS 5. It must, however, be stressed that no human remains have been found at Jebel Faya to identify the hominin who lived there.

A similar lack of human remains in Indian sites rules out drawing a final conclusion on when AMH reached South Asia on their passage further east. There are two conflicting models. One centres on the site of Jawalapuram in Andhra Pradesh Province, where evidence for human presence in the form of stone artefacts has been found under and over the tephra deposited by the Younger Toba eruption (Petraglia et al. 2007). Locality three at this site incorporates a 2.5 m thick deposit of volcanic ash that descended on a lakeside environment. The stone tools found under the ash include scrapers, blades, and burins that represent the Indian Stone Age tradition, with claimed links to African technology that Mellars et al. (2013) have rejected. This context has been dated to 77 ka. Human occupation was also found above the Toba ash, a stone tool assemblage with strong affinities to the earlier artefacts, and dated to about 74 ka. By this time, the colder conditions of GIS4 were in place.

This Middle Palaeolithic model offers a radical contrast to that focussing on the expansion of AMH after the Toba eruption (Mellars 2006; Mellars et al. 2013). This alternative is rooted in the contrast between the stone industry of early Jawalapuram and a widespread South Asian tradition of microlithic stone blades that invariable post-date the Toba eruption. These were probably associated with the bow, and represent such a radical departure from earlier methods that it unlikely to have emerged so rapidly from the Middle Stone Age predecessors, given the absence of any transitional industries. This critical cultural horizon is also characterised by other innovations: ostrich eggshell beads, incised designs, and bone tools all of which are paralleled in African sites (Mellars et al. 2013). The microlithic stone tool tradition has been radiocarbon dated to 35–40 ka at Batadomba-lena and Fahien-lena in Sri Lanka, in association with the bones of AMH. Earlier sites with a coastal orientation will now lie well below the sea, leaving a hiatus in dating the original expansion of AMHs in South Asia according to Paul Mellars's model, which he places broadly between 65 and 55 ka. This is earlier than the expansion of AMHs into Europe and western Asia, but presents a similar set of circumstances, the movement of modern humans, under favourable environmental conditions, into lands long occupied by other archaic human species.

These two models remain compatible only if there are two distinct moves out of Africa, and judging between them will be best achieved through the discovery of South Asian sites containing datable human and cultural remains. However, there are two approaches that can order them in terms of plausibility. One is identifying the presence of AMH further east that predate the Toba eruption, and therefore demonstrate an early exit from Africa during GIS 5, and the second is to consider the evidence from human DNA, with particular reference to the so-called molecular clock that provides possible dates for the coalescence of haplogroups.

### The Evidence from Human Genetics

The analysis of human genetics has revolutionised the study of the human past. It does not necessarily involve extracting DNA from prehistoric individuals, because by identifying modern haplogroups and their geographic distribution, it is possible to trace descent lines. Crucially, an estimate of the rate of genetic mutations then permits an approximate date for the splits between ancestral and descendant DNA haplogroups to be estimated, albeit with very broad ranges of confidence. Essentially, this can be undertaken on the basis of mitochondrial DNA, which represents maternal reproduction, and male and bilateral inherited DNA (Mellars et al. 2013). The first of these has the African foundation haplogroup L3, which gave rise to the original 'African Eve' model (Cann et al. 1987). Three Asian haplogroups, M N and R originated from L3. The key issue is, when did the mutations leading into these new haplogroups occur. Most estimates suggest that the exodus from Africa has a 95% chance of falling within the period 62–79 ka and 50–72 ka for the presence of Hg N in Arabia and 55–70 ka for AMH settlement with Hg M and R in South Asia. However, there has been a significant recent revision of the rate of mutation in nuclear DNA that halves the former figure, and therefore doubles timescales (Scally and Durbin 2012). They have concluded that the split between the African Yoruba population and non-African humans took place between 90 and 130 ka. This result supports a pre-Toba expansion of AMHs out of Africa and suggests that expansion might have occurred in several waves, rather than a single event.

### The Evidence of Archaeology

The second approach to distinguishing between the pre and post Toba models for human expansion into Southeast Asia is archaeological. Is there convincing evidence for the presence of AMSs east of India before 74 ka? When and where do we find the first evidence for the arrival of AMHs in Southeast Asia? Here, we enter a veritable minefield. There is a handful of caves in southern China and Laos that incorporate sediments containing rare human remains, mainly teeth, as well as animal bones and naturally deposited flowstones formed as water moves along the floor of a cave, gradually depositing a hard stone-like gypsum and calcite. The flowstones can be dated by a number of techniques including OSL (Zhang et al. 2015). It would seem straightforward that if you find teeth similar to those of modern humans sealed under a dated flowstone, you have the key to tracing the arrival of AMHs into the region.

Zhiren Cave is located in Guangxi Province, southern China (Figure 3.5). It is rich in faunal remains that reveal the replacement of the Middle Pleistocene Gigantopithecus-Stegodon, assemblage by elephants and small mammals adapted to an open grassland rather than a forested habitat. This latter fauna fits well with GIS 5d climatic conditions. The bones recovered include two human upper molar teeth and part of a jawbone representing two individuals (Wu et al. 2010). A detailed analysis of the form and size of the teeth suggests that they have affinities with early modern humans. The form of the mandible likewise places this bone closer to modern than archaic humans, although it does have some robust features. Dating this faunal assemblage – there are no reports of stone artefacts from Zhiren Cave – is clearly of considerable significance. Early reports describe that the layer containing the teeth and mandible are sealed by flowstone dated by U-series analysis to about 106 ka. Identifying their reverse polarity, leading to an estimate in the vicinity of 116 ka, has recently dated the layers under the human remains. Prima facie, the three Zhiren human bones support a pre-Toba expansion of modern humans into eastern Asia.

Longtanshan cave is located in Yunnan Province of Southwest China. Excavations there have recovered two human teeth, that detailed comparisons of their shape and size, suggest are from AMHs (Curnoe et al. 2016). U-series dating of these two specimens has resulted in a date range of 60–83 ka, which, in conjunction with the associated faunal remains, suggests settlement there during MIS 4-5. At Huanglong Cave in Hubei Province, seven AMH teeth have been indirectly dated by the associated flowstone to 101–81 ka (Shen et al. 2013). Similarly, at Luna Cave in Guangxi, two human teeth ascribed to AMH have been dated by their relationship to flowstones within the span 127–70 ka. A similar range has been published for 47 AMH teeth from Fuyan Cave in Hunan Province, but no stone tools were found in association (Sun et al. 2021). Yangjiapao Cave in Hubei contained 11 AMH teeth associated with the same faunal group as at Huanglong and Luna, and therefore presumably of the same antiquity. Excavations in Sanyou Cave north of the Yangtze River in Hubei Province have recovered a fragment of human skull.

The stratigraphic accumulations at these caves are complex and difficult to interpret. Sun et al. (2021) have critically examined the issues of the relationship between teeth not found in a clearly undisturbed context, such as a living floor, and the dated flowstones, suggesting that the impact of erosion and redeposition severely erodes confidence in the proposed dates. They have, further, applied the acid tests of dating the bones themselves by radiocarbon, and citing the evidence from DNA. Two teeth from Fuyan Cave were radiocarbon dated to ca. 7500 and 500 BC. For Yangjiapao, the sediment samples used for dating the human teeth ranged between 200 and 94 ka. However, radiocarbon dates for an actual human tooth provided a result of about 1300 BC. Whereas sediment samples from Sanyou Cave suggest a date for the human skull fragment of 129–107 ka, the bone itself according to a radiocarbon date, is about 1700 years old. These results were then compared with the clade divergence times for mtDNA extracted from Yangjiapao and Fuyan Cave human teeth that indicated an age of less than 15.6 ka (Sun et al. 2021). The radiocarbon dates and DNA divergence result combine to cast serious doubt on the early dates claimed for the arrival of AMHs in Southern China between 120 and 70 ka

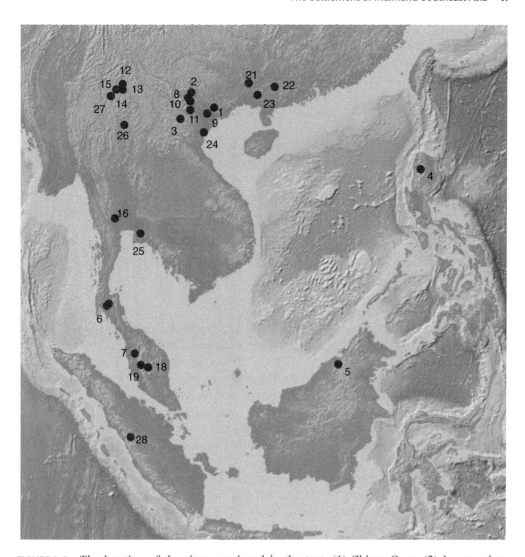

FIGURE 3.5  The location of the sites mentioned in the text. (1) Zhiren Cave, (2) Longtanshan, (3) Tham Pa Ling, (4) Callao Cave, (5) Niah, (6). Lang Rongrien, Moh Khiew, (7) Bukit Bunuh, (8). Xiaodong, Dedan, (9) Nguom, (10) Hang Cho, Son Vi, Xom Trai, (11) Hang Boi, (12) Tham Lod, Ban Rai, (13) Banyan Valley Cave, (14) Steep Cliff Cave, (15) Spirit Cave, (16) Lang Kamnan, (17) Khao Toh Chong, Sakai Cave, (18) Gua Cha, (19) Gua Gunung Runtuh, (20) Gexinqiao, Baida, Kantun, (21) Beidaling, (22) Datangcheng, (23) Dingsishan, (24) Con Co Ngua, Da But, (25) Nong Nor, (26) Doi Pha Kan, (27) Huai Hin, (28) Lida Ajer, (29) Quynh Van, Thach Lac, (30) Ru Diep, (31) Bau Du, (32) Chongtang, (33) Tham Khuong.

Source: Map by C. F. W. Highan. Courtesy: GeoMapApp (www.geomapapp.org), CC by Ryan et al. (2009).

(Hublin 2021). It is, however, noted that the radiocarbon dating protocols employed do not have universal acceptance (Higham and Douka 2021).

Tham Pa Ling cave is located in the Pa Hang upland range of north-eastern Laos, at 1170 m above sea level. The stratigraphic sequence deep inside the cavern is about 4.3 m thick, and at a depth of 2.35 m below the surface, the fragmentary remains of a human skull were recovered, including some of the upper teeth. The absence of any evidence for human occupation suggests that the bones were deposited by natural processes in the recesses of the cave. Charcoal, also probably washed into the cave, has provided an approximate date for the human remains of about 55 ka. Further dating was obtained by thermoluminescence and OSL, providing a date prior to about 46 ka for the cranium, which almost certainly came from one individual. The human frontal bone was further dated by the Uranium series to $63.6 \pm 6$ ka. The skull is the key bone for identifying early AMHs, and there are many aspects to the size and form that allow an assessment of a specimen's place in human evolution. The Tham Pa Ling skull and dentition presents consistent features that place it in the genus *Homo sapiens* (Demeter et al. 2012). For example, it has no shelf of bone running across the top of the eye sockets, a feature known as a supraorbital torus that is characteristic of earlier archaic humans. Like virtually all the mainland sites with minimal and invariably redeposited human remains, there is an element of doubt about the actual status of these bones.

The Punung faunal assemblage, identified from cave deposits on the island of Java, contain all the elements of a rainforest habitat, including orangutan and gibbons. It has been dated between 128 and 118 ka (Westaway et al. 2017). Investigations in the Punung caves before the 2nd World War recovered human teeth, of which one has been traced among the archived collections (Storm et al. 2005). The form and size of this tooth are much more akin with AMHs than *H. erectus*, the latter known to have inhabited Java for over a million years. Moreover, *H. erectus* is an unlikely candidate to inhabit a closed-canopy rainforest. Naturally, one must be cautious in placing any reliance on a single tooth, found decades ago under pre-modern excavation methods.

Lida Ajer is a cave in Western Sumatra examined by Eugene Dubois in the 1880s. It took 60 years before two teeth from the build-up of deposits were identified as human, and by referring back to Dubois's field notes, sediments in which they might have been found have been dated to between 63 and 73 ka. Moreover, the associated faunal remains are typical of the Southeast Asian rainforest. This span brings modern human remains within reach of the Toba eruption (Westaway et al. 2017). Obviously, there are major issues of credibility in this case, particularly since the colour of the two teeth differs from other remains with which they were allegedly associated.

In many respects, the acid test for the arrival of AMHs into Southeast Asia is to be found through the dating of the first human settlement of Australia in the absence of evidence for any preceding occupation by archaic humans. Thus, the likelihood that prehistoric sites in Australia were occupied by AMHs is high: no evidence has yet been identified for the presence of *H. erectus* there. The earliest known settlement is the Madjedbebe rock shelter, located on the western margin of Arnhem Land (Clarkson et al. 2017). The earliest of the three occupation phases there contained an elaborate and in many respects a very large and sophisticated assemblage of stone tools, including edge-ground axes, grinding stones and flakes struck from the parent cores. These first inhabitants used red ochre, and collected seeds and pandanus fruit. The entire sequence has been dated by means 18 OSL dates, that provide a range of 52.7–65 ka. This took place during a period of low sea levels, making the sea passage to Australia shorter, when the climate was wetter and cooler. If this site was occupied by AMHs, no human remains have been identified there yet, this evidence would reveal beyond reasonable doubt that AMHs had already reached mainland Southeast Asia by at least 52.7 ka. However, serious doubts have been cast on this early date (O'Connell et al. 2018). The most recent excavation there covered just 20 m$^2$, and the alleged early layer was found at a depth of 1.9–2.6 m. The upper limit date of 65 ka is earlier by 20 millennia than any comparable site in Australia. No radiocarbon determinations have been obtained from the relevant cultural contexts that show a range beyond the ca. 50 ka upper limit of this technique. There are serious issues of redeposition and disturbances in sites such as Madjedbebe. O'Connell et al. (2018) advise extreme caution in accepting this early context. What we miss in documenting possible settlement of Southeast Asia and Sahul before ca 50 ka, is an undoubtedly undisturbed human occupation site that is rigorously dated. The totality of other Southeast Asian and Sahul dates for the undoubted arrival of AMH are uniformly later than ca. 50 ka.

### Early Anatomically Modern Humans in Mainland Southeast Asia

The shape of mainland Southeast Asia has varied like a concertina. Colder conditions led to a lower sea level and an expansion of the landmass of Southeast Asia, whereas the rising sea with warmer conditions created islands. During the last glacial maximum, Borneo, Sumatra, and Java were all joined with and part of the mainland. Ideally, firm archaeological evidence for the settlement of this vast region should combine the actual remains of AMHs with their artefacts and evidence for subsistence. Niah Cave on the northern shore of Borneo is one site that fulfils all these criteria (Figure 3.6).

Major excavations took place under the direction of Tom and Barbara Harrisson between 1954 and 1967, and it was in 1958 that they discovered a human cranium towards the base of the cultural sequence, that displayed features consistent with it being from an AMH. Dating

FIGURE 3.6   The great cave of Niah on the northern coast of Borneo, where an early Anatomically Modern Human skull has been found.

*Source:* Professor G. Barker.

the bone directly by U-series as well as the contexts in which it lay by radiocarbon is highly relevant. Using the archived site records, it has been possible for Barker and a large team of specialists to revisit Niah, cut back and re-assess the still open excavation sections, and obtain a new series of radiocarbon determinations (Barker and Farr 2016). The U-series direct date on the bone returned a result of 35.2 + 2.6 ka (Pike 2016). This is in close agreement with the preferred radiocarbon results for associated charcoal of 37,360–32,440 ka at 68.3% probability (Higham et al. 2016). Since occupation remains were found under the human skull, occupation of Niah must have begun prior to about 35 ka.

The faunal remains associated with the early occupation phases reflect a rainforest habitat, and a mature adaptation to its exploitation. The bearded pig dominates numerically, with all age ranges represented. Piper and Rabett (2014) have suggested that this probably random nature of trapping rather than the specific targeting of individual animals of a preferred age. Although fewer in numbers, the other species include monkeys, tapir and rhinoceros, sambar deer and muntjak. Turtles and tortoises were also brought back to the cave. The recovery of plant remains supports the conclusions based on the fauna, that the early inhabitants of Niah were well versed in exploiting a forested habitat that was rather drier than at present, with some open areas that attracted deer and bovids. In terms of the plant remains, it is highly likely that the early inhabitants were aware that several local species, such as wild yams, are toxic and require lengthy processing before being edible. Yams, palms, and aroids were collected, as well as nuts and fruits. Shellfish were sought in the local clear streams and other watercourses, but the rarity of marine fish and shellfish, as well as mangrove pollen, suggests that the sea level was lower than at present and some distance from the cave. The cultural remains as a whole are compatible with brief, perhaps seasonal, periods of occupation. Stone tools were designed more for processing wood rather than hunting, and it is highly likely that bamboo played an important role in hunting and gathering.

Lang Rongrien is the principal settlement on the present mainland of Southeast Asia that rivals the antiquity of Niah. It lies near the confluence of the Krabi River and the Khlong Yai Stream in southern Thailand, and presents as a wide and sunny rock shelter fully 36 m wide. Three cultural layers were identified below a thick accumulation of rockfall from the roof (Figure 3.7). The lowest, known as unit 10, lay on top of the bedrock, and included hearths, ash deposits, and chert artefacts that probably date to about 43 ka, while that above it has been radiocarbon dated to 37 ka. It too contained hearths and stone tools, as well as fractured animal bones. The succeeding cultural layer has been dated to about 27 ka. The early stone tools were either made on flakes struck off their parent core, and converted into scrapers and knives, or core tools chipped into the form of choppers and bifacial implements. The cores could have been collected from the bed of the adjacent river that flows past the cave (Anderson 1990). During the earliest phases in the occupation of Lang Rongrien, the sea level was about 85 km from the site. With units 9 and 8, the increasing cold of MIS 2 led to a further fall in the sea level, leaving the coast up to 110 km distant. In contrast to the present tropical lowland rainforest in the area of Lang Rongrien, the climate during the formation of units 8–10 would have been cooler and drier, favouring vegetation of open savannah and patches of forest. The faunal remains from units 8 to 10 reflect proximity to this dry, open forest that attracted deer and bovids. Turtle and or tortoise bones predominated, with nearly half of all bone from unit 8, a remarkable 75% from unit 9, though falling to 10% in the lowest occupation context (Mudar and Anderson 2007). The different species identified indicate visits to ponds, marshes and sluggish streams, as well as their margins. However, there are too few identified mammalian bones to establish the relative

FIGURE 3.7   Excavations at the cave of Lang Rongrien have revealed a long occupation sequence against a backdrop of environmental change.

*Source:* Professor D. Anderson.

frequencies of different species, due largely to their fragmentation. In terms of presence or absence, at least three species of deer were hunted. There are also some bovid bones that could come from the gaur or banteng both of which are adapted to grassland rather than forest. Just one pig bone was found in unit 8. The fragmented bones clustered round hearths, and a significant number exhibit evidence of charring. One of the characteristics of this site, as with Niah, was broad-spectrum exploitation that involved collecting turtles and tortoises, and hunting the local mammalian fauna during periods of relatively brief occupation when the habitat was a mix of open savannah grassland and woodland.

Bukit Bunuh is a quite different site from Niah and Lang Rongrien. Located in the Lenggong Valley in Malaysia, it was a workshop for the manufacture of stone tools. The presence of anvils and hammer stones surrounded by the waste flakes struck from stone cores, indicate that the remains are undisturbed. Stone debitage covers an area of at least 3 km$^2$, and while most of the tools were created on the struck flakes, there are also some core tools in which the removal of flakes created large, pointed artefacts that resemble the widely distributed handaxes of Eurasia. An OSL date for this site places it in the same antiquity as Niah and Lang Rongrien, with an estimate of about 40 ka (Saidin 2006).

## The Hoabinhian

The Hoabinhian is a name given to many sites in Mainland Southeast Asia that display a common tradition of stone tool technology centred on a unifacially flaked axe or chopping tool known as a sumatralith (Figure 3.8).

Other stone tools are known as short axes, choppers, picks, and discoid scrapers. There are also tools fashioned from bone and shell. Most sites are located in caves or rock shelters. The Hoabinhian represents the upland and inland facies of the late Pleistocene and Holocene hunter gatherer tradition, for until about 4300 ka, the sea level was lower than at present, and any

FIGURE 3.8   Sumatraliths, or unifacial discoids are the most widespread of Hoabinhian stone tools.

evidence for coastal occupation has been drowned. It therefore presents only a partial glimpse of the hunter-gatherer adaptation to mainland Southeast Asia. This tradition was first identified in 1906, and was soon followed by cave excavations in Hoa Binh province by the French archaeologist Madeleine Colani. Hence, the name Hoabinhian comes from the eponymous province.

Xiaodong is a large cave, located next to the Hemang River, 1195 m above sea level in southwest Yunnan Province of China. Excavations in 2015 revealed cultural deposits to a depth of nearly 2 m comprising six layers, although the base of the site was not reached. These have been radiocarbon dated, the earliest suggesting occupation began in layer 6 at 43.5 ka, the latest dates for layer 1 being 24.5 ka. Most of the stone tools from Xiaodong come from surface or uncertain stratigraphic provenance, but some were also recovered from the 2015 excavation season. They include several different forms fashioned from the cobbles that are abundant in the nearby river bed. One of the prominent forms was flaked on one side of the cobble, leaving the other side untouched to form an axe-like tool that could have been conveniently held in the hand or possibly also hafted. The assemblage includes heavy-duty choppers, that were probably used to work wood, and scrapers. The unifacially worked chopper tools are widely recognised as characteristic of the "Hoabinhian" hunter gatherer sites of mainland Southeast Asia, all of which are considerably later than basal Xiaodong. Ji et al. (2016) suggest that the Hoabinhian might have originated in the uplands of Yunnan and then spread south.

Dedan is one of ten newly identified Hoabinhian rock shelter sites in this part of Yunnan. It lies 50 km from Xiaodong, and is located close to the Langlong River. The lowest layer is dated to about 35 ka and has yielded just four stone tools. The next two layers are dated to between 18 and 20 ka and have furnished a typical Hoabinhian stone tool assemblage that includes sumatraliths, choppers and modified flake tools (Wu et al. 2022).

On the basis of new radiocarbon determinations, the Hoabinhian in the Vietnamese uplands began about 33 ka at Tham Khuong, and at least 20 ka and possibly as early as 29 ka at the site of Hang Cho (Yi et al. 2008). Lang Vanh cave was occupied by 16.5 ka, and Xom Trai between 18 and 17 ka. Whatever may be the case, it is stressed that the Hoabinhian illuminates the adaptation of AMHs to mainland Southeast Asia over a period when the dry and relatively cold conditions of the late glacial maximum gave way to the warm and humid environment of MIS 1. For the first time too, burials provide evidence for the physical characteristics of the people and the social nature of their mortuary practices.

Excavations at Hang Cho have revealed 13 occupation layers dating between 20 and 8.5 ka, often separated by sterile lenses. Shellfish were very numerous throughout this sequence, doubtless gathered from the stream that formerly flowed past the entrance to this large cavern. Numerically, the sample is dominated by the species *Melanoides tuberculata*. In the lowest layers, dating to MIS 2, the bones of cattle, bears, deer, and pigs were also numerous. As is so often the case, turtle bones were also found. The stone tools include sumatraliths, scrapers, and burins (Yi et al. 2008).

The upper cave of Hang Boi on the margins of the Red River floodplain is barely 15 m wide and deep, and could hardly have accommodated more than an extended family group. The rarity of stone tools in the cultural deposits rules out a definitive attribution to the Hoabinhian, but it seems highly likely. Excavations there have uncovered evidence for occupation within the span of 12–10.5 ka. The settlement was then at least 60 km from the coast, and gave access to freshwater conditions, although it was at this period that the sea level was rising rapidly, bringing more brackish conditions to the area. A remarkable concentration of land snails dominate the cultural deposits, well over 90% coming from the genus *Cyclophorus* (Rabett et al. 2009). Evidently, the best time to collect these snails is during the wet season, and one reason for favouring them is their alleged medicinal qualities. A tiny number of other shellfish come from freshwater habitats. The other faunal remains reflect a broad spectrum approach to subsistence. There are abundant remains of fish, crabs, and turtles, again reflecting the exploitation of the local rivers. Monkeys, including macaques, are the most numerous of the mammalian bones recovered, followed by deer and pigs. Cattle are rare. This assemblage indicates that the occupants lived in a forested environment, probably with open areas that favoured the deer. Although no hearths were identified, the presence of some burnt and fractured bone suggests that animals were brought back to the cave base for consumption. Limestone was the most abundant worked stone, but there is no consistent evidence for tool manufacture. It is as if the stone tools were brought to the site ready-made.

## Northern Thailand

Northwestern Thailand is one of the key regions of Southeast Asia for the examination of hunter gatherer occupation during MIS 1-2. The cave of Tham Lod, located 640 m above sea level, is 30 m wide and 4.5 m deep (Figure 3.9).

It could, again, have only sheltered a small group. Like the other inhabited caves in this area, it had the advantage of proximity to a permanent river, located about 250 m away. Over 4 m of cultural accumulation were identified by excavation, the lowest being dated to 35.7 ka while in the upper deposits, human burials have been dated to 12 ka. Most evidence for occupation in the form of lithics and faunal remains comes from layer 5 in area 1, which is dated to about 22 ka. This equates with the cold period of MIS 2. Here, the stone tools include classic Hoabinhian

FIGURE 3.9   The cave of Tham Lod in Northern Thailand, where early hunter-gatherer occupation has been dated to 35,700 years ago.

*Source:* Dr R. Shoocondej.

sumatraliths and short axes, many of which were manufactured in a workshop within the cave, leading to the accumulation of hammerstones and waste flakes. Shoocondej (2006) has suggested that the freshwater shellfish were probably collected during the dry season. The distribution of artefacts and faunal remains suggest that parts of the cave were set aside for specific activities, with food preparation in one area, stone tool manufacture in another and cooking in a third, seen in the concentration of hearths. After an interval of about ten millennia, the site was used for human burials. The faunal remains include the bones of cattle, water buffalo, pig, and the large sambar deer.

Conrad (2016) has undertaken a detailed analysis of the faunal remains from Tham Lod relative to the daily activities of the Mlabri, present day hunter-gatherers in Northwest Thailand. Ethnographic reports have shown that there is a marked contrast between the activities of the male hunters on the one hand, and the women, children, and the elderly on the other. Whereas men travel away from the base camp to hunt with spears for larger game, such as deer and pigs, the women forage and collect close to home, seeking out the turtles, shellfish, and roots that are more easily collected. By comparing the relative frequency of the larger game that probably reflects male hunting against items more likely to have been collected, Cyler Conrad has identified changes in hunting and gathering activities over three phases of occupation. The faunal spectrum itself is numerically dominated by the large deer, *Cervus unicolor*, other larger mammals including pig, bovids, and the goral, a goat-antelope adapted to hilly terrain. Smaller muntjak deer, macaques, and langurs were also represented. Rhinoceros were rare. Fish, turtles, and tortoises were also abundant, but only in the second of the three phases analysed. If the ethnographic analogy with the Mlabri is a valid yardstick, during the first and third phases, the fauna suggest male dominated hunting while the second phase, numerically dominated by turtles and tortoises, it seems that it was the women, children and the elderly who were to the fore in gathering food.

Ban Rai is located 10 km from Tham Lod. A large cavern measuring 105 by 40 m, it is located on a hillside, next to a stream that flows into a large sinkhole in the limestone (Treerayapeewat

FIGURE 3.10  Most Hoabinhian burials were found in a flexed position with few mortuary offerings. This example comes from Ban Rai in Northern Thailand and dates to about 10,000 years ago.

*Source:* Dr R. Shoocondej.

2005). Hoabinhian occupation began in about 12 ka, the cultural layers containing typical short axes and sumatraliths, together with the flakes and cores that indicate in situ working of stone. The ashy accumulation of occupation remains included mammalian bones, fish, and shellfish. At Tham Lod, the site had also been used for interring the dead, the flexed burial of a man being dated to about 10 ka (Figure 3.10).

A similar period of occupation has been identified at Spirit Cave, a small rock shelter located on a precipitous hillside above the Khong Stream in the same catchment as Tham Lod and Ban Rai. Excavations in the 1960s by Chester Gorman uncovered cultural deposits 75 cm deep, that reflect hunter-gatherer occupation between 13 and 8 ka (Gorman 1972). The rock shelter could barely have accommodated more than a family of hunter gatherers and the occupation layers suggest brief and intermittent visits. The stone artefacts covered the basic range of those typical of the Hoabinhian, including the short axes and sumatraliths thought to have been used to work wood. Indeed, by screening cultural deposits, Gorman pioneered the recovery of very small faunal and plant remains, which has provided a complete list of the hunting and gathering activities that centred on the occupation of this site. The many bat and rat bones probably accumulated naturally. In the earliest occupation layer, which dates towards the end of MIS 2, the small muntjak deer dominates, followed by the larger sambar deer. There are also two macaque bones. The inhabitants sought out turtles and tortoises, fished the Khong stream for carp, even brought frogs back to the rock shelter together with shellfish, crabs, and land snails. Layer 2 dates within the period 10–8 ka, and thus corresponds with MIS 1, the warmer and wetter postglacial. There was a marked change in the faunal spectrum. The number of ground-dwelling mammals fell away, while the range and number of primate bones, including gibbons, macaques, and the slow loris, increased. The number of fish bones also increased markedly.

One of the principal outcomes of the Spirit Cave research has been the recognition of the role played by plant collection. *Canarium* seeds were abundant, and are still eaten in the area at present. This plant can also be used in the manufacture of resin or gum, a necessary constituent for composite hunting gear. Candlenuts can be eaten, or used for illumination. Betel nuts are sought after as a mild stimulant.

Conrad et al. (2016) have turned to the number of bat bones to reinterpret the occupation history of this rock shelter. These mammals roost in caves, but not contemporaneously with humans. Their profusion is thus strong evidence that the site was not as Gorman originally suggested, continuously used as a base but rather, that it was only occasionally and briefly visited. This is in accord with the ethnographic evidence from the Mlabri, who occupy their open campsites only for a matter of days before moving to another locale to continue hunting and foraging. Spirit Cave is therefore significant in that it spans the transition from the late Glacial Maximum into warmer and wetter conditions that would have favoured the spread of canopied rainforest. The local hunter gatherers displayed resilience in adapting to such climatic changes.

If Spirit Cave can be seen as a base for a small and transient group of hunter gatherers, Steep Cliff Cave presents a quite different setting and function. This narrow overhang sheltered Hoabinhian hunter gatherers intermittently between 7.5 and 5.5 ka. The presence of the giant red and the Himalayan striped squirrel indicates a forested environment, as one would expect. However, the bone assemblage is dominated by the burnt and smashed bones of large mammals, including wild cattle, water buffalo, pigs, and deer. The ashy cultural layers, and absence of the wide range of smaller species seen for example at Spirit Cave, suggests that this was a specialised location for the processing of the carcasses. The many flaked stone tools, including the ubiquitous sumatraliths would support this interpretation.

Banyan Valley Cave is the third site excavated during Gorman's fieldwork in this region. This is a considerably larger cave complex than the other two, covering 24 by 14 m, and is strategically located adjacent to a stream as it plunges into a sinkhole (Reynolds 1992). Excavations in 1972 revealed three occupation layers with a maximum depth of just over 2 m. The lowest probably dates to about 6 ka, while radiocarbon determinations place layer 2 between 5.4 and 4 ka. Remarkably, the uppermost occupation has provided a date of just 1 ka. Layers 2 and 3 contained a typical Hoabinhian stone industry, in which hammer stones had been employed in the manufacture of finished artefacts. The numerous waste flakes from this procedure indicate local stone working, including the production of axes, short axes, sumatraliths. However, the stone tools from the uppermost layer were decidedly different, including a bifacially flaked projectile point and ground quadrangular adze. The latest context also contained a few pottery sherds.

Banyan Valley Cave was a base for the manufacture of stone tools, and for general occupation, for the layers contain many hearths and ash lenses. Numerous bones were recovered that represent broad-spectrum hunting and foraging. Small and large deer, bovids, and pigs dominate among the larger hunted species. There are a few bones from langurs and macaques, while otters, turtles, fish, and shellfish were taken, probably from the adjacent stream. Screening has confirmed the exploitation of the surrounding forest, for *Canarium* nuts, gourds, and beans.

**The Khwae Noi Valley, Central Thailand**

The Khwae Noi Valley in west Central Thailand contains numerous rockshelters and caves that were occupied by hunter gatherers. Of these, Lang Kamnan is the most intensely studied (Shoocondej 2000). This site lies about 2 km from the nearest watercourses, in a situation with access to lowland swampy grassland, dry deciduous and upland evergreen forest. There are three cultural phases. The earliest has been dated to 27–11 ka. The cave had been used as the base for stone tool manufacture, seen in the waste flakes and cores as well as the finished sumatraliths, axes, and scrapers. The quartzite used for stone tool manufacture can be obtained within 2.5 km of the cave. Deer bones are particularly abundant, but the inhabitants also brought cattle, squirrel, and water buffalo remains to the cave, as well as many shellfish, turtles, and land snails. *Canarium* nuts would have been available for collection during the rainy season. The hearths indicate a domestic component to the occupation. This presence of bovids suggests that there were open areas in the vicinity of the cave, with patches of woodland. After a long period of abandonment, hunter gatherers returned between 9 and 8 ka, a period of increasing warmth and heavier rainfall. In terms of the lithic industry and the range of mammalian bones, freshwater shellfish, and land snails, there were few obvious developments from the initial settlement phase.

Shoocondej (2000) has concluded that the cave was one of many in the valley that were occupied briefly, during the rainy season, by mobile and small groups of hunter foragers. This closely reflects the observed seasonal rhythm of the Mani hunters of southern Thailand, who occupy the forests during the dry season, but move to the cover of rock shelters during the rains. One such social group comprised 12 adults and 5 children, and occupied an area of just 40 m². There is some patterning in terms of the spatial activities at Lang Kamnan, with one area used to butcher animals, another for cooking and a third for accumulating waste.

**Peninsular Thailand**

No site in Peninsular Thailand is far from the present coast, and unlike the inland sites discussed, the rise and fall of the sea would have had a marked impact on the resources available to hunter-foragers there. Marwick et al. (2017) have identified at the rock shelter of Khao Toh Chong, a sequence that began at least 13.5 ka, when the climate was drier and colder, and the sea level considerably lower than at present. The site has yielded a core-tool stone industry in association with a faunal assemblage in which the large and medium deer and cattle reflect a more open, grassland habitat than is found at present. The inhabitants also collected large quantities of freshwater shellfish and turtles. With ameliorating conditions in the mid-Holocene warm period, however, the sea level rose to be much nearer the site, and the collection of freshwater shells was virtually abandoned.

Further evidence in peninsular Thailand comes from the caves of Sakai, Moh Khiew, and Lang Rongrien. At Sakai Cave, a modern hunter-gatherer occupation overlies prehistoric deposits up to 2 m thick that date back to 10 ka and includes a number of hearths and the stone tools used to process game and to fashion wooden implements. The animals hunted from this base include rainforest species: gibbons, squirrels, macaques, and civets. Freshwater shellfish and some marine shellfish were collected, the latter having to come from a 30 km distance. At Moh Khiew, Hoabinhian stone tools were associated with four inhumation burials dated to 25 ka (Pookajorn 1994). Unfortunately, only part of one upper body has survived. Grave goods consisted of flaked stone tools and quartz pebbles. Upper cultural contexts at Lang Rongrien contain stone choppers and axes dated between 10 and 6 ka.

Further south, the cavern of Gua Cha in Malaysia has hunter gatherer occupation dated to the 7th millennium BP, where the stone industry and biological remains comprise the usual set of flaked tools including bifacially worked discoids (Taha 1991). Young pigs dominate the fauna that includes the bones of squirrels, gibbons, and monkeys indicate a forested habitat. Freshwater shellfish were collected from the nearby stream. Excavations at Gua Gunung Runtuh, a cave in the Lenggong Valley in Perak State, uncovered hunter-gatherer dating back to 13 ka. The site is elevated above the Perak River valley. The freshwater shellfish together with the fragmented and often charred animal bones reflect how broad-spectrum hunting and collecting sustained the hunter-gatherers who used this site from time to time over thousands of years. Among the animal species represented, the wild pig is most abundant, followed by the langur and macaque (Davidson 1994). The large sambar deer and smaller muntjac and bovids were also hunted. The occupants also consumed on-site, tortoise, lizard, and turtle. The freshwater shellfish are adapted to clear rivers and the muddy base of jungle streams.

## Mortuary Remains of Early Hunter Gatherers

Mortuary practices are highly informative. They reflect the cultural traditions of society, and have the potential through the manner of burial and the associated mortuary offerings, to inform on social distinctions. Furthermore, the bones themselves allow the bioarchaeologist to identify the physical characteristics of the social group or groups in question. Hunter gatherer burials in mainland Southeast Asia have been identified from about 20 ka. They have been found principally in caves, but also, in open sites in southern China and coastal settlements when the sea rose above its present level. A flexed position, whether on the side or on the back with the legs raised or in a seated and crouched position is the defining feature of mortuary rituals but grave offerings were sparse.

Most inland cave interments come from northern Vietnam (Figure 3.11). At the site of Du Sang, an old female was buried with stones round the head and over the chest, and three stone axes beyond the feet (Oxenham et al. 2022). Stones were also associated with a seated burial at Hang Chua. Hang Dang burials have been dated to about 6.5 ka. Burial offerings comprised a rhinoceros tooth, a bear's tooth and the jawbone of a monkey. Thirteen burials were recovered from Hang Dong Truong, in flexed or squatting positions with stone artefacts as mortuary offerings. The cave of Hang Lang Gao is remarkable for the deliberate concentration of 20 skulls, with some postcranial bones in their vicinity. Body ornaments are very rare, but at Mai Da Nuoc, a man was interred with a necklace of six sea shells. There is a pattern to these Vietnamese rock shelter burials: some caves became cemeteries with multiple interments in flexed positions, representing men, women and the young, with few mortuary offerings that centred on stone tools and single animal bones.

A remarkable pair of male burials have been examined at the Northern Thai site of Doi Pha Kan (Imdirakphol et al. 2017). This cave has yielded a wealth of artefact and faunal remains, and the walls were painted in red, with depictions of human hands, cattle and other animals and birds. The first burial was found in a flexed position, associated with red ochre within a circle of stones. Mortuary offerings included a stone axe with a polished edge, an adze, the bones of a small deer and a perforated shell pendant. There was also, a singular stone bored through the middle into a circular hole, a type found widely across Southeast Asia and Southern China. The second burial was also found associated with red-ochre-stained stones, in a flexed position. The graves date within the period 13–15 ka.

In Malaysia, Gua Gunung Runtuh contained a complete burial, dated to about 10 ka (Zuraina 1994). The man had been laid out on his back with his legs raised and flexed at the knees. Shells had been scattered under the body, and more were placed over it. Bones from pig, deer, lizard, and monkey, some broken and charred, were found by the left arm, the right shoulder, and the foot. Stone tools, including a sumatralith, a limestone slab, and hammer stones, were placed with

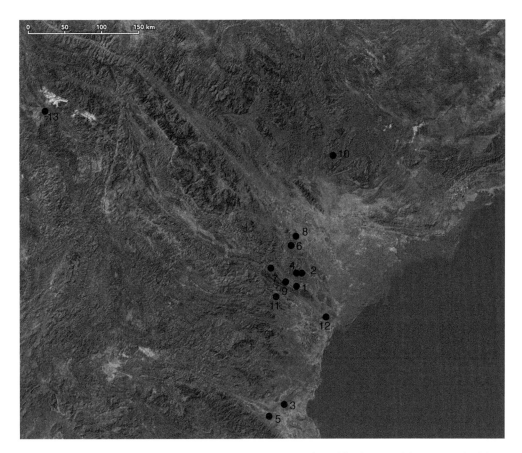

FIGURE 3.11  Distribution map of the Vietnamese sites mentioned in the text. (1) Lang Vanh, (2) Du Sang, (3) Hang Chu, (4) Hang Dang, (5) Hang Dong Truong, (6) Hang Lang Gao, (7) Mai Da Nuoc, (8) Hang Cho, (9) Xom Trai, (10) Nguom, (11) Dieu, (12) Con Co Ngua, (13) Tham Khuong.

the corpse. These showed signs of use-wear, suggesting that they belonged to the dead man, who died between 40 and 45 years of age. A detailed examination of this skeleton has revealed close similarities with those interred at Gua Cha, as well as with Aboriginal Australians. Matsumura and Zuraina (1999) have suggested that the skeleton represents an Australo-Melanesian population of hunter-gatherers of the same stock as those who much earlier crossed into and populated Australia. Gua Cha was also used as a cemetery, that contained at least 15 graves. The dead were interred in a flexed position with few if any mortuary offerings. One young man was buried, however, with his head resting on a large stone. The assemblage includes a teenager, four women, and ten men. Six died as young adults, five when of middle age, and one when an old man (Bulbeck n.d.)

## The Interior Lowlands and Vietnamese Coast

Small rock shelters offer limited insight into the activities of hunter gatherers in Southeast Asia. If the annual round of surviving hunters in peninsular Thailand and Malaysia is a guide to the past, the sheltered forefront of a cave was only occupied briefly during the rainy season. A prehistoric dry season camp would not only be very hard to find, as few structural and artefactual remains would survive, other than possible hearths and rejected stone implements. Throughout much of Southeast Asia, inland settlements other than caves are rare or completely unknown. This might reflect not only their ephemeral nature, but also the changes in the landscape that have followed deforestation and alluviation. However, just south of the Northern Thai sites of Spirit Cave and Tham Lod, intensive site identification surveys along tributaries flowing into the Salween River have identified at Huai Hin, an open Hoabinhian site that provides the vital counter to the many rock shelters in this region (Forestier 2013). The inhabitants of this site had manufactured not only the classic sumatraliths by splitting a large cobblestone and flaking one side only, but also adzes with a transverse cutting edge a range of scrapers through skilfully retouching the edges to form the working surfaces.

Many occupation sites have been found in the southern Chinese province of Guangxi, particularly adjacent to river banks, that present a quite different image of hunter gatherer settlement to that derived from the rock shelters alone. These sites include stone workshops, the remains of subsistence activities and on occasion, cemeteries that evidence complex mortuary behaviour. Gexinqiao (Xie et al. 2003), Baida, and Kantun (Xie and Peng 2006) are located along the course of the Youjiang River, and are dated from about 9 to 5 ka. Excavations at Gexinqiao covering 1,600 m², has recovered a stone industry that includes flaked choppers, points, and scrapers, as well as polished adzes, dated to about 6 ka. All stages of tool manufacture are represented, so it was a workshop site in which the distribution of the stone flakes, hammer stones, and anvils makes it possible to identify the position taken by each artisan. The inhabitants were also familiar with making pottery vessels decorated with cord marking. As with the Vietnamese cave sites, the dead were interred in a flexed position with large river stones as mortuary offerings.

Beidaling is located along the Hongshui River in Central Guangxi (Lin and Xie 2005). It comprises a large stone workshop and eight burials, dated to 8 ka. (Figure 3.12). Stone artefacts include hammer stones, anvils, whetstones, flaked choppers, points, and scrapers, as well as polished adzes and axes in all stages of manufacture. Pottery sherds are rare (Lin and Xie

FIGURE 3.12 The site of Beidaling, along the Honshui River in Central Guangxi.

2005). In eastern Guangxi, five sites have been found along the course of the Xunjiang River. Datangcheng was excavated in 2006 over an area of 2,000 m². Again, we find a stone workshop with two periods of occupation, dated to 8 and 5 ka, respectively. There was a dense accumulation of stone flakes and artefacts in various stages of manufacture, including many adze roughouts, hammer stones, and whetstones. Much pottery was also found at this site, including large vessels with everted rims (Lin et al. 2007). There are several known sites along the course of the Yongjiang River in southern Guangxi, and at Chongtang, a group of 26 human graves has been uncovered in which the dead were interred in a tightly flexed position. Cowrie shells also provide evidence for exchange with coastal communities (He and Chen 2008). The Yongjiang, Zuojiang, and Youjiang River terraces also incorporate many sites of the Dingsishan culture (Zhang and Hung 2010). From 7 to 4 ka, this area of Guangxi was occupied by hunter-gatherers who led a relatively settled, sedentary life in settlements that, similar to Dingsishan itself, included living areas, a cemetery, and middens. The cultural sequence is divided into four phases, with pottery occurring from the initial settlement. During phase 2, pottery was cord marked, or impressed with basketry patterns. Ground stone adzes were fashioned, and nearly half the shell artefacts were used as knives. The 16 burials were placed in a pit in a flexed or squatting position. The 133 burials from phase 3 at this site were interred in a flexed or crouched position, with very few mortuary offerings of stone, bone, or shell (Fu 2002). A particular feature of the phase 3 burials was the dismemberment of the body before burial, different parts of the corpse being carefully placed within the grave. The dismembered body in burial 117 was accompanied by 13 stone slabs. These people had a wide-spectrum subsistence base including hunting, aided by bone spear points and arrowheads. They fished, collected shellfish, and, in terms of their technology, made pottery vessels and used polished stone axes and adzes.

Dingsishan and Da But culture sites in northern Vietnam are so similar that they must have developed in tandem. During the 1930s, Étienne Patte (1932) excavated the shell midden at Da But. This 5 m thick settlement covered an area of only 1500 m², and to judge from the faunal remains, was located in the vicinity of an estuary and salt marshes. Patte recovered polished stone axes markedly similar to those of the inland hunter-gatherer sites. There are also spindle whorls, stone net sinkers, much pottery and 12 burials inhumed in a flexed position. Grave goods included round-based pottery vessels, shell jewellery, stone axes, and red ochre. Recent Vietnamese excavations have revealed evidence for domestic activities in the form of hearths, ceramics and the remains of hunted animals (Vinh 1991). There is also a radiocarbon determination of 4500–5000 BC from a layer 70 cm below the site's surface. As the sea level fell away from Da But, so settlement followed the receding shoreline.

Con Co Ngua is slightly larger than Da But, and recent excavations have greatly enlarged our knowledge of coastal settlement that almost certainly had a long ancestry in the now submerged continental shelves. Excavations there in 2013 documented a complex, large, sedentary hunter-gatherer community dated to ca. 6.9 ka (Oxenham et al. 2018). This was the period of the Holocene thermal maximum, when the sea rose higher than today. Although now 30 km from the shore, Con Co Ngua would then have been close to the sea, with its rich marine resources reflected in the remains of estuarine and marine as well as freshwater fish, turtles, and otters. The inhabitants collected nutritious Canarium nuts, and probably many other plant foods that have not survived. Intriguingly, they also hunted water buffalo and deer, and in doing so probably exposed themselves to injuries seen in a number of healed fractures of the arm and leg bones (Scott et al. 2019). The sedentary nature of this settlement favoured the manufacture of pottery vessels. These had rounded bases and were decorated with parallel impressions similar to the ceramics from Dingsishan and associated sites to the north. They also made shell and bone tools from deer long bones, including points and fishhooks.

Of the 272 individuals in the cemetery there, 30% died when under the age of 15 years, far fewer than in later Neolithic to Iron Age settlements. The dead were interred either in a squatting position looking to the east, or in a flexed posture. Mortuary offerings were virtually absent save for one individual, wearing a bracelet of porcupine teeth. A study of the skulls and dentition places the inhabitants into the group known as Australo-Papuan, with close similarity to modern Melanesians and Australian Aborigines, and confirming descent from the first AMHs to reach Southeast Asia (Matsumura and Oxenham 2014).

A further group of late hunter-gatherer sites takes its name from Quynh Van. About 20 sites are known, clustering behind the present coast in Nghe An and Ha Tinh provinces. Our knowledge of these comes in the main from recent excavations at Ru Diep (Dzung et al. 2020). The cultural deposits comprise compressed lenses of oyster shells interspersed with sandy occupation contexts from which posts, presumably for structures of some sort, were put in place. Occupation is placed between 3300 and 3070 Cal. BC on the basis of a Bayesian analysis of multiple dates. Within this span, it is considered likely that the actual occupation did not extend significantly beyond about 50 years. The inhabitants, who lived near the mangrove shore, concentrated on consuming oyster shells, but also fished, hunted deer and collected turtles. They fashioned pottery vessels, tempered with sand, and used bone as a raw material for their fishing leisters for fishing and spears. There is, however, also an enigmatic aspect to the findings from Ru Diep. Rather than interring the dead in the traditional seated, squatting or the flexed positions, the handful of burials were fully extended, albeit without mortuary offerings. Moreover, a small fraction of the pottery fragments reflect in their decoration, the incised and impressed patterning characteristic of the first incoming rice farming communities. Could it be that this site makes it necessary to add almost a millennium to the first contact between the indigenous hunter gatherers and the new population of farmers? The dates and activities of the Quynh Van affluent foragers are matched in the equivalent cultural context at nearby Thach Lac, where the importance of shellfish collecting and fishing in the coastal lagoons and mangroves has reaffirmed with a major excavation in 2015 (Piper et al. in press).

The enigmatic site of Bau Du lies further south, again in an estuarine environment. It comprises a series of shell middens containing the remains of shellfish, and the bones of deer, monkey, and rhinoceros. Crabs, fish, and turtle are also abundantly represented (Tan 1997). There is no well-documented chronology for this site, and no pottery, nor polished stone tools were encountered. The stone tool industry has a strong Hoabinhian flavour. If this was not a specialised site for initial stages in flaking stone implements, it reflects a marked regionality in these coastal groups.

An analogous settlements has been investigated in the valley of the Bang Pakong River of Central Thailand. Nong Nor was occupied about 4.3 ka, on the shore of a marine embayment (Higham and Thosarat 1998). The inhabitants made pottery vessels and polished stone adzes. They hunted marine mammals and brought back to the site a variety of fish including bull sharks. The midden remains were dominated by one species of marine bivalve, *Meretrix lusoria*. The material culture is the hallmark of newly arrived rice farmers, but the one burial found, that of a woman, was in a seated crouched position so characteristic of hunter gatherers. It seems that the site might have had a mixed population.

In searching for the origins of these complex hunter gatherer communities, it must be recalled that they lived on or near shorelines that formed when the sea level was a few metres higher than at present. These depict the high tide of the MIS 1 rise in sea level following the last glacial maximum, a rise that drowned Sundaland. Surely, the vast, low-lying expanse harboured the ancestral hunter gatherers adapted for many millennia to exploiting the rich marine resources of subtropical Southeast Asia.

## Summary

AMHs evolved in Africa by at least 300 ka ago. When they began to expand territorially into Eurasia, they encountered the descendants of humans who had moved out of Africa much earlier. These included Neanderthals in Europe and the Near East, *H. erectus*, *H. floresiensis* and *H. luzonensis* in Southeast Asia, and the barely known Denisovans in East and Southeast Asia seen in the introgression of Denisovan genes that survive in modern populations. The date and the pathway of the initial expansion of AMHs out of Africa remain controversial. There are hints, but not yet generally accepted evidence, that the initial exodus began over 100 ka ago, well before the eruption of Toba. Mild conditions during MIS 5 would seem to support this. On the other hand, there is also a body of opinion that places the expansion later than 71.6 ka and given the doubtful stratigraphic status of the allegedly early Chinese cave sites, a date in the vicinity of 50 ka is preferred. Only a well-dated site or series of sites in Mainland Southeast Asia predating Toba and containing AMH human remains will resolve this debate.

The archaeological record in mainland Southeast Asia enters solid ground from about 45 ka. At Niah Cave and Lang Rongrien, there is clear evidence for the establishment of AMH hunter-gatherers already well adapted to the environmental conditions, which included near coastal, savannah and rainforest habitats as the world climate fluctuated between glacial and inter-glacial phases. There are three distinct settlement forms. Inland caves or rock shelters were visited on a temporary or seasonal basis, and used as the base for wide-spectrum hunting and foraging, and occasionally, for human burials. During MIS 2, when colder conditions brought diminished rainfall and cooler conditions to Southeast Asia, subsistence was centred on collecting turtles, lands nails, and shellfish, while deer and bovines, which prefer savannah or open forest clearings, were the dominant game. Global warming with MIS 1 led to the spread of rainforest at the expense of savannah grasslands, and hunter gatherer communities adapted by reorientating to secure arboreal game.

Globally warmer conditions with MIS 1 saw a dramatic and swift rise in the level of the sea which had its greatest impact in Southeast Asia as Sundaland was inundated. This doubtless removed a major chapter in the history of hunter gatherer settlement as living sites were lost to science. However, the former shorelines now well inland when the sea rose higher than at present incorporates settlements that reveal, as at Con Co Ngua, sophisticated and complex social communities of hunter gatherers adept at hunting big game animals as well as fishing, foraging for turtles and collecting plant food. Therefore, when the first rice and millet farmers began to expand south from their homelands in the Yangtze and Yellow River valleys, they encountered and integrated with hunter-gatherers whose ancestors had established themselves in Southeast Asia for at least 50,000 years, if not longer still.

## References

Anderson, Douglas. 1990 *Lang Rongrien Rockshelter: A Pleistocene-Early Holocene Archaeological Site from Krabi, Southwestern Thailand.* Philadelphia: University Museum Monograph No. 71.

Armitage, Simon, Sabah, Jasim, Marks, Anthony, Parker, Adrian, Usik, Vitally, and Uerpmann, Hans-Peter. 2011 The southern route "Out of Africa": Evidence for an early expansion of modern humans into Arabia. *Science* 331, 453–456.

Barker, Graeme, and Farr, Lucy. 2016 *Archaeological Investigations in the Niah Caves, Sarawak*. Cambridge: The McDonald Institute.

Barnola, J.-M., Raynaud, D., Korotkevich, Y.S., and Lorius, C. 1987 Vostok ice core provides 160,000-year record of atmospheric $CO_2$. *Nature* 329, 408–414.

Boivin, Nicole, Fuller, Dorian, Dennell, Robin, Allaby, Robin, and Petraglia, Michael. 2013 Human dispersal across diverse environments of Asia during the Upper Pleistocene. *Quaternary International* 300, 32–47.

Bulbeck, David. n.d. *The Gua Cha Burials – Concordance, Chronology, Demography*. Unpublished report. www.keene.edu/library/OrangAsli/guachay.pdf.

Cann, Rebecca, Stoneking, Mark, and Wilson, Allan. 1987 Mitochondrial DNA and human evolution. *Nature* 325, 31–36.

Chappell, J., and Shackleton, N. 1986 Oxygen isotopes and sea level. *Nature* 324, 137–140.

Clarkson, Chris, Jacobs, Zenobia, Marwick, Ben, Fullager, Richard, Wallis, Lynley, Smith, Mike, and Roberts, Rhicard. 2017 Human occupation of Northern Australia by 65,000 years ago. *Nature* 547, 306–310.

Conrad, Cyler. 2016 Ethnographic analogy and the archaeological record of Northern Thailand: Insights from Mlabri hunter-gatherers and the Tham Lod Rockshelter Archaeofauna. *Rian Thai: International Journal of Thai Studies* 9, 71–96.

Conrad, Cyler, Higham, Charles, Eda, Masaki, and Marwick, Ben. 2016 Palaeoecology and forager subsistence strategies during the Pleistocene-Holocene: A reinvestigation of the zooarchaeological assemblage from Spirit Cave, Mae Hong Son Province, Thailand. *Asian Perspectives* 55, 2–27.

Curnoe, Darren, Ji, Xueping, Shaojin, Hu, Tacon, P., and Li, Yanmei. 2016 Dental remains from Longtanshan Cave 1 (Yunnan, China), and the initial presence of anatomically modern humans in East Asia. *Quaternary International* 400, 180–186.

Davidson, G. 1994. Some remarks on vertebrate remains from the excavation of Gua Gunung Runtuh, Perak. In *The Excavation of Gua Gunung Runtuh* ed Zuraina, Majid. Kuala Lumpur: Department of Museums and Antiquity, 141–148.

Demeter, F., Zanolli, C., Westaway, K.E., Joannes-Boyau, R., Duringer, P. et al. 2022. A Middle Pleistocene Denisovan molar from the Annamite Chain of Northern Laos. *Nature Communications*, 2557.

Demeter, Fabrice, Zanolli, Clément, Westaway, Kira, Joannes-Boyau, Renaud, Duringer, Philippe, Morley, Mike, Welker, Frido, Rüther, Patrick, Skinner, Matthew, McColl, Hugh, Gaunitz, Charleen, Vinner, Lasse, Dunn, Tyler, Olsen, Jesper, Sikora, Martin, Ponche, Jean-Luc, Suzzoni, Eric, Frangeul, Sébastien, Boesch, Quentin, Antoine, Pierre-Olivier, Pan, Lei, Xing, Song, Zhao, Jian-Xin, Bailey, Richard, Boualaphane, Souliphane, Sichanthongtip, Phonephanh, Sihanam, Daovee, Patole-Edoumba, Elise, Aubaile, Françoise, Crozier, Françoise, Bourgon, Nicolas, Zachwieja, Alexandra, Luangkhoth, Thonglith, Souksavatdy, Viengkeo, Sayavongkhamdy, Thongsa, Cappellini, Enrico, Bacon, Anne-Marie, Hublin, Jean-Jacques, Willerslev, Eske, and Shackelford, Laura. 2012 Anatomically modern human in Southeast Asia (Laos) by 46 ka. *Proceedings of the National Academy of Science* 109, 14375–14380.

Douka, Katerina, Slon, Viviane, Jacobs, Zenobia, Ramsey, Christopher, Shunkov, Michael, Derevianko, Anatoly, Mafessoni, Fabrizio, Kozlikin, Maxim, Li, Bo, Grün, Rainer, Comeskey, Daniel, Devièse, Thibaut, Brown, Samantha, Viola, Bence, Kinsley, Leslie, Buckley, Michael, Meyer, Matthias, Roberts, Richard, Pääbo, Svante, Kelso, Janet, and Higham, Tom. 2019. Age estimates for hominin fossils and the onset of the Upper Palaeolithic at Denisova Cave. *Nature* 565 (7741), 640–644.

Dzung, Lam, Nguyen, Thi, Quy, Tran, Bellwood, Peter, Higham, Charles, Petchey, Fiona, Grono, Elle, Chieu, Nguyen, and Piper, Philip. 2020 Ru Diep and the Quynh Van culture of central Vietnam. *Archaeological Research in Asia*, 100190. https://doi.org/10.1016/j.ara.2020.100190.

Forestier, Hubert, Zeitoun, Valery, Winayalai, Chinnawut, and Métais, Christophe. 2013 The open-air site of Huai Hin (Northwestern Thailand), chronological perspectives for the Hoabinhian. *Comptes Rendu Palevol* 12, 45–55.

Fu, Xianguo. 2002 The Dingsishan site and the prehistory of Guangxi, Southern China. *Bulletin of the Indo-Pacific Prehistory Association* 22, 63–72.

Gorman, Chester. 1972 Excavations at Spirit Cave, North Thailand: Some interim impressions. *Asian Perspectives* 13, 79–107.

Higham, T.F.G., and Douka, K. 2021. The reliability of late radiocarbon dates from the Paleolithic of southern China. *Proceedings of the National Academy of Sciences* 118 (22), e2103798118. https://doi.org/10.1073/pnas.2103798118.

Higham, T.F.G., Lloyd-Smith, L., Barton, H., Brock, F., and Turney, C. 2016 Radiocarbon dating, in *Archaeological Investigations in the Niah Caves, Sarawak*, ed Barker, Graeme. Cambridge: The McDonald Institute, 217–232.

Higham, C.F.W., and Thosarat, R. (eds) 1998 *The Excavation of Nong Nor, a Prehistoric Site in Central Thailand*. Otago University Studies in Prehistoric Anthropology, 18.

Hublin, Jean-Jacques. 2021 How old are the oldest *Homo sapiens* in far East Asia? *Proceedings of the National Academy of Sciences* 118(10), e2101173118. https://doi.org/10.1073/pnas.2101173118.

Hublin, Jean-Jacques, Abdelouahed, Ben-Ncer, Bailey, Shara, Freidline, Sarah, Neubauer, Simon, Skinner, Matthew, Bergmann, Inga, Le Cabec, Adeline, Benazzi, Stefano, Harvati, Katerina, and Gunz, Philipp. 2017 New fossils from Jebel Irhoud, Morocco and the Pan-African origin of *Homo sapiens*. *Nature* 546, 289–292.

Imdirakphol, Sunisa, Zazzo, Antoine, Auetrakulvit, Prasit, Tiamtinkrit, Chaturaporn, Pierret, Alain, Forestier, H., and Zeitoun, Valery. 2017 The perforated stones of the Doi Pha Kan burials (Northern Thailand): A Mesolithic singularity? *Comtes Rendus Palevol* 16, 351–361.

Ji, Xueping, Kuman, Kathleen, Clarke, R. J., Forestier, Hubert, Li, Yinghua, Ma, Juan, Qiu, Kaiwei, Li, Hao, and Wu, Yun. 2016 The oldest Hoabinhian technocomplex in Asia (43.5 ka) at Xiaodong Rockshelter, Yunnan Province, Southwest China. *Quaternary International* 400, 166–174.

Lin, Q., Xie, G. and Zhu, L. 2007 An important discovery from the excavation of Dangtangcheng Site in Guiping, Guangxi). *China Cultural Relics News* 1534.

Marwick, Ben, Van Vlack, Hannah, Conrad, Cyler, Shoocongdej, Rasmi, Thongcharoenchaikit, Cholawit, and Kwak, Seungki. 2017 Adaptations to sea level change and transitions to agriculture at Khao Toh Chong Rockshelter, peninsular Thailand. *Journal of Archaeological Science* 77, 94–108.

Matsumura, Hirofumi, and Oxenham, Marc. 2014 Demographic transitions and migration in prehistoric East/Southeast Asia through the lens of nonmetric dental traits. *American Journal of Physical Anthropology* 155, 45–65.

Matsumura, H., and Zuraina, M. 1999 Metric analyses of an early Holocene human skeleton from Gua Gunung Runtuh, Malaysia. *American Journal of Physical Anthropology* 109, 327–340.

McDougall, Ian, Brown, Francis, and Fleagle, John. 2005 Stratigraphic placement and age of modern humans from Kibish, Ethiopia. *Nature* 433, 733–736.

Mellars, Paul. 2006 Going east: New genetic and archaeological perspectives on the modern human colonization of Eurasia. *Science* 313, 796–800.

Mellars, Paul, Gori, Kevin, Carr, Martin, Soares, Pedro, and Richards, Martin. 2013 Genetic and archaeological perspectives on the initial modern human colonization of Southern Asia. *Proceedings of the National Academy of Sciences* 110, 10699–10704.

Mudar, Karen, and Anderson, Douglas. 2007 New evidence for Southeast Asian Pleistocene foraging economies: Faunal remains from the early levels of Lang Rongrien Rockshelter, Krabi, Thailand. *Asian Perspectives* 46, 298–334.

O'Connell, James, Allen, Jim, Williams, Martin, Williams, Alan, and Turney, Chris. 2018. When did *Homo sapiens* first reach Southeast Asia and Sahul? *Proceedings of the National Academy of Sciences* 115 (345), 8482–8490.

Oppenheimer, Stephen. 2014 Modern humans spread from Aden to the antipodes with passengers and when? in *Southeast Asia, Australia and the Search for Human Origins*, eds Dennell, Robin, and Porr, Martin. Cambridge: Cambridge University Press, 228–242.

Oxenham, M., Trinh, H.H., Willis, A., Jones, R.K., Domett, K., Castillo, C.C. et al. 2018 Between farming or foraging: Strategic responses to the Holocene thermal maximum in Southeast Asia. *Antiquity* 92, 940–957.

Oxenham, Marc, Willis, Anna, Lan, Nguyen, and Matsumura, Hirofumi. 2022 Hunter-gatherer mortuary variability in Vietnam, in *The Oxford Handbook of Early Southeast Asia*, eds Higham, Charles, and Kim, Nam. New York: Oxford University Press, 229–271.

Penny, Dan. 2001 A 40,000 year palynological record from North-East Thailand: Implications for biogeography and Palaeo-environmental reconstruction. *Palaeogeography, Palaeoclimatology, Palaeoecology* 171, 97–128.

Petraglia, Michael, Korisettar, Ravi, Boivin, Nicole, Clarkson, Christopher, Ditchfield, Peter, Jones, Sacha, Koshy, Jinu, Lahr, Marta, Oppenheimer, Clive, Pyle, David, Roberts, Richard, Schwenninger,

Jean-Luc, Arnold, Lee, and White, Kevin. 2007 Middle Palaeolithic assemblages from the Indian subcontinent before and after the Toba super-eruption. *Science* 317, 114–116.

Pike, Alistair. 2016 Uranium-series dating of the Niah deep skull, *Archaeological Investigations in the Niah Caves, Sarawak*, eds Dennell, Robin et al. Cambridge: The McDonald Institute, 233–234.

Piper, P.J., Nguyen, T.T., Bellwood, P. et al. in press. The significance of Thach Lac archaeological site (Ha Tinh Province) in understanding the cultural sequencing in Central Vietnam between 3000–2000 cal. BC.

Piper, Philip, and Rabett, Ryan. 2014 Late Pleistocene subsistence strategies in Island Southeast Asia, in: *Southeast Asia, Australia and the Search for Human Origins*, eds Dennell, Robin et al. Cambridge: Cambridge University Press, 118–134.

Pookajorn, S. 1994 *Final Report of Excavations at Moh-Khiew Cave, Krabi Province; Sakai Cave, Trang Province and Ethnoarchaeological Research of Hunter-Gatherer Group, So-Called Mani or Sakai or Orang Asli at Trang Province (The Hoabinhian Research Project in Thailand)*. Bangkok: Silpakorn University.

Rabett, Ryan, Barker, Grahame, Hung, G.O., Naruse, T., Piper, P., Raddatz, E., Reynolds, T., Van Son, Nguyên, Stimpson, C., Szabó, K., Tân, Nguyên, and Wilson, J. 2009 The Trang An project: Late-to-post-Pleistocene settlement of the lower Song Hong Valley, North Vietnam. *Journal of the Royal Asiatic Society* 19, 73–109.

Ray, Nicolas, Currat, Mathias, and Excoffier, Laurent. 2008 Incorporating environmental heterogeneity in spatially-explicit simulations of human genetic diversity, in *Simulations, Genetics and Human Prehistory*, ed Matsumura, Hirofumi. Cambridge: The McDonald Institute, 103–117.

Reich, David, Patterson, Nick, Martin, Kircher, Delfin, Frederick, Nandineni, Madhusudan, Pugach, Irina, Ko, Albert, Ying-Chin, Ko, Jinam, Timothy, Phipps, Maude, Saitou, Naruya, Wollstein, Andreas, Kayser, Manfred, Pääbo, Svante, and Stoneking, Mark. 2011 Denisova admixture and the first modern human dispersals into Southeast Asia and Oceania. *The American Journal of Human Genetics* 89, 516–528.

Reynolds, Timothy. 1992 Excavations at Banyan Valley Cave, Northern Thailand: A report on the 1972 season. *Asian Perspectives* 31, 77–98.

Rhodes, Edward. 2011 Optically stimulated luminescence dating of sediments over the past 250,000 years. *Annual Review of Earth and Planetary Sciences* 39, 461–488.

Richter, Daaniel, Grün, Rainer, Joannes-Boyau, Renaud, Steele, Teresa, Amani, Fethi, Rué, Mathieu, Fernandes, Paul, Raynal, Jean-Paul, Geraads, Denis, Ben-Ncer, Abdelouahed, Hublin, Jean-Jacques, and McPherron, Shannon. 2017 The age of the hominin fossils from Jebel Irhoud, Morocco, and the origins of the Middle Stone Age. *Nature* 546, 293–296.

Ryan, William, Carbotte, Suzanne, Coplan, Justin, O'Hara, Suzanne, Melkonian, Andrew, Arko, Robert, Weissel, Rose, Ferrini, Vicki, Goodwillie, Andrew, Nitsche, Frank, Bonczkowski, Juliet, and Zemsky, Richard. 2009 Global multi-resolution topography (GMRT) synthesis data set. *Geochemistry, Geophysics, Geosystems* 10(3), Q03014. https://doi.org/10.1029/2008GC002332.

Saidin, Mohd. 2006 Bukit Bunuh, Lenggong, Malaysia: New evidence of late Pleistocene culture in Malaysia and Southeast Asia, in *Uncovering Southeast Asia's Past*, eds Bacus, Elizabeth et al. Singapore: National University of Singapore, 60–64.

Scally, Aylwyn, and Durbin, Richard. 2012 Revising the human mutation rate: Implications for understanding human evolution, *Nature Reviews Genetics* 13, 745–753. http://dx.doi.org/10.1038/nrg3295.

Scott, Rachel, Buckley, Halllie, Domett, Kate, Tromp, Monica, Hoang Trinh, Hiep, Willis, Anna, Matsumura, Hirofumi, and Oxenham, Marc. 2019 Domestication and large animal interactions: Skeletal trauma in Northern Vietnam during the hunter-gatherer Da But period. *PLoS ONE*. http://dx.doi.org/10.1371/journal.pone.0218777.

Shen, Guanjun, Wu, Xianzhu, Wang, Qian, Tu, Hua, Feng, Yue-Xing, and Zhao, Jian-Xin. 2013 Mass spectrometric U-Series dating of Huanglong Cave in Hubei Province, Central China: Evidence for early presence of modern humans in Eastern Asia. *Journal of Human Evolution* 65, 162–167.

Shoocondej, Rasmi. 2000 Forager mobility organization based on seasonal tropical environments of Western Thailand. *World Archaeology* 32, 14–40.

Shoocondej, Rasmi. 2006 Late Pleistocene activities at the Tham Lod Rockshelter in highland Bang Mapha, Mae Hongson Province, Northwestern Thailand, *Uncovering Southeast Asia's Past*, eds Bacus, Elizabeth et al. Singapore: Singapore University Press, 22–37.

Siddall, M., Rohling, E.J., Thompson, W.J., and Waelbroeck, C. 2008 Marine isotope stage 3 sea level fluctuations: Data synthesis and new outlook. *Revues of Geophysics* 46, RG4003. http://dx.doi.org/10.1029/2007RG000226.

Storm, Paul, Aziz, Fachroel, de Vos, John, Kosasih, Dikdik, Baskoro, Sinung, Ngaliman, and van den Hoek Ostende, Lars. 2005 Late Pleistocene *Homo sapiens* in a tropical rainforest fauna in East Java. *Journal of Human Evolution* 49, 536–545.

Stringer, Chris. 2003 Out of Ethiopia. *Nature* 423, 692–694.

Sun, Xue-feng, Wen, Shao-qing, Lu, Cheng-qiu, Zhou, Bo-yan, Curnoe, Darren, Lu, Hua-yu, Hong-chun, Li, Wang, Wei, Cheng, Hai, Yi, Shuang-wen, Jia, Xin, Du, Pan-xin, Xu, Xing-hua, Lu, Yi-ming, Lu, Ying, Zheng, Hong-xiang, Zhang, Hong, Sun, Chang, Wei, Lan-hai, Han, Fei, Huang, Juan, Edwards, Lawrence, Li, Jin, and Li, Hui. 2021 Ancient DNA and multimethod dating confirm the late arrival of anatomically modern humans in Southern China. *Proceedings of the National Academy of Science* 2021, e2019158118.

Taha, Adi. 1991 Gua Cha and the archaeology of the Orang Asli. *Bulletin of the Indo-Pacific Prehistory Association* 11, 363–372.

Tan, H. V. 1997 The Hoabinhian and before. *Bulletin of the Indo-Pacific Prehistory Association* 16, 35–41.

Treerayapeewat, Cherdsak. 2005 Patterns of habitation and burial activity in the Ban Rai Rockshelter, Northwestern Thailand. *Asian Perspectives* 44, 231–245.

Van Meerbeeck, C.J., Renssen, H., and Roche, D.M. 2009 How did marine isotope stage 3 and last glacial maximum climates differ? – Perspectives from equilibrium simulations. *Climate of the Past* 5, 33–51.

Westaway, K. E., Louys, J., Due Awe, R., Morwood, M., Price, G., Zhao, J., Aubert, M., Joannes-Boyau, R., Smith, M., Skinner, M., Compton, T., Bailey, R., van den Bergh, G., de Vos, J., Pike, A., Stringer, C., Saptomo, E., Rizal, Y., Zaim, J., Santoso, W., Trihascaryo, A., Kinsley, L., and Sulistyanto, B. 2017 An early modern human presence in Sumatra 73,000–63,000 years ago. *Nature* 548, 322–325.

Westaway, K.E., Morwood, M.J., Roberts, R, Rokus, J., Zhao, A.D., Storm, J.X., Aziz, P., van den Bergh, F., Hadi, G., Jatmiko, P., and de Vos, J. 2007 Age and biostratigraphic significance of the Punung rainforest fauna, East Java, Indonesia, and implications for *Pongo* and *Homo*. *Journal of Human Evolution* 53, 709–717.

Wu, Liu, Jina, Chang-Zhu, Zhang, Ying-Qi, Cai, Yan-Jun, Xinga, Song, Wu, Xiu-Jie, Cheng, Hai, Edwards, Lawrence, Pan, Wen-Shi, Qin, Da-Gong, An, Zhi-Sheng, Trinkaus, Erik, and Wu, Xin-Zhi. 2010 Human remains from Zhirendong, South China, and modern human emergence in East Asia. *Proceedings of the National Academy of Sciences* 107, 19201–19206.

Wu, Yun, Qiu, Kaiwei., Luo, Yi, Yang, Qing, Huang, Zhijian., Wen, Jiaxin, Ji, Xueping, Li, Yinghua, and Zhou, Yuduan 2022 Dedan Cave: Extending the evidence of the Hoabinhian technocomplex in Southwest China. *Journal of Archaeological Science Reports* 14. https://doi.org/10.1016/j.jasrep.2022.103524.

Yi, S., Lee, June-Jeong, Kim, Seongnam, Yoo, Yongwook., and Kim, Dongwan. 2008 New data on the Hoabinhian: Investigations at Hang Cho Cave, Northern Vietnam. *Bulletin of the Indo-Pacific Prehistory Association* 28, 73–79.

Zhang, Jia-FuF., Huang, Wei-Wen, Hu, Yue, Yang, Shi-Xia., and Zhou, Li-Ping. 2015 Optical dating of flowstone and silty carbonate-rich sediments from Panxian Dadong Cave, Guizhou, Southwestern China. *Quaternary Geochronology* 30, 479–486.

Zhang, Chi, and Hung, Hsiao-chun. 2010 The emergence of agriculture in Southern China. *Antiquity* 84, 11–25.

Zuraina, Majid. 1994 *The Excavation of Gua Gunung Runtuh*. Kuala Lumpur: Department of Museums and Antiquity.

### References in a Foreign Language from Charles Higham's Bibliography

He, A., and Chen, X. 2008 New discovery from the excavation of Chongtang site in Chongzuo, Guangxi. *China Cultural Relics News* 1, 621, 1 (in Chinese).

Lin, Q., and Xie, G. 2005 An important discovery from the excavation of Beidaling site in Duan, Guangxi. *China Cultural Relics News* 1, 374, 1 (in Chinese).

Patte, É. 1932. Le kjökkenmödding Néolithique de Da-but et ses sépultures.
Vinh, B. 1991 Origins of Neolithic pottery centres in Vietnam. *Khao Co Hoc* 4, 1–8 (in Vietnamese).
Xie, G., Lin, Q., and Peng, C. 2003 Gexinqiao Neolithic site in Baise City, Guangxi. *Archaeology* 12, 3–6 (in Chinese).
Xie, G., and Peng, C. 2006 An important discovery from the excavation of Baida site in Baise, Guangxi. *China Cultural Relics News* 1, 409 (in Chinese).

# 4

# A MIDDLE TO LATE UPPER PLEISTOCENE LITHIC INDUSTRY FROM NORTH VIETNAM

*Anatoly P. Derevianko and Alexander V. Kandyba*

## Introduction

North Vietnam is one of the unique regions in Southeast Asia with regard to the dispersal of early human populations, their cultural development and the evolution of man himself due to its geographical proximity to South China in the north. The waters of the Pacific Ocean, on the other hand, might have encouraged the long maritime migrations in the east.

The earliest Palaeolithic sites that provide the evidence for the first human occupation in Vietnam can be associated with the early Middle Pleistocene (Kahlke and Nghia 1965; Kahlke 1973; Ciochon and Olsen 1986; Olsen and Ciochon 1990; Davidson and Noble 1992; Su 2007). Tham Khuyen and Tham Hai Caves located in Lang Son Province on the border with China have yielded a collection that includes ten teeth attributed to *Homo erectus*, as well as teeth fragments identified as belonging to extinct species of the great apes. The faunal remains associated with the hominin teeth predominantly represent such extinct species as *Ailuropoda*, *Stegodon*, *Pongo* and others. These sites have been dated to 475 ± 125 ka (Marwick 2009).

In Southeast Asia, including Vietnam, lithic industries appear to have evolved convergently throughout the Palaeolithic period since the first appearance of *H. erectus* in the region, without being affected by any massive infiltrations from Western Eurasia. Of course, this does not mean that the mentioned eastern regions of Eurasia were completely isolated from the outside world. Small populations might have migrated repeatedly and these movements were associated with gene flow; however, such small infiltrations would not be able change the overall dynamics in the development of lithic industries in East Asia. And the reason for this was not the backwardness of the local ancient population in the ability to apply innovative lithic reduction technologies, or underdeveloped cognitive capabilities, but specific environmental conditions, such as a lack of major sources that could provide good quality raw material, etc., making hominins use organic materials, including bone, wood and particularly bamboo, more extensively starting from the Lower Palaeolithic. It made the culture of indigenous people fundamentally different from the Palaeolithic traditions that emerged in Western Eurasia (Derevianko 2015).

In eastern Eurasia, neither European nor African criteria allow recognition of Middle Palaeolithic tools. Here, the evolutionary development of lithic industries occurred throughout the

Pleistocene and no innovations in lithic reduction seem to have been brought from other areas for more than 1 million years. For example, evidence shows no indications for the use of Levallois technology. However, it does not mean that the lithic industry recorded across this vast area demonstrates a lack of variety. Archaeologists recognized dozens of cultures that can be characterized by removing flakes from pebble, discoidal, multidirectional and other cores used for manufacturing tools as well as by a large number of choppers and other heavy-duty tools made from cobble. Therefore, there are no well-founded and generally accepted criteria enabling recognition of the Middle Palaeolithic in East and Southeast Asia, unlike the rest of Eurasia and Africa. It should be noted that the lithic industry from East and Southeast Asia does not seem to have been in a state of stagnation for 1.5 million years. This fact is corroborated by the discovery of the Lower Palaeolithic sites with a bifacial industry in Central Vietnam. In Gia Lai Province, near the city of An Khe, the Russian–Vietnamese expedition has found more than 15 Lower Palaeolithic sites with a pebble-flake industry and bifacially worked tools similar to handaxes (Derevianko et al. 2016). $^{40}$K/$^{38}$Ar dating of tektites recovered from the occupation layer together with bifaces and pebble tools has yielded two ages: 806 ± 22 kya and 782 ± 20 kya (Derevianko et al. 2017). These ages indicate that a Lower Palaeolithic industry discovered in Vietnam overlapped chronologically with a lithic industry from the Bose Basin in southern China (Xie and Huang 2003). Bifacially worked tools from southern China and Vietnam differ from handaxes found in Africa and Europe based on the major techno-typological characteristics, and their appearance in Eastern Eurasia can be explained by technological convergence (Derevianko 2014).

In Southeast Asia, including Vietnam, the pebble-flake industry continues to evolve throughout the Middle and Upper Pleistocene, with the ongoing domination of choppers and choppings among heavy duty tools. In the Lower Palaeolithic, bifacially worked tools were a short-term phenomenon in this area. Pebble, discoidal and amorphous cores were found to be dominant among tools manufactured using the primary flaking technique. No evidence for the use of Levallois technology has been documented. Flakes were mainly used as blanks for the manufacture of a diverse tool assemblage. In Vietnam, a significant percentage of implements manufactured from blanks can be traced throughout the Upper Pleistocene, with a predominance of pebble-type tools in general. Over the past 30 years, several Palaeolithic cultures, such as the Nguomian, Sonvian and Hoabinhian, were discovered in the Upper Pleistocene deposits in North Vietnam, dating back between 40 and 10 ka (Figure 4.1). All these cultures retain the major techno-typological features characteristic of the Lower Palaeolithic in Vietnam, suggesting continuity between the Palaeolithic industries throughout the Pleistocene. A study of archaeological sites in North Vietnam shows that the relative stability of the palaeoecological situation with minor species variations in fauna appears to have taken place in the region.

## Nguomian Industry

In North Vietnam, excavations revealed a lithic assemblage recognized as the Nguomian industry with a diagnostic predominance of flake tools. This industry is associated with the middle to late Upper Pleistocene and precedes the previously distinguished Sonvian and Hoabinhian cultures (Nguyen Khac Su 1982). The rock shelter of Mieng Ho located in Bac Thai Province about 120 km north of Hanoi is of great importance for understanding the Stone Age of Vietnam. The site was excavated in 1971 under the direction of Ha Van Tan and Hoang Xuan Tinh. The occupation layer deposited at a depth of about 40 cm from the ground surface yielded no faunal remains. The collection of lithic artefacts includes large cobble tools dominated by scrapers and

A Middle to Late Upper Pleistocene Lithic Industry  71

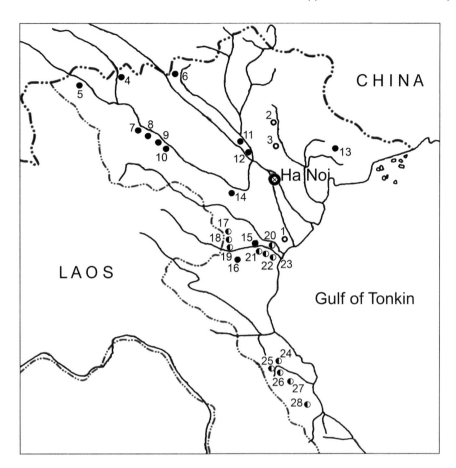

FIGURE 4.1  Distribution of the Palaeolithic sites in Vietnam. Nguomian sites: (1) Nuong, (2) Nguom, (3) Mieng Ho; Sonvian sites, (4) Nam Tun, (5) Tham Khuong, (6) Ben Den, (7) Hang Pong I, Hang Pong II, (8) Ban Cai, (9) Pa Mang, Hang Co, (10) Ban Pho, (11) 98 sites in Vinh Phuc Province, (12) Van Thang, (13) Minh Khai, Khe Tau, (14) Phung Nguyen, (15) Con Moong, (16) Nui Mot; Hoabinhian sites, (15) Con Moong, (17) Anh Ro, Ma Xa, (18) Xom Sat, Thac Son, (19) Lang Bon, (20) Hang Diem, (21) Da Bac, (22) Thac Long, Loc Tinh, (23) Gia Bac, (24) Tham Hoi, (25) Yen Lac, (26) Kim Bang, (27) Xom Thon, (28) Xom Tham.

choppers; some of them show primary flake scars on both surfaces and remind choppings, or may have been used as cores for removing small flakes. The vast majority of the inventory consists of flakes, lithic fragments and tools made from them. Somewhat more than half of the most characteristic flakes reveal smooth, non-faceted striking platforms, occasionally covered with cortex, whereas slightly less than half of them had faceted striking platforms. But most of the other flakes and fragments show evidence of irregular, non-continuous marginal retouch; single and transverse scrapers, as well as notch-denticulate tools of irregular forms, were produced using such type of retouch. Several rectangular flakes trimmed from the dorsal and ventral surfaces and three discoidal cores have been identified.

The Nguom rock shelter, which gave the same name to the Nguomian culture, is located in the limestone massif where a few more rock shelters with the Stone Age sites were found nearby. Three occupation levels were recognized in more than 1 m tick deposits: the upper one that includes two layers associated with the Bacsonian and Hoabinhian cultures; the middle one containing the Sonvian materials; and the lower one with the lithic industry that displays completely different morphological characteristics than those documented in the overlaying units.

Lithic artefacts found in the lower level were manufactured from quartzite, basalt, rhyolite and porphyritic pebbles that appear to have been collected on-site from the river bed. The primary flaking strategy is based on parallel reduction from flat-faced cores. Single and double platform cores resulted from the parallel and convergent flaking (Figure 4.2), as well as amorphous and radial cores, are present. Striking platforms with pebble cortex are predominantly smooth; those showing signs of rejuvenation were found in small numbers. Cortical and primary flakes are dominated by secondary flakes. Blades were found in rather small quantities. Flakes and blades that retain the natural pebble cortex are numerous. It can be explained by the characteristics of a raw material that includes medium-sized pebbles and – very rarely – relatively large cobbles. Although the artefacts were mainly manufactured from different pebbles, this industry cannot be attributed to a traditional pebble tool industry associated with the use of special flaking techniques that make it possible to refer to such a technology as to a 'citrus slice' technique (Ranov 1986, 28–31). The assemblage recovered from the lower layer is characterized

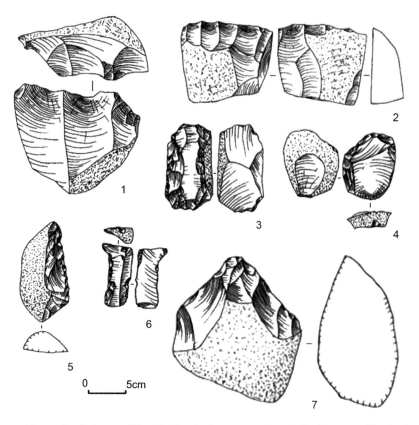

FIGURE 4.2  Nguomian industry: (1) – single platform core, (2 and 7) choppers, (3) single scraper, (4) ventral scraper, (5) single scraper made on cobble, (6) single scraper made on blade flake.

by primary flaking typical of the Middle Palaeolithic tradition based on the manufacturing of flaked blanks from single platform and radial flat-faced cores. The only specific feature is that the striking platforms of the majority of flakes retain natural pebble cortex.

The collection of tools with evidence of secondary treatment from the lower layer Nguom rock shelter is quite numerous. It includes some atypical points with irregular retouch. Denticulate retouch, which is sometimes supplemented by one row, flat or semi-abrupt marginal retouch, occurred frequently. Scrapers and scraper-like tools were present in relatively large numbers. They are dominated by single scrapers made primarily on flakes and, in very rare occasions, on whole pebbles of appropriate forms (see examples in Figure 4.2). The latter are typical of the Sonvian-type assemblages. Atypical double scrapers are also present. There are isolated transverse (oblique) scrapers; however, scrapers that show retouch on the ventral side, which are quite characteristic of this assemblage, occurred relatively often. Their abrupt and semi-abrupt working edges are always extensively retouched and sometimes show a serrate profile. Such kind of treatment is quite characteristic of choppers as well. These scrapers consist of composite tools and implements with chisel-like ends, although the latter may be considered as an element of lithic reduction. The assemblage includes isolated atypical scrapers with abrupt marginal retouch. Scraper-like tools made on small flakes with semi-abrupt marginal denticulate retouch are present. In one instance, a micro-burin scar on the working edge of a bill-hook was observed, but there is a possibility that it may have resulted from utilization of this tool. A point made on elongated flake with a clearly distinguished small tip can be regarded as a borer, albeit tentatively. Notched tools were found in a relatively small number and show differences from typical implements of this kind. Denticulate tools were present in large numbers. This group also includes beaked tools with characteristic working elements separated by notches. One such characteristic implement has two working ends. It should be noted that in Vietnam denticulate retouch is quite typical of tools made on flakes. It was observed not only in the Sonvian and Hoabinhian lithic industries, but also in the Neolithic assemblages.

Of particular interest are chisel-like (adze-like) or axe-like tools. They reveal similar elongated forms and a worked end showing scars from flat flakes removed from both sides, which are sometimes associated with utilization. It was experimentally shown that such traces are characteristic of wood-working (Matyukhin 1983). Very short flakes were commonly used as blanks, whereas longer, but always massive, flakes were exploited rarely. Choppers may have been used as such tools as well. Adze-like and axe-like tools were found in great numbers at Stone Age sites in Vietnam and Southeast Asia. This phenomenon can be easily explained by environmental features of the region, such as tropical forests that served as a permanent habitat for humans.

Although different flake tools show prevalence in the collection, it includes characteristic unifacial and bifacial cobble choppers (Figure 4.2). These implements vary in size, but large specimens were found in small numbers. Unifacial tools that demonstrate long, short and even pointed forms were found to be dominant. The latter are characteristic of the Sonvian pebble tool industry. Similar forms can be observed in the record from Nam Tun Cave (Nguyen Khac Su 1982). Partially bifacially worked tools are present in the collection as well.

Based on techno-typological characteristics, this lithic industry may be attributed to a Middle Palaeolithic tradition that shows specific features. Its specificity is the presence of characteristic heavy-duty tools and some typical choppers.

Another Nguomian site, Nui Nuong, was found on the slope of a basalt mountain, which attains an elevation of about 100 m. The mountain is situated on the flat alluvial plain near the seashore, about 10 km northwest of the city of Thanh Hoa. The accumulation of lithic artefacts was recovered from a small area in the rock massif at the height of 30 m from its base. The preferred raw material for manufacturing the artefacts was basalt. The flake tools are dominated by middle-sized flakes and blades, including isolated large pieces. Cores were found in small numbers; they mainly represent parallel reduction and convergent flaking. The most characteristic tool is a sub-triangle single-platform core showing scars from triangle-shaped flakes. The striking platform was formed by removal of wide flakes. This relatively large core shows evidence of primary flaking.

Dihedral striking platforms occurred more frequently, whereas faceted ones were rarely identified. A very large number of the striking platforms made on pebbles are characteristic of the Sonvian and Hoabinhian industries. The lithic inventory found at Nui Nuong shows considerable differences from these industries and reveals great similarities to the assemblage associated with the bottom layer at the Nguom rock shelter, particularly when flat-faced cores from the collections unearthed at Nui Nuong and Nguom and amorphous cores attributed to the Sonvian and Hoabinhian cultures are compared.

The tool assemblage from the site of Nui Nuong is dominated by flake tools, including notched and denticulate pieces, and scrapers. Single, double, oblique, transverse scrapers and one double-sided scraper are present. However, the latter may have been a heavy-duty tool because the retouch can be an element of lithic reduction, although the tool shows a scraper-like form. Many tools reveal the denticulate working edges, thus making it possible to consider them as notched scrapers. Flakes (and in very rare instances – clastic rocks) were predominantly used as blanks. The collection includes four atypical end-scrapers and a typical borer made on flake. The first are characterized by the presence of irregular coarse retouch. Excavations yielded an indicative short end-scraper similar to end-scraper-like implements from the lower layer at the Nguom rock shelter. The assemblage comprises backed knives made on sub-triangle flakes. Notched and denticulate tools were found in great numbers; as it was mentioned above, many of these pieces are typical denticulate scrapers. It should be recalled that denticulate tools are very characteristic of lithic assemblages (including pebble industries) from Southeast Asia. The collection includes three bifacially worked fragments, which can be identified as blanks for manufacturing axe-like pieces of a relatively large size, and an adze-like (chisel-like) tool made on a large flake fragment.

Excavations produced a few large elongated basalt fragments with a scraper-like lateral edge, which can be classified as backed "cleavers". Two relatively large core-like tools with a sharp edge showing evidence of partial alternating retouch and the untreated back at the opposite end are also distinguished. These implements may be attributed to chopper-like pieces. The lack of original pebble tools was possibly due to the characteristics of raw material.

The Nguom rock shelter appears to have been a seasonally visited site where primary flaking was less important, which is indicated by a small number of cores. Pebble was collected from the river below; after removing primary flakes, the best specimens were brought to the site.

The site of Nui Nuong, located on a large rock massif that elevates over a coastal valley, may be considered as the remains of a lithic workshop located near the outcrops of raw material. Defended from the sea by a mountain, it offered a good view of the area and provided raw material necessary for manufacturing lithic tools. The elevated site may have been the only convenient place in the plain swamp tropical forest where early humans could live in more or less stable conditions during a relatively long time period.

The common feature of the lithic industries under discussion is that the majority of tools showing signs of secondary reduction were made on flakes. As it was mentioned, it makes them different from the Sonvian and Hoabinhian assemblages that appeared later. The lithic industries under discussion show a predominance of the parallel reduction in primary flaking of stones and fashioning tools. The sharp contrast between the stone tools from Nguom and other lithic assemblages presently known in the Indochinese Peninsula closely resembles the Middle Palaeolithic of India (India's Stone Age). The characteristics of flakes and retouch, as well as the major tool types from the rock shelter of Mieng Ho, are similar to those attributed to the Middle Palaeolithic of India. A major difference of the lithic industries recovered from the lower layer at Nguom and from the site of Nui Nuong is that axe-like tools occur occasionally in the Middle Palaeolithic of India, whereas typical chisel-like pieces are common. Such differences may be associated with different environmental conditions.

The age of these sites is currently determined by radiocarbon dates obtained for the layers at the Nguom rock shelter, as well as by the stratigraphic position of the assemblage found below the deposits rich in the Sonvian and Hoabinhian artefacts. A radiocarbon age of more than 32 kya obtained for the overlaying archaeologically sterile deposit defines the uppermost notional boundary of the time period when this assemblage appears in the record. Thus, in the Stone Age of Vietnam, there has been currently recognized a group of distinctive lithic assemblages dominated by flakes, which makes them significantly different from the Sonvian and Hoabinhian industries known in the region. These assemblages were found in both the rock shelters (Nguom, Mieng Ho), and at open-air sites (Nuong). Raw material does not appear to have determined specific features of the lithic industries under discussion as different materials were used here for stone tool production. Primary and secondary flaking techniques, as well as the major tool types, are characteristic of the Eurasian Middle Palaeolithic, revealing the greatest similarities with the Middle Palaeolithic assemblages from India. Analysis indicates that the lithic industries, which emerged in the Asian regions located far apart from each other, seem to have undergone the same development phase at almost the same time period in apparently similar environmental conditions.

The lithic industry recovered from the lower layers of Con Moong Cave is also associated with the earlier phase. The 2010–2014 studies of this site carried out by the joint Russian–Vietnamese expedition under the direction of Academician Anatoly P. Derevianko have made it possible to find evidence for a previously unknown period of human colonization in North Vietnam. Quartzite pebbles were used as the preferred raw material for manufacturing artefacts. The characteristics of the raw material (jointing, friability) enabled specific approaches in lithic reduction such as simple parallel flaking with a minimal preparation of cores, and in many cases no evidence for following any particular flaking strategy has been recognized. The flaking resulted in manufacturing large flakes and numerous stone fragments used as blanks for tool production (typical single scrapers and end-scraper). It is difficult to identify cultural affinity of this industry due to a small number of artefacts in the collection, but lithic analysis suggests selection of a preferred raw material (quartzite pebble) with characteristics that defined flaking strategies (parallel and irregular flaking) and restrained possibilities for developing different tool types, confining them to those that could be easily manufactured. It has been tentatively established that this industry occurred within a time frame ranging from 60 kya to 100 kya.

Pebble tools from Tham Khuyen Cave appear to have occurred earlier than the flake industries discussed above, if it is assumed that they overlap chronologically with the Pleistocene animal fossils recovered from this site (the Ailuropoda-Stegodon faunal complex) and with the teeth from early humans (Anisyutkin and Timofeev 2004). According to the Vietnamese and German palaeontologists, red beds that contained bone remains (and lithic tools) can be associated with a Middle Pleistocene interglacial (Nguyen Lan Cuong 1985). In the collection from Tham Khuyen Cave, flaked pieces are also dominated by pebble tools.

Therefore, "Nguomian-type" lithic industries consisting of the flake tools represent a very interesting phenomenon, breaking the "pebble tradition" and dividing it into two chronological periods. Tool production that emerged in the younger period indicate a definite specialization that appears to have been associated with general changes of climatic conditions during the Holocene, resulting in warmer and more humid environments and therefore in expansion of forests. It is known that climate cooling associated with the Quaternary glaciations caused increased aridity in the tropics and, therefore, a reduction of rainforest areas (for example, in Africa and South America they decreased significantly and repeatedly (Fouli 1990)). However, such an explanation is not applicable to the Sonvian culture that existed in the late Pleistocene when the maximum cooling and climatic deterioration in the Late Peniglacial occurred.

## Sonvian Industries

Studies carried out by Ha Van Tan, Nguyen Khac Su and other Vietnamese researchers have made it possible to identify more than a hundred Upper Pleistocene sites associated with the Sonvian culture. The first sites attributed to this culture were discovered in 1968 (Tan 1971); a total of about 150 localities are known. The Sonvian sites are distributed over a large area that includes the provinces of Lai Chau, Son La, Hoang Lien Son, Ha Bac, Ha Son Binh, Thanh Hoa; most of these sites are concentrated in Vinh Phuc Province, where approximately 100 sites have been found (Tan and Su 1978). They commonly represent localities that yielded surface finds, whereas evidence associated with stratified deposits (Vuon Sao, Con Moong) suggests that this culture can be dated between 30 and 12 kya. The tools were manufactured from river cobbles, mainly of quartz and quartzite. These implements are commonly oval-elongated in shape, and rounded-ellipsoidal in cross-section.

Some tools were produced from bone or shell. The Sonvian reduction strategy is based on rough retouching. The tool assemblage is dominated by roughly retouched cobbles. It comprises various single, transverse and convergent cobble scrapers (Figure 4.3, specimens 3, 6, 7, 9–12), choppers (Figure 4.3, specimens 2, 4, 5, 8) and choppings (Figure 4.3, specimen 1). The other tools in the assemblage include implements made on flakes (retouched flakes, non-standard end-scrapers, burins, etc.). The late Palaeolithic sites yielded pieces (Sumatra-type axes) that were already characteristic of the Hoabinhian culture. Tool assemblages associated with the Sonvian and Hoabinhian sites show domination of roughly retouched cobbles demonstrating a greater degree of perfection and being more accurately worked compared to the early Palaeolithic pebble tools. However, the vast majority of Hoabinhian sites are caves, whereas most of those associated with the Sonvian culture are open-air sites located on hills that commonly rise 10–20 m above the surrounding flood plain. A total of more than 70 such sites have been discovered in Vinh Phuc Province and analysed. Only in Son La and Lai Chau Provinces, excavations undertaken at some cave sites yielded evidence showing features that closely resemble those typical of the Sonvian culture. The Sonvian sites have mostly produced surface finds. Excavations conducted at the site of Vuon Sao in Vinh Phuc Province revealed that lithic tools occur in soil layer at a depth of about 20 cm from the ground surface. Faunal remains, charcoal and ash are not present and no clear indications for the presence of occupation layer have been found; it was possible to recognize only the occurrence level for lithic tools.

The roughly retouched surface in most of the Sonvian tools show a slightly different colour; this phenomenon comparable to patinization of Palaeolithic flints may be considered

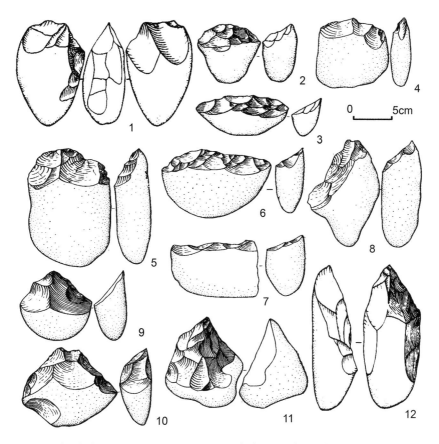

FIGURE 4.3   Sonvian industry: (1) chopping, (2, 4, 5, 8) chopper, (3, 6, 7) transverse scraper made on cobble, (9, 10, 11, 12) convergent convex scrapers.

an indication for antiquity of these implements. Choppers, scrapers produced using 'citrus slice' technique and scrapers with the working edges extending to three-quarters of a cobble perimeter constitute the major categories in the Sonvian lithic inventory. Scrapers were commonly produced from the whole cobbles and only a few of them were manufactured from waste flakes. Long, narrow cobbles that exhibit evidence of rigorous, abrupt and sometimes almost vertically applied rough retouch are specifically diagnostic of the Sonvian culture. Such technique was used for producing original scrapers or choppers with a massive, abruptly retouched edge. The cobble surface beyond the edge retains natural, rounded cortex. In addition to intact tools, those of the same type with one broken end and split transversely occur no less frequently. Scrapers with an angled edge and elongated sub-rectangular tools that also occur in Hoa Binh are characteristic of the Sonvian culture. They show traces of secondary treatment that can be also characterized as rough and less rigorous. Flakes from the Sonvian sites commonly constitute no less than half of all recovered finds. Retouched flakes occurred rarely. Bladelets reveal straight, almost parallel facets; their recognition was primarily based on this feature, rather than only on the length that is twice as long as the width. Elongated bladelets that show a narrow lamellar spall removal scar on a long edge comprise a special group. The scar is very similar to a burin facet, but it does not form a characteristic edge. It is likely that some of these implements include defected burins made on the angle of a broken bladelet, whereas the others consist of non-standard cores used for flaking micro-blades. Atypical burins are present, including regular pieces, those made on the angle of a broken bladelet and truncation burins. Points with a blunt edge and an oblique tip, as well as end-scrapers, were also found. Tools made on bladelets, flake tools, pestles, grindstones, bone points and scrapers made of shell can be recognized in the Sonvian culture as well.

Con Moong Cave is a key site that provides insights into the origin of the Sonvian culture. It is located in northern Vietnam, in Cuc Phuong National Park in Than Hoa Province. This site, with a total area of 230 m$^2$, was discovered in 1974 and studied by the Vietnamese archaeologists in 1975–1977 and 2008 (Nguyen Khac Su 2009). The cave is situated at a height of 147 m above sea level and 32 m above the valley floor of an unnamed seasonal stream that flows in front of the site and joins the Thanh Yen creek that discharges into the Bai River. The site was discovered in a limestone massif at the end of a mountain range that stretches along the Su River in northwest–southeast direction, about 100 km west-south-west of Hanoi.

Vietnamese researchers have initially recognized three cultural and chronological units. Deposits assigned to the earliest cultural period, according to data obtained by the Vietnamese archaeologists, revealed intact snail shells, mainly from such species as *Cyclophorus fulguratus*, *Camaena vayssierei* and *Hybocystis srossei*. Excavations yielded such artefact types as choppers, cobble fragments, retouched flakes and humanly modified animal bones. These tools are characteristic of the Sonvian culture and can be dated to the Upper Palaeolithic (14–17 ka). In 2008, male and female burials containing skeletons have been found. A male individual aged 25–30 years, and a female between the age of 40 and 50 years were buried in the graves. The male's height measured 1.75 m, and that the female was 1.61 m tall. Both individuals were attributed to the Australo-Melanesian phenotype.

A faunal assemblage included the animal remains characteristic of a tropical monsoon climate and identified as belonging to Rhinoceros, *Cervus* sp., *Rusa unicolor*, *Muntiacus muntjac Zimmernann*, Bovidae, *Capricornis sumatraensis* Bechstein, Macaca of mulatta Zimmermann, *Scluridae* sp. Indet, *Canidae* sp. Indet, *Arctonyx collaris F. Cuvier*, *Sus scrofa* L., *Paradoxurus hermaphroditus*, Anser. *Lophura* sp. and *Rattus* sp. Most bones were found broken and sometimes heavily burnt.

In 2010–2014, research works at the site were resumed by a Russian–Vietnamese expedition. A trench of 14 m$^2$ was produced at the entrance zone of the cave. These excavations were a follow-up to the preceding studies and were mainly focused on examination of previously unexplored deposits in the cave. A total area of the exposed deposits is 5.5–6 m$^2$. The structural characteristic of the sediments is that their loose and sometimes calcined texture. The sediments include reddish-brown, occasionally whitish silt sandy loam that has been divided into 21 lithological layers. Large limestone clasts are present in the upper part of the deposits, whereas in the underlying layers they become progressively smaller from the top to bottom. The emergence of a lithic industry associated with the Sonvian culture has been recorded in deposits that may be dated to 40 ka. Quartzite pebbles were used as a raw material. Although the collection of lithic inventory includes a small number of tools and consists of core-shaped fragments and waste flakes, it should be noted that discoidal scraper (sumatralith) characteristic of the younger ages appeared in the record.

Finds recovered from the subsequent layer that can be dated to between 35–40 ka also occurred in small numbers; however, they demonstrate significant changes in raw material selection strategies. Apart from quartzite, andesine and, less frequently, limestone, basalt and a number of sedimentary rocks were exploited for producing tools. It should be noted that all chunks of raw material employed by early humans seem to have originated from alluvial deposits, based on cortex partly preserved on many artefacts. Primary flaking does not appear to have involved preparation of cores. Lithic tools resulted from flaking were large and medium-sized flakes. Such more sophisticated implements as unifacial axe (sumatralith) and borer appear in the tool assemblage. Debitage (flakes, fragments and split cobbles) suggests that a selected strategy aimed at exploiting various raw materials remained in use.

Materials recovered from the two uppermost archaeological layers that may be dated to between 25 and 30 ka comprise the most numerous archaeological collection. Raw material mainly included andesine, whereas basalt, limestone and quartzite were used less frequently. Cobble cores were employed as initial blanks. Based on a prevailing number of natural striking platforms in flakes, flaking technique does not seem to have involved the use of prepared striking platforms. Apart from cores showing evidence of flat parallel reduction, the collection includes radial and amorphous cores. The tool assemblage becomes more diversified. Such group of cobble tools as choppers came into existence. Scrapers became more diverse in types; not only discoidal (sumatralith), but also convergent, single and transverse scrapers were recognized. Of particular note are axes attributed to Hoabinhian (bifacially worked) and Bacsonian (bifacially worked and grinded) types found to be present in the collection along with a unifacial axe (sumatralith). The discovery of such tools as a bone perforator and two grindstones confirms an assumption suggesting that Con Moong Cave began to be intensively used and permanently occupied by early humans.

Accordingly, arguments suggested by the majority of Vietnamese archaeologists, who associate the Sonvian culture with the terminal Pleistocene and consider it a phenomenon that directly preceded the Hoabinhian culture from which the latter originated, seem strong. Types of blade tools recognized at the site of Vuon Sao corroborate such a chronology. No similar blade tools were found in Hoa Binh and Bac Son.

It should be noted that inselbergs, where the site of Vuon Sao (Vinh Phuc Province) are situated, retain scattered alluvial pebbles and cobbles on their surface almost everywhere and represent washed-out stretches of the third Lower-Middle Quaternary terrace located above the floodplain in the present-day foothills. In the Hanoi depression, these inselbergs occupy an intermediate chronological position between a Lower-Middle Quaternary terrace 25–35 m high and an Upper Quaternary terrace 5–8 m high. On that basis, an age of the surface in the inselbergs may be dated to Qal. Such a location of the sites makes it possible to associate them with the terminal Pleistocene.

Also noteworthy are caves excavated by Vietnamese archaeologists in Son La and Lai Chau Provinces in 1973–1975; lithic inventory recovered from these sites shows characteristics similar to those typical of the Sonvian culture, although some special differences have been recognized as well. Of greatest interest are Nam Tun and Hang Pong Caves. The latter has yielded the following radiocarbon dates obtained from shell fragments: 11,915 ± 120 (Bln-1352) and 11,330 ± 180 (Bln-1351) BP. These dates are somewhat older than those provided for the Hoabinhian sites and confirm attribution of the Sonvian culture to the terminal Pleistocene. Archaeological evidence is also supported by associated faunal remains.

Excavations conducted at Nui Mot Cave yielded faunal fossils attributed to the following species: *Pongo* sp., *Sus scrofa*, *Rusa* sp., *Muntiacus muntjac*, Bovidae, Rhinoceros, *Hystrix* sp., *Rattus* sp.; at Phung Quyen Cave: Macaca cf. mulatta Zimmermann, Macaca cf., *Panthera pardus*?, *Arctonyx collaris* F. cuvier, *Paradoxurus hermaphroditus* Pallas, *Ailuropoda melanoleuca fovealis* M u Gr, *Rusa unicolor* Kerr, *Muntiacus muntjac* Zimmerman, *Cervus* sp.

*Bibos* sp., *Sus scrofa* L., Elephantidae gen sp. indet, *Palaeoloxodon* sp. The remains from Nui Mot Cave attributed to Pongo show close resemblance to Pongo from Kėo Leng Cave (Lang Son). The remains of *Ailuropoda melanoleuca fovealis* from Phung Quyen also reveal great similarities with the Ailuropoda remains found at Tham Khuyen Cave (Lang Son). The Sonvian caves contained large accumulations of shells from edible molluscs. They include marine species (*Meretrix meretrix*), but those attributed to gastropods – Melani, *Cyclophorus fulguratus, Camaena vayssierei, Hybocystis crossei, Antimelania* – occurred more frequently. In general, the identified faunal species is similar to the present-day fauna of Central Vietnam, which is typical of the terminal Pleistocene in North Vietnam.

## Hoabinhian Lithic Industries and Issues Related to the Origin of Modern Humans

In North Vietnam, the Pleistocene to Holocene transition is associated with the emergence of such a widespread phenomenon as the Hoabinhian culture that embraced the most part of the Indochinese Peninsula. In 1926–1931, the French researcher M. Colani carried out the first excavations of the cave sites in North Vietnam, enabling recognition of the Hoabinhian assemblage and distinguishing its three periods: the Upper Palaeolithic, Mesolithic and Lower Neolithic (Colani 1927).

In 1070, Solheim noted that the Hoabinhian culture "developed directly out of the chopper-chopping-tool tradition", from the Lower and Middle Palaeolithic. He also made an attempt to distinguish three stages in the development of the Hoabinhian culture. The early Hoabinhian dates to between 50,000 or 40,000 and 20,000 BP; the middle Hoabinhian – 20,000–15,000 BP; the late Hoabinhian – 15,000–2,500 BP (Solheim 1970). Therefore, according to Solheim, the Hoabinhian culture existed in the late Pleistocene – early Holocene.

Currently, the Hoabinhian techno-complex is provisionally dated back to between 16,000–6,000 BP. This time span can be reduced for North Vietnam based on the results of studies undertaken at Con Moong Cave, where the Hoabinhian layer has been recognized between the Sonvian occupation layers and the Bacsonian Neolithic layer. The Hoabinhian layer has yielded a burial with scattered ochre, as well as lithic tools and oyster shells. A skeleton in the grave was found lying in a flexed position and identified as being associated with a male of Australo-Negroid phenotype aged 50–60 years. In contrast to the Sonvian tools recovered from the first cultural layer, the second one yielded almond- and disc-shaped sumatraliths (Figure 4.4, specimens 3, 5, 6), short and long axes (Figure 4.4, specimens 1, 2, 4), bone points and scrapers made of shell, whereas typical convex pebble scrapers still occur in the assemblage (Figure 4.4, specimens 7, 8, 9). These artefacts are characteristic of the Hoabinhian culture, and the tools assemblage is typical of sites associated with the Pleistocene–Holocene transition (9–14 ka) that occur very frequently in this region. Deposits exposed at Diem Cave, containing a Hoabinhian lithic industry and a female human burial similar to the tomb from Con Moong, can be attributed to the same time period.

The Hoabinhian industries were found widespread across the Indochinese Peninsula, Sumatra and southern China. River cobbles appear to have been a dominant raw material selected for tool manufacture using Hoabinhian lithic reduction. After being roughly retouched, they were subsequently used for producing such major categories of tools as Sumatra-type axes, egg-shaped and pointed egg-shaped axes, short axes, rounded axes, rounded or disc-shaped scrapers.

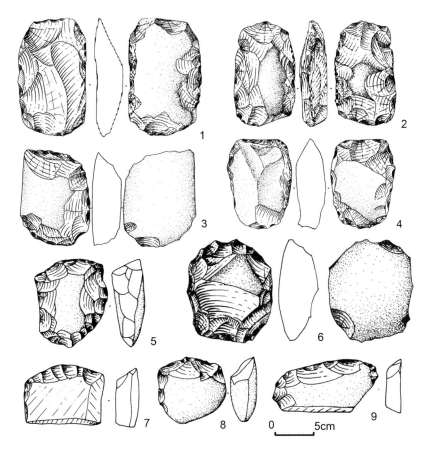

FIGURE 4.4  Hoabinhian industry: (1, 2, 4) Hoabinhian-type axes, (3, 5, 6) sumatraliths, (7, 8, 9) convex scrapers.

It is interesting to note that although in these regions the Hoabinhian assemblages retain the Sonvian tool types such as disc-shaped scrapers and choppers, as well as indications for the use of 'citrus slice' reduction technique, the Sonvian industries reveal only certain features typical of the Hoabinhian culture, for instance, axe-like tools, including polished ones.

Saurin and Fromaget, who studied Indochinese caves, noted that Hoabinhian layers yielded no fossil fauna. These deposits produced the faunal remains attributed only to present-day species (Fromaget 1940; Saurin 1951).

All archaeological evidence that provides insights into the characteristics of Palaeolithic industries from Southeast Asia, including North Vietnam, indicates the development of a techno-typological industry in the area throughout the terminal Pleistocene, showing fundamental differences from those recorded across the rest part of Eurasia.

A pebble-flake industry and the manufacturing of bamboo tools prevailed in lithic industry across Southeast Asia and Vietnam almost throughout the Palaeolithic Age, thus showing the major difference between the culture of indigenous populations and that of Palaeolithic humans from the rest part of Eurasia. A Palaeolithic tool industry appears to have evolved in the area throughout the Pleistocene and no indications for the emergence of fundamentally different innovations in lithic reduction have been documented; evidence for using Levallois primary flaking does not appear in the record for more than one million years.

## The Origin of Anatomically Modern Humans in East and Southeast Asia

The question now arises with regard to taxonomic attribution of populations from East and Southeast Asia that expanded across this region during the Upper Pleistocene. Archaeological, anthropological and paleogenetic data indicate that the genus *Homo* appears to have originated in Africa and about 1.9 (1.8) Ma human populations began to disperse across Eurasia. There are two hypotheses about the origin of anatomically modern humans. According to the "Out-of-Africa" hypothesis, the evolution of *Homo sapiens* occurred in Africa 200,000–150,000 years ago, with its subsequent spread throughout Eurasia and Australia 80,000–60,000 years ago. *H. sapiens* first colonized Eurasia, then Australia, about 60,000–50,000 years ago and more recently – Central Asia and Europe. Proponents of the multiregional hypothesis see the consequences of this process differently. Some of them believe that autochthonous archaic population seems to have been replaced by anatomically modern humans. The others do not rule out the possibility that in some instances *H. sapiens* and *Homo neanderthalensis* coexisted for a long time, for example, in southern Pyrenees. Contacts between newly arrived and local populations may have resulted in diffusion and sometimes in cultural hybridization.

The recent single-origin hypothesis encounters some difficulties. According to its supporters, anatomically modern humans, who dispersed out of Africa, appear to have colonized Australia 60,000–50,000 years ago. However, how can they explain the fact that *H. sapiens* was able to travel a huge distance of more than 10,000 km in 5,000–10,000 years without leaving behind any traces on the way of its movement? In South, Southeast and East Asia, if replacement of autochthonous populations by arrived human groups took place 80,000–30,000 years ago, the lithic industry was expected to be completely replaced, whereas acculturation should have entailed significant changes in techno-typological characteristics of lithic inventory. However, no indications for such processes have been observed in eastern Asia.

A lack of archaeological evidence impelled supporters of the recent single-origin hypothesis to suggest a theory about the existence of a southern migratory flow of modern humans to eastern Eurasia along the seacoast. Thus, Oppenheimer claims that "…the actual colonization of Australia occurred between 65,000 years ago, and Flores and even New Guinea were colonized 75,000 years ago…" (Oppenheimer 2003). When asked why archaeologists cannot find evidence corroborating this process he answers: "As is clear from the sea-level record, however, the beaches our ancestors combed over 60,000–85,000 years ago are now well beneath the sea, so that we should not expect to find much of the evidence…"

Another hypothesis about the multiregional human evolution (polycentric) also includes several versions. Its basic idea can be summarized as follows: *H. sapiens* evolved in areas colonized by *H. erectus*, resulting in the possibility for the emergence of modern humans. This hypothesis is mostly advocated by archaeologists and anthropologists involved in Palaeolithic studies focusing on East and Southeast Asia, being corroborated by the recent discoveries.

A wealth of archaeological and anthropological evidence, as well as data resulted from DNA sequencing, have made it possible to put forward a hypothesis about the existence of four centres where the four sub-species of *H. sapiens* seem to have evolved based on a polytypical ancestry form, *H. erectus sensu lato*, resulting from divergence and gene flow (Derevianko 2011, 2012).

DNA sequencing shows that between 1% and 4% of the genomes of present-day non-African populations are derived from Neanderthals (Green et al. 2010). DNA sequencing of modern human fossils recovered from the cave site of Peștera cu Oase dated 37,000–43,000 years old reveals that 6–9% of the genome of the Oase individual is of Neanderthal origin (Fu et al. 2015). This suggests that a Neanderthal was among his ancestors as recently as four to six generations ago. Therefore, Neanderthals cannot be eliminated from our ancestry and they need to be returned into a sub-species (*H. sapiens neanderthalensis*). The discovery of a new taxon at Denisova Cave in Siberia shows that 5% of the genome of some present-day populations in Southeast Asia came from the Denisovans (Reich et al. 2011). Thus, the Denisovans also appear to have contributed to evolution of anatomically modern humans. In this regard, it was suggested to classify this taxon as a sub-species *H. sapiens altaiensis* (Derevianko 2011).

As mentioned above, the development of lithic industries in East and Southeast Asia during the Palaeolithic seems to have occurred evolutionarily almost throughout the whole period based on a regional tradition. Evidence shows no indications of a sudden shift in a local techno-typological complex, which should be expected to appear if these industries had been replaced by anatomically modern humans who came into this region from Africa. We have no reasons to deny reality of these migrations, but both archaeological and anthropological data suggest that acculturation and miscegenation of newly arrived and autochthonous populations appear to have taken place rather than replacement of indigenous groups. To date, an immense array of factual evidence has been accumulated with regard to human dispersal in China, and on the islands of Southeast Asia, including its mainland areas. The following are some anthropological finds, dating back about 100,000–40,000 years, discovered in these regions.

In East and Southeast Asia, the largest number of sites (over 70) that yielded the Pleistocene human fossils has been discovered in China. These sites provide convincing evidence for continuity in evolution of Pleistocene hominins towards their sedimentation. In addition to the preceding hypotheses about the origin of anatomically modern humans, Chinese researchers suggested the third theory about 'Continuity with Hybridization' based on available palaeoanthropological evidence (Gao et al. 2010). Comprehensive analysis of hominin fossils found in China has made it possible to infer that a continuous evolution of a number of hereditary characteristics suggests no large-scale population replacement of indigenous groups by *H. sapiens* that came from Africa (Ibid.). This conclusion is supported by extensive archaeological evidence associated with Palaeolithic sites dated to between 100,000 and 40,000 years ago, indicating unique and distinguishing features of the lithic industry compared to that from western Eurasia.

Over the last 30 years, Palaeolithic sites, including those associated with palaeoanthropological evidence dated to 70,000–40,000 years ago, have been discovered not only in mainland Southeast Asia, but also on its islands, as well as in Australia and New Guinea (Davidson and Noble 1992; Allen and O'Connell 2014; Clarkson et al. 2015; Westaway et al. 2017).

The fossil remains attributed to *H. sapiens* have been also found in North Vietnam in Hang Hum and Tham Om Caves, dating to about 60,000 years ago. The younger palaeoanthropological finds recovered from the cave sites of Thung Lang and Keo Leng date to 30,000 years ago. Large numbers of fossils identified as belonging to Upper Pleistocene *H. sapiens* were found at Con Moong and Diem Caves. Con Moong Cave demonstrates a continuous sequence in sedimentation during the last 100,000 years, as well as the first evidence for the emergence of early humans in this region. The continued existence of hominins in the region is substantiated by the discovery of a few Palaeolithic cultures in North Vietnam, dating back to the Upper Pleistocene.

With regard to the possibility for the origin of anatomically modern humans, of great importance are the hominin fossils from Tam Pa Ling Cave in Laos recently discovered near Palaeolithic sites in North Vietnam that include the partial cranium from an individual attributed to modern humans (TPL 1) and a largely complete mandible from the other individual (TPL 2), dating back to 63,000–46,000 years ago (Demeter et al. 2015). Like other archaeological evidence from China and Southeast Asia, these finds demonstrate a mosaic pattern in traits characteristic of anatomically modern humans showing plesiomorphic features from the late forms of *H. erectus*. Thus, the TPL 2 mandible reveals the presence of a chin, but it retains a robust lateral corpus and internal corporal morphology typical of archaic hominins. The mosaic morphology of anthropological remains from Tam Pa Ling Cave, like many other finds, shows the possibility of miscegenation between indigenous hominin populations and anatomically modern humans who arrived from Africa.

Based on the continuity between lithic industries from East and Southeast Asia throughout the Palaeolithic Age, and the emergence of a taxon that interbred with anatomically modern humans who arrived from Africa into the region and was able to produce viable offspring, one of the authors of this publication suggested that this population should be attributed to a subspecies of *H. sapiens* and referred to as *H. sapiens orientalensis* (Derevianko 2011, 2012).

Data resulted from DNA sequencing of modern humans, Neanderthals and the Denisovans show that these hominin groups could hybridize and deliver viable descendents. A central, stem-forming role in evolution of anatomically modern humans was indeed played by *H. sapiens* that evolved in Africa and is therefore suggested to be referred to as *H. sapiens africanensis* (Figure 4.5). The dispersal of *H. sapiens africanensis* across Eurasia and Australia resulted in

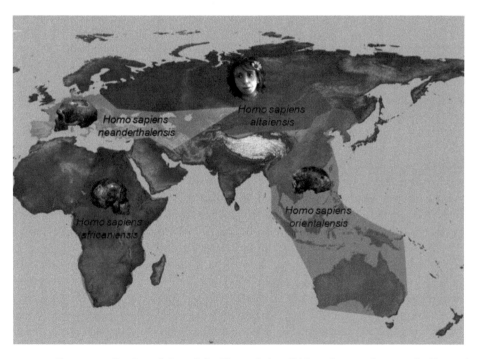

**FIGURE 4.5** Four areas for the origins of the Upper Palaeolithic culture and anatomically modern humans.

acculturation, as well as in assimilation of autochthonous populations by newly arrived hominin groups. Not only had genetic material obtained by *H. sapiens africanensis* from indigenous populations contributed to its adaptation to new environments, but also to some diseases. Thus, the evolutionary history of modern humanity appears to have been a lengthy and complex process. The possibility of new discoveries that may provide additional evidence to address the issue regarding the origin of our species cannot be ruled out.

## References

Allen, Jim, and O'Connell, James. 2014 Both half right updating the evidence for dating first human arrivals in Sahul. *Australian Archaeology* 79, 86–108.

Anisyutkin, N., and Timofeev, I. 2004 *Kamennyie izdeliya iz pescheryi Thamkuen na severe Vetnama*. [*Stone artefacts from the Cave of Tham Khuyen in the North of Vietnam*]. *Arheologicheskie vesti* 11, 13–21.

Ciochon, R.L., and Olsen, J.W. 1986 Paleoanthropological and archaeological research in the Socialist Republic of Vietnam. *Journal of Human Evolution* 15, 623–631.

Clarkson, Chris, Smith, Mike, Marwick, Ben, Fullagar, Richard, Wallis, Lynley, Faulkner, Patrick, Manne, Tiina, Hayes, Elspeth, Roberts, Richard, Jacobs, Zenobia, Carah, Xavier, Lowe, Kelsey, Matthews, Jacqueline, and Florin, Anna. 2015 The archaeology, chronology and stratigraphy of Madjedbebe (Malakunanja II): A site in northern Australia with early occupation. *Journal of Human Evolution* 83, 46–64.

Colani, M. 1927 L'Age de la pierre dans la province de Hoa Binh. *Memoires du service Geologique de L'Indochine*, 14.

Cuong, Nguyen. 1985 Fossile Menschenfunde aus Nordvietnam. *Menschwerdung – biotischer und gesellschafter Entwiklungprocess: Schriften zur Ur- und Fruhgeschichte* 41, 96–101.

Davidson, I., and Noble, W. 1992 Why the first colonization of the Australian region is the earliest evidence of modern human behavior. *Archaeology in Oceania* 27, 135–142.

Demeter, Fabrice, Shackelford, Laura, Westaway, Kira, Duringer, Philippe, Bacon, Anne-Marie, Ponche, Jean-Luc, Wu, Xiujie, Sayavongkhamdy, Thongsa, Zhao, Jian-Xin, Barnes, Lani, Boyon, Marc, Sichanthongtip, Phonephanh, Sénégas, Frank, Karpoff, Anne-Marie, Patole-Edoumba, Elise, Coppens, Yves, and Braga, José. 2015 Early modern humans and morphological variation in Southeast Asia: Fossil evidence from Tam Pa Ling, Laos. *PLoS ONE* e0121193.

Derevianko, A.P. 2011 *Verhniy paleolit v Afrike i Evrazii i formirovanie cheloveka sovremennogo anatomicheskogo tipa*. [*The Upper Palaeolithic in Africa and Eurasia and the Evolution of Anatomically Modern Humans*]. Novosibirsk: Izd-vo IAET SO RAN.

Derevianko, A.P. 2012 *Novyie arheologicheskie otkryitiya na Altae i problema formirovaniya Homo sapiens*. [*Recent Discoveries in the Altai: Issues on the Evolution of Homo sapiens*]. Novosibirsk: Izd-vo IAET SO RAN.

Derevianko, A.P. 2014 *Bifasialnaya industriya v Vostochnoy i Yugo-Vostochnoy Azii*. [*Bifacial Industry in East and Southeast Asia*]. Novosibirsk: Izd-vo IAET SO RAN.

Derevianko, A.P. 2015 *Tri globalnyie migratsii cheloveka v Evrazii. T. 1: Proishozhdenie cheloveka i zaselenie im Yugo-Zapadnoy, Yuzhnoy, Vostochnoy, Yugo-Vostochnoy Azii i Kavkaza*. [*Three Global Human Migrations in Eurasia. V. 1: Human Origins and Early Peopling of Southwestern, Southern, Eastern and Southeastern Asia and the Caucasus*]. Novosibirsk: Izd-vo IAET SO RAN.

Derevianko, A.P., Gladyishev, S.A., Hai, Nguyen, Doi, Nguyen, Su, Nguyen, Kandyba, A. V., Cheha, A.M., Tsybankov, A.A., Toan, Nguyen, and Tuan, Phan. 2017 Novyie dannyie v izuchenii rannego paleolita s bifasialnoy industriey Vietnama. Raskopki stoyanki Roktying-7 v 2017 godu. [New Data from the Study of the Lower Palaeolithic with a Vietnamese Bifacial Industry. The 2017 Excavations of the Roq Tung 7 Site]. *Problemyi arheologii, etnografii, antropologii Sibiri i sopredelnyih territoriy* 22, 79–83.

Derevianko, A.P., Su, N.H., Tsybankov, A.A., and Doi, N.Z. 2016 *Vozniknovenie bifasialnoy industrii v Vostochnoy i Yugo-Vostochnoy Azii*. [*The Emergence of a Bifacial Industry in East and Southeast Asia*]. Novosibirsk: Izd-vo IAET SO RAN.

Fouli, R. 1990 *Esche odin nepovtorimyiy vid: Ekologicheskie aspektyi evolyutsii cheloveka*. [*Another Unique Species: Environmental Aspects of Human Evolution*]. Moskva: Mir.

Fromaget, F. 1940 Les récentes découvertes anthropologiques dans les formations préhistoriques de la chaîne annamitique. *Proceedings of the Third Congress of Prehistorians of the Far East*, 51–59.

Fu, Qiaomei, Hajdinjak, Mateja, Moldovan, Oana, Constantin, Silviu, Mallick, Swapan, Skoglund, Pontus, Patterson, Nick, Rohland, Nadin, Lazaridis, Iosif, Nickel, Birgit, Viola, Bence, Prüfer, Kay, Meyer, Matthias, Kelso, Janet, Reich, David, and Pääbo, Svante. 2015 An early modern human from Romania with a recent Neanderthal ancestor. *Nature* 524, 216–219.

Gao, Xing, Zhang, Xiaoling, Yang, Dongya, Shen, Chen, and Wu, Xinzhi. 2010 Revisiting the origin of modern humans in China and its implications for global human evolution. *Science China, Earth Sciences* 53, 1927–1940.

Green, Richard, Krause, Johannes, Briggs, Adrian, Maricic, Tomislav, Stenzel, Udo, Kircher, Martin, Patterson, Nick, Li, Heng, Zhai, Weiwei, Fritz, Markus, Hansen, Nancy, Durand, Eric, Malaspinas, Anna-Sapfo, Jensen, Jeffrey, Marques-Bonet, Tomas, Alkan, Can, Prüfer, Kay, Meyer, Matthias, Burbano, Good, Schultz, Rigo, Aximu-Petri, Ayinuer, Butthof, Anne, Höber, Barbara, Höffner, Barbara, Siegemund, Madlen, Weihmann, Antje, Nusbaum, Chad, Lander, Eric, Russ, Carsten, Novod, Nathaniel, Affourtit, Jason, Egholm, Michael, Verna, Christine, Rudan, Pavao, Brajkovic, Dejana, Kucan, Željko, Gušic, Ivan, Doronichev, Vladimir, Golovanova, Liubov, Lalueza-Fox, Carles, De La Rasilla, Marco, Fortea, Javier, Rosas, Antonio, Schmitz, Ralf, Johnson, Philip, Eichler, Evan, Falush, Daniel, Birney, Ewan, Mullikin, James, Slatkin, Montgomery, Nielsen, Rasmus, Kelso, Janet, Lachmann, Michael, Reich, David, and Pääbo, Svante. 2010 A draft sequence of the Neandertal genome. *Science* 328, 710–722.

Kahlke, H.D. 1973 A review of the Pleistocene history of the Orangutan (*Pongo Lacepede* 1799). *Asian Perspectives* 1, 5–14.

Kahlke, H.D., and Nghia, Nguyen. 1964 Preliminary report paleontological and anthropological research in North Vietnam 1963–1964. *Tin Tuc Dong Khoa Hoc* 5, 15–33.

Marwick, Ben. 2009 Biogeography of Middle Pleistocene hominins in mainland Southeast Asia. A review of current evidence. *Quaternary International* 202, 51–58.

Matyukhin, A., 1983 Tools of the Early Paleolithic. In: Rogachev A. N. (Editor) *Tekhnologia proizvodsrva v epohupaleolita*. Leningrad: Nauka. 134–187.

Olsen, J., and Ciochon, R. 1990 The paleoanthropology of Middle Pleistocene Vietnam. *Journal of Human Evolution* 19, 761–786.

Oppenheimer, Stephen. 2003 *Out of Eden: the Peopling of the World*. London: Constable.

Ranov, V.A. 1986 Raskopki nizhnepaleoliticheskoy stoyanki Lahuti-1 v 1979 g. [The 1979 excavations at the Lower Palaeolithic site of Lahuti-1]. *Arheologicheskie rabotyi v Tadzhikistane* 19, 11–36.

Reich, David, Patterson, Nick, Kircher, Martin, Delfin, Frederick, Nandineni, Madhusudan, Pugach, Irina, Ko, Albert, Ko, Ying-Chin, Jinam, Timothy, Phipps, Maude, Saitou, Naruya, Wollstein, Andreas, Kayser, Manfred, Paabo, Svante, and Stoneking, Mark. 2011 Denisova admixture and the first modern human dispersals into Southeast Asia and Oceania. *American Journal of Human Genetics*, 89, 516–528.

Saurin, Edmond. 1951 Études Géologiques et préhistoriques. *Bulletin de la Société des études indochinoisestome* 4, 525–539.

Solheim, William. 1970 Northern Thailand, Southeast Asia and world prehistory. *Asian Perspectives* 13, 145–162.

Su, Nguyen. 1982 Kultura Son Vi i ee mesto v kamennom veke Yugo- Vostochnoy Azii. [The Sonvian Culture and its Place in the Stone Age of Southeast Asia]. *Sovetskaya Arheologiya* 3, 5–12.

Su, Nguyen. 2007 Stone age archaeology in Vietnam. *Vietnam Archaeology* 2, 53–64.

Su, Nguyen. 2009 Con Mong cave: New data and new perceptions. *Vietnam Archaeology* 4, 40–52.

Tan, Ha Van. 1971 Van hoa Son Vi [Son Vi culture]. *Khao co hoc*, 11–12.

Tan, Ha Van. 1976 Le Hoabinhian dans le contexte du Vietnam. *Etudes Vietnamiennes* 46, 23–37.

Tan, Ha Van, and Su, Nguyen Khac. 1978 Van hoa Son Vi muoi nam sau khi phat hien. [Son Vi culture after ten years after discovery]. *Khao co hoc* 4, 37–50.

Westaway, K. E., Louys, J., Due Awe, R., Morwood, M., Price, G., Zhao, J., Aubert, M., Joannes-Boyau, R., Smith, M., Skinner, M., Compton, T., Bailey, R., van den Bergh, G., de Vos, J., Pike, A., Stringer, C., Saptomo, E., Rizal, Y., Zaim, J., Santoso, W., Trihascaryo, A., Kinsley, L., and Sulistyanto, B. 2017 An early modern human presence in Sumatra 73,000–63,000 years ago. *Nature* 548, 322–325.

Xie, Guangmao, and Huang, Qishan. 2003 *Baise jiushiqi shidai gongye*. [*The Paleolithic Industry of Baise*]. Beijing: Wenwu.

# 5
# EARLY MODERN HUMANS IN ISLAND SOUTHEAST ASIA

*Daud Tanudirjo*

## Introduction

Straddling the tropics between 95° and 141° longitude, Island of Southeast Asia is the largest archipelago in the world. It consists of more than 25,000 green and lush islands that spread across vast, tranquil seas like a string of emeralds along the equator. It is home to hundreds of ethnic groups with very diverse languages and cultures. Ecologically, this archipelago is also complex. It is among the most active global subduction zones where at least four tectonic plates – the Eurasian, Philippine, Indo-Australian, and Pacific Plates – are colliding to create a vigorous volcanic area known as the Ring of Fire. Inevitably, natural disasters triggered by earthquakes, tsunamis, and volcanic eruptions have become part of people's lives here. Moreover, the flora and fauna of the islands are highly heterogeneous, comprising assortments of species that have dispersed from both mainland Asia and Australia-New Guinea, alongside endemic ones which have evolved in relative isolation.

Attracted by this unique archipelagic environment, the British naturalist A.R. Wallace carried out extensive research here during the mid-19th century. This formed the basis for his independently conceiving the theory of evolution by natural selection, published in 1858 alongside Darwin's own work on the subject. Wallace had also laid the foundation for biogeography and he subdivided Island Southeast Asia into distinct faunal zones. His name was then memorialized by Thomas Huxley who designated the Wallace Line as that which separates the Oriental mammalian fauna in the western areas of the archipelago from the Australasian marsupial fauna in the east. The Wallace Line runs between the islands of Bali and Lombok, through Strait of Makassar, to the east of Palawan, and to the west of Luzon (see Figure 5.1).

The islands of this archipelago are various in size. Larger islands, such as Sumatra, Borneo, Sulawesi, and Java, are mostly situated in the west, while smaller islands, including Maluku and Nusa Tenggara, spread throughout the east. To the eastern end of the archipelago lies the largest island, New Guinea, which is geopolitically divided between Indonesia and Papua New Guinea. In its entirety, Island Southeast Asia comprises five modern nation-states: Malaysia, Brunei, the Philippines, Indonesia, and Timor Leste. For the purpose of this chapter, however, more attention will be given to eastern Malaysia (Sarawak and Sabah), Indonesia, and Timor

DOI: 10.4324/9781003427483-5

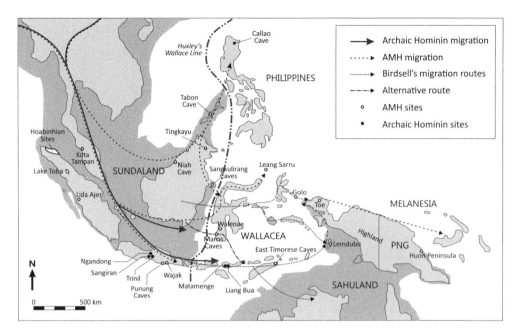

FIGURE 5.1  Locations of important archaeological sites mentioned in the text and reconstructed migration routes followed by archaic hominins and early modern humans in Southeast Asia.

Leste. Literature on the prehistoric archaeology of Brunei is not accessible to the author, while early modern humans in the Philippines is presented in a separate chapter of this volume. From the perspective of early human migration, this archipelago formed important stepping stones which allowed hominins to journey from Mainland Southeast Asia to Australia-New Guinea. This is partly because sea currents and monsoonal winds have proved to be beneficial for the movement of human and animals. Indeed, for some scholars this region is a laboratory for human evolution and migration.

Since the theory of evolution by natural selection was proposed by Charles Darwin and Alfred R. Wallace in the mid-19th century, Island Southeast Asia has been perceived as one of the most important regions in search of the origins of human ancestors. In 1865–1866 a Javanese nobleman and acclaimed painter, Raden Saleh, excavated sites in Java to recover fossils thought locally to belong to giant humans that once lived on the island. His discoveries enticed Eugene Dubois, a Dutch physician and anatomist, to pursue his adamant desire to find the missing link between humans and other primates. Dubois initially researched the limestone caves around Payakumbuh in the Padang Highlands, West-Sumatra (1887–1888).

In one of these caves, Lida Ajer, he excavated abundant fossils of rainforest fauna and human teeth. Nonetheless, all of these findings were deemed to be too young for the missing-link. He then moved to Java when he heard the discovery of a fossilized human skull, later to be known as Wadjak-Man, by geologist B.D. van Rietschoten, in a marble quarry near Tulungagung, East-Java (Theunissen 1989; Shipman 2001).

In 1890–1891, Dubois discovered a fossilized hominin skull cap and a femur at Trinil, a fossil-rich, small village on the bank of Solo River, East Java. He declared these fossils as "the missing-link" and designated it as *Pithecanthropus erectus* ("walking ape-man") after Ernst

Haeckel's hypothetical name for the missing-link (Shipman 2001). This discovery was then followed with more rigorous researches by Margarethe E. Selenka in Trinil (1907–1908), and by G.H.R. von Koenigswald who oversaw almost all palaeoanthropological researches in Solo River Basin, including Ngandong (1931–1933), Punung (1935–1936), Mojokerto (1936), and Sangiran (1936–1941) until the outbreak of World War II. Most of the hominin fossils found at these sites were classified as *Pithecanthropus erectus* – or *Homo erectus* in new taxonomy. The fossils were commonly recovered in contexts alongside Pleistocene faunas and sometimes with simple flake tools labelled as the Sangiran Flake Industry. Another lithic technology often associated with the *H. erectus* includes the pebble tools known as Hallam Movius's chopper-chopping tools. At this stage, very few remains of early *Homo sapiens* were reported from the area. Those that were known include the two Wajak skulls, human teeth from Punung, human skeletal materials from Hoabinhian shell-middens in North Sumatra, and remains from several caves in East Java and South Sulawesi (van Heekeren 1972; Shipman 2001; Storm and de Vos 2006). Unfortunately, none of these individuals were well dated.

After World War II, research on human origins in this archipelago was carried out largely by Indonesian researchers in collaboration with international scholars from various countries. The research area considerably expanded to cover almost the entire archipelago. More *H. erectus* fossils were recovered from Java, while new potential sites with Pleistocene fauna or Palaeolithic flakes and pebble tools were encountered in South Sulawesi, Flores, Borneo, and Timor as well as in Luzon and Mindanao (Evangelista 1969; van Heekeren 1972; Bellwood 2017). A considerable number of prehistoric caves with modern human remains were excavated, but most of them postdated 10,000 years ago, except those from Niah cave in Sarawak (Harrison 1970) and Tabon Cave in Palawan Fox 1970), which were claimed to be c.40,000 and 24,000 years old, respectively.

Since the 1990s, significant progress has been made. New Pleistocene sites have been located and previously researched sites have been re-investigated using modern archaeological techniques. With improvements in radiometric dating, deep-trench excavation strategies, and the archaeological sciences, important advances have been made, including the spectacular discovery of small-bodied hominins – *Homo floresiensis* or "the hobbit" – at Liang Bua cave (Morwood et al. 2004), new dates for the rock art of Sulawesi (Aubert et al. 2014) and Bornean caves (Aubert et al. 2018), and the excavation of another small-bodied hominin at Callao Cave, Luzon (Mijares et al. 2010), up to 40 kya. In eastern Indonesia and Timor Leste, new sites with traces of human occupation exceeding 30 kya are also reported (O'Connor et al. 2017). Meanwhile, reanalysis of previously excavated material has successfully identified further remains of early modern humans, while the reanalysis of site stratigraphy has allowed dating attributions to be refined (Westaway et al. 2017). With these newly available data, the prehistory of early modern humans in Island South East Asia needs to be reassessed.

## Late Pleistocene Settings

In the past 120 kya, Island Southeast Asia has experienced sea level oscillations as a result of changes in the earth's temperature. Beginning with a sharp drop to –60 m relative to present sea-level around 115 kya, sea-levels were then fluctuating between –20 m and –70 m from about 85 kya to 40 kya before declining rapidly to –120 m at the Last Glacial Maximum at 20 kya. Since then, a warmer climate melted the ice-sheets in the higher latitudes, causing sea-level to rise to its present position around 8 kya (Burroughs 2005). During times of compressed sea-level, the islands of Sumatra, Borneo, Java, and Bali amalgamated into the Asian continent to become the landmass of Sundaland, while at the same time the Aru Islands and New Guinea joined to the Australian continent to become Sahulland. Between Sundaland and Sahulland is the so-called Wallacea, an archipelagic area which is surrounded by deep troughs, meaning that it has never been connected with any land bridges to the continents to the east and west. However, the straits between the Wallacean islands and the adjacent continental zones were much narrowed during periods of lower sea level, especially from 67 kya to 61 kya, when the sea was compressed down to –80 m, and certainly during the Last Glacial Maximum when the sea was compressed to –120 m (Burroughs 2005). Most probably it was during these periods of low sea levels and increased island intervisibility (Kealy et al. 2017) that humans and animals from the Asian mainland migrated via land bridges or by crossing narrow straits to the south and east, as they sought warmer environments (Burroughs 2005; van den Bergh et al. 2016a, 2016b, 2016c).

During the Last Glacial Period, the temperature drop in Island Southeast Asia was not as significant as at high latitudes. Furthermore, temperature declines were not uniform in the tropics; in higher altitudes the temperature fell quite substantially between 5°C and 10°C, while close to the sea surface the temperature generally dropped only 2–3°C (Whitmore 1981; Bird et al. 2005). However, these temperature changes were very influential to the environment, especially to vegetation, due to reduced rainfall and humidity. In equatorial areas, rainfall was possibly reduced by 30–50% compared to the present (Allen and Kershaw 1996; Kershaw et al. 2001). As a result, in this region the environment became cooler and drier, which further contracted rainforests and increased the expansion of grasslands in Sundaland and Sahulland alike. It is highly likely that a savanna corridor was formed in central Sundaland, stretching from north to south, about 50–150 km wide, from what is now the South China Sea through the Karimata Strait, to South Sulawesi, Java, and Bali (see Figure 5.2). This savannah corridor thus separated the rainforested areas in Sumatra from that in Kalimantan. Within this more open region, a number of ancient river systems drained the exposed land. Such an environment was surely a suitable area to live in, and probably and ideal migration route for hominins (Bird et al. 2005). Unfortunately, this area is now submerged under the sea, and thus evidence for the presence of Pleistocene humans in this area is difficult to find.

Outside the savanna corridor, rainforests seem to have been predominant in Sundaland during interstadials and were sometimes replaced by more open vegetation during stadials. Tropical rainforests with dense vegetation were widespread throughout much of the Malay Peninsula, Sumatra, and Borneo (van der Kaars and Dam 1995; Rolland 2002). The remains of rainforest fauna such as orangutan (*Pongo pygmaeus*), siamang gibbons (*Hylobates syndactylus*), and sun bear (*Helarctos malayanus*) dated to 73 kya, were reported from archaeological sites in West Sumatra (Westaway et al. 2017), while palaeoecological studies at the Great Cave of Niah, Sarawak, shows rainforest environments were prevalent during the Late Pleistocene (Spehar et al. 2018), although montane forest was sometimes replaced by savanna, and deciduous lowland rainforest with mangroves, during drier periods between 50 kya and 27 kya (Hunt et al. 2012). In West Java, after 100 kya the climate was mostly warm and humid, allowing for the development of swamp forest, although this became slightly drier between 81 and 74 kya (van der Kaas and Dam 1995). Meanwhile, in East Java rainforest habitats were predominant between 120 and 80 kya and became more deciduous as the climate became drier towards the Last Glacial Maximum and even into to the Early Holocene (Westaway et al. 2007).

In general, the Late Pleistocene fauna in Sundaland was characterized by the so-called Punung Fauna (van den Bergh et al. 2001; Storm et al. 2005; Louys 2012) consisting predominantly

Early Modern Humans in Island Southeast Asia 91

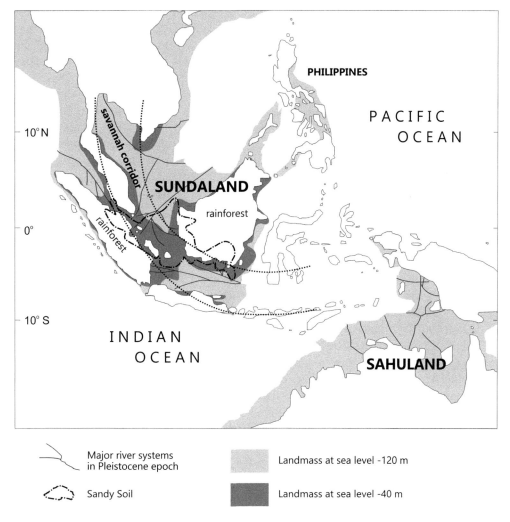

FIGURE 5.2  Palaeoenvironment of Island Southeast Asia during the low sea levels, showing the estimated savanna corridor and possible heath forest area and ancient river system.

of rainforest animals. This included megafauna such as elephants, bovids, rhinoceros, tapirs, tigers, sun bears, deer, and modern humans, as well as medium to small-size species for instance muntjac deer, pigs, monkeys, palm civets, otters, slow lorises, giant pangolins, porcupines, and bats. The Punung Fauna is often considered to be "modern" in its composition and it persisted throughout the Late Pleistocene and Holocene, although some of species experienced local or regional extinction after the Last Glacial Maximum. These included elephants, tapirs, and tigers in Java (Storm and de Vos 2006) and giant pangolins and rhinoceroses in Borneo (Bellwood 2017).

In Wallacea, the Late Pleistocene climate was not much different to that of Sundaland. Prior to the Last Glacial Maximum, the climate at sea level, despite being slightly drier than at present, was still relatively wet. This was then followed by a severe drying period between 33 and 16 kya, though in many parts of Wallacea low rainforest continued to exist. While an expanse of savanna occurred in the most southern part of Sulawesi, from around 80–33 kya, the karstic area of Maros was mainly occupied by evergreen or monsoonal lowland rainforest, with Arenga sp. palms being prominent (Brumm et al. 2018). The long-term perseverance of lowland and montane tropical rainforest is also recorded in the Soroako region to the east of Maros (Hope, 2001), at Lake Towuti (South Sulawesi), Lake Tondano (North Sulawesi), and on Halmahera (North Moluccas) with local variation in species composition (Stevenson 2018). On Flores and Nusa Tenggara generally, a more rapidly fluctuating climate, especially after 50 kya, seems to have been in operation, leading to alternating periods of high rainfall and rainforest, and reduced rainfall which generated open grassland environments (Westaway et al. 2009). On the Sahul side, vegetation data from the northern coastal area of Indonesian Papua, especially in the Cyclops mountain to the west of Jayapura, also supports the long-term existence of montane forest between 60 kya to around 25 kya (Hope and Tulip 1994; Hiscock 2008), which possibly continued into the Early Holocene on the Bird's Head area (Pasveer et al. 2002; O'Connor and Aplin 2007). In contrast, further from the equator, on Timor and at the southern portion of New Guinea and the Aru Islands, which once articulated with Australia, there seems to have been a rather different vegetation regime. In these places, patches of closed-canopy lowland forest may have occurred at least until around 30 kya or later (O'Connor and Aplin 2007), but open woodland, grassland, and savanna were predominant during the Last Glacial Maximum. Following this warmer and wetter climate regenerated the closed lowland forest in the Holocene (Aplin and Pasveer 2007; O'Connor et al. 2007; Hiscock 2008).

Being the largest island in Wallacea, Sulawesi played an important role as a stepping stone for both animal and human dispersals. Moreover, isolation from source population and divergent evolution have resulted in high rates of species endemism. This situation is well reflected in its unique biodiversity. Late Pleistocene fauna of Sulawesi may be best represented by faunal remains from South Sulawesi: at Cabenge, Talepu, and Tanrung sites in Walanae River Valley, and Leang Burung 2 in the Maros area. In the late 1940s, surveys carried out on ancient river terraces along the Walanae River in Cabenge village, revealed fossil remains of now extinct fauna including pygmy elephants (*Archidiskodon celebensis*), *Stegodon* sp., giant pigs (*Celebochoerus heekereni*), and giant tortoise (*Testudo margae*), as well as endemic and still extant Anoa (*Bubalus* sp.), and 'crude' flake tools (van Heekeren 1972). Recently, excavations at another open site called Talepu, adjacent to Cabenge, has expanded on these discoveries, by recovering megafaunal remains in situ and in good stratigraphic position alongside stone artefacts dated from before 200 kya to about 100 kya. *Stegodon* and *Elephas* sp. (elephant) remains were also recovered from the Tanrung site, Walanae Valley (Bartstra 1997; Azis 2000). The date of the Tanrung Fauna is uncertain, but it is possibly younger than Talepu. Another interesting discovery was made during the re-excavation of Leang Burung 2, a cave site in the Maros area, south of Walanae. The site had been excavated in the 1970s, and during this time human occupation layers dated to 31 kya were identified (Glover 1981). The re-excavation of this site in 2011–2013 revealed much older human habitation layers, with a possible age of 82 kya, containing mainly the endemic bovid Anoa (*Bubalus* sp.), babirusa (*Babyrousa* sp.), warty pig (*Sus celebensis*), and an extinct proboscidean (possibly *Elephas* sp.) (Brumm et al. 2018). Simple limestone flake tools were also found within this layer. In the overlaying layers, the remains of Anoa declined significantly after about 45 kya and were replaced by more varied modern animals including macaques, civets, rodents, bats, birds, snakes, and also marsupial cuscus (*Ailurops* sp.), while stone flakes from this period were made of chert and manufactured in a more sophisticated manner (Brumm et al. 2018). These findings suggest there was faunal turnover in South Sulawesi during the Last Glacial Period, during which there were extinctions of megafauna such as stegodon, giant pig, elephants, and giant tortoise, while large endemic animals (anoa, warty pig, and babirusa) declined in the local abundance. These species were then replaced by more a modern fauna after 45 kya.

The small islands of Nusa Tenggara, east of the Wallace Line, tend to support impoverished faunas with some endemic elements. At Leang Bua, Flores, fossils of *H. floresiensis* were found within occupation deposits dated between 100 kya and 18 kya, which also contained a considerable number of lithic artefacts, dwarf stegodon (*Stegodon florensis insularis*), Komodo dragons (*Varanus komodoensis*), smaller monitor lizards (*Varanus hooijeri*), four species of endemic giant rats, bats, and birds (van den Bergh et al. 2009). Other than on Sulawesi and Flores, stegodon fossils were recovered in Sangihe Island (North Sulawesi), Mindanao and Luzon in the Philippines, Sumba, and Timor (Braches and Shutler 1984; Azis 2000) implying that this proboscidean was capable of crossing water barriers and became widely dispersed. Further to the east, marsupial animals were prevalent showing affiliations to the Australia-New Guinea fauna. The human occupation layers of Lemdubu cave in the Aru Islands, dated 30–19 kya, preserve numerous remains of medium to small-bodied marsupials, including savanna grassland dwellers such as agile wallaby (*Macropus agilis*), northern brown bandicoot (*Isoodon macrourus*), and a rat species (*Rattus sordidus*), as well as many rainforest animals like echidna (*Tachyglossus aculeatus*), forest wallaby (*Dorcopsis* sp.), long-nosed spiny bandicoot (*Echymipera rufescens*), tree mouse (*Pogonomys* sp.), cassowary (*Casuarius* sp.), and cuscuses (*Spilocuscus maculatus*, *Phalanger* spp.) (O'Connor et al. 2007).

The Island Southeast Asian environment was not only affected by climate and sea level fluctuations, but also the movement of tectonic plates (Burroughs 2005). Being in an active subduction zone, the region is always impacted by strong earthquakes and volcanism. During the Pleistocene, very strong earthquakes could cause subsidence, severing land bridges between islands. Scholars speculated that a land bridge connecting Sundaland to the southwestern arm of Sulawesi, Flores, and even Timor once existed during the Early and Middle Pleistocene which allowed Stegodons and Geochelone (giant tortoise) to migrate along it (Audley-Charles and Hooijer 1973; Musser 1981).

Another natural phenomenon that is often perceived to have great impact on human dispersal is volcanism. One event that would have had catastrophic implications for nearby human populations was the Toba super-volcano eruption in North Sumatra at 74 kya. The ash cloud from the Toba eruption created a longer winter in higher latitude regions with a corresponding temperature drop of about 5–10°C. This sudden cooling was predicted to have had a great impact on human life, leading to substantial population bottlenecks that changed the course of human evolution (Rampino and Ambrose 2000; Burroughs 2005). However, recent research in India, Malaysia, and Indonesia do not conform this prediction. Archaeological excavations at the Jurerru Valley sites in Andhra Pradesh, South India, uncovered continuities in Palaeolithic stone tool industries both below and above the Younger Toba Tuff deposited by the most recent eruption, suggesting that there was no significant cultural change instigated by the disaster (Haslam et al. 2010; Clarkson et al. 2012; Petraglia et al. 2012). Similarly, in Kota Tampan, Malay Peninsula, identical lithic assemblages were found within and above the thick tuff relating to the 74 kya Toba eruption (Zuraina 1990; Storey et al. 2012). Palaeoecological studies in West Sumatra further testify that vegetation, fauna, and modern humans were not severely impacted by the Toba super eruption. To some extent, the Toba eruption might have had an immediately devastating effect on pine forests in Sumatra, but it created an advantageous condition for the re-establishment of the forest after that (van der Kaars et al. 2012). Likewise, some mammal extinctions might have occurred after the Toba eruption. However, the fact that modern humans, orangutan, and siamang gibbons were still present in West Sumatra post Toba eruption confirms that populations were capable of surviving the calamity Louys 2012). Rather than delay human migration, the cooler climate created by the Toba aftermath might have driven human populations to gradually migrate to the east and reach Australia by island hopping.

### Arrival and Dispersal of Early Modern Humans in Island South East Asia (SEA)

The palaeoenvironment has always been perceived as an important factor in determining the arrival and dispersal of prehistoric people. Certainly, climatic change, natural disaster, island configuration, flora, and fauna would have all affected the movement of people in the past. It is not easy, however, to determine what kind of environment exactly hindered or encouraged early modern human migrations from one place to another because we know very little about human adaptability to the environment. Hence, even if we had a clear picture of the palaeoenvironment, it would be difficult to determine the actual routes of early modern human dispersal. Up to now, there is still no agreement among scholars on when and how early modern humans arrived in, and dispersed across, this region. Undoubtedly, the limited well-dated early human remains are partly responsible for this. Yet other factors should also be taken into account, such as the changing perspective in human evolutionary theory in general, the agreed timing of early modern human out of Africa, and the interpretation of data outside the region especially that of the Sahul.

Until the early 1990s, when hard evidence for early modern humans was very limited and *H. erectus* fossils were quite abundant in Island Southeast Asia, some scholars suggested that the hominin record supported multiregional evolution (Weidenreich 1951; Wolpoff et al. 1984; Thorne and Wolpoff 1992). It was postulated that after their dispersal from Africa around 2 mya, *H. erectus* evolved locally in many regions to become *H. sapiens*. This model hinged especially upon *H. erectus* fossils from Java which exhibited three stages of evolution from archaic *H. erectus Mojokertensis*, via classic *H. erectus*, to progressive *H. erectus soloensis* (Jacob 2001; Widianto 2001). The latter, it was supposed, evolved into *H. sapiens* such as those excavated at Niah, Tabon, and Wajak, which were considered to be the ancestors for indigenous Australians (Thorne and Wolpoff 1992). In view of the bioarchaeological evidence for two different populations of *H. sapiens* in Australia, one exhibiting gracile features and another robust features, it was suggested that there had been two waves of migration into the continent: the first migration by the gracile descendants of East Asian *H. erectus* and the second by the robust descendants of Javanese *H. erectus*. Recently this multiregional hypothesis has been rejected by most scholars as increasingly the evidence favours a replacement hypothesis, which suggests all *H. sapiens* populations descended from groups that initially evolved in Africa and later dispersed across Eurasia, replacing *H. erectus* in many places (Grove 2017).

In the case of *H. sapiens* in Island Southeast Asia, formerly it was widely accepted that there were "two layers" of migration; first by groups of people resemble present day indigenous population of Australia and Papua (Australo-Papuan) and second by groups of Asian population in the Mid Holocene (Bellwood 2017). The Australo-Papuan phenotype dispersed widely across Island Southeast Asia and into Sahul coming to be predominant among inhabitants of this vast region. The "two-layer" model then suggests that around 5 kya, these groups were replaced by, or intermarried with, the "Asian" populations giving rise to the modern composition of populations in the region: the western part of the archipelago was seen to be inhabited primarily Asian groups leaving only some enclaves of Negritos (Australo-Papuan) in Andaman (Onge), Malaysia (e.g. Semang, Senoi, and Jehai), and the Philippines (e.g. Agta, Ayta, Batek, and Mamanwa), whereas the eastern part was seen to be inhabited by populations with various degrees of admixture between Australo-Papuan and Mongoloid features. Since absolute dates were very limited, the timing of the earlier Australo-Papuan migration was only an estimate, lying sometime between the departure of *H. sapiens* from Africa and their arrival in Australia. Formerly, it was believed that early modern humans departed from Africa after 100 kya and most likely arrived in Island Southeast Asia between 70 and 60 kya, then migrating into Sahulland around 45 kya. Such a prediction seemed to be in accord with the estimated arrival of early modern humans in Island Southeast Asia between 70 and 60 kya based on genetic clocks (Anon 2004). This rather late migration was presumed to have been caused by a population bottleneck after the Toba super-eruption. However, in the late 1990s, claims for much earlier dates for the arrival of humans in Australia, ranging from 65 to 110 kya, were published (Fullagar et al. 1996; Thorne et al. 1999). Similarly, the date for early modern humans out of Africa has been suggested to be around 120 kya, if not earlier (Lopéz et al. 2016; Pagani et al. 2016). Thus, the initial arrival of early modern humans in Island Southeast Asia became more open but increasingly difficult to resolve. The discovery of *H. floresiensis* at Leang Bua cave on Flores has complicated the problem.

Fortunately, recent research has shed some light on the arrival of early modern humans in Island Southeast Asia. Remains of early modern humans with more secure dates are reported from a number of Late Pleistocene sites. Reinvestigation of Lida Ajer site and its fossil collection uncovered modern human teeth found in association with rainforest fauna dated to 73 kya (Westaway et al. 2017). In one of the Punung caves, a modern human tooth was recovered from a breccia layer in context with rainforest faunal remains dated at least 115 kya (Strom and de Vos 2006; Westaway et al. 2017). A new date of more than 50 kya is also recently claimed for the existence of early modern human in Niah Cave (Hunt et al. 2012) as well as in Tabon (Détroit et al. 2004). At the Maros caves (South Sulawesi) and Sangkulirang caves (East Kalimantan), rock paintings drawn by modern humans have been dated to 40 kya (Aubert et al. 2014; Brumm et al. 2018). In the North Moluccas, a modern human occupation layer beginning about 35 kya was excavated at Golo cave (Bellwood 2017). Lithic and shell artefacts attributed to modern humans dated to almost 44–35 kya have been found in some caves in Timor, including Jerimalai, Lenehara, Matja Kuru, and Laili (O'Connor et al. 2011; Hawkins et al. 2017; O'Connor et al. 2017). While the remains of another small-statured hominin was excavated from Callao cave (Luzon, Philippines) and Mata Menge (Flores) dating to 67 kya (Mijares et al. 2010) and 700 kya (van den Bergh et al. 2016b), respectively.

All these new discoveries certainly provide a clearer picture of early modern human arrivals and dispersals throughout Island Southeast Asia. Before the arrival of early modern humans, archaic hominins including *H. erectus* and possibly the ancestors of *H. floresiensis* and *Homo luzonensis*, migrated from Africa into Island Southeast Asia since the Early Pleistocene in separate migration waves. *H. erectus* was apparently extinct prior to the Last Glacial Period or slightly later (Westaway et al. 2007; Rizal et al. 2020), but *H. floresiensis* and *H. luzonensis* were able to adapt to island environments by undergoing dwarfism until at least about 60 or perhaps 50 kya in the case of the former. Subsequently, early modern humans arrived to Mainland Southeast Asia before the 74 kya Toba super-eruption and possibly admixted with one population of Denisovan hominins somewhere in Southeast Asia (Reich 2018; Jacobs et al. 2019). They managed to survive from the Toba calamity and migrated across Sundaland, into

Wallacea and Sahulland by island hopping. Although there are suggestions that the widespread dense rainforest and exposed sandy soil with swamps and heath forests within the Sundaland savanna corridor were difficult to pass through (Rolland 2002; Slik et al. 2011), the self-evident capability of early modern human to tackle harsh environments produced by the Toba eruption might have helped them to cope with these so-called 'impenetrable' environments to move further east across the Wallace Line. Indeed, there was not only a single early modern human migration into Island Southeast Asia. Recent genetic studies show that not all Negritos in the region share Australo-Denisovan genetics (Reich et al. 2011). This means that at least three main migrations occurred: (1) the initial migration of early modern humans which admixed with Denisovan populations in Island Southeast Asia, (2) the later migration of early modern humans without Australo-Denisovan ancestry, and (3) later Mid-Holocene migrations of communities that ultimately derived from Taiwan and southern China, who brought Neolithic culture and Austronesian languages. This "three layers" migration hypothesis is in accord with the reconstructions based on wider modern genetic distributions (Cox 2017).

Regarding the migration routes from Sundaland to Sahulland, the earlier two migrations seem to have followed two routes proposed by Joseph Birdsell (1977), which are still favoured by most scholars up to now 74. A southern route passed through Bali and then island hopped along the Nusa Tenggara chain (Lesser Sunda), including Flores and Timor, to land on the shores of what is now northwestern Australia or Aru. Meanwhile, a northern migration route traversed from Borneo through Sulawesi into the small islands of the western Moluccas, then branching out into two sub-routes, which arrived in Sahulland via Waigeo or Aru. Alternatively, from South Sulawesi to Flores, migration could pass north to south through Salayar and the small coral islands of Taka Bone Rate (see Figure 5.1).

## Cultural Aspects of Early Modern Humans (EMH) in ISEA

Tropical rainforest environments are commonly perceived as difficult to penetrate and adapt to by hunter-gatherers without access to cultivated crops to meet subsistence needs (Bailey and Headland 1991). However, the recently available data do not conform this notion. Since their arrival in Island Southeast Asia more than 73 kya, early modern humans have adjusted to tropical rainforests, although they may not have entered into the densest parts of the forest but rather moved along clearings and more open forest (Hunt et al. 2012; Spehar et al. 2018). Evidence for the earliest modern human occupation in this region is mainly recovered from caves that were situated near rainforests during the Last Glacial Period, such as at Lida Ajer, Punung, Tabon, and the Niah caves. Yet only very sparse, simple flaked stone tools and bone implements have preserved to illustrate how humans exploited these "difficult" environments. In fact, both Lida Ajer and Punung caves have no stone tools directly in association with human remains. In Tabuhan, one of the Punung caves, a number of stone flakes appear within a layer dated at least 45 kya (Semah et al. 2004). In Wadjak cave, now dated to 37.4 kya (Storm et al. 2013), two stone microliths are believed to have been made by Wadjak people (Storm 1992, 1995). Subsequently, from around 33 kya, humans occupied a more extensive area in the karstic southern mountains of Central and East Java where many caves containing stone flake-cobble tools and various bone tools, including spatula and diggers, were recovered in association with flexed human burials with Australo-Papuan affinity (Simanjuntak 2002). It is apparent that descendants of these early modern human populations continued to live in Java until the mid-Holocene.

At Tabon cave, a stone flake industry was also recovered throughout occupation layers dated from 50 kya to 9 kya. Basically, it consists of chert flakes of various size and shape manufactured with simple direct percussion. Secondary retouched flakes were sometimes present and quartz hammer stones and basalt choppers are also found. The flake characteristics remain almost unchanged throughout the layers, except that retouching seemed to be more common in the upper layers (Fox 1970). This assemblage is technologically indistinguishable from those described at other Island Southeast Asian flake-cobble sites during the Late Pleistocene.

Multidisciplinary research at the Niah caves in northern Borneo provides a clearer image about how early modern humans adapted to a wide variety of habitats close to rainforest from around 50 kya until the Holocene by practicing broad-spectrum hunting, foraging, fishing, and collecting. Simple flaked stone tools and some pointed- and spatula-shaped bone tools were found throughout the occupation layers (Piper and Rabett 2016). The flakes of metamorphic sandstone were made of shattered pebble without signs of further modification (Majeed-Lowe 1979). Nevertheless, the faunal remains found in archaeological excavations show a wide range of their prey, from the larger species such as wild pigs, tapirs, rhinoceroses, primates, pythons, the now extinct giant pangolin (*Manis javanica*), and porcupines, to smaller species including snakes, bats, lizards, and birds. Fishes and freshwater molluscs were also collected for food. Apparently, the stone flakes were used on bamboo, wood, and possibly fibre for making spears, harpoons, fishing rods, nets, and traps to catch prey. The Niah inhabitants brought and butchered their catches in the cave. Recent studies reveal that fruits, nuts, and plants were consumed as well, including rainforest tuberous plants such as aroids, taro, yam and even sago, some of which need rather complicated preparation before being edible.

Cave paintings occur at the Niah caves, especially in Kain Hitam Cave where red paintings associated with boat-burials date to no more than 2 kya (Pyatt 2005). However, much older cave paintings are recorded from the Sangkulirang area in eastern Borneo, Indonesia. Here, various rock paintings such as hand stencils, decorated hands (likely indicating tattoo-marks), anthropomorphic figures, and possibly an extinct bovid were reported from a complex of karstic caves along the Marang River (Chazine 2005). Based on Uranium series determinations, more recent research at Gua Jeriji Saleh and three other caves recognizes at least three stages of rock painting production: (1) Reddish-orange hand-stencils and figurative animals dating between 52 and 37 kya, (2) dark-purple decorated hand paintings dating between 21 and 14 kya, and (3) black paintings of geometric designs, boats, and dancing or hunting figures about 4 kya in age. Interestingly, an animal figure painted in reddish-orange colour is dated to 40 kya and claimed to be the oldest figurative painting in the world (Aubert et al. 2014). There is no clear explanation about how the three types of cave painting are related to other archaeological material in the caves, except that the caves contain domestic and funerary remains such as food refuse of animal bones and shells, chert flakes, stone tools, and potsherds approximately dated between 12 kya and 4 kya or even later (Chazine 2005).

Beside cave sites, open human occupation sites have been identified in eastern Sabah, especially in the Tingkayu Basin, an extinct Late Pleistocene lake situated around 150 km inland from the Last Glacial Maximum (LGM) shoreline. The occupants of the Tingkayu open sites produced a specialized stone tool industry dated between 28 kya and 18 kya, at a time when the lake was still present. The stone industry consisted of pebble tools, cores, utilized flakes, and particularly pointed or lanceolate bifaces made of locally quarried chert. The manufacturing technique of these bifaces reflects extraordinary skill for that period and there is no comparable stone assemblage known from anywhere else in Island Southeast Asia. The use of the bifaces remains unknown, but they may have functioned as projectile points or knives (Bellwood 1988). Hence, it is rather difficult to fit this industry into the broader regional cultural trajectory. Regardless, this assemblage proves the capability of early modern humans to innovate new ways to live in novel environments.

In Wallacea, more complex cultural innovations seemed to occur following the arrival of early modern humans in this archipelagic environment. In southern Sulawesi, cave sites in the karstic Maros area and open sites on ancient river terraces of the Walanae River Valley have provided interesting information about early modern human behavioural adaptation and culture. The Maros area has attracted scholars since early 1900s, when these caves were still inhabited by the so-called Toala hunter-gatherers (to = people, ala = forest). Archaeological research at numerous caves in the area has also revealed a complex flake assemblage, including flakes with edge-gloss (possibly use-wear from processing silica-rich plants), elongated blade-like flakes or "Levallois-like points", backed flakes, and serrated points known as Maros points, mostly made of cherts. Single- or bi-pointed bones and small spatulas were also found while fragments of pottery were found only in the upper layers. This archaeological material has become the type-assemblage for the 'Toalian culture.'

Fragmentary human remains, mainly teeth, were sometimes present within the deposits, but were dated to the Early Holocene. The first discovery of cave paintings in the area was reported in 1950 with an estimated date of less than 5 kya (van Heekeren 1972). Until a few years ago, the earliest dates for human occupation in Maros caves were around 35 kya and 30 kya in Leang Burung 2 and Leang Sakapao 1, respectively (Bulbeck et al. 2004; Brumm et al. 2018). However, re-excavation of Leang Burung 2 has shown that below the previously dated layer there are older layers possibly up to 82 kya in age. Within these layers, simple limestone flakes are recovered which is rather different to that of the upper layers. The flakes were manufactured from limestone cobbles by hard-hammer percussion producing relatively large flakes (Brumm et al. 2018).

Another interesting area is the Walenae depression where flake tools as well as bifacially flaked cobbles and large worked cores possibly date to the Middle Pleistocene from before 200 kya to about 100 kya (Keates and Bartstra 1992). The Talepu lithic assemblage is considered similar to that of the earliest layers of Leang Burung 2 suggesting a continuous lithic tradition around southern Sulawesi. It is difficult to determine which species of hominin made these tools, whether a late surviving *H. erectus*, *H. floresiensis*, or "Denisovans" (van den Bergh et al. 2016a). Moreover, it is also unclear whether these tool makers lived contemporaneously with *H. sapiens* (Brumm et al. 2018).

What is more certain is the existence of early modern humans in the Maros caves at least 40 kya. This is evident from the dates of the cave paintings (see Figure 5.3) which are widespread within the Maros caves and are dated to almost 40 kya. Detailed analysis of the art identifies generally two different traditions. An earlier art style characterized by red- or mulberry-coloured hand-stencils and figurative paintings of endemic Sulawesi animals such as anoa, babirusa, and warty pig (Figure 5.1), and a later art style consisting of black charcoal paintings of geometric designs, anthropomorphic, and zoomorphic figures. The latter was possibly made by Austronesian-speaking people who inhabited this area around 4.5 kya, whereas Uranium series determinations for the red coloured art, relating to 19 samples collected from 12 hand stencils and two figurative animals from seven sites, give a time range of 39.9 to 17.4 kya. The oldest date of 39.9 kya comes from a hand stencil depicted at Leang Timpuseng, while nearby red infilled paintings of babirusa is dated to 35.4 kya. Another red infilled painting of

FIGURE 5.3  One of the red-colour Cave paintings of possibly warty pig in Maros Cave.

a pig at Leang Barugayya 2 has a minimum age of 35.7 kya (Aubert et al. 2014). The earlier Maros paintings closely resemble those of the early Sangkulirang paintings (see above), thus it may represent the same art tradition produced by broadly related groups of people. The fact that the oldest red paintings were not discovered in Borneo except in the eastern part of (Indonesian) Borneo, which is so close to South Sulawesi, is also thought-provoking. This may be related to the course of early modern human migration from Sundaland into Wallacea. In Bulu Buttue cave some ornamental artefacts, such as beads made from babirusa tooth, perforated cuscus finger bone, and incised stone artefacts stained with red-pigment, are also encountered in a layer dated to 30–22 kya. These kinds of artefact emphasize the symbolic capability of early modern humans in this area (Brumm et al. 2017).

Once early modern humans arrived in Sulawesi, they apparently dispersed further in a variety of directions to inhabit the smaller islands of Wallacea. The Leang Sarru site on Salebabu Island in the Talaud group provides evidence for the oldest human settlement of the small islands north of Sulawesi. To reach this island a sea voyage of more than 150 km was necessary. This small shelter was visited intermittently by humans at least 30 kya. In the Last Glacial Maximum, Salebabu Island merged with a larger island called Karakelong and other small islands in this group to form one larger island, during which time, around 22 kya, human occupation intensified. Humans living on this island depended increasingly on marine resources by collecting shells. No remains of terrestrial animals are recovered here and they made simple flake tools from local cherts with hard hammer percussion. After the LGM, the site was abandoned (Tanudirjo 2001, 2005).

Considering the northern Pleistocene migration route suggested by Birdsell (see Map 5.1), early modern humans would move eastward from Sulawesi along the small island chain comprising the northern Moluccas, and then on to northern Sahul. However, very few traces of pre-LGM human occupation are reported to occur along this route so far. Only on Gebe Island, situated between Halmahera and northern Sahul, is there evidence for early modern humans during the Late Pleistocene. Golo cave and Wetef rockshelter sites on Gebe contained human occupation layers dated to 37 kya and 25 kya, respectively. In Golo Cave, the Pleistocene occupation layers can be divided into two phases. The earliest phase, between 36 and 25 kya, contained flaked stones, coral or volcanic cooking stones, shell scrapers, worked Turbo shell opercula, and shell refuse. The latter phase, between 25 and 11 kya, contained less archaeological material, indicating only intermittent occupation took place. The cave was possibly used solely as ceremonial place as evident from construction of stone circles and alignments towards the end of this phase. The lower occupation layers of Wetef correspond to the latter Golo phase. The inhabitants of these sites depended mainly on marine shellfish for their subsistence by collecting variety of gastropods, limpets, barnacles and oysters (Bellwood et al. 2019). Interestingly, detailed study on the worked shell operculum shows that the shell technology has developed quite separately, and in a more complex manner, than the stone technology. It has also been suggested that this kind of shell technology would have been employed before the initial occupation of Golo cave (Szabo 2019).

Along the southern migration routes (Figure 5.2), the small island chain of Nusa Tenggara, east of Bali, may have been a preferable path taken by archaic hominins migrating to the east. However, there is not much information on early modern human occupation before the Last Glacial Maximum, except on Timor Island. Even on Flores island, where traces of *H. floresiensis* are relatively abundant, archaeological data for early modern human is scarce. Here, *H. floresiensis* inhabited Liang Bua from 100 kya and survived fluctuating climate and abrupt environment changes until 60 kya when they may have become locally extinct. It is only at about 11 kya that there are definite signs of modern human existence. In term of subsistence, they seemed to have relied on small mammals, reptiles, and amphibians. The remains of these animals are deposited in the upper occupation layers of Liang Bua. Imported marine shells for tools and adornment are also encountered in those layers (van den Bergh et al. 2009). Nevertheless, some lithic experts suspect that the Liang Bua flaked tool technology (see Figure 5.4), which is almost identical to that of early modern humans at Timorese cave sites may indicate the existence of early modern humans in this site sometime around 46 kya (Marwick et al. 2016; Sutikna et al. 2018; Shipton et al. 2019). Alternatively, Flores may have only been briefly visited as a stepping island by early modern humans, who passed further eastward due to the impoverished environment on the island. Hence, their vestiges may be archaeologically unobservable.

Cave sites on Timor island provide important data for early modern human settlement in eastern Wallacea. At least three caves in the northeastern part of the island, now Timor Leste, contain human occupation layers more than 40 kya in age: Laili (44 kya), Jerimalai (44 kya), and Lene Hara caves (42 kya), while Matja kuru and Bui Ceri Uato caves have dates of 31 kya and 36 kya respectively. At all of these cave sites, stone artefacts were recovered almost consistently throughout the layers. The stone industry here mostly comprised small flakes and cores made of various siliceous rocks, primarily chert. In principle the stone technology did not change significantly throughout the millennia, although a range of distinctive forms such as single- and multi-platform cores, discoidal cores, cores-made on flakes, burins, and redirecting flakes were produced. Retouched flakes and flakes with edge-gloss were also occasionally recovered. Probably, some flakes were attached to perishable hafting materials to make composite tools (Marwick et al. 2016; Hawkins et al. 2017; Shipton et al. 2019). Most intriguingly, the

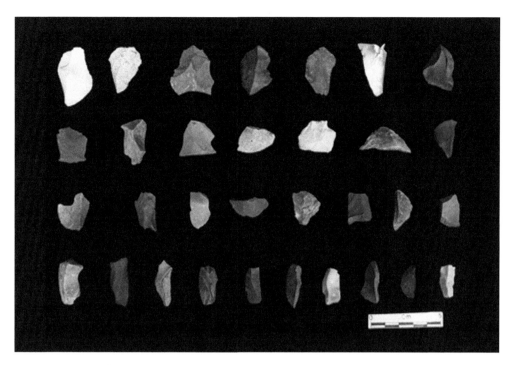

FIGURE 5.4   Stone flakes recovered from Liang Bua resembles to flakes from Timorese Caves produced by early modern human.

*Courtesy:* Tim Peneliti Pusat Penelitian Arkeologi Nasional.

Jerimalai site provides excellent evidence for technological innovation among early modern humans in their shell artefact production. Pieces of worked nautilus shells which were recovered from the lower layer of Jerimalai, showed delicate drilling, pressure flaking, and grinding as well as red pigment staining. Such a technology seemed to be employed to produce similar shell ornaments to those found in other sites on Timor and adjacent islands albeit in younger levels (Langley et al. 2016). Oliva sp. Shell ornaments were also recovered from occupation layers in Timorese sites starting from 42 kya (Langley and O'Connor 2016; Langley et al. 2016). These findings again testify that early modern humans in Wallacea practiced symbolic activities and self-ornamentation reflecting greater needs for material expression of social or personal identity.

The Timorese sites also attest that early modern humans adapted to marine environments as they moved into Wallacea. This is quite different to earlier hominins which, despite managing to cross narrow straits between islands, adapted persistently to terrestrial environments with diminishing returns. Early modern humans in Timor may have developed fishing technology as early as 44 kya. Fish bones make up the majority of food refuse in some sites, of which a significant portion derive from pelagic species and marine turtles. In the earliest layers, there is no evidence for pelagic fishing technology. Considering the small size of the fish, netting rather than angling seems to be more feasible to catch nearshore fish, and this might leave no archaeological traces at all. It is only after 23 kya that one-piece fishhooks made of shell, suitable for angling with bait, appear in Jerimalai (O'Connor et al. 2011) and later on in some other sites, including Alor (Bellwood 2017). Another interesting artefact was recovered from deposits dated to 35 kya in Matja Kuru Cave 2 in the form of a broken serrated projectile point made of a large fish bone. This bone point would have been attached into a shaft as a composite tool (O'Connor et al. 2014).

Certainly, early modern humans on Timor would not have only depended on fish from the sea and they also collected various kinds of rocky shore shellfish. Located about 6 km from the coast today, the Matja Kuru 2 deposits indicate that the inhabitants depended more on terrestrial animals such as giant rats, pythons, lizards, and freshwater turtle (O'Connor et al. 2017). A more broad-spectrum subsistence is observed from occupation layers in Laili cave, inhabited since at least 44 kya. Remains of mollusc and fishes collected from marine, estuarine, and freshwater environments, small-bodied animals such rats, snakes, and lizards as well as birds and bats, were all found in the cave's earliest deposit. It is clear that the inhabitants exploited a wide range of animal habitats close to the cave (Hawkins et al. 2017).

The Timorese caves have also produced various cave paintings and engravings most of which are attributed to Austronesian-speaking population that migrated there in the Mid-Late Holocene. However, red pigment paintings at Lene Hara cave have been Uranium-series dated to possibly 30 kya, and a face engraving from the same site gives a date of 12 kya (Aubert et al. 2007). The occurrence of Pleistocene paintings at these caves is important because it demonstrates the symbolic capacity of early modern humans and allows us to understand the course of human dispersal with consideration to the similar but older cave paintings discovered on Borneo and South Sulawesi. Actually, there are many sites along the Pleistocene migration routes which contain red-pigmented hand stencils and other figurative forms, such as in Muna (Southeast Sulawesi), Seram, Kei, Kisar (Moluccas), Waigeo, Misool, and Berau Gulf (West Papua) among others (Arifin and Delanghe 2004). Unfortunately, those red paintings have no clear dates, so that it is difficult to place them in chronological context. It is not improbable that the red-paintings, especially hand stencils, are Late Pleistocene in age.

In Indonesian Papua, no site with habitation deposits older than 30 kya has been reported. If the northern migration route suggested by Birdsell is correct, it is expected that Indonesian Papua island would produce human settlement sites dated before 40 kya, as the oldest date for human existence in Melanesia is 50 kya derived from the Ivane Valley sites (Summerhayes et al. 2010) and around 40 kya on the Huon Peninsula (Groube et al. 1986). There is a speculation that humans exploited the western highland region of New Guinea since 40 kya based on two lines of evidence: the extinction of large marsupial protemnodon around that time and possible burning activities by human at least 32.5 kya as interpreted from vegetation study (Hope et al. 1993; Hope 1998). However, hard evidence for the earliest human occupation in western New Guinea only stands at 24 kya on Accelerator Mass Spectroscopy (AMS) dating of cassowary egg shells at the Toe cave site on the Bird's Head. Habitation layers in this cave contain simple stone artefacts, pointed bone tools, and the remains of endemic animals such as forest wallaby, tree kangaroo, cuscus, possums, echidna, bandicoot as well as bats and birds. This site is close to a freshwater lake and it is readily apparent that the Toe inhabitants explored the lower montane forests for their living (Pasveer et al. 2002).

## Final Remarks

Recent research has brought new and more reliable data to light that allow us to draw clearer a picture about the life and dispersal of early modern humans in Island Southeast Asia. Certainly, new data will allow for new interpretations, which may even trigger new debate. However, the present available data tend to support the arrival of early modern humans in Island Southeast Asia by 75 kya or even earlier. It is now becoming more obvious that these populations were highly competent at confronting 'difficult situations'. It may be true that these humans only used a basic stone technology of flakes and cobble tools, which are often perceived as indicating an underdeveloped culture. On the contrary, this simple stone tool assemblage has proved efficient and ingenious, functioning as part of a broader technological system to manufacture and maintain more versatile implements made of wood, bamboo, shell, and bone, which have mostly deteriorated in tropical archaeological sites. With those implements, they could have practiced broad-spectrum hunting, foraging, fishing, and collecting plants and animals from different habitats for their subsistence.

It is now becoming evident that early modern humans managed to adapt to tropical rainforests and other harsh environments which were formerly considered impossible to pass through. They even survived throughout the calamity caused by the most disastrous eruption of ancient Toba, which triggered a global prolonged winter and presumably population bottlenecks. During this time, early modern humans persisted in "difficult conditions", and appear to have admixed with Denisovans or their descendants who contemporaneously lived in the region. These descendent populations then moved across Sundaland and into Wallacea and Sahulland where their cultures and adaptive strategies increasingly diverged and changed. Archaeological data discovered at the Wallacean sites demonstrates clearly how innovative and successful these groups were. Undoubtedly, they were capable of sailing to more distant islands and adept at exploring and monopolizing on maritime resources by collecting shellfish and catching pelagic fish. Shell and fish bones then provided even more materials for them to produce novel implements and personal ornamentation. The latter implies the emergence of personal or social identity as well as aesthetic expression.

Artistic expression through cave paintings are also important cultural innovations which were disseminated throughout Island Southeast Asia by early modern humans. Some red coloured hand-stencils and figurative paintings in eastern Borneo and South Sulawesi are claimed to be among the earliest cave art in the world. Besides reflecting human aesthetic capabilities, cave art is often interpreted as being crucial for the reproduction of magic practices, religious activities, or initiation rituals, or can be symbolic signs to denote territoriality. The distribution of these early cave paintings is interesting too, as they are found so far only to the east of the Wallace's Line and in eastern Borneo, immediately to the west of the line.

Whether this distribution is indicative of the migration route of early modern humans in Island Southeast Asia and Sahulland, or plausibly an area where the admixture between early modern humans and more archaic hominins took place is unclear. Nevertheless, strong sea currents that run from the Pacific Ocean to the Indian Ocean along the Wallace Line from the southern Philippines, to northern Borneo, southern Sulawesi and then east to the Flores Sea would have facilitated the migration of early modern humans from Sulawesi to Nusa Tenggara, southern Maluku, and Australia. This may offer an alternative route to the two Pleistocene migration routes suggested by Birdsell (see Figure 5.2). Furthermore, the present distribution of Denisovan genetic markers seems to correspond with this alternative migration route, though certainly it has been affected by waves of later human migration.

In 1999, I wrote an article in an Indonesian newspaper stating that the eastern Indonesian archipelago was a strategic location to search for "the missing link" in human evolution. Throughout that article I tried to encourage Indonesian scholars to carry out more multidisciplinary research there. Otherwise, Indonesia would not only become a place where 'the missing link' is

FIGURE 5.5   Fossils of *Homo floresiensis* excavated in Liang Bua, Flores.
*Courtesy:* Tim Peneliti Pusat Penelitian Arkeologi Nasional.

concealed but also a 'missing link' in itself – a blank spot on the global map of the prehistory of humankind. It was almost 15 years of waiting until the first evidence was announced from Liang Bua in 2004, the discovery of a 'new human' *H. floresiensis* (see Figure 5.5), which has compelled scholars to rethink existing hypotheses on human evolution and dispersal. Since then, by means of collaborative multinational interdisciplinary research, more and more new, surprising evidence has emerged from this area: the world's oldest cave paintings, earliest pelagic fishing technology, human adaptability to rainforests, and the integration of Denisovan genetic markers. This information is obviously important for understanding the course of human evolution both culturally as well as biologically. I still believe that in the future this area in particular, and Island Southeast Asia in general, will continue to contribute significant data to shed light on the long journey of human kind in the past.

## Acknowledgements

I am grateful to Glenn R. Summerhayes for inviting me to participate in this volume and preparing my chapter for publication. I also thank to Dylan Gaffney for his valuable advice and time to proofread my chapter and to Wahyu Saptomo who provides me with some of the photographs used in my chapter. However, all responsibility for errors and mistakes remains with me alone.

## References

Allen, Jim, and Kershaw, Peter. 1996 The Pleistocene-Holocene Transition in Greater Australia, in *Humans at the End of Ice Age*, eds Straus, L.G., Eriksen, B.V., Erlandson, J.M., and Yesner, D.R. London-New York: Plenum, 175–200.

Anon 2004 Studi Genetika Molekul Populasi Austronesia [Molecular genetic study of Austronesian population], in *Polemik tentang Masyarakat Austronesia: Fakta atau Fiksi?* ed. Masinambow, E. Jakarta: Indonesian Institute of Sciences, 103–119.

Aplin, Ken, and Pasveer, Juliette. 2007 Mammals and other vertebrates from Late Quatenary archaeological sites on Pulau Kobroor, in *The Archaeology of the Aru Islands, Eastern Indonesia,* Terra Australis 22, eds O'Connor, Sue, Matthew, Spriggs, and Peter, Veth. Canberra: ANU Press, 57–58.

Arifin, Karina, and Delanghe, Philippe. 2004 *Rock Art in West Papua.* Paris: UNESCO Publishing.

Aubert, M., Brumm, A., Ramli, M., Sutikna, T., Saptomo, E. W., Hakim, B., Morwood, M. J., van den Bergh, G., Kinsley, L., and Dosseto, A. 2014 Pleistocene cave art from Sulawesi, Indonesia. *Nature* 514, 223.

Aubert, Maxime, O'Connor, Sue, McCulloch, Malcolm, Mortimer, Graham, Watchman, Alan, and Richer-LaFleche, Marc. 2007 Uranium-series dating rock art in East Timor. *Journal of Archaeological Science* 34, 991–996.

Aubert, M., Setiawan, P., Oktaviana, A., Brumm, A., Sulistyarto, P., Saptomo, E., Istiawan, B., Ma'rifat, T., Wahyuono, V., Atmoko, F., Zhao, J., Huntley, J., Taçon, P., Howard, D. L., and Brand, H. 2018 Palaeolithic cave art in Borneo. *Nature* 564, 254.

Audley-Charles, Michael, and Hooijer, D. 1973 Relation of Pleistocene Migrations of Pygmy Stegodon to Island Arc Tectonic in Eastern Indonesia. *Nature* 241, 197–198.

Azis, Fachroel. 2000 The Pleistocene Endemic Fauna of the Indonesian Archipelago. *Tropic* 10, 138.

Bailey, Robert, and Headland, Thomas. 1991 The tropical rainforest: Is it a productive environment for human foragers? *Human Ecology* 19, 261–285.

Bartstra, Gert-Jan. 1997. A fifty years commemoration: Fossil vertebrates and Stone tools in the Walanae Valley, South Sulawesi, Indonesia. *Quartar* 47 (48), 29–50.

Bellwood, Peter. 1988 Archaeological research in South-eastern Sabah. *Sabah Museum Monograph* 2, 38–49.

Bellwood, Peter. 2017 *The First Islanders*. Hoboken: Wiley-Blackwell.

Bellwood, Peter, Irwin, Geoffrey, Tanudirjo, Daud, Nitihaminoto, Gunadi, Siswanto, Joko, and Bowdery, Doreen. 2019 Investigations on Gebe Island, in *The Spice Islands in Prehistory. Archaeology in the Northern Moluccas, Indonesia,* ed. Bellwood, Peter. Canberra: ANU Press, 15–44.

Bird, Michael, Taylor, David, and Hunt, Chris. 2005 Palaeoenvironments of insular Southeast Asia during the Last Glacial Period: A savanna corridor in Sundaland? *Quaternary Science Reviews* 24, 2228–2242.

Birdsell, Joseph. 1977. The Recalibration of a Paradigm for the First Peopling of Greater Australia, in *Sunda and Sahul: Prehistoric Studies in Southeast Asia, Melanesia and Australia,* ed. Allen, Jim, Golson, Jack and Jones, Rhys. London: Academic Press, 113–167.

Braches, Friedrich, and Shutler, Richard. 1984 The Philippines and Pleistocene dispersal of mammals in Island Southeast Asia. *Philippine Quarterly of Culture and Society* 12, 108.

Brumm, Adam, Hakim, Budianto, Ramli, Muhammad, Aubert, Maxime, van den Bergh, Gerrit, Li, Bo, Burhan, Basran, Saiful, Andi, Siagian, Linda, Sardi, Ratno, Jusdi, Andi, Abdullah, Mubarak, Andi, Moore, Mark, Roberts, Richard, Zhao, Jian-xin, McGahan, David, Jones, Brian, Perston, Yinika, Szabó, Katherine, Mahmud, Irfan, Westaway, Kira, Jatmiko, Saptomo, Wahyu, van der Kaars, Sander, Grün, Rainer, Wood, Rachel, Dodson, John, and Morwood, Michael. 2018 A reassessment of the early archaeological record at Leang Burung 2, a Late Pleistocene rock-shelter site on the Indonesian island of Sulawesi. *PLoS ONE* 13, 30.

Brumm, Adam, Langley, Michelle C., Moore, Mark W., Hakim, Budianto, Ramli, Muhammad, Sumantri, Iwan, Burhan, Basran, Saiful, Andi, Siagian, Linda, Suryatman, Sardi, Ratno, Jusdi, Andi, Abdullah, Mubarak, Andi, Hasliana, Hasrianti, Oktaviana, Adhi, Adhityatama, Shinatria, van den Bergh, Gerrit, Aubert, Maxime, Zhao, Jian-xin, Huntley, Jillian, Li, Bo, Roberts, Richard, Saptomo, Wahyu, Perston, Yinika, and Grün, Rainer. 2017 Early human symbolic behavior in the Late Pleistocene of Wallacea. *The Proceedings of the National Academy of Sciences* 114, 4105–4110.

Brumm, Adam, Langley, Michelle, Moore, Mark, Hakim, Budianto, Ramli, Muhammad, Sumantri, Iwan, Burhan, Basran, Saiful, Andi, Siagian, Linda, Suryatman, Sardi, Ratno, Jusdi, Andi, Abdullah, Mubarak, Andi, Hasliana, Hasrianti, Oktaviana, Adhi, Adhityatama, Shinatria, van den Bergh, Gerrit, Aubert, Maxime, Zhao, Jian-xin, Huntley, Jillian, Li, Bo, Roberts, Richard, Saptomo, Wahyu, Perston, Yinika, and Grün, Rainer. 2017 Early human symbolic behavior in the Late Pleistocene of Wallacea. *The Proceedings of the National Academy of Sciences* 114, 4105–4110.

Bulbeck, David, Sumantri, Iwan, and Hiscock, Peter. 2004 Leang Sakapao 1, a second dated Pleistocene site from south Sulawesi, in *Quaternary Research in Indonesia, Modern Quaternary Research in Southeast Asia,* eds Bartstra, Gert Jan, and Casparie, Willem. Rotterdam-Boston: A. A. Balkema, 116.

Burroughs, William. 2005 *Climate Change in Prehistory*. Cambridge: Cambridge University Press
Chazine, Jean-Michel. 2005 Rock art, burials, and habitations: Caves in East Kalimantan. *Asian Perspective* 44, 222–226.
Clarkson, Chris, Jones, Sacha, and Harris, Clair. 2012 Continuity and change in the lithic industries of the Jurreru Valley, India, before and after the Toba eruption. *Quaternary International* 258, 165–179.
Cox, Murray. 2017 The genetic history of human populations in Island Southeast Asia during the late Pleistocene and Holocene, in *The First Islanders*, ed. Bellwood, Peter. Hoboken: Wiley-Blackwell, 107–116.
Détroit, Florent, Mijares, Armand, Corny, Julien, Daver, Guillaume, Zanolli, Clément, Dizon, Eusebio, Robles, Emil, Grün, Rainer, and Piper, Philip. 2004 A new species of Homo from the late Pleistocene of the Philippines. *Nature* 568, 181–186.
Evangelista, Alfredo E. 1969 Archaeology in the Philippines to 1950. *Asian Perspectives* 22, 101–103.
Fox, Robert. 1970 *Tabon Caves*. Manila: National Museum.
Fullagar, Richard, Price, David, and Head, Leslie. 1996 Early human occupation of northern Australia: Archaeology and thermoluminescence dating of Jinmium rock-shelter, Northern Territory. *Antiquity* 70, 751–773.
Glover, Ian. 1981 Leang Burung 2: An Upper Palaeolithic rock shelter in south Sulawesi, Indonesia. *Modern Quaternary Research in South East Asia* 6, 1–38.
Groube, Les, Chappell, John, Muke, John, and Price, David. 1986 A 40,000 year-old human occupation site at Huon Peninsula, Papua New Guinea. *Nature* 32, 453–455.
Grove, Colin. 2017 The evolution of Javan *Homo erectus*, in *The First Islanders*, ed. Bellwood, Peter. Hoboken: Wiley-Blackwell, 46–53.
Harrison, Tom. 1970 The prehistory of Borneo. *Asian Perspectives* 13, 17–46.
Haslam, Michael, Clarkson, Chris, Petraglia, Michael, Korisettar, Ravi, Jones, Sacha, Shipton, Ceri, Ditchfield, Peter, and Ambrose, Stanley. 2010 The 74 ka Toba super-eruption and southern Indian hominins: Archaeology, lithic technology and environments at Jwalapuram Locality 3. *Journal of Archaeological Science* 37, 3370–3384.
Hawkins, Stuart, O'Connor, Sue, Maloney, Tim, Litster, Mirani, Kealy, Shimona, Fenner, Jack, Aplin, Ken, Boulanger, Clara, Brockwell, Sally, Willan, Richard, Piotto, Elena, and Louys, Julien. 2017 Oldest human occupation of Wallacea at Laili Cave, Timor Leste, shows broad-spectrum foraging responses to Late Pleistocene Environments. *Quaternary Science Reviews* 171, 58–72.
Hiscock, Peter. 2008 *Archaeology of Ancient Australia*. London-New York: Routledge.
Hope, Geoffrey. 1998 Early fire and forest change in the Baliem Valley, Irian Jaya, Indonesia. *Journal of Biogeography* 25, 456–459.
Hope, Geoffrey. 2001 Environmental change in the late Pleistocene and later Holocene at Wanda site, Soroako, South Sulawesi, Indonesia. *Palaeogeography, Palaeoclimatology, Palaeoecology* 171 (3-4), 129–145.
Hope, Geoffrey, Flannery, Tim, and Boeardi. 1993 A preliminary report of changing quaternary mammal faunas in subalpine new Guinea. *Quaternary Research* 40, 117–126.
Hope, Geoffrey, and Tulip, Jim. 1994 A long vegetation history from lowland Irian Jaya, Indonesia. *Palaeogeography, Palaeoclimatology, Palaeoecology* 109, 39.
Hunt, Chris, Gilbertson, David, and Rushworth, Garry. 2012 A 50,000-year record of late Pleistocene Tropical vegetation and human impact in Lowland Borneo. *Quaternary Science Reviews* 37, 63.
Jacobs, Guy, Hudjashov, Georgi, Saag, Lauri, Kusuma, Pradiptajati, Darusallam, Chelzie, Lawson, Daniel, Mondal, Mayukh, Pagani, Luca, Ricaut, Francois-Xavier, Stoneking, Mark, Metspalu, Mait, Sudoyo, Herawati, Lansing, Stephen, and Cox, Murray. 2019 Multiple deeply divergent Denisovan Ancestries in Papuans. *Cell* 177, 1010–1021.
Jacob, Teuku. 2001 Biological aspects of *Homo erectus* through time-space continuum. In *Sangiran: Man, Culture and Environment in Pleistocene Times*, eds Simanjuntak, Harry, Prasetyo, Bagyo, and Handini, Retno. Jakarta: Yayasan Obor, 19–23.
Kealy, Shimona, Louys, Julien, and O'Connor, Sue. 2017 Reconstructing palaeogeography and inter-Island visibility in the Wallacean Archipelago during the likely period of Sahul Colonization 65-45000 Years Ago. *Archaeological Prospection* 24, 264.
Keates, Susan G., and Gert-Jan, Bartstra. 1992. Island migration of early modern *Homo sapiens* in Southeast Asia: The artefacts from the Depression, Sulawesi, Indonesia. *Palaeohistoria* 33 (34), 19–30.
Kershaw, Peter, Penny, Dan, van der Kaars, Sander, Anshari, Gusti, and Thamotherampillai, Asha. 2001 Vegetation and climate change in lowland Southeast Asia at the Last Glacial Maximum, in *Faunal*

*and Floral Migration and Evolution in Southeast Asia-Australasia*, eds Metcalfe, Ian, Smith, Jeremy, Morwood, Michael, and Davidson, Iain. Lisse: Balkema, 227–236.

Langley, Michelle, and O'Connor, Sue. 2016 An enduring shell artefact tradition from Timor-Leste: Oliva bead production from the Pleistocene to Late Holocene at Jerimalai, Lene Hara, and Matja Kuru 1 and 2. *PLoS ONE* 11, 1–25.

Langley, Michelle, O'Connor, Sue, and Piotto, Elena. 2016 42,000 year-old worked and pigment stained Nautilus shell from Jerimalai (Timor-Leste): Evidence for an early coastal adaptation in ISEA. *Journal of Human Evolution* 97, 1–16.

Lopéz, Saioa, van Dorp, Lucy, and Hellenthal, Garrett. 2016 Human dispersal out of Africa: A lasting debate. *Evolutionary Bioinformatics* 11, 61.

Louys, Julien. 2012 Mammal community structure of Sundanese fossil assemblages from the Late Pleistocene, and a discussion on the ecological effects of the Toba eruption. *Quaternary International* 258, 80–87.

Majeed-Lowe, Zuraina. 1979 The West Mouth, Niah, in the Prehistory of Southeast Asia. PhD Thesis, Yale University: University Microfilms International Ann Arbor.

Marwick, Ben, Clarkson, Chris, O'Connor, Sue, and Collins, Sophie. 2016 Early modern human lithic technology from Jerimalai, East Timor. *Journal of Human Evolution* 101, 45–64.

Mijares, Armand, Détroit, Florent, Piper, Philip, Grün, Rainer, Bellwood, Peter, Aubert, Maxime, Champion, Guillaume, Cuevas, Nida, De Leon, Alexandra, and Dizon, Eusebio. 2010 New evidence for a 67,000-year-old human presence at Callao Cave, Luzon, Philippines. *Journal of Human Evolution* 59, 123–132.

Morwood, M., Soejono, R., Roberts, R., Sutikna, T., Turney, C., Westaway, K., Rink, W., Zhao, J., van den Bergh, G., Due, Rokus, Awe, Hobbs, D., Moore, M., Bird, M., and Fifield, L. 2004 Archaeology and the age of a new hominin from Flores in Eastern Indonesia. *Nature* 431, 1087–1091.

Musser, Guy. 1981 The giant rat of Flores and its relatives east of Borneo and Bali. *Bulletin of the American Museum of Natural History* 169, 67–176.

O'Connor, Sue, and Aplin, Ken. 2007 A matter of balance: An overview of Pleistocene occupation history and the impact of the last glacial phase in East Timor and the Aru Islands, eastern Indonesia. *Archaeology in Oceania* 42, 83.

O'Connor, Sue, Aplin, Ken, Szabó, Katherine, Pasveer, Juliette, Veth, Peter, and Spriggs, Matthew. 2007 Liang Lemdubu: A Pleistocene Cave Site in the Aru Islands, in *The Archaeology of the Aru Islands, Eastern Indonesia*, Terra Australis 22, eds O'Connor, Sue, Spriggs, Matthew, and Veth, Peter. Canberra: ANU Press, 195.

O'Connor, Sue, Louys, Julien, Kealy, Shimona, and Carro, Sofia. 2017 Hominin dispersal and settlement East of Huxley's Line: The role of sea level changes, island size, and subsistence behavior. *Current Anthropology* 58, 1–16.

O'Connor, Sue, Ono, Rintaro, and Clarkson, Chris. 2011 Pelagic fishing at 42,000 years before the present and the maritime skills of modern humans. *Science* 334, 1117–1121.

O'Connor, Sue, Robertson, Gail, and Aplin, Ken. 2014 Are osseous artefacts a window to perishable material culture? Implications of an unusually complex bone tool from the Late Pleistocene of East Timor. *Journal of Human Evolution* 67, 108–119.

Pagani, Luca, Lawson, Daniel John, Jagoda, Evelyn, Mörseburg, Alexander, Eriksson, Anders, Mitt, Mario, Clemente, Florian, Hudjashov, Georgi, DeGiorgio, Michael, Saag, Lauri, Wall, Jeffrey, Cardona, Alexia, Mägi, Reedik, Wilson Sayres, Melissa, Kaewert, Sarah, Inchley, Charlotte, Scheib, Christiana, Järve, Mari, Karmin, Monika, Jacobs, Guy, Antao, Tiago, Mircea, Florin, Iliescu, Kushniarevich, Alena, Ayub, Qasim, Tyler-Smith, Chris, Xue, Yali, Yunusbayev, Bayazit, Tambets, Kristiina, Mallick, Chandana, Saag, Lehti, Pocheshkhova, Elvira, Andriadze, George, Muller, Craig, Westaway, Michael, Lambert, David, Zoraqi, Grigor, Turdikulova, Shahlo, Dalimova, Dilbar, Sabitov, Zhaxylyk, Sultana, Gazi, Lachance, Joseph, Tishkoff, Sarah, Momynaliev, Kuvat, Isakova, Jainagul, Damba, Larisa, Gubina, Marina, Nymadawa, Pagbajabyn, Evseeva, Irina, Atramentova, Lubov, Utevska, Olga, Ricaut, François-Xavier, Brucato, Nicolas, Sudoyo, Herawati, Letellier, Thierry, Cox, Murray, Barashkov, Nikolay, Škaro, Vedrana, Mulahasanovic, Lejla, Primorac, Dragan, Sahakyan, Hovhannes, Mormina, Maru, Eichstaedt, Christina, Lichman, Daria, Abdullah, Syafiq, Chaubey, Gyaneshwer, Wee, Joseph, Mihailov, Evelin, Karunas, Alexandra, Litvinov, Sergei, Khusainova, Rita, Ekomasova, Natalya, Akhmetova, Vita, Khidiyatova, Irina, Marjanovi, Damir, Yepiskoposyan, Levon, Behar, Doron, Balanovska, Elena, Metspalu, Andres, Derenko, Miroslava, Malyarchuk, Boris, Voevoda, Mikhail, Fedorova, Sardana, Osipova, Ludmila, Lahr, Marta, Gerbault, Pascale, Leavesley, Matthew, Migliano,

Andrea, Petraglia, Michael, Balanovsky, Oleg, Khusnutdinova, Elza, Metspalu, Ene, Thomas, Mark, Manica, Andrea, Nielsen, Rasmus, Villems, Richard, Willerslev, Eske, Kivisild, Toomas, and Metspalu1, Mait. 2016 Genomic analyses inform on migration events during the peopling of Eurasia. *Nature* 538, 238–242.

Pasveer, Juliette, Clarke, Simon, and Miller, Gifford. 2002 Late Pleistocene human occupation of inland rainforest, Bird's Head, Papua (Research Reports). *Archaeology in Oceania* 37, 94.

Petraglia, Michael, Ditchfield, Peter, Jones, Sacha, Korisetter, Ravi, and Pal, J. 2012 The Toba volcanic super-eruption, environmental change, and hominin occupation history in India over the last 140,000 years. *Quaternary International* 258, 119–134.

Piper, Philip, and Rabett, Ryan. 2016 Vertebrate fauna from the Niah Caves, in *Rainforest Foraging and Farming in Island Southeast Asia: The Archaeology of the Niah Caves, Sarawak*, eds Barker, Graeme, and Farr, Lucy. Cambridge: McDonald Institute for Archaeological Research, 401–438.

Pyatt, Brian, Wilson, Phillipe, and Barker, Graeme. 2005 The chemistry of tree resins and ancient rock paintings in the Caves, Sarawak (Borneo): Some evidence of rain forest management by early human populations. *Journal of Archaeological Science* 32, 897–901.

Rampino, Michael and Ambrose, Stanley. 2000 Volcanic winter in the Garden of Eden: The Toba Supereruption and the Late Pleistocene Human Population Crash, in *Volcanic Hazards and Disasters in Human Antiquity*, eds McCoy, Ambrose, and Heiken, F. Colorado: Geological Society of America, 71–82.

Reich, David. 2018 *Who We Are and How We Got Here*. New York: Pantheon Books.

Reich, David, Patterson, Nick, Kircher, Martin, Delfin, Frederick, Nandineni, Madhusudan, Pugach, Irina, Ko, Albert, Ko, Ying-Chin, Jinam, Timothy A, Phipps, Maude, Saitou, Naruya, Wollstein, Andreas, Kayser, Manfred, Paabo, Svante, and Stoneking, Mark. 2011 Denisova admixture and the first modern human dispersals into Southeast Asia and Oceania. *The American Journal of Human Genetics* 89, 516–528.

Rizal, Yan, Westaway, Kira, Zaim, Yahdi, van den Bergh, Gerrit, Bettis, Arthur III, Morwood, Michael, Huffman, Frank, Grün, Rainer, Joannes-Boyau, Renaud, Bailey, Richard, Sidarto, Westaway, Michael, Kurniawan, Iwan, Moore, Mark, Storey, Michael, Aziz, Fachroel, Suminto, Zhao, Jian-xin, Aswan, Sipola, Maija, Larick, Roy, Zonneveld, John-Paul, Scott, Robert, Putt, Shelby, and Ciochon, Russell. 2020 Last appearance of *Homo erectus* at Ngandong, Java, 117,000–108,000 years ago. *Nature* 577, 381–385.

Rolland, Nicholas. 2002 The initial hominid colonization of Asia: A survey of anthropic evidence from biogeographic and ecological perspectives. *Indo-Pacific Prehistory Association Bulletin* 22, 1–15.

Semah, Francois, Semah, Anne-Marie, Falguere, Christophe, Detroit, Florent, Gallet, Xavier, Hamea, Sebastien, Molgne, Anne-marle, and Simanjuntak, Truman. 2004 The significance of the Punung Karstic Area (Eastern Java) for the chronology of the Javanese Palaeolithic, with Special Reference to the Song Terus Cave. *Modern Quaternary Research in Southeast Asia* 18, 45–62.

Shipman, Pat. 2001 *The Man Who Found the Missing-Link*. New York: Simon & Schuster.

Shipton, Ceri, O'Connor, S., Jankowski, N., O'Connor-Veth, J., Maloney, T., Kealy, S., and Boulanger, C. 2019 A new 44.000-year sequence from Asitau Kuru (Jerimalai) Timor-Leste indicates long-term continuity in human behaviour. *Archaeological and Anthropological Science* 11, 5717–5741.

Simanjuntak, Truman. 2002 Cave settlement, new trend in the late Pleistocene, in *Gunung Sewu in Prehistoric Times*, ed. Simanjuntak, Truman. Yogyakarta: Gadjah Mada University Press, 89–131.

Slik, Ferry, Aiba, Shin-Ichiro, Bastian, Meredith, Brearley, Francis, Cannon, Charles, Eichhorn, Karl, Fredriksson, Gabriella, Kartawinata, Kuswata, Laumonier, Yves, Mansor, Asyraf, Marjokorpi, Antti, Meijaard, Erik, Morley, Robert, Nagamasu, Hidetoshi, Nilus, Reuben, Nurtjahya, Eddy, Payne, John, Permana, Andrea, Poulsen, Axel, Raes, Niels, Riswan, Soedarsono, van Schaik, Carel, Sheil, Douglas, Sidiyasa, Kade, Suzuki, Eizi, van Valkenburg, Johan, Webb, Campbell, Wich, Serge, Yoneda, Tsuyoshi, Zakaria, Rahmad, and Zweifel, Nicole. 2011 Soils on exposed Sunda shelf shaped biogeographic patterns in the equatorial forest of Southeast Asia. *Proceedings of The National Academy of Sciences* 108, 12343–12347.

Spehar, Stephanie, Sheil, Douglas, Harrison, Terry, Louys, Julien, Ancrenaz, Marc, Marshall, Andrew, Wich, Serge, Bruford, Michael, and Meijaard, Erik. 2018 Orangutans venture out of the rainforest and into the Anthropocene. *Science Advances* 4, e1701422.

Stevenson, Janelle. 2018 Vegetation and climate of the last glacial maximum in Sulawesi, in *The Archaeology of Sulawesi: Current Research on the Pleistocene to the Historic Period*, eds O'Connor, Sue, Bulbeck, D., and Meyer, J. Canberra: ANU Press, 17–29.

Storey, Michael, Roberts, Richard, and Saidin, Mokhtar. 2012 Astronomically calibrated 40Ar/39Ar age for the Toba supereruption and global synchronization of late quaternary records. *The Proceedings of The National Academy of Sciences* 109, 18684–18688.

Storm, Paul. 1992 Two Microliths from Javanese Wadjak Man. *Journal of Anthropological Society of Nippon* 100, 191–203.

Storm, Paul. 1995 The evolutionary significance of the Wajak skulls. *Scripta Geologica* 110, 1–247.

Storm, Paul, Aziz, Fachroel, de Vos, John, Kosasih, Dikdik, Baskoro, Sinung, Ngaliman, and van den Hoek Ostende, Lars. 2005 Late Pleistocene *Homo sapiens* in a Tropical Rainforest Fauna in East Java. *Journal of Human Evolution* 49, 540.

Storm, Paul, and de Vos, John. 2006 Rediscovery of the Late Pleistocene Punung Hominin Sites and the Discovery of a New Site Gunung Dawung in East Java. *Senckenbergiana Lethaea* 86, 271–281.

Storm, Paul, Wood, Rachel, Stringer, Chris, Bartsiokas, Antonis, de Vos, John, Aubert, Maxime, Kinsley, Les, and Grün, Rainer. 2013 U-series and radiocarbon analyses of human and faunal remains from Wajak, Indonesia. *Journal of Human Evolution* 64, 356–365.

Summerhayes, Glenn, Leavesley, Matthew, Fairbairn, Andrew, Mandui, Herman, Field, Judith, Ford, Anne, and Fullagar, Richard. 2010 Human adaptation and plant use in highland New Guinea 49,000 to 44,000 years ago. *Science* 330, 78–81.

Sutikna, Thomas, Tocheri, Matthew, Faith, Tyler, Jatmiko, Awe, Rokus, Meijer, Hanneke, Saptomo, Wahyu, and Roberts, Richard. 2018 The spatio-temporal distribution of archaeological and faunal finds at Liang Bua (Flores, Indonesia) in light of the revised chronology for *Homo floresiensis*. *Journal of Human Evolution* 124, 52–74.

Szabo, Katherine, 2019. Worked shell from the Northern Moluccas, in *The Spice Islands in Prehistory. Archaeology in the Northern Moluccas, Indonesia*, ed. Bellwood, Peter. Canberra: ANU Press, 121–134.

Tanudirjo, Daud. 2001 Islands in Between: Prehistory of the Northeastern Indonesian Archipelago. Ph.D. Thesis, Australian National University.

Tanudirjo, Daud. 2005 Long continuous or short occasional occupation? The human use of Leang Sarru Rockshelter in the Talaud Islands, northeastern Indonesia. *Bulletin of the Indo-Pacific Prehistory Association* 25, 15–19.

Theunissen, Bert. 1989 *Eugene Dubois and the Ape-Man from Java*. Dordrecht: Kluwer Publishers.

Thorne, Alan, Grün, Rainer, Mortimer, G, Spooner, Nigel, Simpson, J, McCulloch, M, Taylor, L, and Curnoe, Darren. 1999 Australia's oldest human remains: Age of the Lake Mungo 3 skeleton. *Journal of Human Evolution* 36, 591–612.

Thorne, Alan, and Wolpoff, Milford. 1992 The multiregional evolution of humans. *Scientific American* 266, 76–83.

van den Bergh, Gerrit, de Vos, John, and Sondaar, Paul. 2001 The late Quaternary Palaoegeography of Mammal Evolution in the Indonesian Archipelago. *Palaeogeography, Palaeoclimatology, Palaeoecology* 171, 387.

van den Bergh, Gerrit, Li, Bo, Brumm, Adam, Grün, Rainer, Yurnaldi, Dida, Moore, Mark, Kurniawan, Iwan, Setiawan, Ruly, Aziz, Fachroel, Roberts, Richard, Suyono, Storey, Michael, Setiabudi, Erick, and Morwood, Michael. 2016a Earliest hominin occupation of Sulawesi, Indonesia. *Nature* 529, 208–226.

van den Bergh, Gerrit, Kaifu, Yousuke, Kurniawan, Iwan, Kono, Reiko, Brumm, Adam, Setiyabudi, Erick, Aziz, Fachroel, and Morwood, Michael. 2016b *Homo floresiensis*-like fossils from the Early Middle Pleistocene of Flores. *Nature* 534, 245–248.

van den Bergh, Gerrit D., Kaifu, Yousuke, Kurniawan, Iwan, Kono, Reiko T., Brumm, Adam, Setiyabudi, Erick, Aziz, Fachroel, and Morwood, Michael J. 2016c *Homo floresiensis*-like fossils from the early middle Pleistocene of Flores. *Nature* 534, 245–248.

van den Bergh, Gerrit, Meijer, H, Awe, Rokhus, Morwood, Michael, Szabó, Katherine, van den Hoek Ostende, L, Sutikna, T, Saptomo, E, Piper, Philip, and Dobney, Keith. 2009 The Liang Bua faunal remains: A 95 kyr sequence from Flores, East Indonesia. *Journal of Human Evolution* 57, 527–537.

van der Kaars, W.A., and Dam, M.A.C. 1995 A 135,000-year record of vegetational and climatic change from the Bandung area, West-java, Indonesia. *Palaeogeography, Palaeoclimatology, Palaeoecology* 117, 55–72.

van der Kaars, Sander, Williams, Martin, Bassinot, Franck, Guichard, François, Moreno, Eva, Dewilde, Fabien, and Cook, Ellyn. 2012 The influence of the ~73 ka Toba super-eruption on the ecosystems. *Quaternary International* 258, 45–53.

van Heekeren, Hendrik. 1972 The stone age of Indonesia. *Verhandelingen van het Koninklijke Instituut voor Taal-, Land-, en Volkenkunde* 61, 70–106.

Weidenreich, Frederich. 1951 Morphology of Solo Man. *Anthropological Paper of the American Museum of Natural History* 43, 205–320.
Westaway, K. E., Louys, J., Due Awe, R., Morwood, M., Price, G., Zhao, J., Aubert, M., Joannes-Boyau, R., Smith, M., Skinner, M., Compton, T., Bailey, R., van den Bergh, G., de Vos, J., Pike, A., Stringer, C., Saptomo, E., Rizal, Y., Zaim, J., Santoso, W., Trihascaryo, A., Kinsley, L., and Sulistyanto, B. 2017 An early modern human presence in Sumatra 73,000–63,000 years ago. *Nature* 548, 322–325.
Westaway, Kira, Morwood, Michael, Roberts, Richard, Rokus, A.D., Zhao, J., Storm, P., Aziz, F., van den Bergh, Gerrit, Hadi, P., Jatmiko, and de Vos, John. 2007 Age and biostratigraphic significance of the Punung Rainforest Fauna, East Java, Indonesia, and implication of Pongo and Homo. *Journal of Human Evolution* 53, 709–717.
Westaway, Kira, Morwood, Michael, Sutikna, T, Moore, Mark, Rokus, A, van den Bergh, Gerrit, Roberts, Richard, and Saptomo, E. 2009 *Homo floresiensis* and the Late Pleistocene environment of Eastern Indonesia: Defining the nature of the relationship. *Quaternary Science Reviews* 28, 2905–2906.
Whitmore, Tim. 1981 Palaeoclimate and vegetation history, in ed. Tim C. Whitmore, *Wallace's Line and Plate Tectonic*. Oxford: Clarendon Press.
Morley, Robert, and Flenley, John. 1987 Late Cainozoic vegetational and environmental changes in the Malay Archipelago, in *The Biogeographical Evolution of the Malay Archipelago*, ed. by Whitmore, Tim C. Oxford: Clarendon Press, 50–59.
Widianto, Harry, eds. 2001 Perspective on the evolution of Javanese *Homo erectus* based on morphological and stratigraphic characteristic, in *Sangiran: Man, Culture and Environment in Pleistocene Times*, eds Simanjuntak, Harry, Prasetyo, Bagyo, and Handini, Retno. Jakarta: Yayasan Obor, 24–45.
Wolpoff, Milford, Wu, Xinzhi, and Thorne, Alan. 1984 Modern *Homo sapiens* Origins: A general theory of hominin evolution involving the fossil evidence from East Asia, in *The Origins of Modern Humans*, eds Smith, Fred H., and Spencer, Frank. New York: Alan R. Liss, 411–483.
Zuraina, Madjid. 1990 The Tampanian problem resolved: Archaeological evidence of a Late Pleistocene lithic workshop. *Modern Quaternary Research in Southeast Asia* 11, 71–96.

# 6
# NORTHERN SAHUL AND THE BISMARCK ARCHIPELAGO

*Glenn R. Summerhayes*

## Introduction

Over the last three years new data focusing on the links between Asia and Australia have been published (Kealy et al. 2016, 2017, 2018, 2019; Norman et al. 2018; Bird et al. 2018), and new dates for occupation of Australia at 70,000–60,000 years are now appearing (Clarkson et al. 2017; Moss et al. 2017; Vannieuwenhuyse et al. 2017; Maloney et al. 2018; McDonald et al. 2018). These have generated new discussions with implications for the Asia/Pacific region as a whole (O'Connell et al. 2018). Archaeological findings of ornamentation at 30,000 years in Island Southeast Asia have now added to the conversation about "modernity" in these early people (Brumm et al. 2017). New evidence has thrown light on the hunting strategies of the earliest colonists in South Asia (Wedage et al. 2019), and indeed for the region as a whole (Roberts and Stewart 2019). The footsteps of humanity are also being found in areas not seen before, such as high-altitude occupation in Tibet (Zhang et al. 2018). Such finds indeed throw light on what it means to be human and to define our general behaviour (Roberts and Stewart 2019).

On top of archaeological data, the last three years have seen major advances in DNA research (Tobler et al. 2017) which impacts on modelling the speed of colonization across the continent of Ancient Sahul, but also on our relationship with other species in our region (Vernot et al. 2016; Slon et al. 2019) and Asia as a whole (Bae et al. 2017). The relationship among Neanderthals, Denisovans, and Modern Humans is a hot topic but primarily based on DNA with little bone found, although pieces are emerging, albeit small including a piece of a cranium (Chen et al. 2019). On top of this new data, studies of craniometric data on existing Modern Human fossils have shed light on prehistoric dispersal in East Asia (Matsumura et al. 2019)

## The First Footsteps

New Guinea was once part of the ancient landmass known as Sahul, which included Australia and Tasmania to the south. In the Pleistocene, sea levels were much lower, reaching 130 metres below present levels during the Late Glacial Maximum, joining these landmasses to form one large continent.

Northern Sahul, the portion comprising today's island of New Guinea, witnessed the first footprints of Humanity by at least 50–45,000 years ago. Occupation could be even earlier, with sites in the south (northern Australia) supposedly dating to between 70 and 60,000 years based on optically stimulated luminescence (Clarkson et al. 2017; Moss et al. 2017; Vannieuwenhuyse et al. 2017; McDonald et al. 2018; Maloney et al. 2018; Florin et al. 2020), although this early date for colonization is disputed by some with a later date for settlement preferred (Allen and O'Connell 2020).

### Where Did They Come from?

The ancestors of the first inhabitants arrived in New Guinea from the west via the Wallacean archipelago, a series of island chains separating Sahul from Sunda, the great landmass comprising what is today Malaysia, Brunei, and parts of western Indonesian. There is debate as to whether one route over the other was used by these early colonists (Kealy et al. 2016, 2017, 2018; Bird et al. 2018; Norman et al. 2018), although it is generally accepted that people moved along both routes (see Allen and O'Connell 2020; Pedro et al. 2020 for updates; see Figure 6.1). One major problem in modelling this migration is the lack of comparable early sites along the Wallacean islands.

Low intensity of occupation is the pattern from Timor sites including Asitau Kuru (Shipton et al. 2019). Here the earliest occupation in Wallacea dates to 41,572+ 939 BP on marine shell *Tectus niloticus*, which calibrates to 46,529–43,085 BP (95.4% probability). Shipton et al. (2019) note the occupation at 44,000 years. This is slightly younger than the earliest occupation in New Guinea to the east. Such low-intensity occupation with evidence of a preponderance of seashore resources suggests impermanent occupation and temporary sedentism, perhaps just proving to be a stepping stone for the populating of the landmass of Sahul to the east. The first evidence of "high intensity" occupation on Timor occurs in the Holocene, although evidence suggests a change of diet to land mammals some 20,000 years after initial occupation and 10,000 years prior to the Holocene (see Roberts et al. 2020). This is based on isotope analysis of teeth from sites in southern Wallacea (Timor and Alor) that indicates exploitation of coastal resources with changes to a terrestrial diet occurring 20,000 years after initial colonization. DNA offers a different insight into this early movement of peoples. The last three years have

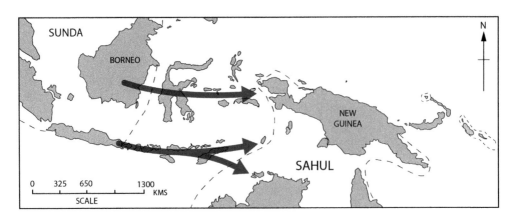

FIGURE 6.1   Migrations of people to Sahul.

seen major advances in DNA research (Tobler et al. 2017) which impacts on modelling the speed of colonization across the continent of Ancient Sahul, but also on our relationship with other species in our region (Vernot et al. 2016; Slon et al. 2019) and Asia as a whole (Bae et al. 2017). The relationship among Neanderthals, Denisovans, and Modern Humans is a hot topic but primarily based on DNA with little bone found, although pieces are emerging, albeit small (Warren 2019) including a piece of a cranium (Viola news report March 1st 2019). Based on DNA it has even been suggested that one population of Denisovans existed east of the Wallace line until the end of the Pleistocene (Jacobs et al. 2019). Despite these finds the basic story for the earliest peopling of Northern Sahul remains unchanged to that based on archaeology. DNA studies supports the model of two groups of people entering Sahul by at least 50,000 years ago with one entering southern Sahul, the other northern Sahul (Pedro et al. 2020).

## The First Inhabitants

The earliest evidence of humanity in the Pacific is found at archaeological sites high in the mountain valleys of Papua, some 2,000 metres above sea level. Within the Ivane Valley a human presence is felt in a number of sites skirting the periphery of the valley dating to between 50,000 and 44,000 years ago (Summerhayes et al. 2010). This valley was first brought to the attention of archaeologists by Catholic priests who uncovered waisted tools when digging for building foundations. Excavations in the 1960s at the Kosipe Mission identified occupation by 27,000 radiocarbon years (calibrated today to 30–32,000 years ago) (White et al. 1970). Return excavations in 2005–2010 identified sites of Vilakuav, Joes Garden site, South Kov, and Airport Mound, which established this valley as an import late Pleistocene landscape (Summerhayes et al. 2010). See Figure 6.2 for the location of the Pleistocene sites mentioned in the text and Table 6.1 for their dates, and Figure 6.3 for the location of Ivane Valley sites.

Temperatures were colder than today during this early occupation, reaching to between −5 and −6°C below modern temperatures during the Last Glacial Maximum (LGM) (Farrera et al. 1999). Occupation would have been close to the tree line, with cooler and wetter conditions

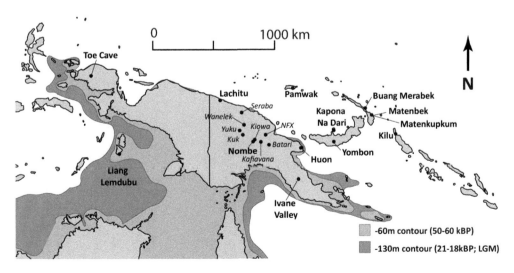

FIGURE 6.2    Pleistocene sites of Papua New Guinea mentioned in text.

114  Glenn R. Summerhayes

TABLE 6.1 The earliest Late Pleistocene sites.

| Archaeological sites | Age (BP) uncalibrated | Lab number | C14 calibrated 95.4% probability | Luminescence | References |
|---|---|---|---|---|---|
| *Mainland PNG* | | | | | |
| *Huon Peninsula* | | | | | |
| Bobongara | | | | >44,000 | Groube et al. (1986) and Chappell (2002) |
| *Owen Stanley Ranges* | | | | | |
| Kosipe Mission | 34,531 + 626 | Wk 17900 | 41,110–37,970 | | Summerhayes et al. (2010) |
| Vilakuav | 41,951 + 1571 | Wk-27072 | 48,690–42,970 | | Summerhayes et al. (2010) |
| South Kov | 40,298 + 956 | Wk 23354 | 45,540–42,760 | | Summerhayes et al. (2010) |
| Airport Mound | 39,836 + 909 | Wk 23356 | 45,170–42,520 | | Summerhayes et al. (2010) |
| *North Coast* | | | | | |
| Lachitu | 34,410 + 1400* | ANU-7610 | 42,225–36,784 | | O'Connor et al. (2011) |
| *Central Highlands* | | | | | |
| Nombe | 20,838 + 139 | Wk-22091 | 25,525>–<19,590 | | Denham and Mountain (2016) |
| | 16,468 + 96 | Wk22090 | | | |
| *West Papua* | | | | | |
| Toe Cave | 25,920 + 180 | OZG063 | 31,040–30,350 | | Pasveer (2004) |
| *Bismarck Archipelago* | | | | | |
| *New Britain* | | | | | |
| Kupona na Dari | | | | 34,000–38,000 | Torrence et al. (2004) |
| Yombon | 35,570 + 480 | Beta-62319 | 41,640–39,400 | | Pavlides and Gosden (1994) |
| *New Ireland* | | | | | |
| Buang Merabak | 40,090 + 550 | ANUA-15809 | 44,890–43,100 | | Leavesley and Chappell (2004) |
| Matenkupkum | 35,410 + 430* | ANU-8178 | 41,100–38,950 | | Allen (1994) |
| Matenbek | 20,430 + 180* | Beta-29007 | 24,400–23,440 | | Allen et al. (1989) |
| *Admiralty Islands* | | | | | |
| Pamwak | 20,900 + ? | ?Unknown | <25,860? | | Spriggs (2001) |
| *Solomon Islands* | | | | | |
| Kilu Cave | 28,740 + 280* | ANU-5990 | 33,365–31,690 | | Wickler (1990, 2001) |

*Source*: Adapted from G.R. Summerhayes and A. Ford (2014).
All terrestrial samples dates calibrated using IntCal09.
* Indicates dates on saltwater shells, calibrated using Marine09.

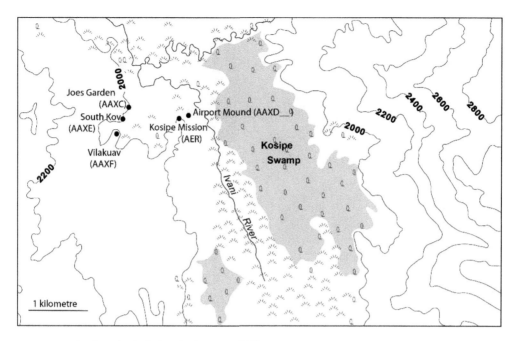

FIGURE 6.3   Archaeological sites in the Ivane Valley.

confirmed by palaeoecological studies (Hope 2009). Pollen studies demonstrated that local vegetation initially comprised swamp forest/sub-alpine forest before shifting to upper montane forest with sub-alpine grassland elements after 45,000 years ago (Hope 2009). These environments would have contained new faunal species, such as now-extinct large mammal species, including Protemnodon and Diprotodontids, which were present in the montane region to between 25,500 and 19,600 years ago at Nombe Cave (Stratum D) (see Denham and Mountain 2016 for updates in the dating of this site).

Exploitation of wild pandanus and yam (*Dioscorea* sp.) is evident from the earliest levels based on starch remains from the stone tools (see Figures 6.4 and 6.5). Macrobotanical remains of pandanus nut are found in all layers, providing a rich source of protein and oil. The presence of *Dioscorea* starch grains on stone tools is all the more significant as it would not have been possible to grow yam at this altitude at this time because of the reduced temperatures. Therefore it would have had to have been brought up from warmer lower altitudes, demonstrating the territorial range of these peoples (Summerhayes et al. 2010).

These early dates indicate that people were moving into the rugged and difficult-to-access montane regions soon after this initial colonization. Only a small number of sites make up the remainder of these early occupations, with four of these found in the islands of the Bismarck Archipelago suggesting rapid movements of people at this time over a number of major water gaps. From the mainland two coastal sites are found. Bobongara is found on the Huon peninsula, on the east coast of mainland New Guinea. Here there is evidence of past shorelines that have been preserved by uplifted coral beds. Stone tools are found on these terraces dated to over 40,000 years based on thermoluminescence (see Groube et al. 1986). Moreover, Lachitu rockshelter is located west of Vanimo on the north coast which dates from 35,000 years ago (see O'Connor et al. 2011). From the Bismarck Archipelago two coastal sites from New Ireland

FIGURE 6.4  Late Pleistocene stone tools, Ivane Valley.

(Buang Merabak and Matenkupkum) and two from New Britain (Kupona na Dari; Yombon) provide evidence for early occupation over 35,000 years (see Summerhayes and Ford 2014 for an update and references; and Figure 6.2 for their location).

Late Pleistocene occupation is evident in other parts of New Guinea, but occurs later in time. From the western half of the island of New Guinea little archaeological work has been undertaken (see Wright et al. 2013 for a review). Excavations at Toe Cave, Ayamaru Region, central Bird's Head, has yielded evidence of occupation dating from 31 to 30,000 years ago. Bones of montane and lowland species of animals have been found at this site (Pasveer 2004).

From the central highlands of eastern New Guinea occupation from 25,500 to 19,600 is found at the site of Nombe (Denham and Mountain 2016, 81); while Kilu Cave located on the east coast of Buka, north Solomons, has occupation from 33 to 32,000 years ago (Wickler 2001). There has also been dates of at least 25,000 years ago associated with occupation from Manus at the site of Pamwak (Spriggs 2001), however, the actual date has yet to be published.

Northern Sahul and the Bismarck Archipelago 117

FIGURE 6.5   Late Pleistocene stone tools, Ivane Valley.

As noted above, the presence of human occupation across mainland New Guinea and the Bismarck Archipelago, with little time separating initial occupation, points to a rapid colonization. During the late Pleistocene, lower sea levels ranged from −56 metres between 44,500 and 46,000 years ago to a maximum depth of −130 metres between 30,000 and 20,000 years (Lambeck and Chappell 2001), yet mainland New Guinea, New Britain, and New Ireland have always remained separated necessitating sea craft to cross these water gaps (see Gaffney 2021). People's skills in seafaring are confirmed by the presence of pelagic fish at the coastal sites. Reef species dominate at Kilu Cave although pelagic fish make up 20% from the earliest levels (Wickler 2001). Developing technologies for pelagic fishing are also found later in time from the Pleistocene cave of Matenbek located in close vicinity to Matenkupkum, where possible fish hook manufacture is evident in the earliest levels dated to between 24,400 and 23,440 years ago (Smith and Allen 1999). At Buang Merabak, the earliest evidence so far recorded for personal adornment during the Pleistocene in Papua New Guinea was also recovered, consisting of a perforated tiger shark tooth, most likely worn as a pendant (Leavesley 2007).

## Life in the Late Pleistocene of New Guinea

Evidence for coastal subsistence is only found in those assemblages from the Bismarck Archipelago sites of New Ireland and north Solomons. Here the evidence suggests that the earliest colonists were small groups of mobile, broad-spectrum foragers that exploited both maritime and terrestrial resources (see Summerhayes and Ford 2014). From New Britain, an indication of high mobility is also indicated by the presence of obsidian (see Summerhayes and Ford 2014; Torrence et al. 2004). The situation is different from coastal mainland New Guinea where heavy large waisted tools were found (Groube et al. 1986) and interpreted to be used in forest clearance allowing the promotion of grasslands which may have been beneficial to hunting or management of economic plant species (Groube 1989). Waisted tools are also found from the Ivane Valley sites (and later Holocene sites as well) (see Figure 6.6). This argument for forest clearance and land management activities can also be found in the pollen record of the Ivane Valley,

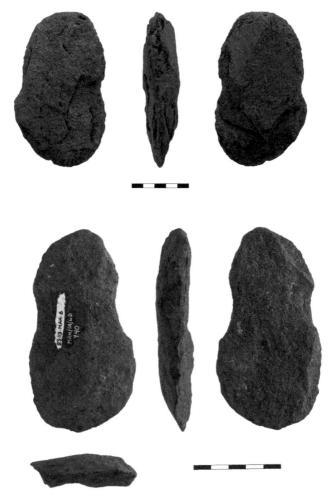

FIGURE 6.6   Waisted tools from Highland New Guinea. Top: Pleistocene contexts from Kosipe, Ivane valley; bottom: Holocene contexts from site of Yuk.

where an increase in charcoal after 45,000 years ago is associated with human firing of the wet montane forest (Hope 2009). Fire would have allowed for the extension of open sub-alpine grasslands into the montane forest areas replacing the forest with grasses, tree ferns, and shrubs.

There are many constraints when assessing subsistence strategies in the islands east of mainland New Guinea. Firstly, it must be noted that sites on New Britain, such as Yombon (Pavlides 2004) and Kupona na Dari (Torrence et al. 2004) contained no faunal remains, a result of the volcanic nature of the landscape and acid soils. Secondly, the native fauna of the Bismarck Archipelago are considered depauperate, with few native mammal species. This is seen in the faunal record from the earliest levels of Buang Merabak which show a low density mixture of both inland and coastal species, including bats, lizards, fish, and shellfish which is consistent with a low intensity use of the cave site by small groups of mobile hunter-gatherers, who visited the cave periodically to hunt bats that used the cave as a roost, but were also utilizing nearby coastal resources (see Leavesley 2005).

Clues about the number of these initial colonizers is indicated by their impact on local resources. Changes in shell collection strategies tell us a lot about the scale of their society. From both Matenkupkum (Allen et al. 1989) and Buang Merabak (Leavesley and Allen 1998) the large-sized shell species *Turbo argyrostoma* predominated, with *Chitons* also found at Buang Merabak. The largest specimens of a narrow range of reef and rocky shore taxa were collected during initial occupation, indicating that shellfish were subject to a targeted foraging strategy. Fish remains are also found at both sites indicating exploitation of the reef zone (reef fish and tropical sharks dominating), albeit found in low numbers. However, human-induced environmental change which is expected with colonizing populations exploiting limited resources is not witnessed till some 30,000 years after initial colonization. From the earliest occupation at Matenkupkum people had targeted the largest shellfish available for eating (*Turbo argyrostoma*). Yet the diminution of shellfish from overexploitation only occurred by 24,400–20,500 years ago, some 25,000 years after initial colonization (Gosden and Robertson 1991). That this overexploitation leading to an environmental impact took so long to manifest within the archaeological record is further testimony to the low population numbers prior to 25,000 years ago.

## Changes in Late Pleistocene Adaptations

Based on the limited data available, the Pleistocene can be characterized by small populations of highly mobile foragers moving across such large areas interacting with similar small mobile groups. After the initial colonization of Sahul, there is no archaeological evidence for subsequent interaction with the west, nor between New Guinea and the islands of the Bismarck Archipelago to the east. Recent DNA studies also suggest that New Guinea was isolated both from southern Sahul and Sunda after initial settlement (Pedro et al. 2020). This scenario changes after some 30,000 years of occupation as the archaeological evidence suggests group boundaries emerged as a result of the filling-up of the landscape (Summerhayes 2007). Changes seen in the archaeological record from 25,000 years ago suggest a widening of social interactions.

Firstly, obsidian from New Britain sources has been identified in southern New Ireland archaeological assemblages from 20,000 years ago, again suggesting a maritime transport strategy to access and procure obsidian from these sources (Summerhayes and Allen 1993). Secondly, from 25,000 years ago there is evidence for the movement of animals by humans from mainland New Guinea to the Bismarck Archipelago, as seen in the introduction of *Phalanger orientalis* (Northern common cuscus) at Buang Merabak and Matenbek (Leavesley 2005) whose addition would have meant an important increase in available animal meat. These introductions occur at the same time as human induced environmental change as noted above with the diminution of shellfish at the site of Matenkupkum. That this overexploitation leading to an environmental impact took so long to manifest within the archaeological record is further testimony to the low population numbers prior to 25,000 years ago. The island of Manus, which was supposedly colonized by this time also witnesses translocation of plants and animals at the site of Pamwak with remains of mainland New Guinea animals and nut trees: cuscus (*Spilocuscus kraemeri*), bandicoot (*Echymipera kalubu*), and *Canarium indicum* nuts.

Thirdly, towards the end of the Pleistocene there is an increase in archaeological sites from highland New Guinea that were occupied for the first time such as NFX, Batari, Wañelek, Yuku, Manim, Kafiavana, and Kiowa (see Summerhayes et al. 2017). These are seen as seasonal camps for hunting and collecting by foragers (Gaffney et al. 2015), with people moving into mountain forests and intermontane valleys following game and perhaps for the collection of Pandanus. This also corresponds with a peak in population after the LGM till the mid-Holocene as evidenced by genetics (Pedro et al. 2020).

The increase in the number of archaeological sites across the landscape, the long-distance exchange/movement of obsidian, and the overexploitation of shellfish all point to the gradual filling up of the landscape at 20–25,000 years ago. It was argued that the population increase contributed to the slow development of group territories with defined boundaries, especially as different groups came into more frequent contact (see Summerhayes 2007), which contributed to the long-distance down-the-line exchange of animals and obsidian. Its appearance by 25–20,000 years ago was argued to be a result of this development for the first time of inter-community contacts: "That is, widespread resource distribution requires the development of dependable exchange links with other communities" (Summerhayes 2007, 16).

## References

Allen, Jim. 1994 Radiocarbon determinations, luminescence dating and Australian archaeology. *Antiquity* 68, 339–343.
Allen, Jim, Gosden, Chris, and White, J. Peter. 1989 Human Pleistocene adaptations in the Tropical Island Pacific: Recent evidence from New Ireland, a Greater Australian Outlier. *Antiquity* 63, 548–561.
Allen, Jim, and O'Connell, Jim. 2020 A different paradigm for the initial colonisation of Sahul. *Archaeology in Oceania* 55, 1–14.
Bae, Christopher J., Douka, Katerina, and Petraglia, Michael. 2017 On the origin of modern humans: Asian perspectives. *Science* 358 (6368), eaai9067. https://doi.org/10.1126/science.aai9067.
Bellwood, Peter, Nitihaminoto, Goenadi, Irwin, Geoff, Gunadi, Waluyo, Agus, and Tanudirjo, Daud. 1998 35,000 years of prehistory in the northern Moluccas. *Modern Quaternary Research in Southeast Asia* 15, 233–73.
Bird, Michael, Beaman, Robin, Condie, Scott, Cooper, Alan, Ulm, Sean, and Veth, Peter. 2018 Palaeogeography and voyage modelling indicates early human colonization of Australia was likely from Timor-Roti. *Quaternary Science Reviews* 191, 431–439.
Brumm, Adam, Langley, Michelle, Moore, Mark, Hakim, Budianto, Ramli, Muhammad, Sumantri, Iwan, Burhan, Basran, Saiful, Andi Muhammad, Siagian, Linda, Suryatman, Sardi, Ratna, Jusdi, Andi, Abdullah, Mubarak, Andi Pampang, Hasliana, Hasrianti, Oktaviana, Adhi Agus, Adhityatama, Shinatria, van den Bergh, Gerrit, Aubert, Maxime, Zhao, Jian-xin, Huntley, Jilliaan, Li, Bo, Roberts, Richard, Saptomo, E. Wahyu, Perston, Yinika, and Grün, Rainer. 2017 Early human symbolic behavior in the Late Pleistocene of Wallacea. *Proceedings of the National Academy of Sciences of the USA* 114, 4105–4110.
Chappell, John. 2002 Sea level changes forced ice breakouts in the last glacial cycle: New results from coral terraces. *Quaternary Science Reviews* 21, 1229–1240.

Chen, Fahu, Welker, Frido, Shen, Chuan-Chou, Bailey, Shara, Bergmann, Inga, Davis, Simon, Xia, Huan, Wang, Hui, Fischer, Roman, Freidline, Sarah, Yu, Tsai-Lue, Skinner, Matthew, Stelzer, Stefanie, Dong, Guangrong, Fu, Qiaomei, Dong, Guanghui, Wang, Jian, Zhang, Dongju, and Hublin, Jean-Jacque. 2019 A late Middle Pleistocene Denisovan mandible from the Tibetan Plateau. *Nature* 569, 409–412.

Clarkson, Chris, Jacobs, Zenobia, Marwick, Ben, Fullagar, Richard, Wallis, Lynley, Smith, Mike, Roberts, Richard, Hayes, Elspeth, Lowe, Kelsey, Carah, Xavier, Florin, S. Anna, McNeil, Jessica, Cox, Delyth, Arnold, Lee, Hua, Quan, Huntley, Jillian, Brand, Helen, Manne, Tiina, Fairbairn, Andrew, Shulmeister, Jamie, Lyle, Lindsey, Salinas, Makiah, Page, Mara, Connell, Kate, Park, Gayoung, Norman, Kasih, Murphy, Tessa, and Pardoe, Colon. 2017 Human occupation of northern Australia by 65,000 years ago. *Nature* 547, 306–310.

Denham, Tim, and Mountain, Mary-Jane. 2016. Resolving some chronological problems at Nombe rock shelter in the highlands of Papua New Guinea. *Archaeology in Oceania* 51 (Suppl 1), 73–83.

Farrera, Isabel, Harrison, Sandy, Prentice, I., Colin, Ramstein, Gille, Guiot, Julie, Bartlein, Patrick J., Bonnelle, Raymonde, Bush, Mark, Cramer, Wolfgang, von Grafenstein, Ulrich, Holmgren, Karen, Hooghiemstra, Henry, Hope, Geoffrey, Jolly, Dyanna, Lauritzen, Stein-Erik, Ono, Yoshiaki, Pinot, Sophie, Stute, Martin, and Yu, Gua. 1999 Tropical climates at the Last Glacial Maximum: A new synthesis of terrestrial palaeoclimate data. I. Vegetation, lake-levels and geochemistry. *Climate Dynamics* 15, 823–856.

Florin, Anna, Fairbairn, Andrew, Nango, May, Djandjomerr, Djaykuk, Marwick, Ben, Fullagar, Richard, Smith, Mike, Wallis, Lynley, and Clarkson, Chris. 2020 The first Australian plant foods at Madjedbebe, 65,000–53,000 years ago. *Nature Communications*. https://doi.org/10.1038/s41467-020-14723-0.

Gaffney, Dylan. 2021 Pleistocene water crossings and adaptive flexibility within the *Homo genus*. *Journal of Archaeological Research* 29, 255–326.

Gaffney, Dylan, Ford, Anne, and Summerhayes, Glenn. 2015 Crossing the Pleistocene-Holocene transition in the New Guinea Highlands: Evidence from the lithic assemblage of Kiowa rockshelter. *Journal of Anthropological Archaeology* 39, 223–246.

Gosden, Chris, and Robertson, Nola. 1991 Models for Matenkupkum: interpreting a Late Pleistocene from Southern New Ireland, Papua New Guinea, in *Report of the Lapita Homeland Project*, eds Allen, J., and Gosden, C. Canberra: Department of Prehistory, Research School of Pacific Studies, The Australian National University, 20–45.

Groube, Les. 1989 The taming of the rainforests: A model for Late Pleistocene forest exploitation in New Guinea, in *Foraging and Farming: The Evolution of Plant Exploitation*, eds Harris, D., and Hillmas, G. London: Unwin Hyman, 292–304.

Groube, Les, Chappell, John, Muke, John, and Price, David. 1986 A 40,000 year-old human occupation site at Huon Peninsula, Papua New Guinea. *Science* 324, 453–455.

Hope, Geoff. 2009. Environmental change and fire in the Owen Stanley Ranges, Papua New Guinea. *Quaternary Science Reviews* 28 (23–24), 2261–2276.

Jacobs, Guy, Hudjashov, Georgi, Saag, Lauri, Kusuma, Pradiptajati, Darusallam, Chelzie, Lawson, Daniel, Mondal, Mayukh, Pagani, Luca, Xavier Ricaut, Francois, Stoneking, Mark, Metspalu, Mait, Sudoyo, Herawati, Lansing, J. Stephan, and Cox, Murray M.P. 2019 Multiple deeply divergent Denisovan ancestries in Papuans. *Cell* 177, 1010–1021.

Kealy, Shimona, Donnellan, Stephan, Mitchell, Kieren, Herrera, Michael, Aplin, Ken, O'Connor, Sue, and Louys, Julien. 2019 Phylogenetic relationships of the cuscuses (Diprotodontia: Phalangeridae) of island Southeast Asia and Melanesia based on the mitochondrial ND2 gene. *Australian Mammalogy*. https://doi.org/10.1071/AM18050.

Kealy, Shimona, Louys, Julien, and O'Connor, Sue. 2016 Islands under the sea: A review of early modern human dispersal routes and migration hypotheses through Wallacea. *The Journal of Island and Coastal Archaeology* 11, 364–384.

Kealy, Shimona, Louys, Julien, and O'Connor, Sue. 2017 Reconstructing palaeogeography and interisland intervisibility in the Wallacean Archipelago during the likely period of Sahul colonisation, 65–45,000 years ago. *Archaeological Prospection* 24, 259–272.

Kealy, Shimona, Louys, Julien, and O'Connor, Sue. 2018 Least-cost pathway models indicate northern human dispersal from Sunda to Sahul. *Journal of Human Evolution* 125, 59–70.

Lambeck, Kurt, and Chappell, John. 2001 Sea level change through the Last Glacial Cycle. *Science* 292, 679–686.

Leavesley, Matthew. 2007 A shark tooth ornament from Pleistocene Sahul. *Antiquity* 81, 308–315.

Leavesley, Matthew G. 2005. Prehistoric hunting strategies in New Ireland, Papua New Guinea: The evidence of the cuscus (*Phalanger orientalis*) remains from Buang Merabak cave. *Asian Perspectives* 44 (1), 207–218.

Leavesley, Matthew, and Allen, Jim. 1998. Dates, disturbance and artefact distributions: Another analysis of Buang Merabak, a Pleistocene site on New Ireland, Papua New Guinea. *Archaeology in Oceania* 33 (2), 63–82.

Leavesley, Matthew and Chappell, John, 2004 Buang Merabak: Additional early radiocarbon evidence of the colonisation of the Bismarck Archipelago, Papua New Guinea. *Antiquity* 78 (301). Project Gallery at http://antiquity.ac.uk/ProjGall/leavesley/index.html.

Maloney, Tim, O'Connor, Sue, Wood, Rachel, Aplin, Ken, and Balme, Jane. 2018 Carpenters Gap 1: A 47,000 year old record of indigenous adaption and innovation. *Quaternary Science Reviews* 191, 204–228.

Matsumura, Hirofuni, Hung, Hsiao-Chun, Higham, Charles, Zhang, Chi, Yamagata, Mariko, Nguyen, Lan Cuon, Li, Zhen, Fan, Xue-chun, Simanjuntak, Truman, Oktaviana, Adhi, He, Jia-nong.m, Chen, Chung-yu, Pan, Chieng-Kuo, He, Gang, Sun, Guo-ping, Huang, Weijii-Huang, Li, Xin-wei, Wei, Xin-tao, Domett, Kate, Halcrow, Sian, Nguyen, Kim Dung, Trinh, Hoang, Hie, Bui, Chi Hoa, Nguyen, Khang Trung Kie, and Reinecke, Andre. 2019 Craniometrics reveal "Two layers" of prehistoric human dispersal in Eastern Eurasia. *Scientific Reports* 9, 1451. https://doi.org/10.1038/s41598-018-35426-z.

McDonald, Jo, Reynen, Wendy, Petchey, Fiona, Ditchfield, Kane, Bryne, Chae, Vannieuwenhuyse, Dorcus, Leopold, Matthias, and Veth, Peter. 2018. *Karnatulul* (Serpents Glen): A new chronology for the oldest site in Australia's Western Desert. *PLoS ONE* 13 (9), e0202511.

Moss, Patrick, Dunbar, Gavin, Thomas, Zoe, Turney, Chris, Kershaw, A. Peter, and Jacobsen, Geraldine. 2017 A 60,000 year record of environmental change for the Wet Tropics of north-eastern Australia based on the ODP 820 marine cores. *Journal of Quaternary Science* 32, 704–716.

Norman, Kasmin, Inglis, Josh, Clarkson, Chris, Faith, J. Tyler, Shulmeister, Jamie, and Harris, Daniel. 2018 An early colonisation pathway into northwest Australia 70-60,000 years ago. *Quaternary Science Reviews* 180, 229–239.

O'Connell, Jim, Allen, F. Jim, Williams, Martin, Williams, Alan, Turney, Chris, Spooner, Nigel, Kamminga, Johan, Brown, Graham, and Cooper, Alan. 2018 When did *Homo sapiens* first reach Southeast Asia and Sahul? *Proceedings of the National Academy of Sciences of America* 115, 8482–8490. https://doi.org/10.1073/pnas.1808385115.

O'Connor, Sue, Barham, Anthony, Aplin, Ken, Dobney, Keith, Fairbairn, Andrew, and Richards, Michelle. 2011. The power of paradigms: Examining the evidential basis for early to mid-Holocene pigs and pottery in Melanesia. *Journal of Pacific Archaeology* 2 (2), 1–25.

Pasveer, Juliette. 2004 *The Djief Hunters: 26,000 years of rainforest exploitation on the Bird's Head of Papua, Indonesia*. London: AA Balkema Publishers.

Pavlides, Christina. 2004 From Misisil Cave to Eliva Hamlet: Rediscovering the Pleistocene in Interior West New Britain. *Records of the Australian Museum, Supplement* 29, 97–108.

Pavlides, Christina, and Gosden, Chris. 1994 35,000-year-old sites in the rainforests of West New Britain, Papua New Guinea. *Antiquity* 68, 604–610.

Pedro, Nichole, Brucato, Nicolas, Fernandes, Veronica, Andre, Mathilde, Saag, Laurant, Pomat, William, Besse, Celine, Boland, Anne, Deleuze, Jean-Francios, Clarkson, Chris, Sudoyo, Herawati, Metspalu, Mait, Stoneking, Mark, Cox, Murray, Leavesley, Mathew, Pereira, Luisa, and Ricaut, Francios-Xavier. 2020 Papuan mitochondrial genomes and the settlement of Sahul. *Journal of Human Genetics*. https://doi.org/10.1038/s10038-020-0781-3.

Roberts, Patrick, Gaffney, Dylan, Lee-Thorp, Julia, and Summerhayes, Glenn R. 2017 Persistent tropical foraging in the Highlands of Terminal Pleistocene-Holocene New Guinea. *Nature, Ecology and Evolution* 1. https://doi.org/10.1038/s41559-016-0044.

Roberts, Patrick, Louys, Julien, Zech, Jana, Shipton, Ceri, Kealy, Shimona, Samper Carro, Sophia, Hawkins, Stuart, Boulanger, Clara, Marzo, Sara, Fiedler, Bianca, Boivin, Nicole, Mahirta, Mahirta, Aplin, Ken, and O'Connor, Sue. 2020 Isotopic evidence for initial coastal colonization and subsequent diversification in the human occupation of Wallacea. *Nature Communications*. https://doi.org/10.1038/s41467-020-15969-4

Roberts, Patrick, and Stewart, Brian. 2019 Defining the "generalist specialist" niche for Pleistocene *Homo sapiens*. *Nature Human Behaviour* 2, 542–550.

Shipton, Ceri, O'Connor, Sue, Jankowski, Nathan, O'Connor-Veth, Jack, Maloney, Tim, Kealy, Shimona, and Boulanger, Clara. 2019 A new 44,000-year sequence from Asitau Kuru (Jerimalai), Timor-Leste, indicates long-term continuity in human behaviour. *Archaeological and Anthropological Sciences* 11, 5717–5741.

Skoglund, Pontus, Posth, Cosimo, Sirak, Kendra, Spriggs, Matthew, Valentin, Federique, Bedford, Stuart, Clark, Geoff, Reepmeyer, Christian, Petchey, Fiona, Fernandes, Daniel, Fu, Qiaome, Harney, Eadaoin, Lipson, Mark, Mallick, Swapan, Novak, Mario, Rohland, Nadin, Stewardson, Kristin, Abdullah, Syafiq, Cox, Murray, Friendlaender, Francois, Friedlaender, Jonathan, Kivisild, Toomas, Koko, George, Kursuma, Pradiptajati, Merriwether, Andrew, Ricaut, Francois-Xavier, Wee, Joseph, Patterson, Nick, Krause, Johannes, Pinhasi, Ron, and Reich, David. 2016 Genomic insights into the peopling of the southwest Pacific. *Nature* 538, 510–513. https://doi.org/10.1038/nature19844.

Slon, Vivane, Mafessoni, Fabrizio, Vernot, Benjamin, de Filippo1, Cesare, Grote, Stefan, Viola, Bence S., Hajdinjak, Mateja, Peyrégne, Stephane, Nagel, Sara, Brown, Samantha, Douka, Katerina, Higham, Tom, Kozlikin, Maxim B., Shunkov, Michael V., Derevianko, Anatoly P., Kelso, Janet, Meyer, Matthias, Prüfer, Kay, and Pääbo, Svante. 2019 The genome of the offspring of a Neanderthal mother and a Denisovan father. *Nature* 561, 113–116.

Smith, Anita, and Allen, Jim. 1999 Pleistocene shell technologies: Evidence from Island Melanesia, Australian Coastal Archaeology, in *Research Papers in Archaeology and Natural History 31, Research School of Pacific and Asian Studies*, eds Jay, Hall, and Ian, McNiven. Canberra: Australian National University, 291–297.

Spriggs, Matthew. 2001 How AMS dating changed my life, in Australasian Connections and New Directions: Proceedings of the 7th Australasian Archaeometry Conference, eds Jones, Michael, and Sheppard, Peter. Auckland: Department of Anthropology, University of Auckland, 365–374.

Summerhayes, Glenn R. 2007 Island Melanesian Pasts – A View from Archaeology, in *Genes, Language and Culture History in the Southwest Pacific*, ed. Friedlaender, Jonathan. New York: Oxford University Press, 10–35.

Summerhayes, Glenn R., and Allen, Jim. 1993 The transport of Mopir obsidian to late Pleistocene New Ireland. *Archaeology in Oceania* 28, 144–148.

Summerhayes, Glenn R., Field, Judith, Shaw, Ben, and Gaffney, Dylan. 2017 The archaeology of forest exploitation and change in the tropics during the Pleistocene: The case of Northern Sahul (Pleistocene New Guinea). *Quaternary International* 448, 14–30.

Summerhayes, Glenn R., and Ford, Anne. 2014. Late Pleistocene colonisation and adaptation in New Guinea: Implications for modeling modern human behaviour, in *Southern Asia, Australia and the Search for Human Origins*, eds Dennell, Robin, and Poor, Martin. Cambridge: Cambridge University Press, 213–227.

Summerhayes, Glenn, Leavesley, Matthew, Fairbairn, Andrew, Mandui, Herman, Field, Judith, Ford, Anne, and Fullagar, Richard. 2010 Human adaptation and use of plants in highland New Guinea 49,000–44,000 years ago. *Science* 330, 78–81.

Swadling, Pamela, Araho, Nick, and Ivuyo, Baiva. 1991 Settlements associated with the inland Sepik-Ramu Sea. *Indo-Pacific Prehistory Association Bulletin* 11, 92–112.

Swadling, Pamela, Chappell, John, Francis, Geoff, Araho, Nick, and Ivuyo, Baiva. 1989 A Late Quaternary inland sea and early pottery in Papua New Guinea. *Archaeology in Oceania* 24, 106–109.

Swadling, Pamela, and Hide, Robin. 2005 Changing landscape and social interaction, looking at agricultural history from a Sepik-Ramu perspective, in *Papuan Pasts: Studies in the Cultural, Linguistic and Biological History of the Papuan Speaking Peoples*, eds Pawley, Andrew, and Golson, Jack. Canberra: Pacific Linguistics, Research School of Pacific and Asian Studies, Australian National University, 289–327.

Swadling, Pamela, and Hope, Geoff. 1992 Environmental change in New Guinea since human settlement, in *The Naive Lands: Prehistory and Environmental Change in Australia and the Southwest Pacific*, ed. Dodson, John. Melbourne: Longman Cheshire, 13–41.

Tobler, Ray, Rohrlach, Adam, Soubrier, Julien, Bover, Pere, Llamas, Bastien, Tuke, Jonathan, Bean, Nigel, Abdullah-Highfold, Ali, Agius, Shane, O'Donoghue, Amy, O'Loughlin, Isabel, Sutton, Peter, Zilio, Fran, Walshe, Keryn, Williams, A., Turney, Chris, Williams, Martin, Richards, Stephan, Mitchell, Robert, Kowal, Emma, Stephen, John, Williams, Lesley, Haak, Wolfgang, and Cooper, Alan. 2017 Aboriginal mitogenomes reveal 50,000 years of regionalism in Australia. *Nature* 544, 180–184.

Torrence, Robin, Neall, Vince, Doelman, Trudy, Rhodes, Ed, McKee, Chris, Davies, Hugh, Bonetti, Robert, Guglielmetti, Alessandra, Manzoni, Alberto, Oddone, Massimo, Parr, Jeff, and Wallace, Cleland. 2004 Pleistocene colonisation of the Bismarck Archipelago: New evidence from West New Britain. *Archaeology in Oceania* 39, 101–130.

Vannieuwenhuyse, Dorcus, O'Connor, Sue, and Balme, Jane. 2017 Settling in Sahul: Investigating environmental and human history interactions through micromorphological analyses in tropical semi-arid north-west Australia. *Journal of Archaeological Science* 77, 172–193.

Vernot, Benjamin, Tucci, Serena, Kelso, Janet, Schraiber, Joshua, Wolff, Aaron, Gittelman, Rachel, Dannemann, Michael, Grote, Steffi, McCoy, Rajiv, Norton, Heather, Scheinfeldt, Laura, Merriwether, David, Koki, George, Friendlaender, Jonathan, Wakefield, Jon, Pääbo, Svante, and Akey, Josh. 2016 Excavating Neandertal and Denisovan DNA from the genomes of Melanesian individuals. *Science* 352, 235–239.

Warren, Matthew. 2019 Biggest Denisovan fossil yet spills ancient human's secrets. *Nature* 569(7754), May 2019, pp. 16+. *News in Focus.*

Wedage, Oshan, Amano, Noel, Langley, Michelle, Douka, Katerina, Blinkhorn, James, Crowther, Alison, Deraniyagala, Siran, Kourampas, Nikos, Simpson, Ian, Perera, Nimal, Picin, Andrea, Boivin, Nicole, Petraglia, Michael, and Roberts, Patrick. 2019 Specialized rainforest hunting by *Homo sapiens* ~45,000 years ago. *Nature Communications* 10, Article number 739.

White, J. Peter. 1972 *Ol Tumbuna: Archaeological Excavations in the eastern Central Highlands, Papua New Guinea.* Canberra: Terra Australis 2. The Australian National University.

White, J. Peter, Crook, Keith A. W., and Ruxton, Bruce P. 1970 Kosipe: A Pleistocene site in the Papua Highlands. *Proceedings of the Prehistoric Society* 36, 152–170.

Wickler, Steve. 1990 Prehistoric Melanesian exchange and interaction: Recent evidence from the Northern Solomon Islands. *Asian Perspectives* 29, 135–154.

Wickler, Steve. 2001 *The Prehistory of Buka: A Stepping Stone Island in the Northern Solomons.* Canberra: Terra Australis 16. Centre of Archaeological Research, Australian National University.

Wright, Duncan, Denham, Tim, Shine, Dennis, and Donohue, Mark. 2013 An archaeological review of Western New Guinea. *Journal of World Prehistory* 26, 25–73.

Zhang, Xiaolin L., Ha, B.B., Wang, Xiaomin, Chen, Zujun, Ge, Junyi, Long, Hao, He, Wei, Da, Wei, Nian, Xiao, Yi, Mingjie, Zhou, Xinying, Zhang, Po, Jin, Yoingshuai, Bar-Yosef, Ofer, Olsen, John, and Gao, Xing. 2018 The earliest human occupation of the high-altitude Tibetan Plateau 40,000 to 30,000 years ago. *Science* 362, 1049–1051.

# 7
# HUMAN DISPERSAL ACROSS SOUTHERN AND CENTRAL SAHUL

*Peter Hiscock and Kim Sterelny*

## Introduction

Humans discovered the ice age continent of Sahul sometime between 50,000 and 70,000 years ago. Their arrival marked a new step for *Homo sapiens*, as this was the first time our species colonised a new continent that was empty of other species of hominids. Humans landing on the continental shores explored lands that were not only unfamiliar but also unoccupied. They encountered no hominids who might compete with them, no environmental niches already constructed by hominid foragers, and no cultural markings of any kind across the landscape. Unlike the many places their ancestors had traversed on the journey from Africa this new land was vacant of hominid history and culture. Colonists found no sites, no artefacts, no marks to guide or limit their behaviour. While the colonists carried with them cultural practices and world views, in many ways this was still a 'new start', creating opportunities and challenges of a kind not met by their ancestors.

Sahul was an enormous, environmentally diverse landmass consisting of modern mainland Australia and the large islands of New Guinea and Tasmania as well as smaller islands, all of which were joined together by the massive exposed continental shelf when sea levels were much lower during the ice age (Figure 7.1). The distance across Sahul is so vast it was almost half as much again as the entire distance from Africa across West, South, East, and Southeast Asia to reach the edge of Sahul. That distance, and the environmental diversity contained within it, reminds us that arrival in Sahul was not the termination of dispersal but one of many nodes in a multi-generational journey of humans across the globe. And yet this node marked a new adaptive experience, as modern human forager groups occupied a land not only devoid of previous hominids but also one that was physically different in many ways from island and tropical Asian environments from which the colonists came. The arrival and spread of people across the diverse environments of central and southern Sahul was built on long-standing economic/social/strategies. Movement on this scale was possible only for agents who were organised, cooperative and technically adept (see Veth et al. 2011). But in the new contexts of Sahul, selection drove local evolution of novel technologies and social networks, a process that resulted in regional differentiation in cultural systems as foragers developed adaptations to diverse niches.

## The Arrival

There is no possibility of establishing the exact location and timing of human arrival in Sahul. All landing sites have been drowned by sea level rise during the deglacial period (roughly 16–7 kya). During the last Ice Age very large areas of the continental shelf were exposed by lower sea levels, which were most commonly 30–90 m below the current level. Across the northern half of what is now Australia (north of about 25°S) the coastline was often 200 km or more out to sea compared to today (see Figure 7.1). Unless colonists first landed on the northern edge of Sahul, they probably first lived somewhere on a coastal plain 1.3–1.4 million square kilometres in area, all of which is now underwater. We may never know where on this plain people first lived and we cannot currently calculate how long they lived exclusively on this plain

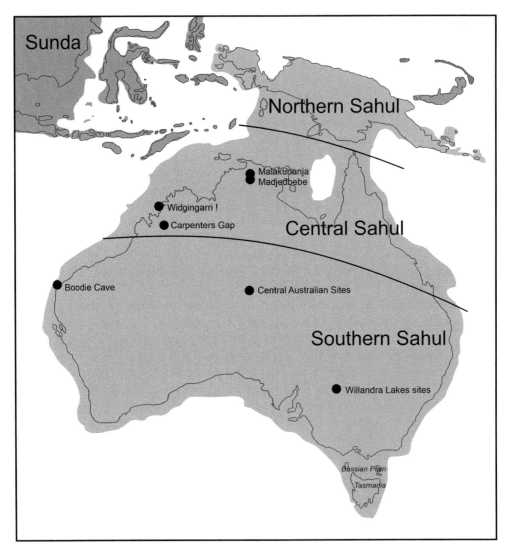

FIGURE 7.1   Location of Central and Southern Sahul, and of sites mentioned in the chapter.

before moving inland to regions that are today dry land. Early sites found on mainland Australia today represent dispersal of people from zones of initial colonisation to local areas. Hence the sites that have been found must represent a lower bound on the presence of humans in Sahul.

A second point about investigations of antiquity is the relatively low resolution of the dating techniques available to us. Luminescence, uranium and radiocarbon systems of age estimation have all been employed to date early traces of occupation in Sahul, and all have large statistical uncertainties of several thousand years associated with calculated estimates. Even when those dates are accurate, they are low resolution, and even in the very best of circumstances we can only argue that an ancient event probably occurred sometime in a window of 5–10,000 years, and circumstances are often less optimal than that. A significant factor complicating any interpretation of radiometric dates is the association between the object being dated and archaeological objects of interest. Most dating technologies that operate in the relevant time period measure alteration to an object (e.g. sand, charcoal) to identify their likely antiquity. But on most occasions, it is not those dated objects we want to interpret, it is nearby objects (e.g. stone, bone, or shell artefacts) that have distinctive cultural properties. In such cases the movement of objects through a deposit can bring cultural material and dated materials into physical association even though they are very different in age. Vertical movement might be common, and is regarded as a significant problem in sandy deposits in northern Australia. Hence the taphonomy of each deposit is scrutinised when discussing the antiquity of initial site occupation.

This potential for physical association to change over time has created extensive disputes about the true age of early sites. While even cautious interpretations accept that people were present in Sahul around 50,000 years ago, bolder interpretations accept substantially older occupation, as early as 60–70 kya. We consider this range of interpretations represent the plausible lower and upper values for the age of human colonisation of Australia. While sites with artefacts securely at levels about 50 kya will underestimate occupation antiquity because they measure local rather than continental occupation, some researchers argue that sites with estimates of 60–70 kya for occupation over-estimate the antiquity because possible downward vertical movement of artefacts may have associated cultural materials with older dated materials. We provide an example of sites in both these categories.

## The Cautious Estimate

A number of sites in Western Australia have provided evidence for human presence at approximately 50 kya (e.g. Veth et al. 2017; Norman et al. 2022). Our example is Boodie Cave on Barrow Island in northwest Australia (Figure 7.1). Barrow Island is the tip of a limestone hill that sat on the continental shelf, some 25–30 km inland from the ocean at 50 kya. At that time Boodie Cave looked out across 2,000 km$^2$ of sloping coastal plains, with the sea just over the horizon to the west. Anyone walking on that narrow coastal plain would have seen 'Barrow Hill', and the cave was probably visited by the earliest human foragers using this coastline. The cave is filled with over 2 m of sediments showing a series of well-defined strata differentiated by colour and texture (Veth et al. 2017). Sediment and geochemical analyses indicate limited vertical movement, and upper sediments indicate that there is little disturbance by biological agents in the internal portions of the deep cave, although luminescence signal indicates some post-depositional movement of grains. The deposit was dated with C14 or radiocarbon and optically stimulated luminescence (OSL) methods, and the base of the deposit was >70 kya. The lowest cultural materials (lithic artefacts and bone and shell) were recovered from strata estimated, with Bayesian analysis, as dating to 46.2–51.1 kya. This age range is considered by the researchers as conservative for the unit containing the lowest artefacts. That calculation excluded two samples that dated somewhat older. If those samples are included the stratigraphic unit containing the oldest artefacts is calculated to have begun accumulating 53,400 ± 6,900 years ago – which at even one standard deviation is a window of 46.5–60.3 kya for the start of that stratigraphic unit.

Dating at Boodie Cave illustrates the effect of large dating uncertainties on the precision of any estimate for occupation of a local region. There are two additional complexities in this case. The first is that the age estimates are for the initial deposition of the dated stratigraphic unit, and that event might not have coincided with the earliest phase of human occupation. If occupation of the cave commenced during the strata 7–8, and if there was also vertical movement of artefacts as seems possible, then the more conservative estimate of 46.2–51.1 kya is a safer conclusion. However, that is an estimate only for local occupation of a kind capable of leaving the faint record that has been discovered, and there is no reason this indicates the age at which humans arrived on the continent, perhaps thousands of kilometres to the north.

**A More Daring Estimate**

Claims for older sites are more complex to make, and are more controversial. We illustrate this by looking at the debate that has raged about the sandy deposits of Nauwalabila and Madjedbebe (also called Malakunanja II) in what is now northern Australia.

For more than three-quarters of a century we have known of the deep deposits found in sandstone rockshelters in Western Arnhem Land. Stone artefacts were found within sediments initially dated by luminescence techniques to about 53,000 years bp (47,500–57,500), and recently redated with samples taken from a new excavation in Madjedbebe (Roberts et al. 1993, 1994; Clarkson et al. 2017). Excavators of the site report a date of 59.3–70.7 kya (mid-point of 65 kya) for the base of the lowest dense band of artefacts, called Phase 2, and 48.4–57 kya (midpoint of 52.7 kya) for the sediments at the top of that band of artefacts (Clarkson et al. 2017). If the artefacts were deposited at the same time as the sediments these dates would indicate their antiquity. If we interpreted these specimens as approximately 53 kya or slightly older this would imply the cultural occupation was about the same age as other early sites reported in Central Sahul (see Norman et al. 2022). But the excavators inferred that at least some cultural debris was associated with the sediments at the base of that band, and therefore can be interpreted as the debris from multiple occupations sometimes between 59,000 and 71,000 years ago. This has been a more challenging claim.

The foundation of that claim is the assertion that artefacts and sediments are in their current association because they were syndepositional. Photographs of the strata show larger rocks associated with numerous artefacts in ways that suggest contemporary deposition as a 'living floor'. But this interpretation has been dismissed as unconvincing (e.g. O'Connell et al. 2018). So how would we know the association of artefacts and sediment samples was credible at Madjedbebe? Several approaches have been used to argue in favour of a syndepositional association. One was to simulate processes of vertical movement through the deposit by experimentally measuring the effects of humans walking on a sandy deposit, to evaluate the potential for human activity to induce downward movement of the artefacts (Marwick et al. 2017). The researchers concluded that specimens were unlikely to have moved more than 20 cm vertically, but their experiments were only 10–15 minutes long and in that short time most artefacts had moved, some more than

5 cm. This evidence gives no reason to think that extensive vertical movement had not happened at Madjedbebe. Moreover, O'Connell et al. (2018) point to artefacts well below the level of Phase 2, in levels the excavators concluded was pre-human – an observation that demonstrates extensive vertical movements of at least some artefacts. Madjedbebe is therefore a deposit in which vertical movement has repositioned artefacts, and so it is possible that artefacts in the Phase 2 band are not syndepositional with dated samples and may be less than 60 kya, a point made at length by O'Connell et al. (2018).

What then is the age of the artefacts in Phase 2 at Madjedbebe? One sceptical view is that they may be only 50 kya and not much older. However, we cannot reliably infer a precise date for every specimen: it is likely that some artefacts have moved downward more than others, and we cannot specify from what level or age each specimen originally derived prior to vertical movement. The result is that we cannot conclude with any confidence that all specimens in Phase 2 moved downwards from levels aged 50 kya or younger, and nor can we conclude that none moved downwards from such levels. We can therefore neither refute nor unambiguously confirm that some artefacts are older than 50–55 kya, and so consider that on current evidence the site is highly likely to indicate human occupation at 50 kya, and possibly at 55 kya or earlier.

Our more general point is that dating must be evaluated independently at each site. Convincing evidence that Nauwalabila dated to earlier than 60 kya would not support a similar interpretation of Madjedbebe, though it would show that it could be as old.

For dated sites to be data, each date must have independent warrant. We do want to identify and not be misled by dates that are inaccurate, but if in the process of doing that we 'disqualify' dates that are accurate we risk entertaining a systemic bias that eliminates some accurate dates merely because they are unlike others. To exclude atypically old or young sites, on the basis of their difference to an apparent general pattern risks potentially disconfirming evidence. This has been a problem for other debates in Australia, where the disqualification from analyses of unexpectedly old dates, ensured that models of rapid and later social/economic/technological changes appeared to be supported (see Hiscock and Attenbrow 1998). In a similar way, elimination of sites for which there are claims of atypically old human occupation in Sahul would have the effect of pseudo-confirming models of relatively late colonisation and very rapid dispersal. Exclusion of sites or dates that contravene general patterns has sometimes been justified as a process that ensures 'chronometric hygiene' (e.g. Spriggs 1989; Anderson 1991; Spriggs and Anderson 1993; Higham and Hogg 2006; Hunt and Lipo 2008; Taché and Hart 2013; Schmid et al. 2019; Napolitano et al. 2019). In reality it ensures conformity to particular models by eliminating data points which are inconsistent with that model, thereby diminishing the potential to refute that model (e.g. Burley et al. 2015). For that reason, we treat sites like Madjedbebe, for which robust interpretation is currently uncertain, as latent tests of existing models.

## Molecular Dating Sets an Upper Limit of Human Arrival in Sahul

Molecular dating involves the study of genetic differences between individuals to estimate elapsed time since past events, such as the last common ancestor of two individuals within a species or the introgression of genes from a different species. These estimates vary because of differences in the component of the genome being used, calculated rate of change in the genome, assumptions built into the calculation, samples being employed, and other factors. Molecular dating is a complex artform and sensitive to many assumptions about population size and structure that create model mis-specification (see Bromham and Penny 2003; Bromham et al.

2017; Scerri et al. 2018; Bromham 2019). That complexity results in different estimates from different research groups, with common estimates changing over time, exactly as we would expect from a rapidly developing field of science. Given the intricacy and dynamics of molecular dating there is an unwise risk in picking a single estimate, and then analysing all data in terms of that estimate. We see that in attempts to constrain Sahul colonisation dates by molecular clock estimates of human movement out of Africa.

Humans could not have arrived in Sahul before they exited Africa. But what age is that? One commonly discussed age-range for modern human dispersal beyond Africa is 50 kya or slightly earlier. That figure has sometimes been used as the maximum possible date for Sahul colonisation. For instance, O'Connell et al. (2018) argue that almost all geneticists had concluded that both 'near-modern' or modern humans were restricted to Africa and nearby portions of Southwest Asia until 50–55 kya. Given the huge distances to be travelled from there to the coasts of East Asia and Australia, those dates imply that East Asia and Australasia could not have been occupied until at least a few thousand years later.

And yet, a 50–55 kya window for modern humans leaving Africa is far from the consensus among genetic researchers, and most estimates in recent literature are larger windows that extend further back in time. For example, some researchers propose an exit from Africa between 45 kya and 65 kya (e.g. Sun et al. 2021), others between 50 kya and 70 kya (e.g. Malaspinas et al. 2016; Hallast et al. 2021), and still others between 60 kya and 80 kya (e.g. Lipson et al. 2020; Montinaro et al. 2021. The common ancestor of non-African people, who carry the L3 lineage of mtDNA, has been estimated as 62.4–94.9 kya (95% HPD, i.e. highest posterior density), and interpreted as the age range in which movement of *H. sapiens* into Eurasia probably occurred (Fu et al. 2013a,b).

These different estimates do not identify a single small window in which global migrations were initiated, instead published estimates for large scale movements from Africa and Western Asia range from 40 kya to 85–90 kya (e.g. Henn et al. 2012; Fu et al. 2013b; Schiffels and Durbin 2014; Mallick et al. 2016; Lipson et al. 2020; Montinaro et al. 2021). These varying estimates are not only different, they all present much larger uncertainties than the one offered by O'Connell et al. (2018).

The situation has become even more challenging for any simple specification of an Out-of-Africa chronology, because evidence is emerging for two or more 'late' migrations from Africa, with movement back into Africa between those phases, and perhaps a global dispersal of modern humans beginning from western Asia about 60 kya (Cabrera et al. 2018). We discuss some of the implications of these interpretations in greater detail in Chapter 1. Here our point is merely that there is no single, high-resolution window for the departure of humans from Africa identified from molecular evidence. While the Out-of-Africa chronology is a constraint on the maximum age of human colonisation of Sahul, that chronology is too open to refute the models being discussed for Australian archaeological evidence. We see no genomic evidence that conflicts with robust archaeological evidence for human presence in Australia approximately 50–55 kya, and the possibility of even older occupation should not be rejected.

## Human Dispersal across Central and Southern Sahul

We have no reliable information about where on the continent the first humans arrived. Researchers commonly assert that the landing places were most likely on the coast of northern or central Sahul, and we agree, but that proposition is based on little more than their geographical proximity to Southeast Asia. In the same way there have been many discussions, over the last half century, of the likely pathways by which humans may have travelled to Australia. These also are based on simple proposition that people might have chosen the shortest, easiest, safest pathways. The assumption that agents minimise costs, including risk costs, is sound. But to minimise travel costs agents need information about landscapes that only comes from traversing them. Moreover, risk and cost is sensitive to agents' technical equipment and ecological knowledge.

After people arrived in Sahul their descendants dispersed across the continent. Several models have hypothesised a directionality and speed for that dispersal. Each model advocates a different dispersal process, each based on a claim that the proposed mode of dispersal required the least economic adjustment to pre-existing strategies. These proposals all suppose that the colonising foragers were adapted to a specific niche, diversifying only when they could not expand within the preferred niche. The logic was the same, but each model substituted a different niche/resource. For example, the coastal first model hypothesised that humans spread around the entire continental margins as these had traditionally targeted marine environments and their resources, expanding inland only after all coastal landscapes were occupied (Bowdler 1977). A 'woodland first' model hypothesised that people dispersed southwards through woodlands, before spreading to southern coasts and deserts (Horton 1981), and a 'waterway' model hypothesised groups dispersed from the north following inlands waterways or surface water availability, before spreading out into other regions (Bird et al. 2016).

There was one contrasting model which was if anything even less nuanced, a saturation model. This hypothesised rapid and nearly linear spreads of people in all directions from the point of landing, irrespective of the kind of environment encountered (Birdsell 1977). This model inverts the logic of other models by presuming there was no difference in learning cost and no variation in economic efficiency for groups adapting to different environments and resources. Birdsell invoked persistent population increase as the mechanism driving saturation, leading to stress on local resources and social lives, and creating group fissioning as portions of the group moved into unoccupied lands. However, differences in resource productivity/accessibility combined with varied costs of movement through environments makes it likely that a simple saturation model will display faster dispersal through some niches.

These models capture genuine possibilities, but which if any is supported by evidence? All make testable predictions, most unable to be tested at the moment. For much of the early history of Sahul, we have few sites, perhaps none, and depending on whether the cautious (c.50 kya) or bold (>55 kya) estimates of known site occupation are employed, we might be looking at five or even ten thousand years of occupation for which we have little evidence. We do not even have a known starting point for dispersal(s), or reliably defined horizons for human appearance in multiple regions, and so models must incorporate multiple variants to accommodate the partial data with which we work. For that reason, we will not nominate a preferred dispersal model.

There are however some constraints on a viable model. There is abundant evidence from many locations of a human presence between 40 and 45,000 year ago; Arnhem Land, the arid centre, desert northwest, arid southeast, forested southwest, inland northeast, Tasmania and so on. These dates set a minimum age for the completion of continent-wide dispersal and eliminate any model which predicts that entire bioregions were not occupied until substantially later. This refutes the original formulation of the coastal model, in which people did not move inland until deglacial sea level rise forced them too, and any coastal-first dispersion model must now be configured as a process completed before 45–50 kya.

Dispersal to most bioregions had largely been completed by 45–50,000 kya, implying that economy and land use had by that date adapted to regionally diverse environments, from tropical woodlands to dense temperate forests, from isolated upland deserts to chains of lakes in semi-arid plains. Tasmania was not occupied until closer to 40 kya, when dropping sea level re-joined it to the mainland, but the dense lowland forests and alpine uplands of Tasmania were quickly occupied once the Bassian Plain connected that island to the mainland. Early ecological breadth tends to count against claims that early economies were single purpose and that people were tethered to one niche such as the coast, or woodlands, or major waterways. It is unlikely that human groups spread across the continent exploiting a single niche. It is more likely that human groups dispersed through multiple very different niches at any one time. That pattern within Sahul would then have shared many similarities with the dispersal of *H. sapiens* from Africa: foragers operating with multiple economic strategies, rather than maintaining a single unvarying adaptive strategy throughout the myriad niches involved.

### Cultural Consequences of Multiple Niches

Early settlement of distinctly different niches across Sahul would have led to diversification. Regional distinctions in mitogenomes suggest long term biological divergence between regions, perhaps involving drift, positive selection and low levels of inter-regional gene flow (Tobler et al. 2017). Cultural diversification is recorded in regional archaeological records. As groups occupying the diverse landscapes across the continent developed economic, technological, and social strategies to more effectively live in the environments in which they were situated, their behavioural systems would have gradually diverged. The result would have been the production of regionally different lifeways and norms, which in turn would have facilitated the emergence of even more novel technologies and economic and social systems. We see this process in novel and geographically bounded technologies in a few early sites that reveal the presence of both novelty and regional differentiation, perhaps even before dispersal was complete. The regionality of technology is maintained, and well documented, for the period 35–45 ka, when preserved site abundance increases.

An earlier generation of scholars imagined early human settlers in Sahul as conservative, employing a uniform, generalised, technology, and foraging strategy in all contexts (see Hiscock 2008). This idea is present in dispersion models that argue early dispersion relied on a single kind of resource/niche across the continent, and it is also embedded in many interpretations of human activities, especially in the well-preserved technology represented by stone artefacts. However the archaeological evidence being recovered from Pleistocene sites does not support uniformity or simplicity, rather it reveals localised development of technologies. A dramatic example of local adaptation, and consequently regional diversification, of tools is the Pleistocene distribution of Ground-Edge Artefacts (GEA), also sometimes called axe or hatchet heads.

We have known for half a century that GEA were present in Central Sahul for far longer than either Southern Sahul or Northern Sahul. It is now clear that GEA are found near the basal layers of archaeological sequences in sites in tropical Australia (Hiscock et al. 2016; Clarkson et al. 2017; Norman et al. 2022; see also Morwood and Trezise 1989; Geneste et al. 2010, 2012). GEA are older in Central Sahul than anywhere else in the world, and are likely to be an invention developed in that area shortly after colonisation. Pleistocene GEA are very similar in size and shape to recent ones in the same region, and are likely to have been hafted rather like recent versions. They are the earliest evidence of composite tools in Australia. Dispersing *H. sapiens* probably had skill in hafting techniques (e.g. Barham 2013; Blinkhorn 2019). Invention of composite ground-edged percussive tools in Central Sahul was likely scaffolded by experimentally adapting existing hafting procedures for a new tool in a new landscape.

Holocene GEA in central and southern Sahul are known to have been hafted and multifunctional (e.g. Attenbrow and Kononenko 2019), and were employed as portable yet extremely long-lived tools that could be used for many resource procurement tasks, making them a means of buffering uncertainty and risk during foraging. Those qualities would have been valuable in the initial settlement of unfamiliar environments, like the woodlands and savannas of central Sahul. GEA may well be one of a number of foundational technologies developed to help initial exploration of unfamiliar niches in the continent.

Ground edged artefacts illustrate regional divergence in Sahul during MIS3 (Marine Isotope Stage 3). From at least c.50 kya until the Holocene GEA were restricted to Central Sahul and were absent from regions both to the south and north. To the north there were large unground but sharp and likely hafted percussive stone heads, and to the south there were no GEA or comparable unground hafted percussive tools that we know of until less than 4 kya (Ford and Hiscock 2021). The axe record shows strikingly stable regional differentiation, with these axes being made in some biogeographical regions but not in adjacent ones for perhaps as long as 45 millennia. Such long-standing cultural differences between regions in Sahul must have been based on persistent differences in not merely tool use and resource use but on broader social differences, perhaps identity based and scaffolded by differences in language and cultural practice. In the historic period these kinds of boundaries existed within Sahul, such as the broad geographical distinction between Pama–Nyungan languages in southern and eastern Australia and Non-Pama–Nyungan languages within north and northwestern historic Australia, or the cultural barriers to technology transmission across Torres Strait that kept bow and arrow technology from New Guinea out of Australia. Those recent cultural differences may not be good proxies for the Pleistocene geographical boundaries, but they emphasise the plausibility of long-lived blocs of culture and technology in a continent of foragers. The persistence of a bounded GEA distribution during the Pleistocene is not explained by physical barriers. A variety of factors probably contributed to the stability of these techno-social blocks, including patterns of technological transmission, population distributions and densities, local functional cost/benefits, and the history of settlement. Investigating the stability of these regional differences will help reveal something of the character of that early period.

Progressive MIS3 regional diversification is also seen in evidence of heat treatment that altered the character of stone materials used in artefact manufacture. Data from three regional sequences in southern Sahul (East coast, Willandra Lakes, and Central Australia) stretch back to 25–40 ka. Early assemblages in each region show high levels of heat treatment. Over time the stoneworking systems in each region evolved differently. In the Willandra lakes heat treatment declined until it all but disappeared (Schmidt and Hiscock 2020a). In Central Australia heat treatment declined somewhat but stayed at moderate levels until the historical period (Schmidt and Hiscock 2002b). On the Eastern seaboard the rate of heat treatment went up over time until in recent millennia it became the typical mode of manufacture (Schmidt and Hiscock 2019). These divergent trends reflect the different optimisation over time of technological process in response to local conditions.

A third example of regional differentiation is the presence of public signalling with shell and bone beads in the northwestern regions of southern Sahul (e.g. Balme and Morse 2015). The beads are made from different materials at different sites but were clearly associated with distinctive, ochre coloured jewellery used to send social signals. Organic beads of this kind have not been found elsewhere in the country during the Pleistocene, despite some locations having excellent organic preservation. Elsewhere is Sahul there was undoubtedly public signalling, with materials such as ochre being found in deposits, used to paint rock surfaces, and scattered on buried bodies in regions such as the Willandra Lakes (e.g. Bowler and Thorne 1976; Bowler et al. 2003; Hiscock 2008). It seems that by 30–40 ka there was regional differentiation in public signalling systems. This use of symbols was common among dispersing humans 40,000–60,000 years ago (Kuhn et al. 2001), and was probably a feature of foragers who colonised Australia. Most likely the differentiation had begun soon after people dispersed across Sahul.

## Conclusion

Archaeological evidence now supports an initial human occupation of Southern and Central Sahul before 50 kya. Based on current archaeological evidence and geographic proximity it is likely that colonisation occurred somewhere in the north or northwest of the continent. Existing dating does not indicate when internal dispersal began or the speed at which people spread across the continent. However, it is clear that most biogeographic regions in central and southern Sahul were occupied before 45 ka, and that dispersing groups were not likely to have spread by filling only one kind of environment or targeting one kind of resource. Instead, it is more likely that foragers dispersed by adapting to adjacent patches with somewhat different environmental profiles, thus progressively but incrementally adapting to multiple very different bioregions. That adaptation to different landscapes was associated with increased behavioural diversity as human groups developed different economic, technological, and social practices. The result seems to have been techno-social blocks of surprisingly longevity.

## References

Anderson, Atholl. 1991 The chronology of colonization in New Zealand. *Antiquity* 65, 767–95.
Attenbrow, Val, and Kononenko, Nina. 2019 Microscopic revelations: The forms and multiple uses of ground-edged artefacts of the New South Wales Central Coast, Australia. *Technical Reports of the Australian Museum Online* 29, 1–100.
Balme, Jane, and Morse, Kate. 2015 Shell beads and social behaviour in Pleistocene Australia. *Antiquity* 80, 799–811.
Barham, Lawrence. 2013 *From Hand to Handle: The First Industrial Revolution.* Oxford University Press.
Bird, Michael, O'Grady, Damien, and Ulm, Sean. 2016 Humans, water, and the colonization of Australia. *Proceedings of the National Academy of Sciences* 113, 11477–82.
Birdsell, Joseph. 1977 The recalibration of a paradigm for the first peopling of greater Australia, in *Sunda and Sahul: Prehistoric Studies in Southeast Asia, Melanesia and Australia*, eds Allen, Jim, Golson, Jack, and Jones, Rhys. London: Academic Press, 113–67.
Blinkhorn, James. 2019 Examining the origins of hafting in South Asia. *Journal of Paleolithic Archaeology* 2, 466–81.
Bowdler, Sandra. 1977 The coastal colonisation of Australia, in *Sunda and Sahul: Prehistoric Studies in Southeast Asia, Melanesia and Australia*, eds Allen, Jim, Golson, Jack, and Jones, Rhys. London: Academic Press, 205–46.
Bowler, Jim, and Thorne, Alan. 1976 Human remains from Lake Mungo: Discovery and excavation of Lake Mungo III, in *The Origin of the Australians*, eds Kirk, Richard and Thorne, Alan. Canberra: Australian Institute of Aboriginal Studies Press, 127–38.
Bowler, Jim, Johnston, Harvey, Olley, John, Prescott, John, Roberts, Richard, Shawcross, Wilfred, and Spooner, Nigel. 2003 New ages for human occupation and climatic change at Lake Mungo, Australia. *Nature* 421, 837–40.

Bromham, Lindell. 2019 Six impossible things before breakfast: Assumptions, models, and belief in molecular dating. *Trends in Ecology and Evolution* 34, 474–86.

Bromham, Lindell, Duchêne, Sebastián, Hua, Xia, Ritchie, Andrew, Duchêne, David, and Ho, Simon. 2017 Bayesian molecular dating: Opening up the black box. *Biology Review: Cambridge Philosophical Society* 93, 1165–91.

Bromham, Lindell, and Penny, David. 2003 The modern molecular clock. *National Review of Genetics* 4, 216–24.

Burley, David, Edinborough, Kevan, Weisler, Marshall, and Zhao, Jian-xin. 2015 Bayesian modeling and chronological precision for Polynesian settlement of Tonga. *PLoS ONE* 10, e0120795. https://doi.org/10.1371/journal.pone.0120795

Cabrera, Vicente, Marrero, Patricia, Abu-Amero, Khaled, and Larruga, Jose. 2018 Carriers of mitochondrial DNA macrohaplogroup L3 basal lineages migrated back to Africa from Asia around 70,000 years ago. *BMC Evolutionary Biology* 18. https://doi.org/10.1186/s12862-018-1211-4

Clarkson, Chris, Jacobs, Zenobia, Marwick, Ben, Fullagar, Richard, Wallis, Lynley, Smith, Mike, Roberts, Richard, Hayes, Elspeth, Lowe, Kelsey, Carah, Xavier, Florin, Anna, McNeil, Jessica, Cox, Delyth, Arnold, Lee, Hua, Quan, Huntley, Jillian, Brand, Helen, Manne, Tiina, Fairbairn, Andrew, Shulmeister, James, Lyle, Lindsey, Salinas, Makiah, Page, Mara, Connell, Kate, Park, Gayoung, Norman, Kasih, Murphy, Tessa, and Pardoe, Colin. 2017 Human occupation of northern Australia by 65,000 years ago. *Nature* 547, 306–310.

Ford, Anne, and Hiscock, Peter. 2021 Axe quarrying, production and exchange in Australia and new Guinea, in *The Oxford Handbook of the Archaeology of Indigenous Australia and New Guinea*, eds McNiven, Ian, and David, Bruno. Oxford: Oxford University Press.

Fu, Qiaomei, Meyer, Matthias, Gao, Xing, Stenzel, Udo, Burbano, Harnan, Kelso, Janet, and Pääbo, Svante. 2013a DNA analysis of an early modern human from Tianyuan cave, China. *Proceedings of the National Academy of Science* 110, 2223–7.

Fu, Qiaomei, Mittnik, Alissa, Johnson, Philip, Bos, Kirsten, Lari, Martina, Ruth, Bollongino, Sun, Chengkai, Giemsch, Liane, Schmitz, Ralf, Burger, Joachim, Ronchitelli, Anna, Martini, Fabio, Cremonesi, Renata, Svoboda, Jiri, Bauer, Peter, Caramelli, David, Castellano, Sergi, Reich, David, Pabo, Svante, and Krause, Johannes. 2013b A revised timescale for human evolution based on ancient mitochondrial genomes. *Current Biology* 23, 553–9.

Geneste, Jean-Michel, David, Bruno, Plisson, Hugues, Clarkson, Chris, Delannoy, Jean-Jacques, Petchey, Fiona, and Whear, Ray. 2010 Earliest evidence for ground-edge axes: 35,400 ± 410 cal BP from Jawoyn country, Arnhem land. *Australian Archaeology* 71, 66–9.

Geneste, Jean-Michel, David, Bruno, Plisson, Hugues, Delannoy, Jean-Jacques, and Petchey, Fiona. 2012 The origins of ground-edge axes: New findings from Nawarla Gabarnmang, Arnhem land (Australia) and global implications for the evolution of fully modern humans. *Cambridge Archaeological Journal* 22, 1–17.

Hallast, Pille, Agdzhoyan, Anastasia, Balanovsky, Oleg, Xue, Yali, and Tyler-Smith, Chris. 2021 A southeast Asian origin for present-day non-African human Y chromosomes. *Human Genetics* 140, 299–307.

Henn, Brenna, Cavalli-Sforza, Luigi, and Feldman, Marcus. 2012 The great human expansion. *Proceedings of the National Academy of Science* 109, 17758–64.

Higham, Thomas, and Hogg, Alan. 2006 Evidence for late Polynesian colonization of New Zealand: University of Waikato radiocarbon measurements. *Radiocarbon* 39(2), 149–192. https://doi.org/10.1017/S0033822200051997

Hiscock, Peter. 2008 *Archaeology of Ancient Australia*. London: Routledge.

Hiscock, Peter, and Attenbrow, Val. 1998 Early Holocene backed artefacts from Australia. *Archaeology in Oceania* 33, 49–63.

Hiscock, Peter, O'Connor, Sue, Balme, Jane, and Maloney, Tim. 2016 World's earliest ground-edge axe production coincides with human colonisation of Australia. *Australian Archaeology* 82, 2–11.

Horton, David. 1981 Water and woodland: The peopling of Australia. *Australian Institute of Aboriginal Studies Newsletter* 16, 21–7.

Hunt, Terry, and Lipo, Carl. 2008 Evidence for a shorter chronology on Rapa Nui (Easter Island). *The Journal of Island and Coastal Archaeology* 3, 140–8.

Kuhn, Steven, Stiner, Mary, Reese, David, and Güleç, Erksin. 2001 Ornaments of the earliest Upper Paleolithic: New insights from the Levant. *Proceedings of the National Academy of Sciences*. 98, 7641–6.

Lipson, Mark, Ribot, Isabelle, Mallick, Swapan, Rohland, Nadin, Olalde, Iñigo, Adamski, Nicole, Broomandkhoshbacht, Nasreen, Lawson, Ann, López, Saioa, Oppenheimer, Jonas, Stewardson,

Kristin, Asombang, Raymond, Bocherens, Hervé, Bradman, Neil, Culleton, Brendan, Cornelissen, Els, Crevecoeur, Isabelle, de Maret, Pierre, Fomine, Forka, Lavachery, Philippe, Mindzie, Christophe, Orban, Rosine, Sawchuk, Elizabeth, Semal, Patrick, Thomas, Mark, Van Neer, Wim, Veeramah, Krishna, Kennett, Douglas, Patterson, Nick, Hellenthal, Garrett, Lalueza-Fox, Carles, MacEachern, Scott, Prendergast, Mary, and Reich, David. 2020 Ancient West African foragers in the context of African population history. *Nature* 577, 665–70.

Malaspinas, Anna-Sapfo, Westaway, Michael, Muller, Craig, Sousa, Vitor, Lao, Oscar, Alves, Isabel, Bergström, Anders, Athanasiadis, Georgios, Cheng, Jade, Crawford, Jacob, Heupink, Tim, Macholdt, Enrico, Peischl, Stephan, Rasmussen, Simon, Schiffels, Stephan, Subramanian, Sankar, Wright, Joanne, Albrechtsen, Anders, Barbieri, Chiara, Dupanloup, Isabelle, Eriksson, Anders, Margaryan, Ashot, Moltke, Ida, Pugach, Irina, Korneliussen, Thorfinn, Levkivskyi, Ivan, Moreno-Mayar, Víctor, Ni, Shengyu, Racimo, Fernando., Sikora, Martin, Xue, Yali, Aghakhanian, Farhang, Brucato, Nicolas, Brunak, Søren, Campos, Paula, Clark, Warren, Ellingvåg, Sturla, Fourmile, Gudjugudju, Gerbault, Pascale, Injie, Darren, Koki, George, Leavesley, Matthew, Logan, Betty, Lynch, Aubrey, Matisoo-Smith, Elizabeth, McAllister, Peter, Mentzer, Alexander, Metspalu, Mait, Migliano, Andrea, Murgha, Les, Phipps, Maude, Pomat, William, Reynolds, Doc, Ricaut, Francois-Xavier, Siba, Peter, Thomas, Mark, Wales, Thomas, Wall, Colleen, Oppenheimer, Stephen, Tyler-Smith, Chris, Durbin, Richard, Dortch, Joe, Manica, Andrea, Schierup, Mikkel, Foley, Robert, Lahr, Marta, Bowern, Claire, Wall, Jeffrey, Mailund, Thomas, Stoneking, Mark, Nielsen, Rasmus, Sandhu, Manjinder, Excoffier, Laurent, Lambert, David, and Willerslev, Eske. 2016 A genomic history of Aboriginal Australia. *Nature* 538, 207–14.

Mallick, Swapan, Li, Heng, Lipson, Mark, Mathieson, Iain, Gymrek, Melissa, Racimo, Fernando, Zhao, Mengyao, Chennagiri, Niru, Nordenfelt, Susanne, Tandon, Arti, Skoglund, Pontus, Lazaridis, Iosif, Sankararaman, Sriram, Fu, Qiaomei, Rohland, Nadin, Renaud, Gabriel, Erlich, Yaniv, Willems, Thomas, Gallo, Carla, Spence, Jeffrey, Song, Yun, Poletti, Giovanni, Balloux, Francois, van Driem, George, de Knijff, Peter, Romero, Irene, Jha, Aashish, Behar, Doron, Bravi, Claudio, Capelli, Cristian, Hervig, Tor, Moreno-Estrada, Andres, Posukh, Olga, Balanovska, Elena, Balanovsky, Oleg, Karachanak-Yankova, Sena, Sahakyan, Hovhannes, Toncheva, Draga, Yepiskoposyan, Levon, Tyler-Smith, Chris, Xue, Yali, Abdullah, Syafiq, Ruiz-Linares, Andres, Beall, Cynthia, Di Rienzo, Anna, Jeong, Choongwon, Starikovskaya, Elena, Metspalu, Ene, Parik, Jüri, Villems, Richard, Henn, Brenna, Hodoglugil, Ugur, Mahley, Robert, Sajantila, Antti, Stamatoyannopoulos, George, Wee, Joseph, Khusainova, Elza, Khusnutdinova, Rita, Litvinov, Sergey, Ayodo, George, Comas, David, Hammer, Michael, Kivisild, Toomas, Klitz, William, Winkler, Cheryl, Labuda, Damian, Bamshad, Michael, Jorde, Lynn, Tishkoff, Sarah, Watkins, Scott, Metspalu, Mait, Dryomov, Stanislav, Sukernik, Rem, Singh, Lalji, Thangaraj, Kumarasamy, Pääbo, Svante, Kelso, Janet, Patterson, Nick, and Reich, David. 2016 The Simons genome diversity project: 300 genomes from 142 diverse populations. *Nature* 538, 201–6.

Marwick, Ben, Hayes, Elspeth, Clarkson, Chris, and Fullagar, Richard. 2017 Movement of lithics by trampling: An experiment in the Madjedbebe sediments, northern Australia. *Journal of Archaeological Science* 79, 73–85.

Montinaro, Francesco, Pankratov, Vasili, Yelmen, Burak, Pagani, Luca, and Mondal1, Mayukh. 2021 Revisiting the Out of Africa event with a deep learning approach. *The American Journal of Human Genetics* 108, 2037–51.

Morwood, Michael, and Trezise, Percy. 1989 Edge-ground axes in Pleistocene Australia: New evidence from southeast Cape York Peninsula. *Queensland Archaeological Research* 6, 77–90.

Napolitano, Matthew, Dinapoli, Robert, Stone, Jessica., Levin, Maureece., Jew, Nicholas, Lane, Brian, O'connor, John, and Fitzpatrick, Scott. 2019 Reevaluating human colonization of the Caribbean using chronometric hygiene and Bayesian modelling. *Science Advances* 5. https://doi.org/10.1126/sciadv.aar7806

Norman, Kasih, Shipton, Ceri, O'Connor, Sue, Malanali, Wudugu, Collins, Peter, Wood, Rachel, Saktura, Wanchese, Roberts, Richard, and Jacobs, Zenobia. 2022 Human occupation of the Kimberley coast of northwest Australia 50,000 years ago. *Quaternary Science Reviews* 288, 107577.

O'Connell, James, Allen, Jim, Williams, Martin, Williams, Alan, Turney, Chris, Spooner, Nigel, Kamming, Johan, Brown, Graham, and Cooper, Alan. 2018 When did homo sapiens first reach Southeast Asia and Sahul? *PNAS* 115, 8482–90.

Roberts, Richard, Jones, Rhys, and Smith, Mike. 1993 Optical dating at Deaf Adder Gorge, Northern Territory, indicates human occupation between 53,000 and 60,000 years ago. *Australian Archaeology* 37: 58–9.

Roberts, Richard, Jones, Rhys, Spooner, Nigel, Head, John, Murray, A., and Smith, Mike. 1994 'The human colonisation of Australia: optical dates of 53,000 and 60,000 years bracket human arrival at Deaf Adder Gorge, Northern Territory', *Quaternary Geochronology, Quaternary Science Reviews* 13: 575–83.

Scerri, Eleanor, Thomas, Mark, Manica, Andrea, Gunz, Philipp, Stock, Jay, Stringer, Chris, Grove, Matt, Groucutt, Huw, Timmermann, Axel, Rightmire, Philip, d'Errico, Francesco, Tryon, Christian, Drake, Nick, Brooks, Alison, Dennell, Robin, Durbin, Richard, Henn, Brenna, Lee-Thorp, Julia, de Menocal, Peter, Petraglia, Michael, Thompson, Jessica, Scally, Aylwyn, and Chikhi, Lounès. 2018 Did our species evolve in subdivided populations across Africa, and why does it matter? *Trends in Ecology and Evolution* 33, 582–94.

Schiffels, Stephan, and Durbin, Richard. 2014 Inferring human population size and separation history from multiple genome sequences. *Nature Genetics* 46, 919–25.

Schmid, Magdalena, Wood, Rachel, Newton, Anthony, Vésteinsson, Orri, and Dugmore, Andrew. 2019 Enhancing radiocarbon chronologies of colonization: Chronometric hygiene revisited. *Radiocarbon* 61, 629–47.

Schmidt, P., and Hiscock, P. 2019 Evolution of silcrete heat treatment in Australia – A regional pattern on the south-east coast and its evolution over the last 25 ka. *Journal of Paleolithic Archaeology* 2, 74–97.

Schmidt, Patrick, and Hiscock, Peter. 2020a The antiquity of Australian silcrete heat treatment: Lake Mungo and the Willandra Lakes. *Journal of Human Evolution*. 142. https://doi.org/10.1016/j.jhevol.2020.102744

Schmidt, Patrick, and Hiscock, Peter. 2020b Early silcrete heat treatment in Central Australia: Puritjarra and Kulpi Mara. *Archaeological and Anthropological Sciences* 12, 188. https://doi.org/10.1007/s12520-020-01163-6

Spriggs, Matthew. 1989 The dating of the Island Southeast Asian Neolithic: An attempt at chronometric hygiene and linguistic correlation. *Antiquity* 63, 587–613.

Spriggs, Matthew, and Anderson, Atholl. 1993 Late colonisation of East Polynesia. *Antiquity* 67, 200–17.

Sun, Xue-feng, Wen, Shao-qing, Lu, Cheng-qiu, Zhou, Bo-yan, Curnoe, Darren, Lu, Hua-yu, Hong-chun, Li, Wang, Wei, Cheng, Hai, Yi, Shuang-wen, Jia, Xin, Du, Pan-xin, Xu, Xing-hua, Lu, Yi-ming, Lu, Ying, Zheng, Hong-xiang, Zhang, Hong, Sun, Chang Wei, Lan-hai, Han, Fei, Huang, Juan, Edwards, Lawrence, Jin, Li, and Li, Hui. 2021 Ancient DNA and multimethod dating confirm the late arrival of anatomically modern humans in southern China. *Proceedings of the National Academy of Science* 2021, e2019158118.

Taché, Karine, and Hart, John. 2013 Chronometric hygiene of radiocarbon databases for early durable cooking vessel technologies in Northeastern North America. *American Antiquity* 78, 359–72.

Tobler, Ray, Rohrlach, Adam, Soubrier, Julien, Bover, Pere, Llamas, Bastien, Tuke, Jonathan, Bean, Nigel, Abdullah-Highfold, Ali, Agius, Shane, O'Donoghue, Amy, O'Loughlin, Isabel, Sutton, Peter, Zilio, Fran, Walshe, Keryn, Williams, Alan, Turney, Chris, Williams, Matthew, Richards, Stephen, Mitchell, Robert, Kowal, Emma, Stephen, John, Williams, Lesley, Haak, Wolfgang, and Cooper, Alan. 2017 Aboriginal mitogenomes reveal 50,000 years of regionalism in Australia. *Nature* 544, 180–4.

Veth, Peter, Stern, Nicola, McDonald, Josephine, Balme, Jane, and Iain, Davidson. 2011 The role of information exchange in the colonisation of Sahul, in *Information and Its Role in Hunter-Gatherer Bands*, eds Whallon, Robert, Lovis, William, and Hitchcock, Robert. Cotsen: Institute of Archaeology Press, 203–20.

Veth, Peter, Ward, Ingrid, Manne, Tiina, Ulm, Sean, Ditchfield, Kane, Dortch, Joe, Hook, Fiona, Petchey, Fiona, Hogg, Alan, Questiaux, Daniele, Demuro, Martina, Arnold, Lee, Spooner, Nigel, Levchenko, Vladimir, Skippington, Jane, Byrne, Chae, Basgall, Mark, Zeanah, David, Belton, David, Helmholz, Petra, Bajkan, Szilvia, Bailey, Richard, Placzek, Christa, and Kendrick, Peter. 2017 Early human occupation of a maritime desert, Barrow Island, North-West Australia. *Quaternary Science Reviews* 168, 19–29.

# 8

# THE PEOPLING OF EAST ASIA

## Perspectives from the Russian Far East

*Andrey V. Tabarev*

## Introduction

The Maritime Region of the Russian Far East (Primorye) is a large area that includes the coast of the Sea of Japan, the Ussuriisk-Khankaiskaya plain, and part of Sikhote-Alin Mountain Range. Archaeologists suggest that the Maritime Region played an important historical role in the migrations and cultural contacts that characterised the Far East as a whole. Primorye includes about 170,000 m² and almost 1,500 km of international frontier with China in the west, with North Korea in the south, and with Japan by sea in the southeast.

Questions about human occupation of the Maritime Region in pre-Upper Palaeolithic times require more detailed research. A handful of finds with particularly archaic technology (Early Middle Palaeolithic) are known from surface collections but unassociated with exact dates or clear stratigraphical context.

The sporo-pollen spectra of the Last Glacial Maximum (circa 22–18,000 years ago) indicates a distribution of medium taiga-type landscapes of patchy spruce/fir and birch/larch forests, which developed in a climate colder than the Riss-Würm interglacial and the present. During the period from 18,000 to 11,000 BP, the climate in the southern Russian Far East became much milder, and dark coniferous and mixed coniferous/broad-leaved forests expanded. Between 13,000 and 11,000 BP most of the tundra and forest-tundra in the Maritime Region was replaced by birch-larch vegetation.

The Palaeolithic sites are mostly located in the south and eastern parts of the Maritime Region and could also be divided into the inland and coastal sites (Figure 8.1). The Upper Palaeolithic in its turn dates to 45,000–11,000 BP and is divided into Early Upper Palaeolithic, Upper Palaeolithic, and Final Palaeolithic (Derevianko and Tabarev 2006; Popov and Tabarev 2017).

### Evidence of Early Upper Palaeolithic Sites in the Maritime Region

The first period of the Upper Palaeolithic of the Primorye is represented by *Osinovka*-type sites that contain distinctive core technologies and developed toolkits. The original *Osinovka* site is one of the best known in Primorye. It is located in the Osinovka River valley, a tributary of the

DOI: 10.4324/9781003427483-8

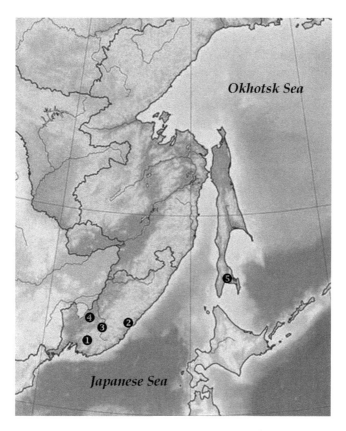

FIGURE 8.1 Territories of the maritime region and Sakhalin Islands, Russian Far East with the group of sites mentioned in the text. (1) Osinovka and Geographical Society Cave; (2) Final Palaeolithic sites in the coastal zone (Ustinovka and Suvorovo groups); (3) Final Palaeolithic sites in the inland zone (Gorbatka 3 and Ilistaya 1); (4) Astrakhanka site; (5) Palaeolithic sites on Sakhalin (Sennaya 1, Ogon'ki 5).

Ilistaya River. The famous Siberian archaeologist, A. P. Okladnikov, discovered the site in 1953, identifying four cultural layers during the excavations. The uppermost layer is early Iron Age. The second layer included Neolithic pottery sherds. The third cultural layer is terminal Pleistocene, and the fourth layer, at the bottom of the Quaternary sequence of *Osinovka*, contains early appearing technology, including choppers and chopping tools, pebble cores, side scrapers, and flake tools exhibiting minimal edge preparation. Several knife/side scrapers with blades 8–15 cm long were also made out of massive flakes. They are to some extent similar to Upper Palaeolithic Siberian side scrapers but differ in size and the type of retouching. Flake artefacts are the most numerous items in the inventory and total 384 items, or 74% of the total. The majority of this assemblage was produced by primary reduction of pebbles for cores and choppers and chopping tools. Blade-like pieces and blades are not as numerous, comprising 64 items, or 13% of the assemblage.

Geological analysis suggests that there were three glacial and two interglacial stages in the Russian Far East during the Late Pleistocene. Thus, people likely came to Osinovka hill during a warm period, which was probably an interglacial stage. Further settlement of the area occurred during the last glaciation, when colluvium trains and the clay-loamy deposits with crudely broken inclusions were formed. The last glaciation is subdivided into two stages, early and late, separated by a warm period dating from 60,000 to 30,000 years ago. If the deposits of the lower *Osinovka* horizons date to an interglacial period, then they could be older than 100,000 years before the present. The *terminus ante quem* of these deposits is 30,000 years ago. Unfortunately, the site was almost totally destroyed by a modern quarry that was active during the 1970s to the 1990s.

Another key Upper Palaeolithic site is the Geographical Society Cave, which is located 25 m above the floodplain of the Partizanskaya River. Excavation of Geographical Society Cave revealed for the first time in the Russian Far East concurrent Late Pleistocene faunal and cultural remains. In the fourth cultural horizon, lithics are represented by a comparatively small number of flakes and tools. From the archaeological patterning at this site, it appears that people occasionally visited the cave during hunting expeditions or to take shelter. The toolkit reveals a distinctive technique of flake removal. Three cores were recovered: one made on a massive sub-rectangular pebble with one platform and several large negative scars of flake removals on one flat side; a core made of a less massive sub-rectangular pebble that has two platforms, one of which retains cortex and has several flake-removal scars; and a third nucleus that was heavily worked with flake scars on all sides. Several retouched flakes may also have been used as tools.

The organic finds include a socket made of elk antler that is grooved at one end to accommodate stone blade insets. The bones of several animals, including mammoth (*Mammuthus primigenius*), horse (*Equus* sp.), rhinoceros (*Coelodonta antiquitatis*), roe deer (*Capreolus capreolus*), elk (*Alces alces*), goral (*Naemorhedus goral*), cave lion (*Panthera leo spelaea*) or tiger (*Panthera tigris*), and brown bear (*Ursus arctos*), were also found. The faunal complex indicates a cool climate that may have been similar to modern conditions or slightly colder. A series of uncalibrated radiocarbon dates between 40,000 and 31,500 BP derived from Geographical Society Cave suggests that the stone tools from the fourth cultural horizon date to an earlier period of the Upper Palaeolithic, but this suggestion needs the confirmation from a clear archaeological context.

The Final Palaeolithic dates to 15,000–11,000 BP and is documented at a number of archaeological sites (more than 150) with very diagnostic lithic assemblages. Taking into consideration the problem of preservation of organic materials in the Far East (soils that are dramatically acidic), archaeologists avoid use of the term "culture" for the Palaeolithic and prefer to employ such terms as "complex" and "industry".

### Palaeolithic Sites in the Coastal Zone of the Maritime Region

One of the most informative groups of sites is located in the Zerkalnaya River valley near the coast of the Sea of Japan (Ustinovka and Suvorovo groups of sites).

Ustinovka 1 is a well-known Upper Palaeolithic site, located on a bluff on the right bank of Bezymyanny Stream near its confluence with the Zerkalnaya River. This stream enters the river approximately 30 km from the point at which it empties into the Sea of Japan. The terrace is 10–12 m above the contemporary river level. The site was discovered in 1954 by geologist V. F. Petrun, who collected a number of artefacts, including cores, blades, and retouched flakes, made from flinty tuff and obsidian. Later, during the 1960s and 1980s the excavated area totalled about 350 m$^2$. Today the collection of stone artefacts, including cores, tools, preforms, blanks, tested pebbles and cobbles, comprises a collection of about 100,000 objects, which is one of the largest in Northeast Asia. Some 15% of the collections from Ustinovka 1 is formal tools and

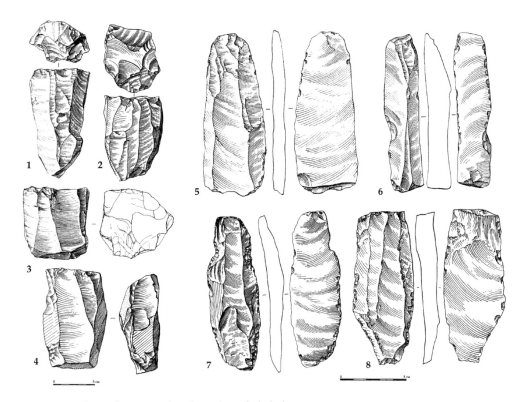

FIGURE 8.2    Coastal zone. Ustinovka 1 site. Blade industry.

85% is by-products of tool manufacture. Large subprismatic cores were made from local flinty tuff. The platforms and dorsal faces of the cores exhibit very simple preparation (Figure 8.2). More than 30–40% of the debris and broken flakes is attributable to preform preparation, and another 30–40% was probably produced during direct percussion of the core face. It appears that only about 20–30% of initial raw material blanks (cortical flakes) was used as preforms for tool production. Different forms of the cores do not constitute different techniques and types. Rather, these forms belong to the same percussive technology but reflect different stages of core reduction. About 90% of all the tools, including end scrapers, burins, knives, gravers, and drills, was made on blades and elongated flakes. There were also a number of bifacial tools present which were mostly located in the upper horizons.

Two possible anthropogenic features, one found in 1968 and another in 1980, were interpreted as the remains of light shelters. The latter feature was an oval depression 3.3 m long and 2 m wide, with the long axis oriented from northwest to southeast. The northeastern side of the hollow is quite steep, the other slopes are gentle. The greatest depth of the depression is 36 cm. The fill was composed of grey-blue clay with a small fraction of ochre clay. Remains of a circular hearth with side slabs measuring 26-by-30 cm in diameter were found along the southeastern wall of the depression. The most intriguing problem concerning the Ustinovka 1 site is its age. Stratigraphy at the site is very complex and does not provide a simple chronology of various levels. The typology of microcores, burins, knives, and other types of stone tools and cores suggests a date of 12,000–10,000 BP. However, some artefacts in the Ustinovka 1 assemblage appear much older. For example, four backed knives on elongated flakes are very similar to "Moro-type" tools of Japan that date to no earlier than 20,000–17,000 BP. In addition, there are two stemmed points on flakes that correlate with similar points known from the Korean Peninsula that date to 25,000–22,000 BP. Some archaeologists suggest that the lithic assemblage from this site may be divided into two periods: 12,000–10,000 BP (upper level) and 20,000–16,000 BP (lower level). Other specialists insist on an older range of 30,000–25,000 BP for the early portion of the cultural level.

Ustinovka 4 site was discovered and intensively studied in the 1980–1990s. The excavated area at this site was close to 1,500 m². The collection is significant and totals 50,000 items. Interpretations of the site's age and palaeoenvironmental context await radiocarbon and palynological determinations. Archaeologists report two cultural layers at this site: fragmentary Bronze Age in the uppermost level, and Final Palaeolithic in the intermediate and lower levels. At least three semi-subterranean dwellings are described in publications. Dwelling 1 is 4.5-by-7.5 m with an elliptical floor dug 20 cm into the ground and a hearth in the centre. Lithic debris and broken tools were concentrated in the northwestern part of the structure. Dwelling 2 has an irregularly shaped subterranean floor that is 6 m long and 2 m wide on the north side and 3.45 m wide on the south side. This dwelling was possibly divided into northern and a southern sections. At the centre of the structure there is a deep posthole for a roof support. Two vestibule-like entrances were built through the northern and southern walls. Dwelling 3 is almost rectangular at four by 6 m and contains traces of two side entrances. The distance between the dwellings is about 10–15 m. The lithic collection includes bifacial tools such as blanks for microcores, points, and knives; burins including transverse burins with various modifications on blades and flakes; and microblades on bifacial and unifacial blanks, with one or two fronts (Figure 8.3). Woodworking tools are rare but some demonstrate partial polishing, a new technique of edge preparation. All other features are common for the local industry and may be dated to the interval 12,000–10,000 BP.

Ustinovka 6 site was discovered in 1961 but was excavated intensively only in the 1990s (Kononenko 2001). Total excavation area is about 60 m² and the collection of artefacts from this site includes almost 10,000 items. The site is located on a cliff terrace about 11–14 m above Zerkalnaya River. All of the findings were concentrated in a 35–40 cm thick layer of brown loam. The assemblage consists of several groups: (1) products and by-products of direct blade percussion (cores, preforms, exhausted forms, blades, and elongated flakes); (2) products of microblade manufacture; (3) tools with evidence of retouching or burination; (4) pebbles with traces of burning; and (5) debitage. Microcores are made on bifaces or on unifaces. Stages of testing and core preparation are documented by different kinds of spalls: platform spalls and ski-spalls. The tool assemblage also includes end scrapers, burins, bifaces, and woodworking tools (adzes). Several points may be interpreted as arrow or dart points similar to those of the Mikoshiba culture in the Japanese archipelago that date to 12,000–11,000 BP. Two radiocarbon dates from a possible hearth feature at Ustinovka 6 are 11,750 ± 620 BP (Siberian Branch of Academy of Sciences (SBAS 3538) and 11,550 ± 240 BP (Geo-1412).

*Suvorovo 3* site was studied from the 1980s to the 2000s. The excavation area is about 250 m², and the artifact collection totals about 5,000 items. The lithic assemblage contains an excellent series of burins with multifaceted modification on blades, flakes, and biface blanks. Initial burin spalls and rejuvenation spalls were also found. Burins are accompanied by gravers, retouched knives on blades, end scrapers, and perforators. Cores in the lithic assemblage are of two main types: (1) a large subprismatic blade technique with direct percussion from a hammerstone, and (2) wedge-shaped microcores produced with pressure flakers. Several examples of thin pressure-flaked blades or bladelets also suggest the appearance of a new, elaborate pressure flaking

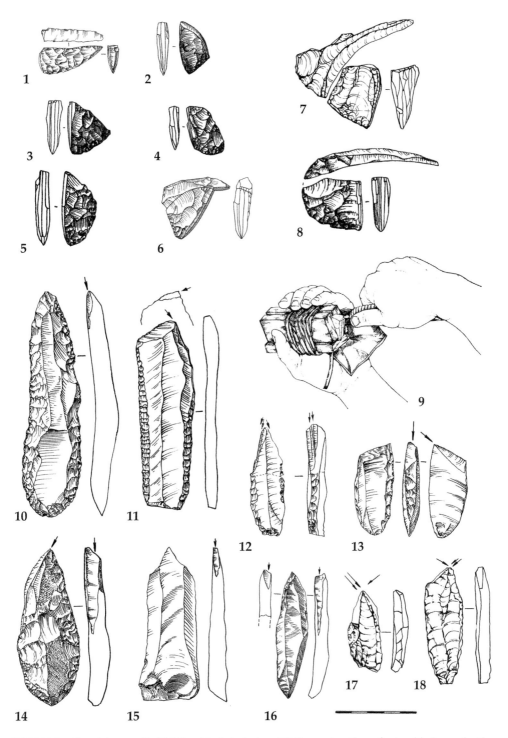

FIGURE 8.3   Coastal zone. (1–8) Microblade industry; (9) Reconstruction of microblade production in a hand device; (10–18) burins.

technique called micro-conical or micro-prismatic. Woodworking tools, including adzes, drills, chisels, and axes, are rare. Detailed use-wear analyses have assisted in the interpretation of the site as a seasonal camp with hunting activity as the focus. Currently, there are no radiocarbon dates from the Final Palaeolithic at Suvorovo 3, but the characteristics of the lithic technology place the site in the 11,500–11,000 BP chronological range.

Suvorovo 4 site was excavated from 1985 to 2000. The excavated area at the site is about 350 m² and the artifact collection includes more than 15,000 lithic items. Given the location of this site between two tributaries of the Zerkalnaya River, it is possible that early inhabitants of the site used the location for seasonal salmon fishing. This activity is suggested in the archaeological assemblage by the presence of numerous woodworking tools that may have been used to manufacture traps, weirs and possibly for small boat construction. Artefacts associated with woodworking at this site include axes, adzes, drills, chisels, gravers, and scrapers. Very distinctive knives that are similar in shape to ethnographically known fishing knives may have been used for butchering and cleaning fish (Tabarev 2011). Burins and other tools relevant to hunting activities are not as numerous as at Suvorovo 3 site. Bifaces made from various raw materials were used as knives, points, and spear tips. Cores are typical subprismatic and micro wedge-shaped forms. In terms of spatial analysis, several areas with intensive flint knapping can be recognised in archaeological deposits by the density of stone flake debitage. Some concentrations of debitage are near fireplaces and around flat stones, which suggest the presence of a light, surface-type wind, and rain shelter not more than 2–3 m in diameter. Four uncalibrated radiocarbon dates between 15,900 and 15,100 BP indicate the time of site occupation.

Suvorovo 6 site was investigated during several field seasons from 1991 to 1996, yielding more than 7,500 stone artefacts recovered from an excavation area of 215 m². The archaeological materials belong to two chronological periods: the Bronze Age and the Final Palaeolithic. The Final Palaeolithic toolkit is typical and contains subprismatic cores for blades and elongated flakes, wedge-shaped microcores on unifacial blanks, microblades, transverse burins, retouched blades, woodworking tools and bifaces. The woodworking tools, including adzes, chisels, and gravers, are technically elaborated and reflect a sophisticated level of woodcraft. Several work areas for core testing and preparation can be recognised in the spatial distribution at the site. Refitting allows the reconstruction of the entire *chaîne opératoire*, which consists of raw material testing, core preparation (platform and front), blade and elongated flake removal (percussion), platform and front rejuvenation, distal face reorientation, and final core exhausting. Depending upon raw material type, it appears as though it was possible to remove 10–20 blade-like blanks from one nucleus. One exceptional artifact found during the 1993 excavations is a large bifacially worked preform that is chipped from siliceous tuff and contains a leaf "print" on one side. Although there are no radiocarbon dates yet for the Final Palaeolithic cultural complex at Suvorovo 6, the tool typology correlates in age with the neighbouring Suvorovo 4 (15,000 BP) site rather than with Suvorovo 3 (11–10,000 BP).

## Final Palaeolithic Sites in the Inland Part of the Maritime Region

Another concentration of Final Palaeolithic sites is known from the continental portion of the Maritime Region in the basin of the Ilistaya River. The most interesting materials from this area were found during the excavation of such sites as Gorbatka 3 and Ilistaya 1. The most abundant raw materials at these sites were large red diabase pebbles and small obsidian pebbles found along riverbanks nearest the sites. Such items as cores, microcores, and debitage from

The Peopling of East Asia  **145**

their manufacture, as well as blades, microblades, and tool preforms were recognised. Although finished tools were not numerous compared to the debitage from this site, finished tools were represented by several dozens to hundreds of artefacts. The microblade cores may be subdivided into three main groups according to their shape: wedge-shaped, conical, or semiconical, and wedge-shaped ones with acute fronts. The platforms of some wedge-shaped cores on flakes were retouched, but usually they have no traces of special preparation. Some of the wedge-shaped cores made on boat-like preforms are very small (about 1 cm in height and 3 cm in length) (Figure 8.4). Conical and semiconical cores were rare in these complexes and comprise

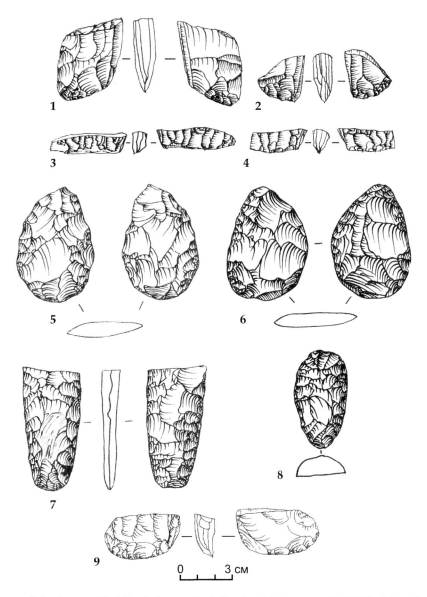

**FIGURE 8.4**   Inland zone. Obsidian industry. (1–4, 9) microblade cores; (5, 6) bifacial preforms for microblade cores; (7) fragment of bifacial point; (8) end scraper.

just 3% of micro-cores at Gorbatka 3 and 3–4% at Ilistaya 1. Most of the cores are quite different from the nuclei of the Suvorovo 3 and 4 sites in the Zerkalnaya River valley, which appears to be due to the effects of raw material on the core configurations and percussion techniques. Both industries belong to the same Final Palaeolithic techno-typological tradition but were developed using different raw material. Wedge-shaped cores with acute fronts share attributes with the previously mentioned core forms from a number of the other Suvorovo sites. There are also many end scrapers on flakes and blades, retouched blades, and flakes. However, bifaces, transversal burins, points, adzes, and perforators were not as numerous. Many foliate bifaces appear to have been used as points. Burins found at these sites include transverse, dihedral, and side varieties.

The stone industries of Gorbatka 3 and Ilistaya 1 are very similar in terms of raw materials, tool types, and technological details. Based on the percentage of raw material, debitage, cores, preforms, and finished tools, these assemblages may be interpreted as workshops and habitation sites. Two uncalibrated radiocarbon age estimates were obtained for *Gorbatka 3*; $2,590 \pm 85$ BP (SBAS-1921) for the light loam level and $13,500 \pm 200$ BP (SBAS-1922) for a black loam lens at the bottom of the dark heavy loam unit. There is also one date for the light loam at *Ilistaya 1* of $7,840 \pm 60$ BP (Ki-3163). Given these age estimates it is quite possible that the small ice wedge visible in the Gorbatka 3 profile dates to the early Holocene because it lies above larger ice wedges that are terminal Pleistocene in age. Therefore, a date of about 13,000 BP for the lens compressed by a large ice wedge does not contradict the age of the cryoturbation formation. A date of about 2,500 BP is thought to be associated with stone tools and early Iron Age pottery that were also found in this layer. Overall, the artefacts at Gorbatka 3 may date to the terminal Pleistocene and early Holocene (11,000–9,000 BP) while the assemblage at Ilistaya 1 is probably early Holocene in age (10,000–8,000 BP) (Derevianko and Tabarev 2006).

Other sites yielding Final Palaeolithic materials are known from the central and western Maritime Region. For example, the *Astrakhanka site*, which was tested with a trench excavation from 1994 to 1996, produced a lithic assemblage similar to that at *Ustinovka 1* and contains subprismatic cores, blades, and elongated flakes with retouching. The site may indicate a western route of migration for microblade industries to the Maritime Region during the Final Palaeolithic.

## Palaeolithic Sites on Sakhalin Island

The study of the Palaeolithic of Sakhalin Island began in the 1960s, but until 1993 it was not possible to find reliably stratified, non-deposited Palaeolithic materials. It has changed only with the investigations of a series of sites in the area of Ogonki village. In 1998 Sakhalin archaeologists reported the discovery of the Sennaya 1 location with possible Lower Palaeolithic age (Vasilevski 2008). However, not all archaeologists consider the stone products found at the Sennaya-1 site as artefacts, and believe that this site requires further geoarchaeological study and argumentation.

Currently, the multi-layer Ogon'ki 5 site, located in the south of the island, is the reference point for the territory of Sakhalin. The authors of the excavations at the site identified three cultural and chronological horizons: Horizon 1 (the uppermost) is connected with the transition from the Palaeolithic to the Neolithic; Horizon 2 is documenting the Final Upper Palaeolithic (18,000–13, 000 BP); and according to the series of Accelerator Mass Spectrometry (AMS) dates, the lithic industry of Horizon 3 – 19,440 ± 140 BP (Beta-115 987), 19,380 ± 190 BP (Beta-115 986), 19,320 ± 145 BP (AA-20 864), and 18,920 ± 150 BP (AA-25 434) – belongs to the earlier period of the Upper Palaeolithic in frames of 19,500–19,000 BP (Vasilevski and Grishchenko 2011; Rudaya et al. 2013).

Cores from Horizons 2 and 3 are represented by narrow-front and amorphous modifications for flakes and blades, along with some examples of the microcores for microblades. The last ones were prepared on boat-shaped preforms up to 10–11 cm long and about 8–10 mm thick. The tool-kit includes end scrapers on blades and flakes, transversal burins, gravers, knives, and unifacial instruments. The researchers of Ogon'ki 5 site underline that most of long blades and their fragments are located in Horizon 3. Taking into consideration the single AMS 14C date – 31, 130 ± 440 BP (AA-23 138), they also suggest the possibility of an earlier Upper Palaeolithic component at the site. Other specialists believe that there is a simple inversion of dates, which is very common for mass dating, when one or two dates fall out of the general series of values (Kuzmin 2016).

## Discussion and Conclusions

In spite of a long history of investigations (since the early 1950s), the Palaeolithic of the Russian Far East has been insufficiently studied. There are not more than 30–35 known sites (only 20 of them excavated sufficiently) with about 20 radiocarbon dates. While the Early and the Middle Palaeolithic of the Maritime Region and Sakhalin Island sites are questionable or non-visible today archaeologically, the Upper Palaeolithic is present with a series of cave and open-air sites that demonstrate the variability of lithic industries, which include percussion of pebble cores for flakes, sub-prismatic cores for blades, and pressure exploration of wedge-shaped/boat-shaped microcores for microblades (Tabarev 2012).

Final Palaeolithic (19–11,000 BP by AMS-dating) sites are known by groups (clusters) of sites on the territory of the Maritime Region and Sakhalin. As shown by the tool-kit, the population was active in hunting-gathering-fishing and in exploration of a wide range of natural resources. The analysis of obsidian samples confirms the high level of mobility (300–100 km from the sources) and raw material procurement (Gillam and Tabarev 2004).

At the moment two scenarios for the appearance of the Palaeolithic groups in the Maritime Region are discussed – directly from the regions of Central Asia (Northern Mongolia in particular), or via the territory of the Korean Peninsula. Some finds of tanged points and backed knives at Ustinovka 1 site help support the latter scenario.

Taking into account the fact that all known and dated Palaeolithic sites in the Maritime Region and on Sakhalin Island are not older than 19,000 BP, these territories cannot be regarded as transitional ones for the initial populations of the Japanese Islands. For the southern part of Sakhalin Island there are no dates older than sites on Hokkaido. Even the single and controversial date from the floor in one of the dwellings at Ogon'ki 5 site (31,130 ± 440 BP) is at most contemporaneous with the earliest complexes on Hokkaido, and much younger than dates on Honshu (Morisaki et al. 2019). The assemblage on Sakhalin does not demonstrate the earliest technological tools documented for the Early Upper Palaeolithic sites on Honshu (trapezoids, knife-tools, and ground axes) (Tsutsumi 2012). All the obsidian on Sakhalin (including the earliest finds at Ogon'ki 5) originates from Hokkaido outcrops, while no distinctive raw materials from Sakhalin were found by archaeologists on Hokkaido (Kuzmin and Glascock 2007). So the initial peopling of Sakhalin is much more possible from the south via Honshu and Hokkaido rather than from the north (Lower Amur) where sites older than 14,000 BP are absolutely unknown.

In terms of basic characteristics of tool-kits and other cultural characteristics of the transitional time from the Palaeolithic to the Neolithic (13–11,000 BP), the Maritime Region and Sakhalin Island demonstrate the same trajectory as the Japanese Islands (Incipient Jomon) and Lower Amur Region (Initial Neolithic) (Yanshina 2019). The only (and still unexplained) difference is the absence of initial pottery technology till 10,000 BP which could be explained both by the degree of knowledge and by the poor preservation of incipient clay containers in acidic soils (Zhushchikhovskaya 1997). Another explanation for the absence of pottery in the Maritime Region may be related to the origin of the Palaeolithic (and alternative decisions for containers) by migration from the territory of the Korean Peninsula where pottery older than 10,000 BP is also not known.

From the other side, Final Palaeolithic industries (15–11,000 BP) of the Northeastern and Northern Japanese Islands along with Sakhalin Island and Kuril Island, which formed the so-called "Paleo-SHK," demonstrate many features (stemmed points, bifacial cores, caches, etc.) similar to the earliest technological characteristics in North America and enlarge the scope of the discussion on the routes of the initial peopling of the New World, which creates intriguing perspectives for further field quests (Kornfeld and Tabarev 2009).

## Acknowledgements

The author is deeply grateful to his Russian colleagues Sergey A. Gladyshev (Novosibirsk) and Alexander A. Krypianko (Vladivostok), and American colleague J.Ch. Gillam (Savanah, South Carolina) for the valuable comments and discussion on the Palaeolithic materials of the Russian Far East. This research was supported by Russian Science Foundation (RSF), *Project #24-28-00003*.

## References

Derevianko, A.P., and Tabarev, A.V. 2006 Palaeolithic of the Primorye (Maritime) Province. In Archaeology of the Russian Far East: Essays in the Stone Age Prehistory. *BAR International Series* 1540, 41–54.

Gillam, J., and Tabarev, A. 2004 On the Path of Upper-Palaeolithic Obsidians in the Russian Far East. *Current Research in the Pleistocene* 21, 3–6.

Kononenko, N. 2001 Ecology of cultural dynamics of archaeological sites in the Zerkalnaya River valley at the Terminal Pleistocene – Early Holocene (the Ustinovka Complex, Russian Far East). *Archaeology, Ethnology and Anthropology of Eurasia* 1, 40–59.

Kornfeld, M., and Tabarev, A. 2009 The French connection? Or is it? *Current Research in the Pleistocene* 26, 90–92.

Kuzmin, Y. 2016 Colonization and early human migrations in the Insular Russian Far East: A view from the mid-2010s. *The Journal of Island and Coastal Archaeology* 11, 122–132.

Kuzmin, Y., and Glascock, M. 2007 Two islands in the ocean: Prehistoric Obsidian Exchange between Sakhalin and Hokkaido, Northeast Asia. *The Journal of Island and Coastal Archaeology* 2, 99–120.

Morisaki, K., Sano, K., and Izuho, M. 2019 Early Upper Palaeolithic blade technology in the Japanese Archipelago. *Archaeological Research in Asia* 17, 79–97.

Popov, A., and Tabarev, A. 2017 The Preagricultural Human Occupation of Primorye (Russian Far East), in *Handbook of East and Southeast Asian Archaeology*, eds Habu, Junko, Lape, Peter V., and Olsen, John W.. New York: Springer, 379–396.

Rudaya, N., Vasilevski, A., Grishchenk, o V., and Mozhaev, A. 2013 Environmental conditions of the late Palaeolithic and early Neolithic sites in Southern Sakhalin. *Archaeology, Ethnology and Anthropology of Eurasia* 41, 73–82.

Tabarev, A.V. 2011 Blessing the Salmon: Archaeological evidences of the transition to intensive fishing in the final Palaeolithic, Maritime Region, Russian Far East. In (eds.) Bicho, N.F. et al. *Trekking the Shore: Changing Coastlines and the Antiquity of Coastal Settlement*, 105–116. New York: Springer.

Tabarev, A. 2012 Blades and microblades, Percussion and pressure: Towards the evolution of Lithic technologies of the Stone age period, Russian far East, in *The Emergence of Pressure Blade Making: From Origin to Modern Experimentation*, ed Desrosiers, P.M.. New York: Springer, 329–346.

Tsutsumi, T. 2012 MIS3 edge-ground axes and the arrival of the first *Homo sapiens* in the Japanese archipelago. *Quaternary International* 248, 70–78.

Vasilevski, A. 2008 *Kamennyj vek ostrova Sahalin* [*Stone Age of Sakhalin Island*]. Yuzhno-Sahalinsk (in Russian)

Vasilevski, A., and Grishchenko, V. 2011 The definition of raw-material centers during the late Palaeolithic, Neolithic and Paleo metal ages of Sakhalin Island, Eastern Russia. *Current Research in the Pleistocene* 28, 11–15.

Yanshina, O. 2019 Understanding the specific nature of the East Asia Neolithic transition. *Documenta Praehistorica* 46, 6–29.

Zhushchikhovskaya, I. 1997 Current data on late-Pleistocene/Early-Holocene Ceramics in Russian Far East. *Current Research in the Pleistocene* 14, 89–91.

# 9

# EARLY PEOPLING IN AND AROUND TAIWAN

Pleistocene through Middle Holocene Groups before the Austronesian Era

*Hsiao-chun Hung, Chin-yung Chao, Hirofumi Matsumura, and Mike T. Carson*

## Introduction

Prior to about 10,000 years ago, Taiwan lay at the eastern end of the Asian continent, connected by dry land to the Chinese coast during the glacial periods of the Pleistocene (Figure 9.1). This land bridge connection existed periodically between about 2 million and 12,000–11,000 years ago, being the most exposed during the peak glacial intervals that occurred about 100,000 years apart from each other. The surface of this ancient land bridge is now submerged beneath the waters of present-day Taiwan Strait. However, its most extensive and stable phase occurred between 26 kya and 20 kya, during the Last Glacial Maximum (LGM), when global sea level was more than 120 m lower than now.

The East Coast Mountain Range in Taiwan has been especially informative about this island's past, in terms of both natural and cultural history (Figure 9.2). It contains several of Taiwan's oldest known archaeological sites, including more than 30 caves and rock shelters of the Baxian Cave Complex. Rapid uplift means that these sites now are located 18–197 m above sea level (asl), and their positions relative to the seashore must have been very different during the LGM. The massive rise in postglacial global sea level already had been underway around 11,700 years ago, at the commencement of the Holocene, but its full effects occurred over an extended period with fluctuations (Chen et al. 2004). Taiwan became an island about 8000 years ago. However, the surrounding waters apparently acted as a barrier during the earlier millennia of the Holocene, during which time little or no evidence has suggested overseas contact.

Preceramic contexts continued in the archaeological record until about 5000 years ago, terminating with the arrival of the Taiwan Neolithic (ca. 5000–4800 BP), presumably associated with the earliest Austronesian-speaking groups (Blust 1984–1985; Bellwood 2017). These people brought pottery, rice and millet farming, dogs, pigs, and numerous other aspects of a Neolithic lifestyle that soon would characterise the people and landscapes of Taiwan (Tsang 2005; Hung and Carson 2014; Deng et al. 2022). During this time, Taiwan Strait facilitated waterborne transportation and communication between Neolithic communities.

Since about 5000 years ago, the coastal zones of Taiwan have grown larger and more stable, due to the accumulation of hillslope erosion and alluvial sediments released by agricultural

DOI: 10.4324/9781003427483-9

Early Peopling in and Around Taiwan    151

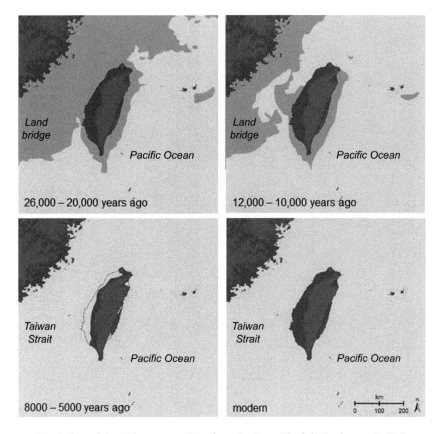

FIGURE 9.1   Evolution of the Taiwan coastline since the Last Glacial Maximum (LGM).

clearance and tillage, as well as by sea level stability. The extensive coastal plain of southwest Taiwan did not exist around 8000 through 5000 years ago, and this entire area was submerged under shallow sea (Chen and Liu 1996; Chen et al. 2004). Most of the present-day coastal plain around Taiwan began to form only during the middle Holocene (Figure 9.1), after the initial period of Austronesian settlement (Carson and Hung 2018).

## Human Remains and Related Fauna from Taiwan Strait

Mammal fossils occasionally have been trawled from the bed of Taiwan Strait by fishermen, mostly around the Penghu Islands in the east and the Taiwan Shoals around Dongshan Island in the west. These areas lie on the East Asian continental shelf, and the topography of the seafloor is level (Chen 2000). Among the large numbers of findings, several human fossils have been collected by fishermen from Taiwan and coastal Fujian waters.

### The Penghu 1 Mandible

The region's oldest known hominin is the mandible of an archaic species of Homo, named "Penghu 1" (Figure 9.3). This mandible was recognised as hominin by amateur fossil collector

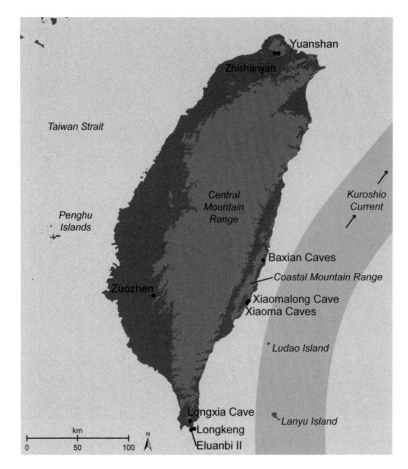

FIGURE 9.2   Major Palaeolithic and Holocene Preceramic sites on the island of Taiwan, noting the location of the Kuroshio Current.

FIGURE 9.3   The Penghu 1 mandible, right half (Photograph by Hsiao-chun Hung, courtesy Kun-yu Tsai and Chun-hsiang Chang).

Early Peopling in and Around Taiwan 153

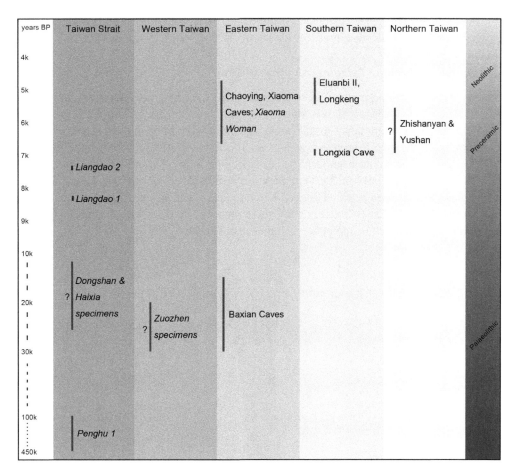

FIGURE 9.4  The chronology of human remains (in italics) and archaeological sites with Palaeolithic and Preceramic associations discussed in this chapter. Note: a possible pottery association is unclear in the cultural layer of Liangdao 2 on Liang Island.

Kun-yu Tsai, who obtained it from fishermen in Tainan. The age of Penghu 1 is claimed to be younger than 450 kya and most likely between 190 kya and 100 kya (Chang et al. 2015) (Figure 9.4). The dating result was based on the limited success of laser-ablation U-series dating, in combination with the relative chronology of Penghu fauna and Penghu 1 hominin mandible through analysis of the contents of fluorine (F) and sodium (Na) in bone samples. Based on bone metrics and dental morphology, connections have been suggested between this mandible and another of a Denisovan from Baishiya Karst Cave in Xiahe County, Gansu in Northwest China (Chen et al. 2019).

## Human Remains from Dongshan Island

The lower part of a right humerus was collected from the seabed next to Dongshan Island, near Zhangzhou in Fujian Province (Chen et al. 2012). This finding often has been referenced as "Dongshan Man" in Chinese archaeological reports. The specimen is light grey in colour, and the remaining part is 57.9 mm in length. A layer of black material has coated the bone, probably manganese. Yuzhu You (1988) estimated that the age of this individual was between the late Pleistocene and early Holocene, probably about 10 kya.

## Other Human and Faunal Remains from Taiwan Strait

A human humerus lacking parts of its capitulum and trochlea was recovered from the Taiwan Strait in 1998 and labelled as "Haixia Man (Strait Man)" by Chinese colleagues. It was found with more than 5000 mammalian fossils, including many with artificial cut and scrape marks, all collected by fishermen from a vast area extending from 23°30′ to 25°00′N and 119°20′ to 120°30′E. This specimen has been identified as belonging to an adult male *Homo sapiens* who stood about 170–172 cm tall (Cai 2001). It measures about 311 mm in surviving length, shows a brown colour, and has been petrified (Figure 9.5). Its age has been estimated as Late Pleistocene, about 26,000–11,000 years BP, based on the approximate association with the ancient Pleistocene land bridge, although no direct dating has been obtained.

FIGURE 9.5 The humerus of "Haixia Man (Strait Man)" (Collection of the Shishi Museum in Fujian, courtesy Xuechun Fan).

The faunal remains from Taiwan Strait have been named variously by different researchers as the "Penghu-Tainan Fauna" (Shikama et al. 1975), the "Penghu Fauna" (Gau 1982; Wei 2007), the "Penghu Channel Fauna" (Ho 2011), and the "Taiwan Land Bridge Fauna" (Ho 2011; Chen 2000). They include several large terrestrial mammals, many now extinct or locally extirpated:

1. elephants: *Palaeoloxodon namadicus*, *P. naumanni penghunensis*, *Mammuthus primigenius*, *Elephas maximus*, and *Elephas* sp.;
2. rhinoceroses: *Dicerorhinus* sp. and/or Rhinocerotidae gen. et sp. indet.;
3. bovids: *Bubalus teilhardi*, *Bubalus youngi*, *Bubalus* sp., *Bison* sp., and *Bos primigenius*;
4. serows: *Capricornis sumatraensis* [note: this species was described as "shrews" instead of "serows" in the source reference (Chen 2000)];
5. cervids: *Cervus (Sika)* cf. *palaeozoensis*, *C. (S.) nippon taiouanus*, *C. unicolor swinhoei* and/or *C. (Rusa) timorensis* (?), *Cervus* sp., *C.* cf. *praenipponicus*, *Elaphurus davidianus*, *Muntiacus reevesi micrurus*;
6. suids: *Sus* cf. *lydekkeri* and *Sus scrofa*;
7. horses: *Equus przewalskii sinensis* and *Equus dalianensis*;
8. tigers: *Panthera tigris*;
9. raccoon dogs: *Nyctereutes procyonoides*;
10. bears: *Ursus arctos* and/or *Ursus* sp.;
11. hyaenas: *Crocuta ultima*;
12. wolves: *Canis lupus* (?).

Additional findings included the remains of whales (*Globicephala macrorhynchus*, *Balaenoptera* sp., Cetacea gen. et sp. indet.) and dolphins (see You et al. 1995; Chen 2000; Wei 2007).

Some of the recovered bones show artificial cut marks (Figure 9.6), and most are estimated to date to the later Pleistocene (You et al. 1995). A few might be late Tertiary, and some could be early Holocene. Kwang-tzuu Chen (2000) suggested a Middle to Final Pleistocene date for the "Taiwan Land Bridge Fauna".

FIGURE 9.6  An antler of Père David's deer (*Elaphurus davidianus*) with intentional cut marks (after Ho (2011: 36), courtesy Chuan-kun Ho).

## The Two Human Burials from Liang Island (Liangdao), Matsu Archipelago

From 2011 to 2013, Chung-yu Chen from Academia Sinica conducted archaeological investigation on Liang Island (Beigan Township, Lianjiang County) in the Matsu Archipelago of Taiwan, located about 30 km from the coast of Mainland China. The team discovered three shell middens, namely Daowei I, Daowei II, and Baishenggang. Two complete human burials were excavated in the Daowei I shell midden; a flexed male (Liangdao 1) dated directly by C14 to 8327–8160 cal. BP, and an extended female (Liangdao 2) directly dated to 7432–7323 cal. BP (Table 9.1, Figures 9.4 and 9.7) (Chen and Chiu 2013).

The Liangdao people probably came to this island at a time when they could cross a shallow sea between the Matsu Archipelago and the mainland of Asia. The craniofacial morphology of these two individuals and the associated archaeology suggest that Liangdao 1 was related to late Palaeolithic populations of Australo-Papuan population affinity (Matsumura et al. 2019). However, ancient DNA analysis of this individual suggests that Liangdao 1 carried a genetic signature of Austronesian ancestry (Ko et al. 2014; Yang et al. 2020). The different interpretations will need to be resolved through analysis of more sets of ancient remains.

## Southwest Taiwan: Human and Faunal Remains from Zuozhen

The first report of ancient human remains in Taiwan was found by amateur fossil collectors in the bed of Cailiao Stream at Zuozhen[1] (written Cho-Chen in Shikama et al. 1976). Zuozhen is located in Tainan, southwest Taiwan (Figure 9.2). These fragmentary human bones were identified by Japanese palaeontologist Tokio Shikama as *Homo sapiens*. According to fluorine and manganese analyses, they could be between 30,000 and 20,000 years old (Shikama et al. 1976). Many Taiwan archaeologists suggest that these remains relate to the Changbin lithic industry of the East Coast of the island (see below) (Sung 1980).

In addition, large numbers of animal bones have been collected from the bed of Cailiao Stream in recent decades. The broadly defined Zuozhen Mammalian Fauna include:

1. stegodonts: *Stegodon sinensis, S.* cf. *orientalis, S. insignis, S. (Parastegodon) akashiensis, S. (P.) aurorae*;
2. elephants: *Mammuthus armeniacus taiwanicus, Elephas hysudricus paramammonteus, Archidiskodon paramammonteus*;
3. rhinoceros: *Rhinoceros sinensis hayasakai*;
4. tapirs: *Megatapirus* cf. *angustus* or *Megatapirus* sp.;
5. hippopotamus: *Hippopotamus* sp. (?);
6. bovids: *Bubalus* sp., *Bibos geron, Bison* sp.;
7. cervids: *Elaphurus formosanus, Cervus (Sika) sintikuensis, C. (S.) nippon taiouanus, C. (S.)* sp., *C. (Rusa)* sp., *Cervus* sp., *C. (Deperetia) kazusensis, Metacervulus astylodon, Muntiacus* cf. *bohlini, Muntiacus* sp., *Eucladoceros* sp., *Capreolus* sp.;
8. suids: *Sus houi, Sus* cf. *australis, Sus* sp., *Sus* cf. *lydekkeri, Potamochoerus* sp.;
9. macaques: *Macaca* sp.;
10. (10) felines: *Panthera* cf. *tigris* or *Panthera* sp., and probably *Felis (Machairodus?)* sp.;
11. dolphins: Delphinidae gen. et sp. indet.;
12. whales: *Pseudorca yunliensis* and other Cetacea (Chen 2000).

TABLE 9.1  C14 dates from Palaeolithic and Preceramic sites in Taiwan.

| Lab. No. | Context | Material Dated | Uncal. BP | Cal. BP | Reference |
|---|---|---|---|---|---|
| *Palaeolithic Phase* | | | | | |
| *Eastern Taiwan: Baxian Caves* | | | | | |
| NTU-135 | | Charcoal | >15,000 | | Hsu et al. (1973) |
| Beta-258291 | LH-7, T2P3 L18 bd | Charred material | 21,320 ± 150 | 25,895–25,360 | Tsang et al. 2009 |
| Beta-260201 | LH-7, T2P3 L19 FP | Organic sediment | 13,330 ± 70 | 16,200–15,450 | Tsang et al. 2009 |
| Beta-260202 | LH-7, T2P3 L20 FP | Organic material | 20,860 ± 130 | 25,495–24,850 | Tsang et al. 2009 |
| Beta-260203 | LH-7, T2P3 L20 FP | Organic sediment | 20,750 ± 100 | 25,285–24,635 | Tsang et al. 2009 |
| Beta-260204 | LH-7, T3P3 L17c | Organic sediment | 25,120 ± 200 | 29,580–28,740 | Tsang et al. 2009 |
| Beta-293014 | LH-24, T1P3 L44.5 F1 | Organic sediment | 17,110 ± 70 | 20,370–20,090 | Tsang et al. (2009) |
| Beta-293015 | LH-24, T1P3 L45 F1 | Organic sediment | 15,510 ± 60 | 18,890–18,750 | Tsang et al. (2009) |
| Beta-376714 | LH-30, P1 L74c | Organic sediment | 17,700 ± 70 | 21,615–21,220 | Tsang et al. (2015) |
| Beta-376713 | LH-30, P1 L621 F7 | Organic sediment | 26,600 ± 110 | 30,975–30,730 | Tsang et al. (2015) |
| Beta-370090 | LH-30, P1 L58.5–62.5 F6 | Organic sediment | 22,400 ± 100 | 27,560–26,730 | Tsang et al. (2015) |
| Beta-370089 | LH-30, P1 L54.5h F5 | Organic sediment | 24,230 ± 120 | 29,400–28,600 | Tsang et al. (2015) |
| Beta-370088 | LH-30, P1 L51 F4 | Organic sediment | 20,0020 ± 80 | 24,130–23,750 | Tsang et al. (2015) |
| Beta-370087 | LH-30, P1 L49Ig, F3 | Organic sediment | 21,520 ± 100 | 36,030–25,500 | Tsang et al. 2015 |
| Beta-370086 | LH-30, P1 L47.5II, F2-1 | Organic sediment | 21,140 ± 100 | 25,530–24,990 | Tsang et al. 2015 |
| Beta-370085 | LH-30, P1 L47 F2 | Organic sediment | 21,390 ± 110 | 25,930–25,150 | Tsang et al. 2015 |
| Beta-370084 | LH-30, P1 L46.5e F2u | Organic sediment | 19,600 ± 90 | 23,660–23,310 | Tsang et al. 2015 |
| Beta-342480 | LH-30, P0II L63.5b F9 | Organic sediment | 22,630 ± 100 | 27,760–26,920 | Tsang et al. 2011 |
| Beta-342480 | LH-30, P0II L62 F9 | Organic sediment | 19,370 ± 80 | 23,390–22,940; 22,770–22,690 | Tsang et al. (2011) |
| Beta-342478 | LH-30, P0II L53.5 F6 | Organic sediment | 20,390 ± 90 | 24,490–24,180 | Tsang et al. 2011 |
| Beta-342477 | LH-30, P0II L52.5 F5 | Organic sediment | 15,790 ± 60 | 18,940–18,830 | Tsang et al. 2011 |
| Beta-339124 | LH-30, P0II L50 F3 | Organic sediment | 21,690 ± 70 | 26,160–25,870 | Tsang et al. 2011 |
| Beta-339123 | LH-30, P0II L49.5 F2 | Organic sediment | 22,600 ± 80 | 27,700–26,930 | Tsang et al. 2011 |
| Beta-339122 | LH-30, P0II L46.5 F1 | Organic sediment | 17,610 ± 60 | 21,270–20,930; 20,680–20,570 | Tsang et al. (2011) |
| Beta-390802 | LH-29, P0 L72.5 F1 | Organic sediment | 23,720 ± 100 | 27,910–27,680 | Tsang et al. 2015 |

(*Continued*)

TABLE 9.1 (Continued)

| Lab. No. | Context | Material Dated | Uncal. BP | Cal. BP | Reference |
|---|---|---|---|---|---|
| Beta-390803 | LH-29, P0 L73c F2 (top) | Organic sediment | 24,820 ± 100 | 29,020–28,670 | Tsang et al. 2015 |
| Beta-390804 | LH-29, P0 L73a | Organic sediment | 24,210 ± 110 | 28,505–27,907 | Tsang et al. 2015 |
| Beta-390805 | LH-29, P0 L74 F5 | Organic sediment | 22,670 ± 80 | 27,215–26,845 | Tsang et al. 2015 |
| **Preceramic Phase** | | | | | |
| *Eastern Taiwan: Chaoyin Cave, in the Baxian Cave Complex* | | | | | |
| NTU-69 | LH-2, T4P2 NE | Charcoal | 5240 ± 260 | 6569–5471 | Sung (1969) |
| NTU-70 | LH-2, T3P1S L13 | Charcoal | 5340 ± 260 | 6678–5585 | Sung (1969) |
| NTU-71 | LH-2, T3P25 (burned area L3) | Charcoal | 4970 ± 250 | 6294–5260 | Sung (1969) |
| Y-2636 | LH-2, K2T2P1N | Charcoal | 4870 ± 300 | 6224–4866 | Chang (1969) |
| Beta-321706 | LH-2, P1-e L52 | Organic sediment | 5090 ± 30 | 5910–5750 | Tsang et al. (2013) |
| *Eastern Taiwan: Xiaoma Caves* | | | | | |
| NTU-1280 | Preceramic layer | Marine shell | 5770 ± 50 | 5996–5725 | Huang (1991) |
| NTU-1311 | Preceramic layer | Marine shell | 5730 ± 50 | 6189–5920 | Huang (1991) |
| *Southern Taiwan: Eluanbi II* | | | | | |
| Beta-6159 | Layer IV (-229 cm), P4, Locus A | Turbo shell | 4820 ± 100 | 5293–4795 | Li (1984) |
| Beta-6727 | Preceramic layer (-100 cm), P3, Locus B | Turbo shell | 4790 ± 120 | 5300–4645 | Li (1984) |
| NTU-4950 | Preceramic layer, L22 (-243 cm), 2006P1 | Turbo shell | 5750 ± 50 | 6080–5680 | Cheng (2009) |
| *Southern Taiwan: Longkeng* | | | | | |
| ? | Preceramic layer | Turbo shell | 5560 ± 90 | 6106–5645 | Li (1987), Tsang (2013) |
| **Others** | | | | | |
| *Taiwan Strait: Daowei I Shell Midden, Liang Island (Liangdao), Matsu* | | | | | |
| Beta-321640 | Liangdao 1 (M01) | Human bone | 7380 ± 40 | 8327–8160 | Chen and Chiu (2013) |
| Beta-336243 | Liangdao 2 (M02) | Human bone | 6490 ± 30 | 7432–7323 | Chen and Chiu (2013) |

*Notes:* (1) Calibrated through OxCal 4.4 to 2-sigma cal. BP; (2) The marine shells were calibrated with the marine reservoir correction ($\Delta R$) of 73 ± 17 years (Yoneda et al. 2007); (3) abbreviations in the table: LH, Loham (Cliff); T, Trench; P, Pit; and L, Level; (4) the precise contexts of the dating samples were not specified in the original site reports.

Early Peopling in and Around Taiwan 159

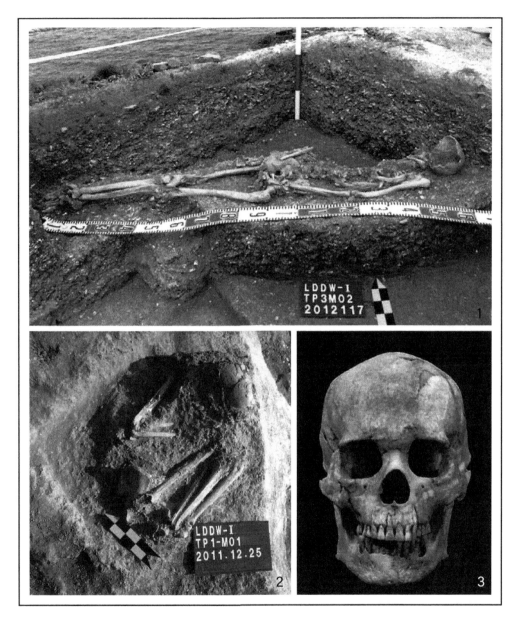

FIGURE 9.7  The two individuals excavated from the Daowei I shell midden on Liang Island In Taiwan Strait. Liangdao 2 (top) is dated to 7300 cal. BP, and Liangdao 1 (bottom) to 8300 cal. BP. Credits: 1 and 2 after Chen and Chiu (2013); 3: Photography by Hsiao-chun Hung, courtesy Chung-yu Chen).

After a comparison of the Zuozhen Fauna with a few representative faunal assemblages in southern China, Chen (2000) concluded that the geological age extended from the middle of the Early Pleistocene into the early Middle Pleistocene.

Scholars disagree about whether the Zuozhen animal fauna was contemporary with the Zuozhen human remains. In 2015, two new AMS (accelerator mass spectrometry) dates of 3215–3060 and

FIGURE 9.8   An undated human skull fragment, shown in two views, collected from the Cailiao Stream in Zuozhen, Tainan, southwest Taiwan (photography by Hsiao-chun Hung, courtesy Kun-yu Tsai).

420–400 years cal. BP were obtained from two human bone specimens (NTM-AH6672 and NTM-AH6674) from Zuozhen (Chiu 2016). These results prompted questions about the reliability of the previous fluorine and manganese analyses by Shikama et al. (1976), and doubts have emerged about whether or not a Palaeolithic Zuozhen hominin existed here.

Additional human remains have been collected by other amateur fossil collectors at Zuozhen during the past decade, but they are undatable by C14 owing to fossilisation (Figure 9.8). Therefore, the possibility that hominins existed at Zuozhen during the Pleistocene cannot be wholly excluded.

## Eastern Taiwan: The Baxian Caves and the Changbin Cobble-tool Industry

In Taiwan, the oldest known sites with Palaeolithic artefacts are in the Baxian Caves complex, located in Changbin Township facing the sea on the eastern side of the Coastal Mountain Range (Figure 9.2). These sites were first discovered in the 1960s, by geologist Chao-chi Lin and archaeologist Wen-hsun Sung from National Taiwan University. "Baxian" means "Eight Spirits" in Chinese literature, and many of these lower caves contain Buddhist shrines today.[2] Individual names refer to several of the larger caves but only extremely few of the smaller caves. The indigenous communities of the Changbin area, the Austronesian-speaking Amis, call the coastal cliffs that contain the caves *Loham*. Therefore, LH, the abbreviation of Loham, has been used for site codes by Taiwanese archaeologists.

During the earliest field surveys from 1968 into the early 1970s, Sung, Lin and colleagues discovered 17 of the Baxian caves. They excavated at four of the largest: Qianyuan Cave, Hailei Cave, Chaoyin Cave, and Kunlun Cave (Sung 1969, 1980; Lien 2015). Between 2008 and 2015, Cheng-hwa Tsang from Academia Sinica in Taipei identified new sites, and now the roster includes 30 caves, 6 rock shelters, and 2 open sites (Tsang et al. 2018) (Figure 9.9).

The Baxian Caves have been carved from volcanic agglomerate by the action of the sea, and now they lie at heights of 18–197 m asl as a result of rapid tectonic uplift, estimated here as averaging 5.8 m per 1000 years (or 5.8 mm per year). This uplift is among the fastest in recent world geological history, due to the subduction of the Philippine Plate beneath the eastern coast of Taiwan. The rate has been calculated by dating marine shells and corals collected from

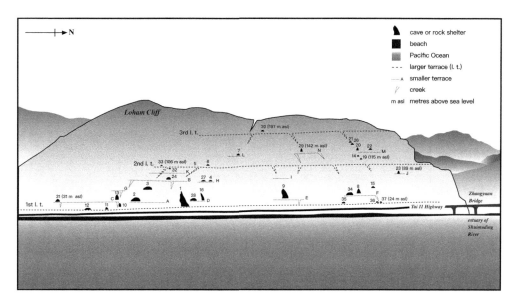

FIGURE 9.9   The distribution of caves and rock shelters sites on the Loham Cliff (abbreviation: LH) in the Baxian Cave Complex, eastern Taiwan. Site codes have a number following "LH", for example, "1" in the figure means site LH-1. Three of the excavated sites (LH-2, 27, and 34; 40–72 m asl) have Holocene Preceramic occupations, ca. 6.7–4.8 kya, whereas nine sites (LH-4, 5, 6, 7, 24, 27, 29, 30, and open terrace B; 72–197 m asl) have Late Pleistocene occupations, ca. 30–15 kya (revised after Tsang (2017: XIII)).

recorded elevations, and is estimated at 2–5 mm per year at the northern end of the East Coast mountain range, and as much as 8–12 mm per year at its southern end (Chen et al. 1991; Liew et al. 1993; Hsieh et al. 2004; Hsieh and Liew 2010; Yang and Chen 2013).

## Chronology, Stratigraphy, and Distribution

During the initial investigations in the 1960s, Lin identified a reddened deposit with *in situ* stone tools and suggested a Pleistocene date. Sung (1969) then announced the discovery of a "Preceramic Culture" in the archaeological record of Taiwan. Prior to this discovery, the archaeological record in Taiwan had been assessed as commencing with the earliest pottery-bearing horizon at about 5000 BP. These Pleistocene findings in the Baxian Caves were termed the *Changbinian* [*Changpinian*] Culture by Ji Li (Sung 1969).

The use of the term "Preceramic Culture" by Sung during the 1960s through 1970s was in line with common practice in Japanese archaeology since the 1950s. Sung regarded the Preceramic Culture as interchangeable with the Changbinian, in this case connecting a rigorously defined Palaeolithic assemblage together with a later non-ceramic assemblage dated to the middle Holocene.

Sung's apparent hesitation to use the term "Palaeolithic" for these assemblages probably reflected an international consensus at the time, wherein a Palaeolithic assemblage usually (but not always) implied a Pleistocene age. All C14 dates from Chaoyin Cave (LH-2 in Figures 9.9 and 9.10), where the richest cultural remains were found, were Middle Holocene and clearly

FIGURE 9.10   Chaoyin Cave (LH-2, 40 m asl), with abundant Preceramic cultural remains dated to 6700–4800 cal. BP (photography by Hsiao-chun Hung).

younger than the Pleistocene. Four dating results of charcoal were 6569–5471 cal. BP (NTU-69), 6678–5585 cal. BP (NTU-70), 6294–5260 cal. BP (NTU-71), and 6224–4866 cal. BP (Y-2636) (see Table 9.1) (Sung 1969; Chang 1969). However, several years later, when the Radiocarbon Dating Laboratory in National Taiwan University announced a date from the higher Qianyuan Cave as older than 15,000 BP (NTU-135) (Hsu et al. 1973), Sung (1980) immediately welcomed the result and even suggested a deeper origin of 50,000 years ago for the "Preceramic Culture" in eastern Taiwan.

Between 2008 and 2015, Cheng-hwa Tsang and colleagues located 13 new caves, six rock shelters, and two large open terrace sites. Test excavations have been conducted in 15 caves (including some previously discovered by Sung et al. in the 1960s), one rock shelter, and one open terrace. Among the 17 excavated sites, nine (including eight caves, LH-4, 5, 6, 7, 24, 27, 29, 30, and the open terrace B) provided Pleistocene Palaeolithic remains, while another three produced only Holocene Preceramic remains (Figure 9.9).

In term of chronology, the Palaeolithic Changbinian context (ca. 30,000–15,000 cal. BP) was followed by a hiatus in C14-dated human activity of more than 8000 years at the Baxian Caves. A new C14 date of 5910–5750 cal. BP (Beta-321706) from Chaoyin Cave (Tsang et al. 2018) now can be added to the four previous dates from this site (Sung 1969; Chang 1969), listed above. These Holocene industries (ca. 6700–4800 cal. BP) are characterised by similar cobble tools as those with Pleistocene dates, but have increasing numbers of small flake tools (Figure 9.11) and bone implements. Similar Holocene artefacts are reported from the Xiaoma Caves (see below) in southeastern Taiwan, about 50 km south of the Baxian Caves (Figure 9.2).

Currently, Taiwanese archaeologists such as Huang (1991) and Tsang (2013) use the term "Preceramic Culture" to refer to the Middle Holocene assemblages that pre-date the arrival

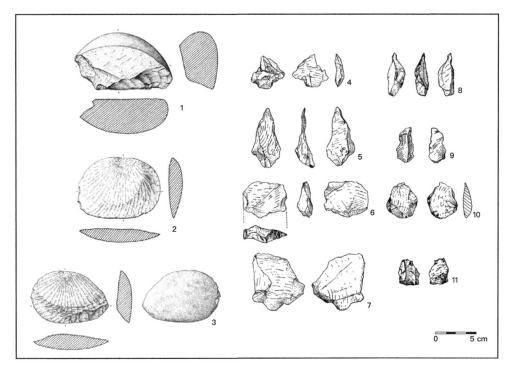

FIGURE 9.11  Preceramic (Holocene) lithics from Chaoyin Cave (LH-2; See location 2 in figure 9.9), ca. 6700–4800 cal. BP, including pebble choppers (1), large flakes (2 and 3), and small quartz flake implements (4–11) (1–3 after Tsang et al. (2015: 407), and 4–11 after Sung (1969); courtesy Wen-hsun Sung and Cheng-hwa Tsang).

of Neolithic farmers (Figure 9.4). Some Taiwanese archaeologists also use the term "Chaoyin Culture" after the initial discoveries in Chaoyin Cave in the 1960s, in order to distinguish these discoveries from the Palaeolithic Changbinian Culture (Tsang et al. 2018, 41–42). So far, three locations on Loham Cliff (LH-2, LH-27, and LH-34) (Figure 9.9) have yielded Preceramic (Holocene) Culture materials, but no human skeletal remains yet have been reported in association.

The oldest assemblage reported from the Baxian Cave comes from the base of "Anonymous Cave 11" (LH-30), located at 197 m asl (Location 30 in Figures 9.9 and 9.12). Among the highest of the Baxian Caves in present-day altitude, this cave originally was situated in the zone of the oldest recorded human activities. The oldest sites have been uplifted the highest, such that the older Palaeolithic deposits now are between 72 m and 197 m asl, while the younger Preceramic deposits now are between 40 m and 72 m asl.

LH-30 contains a Palaeolithic deposit over 2 m in thickness, lying 8 m under the present ground surface. This deposit contains multiple layers of anthropogenic soil rich in organic matter and stone artefacts. At the very bottom, marine sands and gravels overlie the bedrock. A C14 sample retrieved from the lowest anthropogenic layer, just above the marine sands, gave a date of 30,975–30,730 cal. BP (Beta-376713) (Table 9.1), although this sample was not directly associated with cultural remains. However, a date of 29,400–28,600 cal. BP (Beta-370089) comes from another anthropogenic blackened layer associated with stone tools about 80 cm

**164** Hsiao-chun Hung, Chin-yung Chao, Hirofumi Matsumura, et al.

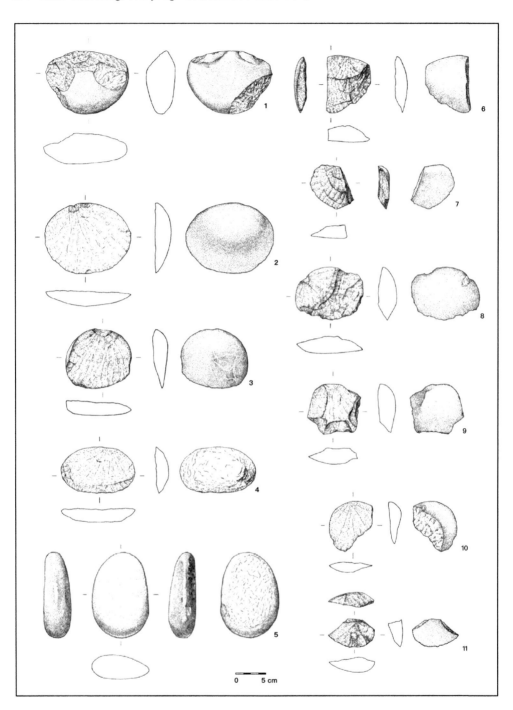

FIGURE 9.12  Palaeolithic (Pleistocene) lithics from Anonymous Cave 11 (LH-30; See location 30 in figure 9.9), ca. 30,000–21,000 cal. BP, including choppers (1), flakes (2–4, 6–11) and a pebble hammer (5) (after Tsang et al. (2015: 86–92); courtesy Cheng-hwa Tsang).

FIGURE 9.13    Cheng-hwa Tsang and Peter Bellwood standing at the base of Anonymous Cave 10 (LH-29), 142 m asl (see location 29 in figure 9.9), with deposits dated to 29,000–22,000 cal. BP. The Palaeolithic remains first appear 7.5 m below the surface (photography by Hsiao-chun Hung).

higher in the profile. Another sample of charred material between these contexts is dated to 27,560–26,730 cal. BP (Beta-370090).

In total so far, 16 AMS dates from the lower deposits in Anonymous Cave 11 (LH-30) range from 30,975 through 18,830 cal. BP (Table 9.1), securing the chronological integrity of the Palaeolithic sequence. In addition, two other AMS dates from Kunlun Cave (LH-7) and Anonymous Cave No. 10 (LH-29) (Figures 9.9, 9.13, and 9.14) calibrate to 29,020–28,670 years BP (Beta-390803) and 29,580–28,740 years BP (Beta-260204).

Further Palaeolithic discoveries include hearth features in several locations, including Anonymous Caves 10 (LH-29), 11 (LH 30) and 4 (LH-24), Kunlun Cave (LH-7), and Chaochen Cave (LH-6). At the bottom of Anonymous Cave 10 (LH-29; 142 m asl), at least five distinct hearth features were recorded through a depth of 40 cm within a single 2 × 2 m² test unit, embedded between basal fluvial sands over the rock floor of the cave and an overlying light brownish gravelly soil. Organic sediment samples from three of these hearths were dated to 27,910–27,680, 29,020–28,570, and 27,215–26,845 cal. BP (Beta-390802, 390803, and 390805). In addition, burnt pebbles and animal bones occurred in association.

In Kunlun Cave (LH-7) (see Location 7 in Figure 9.9), one fireplace (No. 2) is dated to 25,495–15,450 cal. BP by three C14 determinations (Beta-260201, 260202, 260203) (Tsang et al. 2009). In Anonymous Cave 4 (LH-24), two separate fireplaces associated with dense flaking debitage were found at 420–440 cm below the present ground surface (Tsang et al. 2011). Two dates from here are 20,370–20,090 cal. BP (Beta-293014) and 18,890–18,750 cal. BP (Beta-293015).

FIGURE 9.14  The Pacific Ocean from Anonymous Cave 10, 142 m asl (LH-29, see location 29 in figure 9.9) during excavation in 2014 (photography by Hsiao-chun Hung).

On the basis of 95 radiometric dates obtained during 2008 through 2015 (Table 9.1), the Palaeolithic Changbinian Culture began as early as 30,000 BP and lasted until c.15,000 BP. Notably, this time period overlapped with the LGM, when temperatures in Taiwan are estimated to have been colder on average by about 5–9°C (Huang and Zhang 2000), or 8–10°C (Liew and Chung 2001), much colder than modern winter average temperatures in Changbin of about 16–20°C.

The associated burnt pebbles and bones, hearths, and lenses of blackened deposits in the Baxian Caves suggest surprisingly intense Palaeolithic habitation. Most of the caves were restricted in size to under 80 m² behind the drip line, but a few were larger. In terms of the interior space, the largest two caves in this complex are Hailei Cave (LH-4) and Chaochen Cave (LH-6) (see Locations 4 and 6 in Figure 9.9), at 90 and 154 m², respectively. However, small rock shelters often yield rich materials. For example, the small Anonymous Cave 11 (LH-27) (see Location 27 in Figure 9.9), despite being less than 36 m² in size, produced over 10,000 lithic items.

## The Palaeolithic and Preceramic Lithic Assemblages

Comprehensive site reports have not yet been published for the 1969–74 or 2008–2015 excavations in the Baxian Caves, but several preliminary reports (Sung 1969; Tsang et al. 2009, 2011, 2013, 2015) and a catalogue (Tsang 2017) are useful for establishing the basic findings and parameters. Currently, the general term "cobble-tool industry" can be applied to the Changbinian lithic assemblage (Sung 1969; Tsang 2013; Wang 2021). It is characterised by "heavy-duty tools" made from cobbles, such as side- and end-choppers and hammer stones, and "light-duty tools" that are largely used flakes and retouched flake scrapers. The lithics are made of siliceous rocks.

Fine-material lithic of smaller size (<8 cm), mostly made of quartz and few chalcedony and chert, were found in Chaoyin Cave, accounting for several hundreds of the total lithic findings of more than 3,000 items.

### Eastern Taiwan: The Xiaoma Caves

About 50 km south of the Baxian Caves, several limestone caves and rock shelters are located near Xiaoma Village in Donghe Township, southeastern Taiwan. These cave sites contain archaeological remains from Preceramic through Middle Neolithic contexts. Two separate clusters of archaeological sites are: 1) the Xiaoma Caves; and 2) Xiaomalong (Xiaoma Dragon) Cave.

The Xiaoma Caves complex contains more than 10 caves and rock shelters (Figures 9.2 and 9.15), located in the limestone topography on the north bank of the Mawuku River, and facing towards the Pacific Ocean. These caves are about 800 m inland from the modern coastline, and about 400 m north of the Mawuku River. They were documented by Shih-chiang Huang and Dun-shan Wu in 1987, and then from 1988 and 1990 by Shi-chiang Huang, who brought students from National Taiwan University to excavate two of the cave sites, No. 5 (C5) and No. 10 (C10) (Huang and Chen 1990; Huang 1991).

C5 contained a Preceramic layer below 130 cm depth in which no potsherds were found, but instead this layer yielded cobble tools, small flakes of quartz, agate or carnelian, and marine shells (Figure 9.16). Below 200 cm, the excavation encountered marine sand that retained stone tools. A similar Preceramic assemblage was found in C10, excavated in 1990. Two C14 dates on

FIGURE 9.15   The Xiaoma Cave complex along the base of a former sea-cliff, eastern Taiwan (photography by Mike T. Carson).

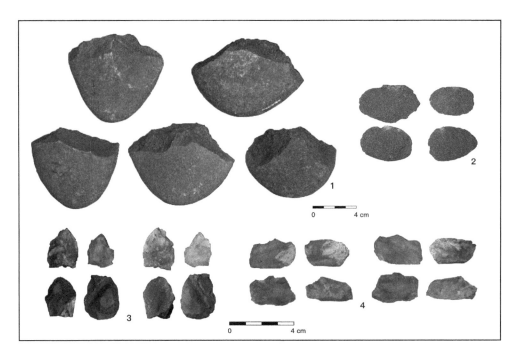

FIGURE 9.16  Preceramic stone tools from the Xiaoma Caves, ca. 6200 to 5700 cal. BP, including cobble chopping tools (1) and flakes (2–4) (after Lee (2004), courtesy Tsuo-ting Lee).

marine shell from Preceramic contexts in the Xiaoma Caves are 6189–5920 and 5996–5725 cal. BP (Table 9.1), similar to the dates from Chaoyin Cave in the Baxian Cave complex.

During the excavation in 1988 by Huang and colleagues, a Preceramic burial was found in C5. The skeleton was placed in a squatting posture (Figure 9.17), and so far it is the only

FIGURE 9.17  The squatting burial of the Xiaoma Woman in Xiaoma C5 (after Huang and Chen (1990), courtesy Shih-chiang Huang).

pre-Neolithic human burial reported from Taiwan. The flexed burial posture equates with other late Palaeolithic and Preceramic burials discovered widely in southern China and Southeast Asia (Higham 2013; Bellwood 2017; Hung et al. 2017).

A craniofacial study by Matsumura and colleagues has confirmed the Xiaoma individual as female, with a small body size. Her closest cranial morphometric affiliation is with Negrito populations in the Philippines (Figure 9.18). This result further confirms legends among indigenous Formosan Austronesian-speaking populations about the former existence of small

FIGURE 9.18  A neighbour joining (NJ) tree generated from Q-mode correlation coefficients based on 13 cranial morphometric measurements from Australia and Melanesia (MEL), Northeast Asia (NEA), Southwest Asia (SWA), Europe (EU), and Africa (AF). This tree has four major clusters, with Australo-Melanesian and African groups clustered together at the bottom. A sub-cluster formed by Xiaoma, Philippine Negritos, and Andaman Islanders lies at the base of the diagram (see Matsumura et al. (2021) for the data sources and analytical methods).

dark-skinned people in Taiwan (for details see Matsumura et al. 2021; Hung et al. 2022; Hung et al. 2024).

Xiaomalong Cave lies about 2.2 km north of the Xiaoma Caves. The small interior slopes steeply downward at least 20 m. A test excavation was conducted here by Yu-pei Chen in 2003. A Neolithic layer at 70–100 cm depth contained potsherds, animal bones, and stone tools, overlaying an older Preceramic deposit with stone artefacts at 100–190 cm depth. In the Preceramic deposit, larger stone objects of hammers, choppers, and flakes were made of sandstone and andesite, while smaller tools were made of quartz, agate, or carnelian (Chen 2004). No direct dating was obtained for the Preceramic layer at Xiaomalong, but the context appeared to be similar to the Preceramic findings at Xiaoma C5.

## Southern Taiwan: Eluanbi II, Longkeng, and Longxia Cave

The southern tip of Taiwan has revealed four major archaeological contexts, according to Kuang-chou Li, wherein "Elunabi [O-Lun-Pi] Prehistoric Cultural Phase I" coincided with the Holocene Preceramic as known in other areas of Taiwan. This Phase is characterised by "a lack of ceramic industry and a lithic industry comprised solely of chipped tools" (Li 1983).

These Preceramic assemblages come from Eluanbi II rock shelter and the Longkeng open site in Pingdong County. Eluanbi II, at about 20–40 m asl, is located in the limestone reef area of Eluanbi Park, within a wider area of numerous limestone rock shelters (Figures 9.2 and 9.19). Excavations by Kuang-chou Li in 1982 targeted a rock shelter (Locus A), a separate cave, and a neighbouring open space (Locus B) (Li 1983, 1984). The archaeological findings include choppers, flake tools, shell scrapers, bone chisels, bone points, marine shells, turtle shells, and

FIGURE 9.19   A rock shelter in Eluanbi II, southern Taiwan (photography by Hsiao-chun Hung).

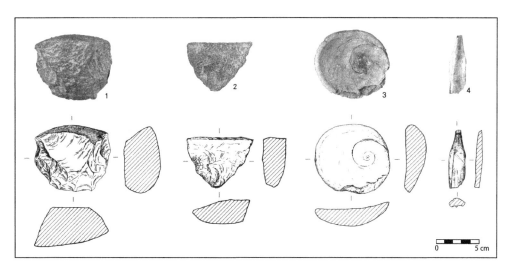

FIGURE 9.20  A cobble tool (1) flake tool (2) shell scraper (3) and bone chisel (4) from Eluanbi II (after Li (1983), courtesy Kuang-chou Li).

bones of land animals and fish (Figure 9.20). Two C-14 dates on marine shell scrapers are 5293–4795 cal. BP (Beta-6159) and 5300–4645 cal. BP (Beta-6727) (Table 9.1). Longkeng is an open site, about 2 km east of Eluanbi II (Figure 9.2). Excavation disclosed a similar cultural assemblage (Li 1984) and a date of 6106–5645 cal. BP (Li 1987; Tsang 2013) (Table 9.1).

A pointed cobble-chopping tool from Longxia Cave (Lobster Cave) in Kending (Figures 9.2 and 9.21) resembles the "oyster picks (*haolizhuo*)" that have been reported from sites dated about 7000–5000 years BP in coastal southern China (Hung 2019). Longxia Cave is located about 240 m asl in a karst landscape, and it contains fossil-bearing deposits that are about 5 m

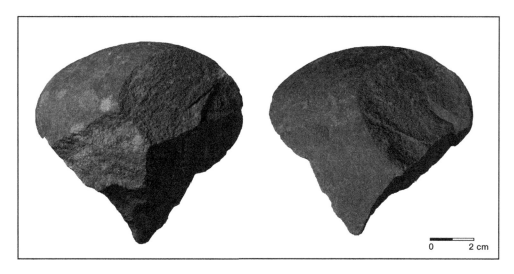

FIGURE 9.21  A pointed cobble chopping tool ("oyster pick", shown from both sides) from Longxia Cave (photography by Chin-yung Chao).

deep. The taphonomy is complex and perhaps involves multiple redepositions, but the excavators estimated an age range for animals such as leopards, deer, and macaques between 500 kya and 12 kya. However, a C14 date on animal bone collagen suggested a much younger date of 7000 years BP (Chi et al. 2021), which may refer to the "oyster pick".

## Other Findings

Besides the aforementioned sites, a few locations in Taiwan have yielded typical late Palaeolithic or Preceramic stone tools, although the associated site contexts have not yet been clarified. For example, a chopper tool was collected at Zhishanyan, a small hill in Taipei City (Sung 1980; Huang 1984). From the lower layer of the Yuanshan site in Taipei, a few chopper tools, flake tools and scrapers were found below the Early Neolithic Dabenkeng cultural layer (Huang 1992).

## Conclusion

This chapter has reviewed hominin and related remains in and around Taiwan from the Middle Pleistocene and continuing until potentially 5 kya (Figure 9.4). Most discoveries come from now-drowned ancient land bridge locations at the west of Taiwan and from now-uplifted caves and rock shelters at the east and south of Taiwan. Human remains include Penghu 1, considered to be an archaic *Homo* or possibly a Denisovan, the two Liangdao Early Holocene burials, and the Xiaoma Cave female. A Palaeolithic record has existed in Taiwan since at least 30,000 BP, followed by Holocene Preceramic sites dated so far between 6700 and 4800 BP. The next major archaeological horizon was the Neolithic, appearing about 5000–4800 BP.

The Changbin cobble tools dated between 30,000 and 15,000 BP represent so far the only Pleistocene and Palaeolithic assemblage in Taiwan. Archaeologists have attempted to locate a homeland for the Changbinian on the Asian Continent through comparisons of lithic technology (e.g., Chang 1969; Solheim 1969; Li and Li 1983; Zhang 1983; Kato 1990, 2003; Huang 1991; Chen 1994; You 1996; Cai 1997; Tsang 2013), but the material is too generic for distinguishing any one specific area apart from another. For instance, proposed origin locations include Guangxi, Hubei, Fujian, Guangdong, and Guizhou in southern China, Henan in northern China, together with Vietnam and the Philippines. Another direction of movement may have been from eastern Taiwan using the Kuroshio Current (Figure 9.2) to reach the southern Ryukyu Islands (Kaifu et al. 2015).

According to craniofacial analyses, the Pre-Neolithic hunter-gatherers who occupied southern China and Southeast Asia between 30,000 and 5000 years BP belonged to the "first layer" of anatomically modern humans (AMH), prior to the period of Neolithic dispersal. They shared the diagnostic skeletal features of dolichocephalic calvaria, large zygomatic bones, prominent glabellae and superciliary arches, concave nasal roots, and low and wide faces. These features relate them to ancestral Australo-Melanesian (Australo-Papuan) populations although additionally Japanese Jomon hunter-gatherers of the Late Pleistocene and Early through Middle Holocene expressed the same features (Matsumura et al. 2019, 2021). Ancient DNA studies focused in the same geographic region have reached a similar conclusion (Lipson et al. 2018; McColl et al. 2018).

Questions persist about the relationship between the Palaeolithic Changbinian cultural group (30,000–15,000 BP) and the later Preceramic cultural group (6700–4800 BP) in Taiwan. Given the time gap between the two periods, definitive conclusions are not yet possible about a sudden shift or a gradual change (Hung et al. 2022).

Preceramic sites contain cultural elements such as small flakes made of quartz and semi-precious stones, plus polished bone tools that appear to have been absent in the older Changbinian sites. The affinity of the Xiaoma female to modern Negrito groups in the Philippines perhaps reflects some degree of population movement on the Kuroshio Current from that region (Kato 2003).

One more question remains to be addressed about the seafaring ability of these Palaeolithic and Preceramic groups. Were people from Taiwan able to reach the Ryukyu Islands by 30,000 years ago, when the first human remains are attested in several of the Ryukyus, especially Okinawa (Kaifu et al. 2015, 2020)? A paddled experimental voyage using a Jomon style of dugout canoe successfully completed a journey from eastern Taiwan to Yonaguni, the westernmost of Japan's Okinawa Islands. This voyage spanned 45 hours and travelled 200 km with the Kuroshio Current across open sea (Normile 2019). Did "Xiaoma Woman" herself, or her ancestors, follow a similar path, borne by the northward-flowing Kuroshio Current from Luzon to Taiwan during a later period?

Another issue involves the persistence of a Preceramic assemblage into the middle Holocene around 5000–4800 years BP, implying a chronological overlap with the arrival of the Neolithic pottery-bearing Dabenkeng Culture. Preceramic hunter-gatherers must have encountered the incoming farmers who crossed Taiwan Strait by 4800 BP. Demographic and cultural admixture would have occurred, as when early rice farmers from southern China first met Hoabinhian hunter-gatherers elsewhere on the mainland of Southeast Asia. Perhaps these interactions are traceable not only through mysterious legends about "little black people" among Formosan populations (Li 1996, Liu 2015; Hung et al. 2022, 2024), but also they could be detectable if ancient DNA samples will become available in Taiwan.

## Acknowledgments

We thank Professors Glenn R. Summerhayes, Takeshi Ueki, and Peter Hiscock for inviting us to write this chapter. Professor Peter Bellwood provided comments to improve this work.

## Notes

1 This chapter uses Pinyin for all site or place names in Mandarin.
2 As "dong" means cave in Mandarin, "Baxian Caves" often is translated into "Baxiandong" or "Baxiandong Caves" in English.

## References

Bellwood, Peter. 2017 *First Islanders: Prehistory and Human Migration in Island Southeast Asia*. Hoboken, NJ: Wiley Blackwell.

Blust, Robert. 1984–1985 The Austronesian homeland: A linguistic perspective. *Asian Perspectives* 26, 45–67.

Cai, B. 1997 Dongshan Luqiao yu Taiwan Zuizao Renlei (Dongshan Land Bridge and the earliest humans in Taiwan). *Zhangzhou Shiyuan Xuebao (Journal of Zhangzhou Teachers College)* 3, 31–36. (In Chinese)

Cai, B. 2001 Taiwan Haixia Wangengxinshi Renlei Gonggu Huashi (Fossil human humerus of late Pleistocene from the Taiwan Strait). *Renlei Xue Xuebao (Acta Anthropologica Sinica)* 20, 178–815. (In Chinese)

Carson, M.T., and Hung, H.C. 2018 Learning from paleo-landscapes: Defining the land-use systems of the ancient Malayo-Polynesian homeland. *Current Anthropology* 59, 790–813.

Chang, K.C. 1969 Changpinian: A newly discovered preceramic culture from the Agglomerate Caves on the east coast of Taiwan (preliminary report). *Wen-hsun Sung. Asian Perspectives* 12, 133–36.

Chang, C, Kaifu, Y, Takai, M, Kono, R, Grün, R, Matsuura, S, Kinsley, L., and Lin, L. 2015 The first archaic Homo from Taiwan. *Nature Communications* 6, 6037.

Chen, G. 1994 Mintai Jiushiqi Shidai Gurenlei yu Gu Wenhua (Ancient humans and ancient culture in the Paleolithic Age in Fujian and Taiwan). *Fujian Shifan Daxue Xuebao (Journal of Fujian Normal University)* 4, 96–102. (In Chinese)

Chen, K. 2000 Shilun Taiwan Ge Shidai de Buru Dongwuqun Ji Qi Xiangguan Wenti-Taiwan Diqu Dongwu Kaoguxue Yanjiu De Jichu Ziliao Zhiyi: Shang Pian) (On Taiwan mammalian faunas in different periods of time and related problems: The background materials for Taiwan zooarchaeological studies: Part I). *Zhongyang Yanjiuyuan Lishi Yuyan Yanjiusuo Jikan (Bulletin of the Institute of History and Philology)* 71, 130–243. (In Chinese)

Chen, Y. 2004 Xiaomalongdong Yizhi Shijue Baogao (Report of test excavations at Xiaomalong Cave site). *Tianye Kaogu (Field Archaeology of Taiwan)* 8, 123–148. (In Chinese)

Chen, C., and Chiu, H. 2013 *Mazu Liangdao Daowei Yizhiqun Fajue ji Liangdaoren Xiufu jihua (Excavation of Liangdao-Daowei Sites Group, Liangdao, Matsu Archipelago and the Treatments of "Liangdao Man" of the Liangdao-Daowei-I Site)*. Liangjian: Liangjian County Government. (In Chinese)

Chen, Y., and Liu, T. 1996 Sea level changes in the last several thousand years, Penghu Islands, Taiwan Strait. *Quaternary Research* 45, 254–262.

Chen, W, Huang, M, and Liu, T. 1991 Neotectonic significance of the Chimei Fault in the Coastal Range, eastern Taiwan. *Proceedings of the Geological Society of China* 34, 43–56.

Chen, W.S., Sung, S., Wu, L., and Hsu, H. 2004 Moci Bingqi Yilai Taiwan Haian Pingyuanqu de Haianxian Bianqian (Shoreline changes in the coastal plain of Taiwan since the last glacial epoch). *Kaogu Renlei Xuekan (Bulletin of the Department of Archaeology and Anthropology)* 62, 40–55. (In Chinese)

Chen, L., Fan, X., and Yang, L. 2012 *Fujian Dongshan Jiushiqi Wenhua Yanjiu (A Study of the Paleolithic Culture in Dongshan, Fujian)*. Fuzhou: Haichao Sheying Yishu Press. (In Chinese)

Chen, F., Welker, F., Shen, C., Bailey, S., Bergmann, I., Davis, S., and Xia, H. 2019 A late middle Pleistocene Denisovan mandible from the Tibetan plateau. *Nature* 569, 409–412.

Cheng, C. 2009 *Taiwan Shiqian Shidai De Wenhua Bianqian Yu Quyu Guanxi- Zie Oluanbi Dier Yizhi Chufa De Fajue Sikao Yu Taolun (Cultural Change and Regional Relationship of Prehistoric Taiwan: A Case Study of Oluanpi II Site)*. PhD diss., National Taiwan University. (In Chinese)

Chi, T., Gan, Y., Yang, T., and Chang, C. 2021 First report of Leopard fossils from a limestone cave in Kenting area, southern Taiwan. *PeerJ* 9, e12020.

Chiu, H. 2016 Zuozhenren de Zaiyanjiu yu Taiwan Jiushiqi Shidai de Xinguancha (Re-study the Zuozhen man and the new perspectives of Taiwan Palaeolithic Age). *Taiwan Bowu Jikan (Taiwan Natural Science)* 35, 12–25. (In Chinese)

Deng, Z., Kuo, S.C., Carson, M.T., and Hung, H.C. 2022 Early Austronesians cultivated rice and millet together: Tracing Taiwan's first Neolithic crops. *Frontiers in Plant Science* 13, https://doi.org/10.3389/fpls.2022.962073.

Gau, J. 1982 Penghu Dongwu Qun (The Penghu fauna). *Haiyang Huikan (Journal of Marine Science)* 27, 123–131. (In Chinese)

Higham, Charles. 2013 Hunter-gatherers in Southeast Asia: From prehistory to the present. *Human Biology* 85, 21–44.

Ho, C. 2011 Shuixia Kaogu yu Taiwan Luqiao Dongwuqun (Underwater archaeology and the Taiwan Land Bridge fauna). *Kexue Fazhan (Science Development)* 458, 32–37. (In Chinese)

Hsieh, M., and Liew, P. 2010 Huadong Haian Quanxinshi Dike Shangsheng Sulu de Zaijiantaoo. (A new version of Holocene tectonic uplift rates along the Hua-Tung coast of eastern Taiwan). *Jingjibu Zhongyang Dizhi Diaochasuo Huikan (Bulletin of the Central Geological Survey, MOEA)* 23, 165–200. (In Chinese)

Hsieh, M., Liew, P., and Hsu, M. 2004 Holocene tectonic uplift on the Hua-tung coast, eastern Taiwan. *Quaternary International* 115–116, 47–70.

Hsu, Y., Chou, M., Hsu, Y., Lin, S., and Lu, S. 1973 National Taiwan University radiocarbon measurements II. *Radiocarbon* 15, 345–9.

Huang, S. 1984 *Taibei Zhishanyan Yizhi Fajue Baogao (Excavation Report of the Zhishanyan Site in Taipei)*. Taipei: Taipei City Archive Committee. (In Chinese)

Huang, S. 1991 Cong Xiaoma Dongxue Tan Taiwan Diqu Xiantao Shiqi Wenhua (Discuss the Preceramic culture in Taiwan from the cave site of Xiaoma). *Tianye Kaogu (Field Archaeology of Taiwan)* 2, 37–54. (In Chinese)

Huang, S. 1992 *Diyiji Guji Yuanshan Yizhi Fanwei Shijue Pinggu Baogao* (Evaluation Report on the Test Excavation of the Yuanshan Site, the First-Class Ancient Relic). Taipei: National Taiwan University. (In Chinese)

Huang, S., and Chen, Y. 1990 *Donghe Diqu Yizhi Shijue ji Shiqian Wenhua Chongjian (Test Excavations in Donghe and Reconstruction of Prehistoric Culture)*. Taipei: National Taiwan University. (In Chinese)

Huang, Z., and Zhang, W. 2000 *Moci Bingqi Shengqi Zhongguo Redai de Bianqian* (The shift of tropical zone during the last glacial maximum in China). *Dili Xuebao (Department of Geography)* 55, 587–95. (In Chinese)

Hung, H.C. 2019 Prosperity and complexity without farming: The South China coast, c. 5000–3000 BC. *Antiquity* 93, 325–341.

Hung, H.C., and Carson, M.T. 2014 Foragers, fishers, and farmers: Origins of the Taiwan Neolithic. *Antiquity* 88, 1115–1131.

Hung, H.C., Zhang, C., Matsumura, H., and Li, Z. 2017 Neolithic transition in Guangxi: A long development of hunting-gathering society on Southern China, in *Bio-Anthropological Studies of Early Holocene Hunter-Gatherer Sites at Huiyaotian and Liyupo in Guangxi, China*, eds Matsumura, H., Hung, H.C., Li, Z., and Shinoda, K. Tokyo: National Museum of Nature and Sciences, 205–228.

Hung, H.C., Matsumura, H., Nguyen, L., Hanihara, T., Huang, S., and Carson, M.T. 2022 Negritos in Taiwan and the wider prehistory of Southeast Asia: New discovery from the Xiaoma Caves. *World Archaeology* 54, 207–228.

Hung, H.C., Matsumura, H., Nguyen, L.C., Hanihara, T., Huang, S.C., and Carson, M.T. 2024 Tracing Negritos and their paths in ancient Taiwan: New findings raise more questions, in *Seeking the Koko' ta'ay*, eds. Openshaw, T. and Karalekas, D. Leiden: Brill, 35–57.

Kaifu, Y., Fujita, M., Yoneda, M., and Yamasaki, S. 2015 Pleistocene seafaring and colonization of the Ryukyu Islands, Southwestern Japan, in *Emergence and Diversity of Modern Human Behavior in Palaeolithic Asia*, eds Kaifu, Y., Izuho, M., Goebel, T., Sato, H., and Ono, A. College Station: Texas A&M University Press, 346–361.

Kaifu, Y., Kuo, T., and Kubota, Y. 2020 Palaeolithic voyage for invisible islands beyond the horizon. *Scientific Reports* 10, 19785.

Kato, S. 1990 Changpinian Wenhua de Ruogan Wenti (Observations on the Changbinian Culture). *Renleixue Xuebao (Acta Anthropologica Sinica)* 9, 16–9. (In Chinese)

Kato, S. 2003 Mintai Diyu Shiqian Wenhua Jiaoliu Wenti (Issues of the cultural interactions between Fujian and Taiwan). *Dongnan Kaogu Yanjiu* (Studies on Southeast China Archaeology) 3, 277–283. (In Chinese)

Ko, A., Chen, C., Fu, Q., Delfin, F., Li, M., Chiu, H., Stoneking, M., and Ko, Y. 2014 Early Austronesians: Into and out of Taiwan. *The American Journal of Human Genetics* 94, 426–436.

Li, K. 1983 Eluanbi *Gongyuan Kaogu Diaocha Baogao (Report of Archaeological Investigations in the Eluanbi Park at the Southern Tip of Taiwan)*. Taipei: Department of Anthropology, National Taiwan University. (In Chinese)

Li, K. 1984 Kending Guojia Gongyuan Suojian de Xiantao Wenhua Jiqi Xiangguan Wenti (On the new discovered preceramic culture in the Kenting National Park in the Southern tip of Taiwan). *Kaogu Renlei Xuekan (Bulletin of the Department of Archaeology and Anthropology)* 44, 79–147. (In Chinese)

Li, K. 1987 *Kending Guojia Gongyuan De Shiqian Wenhua (Prehistoric Cultures in Kending National Park)*. Taipei: Council for Cultural Affairs, Executive Yuan. (In Chinese)

Li, P. 1996 Taiwan Nandao Minzu Guanyu Airen de Chuanshuo (Legends about pygmies among the Formosan natives), in *Zhongguo Shenhua yu Chuanshuo Xueshu Yantaohui Lunwenji (Proceedings of the Conference on Chinese Myth and Legend)*, eds Li, Y., and Wang, C. Taipei: Center for Chinese Studies, 579–604. (In Chinese)

Li, J., and Li, Z. 1983 Taiwan yu Zuguo Dalu de Guanxi yuanyuan Liuchang (The relationship between Taiwan and the motherland mainland has a long history). *Kaogu Yu Wenwu (Archaeology and Cultural Relics)* 1, 1–40. (In Chinese)

Lien, C. 2015 Changpin culture of Taiwan and characteristics of its Lithic Industry, in *Emergence and Diversity of Modern Human Behavior in Palaeolithic Asia*, eds Kaifu, Y., Izuho, M., Goebel, T., Sato, H., and Ono, A. Brazos: Texas A&M University Press, 239–49.

Liew, P., and Chung, N. 2001 Vertical migration of forests during the last glacial period in subtropical Taiwan. *Western Pacific Earth Sciences* 1, 405–14.

Liew, P., Pirazzoli, P., Hsieh, M., Arnold, M., Barusseau, J., Fontugne, M., and Giresse, P. 1993 Holocene tectonic uplift deduced from elevated shorelines, Eastern Coastal Range of Taiwan. *Tectonophysics* 222, 55–68.

Lipson, M., Cheronet, O., Mallick, S., Rohland, N., Oxenham, M., Pietrusewsky, M., Pryce, T.O., Willis, A., Matsumura, H., Buckley, H., Domett, K., Nguyen, G.H., Trinh, H.H., Kyaw, A.A., Win, T.T., Pradier, B., Broomandkhoshbacht, N., Candilio, F., Changmai, P., Fernandes, D., Ferry, M., Gamarra, B., Harney, E., Kampuansai, J., Kutanan, W., Michel, M., Novak, M., Oppenheimer, J., Sirak, K., Stewardson, K., Zhang, Z., Flegontov, P., Pinhasi, R., and Reich, D. 2018 Ancient genomes document multiple waves of migration in Southeast Asian prehistory. *Science* 361, 92–95.

Liu, Y.L. 2015 Taiwan Yuanzhu Minzu Airen Chuanshuo Yanjiu (The Study of the Legend of Pygmy from Taiwanese Indigenous Tribes). PhD dissertation, National Dong Hwa University. (In Chinese)

Lee, T.T. 2004 Xiaoma Dongxue Fajue yu Shiyingzhi Xiaoshiqi Leixing Yanjiu (Typological Investigation of Quartz Lithic from the Xiaoma Caves, Taidong, Taiwan). Master thesis, National Taiwan University. (in Chinese)

Matsumura, H., Hung, H.C., Higham, C., Zhang, C., Yamagata, M., Nguyen, L.C., Li, Z., Fan, X.C., Simanjuntak, T., Oktaviana, A., He, J.N., Chen, C.Y., Pan, C.K., He, G., Sun, G.P., Huang, W.J., Li, X.W., Wei, X.T., Domett, K., Halcrow, S., Nguyen, K.D., Trinh, H.H., Bui, C.H., Nguyen, K.T.K., and Reinecke, A. 2019. Craniometrics reveal 'Two Layers' of prehistoric human dispersal in eastern Eurasia. *Scientific Reports* 9 (1), 12.

Matsumura, H., Xie, G., Nguyen, L.C., Hanihara, T., Li, Z., Nguyen, K.T.K., Ho, X.T., Nguyen, T.N., Huang, S.C., and Hung, H.C. 2021 Female craniometrics support 'Two-layer Model' of human dispersal in eastern Eurasia: Evidence from the Yahuai Cave and other hunter-gatherer sites. *Scientific Reports* 11, 20830.

McColl, H., Racimo, F., Vinner, L., Demeter, F., Gakuhari, T., Moreno-Mayar, V., van Driem, G., Wilken, U., Seguin-Orlando, A., de la Fuente Castro, C., Wasef, S., Shoocongdej, R., Souksavatdy, V., Sayavongkhamdy, T., Saidin, M., Allentoft, M., Sato, T., Malaspinas, A., Aghakhanian, F., Korneliussen, T., Prohaska, A., Margaryan, A., de Barros Damgaard, P., Kaewsutthi, S., Lertrit, P., Nguyen, T., Hung, H.C., Tran, T., Truong, H., Nguyen, G., Shahidan, S., Wiradnyana, K., Matsumae, H., Shigehara, N., Yoneda, M., Ishida, H., Masuyama, T., Yamada, Y., Tajima, A., Shibata, H., Toyoda, A., Hanihara, T., Nakagome, S., Deviese, T., Bacon, A.M., Duringer, P., Ponche, J.L., Shackelford, L., Patole-Edoumba, E., Nguyen, A., Bellina-Pryce, B., Galipaud, J.C., Kinaston, R., Buckley, H., Pottier, C., Rasmussen, S., Higham, T., Foley, R., Lahr, M., Orlando, L., Sikora, M., Phipps, M., Oota, H., Higham, C., Lambert, D., and Willerslev, E. 2018 The prehistoric peopling of Southeast Asia. *Science* 361, 88–92.

Normile, D. 2019 Update: Explorers successfully voyage to Japan in primitive boat in bid to unlock an ancient mystery. Science News, July 2019. Retrieved from https://www.sciencemag.org/news/2019/07/explorers-voyage-japan-primitive-boat-hopes-unlocking-ancient-mystery

Shikama, T., Otsuka, H., and Tomida, Y. 1975 Fossil proboscidea from Taiwan (i). *Science Reports of the Yokohama National University, Section II, Biological and Geological Sciences* 22, 13–35.

Shikama, T., Lin, C., Shimoda, N., and Baba, H. 1976 Discovery of fossil *Homo sapiens* from Cho-Chen in Taiwan. *Journal of the Anthropological Society of Nippon* 84, 131–8.

Solheim, W. II. 1969 Reworking Southeast Asian prehistory. *Paideuma* 15, 125–139.

Sung, W. 1969 Changbin Wenhua: Taiwan Shouci Faxian de Xiantao Wenhua: Jianbao)" (Changpinian: A newly discovered Preceramic Culture from the Agglomerate Caves on the east coast of Taiwan, preliminary report). *Zhongguo Minzuxue Tongxun (Newsletter of Chinese Ethnology)* 9, 1–27. (In Chinese)

Sung, W. 1980 You Kaoguxue Kan Taiwan (Taiwan in archaeological perspectives), in *Zhongguo De Taiwan (Chinese Taiwan)*, ed Chen, Q. Taipei: Zhongyang Wenwu Gongyingshe, 93–220. (In Chinese)

Tsang, C. 2005 Recent discoveries at the Tapenkeng Culture sites in Taiwan: Implications for the problem of Austronesian Origins, in *The Peopling of East Asia. Putting Together Archaeology, Linguistics and Genetics*, eds Blench, R. and Sagart, L. London: Routledge Curzon, 63–73.

Tsang, C. 2013 Baxiandong Kaogu de Xinfaxian Jianlun Taiwan Jiushiqi Wenhua de Niandai yu Leiyuan Wenti (New archaeological discoveries at Baxian Caves and the issues related to the chronology and the affinities of the Palaeolithic Culture in Taiwan, in *Dongya Kaogu De Xinfaxian (New Discoveries from East Asian Archaeology)*, ed Chen, K. Taipei: Academia Sinica, 379. (In Chinese)

Tsang, C. 2017 *Guoding Baxiandong Yizhi Chutu Wenwu Tujian (Illustrated Catalogue of the Artifacts Unearthed from the Nationally Designated Archaeological Site of Baxian Caves)*. Taichung: Bureau of Cultural Heritage, Ministry of Culture. (In Chinese)

Tsang, C., Chen, W., and Li, K. 2009 *Taidongxian Changbinxiang Baxiandong Yizhi Diaocha Yanjiu Jihua (Diyinian) Yanjiu Baogao (Research Report on the Baxian Caves, Changbin Township, Taidong County (First Year))*. Taipei: Academia Sinica. (In Chinese)

Tsang, C., Chen, W., and Li, K. 2011 *Taidongxian Changbinxiang Baxiandong Yizhi Diaozha Yanjiu Jihua (Diernian) Yanjiu Baogao (Research Report on the Baxian Caves, Changbin Township, Taidong County (Second Year))*. Taipei: Academia Sinica. (In Chinese)

Tsang, C., Chen, W., and Li, K. 2013 *Taidongxian Changbinxiang Baxiandong Yizhi Diaozha Yanjiu Jihua (Disannian) Yanjiu Baogao (Research Report on the Baxian Caves, Changbin Township, Taidong County (Third Year))*. Taipei: Academia Sinica. (In Chinese)

Tsang, C., Chen, W., and Li, K. 2015 *Taidongxian Changbinxiang Baxiandong Yizhi Diaozha Yanjiu Jihua (Disinian) Yanjiu Baogao (Research Report on the Baxian Caves, Changbin Township, Taidong County (Fourth Year))*. Taipei: Academia Sinica. (In Chinese)

Tsang, C., Lee, K., Zeng, Y., Chen, W., and by. 2018 Baxiandong Kaogu Yizhi (Baxiandong Archaeological Site), in *Tawian Kaogu Fajue Baogao Jingxuan (Selected Archaeological Reports in Taiwan)*, ed Chen, K. Taichung: Bureau of Cultural Heritage, Ministry of Culture, 1–52. (In Chinese)

Wang, Y.P. 2021 Lishi Gongye Chuantong yu Huanan Jiushiqi Wanqi Wenhua (Cobble-tool tradition and the late Palaeolithic Culture in southern China). *Nanfang Wenwu (Southern Cultural Relics)* 1, 91–97. (In Chinese)

Wei, K.Y. 2007 Taiwan Disiji Buru Dongwu Huashi Yanjiu De Huigu Yu Qianzhan (Quaternary mammalian fossils of Taiwan: An eclectic overview and prospects for future study), in *Jingjibu Zhongyang Dizhi Diaochasuo Tekan Di shiba Hao (Special Issue No. 18 of the Central Geological Survey, Ministry of Economic Affairs)*, ed Wei, K. Taipei: Central Geological Survey, Ministry of Economic Affairs, 261–286. (In Chinese)

Yang, H.C., and Chen, W.S. 2013 Moci Bingqi Yilai Taiwan Dongbu Haian Shanmai Nanduan Zhi Haian Bianqian yu Yizhi Fenbu Zhi Guanxi (The coastline development of the southern part of the coastal range in eastern Taiwan since the last glacial epoch and its relation with the distribution of archaeological sites). *Lingnan Kaogu Yanjiu (Lingnan Archaeological Research)* 13, 89–94. (In Chinese)

Yang, M., Fan, X., Sun, B., Chen, C., Lang, J., Ko, Y.C., Tsang, C., Chiu, H., Wang, T., Bao, Q., Wu, X., Hajdinjak, M., Ko, A., Ding, M., Cao, P., Yang, R., Liu, F., Nickel, B., Dai, Q., Feng, X., Zhang, L., Sun, C., Zeng, C., Zhao, Y., Zhang, M., Cui, X., Reich, David, Stoneking, M., and Fu, Q. 2020 Ancient DNA indicates human population shifts and admixture in Northern and Southern China. *Science* 369, 282–288.

Yoneda, M., Uno, H., Shibata, Y., Suzuki, R., Kumamoto, Y., Yoshida, K., Sasaki, T., Suzuki, A., and Kawahata, H. 2007 Radiocarbon marine reservoir ages in the Western pacific estimated by pre-bomb molluscan shells. *Nuclear Instruments and Methods in Physics Research B* 259, 432–437.

You, Y. 1988 Dongshan Haiyu Renlei Yigu he Buru Dongwu Huashi de Faxian Jiqi Xueshu Jiazhi (The discovery of human remains and mammalian fossils in Dongshan waters and its academic value). *Fujian Wenbo (Fujian Culture Heritage and Museums)* 1, 4–7. (In Chinese)

You, Y. 1996 Shiqian Shiqi Renlei Qianxi Taiwan Zhu Wenti de Tantao (Discussion on the issues of human migration to Taiwan in the prehistoric period). *Wenwu Jikan (Bulletin of Cultural Relics)* 4, 31–36. (In Chinese)

You, Y., Dong, X., Cai, B., and Sun, Y. 1995 Taiwan Haixia Xibu Haiyu Buru Dongwu Huashi (The mammalian fossils from western Taiwan strait). *Gujizhui Dongwu Xuebao (Vertebrata Palasiatica)* 33, 231–237. (In Chinese)

Zhang, S.S. 1983 Woguo Nanfang Jiushiqi Wanqi Wenhua de Ruogan Wenti (Issues on the upper Palaeolithic Cultures in South China). *Renleixue Xuebao (Acta Anthropologica Sinica)* 2, 218–230. (In Chinese)

# 10

# THE ARRIVAL OF MODERN HUMANS IN NORTH CHINA DURING THE LATE PALAEOLITHIC

*Xing Gao and Feng Li*

### Introduction

Since the "Recent Out-of-Africa" model was proposed by geneticists (Cann et al. 1987), research on the origins and evolution of modern humans (*Homo sapiens*) has become a critical issue in the study of human evolution. In particular, the debate over the origins of modern humans has intensified between two competing theories: the "Out-of-Africa" (Single-Place Origin or Total Replacement) theory and the "Multiregional Evolution" paradigm (Stringer 1992, 2002, 2014; Stringer and Andrews 1988; Wolpoff et al. 1984, 2000; Wolpoff 1999; Ke et al. 2001a, 2001b; Templeton, 2002; Wu 1998, 2006; Gao et al. 2010, 2017, 2019). Recently, as more evidence has accumulated, a deeper understanding of these issues has been achieved and models of the origins of modern humans have been revised accordingly. Research on human fossils from Eurasia has demonstrated that various hominin taxa were present there in the Late Pleistocene. Combining fossil evidence of the mosaic characteristics of Neanderthals and early modern humans, some scholars have proposed an assimilation model for modern human origins (Smith et al. 1989). Recent ancient DNA analyses have detected the interbreeding of early modern humans, Neanderthals, and Denisovans which generated various genetic taxa during the formation of modern humans (Green et al. 2010; Fu et al. 2014, 2015; Vernot and Akey 2014; Vernot et al. 2016; Slon et al. 2018). As a result, some of the supporters of the total replacement model of modern human origins have shifted to an assimilation model.

From an archaeological point of view, modern behavior documented in material culture appeared in various regions at different times, which are not always synchronous with the fossil and genetic records. Thus, behavioral modernity is not exclusively associated with anatomically modern humans, consequently some scholars have shifted their research focus increasingly toward behavioral variability (Shea 2011). Increasingly, researchers have realized that the evolution of behavior was more rapid and more variable than changes in phenotypic morphology and the genome, therefore there is no simple one-to-one correlation possible between certain cultural complexes and a particular hominin taxon. In fact, so-called modern human behavior appeared at different times in different regions and among various human groups, and it is not exclusively associated with modern humans; some modern behaviors were clearly expressed by

DOI: 10.4324/9781003427483-10

our Neanderthal cousins (e.g., Zilhão et al. 2010; Caron et al. 2011; Zilhão 2012; Radovčić et al. 2015; Hoffmann et al. 2018). Consequently, archaeologists are not now obsessed solely with identifying modern behavior or behavioral modernity, but seek to trace the behavioral diversity of different hominin groups (Shea 2011).

Meanwhile, new achievements in modern human origins research in China, especially South China, have been made in palaeoanthropology and archaeology. Recent studies have demonstrated that modern human morphological characteristics appeared quite early, as documented by late Middle Pleistocene fossils from Hualongdong Cave in Anhui (Wu et al. 2019), the Dali site in Shaanxi (Wu 2014) and the Panxian Dadong site in Guizhou (Liu et al. 2013), and in the early Upper Pleistocene Zhiren Cave in Guangxi (Jin et al. 2009; Liu et al. 2010), Maba Cave in Guangdong (Wu and Bruner 2016), and the Lingjing site in Henan (Li et al. 2017a,b). Modern morphological features on archaic hominin fossils demonstrate that modern anatomical characteristics appeared at various times rather than as a package at one particular point. New fossils found in Huanglong Cave in Hubei (Liu et al. 2010) and Fuyan Cave in Hunan (Liu et al. 2015), as well as other key sites, indicate that fossil hominins with fully early modern human morphology were present in South and Central China as early as 100 kya (see Liu et al. 2016; Martinón-Torres et al. 2017 for recent reviews).

Evidence from Palaeolithic archaeology indicates continuous development of lithic technology in China and greater East Asia since the Early Palaeolithic. No obvious gap existed from 50 to 100 kya as has been proposed by some geneticists examining the Chinese fossil and archaeological records in support of the "Out-of-Africa" hypothesis (Ke et al. 2001b), which may imply that no total population replacement occurred during this period in the region (Gao 2014). These new finds and research progress, especially achievements gained through carefully coordinated interdisciplinary studies, have made the origins and evolution of modern humans in the region much clearer as more details are revealed (Gao et al. 2017).

For many years, numerous scholars have emphasized on the arrival of modern humans in southern China, and a south-to-north population expansion via several routes has been proposed based on the relatively later age of modern human fossils in northern China (e.g., Liu et al. 2016). However, a detailed comparative study of early modern humans from North and South China that may inform on population affinities has yet to be conducted. Instead of emphasizing discoveries associated with modern humans in southern China, the main goal of this paper is to summarize late Middle Pleistocene and Late Pleistocene palaeoanthropological findings from North China and present the implications of those data with respect to the origins and dispersal of modern humans in northern China.

Geographically, northern China consists of the areas north of Qinling Mountains and Huai River, including North China and Northwest China. Although many sites have been discovered in northern China, few have clear stratigraphic contexts and reliable chronometric dates. Therefore, this paper synthesizes key discoveries dated to approximately 300–30 kya in those regions, including Dali, Jinniushan, Xujiayao-Houjiayao, Lingjing, Shuidonggou, Zhoukoudian Upper Cave, and Tianyuan Cave (Figure 10.1). Although the Tibetan Plateau is geologically distinct, new discoveries on the plateau are also included, since adaptation to high-altitude environments is considered one of the advantages of modern humans.

## Discoveries of Key Late Middle Pleistocene and Early Late Pleistocene Fossils and Lithic Assemblages

The earliest human fossils of modern appearance have been found in Africa and are around 300 kya, such as Jebel Irhoud in Morocco (Hublin et al. 2017). Although scholars have suggested

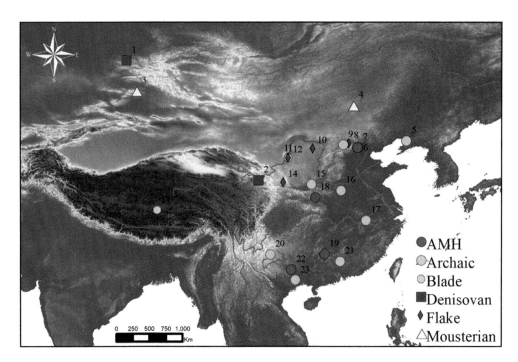

FIGURE 10.1  Geographic locations of sites mentioned in this paper. AMH: anatomical modern human, Archaic: archaic *Homo sapiens*. (1) Denisova cave, (2) Xiahe Baishiya cave, (3) Tongtian cave, (4) Jinsitai cave, (5) Jinniushan, (6) ZKD Upper Cave, (7) Tianyuan Cave, (8) Banjingzi, (9) Xujiayao-Houjiayao, (10) Wulanmulun, (11) Shuidonggou locality 1, (12) Shuidonggou locality 2, (13) Nwya Devu, (14) Xujiacheng, (15) Dali, (16) Lingjing, (17) Hualong cave, (18) Huanglong cave, (19) Fuyan cave, (20) Zhiren cave, (21) Luna cave, (22) Maba, (23) Panxiandadong.

that modern humans arrived in East Asia much later, fossils with modern anatomical characteristics have been found during late Middle Pleistocene and early Late Pleistocene (ca. 300–30 kya) contexts in northern China. Contemporaneous lithic technology shows similar features as the earlier periods with some development and has been considered as representing the "Middle Palaeolithic" of China by some researchers (Qiu 1985; Yee 2012; Li et al. 2018; but see Gao and Norton 2002). Around 40 kya, early modern humans appeared in northern China associated with blade assemblages and ornaments although they were often found in independent sites. In this paper, we will briefly review the key fossils and lithic assemblages in northern China between roughly 300 and 30 kya (Table 10.1).

### Sites Yielding Hominin Fossils Exhibiting a Mosaic Anatomical Morphology in Northern China

Many sites have been discovered in northern China dating to the late Middle Pleistocene and early Late Pleistocene, especially in the Nihewan Basin and the Loess Plateau, among which Dali, Jinniushan, Xujiayao-Houjiayao, and Lingjing have yielded hominin fossils and abundant lithic artifacts.

**TABLE 10.1** Location and age of key sites mentioned in this chapter.

| Site name | Locations | Latitude | Longitude | Age (ka) | Dating method | References |
|---|---|---|---|---|---|---|
| Dali-Tianshuigou | Dali County, Shaanxi | 34°52′N | 109°40′E | 300–247 | U-series, ESR | Yin et al. (2011) |
| Jinniushan | Yingkou City, Liujiang | 40°34′40″N | 122°26′38″E | 190–300 | U-series, ESR | Chen et al. (1994) |
| Xujiayao-Houjiayao | Yangyuan County, Hebei | 40°06′02″N | 113°58′39″E | 160–200 | OSL | Wang and Li (2014) |
| Lingjing | Xuchang County, Henan | 34°04′N | 113°41′E | 105–125 | OSL | Li et al. (2017) |
| Shuidonggou | Lingwu City, Ningxia | 38°17′56″N | 106°30′07″E | 45–27 | AMS, OSL | Li et al. (2019) |
| Upper Cave | Fangshan District, Beijing | 39°41′N | 115°50′E | 33–45 | AMS | Li et al. (2018) |
| Tianyuan Cave | Fangshan District, Beijing | 39°39′28″N | 115°52′17″E | 40 | AMS | Shang et al. (2007) |
| Nwya Devu | Changtang, Tibet | 31°28′19.4″N | 88°48′23.0″E | 40–30 | OSL | Zhang et al. (2018) |

## *The Dali Site*

The Dali site was discovered in 1978 on the third terrace of the Tianshuigou River in Dali County, Shaanxi Province, northern China (34°52′N, 109°40′E). The Dali cranium was initially discovered in a gravel layer in the lower part of the section (Wang et al. 1979; Wu 1981; Wu and Athreya 2013; Athreya and Wu 2017), and subsequent excavations of this layer yielded stone artifacts and animal fossils (Wu and You 1979; Zhang and Zhou 1984). Various dating methods have been applied to date the archaeological layers, such as comparison with the loess-paleosol sequence, electron spin resonance (ESR), and optically stimulated luminescence (OSL) approaches (Yin et al. 2002; Yin et al. 2011; Sun et al. 2017). The initial biostratigraphic analysis suggested a Middle Pleistocene age for the layers bearing hominin fossils and stone artifacts, and this age is supported by recent ESR and OSL results. Overall, the age of the layers yielding archaeological materials and human fossils is estimated to ca. 300–247 kya.

A multivariate morphological assessment considered the Dali cranium as a "transitional" form between Chinese *Homo erectus* and *H. sapiens* (Wu and Athreya 2013; Athreya and Wu 2017). The facial morphology indicates that Dali aligns with Middle Pleistocene *H. sapiens* and is clearly more derived than African or Eurasian Middle Pleistocene *Homo*. However, the neurocranial morphology demonstrates that Dali is most similar to African and eastern Eurasian but not western European Middle Pleistocene *Homo*. When both sets of variables are considered together, Dali exhibits a unique morphology that most closely resembles the earliest *H. sapiens* from North Africa and the Levant. This work has been considered as supporting evidence for Wu's Continuity with Hybridization scenario (Wu and Athreya 2013; Athreya and Wu 2017). In terms of lithic technology, core reduction strategies at Dali are primarily expedient, dominated by simple unifacial unidirectional flaking. In contrast, the retouched tools exhibit relatively sophisticated characteristics including diverse typology and standardized production (Li and Lotter 2018). This trend indicates gradual technological changes from the Early to Middle and early Late Pleistocene.

## The Jinniushan Site

The Jinniushan Cave site is located in Yingkou County, Liaoning Province (45°15′N, 122°30′E). The site was discovered in 1974, and subsequent excavations have been conducted at six localities (A through F) at the site. Near the bottom of the deposits (Layer 7) at the main locality (Locality A) a human skull, together with the vertebrae, ribs, pelvis, patella, and limb bones of a single individual were unearthed in 1984 (Chen et al. 1994). Faunal assemblages from the archaeological layers, including *Macaca robustus*, *Trogontherium* sp., *Megaloceros pachyosteus*, *Dicerorhinus mercki*, and *Microtus brandtioides* suggested a Middle Pleistocene age for the site. U-series dating assigned an age range of 230–300 kya to the layer where the skull was found, and this age has been cross-checked by ESR dating (minimally 195–165 kya) and TL results (197–195 kya) (Chen and Zhang 1991; Chen et al. 1994).

Morphological observations and analyses of the Jinniushan skull show a combination of features of *H. erectus* and *H. sapiens*. Although some features resemble those of *H. erectus*, Wu (1988) suggested that the total morphological pattern is much closer to that of archaic *Homo sapiens*, such as the Dali skull, than to those of the latest *H. erectus* individuals such as the Peking Man skull found in the upper part of Zhoukoudian Locality 1. The number of stone artifacts recovered at the site is small, and most were made on quartz. Scrapers, points, and bipolar products have been reported, as well as evidence for the use of fire (Lü 2004).

## The Xujiayao-Houjiayao Site

The Xujiayao-Houjiayao site (45°60′N, 113°59′), including two localities (73113 and 74093), was discovered in the western Nihewan Basin in the early 1970s. The Houjiayao site (74093) was first excavated in the late 1970s, and two archaeological layers have been identified in a ten meter thick sequence. Twenty pieces of hominin fossils have been discovered along with thousands of stone artifacts and mammalian fossils. The stratigraphy and age of the fossils and archaeological materials have been hotly debated for many years. From 2007 to 2012, excavations conducted by the Hebei Provincial Institute of Cultural Relics yielded new stratigraphic information and additional archaeological remains. An unconformity in the depositional sequence was identified in the 2007–2012 excavation four to five meters under the lower archaeological horizons. The hominin fossils, stone artifacts and mammalian fossils once considered to have been buried in the Nihewan Formation (Jia and Wei 1976) were actually derived from a fluvial deposit above the unconformity which might belong to the third terrace of the Liyigou River (Xie 2008; Wang 2015). By carefully evaluating the results from several independent dating efforts (Li et al. 2014a,b; Tu et al. 2015; Ao et al. 2017), Wang and Li (2019) suggested that the Xujiayao hominins lived in the late Middle Pleistocene, around 200–160 kya.

Early anatomical research suggested that the Xujiayao hominins show mixed characteristics of *H. erectus* and *H. sapiens* (Wu 1986). Recent studies of the mandible (Xujiayao 14) and the temporal labyrinths (Xujiayao 15) also revealed mosaic morphological traits that vary among Old Word Pleistocene *Homo* samples and between Early/Middle Pleistocene archaic humans and Late Pleistocene modern humans in eastern Eurasia (Wu et al. 2014). Some of the traits are found in highest frequency among Neandertals and the morphology of the temporal labyrinths reconstructed via CT-scanned models resembles those of Neandertals (Wu et al. 2014). Although the Neandertal appearance does not necessarily mean there was interbreeding between the Xujiayao hominin and western Eurasian Neandertals, these new studies highlight regional morphological variation among Middle Pleistocene hominins. Using x-ray multiresolution synchrotron phase-contrast microtomography, Xing et al. (2019) recently quantified dental growth and development in a juvenile individual from the Houjiayao site (Xujiayao 1). Despite the archaic morphology of the Xujiayao hominins, most aspects of the dental development of this juvenile fall within modern human ranges (e.g., prolonged crown formation time and delayed first molar eruption) which are comparable to those of equivalently aged modern children (6.5 years) (Xing et al. 2019).

More than 30,000 stone artifacts have been unearthed but have not yet been fully published. In general, the artifacts are made primarily of quartz, and are typical flake-based assemblages. Direct hard hammer percussion is the principal stone knapping and retouching technique. The assemblage is dominated by simple unifacial unidirectional flaking, followed by bifacial discoidal reduction. The retouched tools exhibit relatively sophisticated characteristics including diverse retouched tool types and standardized production including various scrapers and points (Jia and Wei 1976). Additionally, approximately 1000 well-shaped spheroids were found at the site during the 1970s excavations (Li 1994). Although the function of the spheroids requires more analysis, the numerous specimens show higher technological standardization and significant investment in their production.

## *The Lingjing Site*

The Lingjing site, discovered in 1965, is located on the western margin of Lingjing Town in Xuchang City, Henan Province, northern China (34°04′N, 113°41′E). The open-air Lingjing site consists of a series of horizontal strata around a spring, extending from the earliest Late Pleistocene to the early Holocene. Two human crania dispersed within a circumscribed horizontal area within Layer 11 were found at the site along with many lithic artifacts and faunal remains. The hominin fossils were associated with a diverse macromammalian faunal assemblage, rich in *Equus*, *Bos*, *Megaloceros*, *Procapra*, *Cervus*, and *Coelodonta*. Layer 11 has produced a consistent series of OSL ages, placing the human remains between about 105 and 125 kya, and the overlying Layers 10 and 9 have provided ages of about 100 and 90 kya (Li et al., 2017a,b). The human crania are therefore securely dated to Marine Isotope Stage (MIS) 5. The two crania exhibit a mosaic morphological pattern with differences from and similarities with their western contemporaries (Li et al. 2017a,b). They share pan–Old World trends in encephalization and in supraorbital, neurocranial vault, and nuchal gracilization. They reflect eastern Eurasian ancestry in having low, sagittally flat, and inferiorly broad neurocrania. They share occipital (suprainiac and nuchal torus) and temporal labyrinthine (semicircular canal) morphology with Neandertals. Li et al. (2017a,b) have argued both for substantial regional continuity in eastern Eurasia into the early Late Pleistocene population and for some level of east-west population interaction across Eurasia.

More than 10,000 stone artifacts, mainly made of quartz, have been excavated at the Lingjing site. A detailed analysis of stone artifacts conducted by Li et al. (2018) shows increased technological advancement and sophistication in the technological organization of the Lingjing humans, including bi-conical discoidal core reduction strategies, discrete small-sized tool types, and refined retouch on blanks. Formal bone tools, including retouchers, have also been identified at the site (Doyon et al. 2018).

## Sites Yielding Early Modern Human Fossils or Early Upper Palaeolithic Artifacts in Northern China

Although modern humans appeared in southern China as early as MIS 5 (Liu et al. 2010, 2015; Bae et al. 2014), anatomically modern human fossils appeared in northern China by approximately 40 kya. Sites yielding early Upper Palaeolithic assemblages have been discovered in northern China during the late Late Pleistocene. Here, we introduce the main finds associated or supposedly associated with modern humans in northern China from Tianyuan Cave, Zhoukoudian Upper Cave, the Shuidonggou site complex, and the Nwya Devu site in northern Tibet.

### Tianyuan Cave

Tianyuan Cave (Tianyuandong) is located on the Tianyuan Tree Farm in Zhoukoudian Town, Fangshan County, Beijing, North China (39°39′N, 115°52′E), 6 km southwest of the Zhoukoudian Peking Man site (Locality 1). The site was discovered in 2001 and was subsequently investigated and excavated in 2003 and 2004. The cave deposits consist of four layers, and 34 fossil elements of an early modern human were found in Layer 3 along with numerous mammalian fossils. However, no archaeological materials have been found at the site to date. A sample from one of the human femora provided an age of 34,430 ± 510 $^{14}$C BP, placing the human partial skeleton securely between 42 and 39 kya (Shang et al. 2007).

Morphological comparison (Shang et al. 2007) shows Tianyuan 1 exhibits a series of derived modern human characteristics, including a projecting tuber symphyses, a high anterior symphyseal angle, a broad scapular glenoid fossa, a reduced hamulus, a gluteal buttress, and a pilaster on the femora. However, Tianyuan 1 also exhibits several late archaic human features, such as its anterior to posterior dental proportions, a large hamulus length, and a broad and rounded distal phalangeal tuberosity. Recent nuclear DNA sequences reconstructed for this specimen reveal that the Tianyuan individual derived from a population that was ancestral to many present-day Asians and Native Americans but postdated the divergence of Asians from Europeans (Fu et al. 2013). They also show that this individual carried proportions of DNA variants derived from archaic humans similar to present-day populations in mainland Asia. An updated genome-wide dataset (Yang et al. 2017) confirmed that the Tianyuan individual is more closely related to present-day and ancient Asians than to Europeans, but suggested the individual shares more alleles with a 35,000-year-old European than with other ancient Europeans. Studies of the Tianyuan individual highlight the complex migration, interbreeding, and subdivisions of early modern human populations in Eurasia.

### Zhoukoudian Upper Cave (ZKD UC)

ZKD UC (39°41′N, 115°55′E) is the second-best known locality at Zhoukoudian, after Locality 1, and is located 50 km southwest of Beijing. It was discovered in 1930 during excavations at Locality 1 and was later excavated in 1933 and 1934 (Pei 1934, 1939). Four spatial subdivisions (Entrance, Upper Room, Lower Room, and Lower Recess) and five "cultural layers" (L1–L5) with a total thickness of over 10 meters were identified by Pei (1939). Two aspects of ZKD UC that are especially important to palaeoanthropology are the early modern human fossils, considered to have been intentionally interred, and associated archaeological materials, including ornaments, that are thought to represent evidence of behavioral modernity.

Unfortunately, uncertainty regarding the Upper Cave's chronology has long hindered determination of its importance in the debate over modern human dispersals. Recently, Li et al. (2018) presented a new set of accelerator mass spectrometry radiocarbon dating results from ZKD UC. Based on this new set of dates and reevaluations of the previous dating analyses, archaeological materials, published excavation reports, and stratigraphy, they concluded that the ZKD UC archaeological layers minimally date to 35.1–33.5 kya.

The human fossils have contributed to debates focusing on population affinities, particularly whether *in situ* evolution occurred or whether the fossils may have originated from a different region or regions of western Eurasia (Weidenreich 1939a,b; Wu 1961; Kamminga and Wright 1988; Brown 1999; Cunningham and Wescott 2002; Liu et al. 2006; Harvati 2009). Wu (1961) suggested that the ZKD UC human fossils represent a primitive Mongoloid type closely related to the ancestors of modern Chinese, Inuit, and Amerindians. However, many researchers disagree with this opinion. Recent geometric morphometric analysis of the Upper Cave 101 and 103 crania found morphological similarities with Upper Palaeolithic Europeans, especially Předmostí 3 and Mladeč 1 from the Czech Republic in Central Europe (Harvati 2009). Despite the fact that only 25 stone artifacts were recovered from ZKD UC, 141 ornaments were excavated, including perforated mammal teeth, stone beads, perforated *Arca* shells, bone pendants, a perforated fish supraorbital bone, and a pierced pebble (Pei 1939). Combining the similarities between the human fossils and archaeology between ZKD UC and western Eurasia, Li et al. (2018) proposed that the Upper Cave human foragers were part of dispersal events across northern Eurasia toward Siberia and eventually reaching into northern China. Considering the high within-group variation (Cunningham and Wescott 2002; Cunningham and Jantz 2003) and the higher archaic morphological trait frequency (Liu et al. 2006), interbreeding during dispersal with other archaic hominin groups could have occurred in the Zhoukoudian Upper Cave hominin population.

### *Shuidonggou (SDG) Site Complex*

The Shuidonggou complex is located in the Ningxia Hui Autonomous Region of northern China, 18 km east of the Yellow River on the margins of the Mu Us (Maowusu) Desert. The Palaeolithic site cluster at Shuidonggou was first located and investigated by the French palaeontologists Émile Licent and Pierre Teilhard de Chardin in 1923 (Licent and Teilhard 1925). They initially recorded five distinct localities (F1–F5, now SDG 1–5) in the Shuidonggou Valley, and excavated an area of around 80 m$^2$ at Locality 1. Locality 1 was subsequently re-excavated and studied intensively in 1960, 1963, and 1980 (Jia et al. 1964; Ningxia Museum et al. 1987). During the 1963 excavations at Locality 1 a surface site named Xiaokouzi (SDG 6), 500 m northwest of Locality 1 was also investigated (Zhang 1999).

A new research program has been underway at Shuidonggou since 2002. This most recent program of research has resulted in the discovery of another six Palaeolithic localities (SDG 7–12) (Gao et al. 2004; Liu et al. 2008). The Shuidonggou site cluster is often equated with Locality 1, the first site to be discovered and excavated. Since its discovery in 1923, the Shuidonggou site cluster has been interpreted in terms of large-scale diffusion of European Upper Palaeolithic technology, based mainly on the large blade assemblage found at SDG locality 1 (Boule et al. 1928; Brantingham et al. 2001; Madsen et al. 2001). However, a wide range of assemblages exhibiting different technologies and ages has been identified during subsequent research in the area (Pei et al. 2012; Li et al. 2013a; Gao et al. 2013a,b). Among the 12 currently known localities, Localities 1 and 2 are the most important and are briefly summarized here.

The stratigraphic sequence at SDG 1 is usually divided into two parts, corresponding with Late Pleistocene (lower cultural layer) and Holocene (upper cultural layer) deposits. More recently, earlier ages for the Palaeolithic sequence at this locality have been suggested: ~41 kya based on a single charcoal sample (Morgan et al. 2014), and 33–46 kya from more systematic OSL analysis (Nian et al. 2014). The majority of the material collected from the lower cultural layers at SDG 1 is representative of a blade-based technology. The often-described lithic assemblage from the lower cultural layer at SDG 1 was the product of systematic Levallois and prismatic blade reduction. Two independent studies of the lithic artifact sample from the 1980 excavation have been conducted and their results agree closely (see Brantingham et al. 2001; Peng et al. 2014 for details). Most of the cores produced blades or elongated flakes, and nearly 30% of the blanks are blades. Retouched tools include various scrapers, denticulates, and notches. Both flakes and blades were retouched and points and end scrapers were most often made on blades.

The stratigraphic sequence at SDG 2, with a total thickness of 12.5 m, contains 18 layers, seven of which yielded Palaeolithic remains. A total of 29 dates have published from Locality 2 including accelerator mass spectrometry (AMS) $^{14}$C and OSL dates, although some controversy concerning the ages remains (Keates and Kuzmin 2015; Li et al. 2015). The combined radiocarbon and OSL dates show that the first cultural layer (CL7) falls within the period from 41.5 to 40.5 kya; the second and third (CL6 and 5) are thought to date from 34.4–32.6 kya (based on ages of strata above and below); the fourth and fifth (CL4 and 3) 32.6–31 kya; the sixth (CL2), 31–29 kya; and the seventh (CL1) 27 kya (Li et al. 2013). Lithic assemblages from the different archaeological layers at SDG 2 can be divided into two broad groups (see Li et al. 2013b for details). AL7 and AL5a yielded two blade cores similar to those described from SDG 1. The assemblages from AL6, AL5b, and AL4-AL1 show consistent features, which include comparatively simple flake production and side-scraper-dominated tool assemblages. These core and flake assemblages contain no evidence of systematic production of blades or Levallois elements. However, some technological changes and other innovations are documented within the sequence of core and flake assemblages (Li et al. 2019). In AL2, some high quality raw materials were transported to the site and soft-hammer percussion may have been used for the reduction of this material (Li et al. 2016a,b). Small bladelet size blanks manufactured on high quality material were also present, although no counterpart cores were found. AL1a shows a high frequency of bipolar reduction on small, local high-quality chert pebbles and, as a result, small elongated blanks are much more common than in other layers. Well-retouched end scrapers, made mainly on flakes, are present in assemblages from AL2 and AL1a but not in earlier layers. One fragment of a grinding tool was discovered from AL1a. Ornaments and bone tools are present in AL3 and AL2: one freshwater shell bead fragment was found in AL3 (Wei et al. 2016), and more than 70 ostrich (*Struthio*) eggshell beads and a bone needle fragment were recovered from AL2 (Li et al. 2014a,b; Martí et al. 2017).

*Nwya Devu Site*

The Nwya Devu (ND) site was discovered in 2013 during archaeological investigation of the eastern Changtang region in northern Tibet, which averages 5000 m asl. The site is situated south of Siling Co and Co Ngoin lakes, ~300 km northwest of the Tibet Autonomous Region capital, Lhasa, encompassing an area of ~1 km east-west by 2 km north-south. The ~170-cm-thick ND sedimentary sequence in the excavation pit which has a surface elevation of ~4600 m asl is divided into three layers from top to bottom. Anthropogenic stone artifacts have been recovered from the upper 138 cm of the sequence, including 3124 artifacts from Layer 1, 223 from Layer 2, and 336 from Layer 3. A total of 24 OSL and two AMS dates for samples from three sections in the excavation unit has been obtained which provide bracketing ages for the artifacts: Layer 3 yields ages of ~45 to 30 kya; the ages of Layer 2 fall within a narrow range of ~25 to 18 kya; and ages of Layer 1 range from ~13 kya to ~4 kya (Zhang et al. 2018).

The lithic assemblages at the ND site include blade cores, flake cores, blades, flakes, chunks, and tools. There are no significant differences among assemblages from the different archaeological layers. A distinctive feature of the assemblage is the production of blades and blade tools. Such blades were made mainly on prismatic cores, and most of the blades were detached from the cores' long and narrow faces. Unidirectional flaking dominates the blade production in the assemblages (72 of 91 cores), and blade size varies considerably. Retouched tools include scrapers, awls, choppers, notches, and burins. Finely retouched formal pieces are rare, and most modifications are expedient (Zhang et al. 2018).

The Nwya Devu site is the first excavated stratified Palaeolithic site in high-elevation Tibet. The extreme environment characterized by a pervasively cold, dry climate and atmospheric hypoxia presumably greatly constrained early human settlement in the region. The age and typological characteristics of the lithic assemblage at ND indicate that modern humans bearing an advanced blade technology occupied this high-altitude area at least ~40–30 kya ago. This evidence establishes a record for the prehistoric occupation of this high-altitude environment, much earlier than current evidence, and indicates hitherto-unknown capacities for the survival of early modern humans (Zhang et al. 2018).

## Implications of the Discoveries of Late Middle and Early Late Pleistocene Fossils in China

Hominin fossils found in late Middle Pleistocene contexts reflect many combinations of archaic and modern anatomical characteristics between approximately 300 and 100, including specimens from Dali, Jinniushan, Xujiayao, and Lingjing. This mosaic morphology indicates a pattern of continuity with earlier, Middle Pleistocene eastern Eurasia humans, such as *H. erectus*. On the other hand, some features which associate them with Neandertals are also observed on the fossils from Xujiayao and Lingjing. This demonstrates certain population interactions across Eurasia during the late Middle and early Late Pleistocene. Based on the morphology of hominin fossils, current evidence tends to support the Continuity with Hybridization scenario proposed by Wu (1998), at least until the very early Late Pleistocene (ca. 100 kya).

In terms of technology, the basics remain the same although some innovations did take place. The major core reduction sequences were aimed at producing various flake blanks by means of free-hand hammer stone percussion. Some sites include many discoidal nuclei, which exhibit definite organization of core surfaces, however, little attention was paid to the maintenance of platforms and the control of blank morphology. A more striking difference from western Eurasian Middle Palaeolithic industries is that no Levallois technology has been discovered in the East Asian late Middle and early Late Pleistocene record despite a few not-widely accepted arguments (see Li et al. 2019). In addition, no systematic manufacture of blades, which are often observed in the Middle Palaeolithic of western Eurasia and Africa, has been found during the late

Middle Pleistocene and early Late Pleistocene in China. The retouched tool assemblages demonstrate many developments in comparison with the early Lower Palaeolithic (ca. 2–0.3 Ma). More formal retouched tools, including various scrapers, points, and other types, are commonly present in Chinese late Middle and early Late Pleistocene sites. In sum, no abrupt technological shift has been observed in the Palaeolithic record before 100 kya in China, although certain technological innovations were definitely manifest in the Middle and early Late Pleistocene.

Other types of material culture also demonstrate developments in human behavior during the late Middle and early Late Pleistocene. Formal bone tools such as retouching implements are reported from the Lingjing site (Doyon et al. 2018), although it remains the only such evidence from the Middle and early Late Pleistocene in East Asia. Although detailed zooarchaeological analyses have not been commonly undertaken at Early Palaeolithic sites in northern China, well-developed hunting abilities have been recorded at the Xujiayao-Houjiayao site (Norton and Gao 2008; Li et al. 2017a,b) and the Lingjing site (Zhang et al. 2009, 2011).

Less evidence of human activities in China from approximately 100 to 50 kya has been used as part of the evidence for a local distinction of archaic hominins in China (Jin and Su 2000). Although this argument currently has little basis owing to the large number of Pleistocene archaeological and human palaeontological discoveries reported recently in China (Gao 2014; Liu et al. 2016; Wu and Xu 2016), it is worth mentioning that no hominin fossils have been discovered dating to the period from around 100 to 45 kya in northern China. However, many sites with archaeological remains dating to the early Late Pleistocene have been discovered, including the Banjingzi, Wulanmulun, and Xujiacheng sites (Gao 2014). For example, the Banjingzi site in the Nihewan Basin has been dated to around 80–89 kya by OSL (Guo et al. 2016), and a lithic assemblage which closely resembles the Lingjing and Xujiayao-Houjiayao sites was reported, consisting of flake production without predetermination and a scraper-dominated tool inventory (Ren et al. 2018). In conclusion, the lithic technology of sites dating to 100–50 kya may indicate a pattern of continuity with earlier industries in the late Middle and early Late Pleistocene.

## Evidence of Modern Human Dispersals into Northern China and Interactions with Other Archaic Hominins

For a long time, a south to north route of early modern human dispersals in eastern Asia, particularly China, was proposed by early genetic studies (Chu et al. 1998; Su et al. 1999; Jin and Su 2000; but see Gao et al. 2010; Rosenberg and Wu 2013). The current hominin fossil record from China seems to lend support to this hypothesis (Liu et al. 2016; Martinon-Torres et al. 2017) in terms of chronology. For instance, all of the earliest modern human fossils are located in the south or central part of China, such as Fuyan Cave (Liu et al. 2015; but see Michel et al. 2016), Zhiren Cave (Liu et al. 2010a), Luna Cave (Bae et al. 2014), and Huanglong Cave (Liu et al. 2010b), all with provisional dates ranging between 120 and 70 kya. The earliest modern human fossils found in north China are from Tianyuan Cave, directly dated to 40 kya (Shang et al. 2007). A recently revised chronology for the Zhoukoudian Upper Cave indicates the ZKD UC modern humans minimally date to 35.1–33.5 kya.

However, some comparative studies of the Chinese Late Pleistocene hominin fossil record from ZKD UC and Tianyuan Cave (ZKD Locality 27) suggest relationships with coeval groups from western Eurasia (Shang et al. 2007; Harvati 2009). A recent genetic study found the Tianyuan individual shared more alleles with a 35,000-year-old European individual from Belgium, but not with other ancient Europeans (Yang et al. 2017). Combining similarities between hominin palaeontology and the archaeology, Li et al. (2018) provisionally conclude that ZKD UC and, probably, the Tianyuan modern humans were part of dispersal events across Eurasia following a northern route, as others have suggested (e.g., Fu et al. 2014; Kaifu et al. 2015; Buzhilova et al. 2017; Bae et al. 2017a,b), eastward toward Siberia and eventually south into northern China.

Other evidence potentially indicating modern human dispersal through a northern route comes from the Shuidonggou complex and the Nwya Devu site. An assemblage consisting of large blade production was found in the lower cultural layer at SDG1, AL7 and AL5a of SDG2, and SDG9. These blade techno-complexes, dating to approximately 35–45 kya, have been affiliated with the Initial Upper Palaeolithic in eastern Eurasia in that it combines the Levallois technique and a prismatic method to manufacture blades. Considering similar and earlier finds from west of Shuidonggou area, scholars have concluded that this techno-complex is intrusive from the Siberian Altai and/or northern Mongolia (Brantingham et al. 2001; Peng et al. 2014; Li et al. 2014a,b; Gao et al. 2013a,b; Li et al. 2016b).

Although linking a lithic industry with a specific hominin group is problematical at best and is always controversial, some authors believe Initial Upper Palaeolithic (IUP) industries were made by early modern humans (Gao et al. 2013a,b; Li et al. 2019, but see Bar-Yosef and Belfer-Cohen 2013). Therefore, the presence of the IUP in northern China implies a northern dispersal of modern humans across Eurasia. Interestingly, IUP assemblages lasted for only a short time and their distribution was limited to northwestern China, never appearing in the eastern part of North China. Instead, the core and flake technology dominated the late Late Pleistocene record there until the emergence of microblade technology after ca. 30–25 kya. Based on this geographic distribution of blade and core-flake assemblages, Li et al. (2014a,b; 2016a,b) have proposed a demographic model of diverse lithic technologies in the late Late Pleistocene: early UP assemblages indicate hominin groups dispersed from the west, while core-flake assemblages imply the continuous evolution of local hominin groups in northern China. The blade assemblage at the Nwya Devu site is based mainly on the prismatic production of blades typical of the Upper Palaeolithic. Due to the scarcity of this technology in northern China, scholars tend to link the blade assemblage at ND with similar finds in the Siberian Altai and Mongolia where prismatic blade production appeared earlier (Zhang et al. 2018). Occupying the high-elevation area of Tibet required great adaptive abilities among hominin groups. For many years, the earliest evidence of hominin occupation in high-elevation Tibet has been controversial and the later arrival of modern humans after the Last Glacial Maximum was commonly accepted (Brantingham and Gao 2006). The discovery of the Nwya Devu site indicates modern humans carrying a blade technology arrived on the high plateau at least 30 kya, if not substantially earlier.

Some population interactions across Eurasia have been inferred from the presence of Neandertal ancient DNA and morphological similarities in the Tianyuan 1 early modern humans (Shang et al. 2007; Fu et al. 2013). Recent archaeological finds from Jinsitai Cave (Li et al. 2018) and Tongtian Cave (Yu et al. 2018) have added more evidence of MP (specifically Mousterian) dispersal by means of lithic technology. Mousterian assemblages have been found in these sites, including a typical Levallois component and Middle Palaeolithic retouched tool typology. Classic Mousterian industries are associated with Neanderthal remains at dozens of sites in Europe, the Caucasus, and Central Asia (Stringer 2002; Hublin 2007; Krause et al. 2007; Slimak et al. 2011). Comparison of the Jinsitai Mousterian assemblages with adjacent regions, such as the Siberian Altai, suggests that Mousterian assemblages in northern China were probably also made by Neandertals (Li et al. 2018). Research on the genetically determined new population Denisovans in Siberian Altai have demonstrated intriguing complex interactions with modern humans and Neandertals (Krause et al. 2010; Reich et al. 2010; Slon et al. 2017, 2018). And new study on the present-day individuals found Denisovan ancestry in populations broadly from East and South Asia (Browning et al. 2018) beyond the previous evidence in Oceanic populations (Vernot et al. 2016). Two distinct instances of Denisovan admixture into modern humans occurred, involving Denisovan populations that had different levels of relatedness to the sequenced Altai Denisovan (Browning et al. 2018). New hominin mandible found in Xiahe County on the eastern Tibet Plateau of China is identified as a Denisovan by ancient protein analysis indicating that Denisovans may have also lived in China in 160 kya (Chen et al. 2019). Although determining the presence of Neandertals and persistence of Denisovans in northern China requires more evidence, the discoveries of Mousterian lithic assemblages, the presence of Neandertal morphological features on some fossil specimens (such as Lingjing and Xujiayao), and the Xiahe Denisovan all indicate a much more complex picture for Late Pleistocene hominin dispersals and possible physical and technological interactions among different hominin groups in northern China. Apparently, simple replacements by modern humans can't interpret the current Palaeoanthropological data in northern China. In consequence, we should pay more attention on the Denisovan-Neandertal-Archaic *H. sapiens* dynamics in the discussion of modern human origins and dispersals in East Asia.

## Future Directions in Exploring Modern Human Origins and Dispersals in Northern China

Fully modern humans arrived in northern Eurasia around 45 kya which is much later than in southern Eurasia and Africa. This scenario also seems valid in China. Several sites yielding modern human fossils have been reported recently in southern China, including Fuyan Cave, Zhiren Cave (Liu et al. 2010a), Luna Cave (Bae et al. 2014), and Huanglong Cave (Liu et al. 2010b). Those sites date to MIS 5, however modern humans did not appear in northern China until 45–40 kya (Figure 10.2). Therefore, one of the most intriguing problems concerning modern human evolution in China is to test the validity of the hypothetical temporal gap between modern human occupations in southern and northern China, and if true, how to explain it. Many archaic hominins exhibiting modern morphological characteristics were in northern China during MIS 6-5. Did they evolve into the modern humans of MIS 3 or not? If they did, is it possible they moved to southern China because of a colder climate during MIS 4 and then moved back during mid-MIS 3? If not, why? Does the temporal gap mean that modern humans did not disperse into northern China because the region was already occupied by archaic hominins like western Europe (Liu et al. 2016a,b) or the region was not suitable for living during MIS 4 and early MIS 3? Of course, we cannot answer those questions yet, but the asynchronous evolution of modern humans in southern and northern China remind us of the significance of a regional perspective and the emphasis on research on the interactions of climate fluctuation and demographic change in China. China is a vast region, and archaeological data in different regions may have different implications for the dispersal and origins of modern humans and their material culture (Dang, this issue).

Many sites dating to the late Late Pleistocene have been discovered in northern China, however, only two associated with relatively reliable dates have yielded hominin fossils: Zhoukoudian Upper Cave and Tianyuan Cave. If to these we add the Shuidonggou sites with early Upper Palaeolithic large blade assemblages possibly made by modern humans, the richness of the archaeological data is still very low considering the large area of northern China. Therefore, one

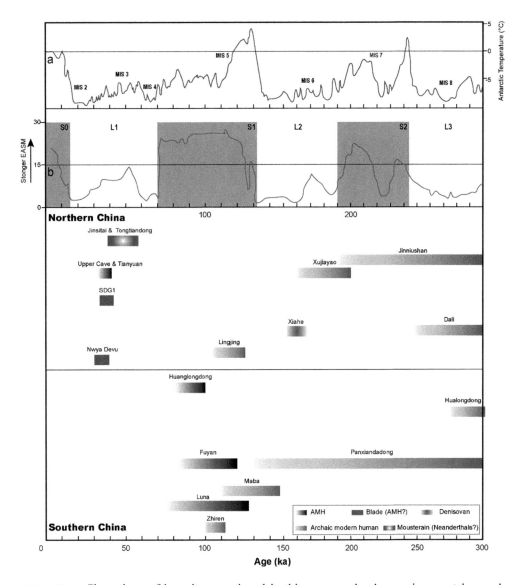

FIGURE 10.2  Chronology of key sites mentioned in this paper and palaeoenvironmental records. (a) Temperature anomaly record derived from the EPICA Dome C (EDC) ice-core deuterium record (Lowe and Walker, 2015). (b) $x_{fd}$ ($10^{-8}$ m$^3$ kg$^{-1}$) data in the Luochuan loess section in northern China (Hao, 2012). AMH: anatomical modern human.

of our main tasks in undertaking Palaeolithic studies in northern China is to discover more sites and enlarge the database for modern human evolution research. Together with new discoveries made in southern China, we may in future draw a relatively complete picture of modern human dispersals in China.

As we have mentioned, linking a specific hominin group with a particular lithic assemblage is always controversial, especially when the archaeological materials were not found in direct association with human fossils. In northern China, a few archaeological materials including

23 stone artifacts and a handful of ornaments and bone artifacts, have been found in the Zhoukoudian Upper Cave. No archaeological material has yet been discovered with the Tianyuan human fossils. At the Shuidonggou sites, Initial Upper Palaeolithic large blade assemblages have been found but no contemporaneous hominin fossils have yet been discovered. If we look at a broad geographic area, more early Upper Palaeolithic assemblages have been found in the Siberian Altai, northern Mongolia, and the Transbaikal regions, but no associated modern human fossils. Recently, a re-dated human skull from Salkhit, northern Mongolia (33–34 kya) has added one more case to the early modern human fossil database of East Asia, however no archaeological materials were found at the site (Devièse et al. 2019). Therefore, it is currently difficult to combine evidence of archaeological materials and human fossils to fully address issues of modern human dispersals in northern China. The continuous evolution of simple core-flake technologies was considered evidence supporting the *in situ* evolution of modern humans. Nevertheless, the simple correspondence of late Late Pleistocene sites with modern humans can be questioned. Many sites yielding core-flake assemblages are widely distributed in northern China, however human fossils associated with them are few, if any. Admittedly it is not an easy task, but clear associations between variable material culture and specific hominin groups in the late Late Pleistocene will be very helpful in understanding the origins and dispersals of modern humans in northern China.

## Conclusions

In the past two decades, new human fossil and Palaeolithic archaeological discoveries have drastically changed our theoretical perspectives on modern human origins, evolution and adaptations. Currently, archaic *H. sapiens* fossils from sites including Dali, Jinniushan, Xujiayao, and Xuchang, exhibiting mosaic or transitional features and possible admixture with Neanderthals and Denisovans, have been found in northern China. Together with the *in situ* evolution of simple core-flake technologies, this evidence provides support for the "Continuity with Hybridization Model" of modern human evolution in China (Wu 1998, 2006; Gao et al. 2010, 2017, 2019). However, the anatomical and genetic evidence of early modern humans from Zhoukoudian Upper Cave and Tianyuan Cave reveals a very complicated history of genetic inheritance and hybridization with other hominin groups in western Eurasia, including both modern and archaic groups. Blade techno-complexes appeared at some sites in northern China by at least ca. 40 kya, indicating possible technological ties with lithic industries in Siberia and Central Asia and a possible northwest-to-southeast migration route before the Last Glacial Maximum. Nevertheless, many persisting problems could weaken this model, including scant data regarding modern human origins and dispersals in northern China, the hypothetical temporal gap in the human fossil record between 100 and 50 kya, and the uncertain relationships between specific archaeological assemblages and particular hominin groups. It is clear that one of the principal tasks in northern China is the discovery of more sites and fossils dating to 100–30 kya that will help us better understand the origins and dispersals of modern humans.

## Acknowledgments

We are grateful to John W. Olsen (University of Arizona, United States) for providing constructive comments and improving the English. Any shortcomings contained within are our own. Feng Li thanks the Youth Innovation Promotion Association, Chinese Academy of Sciences

(2017102) facilitating this study. This research was supported by the Strategic Priority Research Program of Chinese Academy of Sciences (Grant No. XDB26000000) and the National Natural Science Foundation of China (Grant No. 41502022 and 41672024).

## References

Ao, Hong, Liu, Chun-Ru, Roberts, Andrew, Zhang, Peng, and Xu, Xinwen. 2017 An updated age for the Xujiayao hominin from Nihewan Basin, North China: Implications for middle Pleistocene human evolution in East Asia. *Journal of Human Evolution* 106, 54–65.

Athreya, Sheela, and Wu, Xinzhi. 2017 A multivariate assessment of the Dali hominin cranium from China: Morphological affinities and implications for Pleistocene evolution in East Asia. *American Journal of Physical Anthropology* 164, 679–701.

Bae, Christopher, Petraglia, Michael, and Douka, Katerina. 2017a Multidisciplinary perspectives on the human evolution in Late Pleistocene Asia: Introduction to supplement 17. *Current Anthropology* 58, S373–S382.

Bae, Christopher, Petraglia, Michael, and Douka, Katerina. 2017b On the origin of modern humans: Asian Perspectives. *Science* 358, eaai9067.

Bae, Christopher, Wang, Wei, Zhao, Jianxin, Huang, Shengming, Tian, Feng, and Shen, Guanjun. 2014 Modern human teeth from Late Pleistocene Luna Cave (Guangxi, China). *Quaternary International* 354, 169–183.

Bar-Yosef, Ofer, and Belfer-Cohen, Annette. 2013 Following Pleistocene road signs of human dispersals across Eurasia. *Quaternary International* 285, 30–43.

Boule, Marcellin, Breuil, Henri, Licent, E, and Teilhard de Chardin, Pierre. 1928 *Le Paléolithique de la Chine*. Paris: Archives de l'Institut de Paléontologie Humaine.

Brantingham, Jeffrey, Krivoshapkin, Andre, Li, Jinzeng, and Tserendagva, Yadmaa. 2001 The initial upper Palaeolithic in Northeast Asia. *Current Anthropology* 42, 735–747.

Brantingham, Jeffrey, and Xing, Gao. 2006 Peopling of the northern Tibetan Plateau. *World Archaeology* 38, 387–414.

Brown, P. 1999 The first modern East Asians? Another look at Upper Cave 101, Liujiang and Minatogawa 1, in *Interdisciplinary Perspectives on the Origins of the Japanese*, ed Omoto, K.. Kyoto: International Research Center for Japanese Studies, 105–124.

Browning, Sharon, Browning, Brian, Zhou, Ying, Tucci, Serena, and Akey, Joshua. 2018 Analysis of human sequence data reveals two pulses of archaic Denisovan admixture. *Cell* 173, 53–61.

Buzhilova, Alexandra, Derevianko, Anatoly, and Shunkov, Michael. 2017 The northern dispersal route: Bioarchaeological data from the Late Pleistocene of Altai, Siberia. *Current Anthropology* 58, S491–S503.

Cann, Rebecca, Stoneking, Mark, and Wilson, Allan. 1987 Mitochondrial DNA and human evolution. *Nature* 325, 31–36.

Caron, François, d'Errico, Francesco, del Moral, Pierre, Santos, Frédéric, and Zilhão, João. 2011 The reality of Neandertal symbolic behavior at the Grotte du Renne, Arcy-sur-Cure, France. *PLoS ONE* 6, e21545.

Chen, Fahu, Welker, Frido, Shen, Chuan-Chou, Bailey, Shara, Bergmann, Inga, Davis, Simon, Xia, Huan, Wang, Hui, Fischer, Roman, Freidline, Sarah, Yu, Tsai-Luen, Skinner, Matthew, Stelzer, Stefanie, Dong, Guangrong, Fu, Qiaomei, Dong, Guanghui, Wang, Jian, Zhang, Dongju, and Hublin, Jean-Jacques. 2019 A late Middle Pleistocene Denisovan mandible from the Tibetan Plateau. *Nature* 569, 409–412.

Chen, T., and Zhang, Y. 1991 Palaeolithic chronology and possible coexistence of *Homo erectus* and *Homo sapiens* in China. *World Archaeology* 23, 147–154.

Chen, T. M., Quan, Y., and En, W. 1994 Antiquity of *Homo sapiens* in China. *Nature* 368, 55–56.

Chu, J., Huang, W., Kuang, S., Wang, J., Xu, J., Chu, Z., Yang, Z., Lin, K., Li, P., Wu, M., Geng, Z., Tan, C., Du, R., and Jin, L. 1998 Genetic relationship of populations in China. *Proceedings of the National Academy of Sciences USA* 95, 11763–11768.

Cunningham, Deborah, and Wescott, Daniel. 2002 Within-group human variation in the Asian Pleistocene: The three Upper Cave crania. *Journal of Human Evolution* 42, 627–638.

Cunningham, Deborah., and Jantz, Richard. 2003 The morphometric relationship of upper cave 101 and 103 to modern *Homo sapiens*. *Journal of Human Evolution* 45, 1–18.

Devièse, Thibaut, Massilani, Diyendo, Yi, Seonbok, Comeskey, Daniel, Nagel, Sarah, Nickel, Birgit, Ribechini, Erika, Lee, Jungeun, Tseveendorj, Damdinsuren, Gunchinsuren, Byambaa, Meyer, Matthias,

Pääbo, Svante, and Higham, Tom. 2019 Compound-specific radiocarbon dating and mitochondrial DNA analysis of the *Pleistocene hominin* from Salkhit Mongolia. *Nature Communications* 10, 274.

Doyon, L., Li, Z., Li, H., and d'Errico, F. 2018 Discovery of circa 115,000-year-old bone retouchers at Lingjing, Henan, China. *PLOS ONE* 13, e0194318.

Fu, Qiaomei, Hajdinjak, Mateja, Moldovan, Oana, Constantin, Silviu, Mallick, Swapan, Skoglund, Pontus, Patterson, Nick, Rohland, Nadin, Lazaridis, Iosif, Nickel, Birgit, Viola, Bence, Prüfer, Kay, Meyer, Matthias, Kelso, Janet, Reich, David, and Pääbo, Svante. 2015 An early modern human from Romania with a recent Neanderthal ancestor. *Nature* 524, 216–219.

Fu, Qiaomei, Li, Heng, Moorjani, Priya, Jay, Flora, Slepchenko, Sergey, Bondarev, Aleksei, Johnson, Philip, Aximu-Petri, Ayinuer, Prüfer, Kay, de Filippo, Cesare, Meyer, Matthias, Zwyns, Nicolas, Salazar-García, Domingo, Kuzmin, Yaroslav, Keates, Susan, Kosintsev, Pavel, Razhev, Dmitry, Richards, Michael, Peristov, Nikolai, Lachmann, Michael, Douka, Katerina, Higham, Thomas, Slatkin, Montgomery, Hublin, Jean-Jacques, Reich, David, Kelso, Janet, Viola, Bence, and Pääbo, Svante. 2014 Genome sequence of a 45,000-year-old modern human from western Siberia. *Nature* 514, 445–449.

Fu, Qiaomei, Meyer, Matthias, Gao, Xing, Stenzel, Udo, Burbano, Harnan, Kelso, Janet, and Pääbo, Svante. 2013 DNA analysis of an early modern human from Tianyuan Cave, China. *Proceedings of the National Academy of Science* 110, 2223–2227.

Gao, X., Li, F., Guan, Y., Zhang, X., and Olsen, J. 2019 An archaeological perspective on the origins and evolution of modern humans in China. *Acta Anthropologica Sinica* 38, 317–334. (In Chinese).

Gao, X., Peng, F., Fu, Q., and Li, F. 2017 New progress in understanding the origins of modern humans in China. *Science China Earth Sciences* 60, 2160–2170.

Gao, X., Zhang, X., Yang, D., Shen, C., and Wu, X. 2010 Revisiting the origin of modern humans in China and its implications for global human evolution. *Science China Earth Sciences* 53, 1927–1940.

Gao, X. 2014 Gengxinshi Dongya Renqun Lianxu Yanhua De Kaogu Zhengju Ji Xiangguan Wenti Lunshu [Archaeological evidence for evolutionary continuity of Pleistocene humans in China and East Asia and related discussions]. *Acta Anthropologica Sinica* 33, 237–253. (In Chinese).

Gao, X., and Norton, C. 2002 A critique of the Chinese 'Middle Palaeolithic. *Antiquity* 76, 397–412. (In Chinese).

Gao, X., Pei, S., Wang, H., and Zhong, K. 2004 Ningxia Jiushiqi Kaogu Diaocha Baogao. [A report on Palaeolithic reconnaissance in Ningxia, north China]. *Acta Anthropologica Sinica* 23, 307–325. (In Chinese).

Gao, X., Wang, H., and Guan, Y. 2013a Shuidonggou Jiushiqi Kaogu Yanjiu De Xinjinzhan Yu Xinrenshi. [Research at Shuidongou: New advance and new perspective]. *Acta Anthropologica Sinica* 32, 121–132. (In Chinese).

Gao, X., Wang, H., and Pei, S. 2013b *Shuidonggou: 2003-2007 Niandu Kaogu Fajue Yu Yanjiu Baogao.* [Shuidonggou: Excavation and Research Report (2003–2007)]. Beijing: Science Press. (In Chinese).

Green, Richard, Krause, Johannes, Briggs, Adrian, Maricic, Tomislav, Stenzel, Udo, Kircher, Martin, Patterson, Nick, Li, Heng, Zhai, Weiwei, Fritz, Markus, Hansen, Nancy, Durand, Eric, Malaspinas, Anna-Sapfo, Jensen, Jeffrey, Marques-Bonet, Tomas, Alkan, Can, Prüfer, Kay, Meyer, Matthias, Burbano, Hernán, Good, Jeffrey, Schultz, Rigo, Aximu-Petri, Ayinuer, Butthof, Anne, Höber, Barbara, Höffner, Barbara, Siegemund, Madlen, Weihmann, Antje, Nusbaum, Chad, Lander, Eric, Russ, Carsten, Novod, Nathaniel, Affourtit, Jason, Egholm, Michael, Verna, Christine, Rudan, Pavao, Brajkovic, Dejana, Kucan, Željko, Gušic, Ivan, Doronichev, Vladimir, Golovanova, Liubov, Lalueza-Fox, Carles, de la Rasilla, Marco, Fortea, Javier, Rosas, Antonio, Schmitz, Ralf, Johnson, Philip, Eichler, Evan, Falush, Daniel, Birney, Ewan, Mullikin, James, Slatkin, Montgomery, Nielsen, Rasmus, Kelso, Janet, Lachmann, Michael, Reich, David, and Pääbo, Svante. 2010 A draft sequence of the Neandertal genome. *Science* 328, 710–722.

Guo, Yu-Jie, Li, Bo, Zhang, Jia-Fu, Yuan, Bao-Yin, Xie, Fei, and Roberts, Richard. 2016 Luminescence ages for three 'Middle Palaeolithic' sites in the nihewan basin, Northern China, and their archaeological and palaeoenvironmental implications. *Quaternary Research* 85, 456–470.

Hao, Qingzhen, Wang, Luo, Oldfield, Frank, Peng, Shuzhen, Qin, Li, Song, Yang, Xu, Bing, Qiao, Yansong, Bloemendal, Jan, and Guo, Zhengtang. 2012 Delayed build-up of Arctic ice sheets during 400,000-year minima in insolation variability. *Nature* 490, 393–396.

Harvati, Katerina. 2009 Into Eurasia: A geometric morphometric reassessment of the Upper Cave (Zhoukoudian) specimens. *Journal of Human Evolution* 57, 751–762.

Hoffmann, D. L., Standish, C. D., García-Diez, M., Pettitt, P. B., Milton, J. A., Zilhão, J., Alcolea-González, J., Cantalejo-Duarte, P., Collado, H., de Balbín, R., Lorblanchet, M., Ramos-Muñoz, J., Weniger, G., and Pike, A. 2018 U-Th dating of carbonate crusts reveals Neandertal origin of Iberian cave art. *Science* 359, 912–915.

Hublin, Jean-Jacques, Ben-Ncer, Abdelouahed, Bailey, Shara, Freidline, Sarah, Neubauer, Simon, Skinner, Matthew, Bergmann, Inga, Le Cabec, Adeline, Benazzi, Stefano, Harvati, Katerina, and Gunz, Philipp. 2017 New fossils from Jebel Irhoud, Morocco and the pan-African origin of *Homo sapiens*. *Nature* 546, 289–292.

Hublin, Jean.-Jacques. 2007 What can Neanderthals tell us about Modern Origins? in *Rethinking the Human Revolution: New Behavioural and Biological Perspectives on the Origin and Dispersal of Modern Humans*, eds Mellars, Paul., Boyle, Katie., Bar-Yosef, Ofer., and Stringer, Chris.. Cambridge: McDonald Institute for Archaeological Research, 235–248.

Jia, L., Gai, P., and Li, Y. 1964 Shuidonggou Jiushiqi Shidai Yizhi De Xincailiao. [New materials from the Palaeolithic site of Shuidonggou]. *Gujizhuidongwu Yu Gurenlei* 8, 75–86. (In Chinese).

Jia, L.P. and Wei, Q. 1976 Xujiayao Palaeolithic site, in Yanggao County, Shanxi Province. *Archaeology Bulletin*, 2, 97–114.

Jin, ChangZhu, Pan, WenShi, Zhang, YingQi, Cai, YanJun, Xu, QinQi, Tang, ZhiLu, Wang, Wei, Wang, Yuan, Liu, JinYi, Qin, DaGong, Edwards, Lawrence, and Cheng, Hai. 2009 The *Homo sapiens* Cave hominin site of Mulan Mountain, Jiangzhou District, Chongzuo, Guangxi with emphasis on its age. *Chinese Science Bulletin* 54, 3848–3856.

Jin, Li., and Su, Bing. 2000 Natives or immigrants: Modern human origin in East Asia. *Nature Reviews Genetics* 1, 126–133.

Kaifu, Yousuke, Izuho, Masami, and Goebel, Ted. 2015 Modern human dispersal and behavior in Palaeolithic Asia: summary and discussion, in *Emergence and Diversity of Modern Human Behavior in Palaeolithic Asia*. (eds.) Kaifu, Yousuke., Izuho, Masami., Goebel, Ted., Sato, Hiroyuki., Ono, Akira College Station: Texas A&M University Press, 535–566.

Kamminga, Johan, and Wright, Richard. 1988 The Upper Cave at Zhoukoudian and the origins of the Mongoloids. *Journal of Human Evolution* 17, 739–767.

Ke, Yuehai, Su, Bing, Song, Xiufeng, Lu, Daru, Chen, Lifeng, Li, Hongyu, Qi, Chunjian, Marzuki, Sangkot, Deka, Ranjan, Underhill, Peter, Xiao, Chunjie, Shriver, Mark, Lell, Jeff, Wallace, Douglas, Wells, Spencer, Seielstad, Mark, Oefner, Peter, Zhu, Dingliang, Jin, Jianzhong, Huang, Wei, Chakraborty, Ranajit, Chen, Zhu, and Jin, Li. 2001a African origin of modern humans in East Asia: A Tale of 12,000 Y chromosomes. *Science* 292, 1151–1153.

Ke, Yuehai, Su, Bing, Li, Hongyu, Chen, Lifeng, Qi, Chunjian, Guo, Xinjun, Huang, Wei, Jin, Jianzhong, Lu, Daru, and Jin, Li. 2001b Y-chromosome evidence for no independent origin of modern human in China. *Chinese Science Bulletin* 46, 935–937.

Keates, Susan, and Kuzmin, Yaroslav. 2015 Shuidonggou localities 1 and 2 in northern China: Archaeology and chronology of the Initial Upper Palaeolithic in north-east Asia. *Antiquity* 89, 714–720.

Krause, Johannes, Fu, Qiaomei, Good, Jeffrey, Viola, Bence, Shunkov, Michael, Derevianko, Anatoli, and Pääbo, Svante. 2010 The complete mitochondrial DNA genome of an unknown hominin from southern Siberia. *Nature* 464, 894–897.

Krause, Johannes, Orlando, Ludovic, Serre, David, Viola, Bence, Prüfer, Kay, Richards, Michael, Hublin, Jean-Jacques., Hänni, Catherine, Derevianko, Anatoly, and Pääbo, Svante. 2007 Neanderthals in Central Asia and Siberia. *Nature* 449, 902–904.

Li, C. 1994 Shiqiu De Yanjiu. [The study of stone bola]. *Wenwu Shijie* 3, 103–108. (In Chinese).

Li, Hao, and Lotter, Matt. 2018 Lithic production strategies during the late Middle Pleistocene at Dali, Shaanxi Province, China: Implications for understanding late archaic humans. *Archaeological and Anthropological Sciences* S8, 1–12.

Li, Hao, Li, Zhan-yang, Gao, Xing, Kuman, Kathleen, and Sumner, Alexandra. 2019 Technological behavior of the early Late Pleistocene archaic humans at Lingjing (Xuchang, China). *Archaeological and Anthropological Sciences* 11, 3477–3490.

Li, J, Bunn, H., Zhang, S, and Gao, X. 2017 Equid prey acquisition and archaic *Homo* adaptability at the Early Late Pleistocene site of Xujiayao. China. *International Journal of Osteoarchaeology* 28, 75–82.

Li, Zhan-yang, Wu, Xiu-Jie, Zhou, Li-ping, Liu, Wu, Gao, Xing., Nian, Xiao-mei, and Trinkaus, Erik. 2017 Late Pleistocene archaic human crania from Xuchang, China. *Science* 355, 969–972.

Li, Zhengtao, Xu, Qinghai, Zhang, Shengrui, Hun, Lingyun, Li, Manyue, Xie, Fei, Wang, Fagang, and Liu, Liangiang. 2014 Study on stratigraphic age, climate changes and environment background of Houjiayao Site in Nihewan Basin. *Quaternary International* 349, 42–48.

Li, Feng, Chen, Fu-you, Wang, Yinghua, and Gao, Xing. 2014 Modern behaviors of ancient populations at Shuidonggou Locality 2 and their implications. *Quaternary International* 347, 66–73.

Li, F., Chen, F., Wang, Y., and Gao, X. 2016b Technology diffusion and population migration reflected in blade techniques in Northern China in the Late Pleistocene. *Science China Earth Sciences* 59, 1–14.

Li, Feng, Gao, Xing, Chen, Fu-you, Pei, Shuwen, Zhang, Yue, Zhang, Xiaoling, Liu, Decheng, Zhang, Shuangquan, Guan, Ying, and Wang, Huimin. 2013a The development of Upper Palaeolithic China: New results from the Shuidonggou site. *Antiquity* 87, 368–383.

Li, Feng, Li, Yinghua, Gao, Xing, Kuhn, Stephen, Boda, Eric, and Olsen, John. 2019 A refutation of reported Levallois technology from Guanyingdong Cave in South China. *National Science Review* 6, 1094–1096.

Li, Feng, Kuhn, Steven., Chen, Fu-you, and Gao, Xing. 2016a Raw material economies and mobility patterns in the Late Palaeolithic at Shuidonggou locality 2, North China. *Journal of Anthropological Archaeology* 43, 83–93.

Li, Feng, Kuhn, Steven, and Gao, Xing. 2015 A response to Keates and Kuzmin. *Antiquity* 89, 721–723.

Li, Feng, Kuhn, Steven, Gao, Xing, and Chen, Fu-you. 2013b Re-examination of the dates of large blade technology in China: A comparison of Shuidonggou Locality 1 and Locality 2. *Journal of Human Evolution* 64, 161–168.

Li, Feng, Bae, Christopher, Ramsey, Christopher, Chen, Fuyou, and Gao, Xing. 2018 Re-dating Zhoukoudian Upper Cave, northern China and its regional significance. *Journal of Human Evolution* 121, 170–177.

Li, Feng, Vanwezer, Nils, Boivin, Nicole, Gao, Xing, Ott, Florian, Petraglia, Michael, and Roberts, Patrick. 2019 Heading north: Late Pleistocene environments and human dispersals in central and eastern Asia. *PLoS ONE* 14, e0216433.

Licent, E., and Teilhard, Pierre de Chardin. 1925 Le Paléolithique de la Chine. *L'Anthropologie* 25, 201–234.

Liu, Wu, Jin, Chang-Zhu, Zhang, Ying-Qi, Cai, Yan-Jun, Xing, Song, Wua, Xiu-Jie, Cheng, Hai, Edwards, Lawrence, Pan, Wen-Shi, Qin, Da-Gong, An, Zhi-Sheng, Trinkausg, Erik, and Wu, Xin-Zhi. 2010 Human remains from Zhirendong, south China, and modern human emergence in East Asia. *Proceedings of the National Academy of Science* 107, 19201–19206.

Liu, Wu, Martinón-Torres, María, Cai, Yan-jun, Xing, Song, Tong, Hao-wen, Pei, Shu-wen, Sier, Mark, Wu, Xiao-hong, Edwards, Lawrence, Cheng, Hai, Li, Yi-yuan, Yang, Xiong-xin, Bermúdez de Castro, José, and Wu, Xiu-jie. 2015 The earliest unequivocally modern humans in southern China. *Nature* 526, 696–699.

Liu, Wu, Schepartz, Lynne, Xing, Song, Miller-Antonio, Sari, Wu, Xiujie, Trinkaus, Erik, and Martinón-Torres, María. 2013 Late Middle Pleistocene hominin teeth from Panxian Dadong, South China. *Journal Human Evolution* 64, 337–355.

Liu, W, Xing, S, and Wu, X. 2016 Zhonggengxinshi Wanqi Yilai Zhongguo Gurenlei Huashi Xingtai Tezheng De Duoyangxing, [Morphological diversities of the Late-Middle and Late Pleistocene human fossils in China]. *Zhongguo Kexue Diqiu Kexue* 46, 906–917. (In Chinese).

Liu, D., Chen, F., Zhang, X., Pei, S., and Gao, X. 2008 Shuidonggou 12 Didian De Guhuanjing Yanjiu [Preliminary comments on the paleoenvironment of the Shuidonggou Locality 12]. *Acta Anthropologica Sinica* 27, 295–303. (In Chinese).

Liu, Wu, Wu, Xianzhu, Pei, Shuwen, Wu, Xiujie, and Norton, Christopher. 2010 Huanglong cave: A Late Pleistocene human fossil site in Hubei Province, China. *Quaternary International* 211, 29–41.

Liu, Wu, Vialet, Amelie, Wu, Xiujie, He, Jianing, and Lu, Jinyan. 2006 Comparaison de l'expression de certains caractères crâniens sur les hominidés chinois du Pléistocène récent et de l'Holocène (grotte supérieure de Zhoukoudian, sites de Longxian et de Yanqing). *L'Anthropologie* 110, 258–276.

Lü, Z. ed. 2004 *Zhongguo Kaoguxue Yanjiu De Shiji Huigu: Jiushiqi Shidai Kaogu Juan.* [A Century Review of the Chinese Archaeology: Palaeolithic]. Beijing: Kexue Chubanshe. (In Chinese).

Lowe, John, and Walker, Michael. 2015 *Reconstructing Quaternary Environments.* London and New York: Taylor & Francis Group.

Madsen, David, Li, Jingzen, Brantingham, Jeffrey, Gao, Xing, Elston, Robert, and Bettinger, Robert. 2001 Dating Shuidonggou and the Upper Palaeolithic blade industry in North China. *Antiquity* 75, 706–716.

Martí, A., Wei, Y., Gao, X., Chen, F., and d'Errico, F. 2017 The earliest evidence of coloured ornaments in China: The ochred ostrich eggshell beads from Shuidonggou Locality 2. *Journal of Anthropological Archaeology* 48, 102–113.

Martinón-Torres, María, Wu, Xiujie, Castro, Jose, Xing, Song, and Liu, Wu. 2017 *Homo sapiens* in the eastern Asian Late Pleistocene. *Current Anthropology* 58, S434–S448.

Michel, Véronique, Valladas, Hélène, Shen, Guanjun, Wang, Wei, Zhao, Jian-xin, Shen, Chuan-Chou, Valensi, Patricia, and Bae, Christopher. 2016 The earliest modern *Homo sapiens* in China? *Journal of Human Evolution* 101, 101–104.

Morgan, Christopher, Barton, Loukas, Yi, Mingjie, Bettinger, Robert, Gao, Xing, and Peng, Fei. 2014 Redating Shuidonggou Locality 1 and implications for the Initial Upper Palaeolithic in East Asia. *Radiocarbon* 56, 165–179.

Nian, X, Gao, X, and Zhou, L. 2014 Chronological studies of Shuidonggou (SDG) Locality 1 and their significance for archaeology. *Quaternary International* 347, 5–11.

Ningxia Museum, Ningxia Bureau of Geology, and Chu Cheng Geological Research Team. 1987 1980 Nian Shuidonggou Yizhi Fajue Baogao. [A report on the 1980 excavation at Shuidonggou]. *Kaogu* 4, 439–449.

Norton, C., and Gao, X. 2008 Hominin–carnivore interactions during the Chinese Early Palaeolithic: Taphonomic perspectives from Xujiayao. *Journal of Human Evolution* 55, 164–178.

Pei, Shuwen, Gao, Xing, Wang, Huimin, Kuman, Kathleen, Bae, Christopher, Chen, Fuyou, Guan, Ying, Zhang, Yue, Zhang, Xiaoling, Peng, Fei, and Li, Xiaoli. 2012 The Shuidonggou site complex: New excavations and implications for the earliest Late Palaeolithic in North China. *Journal of Archaeological Science* 39, 3610–3626.

Pei, W. 1934 A preliminary report on the Late Palaeolithic cave of Choukoutien. *Bulletin of the Geological Society of China* 13, 327–258.

Pei, W. 1939 On the Upper Cave industry. *Palaeontologica Sinica* 9.

Peng, F., Wang, H., and Gao, X. 2014 Blade production of Shuidonggou Locality 1 (Northwest China): A technological perspective. *Quaternary International* 347, 12–20.

Qiu, Z. 1985 The Middle Palaeolithic of China, in *Paleoanthropology and Palaeolithic Archaeology in the People's Republic of China*, eds Wu, R., and Olsen, J.. Orlando: Academic Press, 187–210.

Radovčić, D, Sršen, A., Radovčić, J., and Frayer, D. 2015 Evidence for Neandertal jewelry: Modified white-tailed eagle claws at Krapina. *PLoS ONE* 10, e0119802.

Ren, J., Li, F., Wang, X., Chen, F., and Gao, X. 2018 Hebei Nihewan Pendi Banjingzi Jiushiqishidai Yizhi 2015 Nian Fajue Jianbao [A preliminary field report on 2015 excavation at the Banjingzi site of Nihewan Basin in Hebei]. *Kaogu* 11, 3–14. (In Chinese).

Reich, David, Green, Richard, Kircher, Martin, Krause, Johannes, Patterson, Nick, Durand, Eric, Viola, Bence, Briggs, Adrian, Stenzel, Udo, Johnson, Philip, Maricic, Tomislav, Good, Jeffrey, Marques-Bonet, Tomas, Alkan, Can, Fu, Qiaomei, Mallick, Swapan, Li, Heng, Meyer, Matthias, Eichler, Evan, Stoneking, Mark, Richards, Michael, Talamo, Sahra, Shunkov, Michael, Derevianko, Anatoli, Hublin, Jean-Jacques, Kelso, Janet, Slatkin, Montgomery, and Pääbo, Svante. 2010 Genetic history of an archaic hominin group from Denisova Cave in Siberia. *Nature* 468, 1053–1060.

Rosenberg, K., and Wu, X. 2013 A River runs through it: Modern human origins in East Asia, in *The Origins of Modern Humans: Biology Reconsidered*, Second Edition, eds Smith, Fred. and Ahern, James, John Wiley & Sons: New York, 89–121.

Shang, H., Tong, H., Zhang, S., Chen, F., and Trinkaus, E. 2007 An early modern human from Tianyuan Cave, Zhoukoudian, China. *Proceeding of National Academy of Sciences USA* 104, 6573–6578.

Shea, J. 2011 *Homo sapiens* is as *Homo sapiens* was: Behavioral variability versus "behavioral modernity" in Palaeolithic Archaeology. *Current Anthropology* 52, 1–35.

Slimak, Ludovic, Svendsen, John, Mangerud, Jan, Plisson, Hugues, Heggen, Herbjørn, Brugère, Alexis, and Pavlov, Pavel. 2011 Late Mousterian persistence near the Arctic Circle. *Science* 332, 841–845.

Slon, Viviane, Mafessoni, Fabrizio, Vernot, Benjamin, de Filippo, Cesare, Grote, Steffi, Viola, Bence, Hajdinjak, Mateja, Peyrégne, Stéphane, Nagel, Sarah, Brown, Samantha, Douka, Katerina, Higham, Tom, Kozlikin, Maxim, Shunkov, Michael, Derevianko, Anatoly, Kelso, Janet, Meyer, Matthias, Prüfer, Kay, and Pääbo, Svante. 2018 The genome of the offspring of a Neanderthal mother and a Denisovan father. *Nature* 561, 113–116.

Slon, Viviane, Hopfe, Charlotte, Weis, Clemens, Mafessoni, Fabrizio, De La Rasilla, Marco, Lalueza-Fox, Carles, Rosas, Antonio, Soressi, Marie, Knul, Monika, Miller, Rebecca, Stewart, John, Derevianko, Anatoly, Jacobs, Zenobia, Li, Bo, Roberts, Richard, Shunkov, Michael, de Lumley, Henry, Perrenoud, Christian, Gušić, Ivan, Kućan, Željko, Rudan, Pavao, Aximu-Petri, Ayinuer, Essel, Elena, Nagel, Sarah, Nickel, Birgit, Schmidt, Anna, Prüfer, Kay, Kelso, Janet, Burbano, Hernán, Pääbo, Svante, and Meyer, Matthias. 2017 Neandertal and Denisovan DNA from Pleistocene sediments. *Science* 356, 605–608.

Smith, F., Falsetti, H., and Donnelly, S. 1989 Modern human origins. *Yearbook of Physical Anthropology* 32, 35–68.
Stringer, Chris, and Andrews, Peter. 1988 Genetic and fossil evidence for the origin of modern humans. *Science* 239, 1263–1268.
Stringer, Chris. 1992 Reconstructing recent human evolution. *Philosophical Transactions of the Royal Society B: Biological Sciences* 337, 217–224.
Stringer, Chris. 2002 Modern human origins: Progress and prospects. *Philosophical Transactions of the Royal Society B: Biological Sciences* 357, 563–579.
Stringer, Chris. 2014 Why we are not all multiregionalists now. *Trends in Ecology & Evolution* 29, 248–251.
Su, Bing, Xiao, Junhua, Underhill, Peter, Deka, Ranjan, Zhang, Weiling, Akey, Joshua, Huang, Wei, Shen, Di, Lu, Daru, Luo, Jingchun, Chu, Jiayou, Tan, Jiazhen, Shen, Peidong, Davis, Ron, Cavalli-Sforza, Luca, Chakraborty, Ranajit, Xiong, Momiao, Du, Ruofu, Oefner, Peter, Chen, Zhu, and Jin, Li. 1999 Y-chromosome evidence for a northward migration of modern humans into Eastern Asia during the Last Ice Age. *The American Journal of Human Genetics* 65, 1718–1724.
Sun, X., Yi, S., Lu, H, and Zhang, . 2017 TT-OSL and post-IR IRSL dating of the Dali Man site in central China. *Quaternary International* 434, 99–106.
Templeton, A. 2002 Out of Africa again and again. *Nature* 416, 45–51.
Tu, H., Shen, G., Li, H., Xie, F., and Granger, D. 2015 $^{26}$Al/$^{10}$Be burial dating of Xujiayao-Houjiayao site in Nihewan Basin, northern China. *PLoS One* 10, e0118315.
Vernot, Benjamin, and Akey, Joshua. 2014 Resurrecting surviving Neandertal lineages from modern human genomes. *Science* 343, 1017–1021.
Vernot, Benjamin, Tucci, Serena, Kelso, Janet, Schraiber, Joshua, Wolf, Aaron, Gittelman, Rachel, Dannemann, Michael, Grote, Steffi, Mccoy, Rajiv, Norton, Heather, Scheinfeldt, Laura, Merriwether, David, Koki, George, Friedlaender, Jonathan, Wakefield, Jon, Pääbo, Svante, and Akey, Joshua. 2016 Excavating Neandertal and Denisovan DNA from the genomes of Melanesian individuals. *Science* 352, 235–239.
Wang, F., and Li, F. 2019 Xujiayaoren Maicang Diceng Yu Shidai Tantao [Discussions on the stratigraphy and age of the Xujiayao hominin]. *Acta Anthropologica Sinica* DOI: 10.16359/j.cnki.cn11-1963/q.2019.0000. (In Chinese).
Wang, Y., Xue, X., Zhao, J., Yue, L., and Liu, S. 1979 Discovery and preliminary study of Dali cranium from Shaanxi Province. *Chinese Science Bulletin* 24, 303–306.
Wang, F. 2015 Houjiayao Yizhi 2007–2012 Fajue Diceng De Xinrenshi, [New perspectives on the stratigraphy of 2007–2012 excavation at the Houjiayao site]. *Wenwu Chunqiu* 6, 15–22. (In Chinese).
Wei, Y., d'Errico, F., Vanhaeren, M., Li, F., and Gao, X. 2016 An early instance of upper Palaeolithic personal ornamentation from China: The freshwater shell bead from Shuidonggou 2. *PLoS One* 11, e0155847.
Weidenreich, F. 1939a The duration of life of fossil man in China and the pathological lesions found in his skeleton. *Chinese Medical Journal* 45, 33–44.
Weidenreich, F. 1939b On the earliest representatives of modern mankind recovered on the soil of East Asia. *Peking Natural History Bulletin* 13, 161–174.
Wolpoff, M. H., Hawks, J., and Caspari, R. 2000 Multiregional, not multiple origins. *American Journal of Physical Anthropology* 112, 129–136.
Wolpoff, M. H., Wu, X., and Thorne, A. G. 1984 Modern *Homo sapiens* origins: A general theory of hominid evolution involving the fossil evidence from East Asia, in *The Origins of Modern Humans: A World Survey of the Fossil Evidence*, eds Smith, F. H., and Spencer, F.. New York: Alan R Liss Inc, 411–483.
Wolpoff, M. 1999 *Paleoanthropology*. New York: McGraw-Hill.
Wu, R. 1988 Liaoning Yingkou Jinniushanren Huashi Tougu De Fuyuan Jiqi Zhuyao Xingzhuang. [The reconstruction of the fossil human skull from Jinniushan, Yinkou, Liaoning Province and its main features]. *Acta Anthropologica Sinica* 7, 97–101. (In Chinese).
Wu, X. 1981 Shannxi Dalixian Faxian De Zaoqizhiren Gulaoleixing De Yige Wanhao Tougu. [A well-preserved cranium of an archaic type of early *Homo sapiens* from Dali, China]. *Zhongguokexue* 14, 530–539. (In Chinese).
Wu, X. 1998 Cong Zhongguo Wanqizhiren Luya Tezheng Kan Zhongguo Xiandairen Qiyuan. [Origin of modern humans of China viewed from cranio-dental characteristics of Late *Homo sapiens* in China.]. *Acta Anthropologica Sinica* 17, 276–282. (In Chinese).

Wu, X. 2006 Xiandairen Qiyuan De Duodiqu Jinhua Xueshuo Zai Zhongguo De Shizheng. [Evidence of multiregional human evolution hypothesis from China]. *Disiji Yanjiu* 26, 702–709. (In Chinese).
Wu, X. 2014 Dali Lugu Zai Renlei jinhuazhong De Weizhi. [The Place of Dali cranium in human evolution]. *Acta Anthropologica Sinica* 33, 405–426. (In Chinese).
Wu, X., and Bruner, E. 2016 The endocranial anatomy of Maba 1. *American Journal of Physical Anthropology* 160, 633–643.
Wu, Xiu-Jie, Crevecoeur, Isabelle, Liu, Wu, Xing, Song, and Trinkaus, Erik. 2014 Temporal labyrinths of eastern Eurasian Pleistocene humans. *Proceedings of the National Academy of Sciences USA* 111, 10509–10513.
Wu, Xiu-Jie, Pei, Shu-Wen, Cai, Yan-Jun, Tong, Hao-Wen, Li, Qiang, Dong, Zhe, Sheng, Jin-Chao, Jin, Ze-Tian, Ma, Dong-Dong, Xing, Song, Li, Xiao-Li, Cheng, Xing, Cheng, Hai, de la Torre, Ignacio, Edwards, Lawrence, Gong, Xi-Cheng, An, Zhi-Sheng, Trinkaus, Erik, and Liu, Wu. 2019 Archaic human remains from Hualongdong, China, and Middle Pleistocene human continuity and variation. *Proceedings of the National Academy of Sciences* 116, 9820–9824.
Wu, X., and Athreya, S. 2013 A description of the geological context, discrete traits, and linear morphometrics of the Middle Pleistocene hominid from Dali, Shaanxi Province, China. *American Journal of Physical Anthropology* 150, 141–157.
Wu, X., and You, Y. 1979 Daliren Yizhi De Chubu Guancha [Preliminary study of the Dali hominid site]. *Gujihuzidongwu Xuebao* 17, 294–303. (In Chinese).
Wu, X., and Xu, X. 2016 Cong Zhongguo He Xiya Jiuishiqi Ji Daoxian Renya Huashi Kan Zhongguo Xiandairen Qiyuan [The origin of modern humans in China viewed from the palaeolithic data and Daoxian human fossils]. *Acta Anthropologica Sinica* 35, 1–13. (In Chinese).
Wu, M. 1986 Xujiayaoren Niegu Yanjiu [Study of temporal bone of Xujiayao Man]. *Renleixuexuebao* 5, 220–226. (In Chinese).
Wu, X. 1961 Zhoukoudian Shandingdongren Huashi Yanjiu [Study on the Upper Cave man of Choukoutien]. *Gujizhuidongwu Yu Gurenlei* 3, 181–203. (In Chinese).
Xie, F. 2008 Houjiayao Yizhi Chutu De Renlei Huashi Ji Wenhua Yiwu Bushi Chanzi Nihewanceng. [The Hominin Fossils and Cultural Remains are not from the Nihewan Formation]. *Zhongguo Wenwubao*, 23 May. (In Chinese).
Xing, Song, Tafforeau, Paul, O'hara, Mackie, Modesto-Mata, Mario, Martín-Francés, Laura, Martinón-Torres, María, Zhang, Limin, Schepartz, Lynne, Bermúdez De Castro, José, and Guatelli-Steinberg, Debbie. 2019 First systematic assessment of dental growth and development in an archaic hominin (genus, *Homo*) from East Asia. *Science Advances* 5, eaau0930.
Yu, J., Wang, Y., He, J., Feng, Y., and Li, Y. 2018 Xinjiang Jimunaixian Tongtiandong Yizhi [Tongtiandong Site in Jimunai County of Xinjiang]. *Kaogu* 7, 3–14. (In Chinese).
Yang, Melinda, Gao, Xing, Theunert, Christoph, Tong, Haowen, Aximu-Petri, Ayinuer, Nickel, Birgit, Slatkin, Montgomery, Meyer, Matthias, Pääbo, Svante, Kelso, Janet, and Fu, Qiaomei. 2017 40,000-Year-Old individual from Asia provides insight into early population structure in Eurasia. *Current Biology* 27, 3202–3208.
Yee, M. K. 2012 The Middle Palaeolithic in China: A review of current interpretations. *Antiquity* 86, 619–626.
Yin, Gongming, Bahain, Jean-Jacques, Shen, Guanjun, Tissoux, Hélène, Falguères, Christophe, Dolo, Jean-Michel, Han, Fei, and Shao, Qingfeng. 2011 ESR/U-series study of teeth recovered from the palaeoanthropological stratum of the Dali Man site (Shaanxi Province, China). *Quaternary Geochronology* 6, 98–105.
Yin, G., Zhao, H., Yin, J., and Lu, Y. 2002 Chronology of the stratum containing the skull of the Dali Man. *Chinese Science Bulletin* 47, 1302–1307.
Zhang, S., Gao, X., Zhang, Y., and Li, Z. 2011 Taphonomic analysis of the Lingjing fauna and the first report of a Middle Palaeolithic kill-butchery site in North China. *Chinese Science Bulletin* 56, 3213–3219.
Zhang, S., Li, Z., Zhang, Y., and Gao, X. 2009 Mortality profiles of the large herbivores from the Lingjing Xuchang Man Site, Henan Province and the early emergence of the modern human behaviors in East Asia. *Chinese Science Bulletin* 54, 3857–3863.
Zhang, S., and Zhou, C. 1984 Daliren Hushi Didian Dierci Fajue Jianbao, [A preliminary study of the second excavation of Dali Man locality]. *Acta Anthropologica Sinica* 3.1–29. (In Chinese).
Zhang, S. 1999 Xiaokouzi Shiqian Didian Faxian De Shizhiping Yanjiu, [A study of stone artefacts found at the Xiaokouzi prehistoric site]. *Acta Anthropologica Sinica* 18, 81–100. (In Chinese).

Zhang, X., Wang, S., Chen, Z., Ge, J., Long, H., He, W., Da, W., Nian, X., Yi, M., Zhou, X., Zhang, P., Jin, Y., Bar-Yosef, O., Olsen, J., and Gao, X. 2018 The earliest human occupation of the high-altitude Tibetan Plateau 40 thousand to 30 thousand years ago. *Science* 362, 1049–1051.

Zilhão, J. 2012 Personal ornaments and symbolism among the Neanderthals. *Developments in Quaternary Sciences* 16, 35–49.

Zilhão, João, Angelucci, Diego, Badal-García, Ernestina, d'Errico, Francesco, Daniel, Floréal, Dayet, Laure, Douka, Katerina, Higham, Thomas, Martínez-Sánchez, María, Montes-Bernárdez, Ricardo, Murcia-Mascarós, Sonia, Pérez-Sirvent, Carmen, Roldán-García, Clodoaldo, Vanhaeren, Marian, Villaverde, Valentín, Wood, Rachel, and Zapata, Josefina. 2010 Symbolic use of marine shells and mineral pigments by Iberian Neandertals. *Proceedings of the National Academy of Sciences* 107, 1023–1028.

# 11

## THE PHILIPPINES

Origins to the End of the Pleistocene

*Alfred Pawlik and Philip Piper*

### Introduction

The Philippine archipelago lies at a geographically strategic location between the Asian mainland and islands of Southeast Asia within latitudes 4°30′ to 21°12′N and longitudes 119° to 127°E. It straddles two distinct biogeographic zones, with Palawan forming the north-eastern edge of the Sundaic region, and the main islands of Luzon, the Visayas and Mindanao located east of Huxley's modification of Wallace's Line in the island realm of Wallacea. This unique island-scape has now produced an archaeological and palaeontological record that extends back around 1–0.7 mya and includes a record of hominin colonisation and habitation from the Middle Pleistocene into the Late Pleistocene. This is supported by some marked similarities between lithic assemblages from Northern and Central Luzon, not only with several sites on Mainland Southeast Asia and South China, but also with stone implements recovered from Java and Flores, that also suggest the migration of hominins into the Philippines as early as 1 mya. These hominins appear to have inhabited the islands with a megafaunal community, of which most species are now extinct. As on Flores (and perhaps Sulawesi), it is possible that hominins in the Philippines survived until the arrival of anatomically modern humans (AMH) during regional expansion between the biogeographic regions of Sunda, Wallacea, and Sahul between 60–50 kya (if not slightly earlier).

Recently, the Philippine archaeological record has produced some significant insights into the economic strategies and the technological capabilities of the early modern human inhabitants of the archipelago. Excavations on Mindoro Island, for example, have delivered evidence of sophisticated implements in shell and bone. These technologies parallel those observed to the southeast in Sulawesi and Timor in their sophistication but are morphologically different. The developing evidence suggests that modern human communities likely arrived in Southeast Asia with a number of shared (though potentially already divergent) technologies, skills, and social behaviours (and no doubt ideologies). Once these populations had radiated out and occupied the various islands and archipelagos across Southeast Asia (SEA), they became relatively isolated. Thereafter, island communities developed their own complex innovations and techniques of coping with the diverse environments they encountered, and their own interdependent social

DOI: 10.4324/9781003427483-11

and cultural interactions. Towards the end of the Pleistocene, probably with the assistance of improved boat technology and greater mobility, we see regional convergence and the dispersal of ideological and technological innovation over the broader Southeast Asian region.

## In the Beginning: Early Hominin Colonization of the Philippines

The Philippines formed as part of the north-south aligned 'ring of fire' that extends along the southern and western margins of the Indonesian islands of Sumatra and Java, north through Sulawesi and onwards beyond the Philippines along the east coast of Japan. Two major processes have resulted in the island configuration of the Philippine Archipelago; the landforms of northern Luzon started to emerge around 30 million years ago due to volcanic activity forced by the subduction zones. The second was the gradual southwards movement of a piece of the earth's crust from the southern China region that eventually contributed a substantial portion to the karst limestone landmasses of Palawan and Mindoro (Heaney 1993).

Over the following 25 million years, various landforms were produced through volcanic activity and the compression caused by contact between the crustal formation that would eventually become Palawan and Mindoro moving southwards, and the island formations of the rest of the Philippine archipelago. Many of the islands such as Luzon have portions that developed independently, and finally became conjoined as late as 3 million years ago into larger landscape formations. Thus, much of the Philippine archipelago remained as small, isolated islands until fairly recently in geological time, and this likely had considerable impacts on the high rates of plant and animal diversity and observed island endemism (Heaney et al. 2016).

Four possible routes have been postulated as points of entry for various plants, animals, and hominins into the Philippine archipelago (Figure 11.1); from Taiwan to Luzon, from Borneo via Palawan to Mindoro or via the Sulu archipelago into western Mindanao, as well as northwards from Sulawesi into southern Mindanao (Hughes et al. 2015; Ono et al. 2023a,b). Palawan shares a considerable amount of its terrestrial vertebrates with Borneo (Esselstyn et al. 2010) suggesting migration between the two islands, and to a lesser extent onwards to Mindoro and then Luzon. This was certainly one active route and is the only colonization route that might have been facilitated by an initial stage land bridge connection between Borneo and Palawan during the Middle Pleistocene (Heaney 1993), and possibly again in the Late Pleistocene during the Last Glacial Maximum (LGM) after a gradual drop of the eustatic sea level to its lowest value of c.−134 m at the end of this interval around 21,000 BP (Earl of Cranbrook 2000;Lambeck et al. 2014). Considering the current reconstructed depth of c.−135 m for the Balabac Strait that separates Borneo and Palawan today, a land bridge of c.2 km width between the two islands could have opened during the LGM (Robles et al. 2015). The rest of the Philippines have never been physically conjoined to any mainland and a sea crossing has always been required to reach the islands (Heaney 1993; Oliver and Heaney 1996).

During periods of lowered sea level several of the larger and smaller islands were intermittently conjoined. For example, Palawan merged with Culion and Busuanga to form the Greater Palawan region, the Visayan islands of Cebu, Panay, and Negros combined, and Mindanao joined with many of the smaller islands in the Sulu Sea, and Luzon (Voris 2000; Hanebuth et al. 2000; Sathiamurthy and Voris 2006, 2009; Piper et al. 2008; Pawlik et al. 2014; Robles et al. 2015). But these larger island groups remained separated from each other by deep ocean channels. The geographic isolation of the main Philippine archipelago and the continuous separation of Greater Palawan from Greater Luzon, Mindanao, and the Visayan region is evident in the

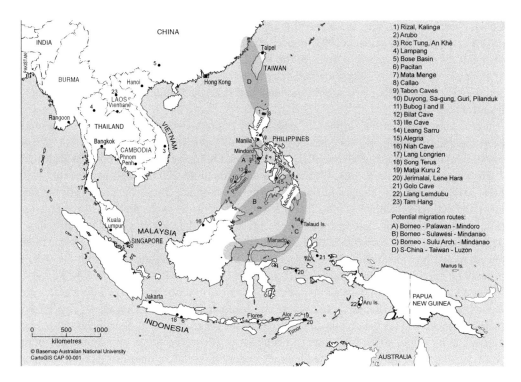

**FIGURE 11.1** Geographical location of the Philippines with potential migration routes and relevant sites.

impoverished nature of the modern faunas, and the high levels of endemism and speciation they demonstrate on the different island groups across the archipelago. Rats, for example appear to have been early colonizers of the Philippine archipelago, arriving as much as 18 mya (Heaney et al. 2016). Finding a broad range of 'empty' ecological habitats they rapidly radiated to occupy a variety of niches that on the mainland, to the west, would commonly have been occupied by various taxa such as squirrels and shrews. The different island groups of the Philippines all possess their own diverse range of endemic species (Heaney 1993; Oliver and Heaney 1996; Jansa et al. 2006).

High rates of endemism and low diversity (relative to a mainland) is also reflected in the earliest known terrestrial vertebrate faunas of the Middle Pleistocene recorded in the Philippines. The island of Luzon for example, was inhabited by a range of large mammals and reptiles that are considered to be good colonizers of even quite remote islands. Several sites in Kalinga, Pangasinan, La Union, but also in the Metro Manila area have produced fossil evidence of giant tortoise (Geochelone), large lizards and the proboscideans *Stegodon* and *Elephas* (Teves and Gonzales 1950; Foronda et al. 1987; Bautista 1995; Ingicco et al. 2018). Fossil records from the Visayan and Mindanao regions are sparse but they have produced *Stegodon* and *Elephas* (De Vos and Bautista 2003). Giant tortoises, lizards, rats and proboscideans are also found across the broader Wallacean region – Flores and Timor (Morwood and Oosterzee 2007). The Philippines (and Sulawesi), however, vary from many of the more isolated islands in the Wallacean region such as Flores, Timor, and the Maluku Islands in that they also possess(ed) a much greater diversity of large mammals that included bovines, cervids, and suids (including a variety of

*Celebochoerus*), and in the case of the Philippines specifically, a rhinoceros (*Rhinoceros philippinensis*; de Vos and Bautista, 2003; Ingicco et al. 2017, 2018). The higher diversity of large mammal taxa that managed to cross to the Philippines and Sulawesi is probably a reflection of their closer proximity, larger overall size, and greater accessibility from the Sundaic biogeographic region to the west and/or mainland to the north, than the more isolated Wallacean islands to the east.

Fossil vertebrate remains in the Cagayan Valley region of northern Luzon had occasionally been reported as being associated with lithic artefacts labelled as the *Cabalwanian*, and the presence of hominins in the Middle Pleistocene of the Philippines had been postulated since the 1950s (Koenigswald 1958; Fox 1978; Pawlik and Ronquillo 2003; Dizon and Pawlik 2010). Fox (1978) for instance, suggested, based on inferred chronological associations between stone tools and extinct vertebrate faunas, that the lithic assemblages were produced by a precursor to modern humans who had reached Luzon during the Middle Pleistocene. Unequivocal evidence though, of an association between the artefacts and Middle Pleistocene vertebrate faunas has, until recently, been difficult to prove. Now, ongoing investigations close to the old Fox excavation sites in the municipality of Rizal in the Cagayan Valley have uncovered a variety of vertebrate fossils, including an almost complete *in situ* rhinoceros (*R. philippinensis*) skeleton (Ingicco et al. 2018, 2020). Cut marks and hammer stone percussion marks clearly show that the rhinoceros was disarticulated and some of the bones smashed, presumably for marrow extraction, by a tool using hominin. The deposits in which the bones and tools were buried were dated through optical stimulated luminescence (OSL) and argon-argon (Ar/Ar) to around 700 kya (Ingicco et al. 2018) demonstrating that the initial assumptions of Koenigswald (1958) and Fox (1978) were correct. The 57 stone artefacts recovered include six cores, 49 flakes, and two possible hammer stones. The knapping strategy is described as rather unorganized core reduction that resulted in non-standardized flakes and an absence of retouch, but nevertheless the tool repertoire is relatively diverse in its technology and final products (Ingicco et al. 2018). The authors stated a technological similarity with the Arubo assemblage found in Nueva Ecija. However, the generally small sizes of the Rizal artefacts and the absence of unifacial and bifacial forms stands in remarkable contrast to the lithic repertoire reported from Arubo, with its core tools, unifacial, and bifacial modifications (Pawlik 2002, 2004; Dizon and Pawlik 2010). Arubo is located south of Rizal, in the municipality of General Tinio in Nueva Ecija, Central Luzon. The site produced an assemblage of surprisingly 'formal' lithic artefacts of possible Middle Pleistocene origin (Pawlik 2002, 2004). The assemblage included several tool forms typical of the early Palaeolithic. While the assemblages from northern Luzon and Mindanao are mainly composed of simple Mode 1 pebble tools, the Arubo assemblages incorporate unifacial and bifacial Mode 2 artefacts (Figure 11.2A–C), including a handaxe, choppers, and retouched flakes (Pawlik 2002, 2004; Pawlik and Ronquillo 2003; Dizon and Pawlik 2010). The presence of large amounts of chert in close proximity to Arubo might suggest it was frequented for the acquisition of raw material and for tool production. Variability in preparation and reduction techniques is indicated by the presence of a diversity of cores, including a large flake core and a so-called horse-hoof core (Figure 11.2D and E), similar to cores recorded in early Palaeolithic assemblages in Java (Koenigswald 1936; Van Heekeren 1972; Bartstra 1984; Soejono 1984; Sémah et al. 1992; Simanjuntak et al. 2001). Multiple uses of tools and curation were recognized through microscopic use-wear analyses (Pawlik 2002; Teodosio 2005). Unfortunately, the Arubo site was already heavily disturbed prior to excavation, caused by the dredging of a fishpond. Although that activity led to the discovery of the site, most of the artefacts were

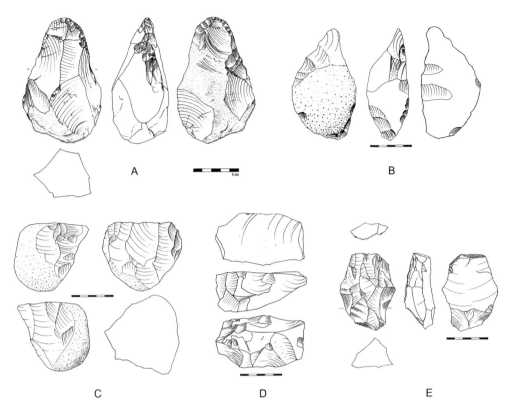

FIGURE 11.2  Lithic artefacts from Arubo, Nueva Ecjia. (A) handaxe; (B) large flake with pointed retouch; (C) 'horse-hoof' core; (D) core on a larger flake with striking platform on ventral; (E) unifacially modified flake tool with distal reduction on ventral (after Pawlik 2004; Teodosio 2005).

recovered from on or close to the ground surface, making it impossible to get a reliable chronometric date. On the mainland of Southeast Asia, early Palaeolithic sites like Roc Tung/An Khê in Vietnam, Lampang in Thailand, and in the Bose Basin in Guangxi, South China (Huang 1989; Xiang 1990; Xie 1990; Schick and Dong 1993; Leng Jian and Shannon 2000; Yamei et al. 2000; Zeitoun et al. 2013; Derevianko et al. 2016), and also sites in Island Southeast Asia (ISEA) like Pacitan in Java (Sémah et al. 2000) and Mata Menge on Flores (van den Bergh et al. 1996; Morwood et al. 1998; Simanjuntak et al. 2010) are all sites variously dated to between c.1.0 and 0.5 mya. They have produced handaxes and other bifacial and unifacial forms similar to Arubo, providing a potential age range for its lithic assemblage.

Although, both the Rizal and Arubo sites seem to share similar core preparation technology and lithic raw material (Pawlik 2004; Ingicco et al. 2018) the differences between stone technologies at the two sites are clear, and this raises a number of important questions that are currently difficult to resolve. For example, although undated the Arubo artefacts are potentially considerably older than the archaeological remains from Rizal. Another possibility is that the two assemblages were produced by different species of Middle Pleistocene hominin. Over the last two decades or so it has become evident that two or more species of hominin have overlapped both chronologically and geographically in several regions of the world (Gibbons 2015;

Brown et al. 2016; Schroeder et al. 2017; Slon et al. 2017; Larena et al. 2021a), and the Philippines might have been no exception.

Following the Middle Pleistocene there is a considerable gap in the archaeological record of the Philippines, between c.700 and 70 kya and there is currently no record for a hominin presence during that period. After 70 kya a single site, Callao Cave in the Peñablanca region of northern Luzon provides evidence of a late hominin presence in the Philippines. Here, a third right metatarsal was discovered in 2007 and was initially identified as AMH (Mijares et al. 2010). A direct U-series ablation date produced a minimum age of 66,700 ± 1,000 BP while two associated cervid teeth returned U-series ages of 52,000 ± 1,400 BP and 54,300 ± 1,900 BP, respectively. Further excavations in 2011 and 2015 produced a total of 12 fossil remains, including the entire post-canine dentition from the right side of a maxilla, a second right maxillary third molar and a juvenile femur shaft fragment, indicating the presence of at least three individuals in the Callao hominin fossil assemblage. Laser ablation U-series analysis of one of the human teeth produced a date of around 50,000 BP and younger than the U-series date of the human MT3, but consistent with the dates obtained from the cervid teeth (Grün et al. 2014). The morphological uniqueness of these hominin remains warranted a new species designation, *Homo luzonensis* (Détroit et al. 2019). The origins of *H. luzonensis* remain somewhat enigmatic. However, based on the morphological shape and microstructure of the teeth, Zanolli et al. (2022) have argued that *H. luzonensis* is likely an island endemic with an Indonesian *Homo erectus* ancestry.

The human fossils, from Layer 14, were associated with a relatively large faunal assemblage. While no lithic or other artefacts were found associated with the fossil remains, cut marks observed on some bones might suggest that at least some of the bone accumulation had resulted from the butchering activities of a hominin (Mijares et al. 2010; Manalo 2011). The bone accumulation in Layer 14 of Callao consisted predominantly of the deer *Rusa marianna*, some pig (*Sus philippensis*), and a few fragments of an extinct bovine, probably similar to *Bubalus mindorensis* (Tamaraw) that today only inhabits the island of Mindoro (Mijares et al. 2010). There was no evidence of *Stegodon*, giant tortoise, rhinoceros, or any of the other large megafauna found in the Middle Pleistocene of the Cagayan Valley at Callao, perhaps indicating that they were already extinct before the earliest recorded phases of hominin occupation in the cave.

A genetic study has hinted at the possible presence of a third enigmatic hominin, if not in the Philippines, certainly within Island Southeast Asia. It has been suggested that the original modern human colonizers of the Philippines possess(ed) relatively high traces of Denisovan admixture (Jinam et al. 2017). High proportions of Denisovan genomic content in the most ancient human populations east of Wallace's Line, such as the Australo-papuans and Philippine Negritos suggests a shared ancestry as the first forager communities to migrate across the region (Lipson et al. 2018). However, different proportions of Denisovan genes are recorded in Philippine Negrito groups, compared to Australo-papuans, suggesting independent introgression with Denisovans following separation of the two population lineages (Teixeira and Cooper 2019). It has been argued that at least some of the interaction with Denisovans must have occurred once human populations had crossed Wallace's Line, and perhaps even reached the Philippines (Reich et al. 2011; Jinam et al. 2017) – suggesting a presence of Denisovans in the Philippines, prior to the arrival of modern humans. This argument, based on small human sample sizes is extremely speculative, and it assumes that the earliest human populations who eventually arrived in the Philippines and those that travelled to Australia and New Guinea were from a single coherent mainland population, before they dispersed across Wallace's Line – there appears to be no reason to believe that this was the case. Instead, recent genetic studies have argued that the first modern human populations to arrive in the Philippines, commonly referred to as the Ayta or Negritos, and especially those from Central Luzon possess the highest level of Denisovan ancestry in the world, about 30–40% greater than that of Australians and Papuans. The data are consistent with an independent admixture event between Negritos from Denisovans (Larena et al., 2021a). Together with the recently described *H. luzonensis*, the authors of the study suggest that before the arrival of modern humans the Philippines were inhabited by multiple archaic species of hominin that may have been genetically related. Genetic data also suggests that early colonization of the Philippines by Ayta/Negrito communities happened in at least five major events over the last 50,000 years. The first colonizers are related to the Northern and Southern Negritos. This was then followed by the arrival of the Manobo, Sama, Papuan, and Cordilleran-related populations (Larena et al. 2021b).

**Arrival of Anatomically Modern Humans in The Philippines**

Despite a timeline for AMH migration of 50,000 years suggested by genetic studies, few sites with archaeological records dating to the Late Pleistocene, and especially pre-dating 30 kya, have been identified in the Philippines – and all of these have been along the Palawan, Mindoro and Luzon route of colonization. The paucity of archaeological data from the southern Philippines is likely related to the small number of archaeologists working in the country as well as limitations in field research due to ongoing political and social instability in certain areas.

The earliest known AMH fossils recovered in the Philippines so far are those from Tabon Cave in Quezon Province, Palawan. The human remains from Tabon include a frontal bone, two mandibular fragments and several teeth, as well as fragments of post-cranial skeleton from a number of individuals. However, a reliable date for the fossils has been difficult to achieve. Charcoal from the layer which supposedly produced the human fossils (Fox 1970, 40–44) produced a somewhat younger date of 23,200 ± 1000 uncal. BP or 29,657–25,157 cal. BP (UCLA 699). The earliest date recorded by Fox (1970, 24) on charcoal, apparently associated with what he called 'Flake Assemblage IV' was 30,500 ± 1100 uncal. BP or 36,731–31,814 cal. BP (UCLA-958), but in a rough estimate of sedimentation and 'age–depth' relationships, Fox concluded that the oldest deposits and 'Flake Assemblage V' would probably be c.40 kya (Fox 1970, 28). More recently, the frontal bone from Tabon was directly dated by uranium gamma ray counting at the Institut de Paléontologie Humaine of the Muséum national d'Histoire naturelle in Paris, and this corrected the date to 16,500 ± 2000 BP (Dizon et al. 2002). A human tibia found 21 cm below modern ground surface in a disturbed layer excavated during a re-investigation of Tabon Cave by the National Museum of the Philippines and the Institut de Paléontologie Humaine, Paris, delivered another uranium series date of 47,000 + 11,000/−10,000 BP, while a right mandible fragment from the Fox excavation found in a disturbed context outside the main excavation area produced a uranium series date of 31,000 +8,000/−7,000 BP (Détroit et al. 2004). Although these dates are relatively consistent with the estimate of Fox for the lowest cultural layer in Tabon Cave to ~40 kya, the very high standard error in the U-series dates demands a cautionary consideration of the absolute dates of the Tabon human fossils (Pawlik 2021). Probably, a more reliable age estimation is provided by several radiocarbon dates on hearth features found in the cave of around 32–39 kya (Choa et al. 2016; Xhauflair et al. 2023).

Palawan Island is c.425 km long, 40 km wide, and it covers approximately 11,857 km². But what is currently above sea level, is the mountainous spine that runs down the middle of the island. During most of the Pleistocene, and especially during the LGM, when sea levels were c.134 m below present (Lambeck et al. 2014), Palawan had a much greater landmass, of approximately 79,440 km² (Robles et al. 2015). Instead of the tropical rainforests that characterize the contemporary vegetation of the Sundaic biogeographic zone, of which Palawan is part, the island was considerably drier and cooler, and covered with an open grassland/woodland vegetation (Bird et al. 2005, 2007).

At present the upstanding karst limestone formations of Lipuun Point around Tabon Cave protrude into the shallow South China seas. During the early occupation of Tabon it is estimated that sea levels would have been 60–80 m below modern levels and the coast would have been at a considerable distance, c.32–36 km away from the cave (Robles et al. 2015). This is supported by the absence of shell midden deposits in Tabon, in contrast to the Mid- to Late Holocene sites close to Tabon such as Guri Cave, Sa'gung and Duyong (Piper and Rabett 2014). The inhabitants of Tabon therefore relied on terrestrial resources. Hunting is likely to have focused on *Axis calamianensis* and another extinct species of deer, along with the wild boar (*Sus ahoenobarbus*), the macaque *Macaca fascicularis philippinensis* and a variety of smaller mammals such as the Palawan porcupine (*Hystrix pumila*) and Palawan pangolin (*Manis culionensis*), as they did towards the end of the Pleistocene and into the early Holocene (Piper and Rabett 2014; Ochoa and Piper 2017).

Mindoro Island is approximately 80 km in a straight line from Coron, a small island that would have been connected to the north of Palawan, as part of the greater Palawan region, during glacial sea level regression (Pawlik et al. 2014; Pawlik and Piper 2019). Here, excavations at three sites, two rockshelters (Bubog I + II) on Ilin Island, just off the southeast coast of Mindoro (though the island would have been joined to Mindoro during the Pleistocene) and one cave in Sta. Teresa (Bilat) at the southwestern end of Mindoro, have produced a much more securely dated record for modern human presence during the Late Pleistocene and Early Holocene. Excavation of a unique, well-stratified shell midden in Bubog I (Pawlik et al. 2014) produced a series of Accelerator Mass Spectrometry (AMS) 14-C dates on charcoal and marine shell from as early as c.33 kya to around 4 kya (Pawlik and Piper 2019; Pawlik 2021). The LGM and the period between 28 and 12 kya appears to be missing from the archaeological record, with Late Pleistocene strata immediately succeeded by the Terminal Pleistocene at c.12 kya. This is a relatively common feature of cave and rock shelter sequences in ISEA (O'Connor 2015). The shell middens overlay further, earlier, occupation layers of Late Pleistocene age that are proving difficult to accurately date.

Prior to c.33 kya there is evidence for use of technologies to capture open reef fishes where Ilin shelves rapidly into deep ocean, off the south end of the island, and for the hunting of the endemic pig (*Sus oliveri*), the endemic dwarf buffalo *Bubalus mindorensis* (Tamaraw), and the extinct giant rat *Crateromys paulus* (Pawlik et al. 2014; Boulanger 2021; Ingicco et al. 2017; Reyes et al. 2017; Boulanger et al. 2019, 2023; Pawlik and Piper 2019). Around 33 kya the first shell deposits accumulated. The Bubog I foragers collected a variety of molluscs and crabs in the mangroves that existed directly below the cave entrance (Pawlik et al. 2014, 2015). Fishing in reefs continued into the Holocene, including the exploitation of poisonous pufferfish, possibly to extract their toxin for use in hunting, as well as hunting a variety of island vertebrates.

Archaeological sites that straddle the LGM between c.26 and 15 kya are rare in the Philippines. On Palawan, Pilanduk Cave c.11 km distant from Tabon Cave has been dated to the Last Glacial Maximum. It was first excavated in 1969 by Jonathan Kress (1978), who suggested that its initial occupation phase dated to between 26 and 18ka BP. This timeline was confirmed through radiocarbon-dating to 25–20 ka cal. BP (Ochoa 2019). Excavations delivered lithic artefacts and faunal remains, mainly deer and pig. After the LGM, no occupation is recorded for Pilanduk until it was used during the metal-using period for secondary jar burials (Kress 1978). The only lowland coastal site in the Wallacean part of the Philippines is Bilat Cave located in southern Mindoro, across the Ilin Strait from Bubog I and II (Pawlik and Piper 2019). The cave is presently situated at a height of c.3 m amsl, (above mean sea level) and has openings to the sea, facing the Ilin Strait. A dense but shallow shell midden has been dated to c.8 kya until recent times. The archaeological deposits below the shell midden containing a few chert flakes are associated with AMS $^{14}$C dates on charcoal and *Melanoides* shells dating to between 13 and 22 kya (Pawlik and Piper 2019; Pawlik and Fuentes 2023). Despite the absence of an LGM record at Bubog, the Bilat site provided evidence for a human presence in southern Mindoro during the LGM and demonstrates that human communities continued to collect mangrove and estuarine shell fish along the coasts, and hunt a variety of local fauna.

Another region where there has been fairly intensive archaeological research is the Peñablanca limestone formations in northern Luzon. At least a dozen caves and rock shelters have been excavated – all but one site, Callao only have archaeological sequences dating from the mid-Holocene onwards (Thiel 1987, 1990; Mijares 2007; Pawlik et al. 2014; Fuentes 2015). At Callao, Layer 8 (105–110 cm below surface) produced chert flakes, fragmentary animal bones and possible evidence for the remnants of a hearth. A single AMS C$^{14}$ determination on charcoal from this layer returned a date of 25,968 ± 373 BP (Wk-14881), confirming that human populations had reached the north of Luzon Island during the Late Pleistocene (Mijares 2007).

## Late Pleistocene Technologies

In the Late Pleistocene lithic technologies consist predominantly of unretouched and mostly small-sized flaked artefacts. This lithic industry appears to have remained remarkably uniform across Southeast Asia, until the introduction of fully ground stone tool technologies at c. 4500–4000 BP, or even later (Pawlik and Ronquillo 2003; Haidle and Pawlik 2009; Pawlik 2010, 2012, 2021; Patole-Edoumba et al. 2012; Pawlik and Piper 2019). These flakes were commonly produced informally using straightforward manufacturing techniques without complex core preparation. There is no conclusive evidence for the intentional production of formal tools, and advanced knapping technologies, such as blade production, with the exception of Arubo in Nueva Ecija.

The broad absence of 'modern' tool types and formal tools in Southeast Asia's Palaeolithic industries in general, and especially in comparison to the European lithic record was initially considered to be due to the limited ability of early humans in eastern Asia to make sophisticated tools (Colani 1927; Movius 1944; Mijares 2002). Later it was explained by the hypothetical existence of a wooden or bamboo tool industry replacing formal stone tools and/or the poor availability and difficult acquisition of lithic raw material (e.g. Narr 1966; Solheim 1970; Pope 1989; Schick and Dong 1993; Reynolds 1993; Mijares 2002; Dennell 2009; Xhauflair and Pawlik 2010; Xhauflair 2014; Xhauflair et al. 2016). No prehistoric tools made of bamboo and wood have been found in the Late Pleistocene archaeological record of SEA so far. Explaining the pervasive absence of formal lithic tool types by supposing an advanced organic tool industry that is even more elusive, is an unconvincing way to argue for innovation in Southeast Asian tool technology (Haidle and Pawlik 2010; Pawlik 2010). Furthermore, the argument that the production of vegetal tools led to a simplification of lithic industries has not been convincingly explained, and it does not take into consideration the need for stone tools to produce organic implements in the first place (Pawlik 2002; 2004, 2012; Mijares 2002; 2007; Reepmeyer et al. 2011; Neri et al. 2015). Almost certainly, Pleistocene AMH in SEA produced a broad range of organic tools and utilitarian objects, including those manufactured from bamboo and wood (Xhauflair 2014), but they had their own specific functions (e.g. storage vessels, carriers, mats, digging implements, bindings etc.) and most likely complemented lithic toolkits in most cases, rather than acting as replacements or alternatives. The bone and shell tools that have been found across SEA in Pleistocene deposits are a good example of the types and diversity in raw material utilization in the Late Pleistocene and Early Holocene (see below, Barton et al. 2009; Pawlik 2009; Bar-Yosef et al. 2012; Pawlik et al. 2014; 2015; Fuentes et al. 2019).

The best chrono-stratigraphic sequence of stone artefacts in the Philippines still comes from Tabon Cave, Palawan (Fox 1970; Patole-Edoumba 2002; Xhauflair and Pawlik 2010; Patole-Edoumba et al. 2012; Pawlik and Piper 2019). Fox (1970, 17f.) estimated the age of the lithic deposits (Flake Assemblages I-A – V) to between 50,000 BP and 8,500 BP. $^{14}$C assays produced on associated charcoal were used to date Flake Assemblage IV (30,500 ± 1,100 uncal. BP or 36,731–31,814 cal. BP; UCLA 958), Flake Assemblage III (23,200 ± 1,000 uncal. BP or 29,657–25,157 cal. BP; UCLA 699), and Flake Assemblage I-B (9,250 ± 250 uncal. BP or 11,182–9,768 cal. BP; UCLA-284) (Fox 1970, 40–44). They are all composed of simple unretouched flakes that seem to continue unchanged into the Holocene and in caves and rock-shelters such as Duyong, Guri and Pilanduk in central Palawan (Fox 1970, 1978; Kress 1977; Patole-Edoumba 2002), and in Ille Cave, northern Palawan, dating to the Terminal Pleistocene and Early/Mid-Holocene (Lewis et al. 2008; Pawlik 2012, 2015). However, the few use-wear and residue analyses undertaken so far on Philippine lithic materials have illustrated some interesting technological features that suggest complex use-contexts existed that are not evident in the basic production attributes of flakes. For example, at Tabon Cave, Xhauflair et al. (2020) identified flakes with notched edge modifications associated with a particular plant processing technique – splitting of bamboo. The use of artefacts with notched retouch for specialized plant processing during the Late Pleistocene and Early Holocene has also been reported from Leang Sarru Rockshelter in northern Sulawesi (Ono et al. 2010; Fuentes et al. 2019). Here, a multi-stage use-wear and residue analysis using optical and scanning electron microscopy coupled with energy-dispersive X-ray analysis revealed the consistent use of notched flake tools for the extraction of fibrous plant matter, used for instance to produce cords, bindings and woven materials, such as baskets, nets and ropes from at least c.35 kya onwards (Fuentes et al. 2020). Early evidence for hafting and composite tool making has been observed in the same site at c.22–17 kya (Ono et al. 2010; Fuentes et al. 2019) and from Ille Cave, Palawan dating between 14 and 12 kya (Pawlik 2012).

The almost complete absence of a 'formal' lithic technology in much of the shell midden deposits of Bubog I is remarkable. No flaked lithic artefacts other than the few obsidian chips in the lowest shell midden layer were found (see below). The only other lithic tools are beach-rounded igneous pebbles used as unmodified hammerstones to access the soft fleshy parts of large marine shells such as *Strombus*, *Trochus*, and *Lambis* (Figure 11.3A–C; Pawlik et al. 2014). This repetitive percussion was clearly evident in the pitted stone surfaces. If a hammerstone broke, producing sharp edged fragments, they were utilized as implements to work hard organic materials such as wood, bone, and bamboo (Figure 11.3D–F; Fuentes and Pawlik 2015). Some hammer stones had flakes removed resulting in a characteristic notched modification rather similar to the waisted axes reported from New Guinea (Anderson and Summerhayes 2008). However, the specimens from Ilin Island demonstrate no evidence for the manufacture

FIGURE 11.3  Pebbles used as hammerstones (A–C) and fragments thereof with use traces (D–F); (G, H) Hammerstones with waisted modification re-used as Netsinkers. Bubog I and II, Ilin Island (Photos: A. Pawlik).

of a 'cutting-edge', and it is more likely the notches were produced to attach them as weights on fishing nets and/or traps (Figure 11.3G and H). The lithic assemblage from Bubog neatly demonstrates that simple large pebbles and fragments following their breakage could be used for various, and successive complex tasks.

A small lithic flake assemblage was, however, found in terrestrial silty sediments below the stratified shell midden deposits at Bubog I. While no datable materials are directly associated with the artefacts, five AMS $^{14}$C dates on shell between 28 and 33,000 cal. BP from the overlying shell midden layer provides a *terminus ante quem* of over c.33 kya for this assemblage (Pawlik and Piper 2019). Obsidian débitage was recovered from both the lowest Late Pleistocene shell midden layer, and the silty layer below. Portable X-ray fluorescence analysis on the Ilin samples demonstrated a chemical match with Obsidian artefacts from Ille Cave in northern Palawan, dated to c.11–9 kya, and undated Obsidian flakes from open sites in Alegria, Cebu Island (Reepmeyer et al. 2011; Neri et al. 2015). No obsidian sources are known on any of these islands, and the obsidian must have been introduced from elsewhere. One potential

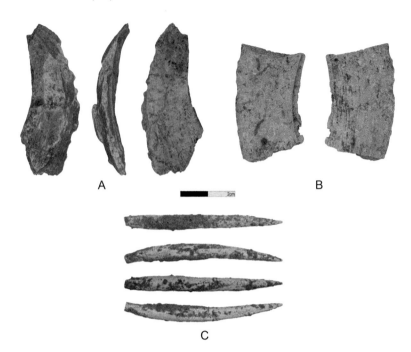

FIGURE 11.4  Bone and shell tools. (A, B) Flaked and modified Geloina shells from Bubog I; (C) bone fishing gorge from Bubog I (Photos: A. Pawlik).

source is Melanesia, from where obsidian was already being sourced and traded by the end of the Pleistocene (Reepmeyer et al. 2011).

In the Philippines, the use of flaked shell artefacts derives from the Late Pleistocene onwards (Pawlik and Piper 2019). Several bivalves of *Geloina (erosa) coaxans* recovered from the basal shell midden Layer 9 at Bubog I onwards demonstrated striking damage to the umbo as well as flaking and denticulation of shell margins, visible scarring, serration, and edge rounding (Figure 11.4A and B). These modifications probably resulted from activities that utilized longitudinal and transverse motions such as scraping and sawing of various middle and harder contact materials. The *Geloina* valves might even have been used as chisel-like implements (Benz 2016; Pawlik and Piper 2019). Comparable modifications were attained by AP through experimental use of modern *Geloina* shells as chisel-like implements or wedges to split woody materials such as bamboo. What the analytical research at Bubog has demonstrated is that shells had considerably more diverse uses than as simple 'scrapers' (Mansur and Clemente 2009; Douka 2010; Solana et al. 2011; Szabó and Koppel 2015) and could be utilized for functions and activities where lithic tools would more commonly have perhaps been employed. Direct AMS dates on two *Geloina* shell tools, and on *Conus* and *Strombus* shells from the same stratigraphic horizon for comparative dating purposes provided ages of between c.28 and 31 kya (Pawlik and Piper 2019).

Compared to the lithic and shell technologies in the Philippines, implements manufactured from bone are relatively scarce in the Pleistocene. A fully worked fragmented bone point that has been interpreted as a fishing gorge (Figure 11.4C) was recovered from Bubog I from deposits below the basal shell layer dated to 33,000–28,000 cal. BP (Boulanger et al. 2019; Pawlik and Piper 2019).

Despite the artefactual scarcity, the antiquity of bone tools and the emergence of bone technology in the Late Pleistocene is demonstrated across Southeast Asia. Early examples for the manufacture of bone tools have been recorded at Niah Cave, Borneo dating to c.40 kya (Rabett and Piper 2012), Lang Longrien in Peninsula Malaysia at c.42 kya (Anderson 1990, 1997), in the 'Tabuhan' layers of Song Terus dating to between 80 and 30 kya (Kusno 2009), at Topogaro 2 on the east coast of Central Sulawesi at c.26 kya (Ono et al. 2021) and at Matja Kuru 2 in East Timor, where the base of a hafted point was recorded dating to c.34 kya (O'Connor et al. 2014).

## The Philippines in the Archaeology of Island Southeast Asia

Although the early Palaeolithic record of the Philippines is still fragmentary, and evidence for a continuous human presence during the Middle Pleistocene needs further verification, the early Palaeolithic artefacts from Arubo in Nueva Ecija and especially, the discovery of a rhinoceros skeleton in Rizal, Kalinga demonstrating butchery, and the associated lithic artefacts support the argument for a likely migration of hominins into the oceanic part of the Philippines around c.0.7–1.0 mya (Dizon and Pawlik 2010; Ingicco et al. 2018). This adds another piece to the puzzle in our understanding of the initial colonization of Wallacea, and illustrates that archaic hominins managed to reach the large island archipelagos of the Philippines and Sulawesi (Simanjuntak et al. 2010; Ingicco et al. 2018; van den Bergh et al. 2016; Brumm et al. 2017; Ono et al. 2023), and the lesser Sunda chain as far as Flores Island (Morwood et al. 1998, 2008; van den Bergh et al. 2009; Brumm et al. 2010) by making multiple sea-crossings during the Middle Pleistocene.

The earliest hominin inhabitants of the Philippines, as well as Sulawesi and Flores shared the islands with a range of predominantly extinct large vertebrate faunas. The 'core' of these vertebrate communities on all islands, the proboscideans and giant tortoises, as well as rats are considered to be excellent island colonizers capable of making substantial sea-crossings. There is no material evidence that any of the endemic island hominins were capable of designing and constructing a watercraft of any kind, nevertheless, they must have managed to drift/raft, either deliberately or inadvertently, between islands. Either way, in SEA hominins must now be considered amongst some of the most adept Middle Pleistocene terrestrial island colonizers.

The close proximity of the large Pleistocene landmasses of Luzon, Mindanao, the Visayas, and Mindoro to each other raises the possibility that archaic hominins spread across the Philippine archipelago, became isolated and diversified. Eventually, each landmass could have been inhabited by its own hominin species – as has been observed in many other mammal radiations across the Philippines (Heaney 1993; Heaney et al. 2016). Only future research will provide definitive evidence of whether hominin radiation and speciation really did occur across the Philippine archipelago.

Unlike, Flores (and Timor) to the Southeast of the Philippines, which were inhabited by extremely impoverished vertebrate faunas that consisted of stegodon, giant tortoise, komodo dragons, rats, and large birds. Luzon was home to a relatively diverse community of large mammals including proboscideans (*Elephas* and *Stegodon*), deer, pigs, bovines, rhinoceros, and rats (Koenigswald 1958; Bautista 1995; Piper et al. 2011; Ingicco et al. 2018) though it is still unclear whether they all inhabited the Middle Pleistocene Luzon at the same time). This would probably have provided much greater foraging opportunities than on smaller, more isolated islands, and potentially supported larger hominin populations.

Like Flores, there is a considerable gap in the Philippine archaeological record following the early Middle Pleistocene occupation in Rizal, Kalinga, and the Late Pleistocene (Sutikna et al. 2017; Ingicco et al. 2018). Here, the record resumes again at Callao Cave in the Penablanca region of northern Luzon, at shortly after 70 kya (Mijares et al. 2010; Détroit et al. 2019). The Callao fossils suggest that an archaic hominin, *H. luzonensis* continued to inhabit Luzon into the Late Pleistocene. By this time, it appears that much of the ancient vertebrate faunas that inhabited the broad open plains of the Cagayan Valley were already extinct, with the exception of an endemic pig, deer, and bovine (now extinct). At present, there is no evidence that *H. luzonensis* existed elsewhere in the Philippines nor survived beyond about 50 kya.

There is currently no solid evidence for an AMH presence in the Philippines prior to c.40 kya (Pawlik and Piper 2019) though the new genetic data and the archaeological records in Island Southeast Asia and Australia might suggest earlier colonization was possible (Clarkson et al. 2015; Westaway et al. 2017; Aubert et al. 2019; Shipton et al. 2019a; Ono et al. 2023a). On arrival, the Late Pleistocene archaeological record of the Philippines suggests that communities were well adapted to a variety of landscapes and environments where they hunted a diversity of large and small mammals and reptiles, fished and foraged along coastlines and processed a variety of economically useful plants. As already noted, unlike most of the other isolated islands east of Huxley's modification of Wallace's Line (except Sulawesi), the larger Philippine islands possess relatively diverse vertebrate faunas including pigs, deer and bovines. Colonizing modern human populations would not have necessarily needed to adapt their economic strategies to compensate for the impoverished nature of islands such as Flores and Timor that possessed no large-bodied mammals.

Enhanced use of coastal exploitation might have been one way that the absence of terrestrial resources was compensated for on small islands – as is evidenced on islands such as Talaud, Timor Leste, and surrounding islands where sophisticated fishing technologies were already in use during the Late Pleistocene (Ono et al. 2010; O'Connor et al. 2011; Samper-Carro 2016; Boulanger et al. 2019; Fuentes et al. 2019; Boulanger 2021). The ability to employ such strategies, however, was likely already developed before human dispersal across Island Southeast Asia. On Ilin Island for example, the presence of net sinkers suggests the inhabitants of Bubog had relatively well-developed fishing technologies that included the manufacture and maintenance of nets or traps. Local innovation in the Philippines is perhaps evident at Bubog I with the use and manufacture of fishing gorges, a technique of capturing carnivorous fishes. These are different fishing techniques to those observed in locales to the east such as Alor Island and Timor Leste where the sites of Jerimalai and Lene Hara have produced evidence for the manufacture of shell fishhooks (O'Connor and Veth 2005; O'Connor et al. 2011, 2017), a technology absent from the Late Pleistocene Philippines.

How terrestrial game was hunted remains somewhat elusive, but it is likely that besides weaponry a variety of traps and snares may have been employed (Piper and Rabett 2009). The earliest evidence of range weapon technology in the Philippines is in the terminal Pleistocene at c.12 kya when we have the first projectile tips manufactured on stone (Pawlik 2010, 2012). The Terminal Pleistocene is also when projectiles first appear at Niah Cave, Borneo (Barton et al. 2009), but these are produced on bone rather than stone. Projectile technologies have been recorded much earlier at c.35 kya at Leang Sarru on Sulawesi (Ono et al. 2010; Fuentes et al. 2019) and this might be a learned technology transferred across Southeast Asia. Implements manufactured from different raw materials but designed for similar functions imply the know-how to transfer technological skills between raw materials.

In fact, Pleistocene communities in the Philippines appear to have utilized stone, bone, and shell in the production of various implements, probably from the time of initial colonization onwards. Bone technology seems to have been a part of the AMH toolkit during initial expansion across ISEA, though it is relatively scarce and sporadic before the end of the Pleistocene. And use contexts appear to have been limited prior to the LGM, but somewhat varied across the region (Rabett and Piper 2012).

The significance of mollusk shell was probably underemphasized in Southeast Asian prehistory. Shell appears to have been a manufacturing medium from very early in human history (Douka and Spinapolice 2012; Joordens et al. 2015). In the Philippines, currently, the earliest evidence of shell tool manufacture dates to between 28 and 33 kya at Bubog I, Ilin Island where modifications to the mangrove shell *Geloina coaxans* suggest they were potentially utilized as chisels, scrapers, and saw-like implements (Pawlik et al. 2014; Pawlik and Piper 2019). In the absence of suitable lithic raw material sources on Ilin Island, an alternative strategy appears to have been the reduction of *Tridacna/Hippopus* valves to produce sharp-edged flake tools, recorded from at least 9,000 BP onwards (Pawlik et al. 2014). The only other locations where shell flaking has so far been recorded is at Golo Cave in the Maluku Islands around c.30 kya, where the opercula of *Turbo marmoratus* was utilized for similar purposes, rather than the valves of large clams (Szabó et al. 2007; Szabó and Koppel 2015), and *Trochus* fishhooks at Jerimalai in Timor Leste dated to between c.23–16 kya (O'Connor et al. 2011; O'Connor 2015). There is, however, the likelihood that shell-flake tool production has been overlooked within dense shell middens at other archaeological sites in the region, including the Philippines where the flaking of shell could have considerably greater antiquity than is presently recorded. It is possible that shell as a raw material became significant in the Late Pleistocene in the Wallacean region on islands with limited resources of knappable rocks, while marine shell was readily available. New technologies in bone, stone, shell, and organic materials were added to the repertoire, and these expanded across the region at various times throughout the Late Pleistocene and Holocene.

Maritime interaction across the Philippines, and the broader SEA region is supported by the recovery of chemically matching obsidian artefacts from three sites on Ilin/Mindoro, Palawan, and Cebu, that might have its origins in Near Oceania (Reepmeyer et al. 2011, 2016; Neri et al. 2015). The age of over 30 kya BP for the Obsidian flakes from Ilin Island suggests that inter-island voyaging to acquire 'valuable' raw materials was possible during the Late Pleistocene and possibly also indicates a socio-cultural linkage between populations in different island regions (Pawlik and Piper 2019). Similar connectivity through the distribution of obsidian has been identified for Kisar and surrounding islands in the eastern part of the Wallacean chain in the Terminal Pleistocene (O'Connor et al. 2019), and possibly between Sabah, Borneo, Talaud Islands in eastern Indonesia and Mindanao in the southern Philippines in the mid-Holocene (Tykot and Chia 1997; Reepmeyer et al. 2011; Neri et al. 2015). These more localized networks likely expanded during the Holocene as boat technology potentially improved. For example, Golson (2005, 484) has suggested that the shell adze was an implement specifically designed for the manufacture of canoes. Shell adzes emerge during the Terminal Pleistocene/early Holocene, probably starting in the region of Melanesia and northern Maluku Islands, before expanding to the west as far as the Sulu Archipelago, and Timor Leste in the south (Pawlik et al. 2015; Shipton et al. 2019b).

Further evidence for increasing mobility and the spread of socio-cultural ideas is reflected in the emergence of burial traditions across Southeast Asia. Although anatomically modern humans have been present in Southeast Asia for at least c.65,000 years (Westaway et al. 2017), the first clear evidence for the deliberate interment of the dead has been identified at just a few locations across Mainland and Island Southeast Asia (Piper 2016). These include sites such as Liang Lemdubu in the Aru Islands at c.19–22 kya (Bulbeck 2006, 2008) and Tam Hang Cave in Laos at 14 kya (Shackelford and Demeter 2012). At the end of the Pleistocene burials start to appear across Southeast Asia suggesting transmission of new ideological perspectives. The diversity of interment practices observed across the region implies that various hunter-gatherer communities adopted and adapted these new cultural perceptions to their own ways of perceiving this world and the next – as they also tailored new, introduced technologies and raw materials to fulfil their own specific requirements (Lloyd-Smith 2012; Pawlik and Piper 2019; Pawlik et al. 2019).

## Conclusion

The archaeological record of the Cagayan Valley, northern Luzon indicates that the Philippines was initially colonized by a species of hominin during the early Middle Pleistocene by at least c.700 kya. These archaic humans must have made several sea crossings either southwards via Taiwan and Batanes, northeastwards via Borneo and Palawan, or northwards from Sulawesi. These colonization routes would have potentially led to occupation of numerous Philippine islands where the effects of island isolation could have led to diversification and speciation as has been observed in several Philippine terrestrial mammals. With the identification of hominins in the Philippines, Flores and potentially on Sulawesi, it appears that they were one of the best large terrestrial vertebrate island colonizers. There is currently no evidence to suggest our early ancestors could conceive and build watercraft, but this does not negate intentionality in attempting, and as is clear from the Philippines, Sulawesi, and Flores, successfully negotiating sea crossings and colonizing new landscapes.

The first Philippine inhabitants co-existed with a variety of large terrestrial vertebrates that included some notoriously good island colonizers found throughout the Wallacean region such as proboscideans and giant tortoises, and others that seem more restricted to the large landmasses to the west side of Huxley's modification of Wallace's Line such as archaic suids and bovids. Evidence of rhinoceros butchery from Rizal and early Palaeolithic stone tools at Arubo (and elsewhere in the Philippines) indicates that the initial colonizers were tool-using hominins.

At least one species of hominin, *H. luzonensis* survived on Luzon until c.50 kya. This diminutive species of human appears to have outlived much of the Middle Pleistocene megafauna but continued to hunt/scavenge deer and pig. How long *H. luzonensis* (and perhaps other hominins) continued to survive in the Philippines is unclear, but, as yet there is currently no indication that they encountered or interacted with AMH.

The first evidence for the arrival of AMH in the Philippines at around 40 kya (or shortly after) has been recovered from Tabon Cave, Palawan, and Ilin Island, Mindoro, suggesting they originated from the Sundaic biogeographic region. By the time AMH reached the Philippine archipelago they could be considered broad spectrum inland and coastal foragers capable of employing a wide range of hunting and gathering strategies within rapidly changing woodland and rainforest environments. Fishing technologies appear to have been well-developed and diverse, and included the production of nets with sinkers and lines with baited fishing gorges. These methods of catching fish vary from equally early strategies observed in Timor Leste and Alor, perhaps implying '*in situ*' innovation across the Wallacean region following initial dispersal from ISEA. Terrestrial hunting repertoires appear to have included range weaponry from the Terminal Pleistocene onwards, consistent with evidence of similar modes of capturing arboreal prey observed in other regions of ISEA.

The seemingly unsophisticated Late Pleistocene stone technologies characteristic of ISEA are rather deceptive in terms of their general manufacturing techniques. Traceological studies on Philippine (and Sulawesi) stone implements are demonstrating that informal lithic flake tools could be utilized for a diverse range of tasks. Some implements appear to have been deliberately manufactured as components in complex composite tool technologies. Artefact repertoires from the Late Pleistocene onwards appear to have also included implements produced from bone and shell suggesting that the core techniques of manufacturing in these media probably entered ISEA with the earliest modern human populations. Technological innovation is also evident in the increasing diversity of artefacts produced in bone, stone and shell recorded in the Philippines from c.30 kya onwards. This appears to be a combination of factors, driven by local innovation and the development of artefact repertoires best suited to the range of tasks and challenges required by local communities, and the dispersal of new knowledge and technologies through inter-island communication and contact. Some of these technologies and interaction spheres appear to have been relatively broad and incorporated communities from across ISEA, whereas others, for instance shell flaking and the use of fishing gorges for bait fishing, were perhaps much more geographically distinct (see also Bulbeck 2008). The appearance of composite tool technologies with similar functions produced in stone and bone suggests flexible ability to transfer knowledge between manufacturing raw materials. The successful adaptation of these early islanders to the changing maritime environment by that time is reflected in the increase in technological innovation, the acquisition of nautical and navigational skills that allowed deep-sea fishing and the colonization of remote islands.

Towards the end of the Pleistocene diversification in subsistence strategies, material culture, and technology seem to have been blended with new social and ideological concepts of the living, the dead and the afterlife, manifest in new burial practices. The emergence of burial practices suggests that a diversity of intangible social and cultural information was being transmitted between island communities along with the more tangible evidence of material culture exchange.

## Acknowledgements

The authors wish to thank the funding institutions that have greatly supported their research and fieldwork in Mindoro: The National Geographic Society, Global Exploration Fund; the POSCO Asia Forum of POSCO TJ Park Foundation; the University of the Philippines OVPAA Enhanced Creative Work and Research Grant and Emerging Interdisciplinary Research Programs; and the University of the Philippines Diliman OVCRD Outright Research Grant. Alfred Pawlik received support through the Ateneo de Manila University Loyola Schools Scholarly Work Faculty Grant, entitled 'Archaeological Explorations in the Central and Southern Philippines', and the Ateneo de Manila University Research and Creative Work Faculty Grant, entitled 'Traces ASIA – A Deep Time Archaeological Collaboratory and Cultural Resource Management Space of the Anthropological and Sociological Initiatives of the Ateneo (ASIA)'. Philip Piper received support through the Australian Research Council Grant entitled 'Landscape, resources and human migration during the Southeast Asian Neolithic'. We thank the National Museum of the Philippines for permission to excavate in Mindoro and to analyse the archaeological materials from the Philippines reported in this paper. We are grateful to the members of the Mindoro Archaeological Research Team, and the municipalities and people of San Jose and Magsaysay for their help and support of our fieldwork.

## References

Anderson, Douglas. 1990 *Lang Rongrien, a Pleistocene rockshelter: A Pleistocene-Early Holocene archaeological site from Krabi, Southwestern Thailand. The University Monograph Museum* 71. Philadelphia: University of Pennsylvania Press.

Anderson, Douglas. 1997 Cave archaeology in Southeast Asia. *Geoarchaeology* 12, 607–638.

Anderson, Douglas, and Summerhayes, Glenn. 2008. Edge-Ground and Waisted Axes in the Western Pacific Islands: Implications for an example from the Yaeyama Islands, Southernmost Japan. *Asian Perspectives* 47 (1), 45–58.

Aubert, Maxime, Lebe, Rustan, Oktaviana, Adhi, Tang, Muhammad, Burhan, Basran, Hamrullah, Jusdi, Andi, Abdullah, Hakim, Budianto, Zhao, Jian-xin, Geria, Made, Sulistyarto, Priyatno, Sardi, Ratno, and Brumm, Adam. 2019 Earliest hunting scene in prehistoric art. *Nature* 576, 442–445.

Barton, Huw, Piper, Philip, Rabett, Ryan, and Reeds, Ian. 2009 Composite hunting technologies from the terminal pleistocene and early Holocene, Niah Cave, Borneo. *Journal of Archaeological Science* 36, 1708–1714.

Bartstra, G. 1984 Some remarks upon: Fossil man from java, his age, and his tools, in *Prehistoric Indonesia: A Reader*, ed van de Velde, P.. Dordrecht: Foris, 121–162.

Bar-Yosef, Ofer, Eren, Metin, Yuan, Jiarong, Cohen, David, and Li, Yiyuan. 2012 Were bamboo tools made in prehistoric Southeast Asia? An experimental view from South China. *Quaternary International* 269, 9–21.

Bautista, Angel. 1995 Fossil remains of rhinoceros from the Philippines. *National Museum Papers* 5, 1–9.

Benz, A. 2016 *Shell Tool Technology in Southeast Asia. Considerations on Function and Significance of Early Holocene Geloina Artefacts from Bubog 1, Mindoro Occidental, Philippines*. Bachelor of Arts Thesis, University of Bonn.

Bird, Michael, Taylor, David, and Hunt, Chris. 2005 Palaeoenvironments of insular Southeast Asia during the last glacial period: A savanna corridor in Sundaland? *Quaternary Science Reviews* 24, 2228–2242.

Bird, Michael, Boobyer, Ella, Bryant, Charlotte, Lewis, Helen, Paz, Victor, and Stephens, Edryd. 2007 A long record of environmental change from bat guano deposits in Makangit Cave, Palawan, Philippines. *Earth and Environmental Science Transactions of the Royal Society of Edinburgh* 98, 59–69.

Boulanger, C. 2021 *Aquatic resources exploitation and adaptation of Anatomically Modern Human in Island Southeast Asia: palaeoenvironmental and cultural implications*. PhD dissertation. Muséum National d'Histoire Naturelle, Paris, and Australian National University, Canberra.

Boulanger, Clara, Ingicco, Thomas, Piper, Philip, Amano, Noel, Grouard, Sandrine, Ono, Rintaro, Hawkins, Stuart, and Pawlik, Alfred. 2019 Coastal subsistence strategies and mangrove swamps evolution in bubog i rockshelter (Ilin island, mindoro, Philippines) from the late pleistocene to the mid-holocene. *The Journal of Island and Coastal Archaeology* 14, 584–604.

Boulanger, Clara, Pawlik, Alfred, O'Connor, Sue, Semah, Anne-Marie, Reyes, Marian, and Ingicco, Thomas. 2023 The exploitation of toxic fish from the terminal Pleistocene in Maritime Southeast Asia: A case study from the Mindoro Archaeological Sites, Philippines. *Animals* 13, 1–19.

Brown, Samantha, Higham, Thomas, Slon, Viviane, Pääbo, Svante, Meyer, Matthias, Douka, Katerina, Brock, Fiona, Comeskey, Daniel, Procopio, Noemi, Shunkov, Michael, Derevianko, Anatoly, and Buckley, Michael. 2016 Identification of a new hominin bone from Denisova Cave, Siberia using collagen fingerprinting and mitochondrial DNA analysis. *Scientific Reports* 6, 23559.

Brumm, Adam, Langley, Michelle, Moore, Mark, Hakim, Budianto, Ramli, Muhammad, Sumantri, Iwan, Burhan, Basran, Saiful, Andi, Siagian, Linda, Suryatman, Sardi, Ratno, Jusdi, Andi, Abdullah, Mubarak, Andi, Hasliana, Hasrianti, Oktaviana, Adhi, Adhityatama, Shinatria, van den Bergh, Gerrit, Aubert, Maxime, Zhao, Jian-xin, Huntley, Jillian, Li, Bo, Roberts, Richard, Saptomo, Wahyu, Perston, Yinika, and Grün, Rainer. 2017 Early human symbolic behavior in the Late Pleistocene of Wallacea. *PNAS* 114, 4105–4110.

Brumm, Adam, Jensen, Gitte, van den Bergh, Gert, Morwood, Michael, Kurniawan, Iwan, Aziz, Fachroel, and Store, Michael. 2010 Hominins on Flores, Indonesia, by one million years ago. *Nature* 464, 748–753.

Bulbeck, David. 2006 The last glacial Maximum human burial from Liang Lemdubu in northern Sahulland, in *The Archaeology of Aru Islands, Eastern*, ed O'Connor, Sue.. Canberra: Australian National University Press, 255–294.

Bulbeck, David. 2008 An integrated perspective on the Austronesian diaspora. *Australian Archaeology* 67, 31–51.

Choa, O., Lebon, M., Gallet, X., Dizon, E., Ronquillo, W., Jago-on, S., Détroit, F., Falguères, C., Ghaleb, B., and Sémah, F. 2016 Stable isotopes in guano: Potential contributions towards palaeoenvironmental reconstruction in Tabon Cave, Palawan, Philippines. *Quaternary International* 416, 27–37.

Clarkson, Chris, Smith, Mike, Marwick, Ben, Fullagar, Richard, Wallis, Lynley, Faulkner, Patrick, Manne, Tiina, Hayes, Elspeth, Roberts, Richard, Jacobs, Zenobia, Carah, Xavier, Lowe, Kelsey, Matthews, Jacqueline, and Florin, Anna. 2015 The archaeology, chronology and stratigraphy of Madjedbebe (Malakunanja II): A site in northern Australia with early occupation. *Journal of Human Evolution* 83, 46–64.

Colani, M. 1927 *L'âge de la pierre dans la province de Hoa Binh, Tonkin. Mémoires du Service Géologique de l'Indochine XIV*. Hanoi: Imprimé d'Extrême-Orient.

Dennell, Robin. 2009 *The Palaeolithic Settlement of Asia*. New York: Cambridge University Press.

Derevianko, A., Su, N., Tsyvbankov, A., and Doi, N. 2016 *The Origin of Bifacial Industry in Southeast Asia*. Novosibirsk: IAET SB RAS Publishing.

Détroit, Florent, Dizon, Eusebio, Falguères, Christophe, Hameau, Sébastien, Ronquillo, Wilfredo, and Sémah, François. 2004 Upper Pleistocene *Homo sapiens* from The Tabon cave (Palawan, The Philippines): Descriptions and dating of new discoveries. *Comptes Rendus Palevol* 3, 705–712.

Détroit, Florent, Mijares, Armand, Corny, Julien, Daver, Guillaume, Zanolli, Clément, Dizon, Eusebio, Robles, Emil, Grün, Rainer, and Piper, Philip. 2019 A new species of Homo from the Late Pleistocene of the Philippines. *Nature* 568, 181–188.

De Vos, J., and Bautista, A. 2003 Preliminary notes on the vertebrate fossils from the Philippines. *Proceedings of the Society of Philippine Archaeologists, Semantics and Systematics: Philippine Archaeology* 1, 42–62.

Esselstyn, J.A., Oliveros, C.H., Moyle, R.G., Peterson, A.T., J.A. McGuire, and Brown, R.M. 2010. Integrating phylogenetic and taxonomic evidence that illuminates complex biogeographic patterns along Huxley's modification of Wallace's line. *Journal of Biogeography* 37, 2054–2066.

Dizon, Eusebio, and Pawlik, Alfed. 2010 The lower palaeolithic record in the Philippines. *Quaternary International* 223–224, 444–450.

Douka, Katerina. 2010 An upper palaeolithic shell scraper from Ksar Akil (Lebanon). *Journal of Archaeological Science* 38, 434.

Douka, Katerina, and Spinapolice, Enza. 2012 Neanderthal shell tool production from middle Palaeolithic Italy and Greece. *Journal of World Prehistory* 25, 45–79.

Earl of Cranbrook. 2000 Northern Borneo environments of the past 40,000 years, archaeological evidence. *Sarawak Museum Journal* 76, 61–110.

Foronda, J., Schoell, W., Jagolino, O., and Alfane, S. 1987 Facies of the resedimented volcaniclastic units of the Laguna Formation, Rizal Province, Luzon, Philippines, in *Proceedings of the Workshop on Economic Geology, Tectonics, Sedimentary Processes and Environment of the Quaternary in Southeast Asia*. Bangkok: Department of Geology, Chulalongkorn University, pp. 53–64.

Fox, Robert. 1970 *The Tabon Caves*. Manila: National Museum of the Philippines.

Fox, Robert. 1978 The Philippine Palaeolithic, in *Early Palaeolithic in South and East Asia*, ed Ikawa-Smith, F. Paris: Moutton, 59–85.

Fuentes, Riczar. 2015. *Use-Wear Analysis of Lithic Artefacts from Vito Cave in Peñablanca, Cagayan, Northern Luzon, Philippines*. Master thesis. Quezon City: University of the Philippines Diliman.

Fuentes, Riczar, and Pawlik, Alfred. 2015 Not formal but functional: Traceology and the Lithic Record in the Philippines, in *Hunter-Gatherers Tool Kit: a Functional Perspective, Ed Gibaja-Bao*, Juan. Newcastle upon Pyne: Cambridge Scholars Publishing, 2020, 290 308.

Fuentes, Riczar, Ono, Rintaro, Nakajima, Naoki, Nishizawa, Hiroe, Siswanto, Joko, Sriwigati, Sofian, Harry, Miranda, Tatiana, and Pawlik, Alfred. 2019 Technological and behavioural complexity in expedient industries: The importance of use-wear analysis for understanding flake assemblages. *Journal of Archaeological Science* 112, 105031.

Fuentes, Riczar, Ono, Rintaro, Carlos, Jane, Kerfant, Celine, Sriwigati, Aziz, Nasrullah, Miranda, Tatiana, Aziz, Nasrullah, Sofian, Harry, and Pawlik, Alfred. 2020 Stuck within notches: Direct evidence of plant processing during the last glacial maximum to Holocene in North Sulawesi. *Journal of Archaeological Science: Reports* 30, 102207.

Gibbons, Ann. 2015 Ancient DNA pinpoints Paleolithic liaison in Europe. *Science* 348, 847–847.

Golson, Jack. 2005 The middle reaches of new Guinea history, in *Papuan Pasts: Cultural, Linguistic and Biological Histories of Papuan-Speaking Peoples*, eds Andrew, Pawley, Robert, Attenborough, Jack, Golson, and Hide, Robin.. Canberra: Australian National University, 451–491.

Grün, Rainer, Eggins, Stephen, Kinsley, Leslie, Moseley, Hannah, and Sambridge, Malcolm. 2014 Laser ablation u-series analysis of fossil bones and teeth. *Palaeogeography, Palaeoclimatology, Palaeoecology* 416, 150–167.

Haidle, Miriam, and Pawlik, Alfred. 2009 Missing types: Overcoming the typology dilemma of lithic archaeology in Southeast Asia. *Bulletin of the Indo-Pacific Prehistory Association 29*, 2–5.

Haidle, Miriam, and Pawlik, Alfred. 2010 Pleistocene modernity: An exclusively Afro-European issue? *Bulletin of the Indo-Pacific Prehistory Association 30*, 3–8.

Hanebuth, T., Stattegger, K., and Grootes, P.M. 2000 Rapid flooding of the Sunda Shelf: A Late-glacial sea-level record. *Science 288*, 1033–1035.

Hanebuth, T., Stattegger, K., and Bojanowski, A. 2009 Termination of the last glacial maximum sea-level lowstand: The Sunda-Shelf data revisited. *Global and Planetary Change* 66, 76–84.

Heaney, Awrence. 1993 Biodiversity patterns and the conservation of mammals of the Philippines. *Asia Life Sciences* 2, 261–74.

Heaney, Lawrence, Balete, Danilo, and Rickart, Eric. 2016 *The Mammals of Luzon Island*. Baltimore: John Hopkins University Press.

Huang, W. 1989 Bifaces in China. *Human Evolution* 4, 87–92.

Hughes, Mark, Rubite, Rpsario, Blanc, Patrick, Chung, Kuo-Fang, and Peng, Ching-I. 2015 The Miocene to Pleistocene colonization of the Philippine archipelago by Begonia sect. Baryandra (Begoniaceae). *American Journal of Botany 102*, 695–706.

Ingicco, Thomas, Piper, Philip, Amano, Noel, Paz, Victor, and Pawlik, Alfred. 2017 Biometric differentiation of Wild Philippine Pigs from introduced *Sus scrofa* in modern and archaeological assemblages. *International Journal of Osteoarchaeology* 27, 768–784.

Ingicco, Thomas, van den Bergh, G., Jago-on, C., Bahain, J.-J., Chacón, M., Amano, N., Forestier, H., King, C., Manalo, K., Nomade, S., Pereira, A., Reyes, M. C., Sémah, A.-M., Shao, Q., Voinchet, P., Falguères, C., Albers, P., Lising, M., Lyras, G., Yurnaldi, D., Rochette, P., Bautista, A., and de Vos, John. 2018 Earliest known hominin activity in the Philippines by 709 thousand years ago. *Nature* 557, 233–237.

Ingicco, T., Reyes, M., de Vos, J., Belarmino, M., Albers, P., Lipardo, I., Gallet, X., Amano, N., van den Bergh, G., Cosalan, A., and Bautista, A. 2020 Taphonomy and chronosequence of the 709 ka kalinga site formation (Luzon island, Philippines). *Scientific Reports* 10, 11081.

Jansa, Sharon, Barker, Keith, and Heaney, Lawrence. 2006 The pattern and timing of diversification of Philippine endemic rodents: Evidence from mitochondrial and nuclear Gene sequences. *Systematic Biology* 55, 73–88.

Jinam, Timothy, Phipps, Maude, Aghakhanian, Farhang, Majumder, Partha, Datar, Francisco, Stoneking, Mark, Sawai, Hiromi, Nishida, Nao, Tokunaga, Katsushi, Kawamura, Shoji, Omoto Keiichi, and Saitou, Naruya. 2017 Discerning the origins of the Negritos, first Sundaland people: Deep divergence and archaic admixture. *Genome Biology and Evolution* 9, 2103–2122.

Joordens, Josephine, d'Errico, Francesco, Wesselingh, Frank, Munro, Stephen, de Vos, John, Wallinga, Jakob, Ankjærgaard, Christina, Reimann, Tony, Wijbrans, Jan, Kuiper, Klaudia, Mücher, Herman, Coqueugniot, Hélène, Priel, Vincent, Joosten, Ineke, van Os, Bertil, Schulp, Anne, Panuel, Michel, van der Haas, Victoria, Lustenhouwer, Wim, Reijmer, John, and Roebroeks, Wil. 2015 Homo erectus at Trinil on Java used shells for tool production and engravings. *Nature* 518, 228–231.

Koenigswald, Gustav. 1958 Preliminary report on a newly discovered Stone age culture from Northern Luzon, Philippine Islands. *Asian Perspectives* 2, 69–71.

Kress, Jonathan. 1977 Tom Harrison, north Borneo, and Palawan: A preliminary assessment. *Asian Perspectives* 20, 75–86.

Kress, Jonathan. 1978 The ceramics from Pilanduk Cave and Sa'gung Rockshelter, Quezon Municipality, Palawan Island, Philippines. *Asian Perspectives* 21, 58–85.

Kusno, A. 2009 Archaeological contribution to the characterization of the stratigraphy of the Upper Pleistocene in Tabuhan Layers. Master's Thesis Erasmus Mundus Quaternary and Prehistory, Paris: Muséum national d'Histoire naturelle.

Lambeck, Kurt, Rouby, Helene, Purcell, Anthony, Sun, Yiying, and Sambridge, Malcolm. 2014 Sea level and global ice volumes from the last glacial maximum to the holocene. *PNAS* 111, 15296–15303.

Larena, Maximilian, McKenna, James, Sanchez-Quinto, Federico, Bernhardsson, Carolina, Ebeo, Carlo, Reyes, Rebecca, Casel, Ophelia, Huang, Jin-Yuan, Hagada, Kim, Guilay, Dennis, Reyes, Jennelyn, Allian, Fatima, Mori, Virgilio, Azarcon, Lahaina, Manera, Alma, Terando, Celito, Jamero, Lucio, Sireg, Gauden, Manginsay-Tremedal, Renefe, Labos, Maria, and Jakobsson, Mattias. 2021a Philippine Ayta possess the highest level of Denisovan ancestry in the world. *Current Biology* 31, 1–12.

Larena, Maximilian, Sanchez-Quinto, Federico, Sjödin, Per, McKenna, James, Ebeo, Carlo, Reyes, Rebecca, Casel, Ophelia, Huang, Jin-Yuan, Hagada, Kim, Guilay, Dennis, Reyes, Jennelyn, Allian, Fatima, Mori, Virgilio, Azarcon, Lahaina, Manera, Alma, Terando, Celito, Jamero, Lucio, Sireg, Gauden, Manginsay-Tremedal, Renefe, Labos, Maria, Vilar, Richard, Latiph, Acram, Saway, Rodelio, Marte, Erwin, Magbanua, Pablito, Morales, Amor, Java, Ismael, Reveche, Rudy, Barrios, Becky, Burton, Erlinda, Salon, Jesus, Kels, Ma, Albano, Adrian, Cruz-Angeles, Rose, Molanida, Edison, Granehäll, Lena, Vicente, Mário, Edlund, Hanna, Loo, Jun-Hun, Trejaut, Jean, Ho, Simon, Reid, Lawrence, Malmström, Helena, Schlebusch, Carina, Lambeck, Kurt, Endicott, Phillip, and Mattias, Jakobsson. 2021b Multiple migrations to the Philippines during the last 50,000 years. *PNAS* 118, e2026132118.

Lewis, Helen, Paz, Victor, Lara, Myra, Barton, Huw, Piper, Philip, Ochoa, Janine, Vitales, Timothy, Carlos, Jane, Higham, Tom, and Ner, Leee. 2008 Terminal Pleistocene to mid-Holocene occupation and an early cremation burial at Ille Cave, Palawan, Philippines. *Antiquity* 82, 318–335.

Lipson, Mark, Cheronet, Olivia, Mallick, Swapan, Rohland, Nadin, Oxenham, Marc, Pietrusewsky, Michael, Pryce, Thomas, Willis, Anna, Matsumura, Hirofumi, Buckley, Hallie, Domett, Kate, Nguyen, Giang, Trinh, Hoang, Kyaw, Aung, Win, Tin, Pradier, Baptiste, Broomandkhoshbacht, Nasreen, Candilio, Francesca, Changmai, Piya, Fernandes, Daniel, Ferry, Matthew, Gamarra, Beatriz, Harney, Eadaoin, Kampuansai, Jatupol, Kutanan, Wibhu, Michel, Megan, Novak, Mario, Oppenheimer, Jonas, Sirak, Kendra, Stewardson, Kristin, Zhang, Zhao, Flegontov, Pavel, Pinhasi, Ron, and Reich, David. 2018 Ancient genomes document multiple waves of migration in Southeast Asian prehistory. *Science* 361, 92–95.

Lloyd-Smith, Lindsay. 2012 Early holocene burial practice at niah cave, Sarawak. *Journal of Indo-Pacific Archaeology* 32, 54–69.

Manalo, M. 2011 Preliminary Identification of Cut Mark Morphology on Animal Bones: Methods and Applications. Master Thesis, Quezon City: University of the Philippines Diliman.

Mansur, M.E., and Clemente, Conte I. 2009 ¿Tecnologías invisibles? Confección, uso y conservación de instrumentos de valva en Tierra del Fuego, in *Arqueología Argentina los inicios de un nuevo siglo, XIV Congreso Nacional de Arqueología Argentina, Tomo II*, eds. Oliva, F., de Grandis, N., and Rodriguez, J. Rosario: National University of Rosario, 359–367.

Mijares, Armand. 2002 *The Minori Cave Expedient Lithic Technology*. Contributions to Archaeology Series. Quezon City: University of the Philippines Press.

Mijares, Armand. 2007 Unearthing prehistory: The archaeology of Northeastern Luzon, Philippine Islands. *British Archaeological Report International Series 1613*, Oxford: Hedges, Ltd.

Mijares, Armand, Détroit, Florent, Piper, Philip, Grün, Rainer, Bellwood, Peter, Aubert, Maxime, Champion, Guillaume, Cuevas, Nida, De Leon, Alexandra, and Dizon, Eusebio. 2010 New evidence for a 67,000-year-old human presence at Callao Cave, Luzon, Philippines. *Journal of Human Evolution* 59, 123–32.

Morwood, Michael, O'Sullivan, P., Aziz, F., and Raza, A. 1998 Fission-track ages of stone tools and fossils on the east Indonesian island of Flores. *Nature* 392, 173–76.

Morwood, Michael, and Oosterzee, Penny. 2007 *The Discovery of the Hobbit: The Scientific Breakthrough that Changed the Face of Human History*. Sydney: Random House.

Morwood, Michael, Sutikna, T., Saptomo, E., Westaway, K., Jatmiko, Due, Awe, Moore, M., Yuniawati, Dwi, Hadi, P., Zhao, J.-X., Turney, C., Fifield, K., Allen, H., and Soejono, R. 2008 Climate, people and faunal succession on Java, Indonesia: Evidence from Song Gupuh. *Journal of Archaeological Science* 35, 1776–1789.

Movius, Halam. 1944 *Early man and Pleistocene stratigraphy in Southern and Eastern Asia*. Cambridge (MA): Papers of the Peabody Museum of American Archaeology and Ethnology 19(3).

Narr, K. 1966 *Die frühe und mittlere Altsteinzeit Süd- und Ostasiens. Handbuch für Urgeschichte*. Munich: Francke.

Neri, L.A, Pawlik, A.F., and Reepmeyer, C. et al. 2015 Mobility of Early Islanders in the Philippines during the Terminal Pleistocene/Early Holocene Boundary: PXRF-Analysis of Obsidian Artefacts. *Journal of Archaeological Science* 61, 149–157.

Ochoa, Janine. 2019. Island Biodiversity and Human Palaeoecology in the Philippines: A zooarchaeological study of Late Quaternary faunas. PhD thesis, University of Cambridge.

Ochoa, Janine, and Piper, Philip. 2017 Holocene large mammal extinctions in Palawan Island, Philippines, in *Climate change and human responses: A zooarchaeological perspective*, ed Monks, Gregory G. Vertebrate Paleobiology and Paleoanthropology Series. Dordrecht: Springer, 69–87.

O'Connor, S. 2015 Crossing the Wallace Line: The Maritime Skills of the Earliest Colonists in the Wallacean Archipelago, in *Emergence and Diversity of Modern Human Behavior in Paleolithic Asia*, eds Kaifu, Yousuke, Izuho, Masami, Goebel, Ted, Sato, Hiroyuki, and Akira, Ono. Post Station: Texas A&M University Press, 214–224.

O'Connor, S., and Veth, P. 2005 Early Holocene shell fish hooks from Lene Hara Cave, East Timor establish complex fishing technology was in use in Island South East Asia five thousand years before Austronesian settlement. *Antiquity* 79, 249–56.

O'Connor, Sue, Ono, Rintaro, and Clarkson, Chris. 2011 Pelagic fishing at 42,000 years Before the present and the maritime skills of modern humans. *Science* 334, 1117–1121.

O'Connor, Sue, Robertson, Gail, and Aplin, Ken. 2014 Are osseous artefacts a window on perishable material culture? Implications of an unusually complex bone tool from the late pleistocene of East Timor. *Journal of Human Evolution* 67, 108–19.

O'Connor, Sue, Mahirta, and Wood, Rachael. 2017 Fishing in life and death: Pleistocene fish-hooks from a burial context in Alor Island, Indonesia. *Antiquity* 91, 1451–1468.

O'Connor, Sue, Mahirta, Kealy, Shimona, Boulanger, Clara, Maloney, Tim, Hawkins, Stuart, Langley, Michelle, Kaharudin, Hendri, Suniarti, Yuni, Husni, Muhammad, Ririmasse, Marlon, Tanudirjo, Daud, Wattimena, Lucas, Handoko, Wuri, Alifah, and Louys, Julien. 2019 Kisar and the archaeology of small islands in the Wallacean archipelago. *Journal of Island and Coastal Archaeology* 14, 198–225.

Oliver, W., and Heaney, L. 1996 Biodiversity and conservation in the Philippines. *International Zoo News* 45, 329–337.

Ono, Rintaro, Soegondho, S., and Yoneda, M. 2010 Changing marine exploitation during Late Pleistocene in northern Wallacea: Shell remains from Leang Sarru Rockshelter in Talaud Islands. *Asian Perspectives* 48, 318–341.

Ono, Rintaro, Fuentes, Riczar, Amano, Noel, Sofian, Harry, Sriwigati, Aziz, Nasrullah, and Pawlik, Alfred. 2021 Development of bone and lithic technologies by anatomically modern humans during the late Pleistocene to Holocene in Sulawesi and Wallacea. *Quaternary International* 596, 124–143.

Ono, Rintaro, Sofian, Harry, Fuentes, Riczar, Aziz, Nasrullah, and Ririmasse, Marlon. 2023a Early modern human migration into Sulawesi and Island adaptation in Wallacea. *World Archaeology* 54, 229–243.

Ono, Rintaro, Sofian, Harry, Fuentes, Riczar, Aziz, Nasrullah, and Pawlik, Alfred. 2023b The Goa topogaro complex and traces of human migration and mortuary practice in Sulawesi during the Late Pleistocene and Holocene. *L'Anthropologie*, 103155.

Patole-Edoumba, Elise. 2002 L'industrie Lithique Préhistorique de Débitage des Philippines de la Fin du Pleistocène à l'Holocène Moyen. PhD thesis, Marseille: University of Aix-Marseille I.

Patole-Edoumba, Elise, Pawlik, Alfred, and Mijares, Armand. 2012. Evolution of prehistoric lithic industries of the Philippines during the Pleistocene. *Comptes Rendus Palevol* 11 (2–3), 213–30.

Pawlik, Alfred. 2002 Is there an early Palaeolithic in the Philippines? New approaches for lithic analysis in the Philippines, in *Australasian Connections and New Directions: Proceedings of the 7th Australasian Archaeometry Conference. Research in Anthropology and Linguistics 5*, eds Mark, Horrocks, and Peter, Sheppard. Auckland: University of Auckland, 255–270.

Pawlik, Alfred. 2004 The Palaeolithic Site of Arubo 1 in Central Luzon, Philippines. *Bulletin of the Indo-Pacific Prehistory Association* 24, 3–12.

Pawlik, Alfred. 2009 Is the functional approach helpful to overcome the typology dilemma of Lithic Archaeology in Southeast Asia? *Bulletin of the Indo-Pacific Prehistory Association* 29, 6–14.

Pawlik, Alfred. 2010 Have we overlooked something? Hafting traces and indications of modern traits in the Philippine Palaeolithic. *Bulletin of the Indo-Pacific Prehistory Association* 30, 35–53.

Pawlik, Alfred. 2012 Behavioural complexity and modern traits in the Philippine Upper Palaeolithic. *Asian Perspectives* 51, 22–46.

Pawlik, Alfred. 2021 Technology, adaptation, and mobility in maritime environments in the Philippines from the late Pleistocene to Early/Mid-Holocene. *Quaternary International* 596, 109–123.

Pawlik, Alfred, and Ronquillo, Wilfredo. 2003 The Palaeolithic in the Philippines. *Lithic Technology* 28, 79–93.

Pawlik, Alfred, and Piper, Philip. 2019 The Philippines from c. 14,000 to 4,000 cal. BP in regional context. *Cambridge Archaeological Journal* 29, 1–22.

Pawlik, Alfred, and Fuentes, Riczar. 2023 Prehistoric Hunter-Gatherers in the Philippines-Subsistence strategies, adaptation, and behaviour in maritime environments. *Frontiers in Earth Science* 11, 1110147.

Pawlik, Alfred, Piper, Philip, Faylona, Marie, Padilla, Sabino, Carlos, Jane, Mijares, Armand, Vallejo, Benjamin, Reyes, Marian, Amano, Noel, Ingicco, Thomas, and Porr, Martin. 2014 Adaptation and foraging from the Terminal Pleistocene to the Early Holocene: Excavation at Bubog on Ilin Island, Philippines. *Journal of Field Archaeology* 39, 230–47.

Pawlik, Alfred, Piper, Philip, Wood, Rachel, Lim, Kristine, Faylona, Marie, Mijares, Armand, and Porr, Martin. 2015 Shell tool technology in Island Southeast Asia, an early Middle Holocene Tridacna adze from Ilin Island, Mindoro, Philippines. *Antiquity* 89, 292–308.

Pawlik, Alfred, Crozier, Rebecca, Fuentes, Riczar, Wood, Rachel, and Piper, Philip. 2019 Burial traditions in early Mid-Holocene Island Southeast Asia: New evidence from Bubog-1, Ilin Island, Mindoro Occidental. *Antiquity* 93, 901–918.

Piper, Philip. 2016 Human cultural, technological and adaptive changes from the end of the Pleistocene to the mid-Holocene in Southeast Asia, in *The Routledge Handbook of Bioarchaeology in Southeast Asia and the Pacific Islands*, eds Marc, Oxenham, and Hallie, Buckley. London: Routledge, 24–44.

Piper, Philip, and Rabett, Ryan. 2009 Hunting in a tropical rainforest: Evidence from the terminal Pleistocene at Lobang Hangus, Niah Caves, Sarawak. *International Journal of Osteoarchaeology* 19, 551–565.

Piper, Philip, and Rabett, Ryan. 2014 Late Pleistocene subsistence strategies in Southeast Asia and their implications for understanding the development of modern human behaviour, in *Southern Asia, Australasia and the Search for Modern Human Origins*, eds Robin, Dennell, and Martin, Porr. Cambridge: Cambridge University Press, 118–134.

Piper, Philip, Ochoa, Janine, Lewis, Helen, Paz, Victor, and Ronquillo, Wilfredo. 2008 The first evidence for the past presence of the tiger *Panthera tigris* (l.) on the island of Palawan, Philippines: Extinction in an island population. *Palaeoclimatology, Palaeogeography, Palaeoecology* 264, 123–127.

Piper, Philip, Ochoa, Janine, Robles, Emil, Lewis, Helen, and Paz, Victor. 2011 Palaeozoology of Palawan Island, Philippines. *Quaternary International* 233, 142–158.

Pope, Geoffrey. 1989 Bamboo and human evolution. *Natural History* 98, 1–15.

Rabett, Ryan, and Piper, Philip. 2012 The emergence of bone technologies at the end of the Pleistocene in island and mainland Southeast Asia and their regional implications. *Cambridge Archaeological Journal* 22, 37–56.

Reepmeyer, Christian, Spriggs, Matthew, Anggraeni, Lape, Peter, Neri, Leee, Ronquillo, Wilfredo, Simanjuntak, Truman, Summerhayes, Glenn, Tanudirjo, Daud, and Tiauzon, Archie. 2011 Obsidian sources and distribution system in Island southeast Asia: New results and implications from geochemical research using LA-ICPMS. *Journal of Archaeological Science* 38, 2995–3005.

Reepmeyer, C., O'Connor, S., Mahirta, Maloney, T., and Kealy, S., 2016. Late Pleistocene/Early Holocene maritime interaction in Southeastern Indonesia—Timor Leste. *Journal of Archaeological Science* 76, 21–30.

Reich, David, Patterson, Nick, Kircher, Martin, Delfin, Frederick, Nandineni, Madhusudan, Pugach, Irina, Ko, Albert, Ko, Ying-Chin, Jinam, Timothy, Phipps, Maude, Saitou, Naruya, Wollstein, Andreas, Kayser, Manfred, Pääbo, Svante, and Stoneking, Mark. 2011 Denisova admixture and first modern human dispersals into Southeast Asia and Oceania. *American Journal of Human Genetics* 89, 516–28.

Reyes, M.C., Ingicco, T., Piper, P.J., Amano, N., and Pawlik, A. 2017 First fossil evidence of an extinct cloud rat (*Crateromys paulus*) (Chordata: Mammalia: Rodentia, Muridae) from Ilin Island, Mindoro (Philippines): Insights on *Crateromys paulus* diversity and *Crateromys* systematics. *Proceedings of the Biological Society of Washington* 130, 84–97.

Reynolds, T. 1993 Problems in the Stone age of South-East Asia. *Proceedings of the Prehistory Society* 59, 1–15.

Robles, Emil, Piper, Philip, Ochoa, Janine, Lewis, Helen, Paz, Victor, and Ronquillo, Wilfredo. 2015 Late quaternary sea level changes and the palaeohistory of Palawan Island, Philippines. *Journal of Island and Coastal Archaeology* 10, 76–96.

Samper Carro, Sofia, O'Connor, Sue, Louys, Julien, Hawkins, Stuart, and Mahirta, Mahirta. 2016 Human maritime subsistence strategies in the Lesser Sunda Islands during the terminal Pleistocene-early Holocene: New evidence from Alor, Indonesia. *Quaternary International* 416, 64–79.

Sathiamurthy, Edlic, and Voris, Harold. 2006 Maps of Holocene Sea level transgression and submerged lakes on the sunda shelf. *The Natural History Journal of Chulalongkorn University* Supplement 2, 1–43.

Schick, Kathy, and Zhuan, Dong. 1993 Early Paleolithic of China and Eastern Asia. *Evolutionary Anthropology* 2, 22–35.

Schroeder, Lauren, Scott, Jill, Garvin, Heather, Laird, Myra, Dembo, Mana, Radovčić, Davork, Berger, Lee, de Ruiter, Darryl, and Ackermann, Rebecca. 2017 Skull diversity in the Homo lineage and the relative position of Homo naledi. *Journal of Human Evolution* 104, 124–135.

Sémah, Francois, Sémah, A.-M., Diubiantono, Tony, and Simanjuntak, H.T. 1992 Did they also make stone tools? *Journal of Human Evolution* 23, 439–446.

Sémah, Francois, Saleki, Hassane, Falguères, Christophe, Féraud, Gilbert, and Djubiantono, Tony. 2000 Did early man reach Java during the late Pleistocene? *Journal of Archaeological Science* 27, 763–769.

Shackelford, Laura, and Demeter, Fabrice. 2012. The place of Tam Hang in Southeast Asian human evolution. *Comptes Rendus Palevol* 11 (2–3), 97–115.

Shipton, Ceri, O'Connor, Sue, Jankowski, Nathan, O'Connor-Veth, J, Maloney, Tim, Kealy, Shimona, and Boulanger, Clara. 2019a. A new 44,000-year sequence from Asitau Kuru (Jerimalai), Timor-Leste, Indicates long-term continuity in human behaviour. *Archaeological and Anthropological Sciences* 11, 5717–5741. DOI: 10.1007/s12520-019-00840-5.

Shipton, Ceri, O'Connor, Sue, Reepmeyer, Christian, Kealy, Shimona, and Jankowski, Nathan. 2019b Shell adzes, exotic obsidian and inter-island voyaging in the early and middle Holocene of Wallacea. *Journal of Island and Coastal Archaeology* 15, 525–546.

Simanjuntak, Truman, Prasetyo, Bagyo, and Handini, Retno. 2001 *Sangiran: Man, Culture, and Environment in Pleistocene Times*. Jakarta: Yayasan Obor Indonesia/The National Research Centre of Archaeology/EFEO.

Simanjuntak, Truman, Sémah, Francois, and Gaillard, Claire. 2010 The palaeolithic in Indonesia: Nature and chronology. *Quaternary International* 223–224, 418–21.

Slon, Viviane, Hopfe, Charlotte, Weis, Clemens, Mafessoni, Fabrizio, de la Rasilla, Marco, Lalueza-Fox, Carles, Rosas, Antonio, Soressi, Marie, Knul, Monika, Miller, Rebecca, Stewart, John, Derevianko, Anatoly, Jacobs, Zenobia, Li, Bo, Roberts, Richard, Shunkov, Michael, de Lumley, Henry, Perrenoud, Christian, Gušić, Ivan, Kućan, Željko, Rudan, Pavao, Aximu-Petri, Ayinuer, Essel, Elena, Nagel, Sarah, Nickel, Birgit, Schmidt, Anna, Prüfer, Kay, Kelso, Janet, Burbano, Hernán, Pääbo, Svante, and Meyer, Matthias. 2017 Neandertal and Denisovan DNA from Pleistocene sediments. *Science* 356, 605–608.

Soejono, R.P. 1984 Prehistoric Indonesia, in *Prehistoric Indonesia. A Reader*, ed Van de Velde, Piet.. Dordrecht: Foris, 49–78.

Solana, David, Zugasti, Ivan, and Conte, Ignacio. 2011 the use of mollusc shells as tools by coastal human groups, the contribution of ethnographical studies to research on Mesolithic and early Neolithic technologies in Northern Spain. *Journal of Anthropological Research* 67, 77–102.

Solheim, William. 1970 Prehistoric Archaeology in Eastern Mainland Southeast Asia and the Philippines. *Asian Perspectives* 13, 47–58

Sutikna, Thomas, Tocheri, Matthew, Morwood, Michael, Saptomo, Wahyu, Jatmiko, Awe, Rokus, Wasisto, Sri, Westaway, Kira, Aubert, Maxime, Li, Bo, Zhao, Jian-xin, Storey, Michael, Alloway, Brent, Morley, Mike, Meijer, Hanneke, van den Bergh, Gerrit, Grün, Rainer, Dosseto, Anthony, Brumm, Adam, Jungers, William, and Roberts, Richard. 2017 Revised stratigraphy and chronology for *Homo floresiensis* at Liang Bua in Indonesia. *Nature* 532, 366–369.

Szabó, Katherine, and Koppel, Bernard. 2015 Limpet shells as unmodified tools in Pleistocene Southeast Asia: An experimental approach to assessing fracture and modification. *Journal of Archaeological Science* 54, 64–75.

Szabó, Katherine, Brumm, Adam, and Bellwood, Peter. 2007 Shell artefact production at 32,000–28,000 BP in Island Southeast Asia: Thinking across media. *Current Anthropology* 48, 701–23.

Teixeira, Joao, and Cooper, Alan. 2019 A 'Denisovan' genetic history of recent human evolution. *PeerJ Preprints* 7, e27526v1

Teodosio, S. 2005 A Functional Analysis of the Arubo Stone Tools. Master thesis. Quezon City: University of the Philippines Diliman.

Teves, J.S., and Gonzales, M.L. 1950. The geology of the University – Balara area, Quezon City. *Philippine Geology* IV (3), 1–10.

Thiel, Barbara. 1987. Excavations at the Lal-Lo Shell middens, Northeast Luzon, Philippines. *Asian Perspectives* 27 (1), 71–94.

Thiel, Barbara. 1990 Excavations at Musang Cave, Northeast Luzon, Philippines. *Asian Perspectives* 28, 61–81.

Tykot, Robert, and Chia, Stephen. 1997 Long-distance obsidian trade in Indonesia. *Materials Research Society Symposium Proceedings* 462, 175–180.

Van Heekeren, Robert. 1972 *The Stone Age of Indonesia*. Second edition. The Hague: Martinus Nijhoff.

van den Bergh, Gerrit, Mubroto, B., Aziz, F., Sondaar, P., and De Vos, Jon. 1996 Did Homo erectus reach the Island of Flores? *Bulletin of the Indo-Pacific Prehistory Association* 14, 27–36.

van den Bergh, Gerrit, Meijer, H, Awe, Rokhus, Morwood, Michael, Szabó, Katherine, van den Hoek Ostende, L, Sutikna, T, Saptomo, E, Piper, Philip, and Dobney, Keith. 2009 The Liang Bua faunal remains: A 95 k. yr. sequence from Flores, East Indonesia. *Journal of Human Evolution* 57, 527–37.

van den Bergh, Gerrit, Li, Bo, Brumm, Adam, Grün, Rainer, Yurnaldi, Dida, Moore, Mark, Kurniawan, Iwan, Setiawan, Ruly, Aziz, Fachroel, Roberts, Richard, Suyono, Storey, Michael, Setiabudi, Erick, and Morwood, Michael. 2016 Earliest hominin occupation of Sulawesi, Indonesia. *Nature* 529, 208–26.

Voris, Harold. 2000 Maps of the Pleistocene sea levels in Southeast Asia: Shorelines, river systems and time durations. *Journal of Biogeography* 27, 1153–67.

Westaway, K. E, Louys, J., Due Awe, R., Morwood, M., Price, G., Zhao, J., Aubert, M., Joannes-Boyau, R., Smith, M., Skinner, M., Compton, T., Bailey, R., van den Bergh, G., de Vos, J., Pike, A., Stringer, C., Saptomo, E., Rizal, Y., Zaim, J., Santoso, W., Trihascaryo, A., Kinsley, L., and Sulistyanto, B. 2017 An early modern human presence in Sumatra 73,000–63,000 years ago. *Nature* 548, 322–325.

Xiang, Anqiang. 1990 Palaeolith discovered in the Lishui Basin, the Dong-ting Lake region. *Southern Ethnology and Archaeology* 3, 249–70.

Xie, Guangmao. 1990 Relation between the stone tools from Baise and the lower Palaeolithic cultures from South and Southeast Asia. *Southern Ethnology and Archaeology* 3, 237–47.

Xhauflair, Hermine. 2014 Plant use in the subsistence strategies of prehistoric hunter-gatherers in Palawan Island assessed from the lithic industry. PhD thesis. Paris: Muséum national d'Histoire naturelle.

Xhauflair, Hermine, and Pawlik, Alfred. 2010 Usewear and residue analysis, contribution to the study of the lithic industry from Tabon Cave, Palawan, Philippines. *Annali dell'Università di Ferrara Museologia Scientifica e Naturalistica* 6, 147–54.

Xhauflair, Hermine, Pawlik, Alfred, Gaillard, Claire, Forestier, Hubert, Vitales, Timothy, Callado, John, Tandang, Danilo, Amano, Noel, Manipon, Dante, and Dizon, Eusebio. 2016 Characterisation of the use-wear resulting from bamboo working and its importance to address the hypothesis of the existence of a bamboo industry in prehistoric Southeast Asia. *Quaternary International* 416, 95–125.

Xhauflair, Hermine, Jago-on, Sheldon, Vitales, Timothy, Manipon, Dante, Amano, Noel, Callado, John, Tandang, Danilo, Kerfant, Céline, Choa, Omar, and Pawlik, Alfred. 2020 Plant processing experiments and use-wear analysis of Tabon Cave artefacts question the intentional character of denticulated stone tools in prehistoric Southeast Asia. *Journal of Archaeological Science: Reports* 32, 102334.

Xhauflair, H., Jago-on, S., and Pawlik, A., et al. 2023 The invisible plant technology of Prehistoric Southeast Asia: Indirect evidence for basket and rope making at Tabon Cave, Philippines, 39–33,000 years ago. *PLoS ONE* 18(6), e0281415.

Yamei, Hou, Potts, Richard, Baoyin, Yuan, Zhengtang, Guo, Deino, Alan, Wang, Wei, Clark, Jennifer, Xie, Guangmao, and Weiwen, Huang. 2000 Mid-Pleistocene Acheulean-like stone technology of the Bose Basin, South China. *Science* 287, 122.

Zanolli, Clément, Kaifu, Yousuke, Pan, Lei, Xing, Song, Mijares, Armand, Kullmer, Ottmar, Schrenk, Friedemann, Corny, Julien, Dizon, Eusebio, Robles, Emil, and Détroit, Florent. 2022 Further analyses of the structural organisation of *Homo luzonensis* teeth: Evolutionary implications. *Journal of Human Evolution* 163, 103124.

Zeitoun, Valery, Forestier, Hubert, Rasse, Michel, Auetrakulvit, Prasit, Kim, Jeongmin, and Tiamtinkrit, Chaturaporn. 2013 The Ban Don Mun artifacts: A chronological reappraisal of human occupations in the Lampang province (Northern Thailand). *Journal of Human Evolution* 65, 10–20.

# 12
# EMERGENCE OF PLEISTOCENE MODERNITY AND ITS BACKGROUND IN THE KOREAN PENINSULA

*Yongwook Yoo*

## Introduction

Outlining the nature of anatomically modern humans (AMH) in the Korean Peninsula is a difficult job since the geographic area under review should be extended beyond the current boundary of modern political units. In addition, Korea is a unique territory affected by a tattered modern history represented by colonisation and separation out of a cold-war doctrine (Yoo 2017). As a result, the history and archaeology of Korea have been narrated in a totally different mode in the North and the South respectively. The North was seeking a political propaganda to hail its nationalistic spirits and to secure its autonomous land tenure by taking a reclusive and dogmatic pace in interpreting archaeological data (Yoo 2017). It is, therefore, of a premature notion that Korean data can significantly contribute to the problem of modern human emergence and dispersals in a global scale.

In spite of these innate limitations, this chapter will seek to briefly demonstrate the *status quo* of Korean Palaeolithic research with an "aloof but critical" tone. The reason for this is twofold. First, although the nature of data is to be examined, the current situation involved in those data needs to be introduced, summarized, and exposed to a wider audience. In other words, by evading and overcoming biased interpretations, the factual data at least should be exhibited for future research since most researchers, especially Westerners, are yet to be exposed to the true characteristics of the Korean Palaeolithic data.

The second reason is to modulate or reduce the emotional tone and minimize the subjectivity of the narratives. This is probably associated with the research attitudes of local archaeologists, and so is not unique to the Korean case alone. Because of historically rooted emphasis on their ancestral territory, Koreans highly value the prolonged age and originality of their long-standing folk lineage; this value has continuously influenced the research attitude of Korean Palaeolithic studies, and the instant result is some overestimated ages of Palaeolithic remains that are far older than their actual chronometric dates. Moreover, the quality of data itself is liable to be exaggerated and utilized as media to convey the idea that Korean ancestors commanded (or "flourished with") *magnificent* and *remarkable* prehistoric *cultures*. As a result, this value-added prehistory of Korea has been gaining considerable popularity with the public, but the academic reality cannot but be compensatedly compromised.

In order to assess and overcome this old research bias, this chapter will be more focused on the illustration of currently available data and discuss its validity. This task will be the starting point of understanding the current issue: the emergence of Pleistocene modernity in Korea. It is not an overstatement that most of Korean Palaeolithic data are the behavioural imprint of anatomically modern humans (AMH from now) who resided in the Peninsula since the Late Pleistocene. With some controversial data ruled out, Korean fossil remains and lithic assemblages, as well as a handful of faunal data, predominantly belong to the latter half of the Late Pleistocene, context and more high-resolution data are from the full-fledged Late Palaeolithic period.

This chapter will be devoted to (1) introduce those archaeological/palaeoanthropological data from the Korean Peninsula, (2) associate them with the Pleistocene environmental background, and (3) discuss their cultural/technological significance on the local (Korean), regional (East Asian), and global scale respectively. In order to perform these tasks, some general remarks will be addressed on the environmental and archaeological background of the Pleistocene Korean Peninsula. For the sake of convenience, this chapter, from now on, refers to the whole of Korea as "the Peninsula," China and other inland areas as "the Continent," Siberian Russia as "the North" and Japan as "the Archipelago," evading any modern political connotations.

## Pleistocene Environment of East Asia in General

The global environment had seriously changed since the final Tertiary (ca 2.5 mya) and the ice ages has cycled in a tempo of 0.1 million years during the Pleistocene era. Each glacial/interglacial period had been marked with stadial and interstadial subdivisions of hundreds or thousands of years. Palaeolithic people had unexpectedly undergone numerous environmental changes and adjusted their lifeways alongside. These diverse lifeways yielded the currently available archaeological record under totally different environmental conditions.

Analysis of deep-sea marine isotope oxygen has furnished a panorama of global Pleistocene environmental change. More information has become available by the study of polar ice caps from Greenland and the Antarctic since the 1970s. This long-term climatic evidence indicates that the Peninsula was free of the Asiatic continental ice sheet from the North (Yi 1989). The seasonal monsoon which emerged as a result of uplifting Asian terrains during the Tertiary was one of the major factors responsible for the East Asian climatic change; locally rugged terrain and anastomosing river channels in the Peninsula turned different microenvironments into niches for local fauna/flora and hominin populations.

It can be generally summarized that a relatively mild environment reduced hominin survival stress during the latter part of the Middle Pleistocene in the Peninsula and adjacent Continent (Pu 1991; Shi 1991). Since the beginning of the Marine Isotope Stage (MIS) 6, however, somewhat abrupt climatic deterioration began to occur in the northern East Asia. Affected by more severed climatic conditions, the early hominin population size did not expand, and the relevant archaeological record is accordingly scarce. Some evidence of the earliest hominin occupation is sparsely distributed inside the Peninsula, though (e.g. the *Jangsanri* site of the Imjin-Hantan River Area (IHRA); Yoo 2008).

Several sub-stages of warm/cold cycles of the MIS 5e can be observed from the Continental data in a macro-geographical scale. Notwithstanding the climatic fluctuation, the general temperature was reduced across the entire Continent since the MIS 5a, and ecologically favourable areas for hominin survival were centripetally constricted around the middle-eastern part of the

Continent until the Last Glacial Maximum (LGM ca 20 ka, Pu 1991; Shi 1991). This global climatic deterioration since the MIS 5a was possibly accelerated by several huge volcanic eruptions recorded both in the Archipelago and *Sunda* area (Rampino and Self 1993; Ambrose 1998; Takarada and Hoshizumi 2020; Doughty et al. 2021).

Ironically, as a result of hominin resilient actions, more vigorous migration and propagation of survival technology was triggered and instigated by the gradual ecological crisis within the Continent. As such, the continuous environmental deterioration could not entirely hinder the gradual expansion of the hominin habitat, and the influx of hominin populations towards the Peninsula was accelerated during the Late Pleistocene. The area below 40° N did not constitute extremely harsh conditions for the positive adaptation of the Asian hominins (Yi 1989, 112). Except for the North (e.g. Manchuria) and some high alpine areas (e.g. the Tibetan Plateau) with tremendously low productivity, almost every part of the eastern Continent and the Peninsula was occupied by hominins who modified their survival strategy, as exemplified by several unique localized lithic technologies.

## Topography and the Fluvial System of the Korean Peninsula

In order to elucidate the population history of the Peninsula, some geographic factors should be taken into closer consideration. The northern part is connected to the Continent and currently occupied by North Korea. The whole Peninsula ranges between 33°06′ and 43°01′ latitude and between 124°11′ and 131°53′ longitude. Total area is about 221,000 km² including all adjacent islands. The Peninsula is a part of the stable Asian land mass but located at the margin of the Circum-Pacific Orogen where vigorous orogenic movement is still under way. As a result, the Peninsula is characterized by diverse mountainous topography like the Archipelago. The general topography of the Peninsula was formed by the "*Daebo* Orogeny" from the early Jurassic to the Cretaceous Period (ca 180–120 Mya, Soh 1980). Violent thrusting and innumerable folds accompanied by large-scale faulting produced a series of high mountains. This movement occurred mainly in the middle and southern parts of the Peninsula, and the consequences are well observed by the syntactic granites across the "Okchon Geosyncline Belt" (I of Figure 12.1) which traverses from northeast to southwest.

The land surface consists of generally low mountain ranges with only 5% being above 1,000 m. However, the topography is much dissected and even low mountains have steep slopes associated with a relatively early stage of the topographic developmental cycle (Bartz 1972). Two linear mountain ranges traverse the Peninsula like a spine: the *Nanglim* and *Taebaek* Mountains. Several other tributary mountain shoots erupt from these two ranges (1 of Figure 12.2). Because of its extensive mountainous area, the Peninsula is populated primarily in the midwestern and southwestern regions. Archaeological evidence tends to occur sporadically, but its distribution shows a highly clustered pattern dispersed among these mountain ranges.

Palaeolithic sites are located within the altitude range of 20–70m above sea level which is the same location for current populations in the Peninsula. They generally follow along the outskirts of steep mountain slopes. In some cases, Palaeolithic sites have been discovered in several regions of limestone caves which extend far above the slope range. The *Okchon* Belt mentioned above, is a well-developed calcareous land mass with various escarpments and cavities which provide an ideal habitat both for hominins and animals. Because of the calcareous alkali environment, fossil remains are well-preserved in these cave sites, but most of the other open-air sites rarely produce animal or hominin fossils.

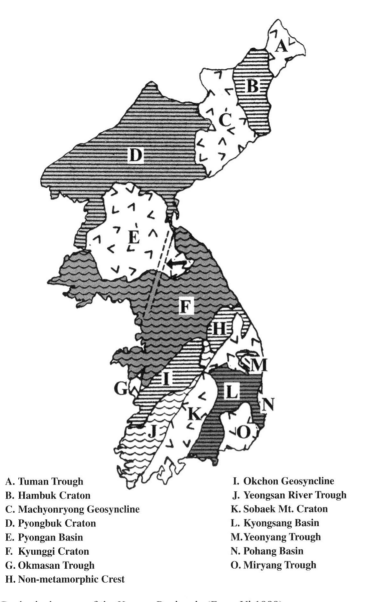

A. Tuman Trough
B. Hambuk Craton
C. Machyonryong Geosyncline
D. Pyongbuk Craton
E. Pyongan Basin
F. Kyunggi Craton
G. Okmasan Trough
H. Non-metamorphic Crest
I. Okchon Geosyncline
J. Yeongsan River Trough
K. Sobaek Mt. Craton
L. Kyongsang Basin
M. Yeonyang Trough
N. Pohang Basin
O. Miryang Trough

FIGURE 12.1  Geological zones of the Korean Peninsula (From Yi 1989).

The majority of Korean open-air sites are distributed along the major river channels. Since the Peninsula is predominantly a mountainous area, the river channel systems largely have anastomosing modes, and their alluvial area is towards the Yellow Sea because the Peninsula has a west-slanting topography. At the northernmost border of the Peninsula, two channels, the *Amnok* (*Yalu* in Chinese) and the Tuman River, originate from *Baekdu* (*Changbai* in Chinese) Mountain and demarcate the Peninsula from the Continent. Below the Amnok and Tuman, numerous river channels run from east to west, parallel to the direction of most mountain ranges (2 of Figure 12.2). In the southern part of the Peninsula, three major channels: the *Nakdong,*

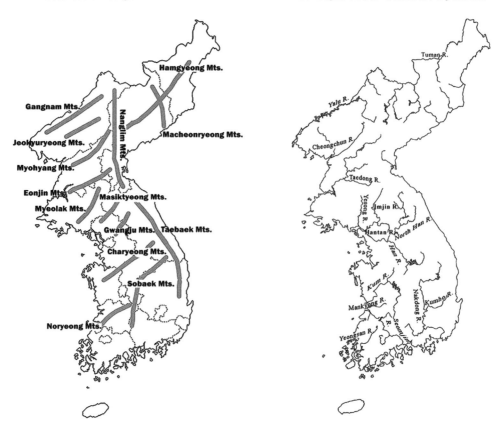

FIGURE 12.2   Mountain ranges and major river channel systems of the Korean Peninsula.

*Seomjin,* and *Yeongsan,* flow southward through deeply entrenched valleys, developing a complex network of streams. The accessibility of water was always a critical concern, and most Palaeolithic sites are located adjacent to the hydraulic sources such as a major channel system.

## Pleistocene Hominin Occupation in the Peninsula

The population history during the Pleistocene is not well-documented but it has become axiomatic that the Peninsula was initially populated by hominins who migrated from the Continent, possibly from the Manchuria. Especially, since the eastern part of the Continent was connected to the Peninsula until the Last Glacial Maximum (LGM; Han 2003), the land bridge enabled frequent population influx during the Late Pleistocene until the Yellow Sea was finally formed from the beginning of the Holocene. It should not, however, be thought that the Continental hominin population preferred the Peninsula, voluntarily moving eastward in search of more favourable habitats. The Peninsula is interspersed with very rugged terrains, and small-scale fluvial channels did not furnish surplus productivity to host large and ubiquitous hominin groups. This might be a partial reason for the fact that most Palaeolithic assemblages are small-scale and rarely display the evidence of long-term occupation to the extent that temporal changes in lithic technological adaptation can be well-documented.

Although far older evidence of hominin occupation is reported from the Continent, Palaeolithic evidence dated as old as Early/Middle Pleistocene is yet to be identified in the Peninsula as well as in the Archipelago. Age determination of Palaeolithic assemblages is still controversial and reliable dating samples are hard to obtain because of extremely acidic sediments. It is, therefore, an unproven claim that the Peninsula was occupied/populated simultaneously with the Continent and that their lithic assemblages are coeval. According to the recent knowledge about the Pleistocene environment and relevant chronometric dates (TKAS 2007), it is undisputed that the majority of Palaeolithic assemblages discovered in the Peninsula are chronologically bracketed into the Late Pleistocene (125–12 ka). As has been stated before, the Late Pleistocene is characterized by gradual deterioration of climate and biomass, and this condition coincided with the development of local lithic technology and population migration into and out of the Peninsula in response to changes in the environment through the connected land bridge. An example of hominin fossils from the Peninsula and their general characteristics are presented in Table 12.1.

Hominin fossils are usually discovered in the same context with faunal remains. Until 2024, 11 cave sites, one rock shelter and one open-air site have yielded hominin fossils. Seven of those 11 cave sites (*Yeokpori, Seungnisan, Ryonggok Cave, Mandalri, Geumcheon, Chongpadae Cave,* and *Laengjeong Cave*) and one open site (*Hwadaeri*) are located in North Korea, while the remaining cave sites (*Jeommal Cave, Gunang Cave,* and *Heungsu Cave at Durubong*) and the one rock shelter site (*Sangsiri*) are located in the limestone area at the central part of South Korea. An almost complete skeleton of a single juvenile individual (the "Heungsu Boy") from the *Heungsu Cave* of *Durubong site* has been recently estimated to be a possible Holocene specimen (de Lumley et al. 2011). In addition, the extent to which his dental decay had progressed is a typical indication of post-agricultural diets, plus there is no geological correlation between the original Pleistocene strata and the horizon where the skeleton was found.

Except for this controversial *Heungsu* Boy case, the rest of the hominin fossils are mostly composed of fragments of various body parts. It is notable that, other than unconfirmed data from *Hwadaeri* site (Table 12.1), most hominin fossils of the Peninsula are AMH. Two skulls and post-cranial bones discovered from *Ryonggok Cave*, originally reported to be *Homo erectus*, have now been re-interpreted as anatomically modern humans based on their prominent modern-looking morphology and the dimensions of the crania (Park and Lee 2003). While three cranial fragments from the *Yeokpori* Cave are arguably believed to be in the category of more archaic species (i.e. possibly *H. erectus*; Norton 2000, 818), it is still unclear to conclude that the Peninsula was inhabited by hominins as old as that archaic form of *H. sapiens*. In spite of some speculation that very old hominin species resided in the Peninsula and their uncontested fossils will be discovered in the future, we cannot go further beyond the fact that discovered hominin fossils show, whether partially or fully, anatomically modernized features.

## Palaeolithic Assemblages and Their Periodization

Archaeological assemblages are rarely associated with hominin fossils. In fact, only three hominin fossils from *Mandalri* (Figure 12.3; Han 1990, 380–9), *Chongpadae* (Choe et al. 2020; Chol et al. 2023), and *Laengjeong* were discovered in primary context with portable artefacts. The *Mandalri* site yielded 13 lithic specimens made of quartzite and obsidian, most of which are examples of microblade cores representative of terminal Late Palaeolithic technology (1 of Figure 12.3).

TABLE 12.1 Hominin fossils discovered in the peninsula.

| Location | Age (est.) | Parts | Species |
|---|---|---|---|
| Yeokpori | Middle/Late Pleistocene | frontal, occipital, parietal | *H. erectus* (?) |
| Seungnisan | Middle/Late Pleistocene | two molars, scapula, mandible | Archaic *H. sapiens* |
| Ryonggok Cave | Layer 9 (46–48 ka by U-series dating) | cranium (No.7), mandibles (No.1, 2, 6) | Modern *H. sapiens* (?) |
| Ryonggok Cave | Layer 10 | cranium (No.3), mandibles (No. 4, 6) femur | Modern *H. sapiens* (?) |
| Ryonggok Cave | Layer 11 | temporal, frontal, mandible (fr.), 3 humerus (fr.), 8 vertebrae, 3 innominate, 2 femur (fr.) | Modern *H. sapiens* |
| Ryonggok Cave | Layer 12 | maxilla (No. 8) | Modern *H. sapiens* |
| Mandalri | Late Pleistocene | calvaria, mandible (fr.), humerus, femur, innominate | Modern *H. sapiens* |
| Geumcheon | 30 ka | mandible, inciser, axial (fr.) | Modern *H. sapiens* |
| Hwadae | 0.3 ma (?) | unidentified skeletal (fr.) | Archaic *H. sapiens* (?) |
| Chongphadae Cave *(8th layer)* | 61, 67, 69 ka (TL)XX61.5 ± 9.8 ka(U-series) | maxilla (fr., No.1) | Archaic *H. sapiens* (?) |
| Chongphadae Cave *(12th layer)* | cal 24,980–21,340 BP | mandible (No.9) | Modern *H. sapiens* |
| Chongphadae Cave *(13th layer)* | cal 34,770–27,340 BP | mandible, occipital, radius (No.2) XX maxilla (No.6) | Modern *H. sapiens* |
| Laengjeong Cave *(10th layer)* | 43 ka (TL), 53 ka (ESR) XX 46 ± 1 ka(U-series) | mandible (fr.), frontal (fr.) | Modern *H. sapiens* |
| Cheomnal Cave | 40–60 ka | phalanx, metatarsal | Modern *H. sapiens* |
| Sangsiri | 30 ka | left parietal, occipital (fr.), radius, right scapula, right humerus, teeth | Modern *H. sapiens* |
| Gunang Cave | Late Pleistocene | talus, metatarsal, phalanx | Modern *H. sapiens* |
| Heungsu Cave at Durubong | controversial | nearly complete single juvenile individual (possibly Holocene specimens) | Modern *H. sapiens* |

*Sources:* From Norton (2000: 74) and Park and Lee (2003: 42).

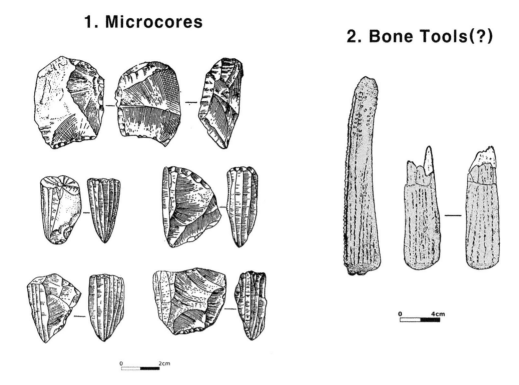

FIGURE 12.3  Microcores and presumed bone tools discovered at *Mandalri* site.

In addition, a fluted antler shaft and a partly ground antler spatula were discovered with lithic assemblages. These arguable "bone tools" seem to have been used as a stone knapping implements (2 of Figure 12.3). In spite of their seemingly artificial features, the provenance of these tools is not secured and their arguable contemporaneity with the hominin fossil is compromised.

The Palaeolithic data of the Peninsula are local variations of the East Asian technocomplex entity; but they are not so easily classified into Early-Middle-Late chronological subunits. This is due to two main facts. (1) The Peninsula lacks evidence of chronologically and geologically solid hominin species which can be employed to demarcate the cultural/technological evolution at the local level. (2) Technological repertoires of Palaeolithic assemblages are very dull and monotonous; they scarcely show temporal dynamics, and any visible changes do not seem to occur for a considerably long time before the emergence of Late Palaeolithic technology. It is hardly to be expected that any clear-cut scheme can be substantiated in the Peninsula, and even in the Asian Palaeolithic, by employing such classic cultural industrial terms as "Acheulian," "Mousterian," and "Aurignacian." This lack of cultural and temporal markers will be a unique inlaid characteristic of technological evolution in the Palaeolithic record of the Peninsula and other parts of Asia.

However, while assemblages display little technological development, the hominin basic mind-set and attitude concerning the manufacture and use of lithic tools should not be much different from the Western equivalents brought about by Neanderthals though. Because lithics are "susceptibly produced by dint of technological provisioning strategies" (Kuhn 1995, 9), hominins were coping with their environmental stress and solving germane problems by modifying their available resources in their immediate vicinity. In a sense, the difficulty in characterizing and documenting the Palaeolithic assemblages of East Asia principally lies in the less variable-displaying capacity under relatively mild and tranquil living conditions rather than in the "monotone" of the technological strategies themselves. Morphological changes incurred by technological variation as a mode of adaptation to the local environment will not be easily detected, at least enough to demonstrate the high-fidelity of technical susceptibility in cases of relatively stress-free conditions. This kind of dynamics in lithic technological evolution tends to appear simple and unsophisticated materiality within assemblages, leading observers to believe too easily that they are simply crude and under-developed and even for some who are more gullible observers to argue that East Asian Palaeolithic data are the output of culturally retarded local hominins (e.g. Movius 1944).

Taken the monotonous characteristics of the Palaeolithic of the Peninsula in general, a substantial conclusion can be made that its periodization and/or chronology need not follow the Westernized scheme. The widely accepted East Asian Palaeolithic scheme (Gao and Norton 2001; Ikawa-Smith 1978) employs a dichotomic Early/Late Palaeolithic. The Early Palaeolithic incorporates whole lithic assemblages produced during the pre-modern sapiens phase. Its time span is from the Middle to the earlier part of the Late Pleistocene.

The earliest published ages of the palaeolithic localities are the *Geomeunmoru* site of North Korea with controversial chronometric dates of 1.0–0.5 mya, and in South Korea, the *Mansuri* site, is the oldest locality dated around 0.5 mya (NRICHK 2014). Except for these several "far-old" dates, the chronometric dates for Palaeolithic sites in the Peninsula commonly indicate that the hominin occupation was initiated no earlier than the latter half of the Middle Pleistocene, as late as MIS 6. This leads to a speculation that the hominin occupation of the Peninsula was significantly later than the Continent because of its location at the far eastern corner where the presumed migratory route of the hominin groups reached at its latest phase.

### Archaeological Evidence Before the Pleistocene Modernity

The Early Palaeolithic assemblages of the Peninsula are mostly composed of crude simple tools like choppers, picks and amorphous large flakes made of quartz and quartzite. What is noteworthy is that some Acheulian-like handaxes and cleavers have been recurrently discovered around the *Imjin and Hantan River Area* (the IHRA, Yoo 2008). Upon their first discovery in 1978, they were regarded as the ultimate counterevidence against Movius' (1944) early claim that East Asian early lithic technology is devoid of Acheulian characteristics and predominantly composed of such simple tools as choppers and chopping-tools. In recent years, however, the nature of the IHRA handaxes has been re-examined apart from Movius' culture-historical dogma because their dates are much younger than the presumed Middle Pleistocene age and their technological features are totally different from the genuine Acheulian ones (see Yoo 2008, 2009).

In this chapter, some important evidence before the emergence of the Pleistocene modernity will be enumerated and reviewed in the context of their cultural/technological significances (see Figure 12.4).

### *Gulpori*

It is the first Palaeolithic site discovered (1962) in the Peninsula, which is located at *Seonbong* County, Northern *Hamgyeong* Province in North Korea. Two artefact layers were identified within the Pleistocene sediments. The lower layer (*Gulpo I*) yields simple quartz tools and the

FIGURE 12.4  Major Palaeolithic localities mentioned in this chapter.

upper layer (*Gulpo II*) includes end scrapers and other small tools made of shale. *Gulpo I* is estimated ca 10 ka and *Gulpo II* is ca 40–30 ka with no chronometric dates (NRICHK 2014).

## Geomeunmoru

It was discovered near Pyongyang City and excavated in the 1960s by the Institute of Archaeology of North Korea. It is a cave site located on the escarpment of a shallow rock inselberg. Some subtropical faunal remains were discovered with very crude lithic artefacts, and their ESR dates are around ca 1.0 ma. Considering its unstable age and the nature of the formation

**236** Yongwook Yoo

process of cave deposits, the archaeological context of *Geomeummoru* is not believed to be intact (NRICHK 2014).

### Jeongokri and the IHRA Handaxe Sites

The first discovery of handaxes in East Asia was reported in 1978 at the *Jeongokri* site, and other IHRA localities—*Geumpari, Juweolri, Namgyeri*, etc.—located around the DMZ area between North and South Korea along the *Imjin and Hantan* River channels (Figure 12.5). The IHRA sites are commonly distributed above volcanic lava and their K-Ar dates (ca 0.5–0.3 mya) indicate the maximum oldest date of artefact layers. Their whole lithic assemblages including handaxes were formed considerably later than the volcanic eruption, though. Some chronometric dates (OSL and C14) of artefact layers are predominantly of MIS 4 or younger. The dates of Aira Tanzawa (AT)

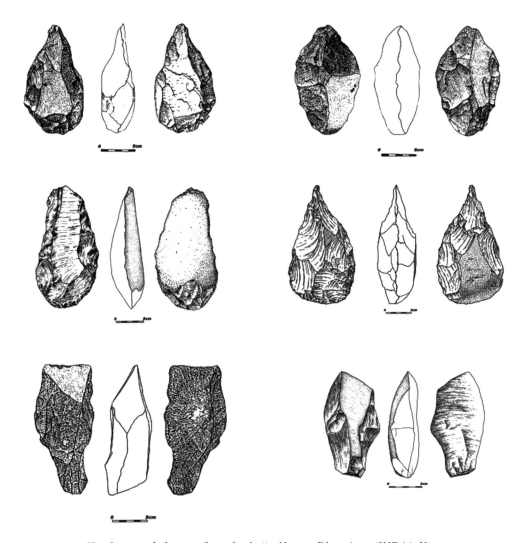

**FIGURE 12.5** Handaxes and cleavers from the *Imjin-Hantan* River Area (IHRA), Korea.

tephra (ca 28 ka) discovered above the artefact horizon demonstrate the possible youngest date of handaxes (Yoo 2008, 2009; Yi 2011).

Given these dates and the geological context of the artefact horizons, the IHRA handaxe are younger than typical Acheulian ones and sheds a light on an alternative position that they are not directly associated with the Acheulian acculturation from the West. More discussion on the Mode 2 technology in East Asia needs to be developed in the future (NRICHK 2014; White 2022).

## Late Palaeolithic Assemblages Reflecting the AMH's Occupation

The issue of the emergence of AMH in the Peninsula is a hot debate and still needs valid archaeological data to corroborate. If blade and laminar lithic technology are an output of technological innovation accomplished by AMH, the emergence of the Korean Late Palaeolithic in the Peninsula is believed to be around 40 ka when initial blade technology was globally propagated along with the migration of AMH. As a sufficient condition for making effective blade-based toolkits, the raw material is shifted from low quality stone (quartz and quartzite) to high quality ones (chert, rhyolite, obsidian, etc.). *Suyanggae*, *Seokjangri*, *Hopyeongdong*, and *Yongsandong* sites are examples of local Late Palaeolithic industry and they share some common features: (1) lithic assemblages were composed of blade-dominant debitages and highly retouched tools; (2) locally available high-quality raw materials were extensively exploited; (3) some unprecedented such cultural features such as house-pits, hearths, and engraved objects emerged as a result of local adaptation and human agency.

The Late Palaeolithic witnessed its final phase characterized by microlithic technology during the terminal Pleistocene. Around the LGM (ca 30,000 BP or MIS 2), the environmental productivity of the Peninsula reached its minimum, and highly economizing technological solutions were sought and devised (Han 2003). Production of microblades and composite toolkits seem to be some of these solutions for successfully responding to the daily requirements in a more compromised resource management background. This type of technology enabled the AMH groups to survive during the harsh cold period and to welcome the beginning of the Holocene period (after 12 ka) when temperatures began to recover and sea levels began to rise, creating the current coastline of the Peninsula.

Now, more than 200 Palaeolithic localities have been discovered, most of them are open air sites discovered near river banks, though caves and rock shelters in the mountainous areas have also been found. The important Late Palaeolithic localities and their cultural remains are briefly introduced hereafter.

### *Yonggok Cave*

This site is located in *Sangwon* County, *Pyongyang* City in North Korea. Composed of two adjacent caves, it was excavated by Kim Il-Sung University during 1980–1981. Exact chronometric dates are not available because of the complicated formation process of cave deposits but faunal fossils include some warm-climate species. Two individuals of AMH skeletons were discovered with simple quartz tools, fragmented bones and remains of a hearth. Although *Yonggok Cave* is a definite prehistoric shelter resided in by local hominins during the Late Pleistocene, the exact date and technological/cultural characteristics of lithic specimens are not yet clearly understood yet (NRICHK 2014).

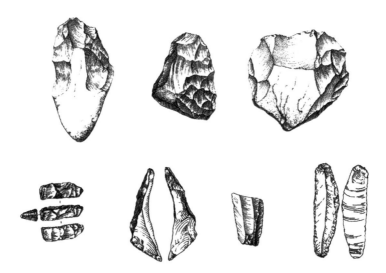

FIGURE 12.6    Lithic specimens from the *Seokjangri* site (No scales).

## *Seokjangri*

The *Seokjangri* site is located along *Geum* River which traverses the midwestern part of South Korea (Yoo 2015). Originally it was reported in 1964 to have a long stratigraphic sequence from Early to Late Palaeolithic, but its validity was highly contested by the fact that the site is located at the immediate vicinity of current channel flow. The layers are believed to have been influenced by subsequent alluvial deformation and re-deposition until original artefact horizons were seriously washed out. The intact archaeological horizon in the whole sequence is the uppermost layer of the Late Palaeolithic phase, which yielded small scrapers, microliths and some arguable engraved portable arts (Figure 12.6; NRICHK 2014).

## *Hopyeongdong*

Located in *Namyangju* City in South Korea, the *Hopyeongdong* site is in a bowl-shaped basin surrounded by shallow hills. Its sediments are largely composed of colluvium. About 10,000 lithic artefacts were discovered, and their raw materials are quartz, tuff, and rhyolites; some obsidian of external origins was also discovered from the upper cultural layer (Figure 12.7). The OSL and C14 dates of artefact layers are distributed between late MIS 3 and MIS 2. The lithic assemblage exhibits typical Late/Terminal Palaeolithic tool types made of blades and microblades (NRICHK 2014).

## *Suyanggae*

This locality is a vast open-air site of scattered lithic specimens on the river bank of the southern *Han* River. A series of excavations were conducted from 1983 to 2014, and diverse cultural layers were found distributed on the river terrace. Raw material is mostly the high-quality microcrystalline shale easily accessible in the vicinity. Tool types include endscraper, stemmed point, handaxe, and various retouched blades. The stemmed point, a unique hunting weapon type of the Peninsula,

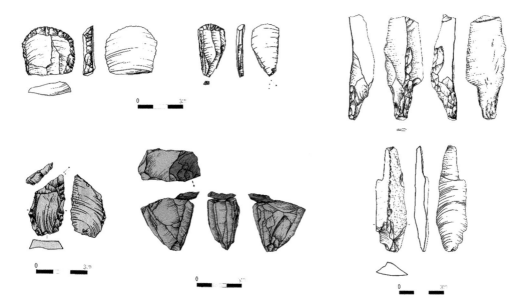

FIGURE 12.7   Late palaeolithic specimens from the *Hopeongdong* site.

is believed to be dominant between MIS 3 and 2. A C14 date (18–16 ka) of terminal Pleistocene was obtained from the upper cultural layer of the original excavation in 1983 (NRICHK 2014).

Some up-to-date results of recent excavations at *Suyanggae* will be published in the near future. The whole site area is now submerged by the construction of large-scaled dams and reservoirs, and originally excavated lithic specimens are yet to be officially reported and published.

## *Yongsandong*

Located inside the metropolitan area of *Daejeon* city near the big tributary channel of *Geum* River, the *Yongsandong* site yielded typical Late palaeolithic assemblages. The assemblage horizons are very limited and their AMS dates are around MIS 2 (19,310±790 BP and 24,430±870 BP; Yoo 2014, 33).

It is noteworthy that the *Yongsandong* site has a number of stemmed points and small scrapers made of fine-grained hornfels. The majority of those small tools are found broken and fractured without any hints of provisioning/recycling strategies. It is speculated that the stemmed points and scrapers were used for highly schemed hunting and animal resource modification tasks including instant hiding and butchering inside the site area (Figure 12.8). The lithic assemblage also indicates that the *Yongsandong* site area was repetitively visited as a sort of base camp where ready-made tools were imported from outside and consumed/discarded on the spot (Yoon and Jo 2007, 115).

## *Jingeuneul*

This site is located at the far upper stream area of *Geum* River, in the central high-altitude mountainous area of South Korea. The altitude of the *Jingeuneul* site is about 247m, and it is

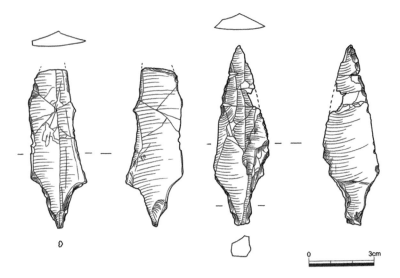

FIGURE 12.8  Stemmed points discovered from the *Yongsandong* site.

surrounded by higher slopes of steep mountain ranges. Around 12,000 lithic specimens were discovered with almost 20 residues of workshops and hearths (Lee 2004). The highly modified stemmed points and debitages with well-preserved in-situ lithic manufacturing areas indicate the *Jingeuneul* site is an example of hominins' intended occupation of this high mountainous area in favour of animal exploitation (Figure 12.9). Its AMS dates (22,850±350 BP; Lee 2004, 11–4) of charcoal retrieved from the hearths corresponds to the terminal MIS 3 and MIS 2 when the productivity of the Peninsula was minimal and the residential movement of hominins reached up to the higher altitudes so that they could obtain crucial animal resources by way of appropriate hunting strategies (e.g. Yoo 2014).

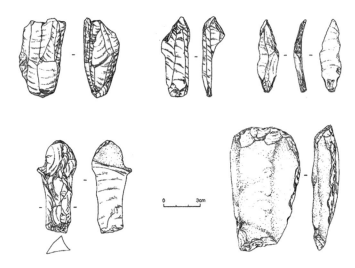

FIGURE 12.9  Lithic types discovered from the *Jingeuneul* site.

## Goryeri

Few Palaeolithic sites have been reported down the *Sobaek* Mts, in the southeastern part of the Peninsula. Some reasons for this are to be: (1) the lack of populous areas during the Pleistocene due to the natural barriers of the complex mountain systems, and (2) that the evidence of Palaeolithic hominin occupation was largely erased by subsequent human occupations during the historical period. In either case, the scanty Palaeolithic record in the southeastern part of the Peninsula remains an intriguing archaeological phenomenon for researchers. Up until now, there have been only a handful of excavated localities in this area, though recent discoveries of Palaeolithic assemblages have attracted researchers' attention due to cultural/technological intimacy with the Palaeolithic record from the Archipelago.

Among these discoveries, the *Goryeri* site has one of the most outstanding lithic assemblages to shed light on the hominins' local adaptation during the final phase of the Late Pleistocene. Discovered and excavated in 1993, the *Goryeri* site abounds in well-made blades/blade-cores and several typical Late Palaeolithic tools. Some local high-quality raw materials such as shales, hornfels, and andesite (Chang 2016, 23) were intensively procured, and the diversity of toolkits is remarkable. As with the cases of both *Yongsandong* and *Jingeuneul*, *Goryeri* boasts stemmed points made of blade blanks as well as some amorphous scrapers and knife-shaped retouched pieces. The age of the assemblage could not be measured because a reliable dating source was not available; only AT volcanic ashes which has a solid date of ca 27 ka was discovered within the assemblage layer.

The *Goryeri* assemblage indicates important archaeological facts about the hominin occupation of the Peninsula during the Late Pleistocene: 1) by the age of MIS 2, almost every part of the Peninsula was occupied, possibly by AMH groups; 2) the lithic assemblages were based on blade technology using diverse local raw materials; 3) some specialized toolkits like stemmed point and MIS cellaneous scrapers/burins became wide-spread, reflecting more intensive exploitation of available resources, which was never witnessed before the MIS 2.

## Conclusion: the AMHs' Lifeways in the Peninsula

It is still not crystal-clear that the Late Pleistocene hominin groups of the Peninsula were exclusively an AMH population (Norton and Braun 2011). The recent discoveries of the Denisovans at the marginal Continent strongly indicate that multiple groups with different genetic origins possibly co-habited in East Asia. There is no solid evidence that specific tool types such as stemmed points and elaborate microliths are exclusively indicative of the AMH-patented technology. It is intriguing that the emergence of modernity in the Peninsula is in accordance with several drastic shifts from the previous technologies, though. This shift was, while many other factors are to be considered, caused by the changes in the global environment and relevant population dynamics in the Continent, these changes possibly substantiated by both the arrival of new hominin species and apparent deterioration of the environment during MIS 3. If this shift was not accomplished until the onset of population changes but was already underway during the initial phase of the Late Pleistocene, we can safely presume that there was not such an abrupt shift as to be labelled a "revolution" (McBrearty and Brooks 2000).

Nevertheless, rather than gradual, steady, and recurrent, the tempo and velocity of this change, however, seems to be punctuated, abrupt, and accelerated within a relatively short time span in the Peninsula. For example, a very crude and monotonous mode of lithic technology based on quartz and quartzite became entirely replaced by a blade-dominant, highly effective toolkits. Their raw materials were composed of excellent microcrystalline rock, some of it (e.g. obsidians from *Baekdu* Mt.; Yi and Jwa 2015) are exotic rocks exclusively obtained by a long-distance exchange network. In addition, the highly effective weapon-like tools were greatly increased and were intensively manufactured/utilized. Their technological origin is not well-documented but became widespread across the entire Peninsula within a relatively short span of time.

It is highly probable that these tools were immediately devised and rapidly traditionalized as a result of effective technological "character displacement." This was done in the course of repetitive animal hunting and the mutual use of violence under harsher environmental conditions. Unless otherwise narrated with the increasingly available archaeological record and its dates, the emergence of Pleistocene modernity, in other words the "Emergence of the Late Palaeolithic," was triggered, inspired and motivated by the arrival and propagation of the AMH in the Peninsula. In the course of this change in population dynamics, the environmental changes also played a significant role as a catalyst of these revolutionary changes.

The hominins of the Peninsula during the Late Pleistocene, including the AMH, were both hunters and gatherers, but direct evidence of their active animal resource exploitation has not survived in the harsh preservatory conditions of the Peninsula. Some faunal remains from caves and limestone environments hint at the interactions between humans and animals, especially the employment of hunting technology and butchering skills (TKAS 2007). Because the AMHs were not sedentary and continuously migrated in line with the availability of resources, their residential structures took the form of ephemeral and temporary shelters like caves and simple huts made of shrubs and stones. Remains of open-air hearths from *Hopyeongdong* and *Jingeuneul* sites demonstrate the use of temporary working places, and some claimed pit-houses discovered at the *Seokjangri*, *Changnae*, and *Nobong* sites are not suggestive of patterned behaviours for the regular construction of residential structures.

In essence, according to the amount of undisputed archaeological data, the population level of the Pleistocene Peninsula was very low, too low for any cultural sphere to be created and maintained from generation to generation. In addition, since the Peninsula is highly mountainous and not an easy domain to navigate around, the human interrelationship and any strategic formation of social network could hardly be expected.

The Palaeolithic living conditions in the Peninsula seem to have been neither harsh nor affluent; they generally did not entail any severe environmental constrains such as glaciers and desert, for example. They did not allow, however, any proper physical conditions favorable enough to enable a large hominin population to flourish within each limited locality even after the arrival of the AMH groups. Because of the low resolution of archaeological data, only speculation can be put forth about what they lived on and how they produced and utilized relevant materials. It is quite clear that the population distribution was uneven across the Peninsula, and interactions among local groups were not highly motivated because of the lack of mutual exposure. As a result, the emergence of any "regional tradition", whether it is cultural or merely technological, could not be anticipated until the global-wide warming period, a. k. a. the Holocene.

As Clark (2014, 21) properly put it, the East Asia "experienced a complex series of dispersals, back migrations, regional diversification, isolation, reintegration, local extinctions, range extensions, displacements, replacements, radiations, continuity and discontinuity, all set against the backdrop of climatic change extending far back into the Miocene." Addressing the emergence of Pleistocene modernity in terms of the global AMH occupation is rather re-encoding this complexity than decoding the separate individual processes. The emergence of the AMH and their arrival in the Peninsula is a very tiny piece of the puzzle that can hardly contribute to reconstructing the big and original picture of the Pleistocene population dynamics in Asia. In particular, illustrating the emergence of Pleistocene modernity with only the archaeological data is like trying to behold the real world "through a glass darkly." What is rather important is to acknowledge the existence of this glass, which is also known as the bias, than to argue that the glass is limpid enough to render a virtual image lucidly.

## Acknowledgments

The author appreciates many anonymous reviewers and helpers writing the final draft of this chapter. This work was supported by the Ministry of Education of the Republic of Korea and the National Research Foundation of Korea (NRF-2024S1A5A2A01019918).

## References

Ambrose, Stanley. 1998 Late Pleistocene human population bottlenecks, volcanic winter, and differentiation of modern humans. *Journal of Human Evolution* 34, 623–651.

Chang, Y. 2016 Miryang Goryeriwa Jinju Jiphyeon Yujeokeui Guseokgi Yeongu [A study of Milyang Gorye-ri and Jinju Jiphyeon sites in the Late Paleolithic in Korea]. *Hanguk Guseokgi Hakbo* [*Journal of the Korean Palaeolithic Society*] 34, 20–49.

Choe, Rye, Han, Kum, Kim, Se, Chol, U., Ho, Chol, and Kang, Il. 2020 Late Pleistocene fauna from Chongphadae Cave, Hwangju County, Democratic People's Republic of Korea. *Quaternary Research* 97, 42–54.

Chol, U., Choe, Rye, Ri, Jae, Han, and Myong, G. 2023 Paleoenvironment and human activity on the central Korean Peninsula during the late MIS 3 and MIS 2. *Quaternary Research* 112, 67–77.

Clark, G. 2014 Paleolithic archaeology and human Paleontology in East Asia – A view from the west. *Hanguk Guseokgi Hakbo* [*Journal of the Korean Palaeolithic Society*] 30, 3–24.

de Lumley, H., Cauche, D., Celberti, V., Khatib, S., Lartigot-Campin, A.-S., Lebatard, A.-É., Lebègue, F., Menras, C., Mestour, B., Moigne, A.-M., Moles, V., Moullé, P.-É., Notter, O., Perrenoud, C., Rochette, P., Rossini, E., Saos, T., Vialet, A., Wengler, L., Bourlès, D., Braucher, R., Lee, Y-J., Park, Y-C., Han, C-G., Bae, K., Yi, S., Hong, M-Y., Cho, T-S., Kong, S., Choi, M-C., Cho, S-Y., and Jung, S-E. 2011 *les industries du Paléolithique ancien de la Corée du Sud dans leur contexte stratigraphique et paléoécologiques: leur place parmi les cultures du Paléolithique ancien en Eurasie et en Afrique*. Paris: CNRS Éditions.

Doughty, Alice, Kaplan, Michael, Peltier, Carly, and Barker, Stephen. 2021 A maximum in global glacier extent during MIS 4. *Quaternary Science Reviews* 261, 1–16.

Gao, Xing, and Norton, Christopher. 2001 A critique of the Chinese 'Middle palaeolithic. *Antiquity* 76, 397–412.

Han, C. 1990 *Bukhaneui Seonsa Gogohak* [*Prehistoric Archaeology of North Korea*]. Seol: Baeksan Munhwasa.

Han, C. 2003 Hanguk Guseokgi Yuseokeui Yeondae Munjee Daehan Gochal' [On the problems of the dates of Korean palaeolithic sites]. *Hanguk Guseokgi Hakbo* [*Journal of the Korean Palaeolithic Society*] 7, 1–39.

Ikawa-Smith, Fumiko. 1978 Introduction: The early palaeolithic tradition of East Asia, in *Early Palaeolithic in South and East Asia*, ed Ikawa-Smith, Fumiko.. The Hague: De Gruyter Mouten, 1–11.

Kim, W. 1986 *Hanguk Gogohak Gaeseol* [*Introduction to the Korean Archaeology*]. Seoul: Iljisa.

Kuhn, S. L. 1995 *Mousterian Lithic Technology: an Ecological Perspective*. Princeton: Princeton University Press.

Lee, G. 2004 Jinan Jingeuneul Yujeok Guseokgi Munhwacheungeui Seonggyeokgwa Euimi [The Jingeuneul Late palaeolithic Site in Jinan County of submerged area around The Yongdam Dam and its significance]. *Honam Gogohakbo* [*Journal of the Honam Archaeological Society*] 19, 5–23.

McBrearty, Sally, and Brooks, Alison. 2000 The revolution that wasn't: A new interpretation of the origin of modern human behavior. *Journal of Human Evolution* 39, 453–563.

Movius, Halam Jr. 1944 *Early Man and Pleistocene Stratigraphy in Southern and Eastern Asia*. Cambridge: Papers of the Peabody Museum of American Archaeology and Ethnology.

National Research Institute of Cultural Heritage Korea (NRICHK). 2014 *Hanguk Gogohak Sajeon-Guseokgi Sidae* [*Dictionary of Korean Archaeology- The Paleolithic Age*]. Daejeon: Publication Department of NRICHK.

Norton, Christopher. 2000 The current state of Korean paleoanthropology. *Journal of Human Evolution* 38, 803–825.

Norton, Christopher, and Braun, David. eds. 2011 *Asian Paleoanthropology - from Africa to China and Beyond*. New York: Springer.

Park, S., and Lee, E. 2003 Hanbandoeui Goinryu [Hominins of the Peninsula]. *Hanguk Guseokgi Hakbo* [*Journal of the Korean Palaeolithic Society*] 7, 41–51.

Pu, Q. 1991 Quaternary glaciers in China in *The Quaternary of China*, ed. Z. Zhang. Beijing: China Ocean Press, 240–274.

Rampino, Michael, and Self, Stephen. 1993 Climate–Volcanism Feedback and the Toba Eruption of ~74,000 years ago. *Quaternary Research* 40, 269–280.

Shi, Y. 1991 Glaciers and glacial geomorphology in China, in *Quaternary Geology and Environment in China*, ed Liu, T. Beijing: Science Press, 16–27.

Takarada, Shinji, and Hoshizumi, Hideo. 2020. Distribution and eruptive volume of Aso-4 pyroclastic density current and Tephra fall deposits, Japan: A M8 super-eruption. *Frontiers in Earth Science* 8(170), 1–16.

The Korean Archaeological Society (TKAS). 2007 *Han Guk Go Go Hak Gang Eui* [*Lectures on Korean Archaeology*]. Seoul: Sahwoepyeongron Publishing.

White, Mark. 2022 *A Global History of the Earlier Palaeolithic: Assembling the Acheulian World, 1673–2020s*. London: Routledge.

Yoo, Y. 2008 *Beyond the Movius Line, BAR International Series 1772*. Oxford: Hadrian Books.

Yoo, Y. 2009. Jeongokri Jumeokdokieui Siganjeok Wichie Daehan Siron [A Speculation on the Temporal Horizon of Handaxes from the Chongokni Site: A Heuristic Approach]. *Gogohak* [*Archaeology*] 8 (1), 5–25.

Yoo, Y. 2014 Seoul Mit Hangang Bonryuyeok Guseokgi Yujeokeui Ipjiwa Seongyeok [palaeolithic settlement patterns and lithic diversities in Seoul and mainstream Han River Area]. *Hyangto Seoul* 88, 5–67.

Yoo, Y. 2015 Geumgang Yuyeok Guseokgi Yujeokeui Hyeongseong Gwajeonggwa Goinryu Jeongeo Gwajeong Siron [A speculation on the formation process of Palaeolithic sites and hominin occupation in the Geum River Area, Korea]. *Hoseo Gogohakbo* [*Journal of Hoseo Archaeological Society*] 33, 4–39.

Yoo, Y. 2017 A Story of Their Own: what happened and what is going on with North Korean archaeology? in *Archaeology of the Communist Era: a Political History of the 20th Century*, ed Lozny, R.. New York: Springer, 275–294.

Yoon, S., and Jo, S. 2007 *Daejeon Yongsandong Yuseok: Daedeok Techno-Valley Yidangye Joseongsaeop Bujinae* [*Excavation Report of the Yongsandong Site Within the 2nd Phase Development Area of Daedeok Techno-Valley*]. Darjeon: Central Institute of Cultural Heritages.

Yi, Seonbok. 1989 *Dongbuk Asia Guseokgi Yeongu* [*A Study of Northeast Asian Palaeolithic*]. Seoul: Seoul National University Press.

Yi, Seonbok. ed. 2011 *Handaxes in the Imjin Basin*. Seoul: Seoul National University Press.

Yi, Seonbok, and Jwa, Y. 2015 Heukyoseok Sanji Chujeong Yeongueui Jaegeomto [On Provenance of the Prehistoric Obsidian Artifacts in Korea]. *Hanguk Guseokgi Hakbo* [*Journal of the Korean Palaeolithic Society*] 31, 156–180.

# 13

# ANALYZING JAPANESE SITES BELONGING TO THE INITIAL PERIOD OF THE UPPER PALAEOLITHIC

## Creating Macro-Models

*Takeshi Ueki*

## Introduction

What can we know about the first Modern Humans (*Homo sapiens*) who made their way to the Japanese Archipelago? From this great distance in time, perhaps the most useful approach would be to use the many excavation monographs available to analyze the types of environment in which they chose to settle and the types and numbers of occupation traces and implements they left behind.

It has been common for archaeologists everywhere to select a particular artifact or feature and compare the presence or absence of this in a series of other sites, the micro-model approach. My aim instead became to look at everything found at my selected sites and then make models based on groups of artifacts and features that were common to them all, a macro-model approach new to Japan. Such models would be useful hereafter in analyzing both old and new sites in Japan, but more than that, they could be used for comparisons with Modern Human sites found in Korea, China, Russia, the Philippines, and Southeast Asia, looking for similarities and differences. In that way we would have a new method to trace our ancestors' footprints after they departed Africa and reached Eastern Asia and the offshore island groups, including Japan.

In Japan the Upper Palaeolithic Age lasted between approximately 39,000 (or 38,000) cal BP and 16,000 cal BP (Inada and Sato eds. 2010a,2010b). There are a great many sites presumed to be from the previous Early or Middle Palaeolithic (examples include Kanadori, Sunahara, Hoshino, Tsujita, Iriguchi, Souzudai, and Niu), but long-continued debate notwithstanding, many researchers still cannot agree on their age. To avoid this sort of controversy, the 12 sites selected were those unequivocally recognized by all to be the oldest created by Modern Humans during the Initial Period of the Upper Palaeolithic Age (39,000 cal BP to 34,000 cal BP).

But first, let us look briefly at what sort of place these early people encountered. What was prehistoric Japan like?

DOI: 10.4324/9781003427483-13

## Natural Environment

### Climate and Sea Level

The Upper Palaeolithic Age in Japan is dated variously, but began about 39,000–38,000 calibrated dates before the present time, an age that coincided with the latter half of MIS 3 (Marine Isotope Stage 3) when conditions were still marginally warmer than the next stage. This was a period of repeated cooling and warming before the onset of the extended extreme cold of MIS 2. The point of the Last Glacial Maximum (LGM) is also variously dated, but here let us use the ice core dates of 28,000–24,000 before the present (Kudo 2010, 134; 2012, 42). At the coldest point of stage MIS 2, sea level is estimated to have been between 100 and possibly up to 120 m lower than today. Figure 13.1 shows the extent of the exposed land at that time with the sea down 120 m (Machida 2007).

At 39,000 years ago, there were several routes that Modern Humans might have taken to reach Japan. Studies by archaeologists, DNA researchers, and palaeoanthropologists have identified six possibilities (Nakazawa 2017), but here we will look at the three most likely. The first was from Siberia, over Sakhalin Island, to Hokkaido. The second was from the Korean Peninsula into northern Kyushu. The third was from Okinawa into southern Kyushu. That said, despite a great number of Palaeolithic sites found, so far no Initial Period sites have been identified in Hokkaido, while only one (Yamashitacho, Cave No. 1) has been found in Okinawa. Thus many Palaeolithic researchers presume that the second route via the Korean Peninsula into northern Kyushu was the most likely crossing place. Despite the Initial Period sea level being much lower than the present day, the Japanese Archipelago was not actually

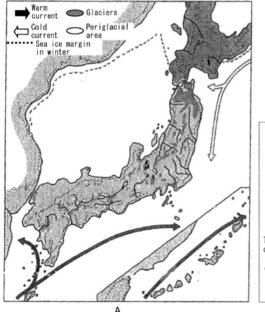
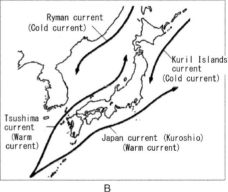

**FIGURE 13.1** (A) Shoreline 24,000 years BP, 120 m lower (Machida 2007, 27). (B) Present day shoreline and sea currents.

joined to the Asian mainland. It has been thought that these early people arrived by raft or paddled over in small canoes.

## Tephra

"Tephra," from the Greek for "ash," is the general name for pyroclastic flow, surge, and fall deposits, variously named for the way they exit an erupting volcano. Flows and surges are both very hot collections of ash, rock debris, and gas that run down the sides of a volcano, flows being denser, which slows their movement slightly so that they tend to follow the topography of the surrounding land, and surges having a higher gas content, making them more fluid, faster, and capable of surmounting obstacles such as nearby hills. These may occur separately or together, and deposits from both spread along the surrounding ground, sometimes for great distances. Pyroclastic fall deposits result from the explosive plume of hot gas, ash, and debris blasted upward, heavier blocks of rock falling close to the volcano, and the lightest material reaching the upper atmosphere and distributed by the prevailing wind, even encircling the earth after the most massive eruptions. The raining ash is what many people think of as volcanic deposits, but all three types of pyroclastic deposits should be taken into account as tephra (Machida and Arai 2003, 7).

The content of ash falls is further divided by the characteristics of the materials they contain, ash itself being the smallest at 2–4 mm, while anything from pebbles to large blocks of rock may be ejected. Rocks of basalt, dense and dark-colored, are called scoria. Those of rhyolite, lightweight, and light-colored, are pumice. Both are pocked with bubbles from exploded gas, pumice having more of these.

From the standpoint of the archaeologist, at excavations where cultural layers are mixed with naturally accumulating tephra layers, dating of the latter through other research leads to dating of the sites. Local tephra accumulations are of course useful, but of particular importance is widespread tephra, which may cover huge areas. An example is the Aira-Tn (AT) tephra layer from the first half of the Upper Palaeolithic Age (29,000–30,000 $^{14}$C cal BP), deposited over all of Japan except the eastern part of Hokkaido and all of the Korean Peninsula except a small part in the north. Sites excavated in Japan from beneath Aira-Tn will be no later than the Early Period of the Upper Palaeolithic, while those from above it will belong to the Late Period, an extremely important index for excavators (see Figure 13.2).

## Flora

The Japanese Archipelago lies in the temperate zone, but since it stretches over 3,000 km north-to-south there are marked climatic divisions. In the far north there is subarctic coniferous forest, then moving down there are cold-temperate deciduous forest, warm-temperate evergreen broad-leaved forest, and finally subtropical broad-leaved forest. During the Initial Period of the Upper Palaeolithic the climate was considerably colder than today, though not yet extremely cold. Fairly severe temperature fluctuations marked those times, however, as the overall climate slid toward the period of greatest cold. In Figure 13.3A we can see a diagram of the vegetation throughout Japan and the eastern edge of Asia about 6,000 years after the Initial Period ended and the start of the LGM (Sugiyama 2010, 168). Focusing on evergreen broad-leaved forest (No.5 in the list), at that time this was limited to the southernmost parts of Shikoku and Kyushu, today under the sea, as well as on the islands of Amami and Okinawa. Figure 13.3B shows

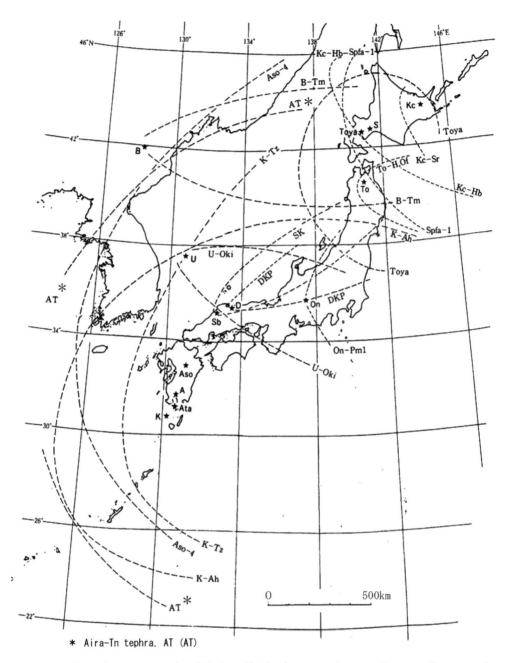

**FIGURE 13.2** Late Quaternary regional Tephra distributions over Japan and surrounding countries (Machida and Arai 2003, 54, partially revised).

us the theoretical vegetation zones today (Numata and Iwase 2002, 20) if there were only the present-day environment with its natural degrees of temperature and humidity and no artificial changes wrought by human activity. From this it is evident that, excepting alpine areas, all of the easternmost area of the country would be in the zone of evergreen broad-leaved forest. One

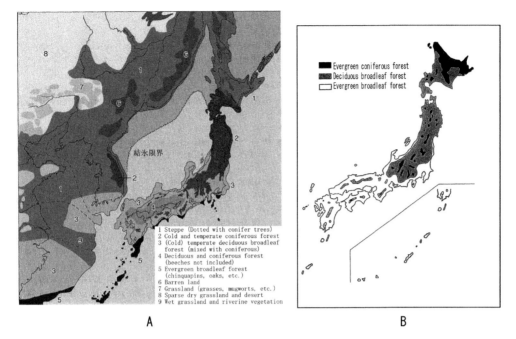

FIGURE 13.3  (A) Vegetation zones in East Asia during the Last Glacial Maximum (from Sugiyama 2010, 168) and (B) potential vegetation zones in present day Japan (from Numata and Iwase 2002, 20).

theory holds that the difference in average yearly temperature between the LGM and today is about 7–8 degrees Celsius. This dramatic difference in vegetation is the result of just that much change in the climate.

Figure 13.4 shows that during the LGM northeastern Japan was covered by coniferous trees while the southwest had temperate mixed forests of conifers and broad-leaved trees such as pine, oak, fir, Japanese hemlock, and cedar. At the same time we can appreciate that all the coastal settlements of the time are now sunk below 100–120 m of rising seawater as the glaciers melted.

## Fauna

The study of palaeo-mammals in Japan was spurred by the widespread discovery of Pliocene animal bones (Kamei, Kawamura and Taruno 1988). However, here we will focus on the animals of the last stage of the Late Pleistocene, roughly comparable to the Upper Palaeolithic stage of Modern Human development. Figure 13.5 illustrates the mammals of that age: small-sized (mice and rats, moles, Japanese dormice), and medium- to large-sized (Japanese macaques, tanuki [raccoon dogs], foxes, wolves, Asiatic black bears, brown bears, leopards, tigers, Naumann elephants, giant Japanese elk, elk, steppe bison, aurochs) (Kawamura 2005). It has been conjectured that these animals migrated from the Asian mainland over the land bridge connecting it to the archipelago during the Middle Pleistocene, newly dated to approximately 0.77–0.13 million years ago.

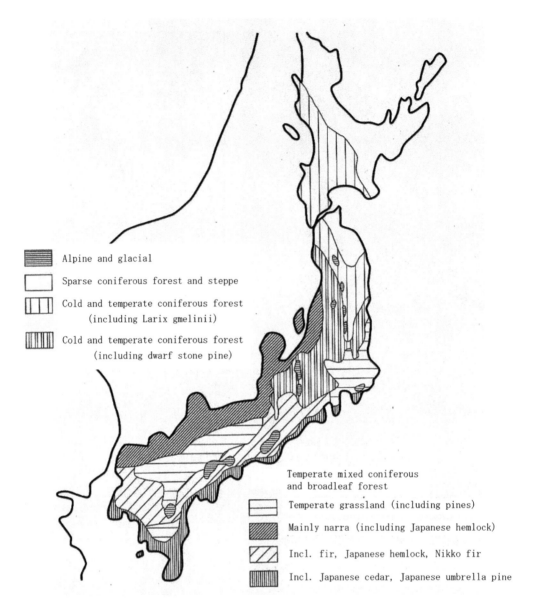

FIGURE 13.4   Palaeo-vegetation in Japan during the Last Glacial Maximum (Okamura et al. 1998, 167).

Unfortunately, bones of these Palaeo-mammals have not been found during excavations of Palaeolithic sites in Japan, though fossils in rocks have revealed their presence. Where they have very occasionally been found at excavation sites, this was from the bedrock of caves or in limestone caves, all in Okinawa. In the highly acidic soil of typical open land excavation sites in the more northerly islands, everything including the bones and teeth of animals has dissolved

FIGURE 13.5   Late Pleistocene mammals of Honshu, Shikoku, and Kyushu, Japan (Kawamura 2005, 53).

away. This was true as well for the 12 sites chosen for the current study. No bones, whether of people or hunted animals, were found.

## Model Formation

Modern Humans first arrived in the Japanese Archipelago approximately 39,000 cal BP ago, according to the most recent findings (see Table 13.1). For our purpose here, let us consider the very oldest known sites and draw an arbitrary line at the 5,000 year mark, designating 39,000–34,000 cal BP the Initial Period of the Upper Palaeolithic Age. The specific data considered were features and artifacts excavated from these sites, types of stone used to make them, as well as climate and vegetation. Since the unclear dates of possibly older sites from the Early and Middle Palaeolithic make them unsuitable for inclusion, the general model formation for these established Upper Palaeolithic sites constitutes the oldest macro-models for Japan.

### Sample Site Selection

According to the Japanese Palaeolithic Research Association, as of 2010 there were some 10,200 Upper Palaeolithic sites in Japan. Since that count was made, still others have been discovered (Nihon Kyusekki Gakkai 2010). From this long list, cal$^{14}$C specialist Yuichiro Kudo checked the lab reports for those that have been excavated (possibly 20–30%) and listed up the $^{14}$C dates for 686 carbon samples from 146 sites, excluding Hokkaido (Kudo 2012,

TABLE 13.1 Twelve oldest sites with cal $^{14}$c dates from the Initial Period of the Upper Palaeolithic Age in Japan.

| Site name* | Lowest cultural layer | $^{14}$C BP ($^{14}$C cal BP) [Laboratory Sample No.] | | Ranking* |
|---|---|---|---|---|
| 1 Takaidohigashi | X | 32,000 ± 170 BP (36,520 cal BP) [IAAA-51557] <br> 31,780 ± 200 BP (36,220 cal BP) [IAAA-51559] | 31,790 ± 160 BP (36,260 cal BP) [IAAA-51558] | 5 |
| 2 Musashidai | Xb | 30,400 ± 400 BP (35,110 cal BP) [Beta-156135] | 29,860 ± 150 BP (34,590 cal BP) [Beta-182638] | 10 |
| 3 Umenokizawa** | Lower BB IV~ Upper BB VI | 29,650 ± 340 BP (34,210 cal BP) [Beta-156808] <br> 29,970 ± 320 BP (34,540 cal BP) [Beta-156810] | 29,630 ± 300 BP (34,170 cal BP) [Beta-156809] | 12 |
| 4 Fujiishi | BBVII(31) | 31,620 ± 190 BP (35,500 cal BP) [IAAA-90634] <br> 32,550 ± 190 BP (36,500 cal BP) [IAAA-90636] <br> 31,930 ± 180 BP (35,800 cal BP) [IAAA-90638] | 32,500 ± 180 BP (36,400 cal BP) [IAAA-90635] <br> 31,840 ± 180 BP (35,750 cal BP) [IAAA-90637] | 3 |
| 5 Nishiboru (b-1) | Surface BBVIO | 30,200 ± 360 BP (34,300 cal BP) [Beta-122043] <br> 30,400 ± 230 BP (34,400 cal BP) [Beta-122045] | 29,700 ± 210 BP (33,850 cal BP) [Beta-122044] | 11 |
| 6 Idemaruyama | BBVII~SCIV | 32,700 ± 190 BP (36,800 cal BP) [IAAA-63169] <br> 33,000 ± 190 BP (37,210 cal BP) [IAAA-63171] | 32,390 ± 200 BP (35,300 cal BP) [IAAA-63170] <br> 33,200 ± 180 BP (37,415 cal BP) [IAAA-63172] | 2 |
| 7 Oiwakegun (No.1) | Layer 42 | 31,039 ± 298 BP (35,000 cal BP) [TERRA-b030501c19] | 30,635 ± 296 BP (34,600 cal BP) [TERRA-b030501c23] | 7 |
| 8 Yamada | LowerXb~ Upper XI | 30,630 ± 230 BP (35,200 cal BP) [Beta-183469] | 30,550 ± 220 BP (35,100 cal BP) [Beta-184680] | 9 |
| 9 Setaikenohara | XVIc~XVIIa | 30,260 ± 170 BP (34,840 cal BP) [IAAA-72245] <br> 31,830 ± 170 BP (36,310 cal BP) [IAAA-72247] | 30,340 ± 170 BP (34,880 cal BP) [IAAA-72246] <br> 32,210 ± 180 BP (36,710 cal BP) [IAAA-72248] | 4 |
| 10 Ishinomotogun (Nos.8,54,55) | Vg, VIa, VIb | 32,750 ± 1,060 BP (38,000 cal BP) [Beta-84289] <br> 33,180 ± 550 BP (37,870 cal BP) [Beta-84291] | 33,710 ± 430 BP (38,500 cal BP) [Beta-84290] <br> 31,600 ± 270 BP (35,880 cal BP) [Beta-84292] | 1 |
| 11 Tachikiri | XIII | 30,360 ± 120 BP (34,750 cal BP) [IAAA-110766] <br> 30,390 ± 600 BP (35,160 cal BP) [Beta-169709] | 30,910 ± 120 BP (35,975 cal BP) [IAAA-110767] | 8 |
| 12 Yokomine (C) | XIIIa | 31,290 ± 690 BP (35,910 ± 827 cal BP) [Beta-102399] | 29,660 ± 540 BP (34,200 ± 698 cal BP) [Beta-102400] | 6 |

* One very old site (50 ka cal BP), Nojiriko Tategahana, is not included here. Findings there were limited to molars of the Naumann elephant with no stone tools or carbon recovered. All sites in this list were dated from carbon samples with the column on the right giving their ages, the oldest as No. 1.
** At Umenokizawa, a deeper undated layer (BB VII) had 1 feature, 14 artifacts, and 10 natural stones. All other sites were from the deepest cultural layer.

126–146). Using his sample sites, target sites for my cluster analysis were selected based on the following four criteria.

- First, the oldest sites carbon dated to between 39,000 and 34,000 cal BP were picked up (30 sites).
- Next, those sites among the 30 from which there were two or more Initial Period dates from the oldest cultural layer were singled out (21 sites).
- After reading the monographs prepared by the excavators for the 21 sites, I looked for those with very clear descriptions of the oldest cultural layer and newer layers above (all 21).
- Of these, for the sake of quantitative analysis, large-scale excavations which produced a large number of features and artifacts from the oldest cultural layer, all of which were counted down to stone flakes and chips, were chosen (10 sites).

These ten satisfied all four criteria and could be used for the model formation, but the list from which Kudo worked was already several years old. Perhaps there were newer discoveries that might be included. Searching the literature did produce two more sites (at Fujiishi and Idemaruyama), bringing the total to 12 as our analysis targets. Table 13.1 shows the $^{14}$C dates obtained for each, and composites of these were ranked in the column on the right in order of oldest to newest. The oldest was Ishinomotogun site in Kumamoto Prefecture, while the most recent was Umenokizawa site in Shizuoka Prefecture.

## Site Locations and Conditions

Checking the location of the 12 oldest sites fulfilling the four criteria, they turned out to be clustered in two locations, one on the Pacific side of central Honshu and the other on Kyushu's main island and one offshore island (see Figure 13.6). This is not to say that there are no Initial Period sites elsewhere. There are indeed other fine sites in northern Honshu and in western Honshu facing the Japan Sea, but none was found that fulfilled all four criteria and so they could not be included.

Table 13.2 lists the groups responsible for site excavation and their reasons for undertaking this. It's immediately evident that, excepting one private group that investigated Takaidohigashi, all the excavations were carried out by municipal boards of education or the Buried Cultural Property Research Centers set up by prefectural governments. Excavations were undertaken as a result of site discovery during preliminary surveys prior to road construction or road maintenance afterward in seven of the 12 cases. The remaining five sites were found and investigated in the course of construction of various types of public facility.

The area excavated depended more on the decision of each investigating group than on the nature of the sites. However, in order to create Palaeolithic cultural models for sites located in plains and other open land, it's important to excavate a considerable area in order to grasp the whole picture of the site. Short-term, small-scale excavations of under 1,000 m² can't accomplish this.

Table 13.3 gives more details on site locations. The three shaded areas are compilations of data on the lowest cultural layer gathered by different groups excavating neighboring sites. The first two in the list, located in Tokyo, have in common Layer X as the oldest, particularly Xb. The next four, 3–6, located in Shizuoka Prefecture, straddle Layers BBIV-SCIV, though it appears from their monographs that BBVII was the main layer. Number 7 is in Nagano Prefecture. Numbers 8–10 in central Kyushu were notably varied in their oldest strata. In contrast, 11 and 12 on Tanegashima Island had in common Layer XIII as the oldest.

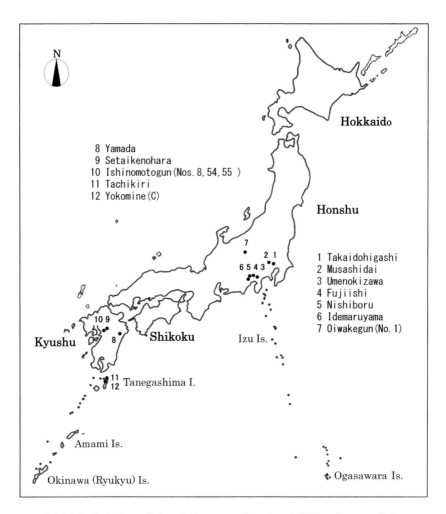

**FIGURE 13.6** Initial Period Upper Palaeolithic excavation sites fulfilling four conditions.

All but one of the 12 sites were lowland types, but the single site at higher elevation (Oiwakegun No.1) pushed up the average elevation to the misleading 221 m. If that site were disregarded, the average was 116 m. The depth of the oldest layer from the present land surface varied from 1.2 to 4.5 m (average 2.4 m). Distance to freshwater refers to distance to present-day rivers except for Nos. 8 and 11 which are close to natural springs. It's unknown whether these existed in the distant past, but here it is assumed so. Average distance to fresh water was 379 m. Given the importance of water in daily life and the danger of flooding from rivers, we may posit the existence of now-vanished springs much closer to living sites in the past.

### Features, Artifacts, and Natural Stones

First a word about the definitions of features and artifacts used by researchers of Palaeolithic culture in Japan. Starting with excavation of the famous Iwajuku site in the postwar period, the

TABLE 13.2 Investigation groups and excavation reasons.

| Site name | Investigation group | Excavation reason | Excavated area (m²) |
|---|---|---|---|
| 1 Takaidohigashi | Private survey group | Garbage incinerator construction | 5,000 |
| 2 Musashidai | Buried Cultural Property Investigation Center | Municipal medical center construction | 7,000 |
| 3 Umenokizawa | Buried Cultural Property Investigation Center | Highway construction | 4,500 |
| 4 Fujiishi | Buried Cultural Property Investigation Center | Highway construction | 3,000 |
| 5 Nishiboru (b-1) | Municipal Board of Education | Archaeological site confirmation; public exercise park | 9,000 |
| 6 Idemaruyama | Municipal Board of Education | City road construction | 1,519 |
| 7 Oiwakegun (No.1) | Municipal Board of Education | National road construction | 2,820 |
| 8 Yamada | Buried Cultural Property Investigation Center | National road construction | 4,400 |
| 9 Setaikenohara | Municipal Board of Education | Dam construction | 1,000 |
| 10 Ishinomotogun (Nos. 8, 54, 55) | Municipal Board of Education | National Athletic Meet site construction | 6,220 |
| 11 Tachikiri | Municipal Board of Education | Farm road maintenance | 4,793 |
| 12 Yokomine (C) | Municipal Board of Education | Farm road and farmland maintenance | 1,700 |
| | | Total | 50,952 |
| | | Average | 4,246 |

TABLE 13.3 Elevation and distance to fresh water by site.

| Site name | Lowest cultural layer* | Elevation (m) | Depth of oldest layer (m) | Distance to fresh water (m) |
|---|---|---|---|---|
| 1 Takaidohigashi | X (Xb)** | 47 | 2.5 | 100 |
| 2 Musashidai | | 78 | 3.5 | 1,200 |
| 3 Umenokizawa | BBIV–SCIV | 170 | 2.5 | 50 |
| 4 Fujiishi | | 195 | 3.5 | 500 |
| 5 Nishiboru (b-1) | (BBVII)** | 170 | 1.2 | 20 |
| 6 Idemaruyama | | 47 | 1.3 | 80 |
| 7 Oiwakegun (No.1) | Layer 42 | 1,370 | 4.5 | 30 |
| 8 Yamada | LowerXb–UpperXI | 50 | 1.5 | (spring) 15 |
| 9 Setaikenohara | XVIc–XVIIa | 210 | 3.0 | 150 |
| 10 Ishinomotogun (Nos. 8, 54, 55) | Vg, VIa, VIb | 75 | 1.7 | 1,800 |
| 11 Tachikiri | XIII** | 114 | 1.7 | 250 |
| 12 Yokomine (C) | | 120 | 1.7 | (spring) 350 |
| | Total | 2,646 | 28.6 | 4,545 |
| | Average | 221 | 2.4 | 379 |

\* All sites are from the deepest, oldest cultural layer with the exception of Umenokizawa, as explained in Table 13.1, footnote \*\*.
\*\* The labels of the lowest cultural layers in the shaded columns are consolidations of those used by different excavating groups.

typology used was basically borrowed as is from Europe, particularly England. Pioneer archaeologists Sosuke Sugihara and Chosuke Serizawa, who were responsible for the Iwajuku excavation, visited the Kanda used book district in Tokyo where they acquired books on archaeology in English, and from these studied lithic terminology from zero, an anecdote the present author heard from the late Professor Sugihara. The terms were gradually somewhat modified, however, to better describe the materials excavated in Japan. In every country over years of research, traditions are built up, so the judgments and standards in each place do not necessarily agree. In Japan, too, some researchers now prefer the French typology, adding a layer of difficulty in deciding tool type (Takeoka 2019, 27–29). That said, in the nearly 80 years since World War II, Japanese Palaeolithic terminology has basically solidified, so we are able to give simple definitions of features and artifacts on which most researchers here agree. Representative examples and their types are shown in Figures 13.8–13.10.

In deciding the types and definitions to use, the terminology of a number of research groups was investigated and combined (Naganoken Buried Cultural Property Center 2000, 2004; Naganoken Nagatomachi Board of Education 2001; Miyazakiken Kawaminamicho Board of Education 2002; Shimaneken Board of Education 2008). When assigning a type to each artifact, its shape and estimated function were used, and where this proved impossible, shape alone was used. Researchers always feel conflicted when this sort of problem arises. Working in the lab, some archaeologists are very strict in their analysis and put a lot of thought into deciding on assigning a type to an artifact, while others interpret more broadly. Take, for example, a feature such as a flake cluster, which many will recognize as a result of human activity (stone gathering, preliminary working, tool manufacturing or use). The writer of the site monograph might simply see a scattering of flakes and chips, count every one, and report a much larger number than the clusters shown on the site map. Or, again, consider the trapezoids. During the Initial Period of the Upper Palaeolithic in Japan, this artifact was as important an index of Modern Human activity as the edge-ground adze, but one researcher will positively identify it as a trapezoid while another will call the same thing a backed point or even simply a flake. This is an illustration of the actual situation at sites where several people take charge, each with his own judgment.

### Definition of Features (See Table 13.4)

In archaeology, a feature is a trace of some usually non-movable human facility or activity. If you picked up all or part of the feature, its shape would disappear and its function become unrecognizable. Figure 13.7 gives several examples.

- Fist-sized pebble cluster (Figure 13.7, specimen 1). A 1–3 m flat circle of fist-sized rocks (0.3–1 kg) which may show evidence of burning, though many do not.
- Flake cluster (Figure 13.7, specimen 2). Conventionally this grouping was called a block or unit in Japan, but here we will call this lithic concentration of stone tools and flakes a cluster. Some clusters may be very small, only 0.3 m, but they may range up to circles 10 m in diameter, comprising a few stone tools, many stone flakes, and hundreds of chips. Those assumed to be full-fledged tool manufacturing sites may take the shape of ring of clusters.
- Areas of carbon concentration (Figure 13.7, specimen3). Bits of carbon from two to several millimeters in size and numbering from the 10s to 1,000 or more are found in one concentrated circular or oval-shaped area 0.3–3 m in diameter, evidence of wood being burned,

Analyzing Japanese Sites of the Upper Palaeolithic  **257**

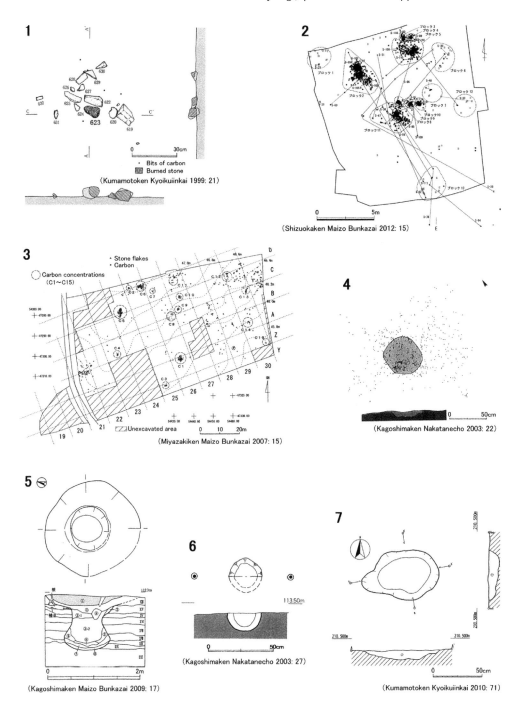

FIGURE 13.7  All types of features. **Fist-sized pebble cluster** (1): Only the shaded stone 623 was clearly burned; **Flake Clusters** (2): Small ring of flake clusters; **Areas of carbon concentration** (3): In a 50 × 100 m area, 15 carbon clusters were scattered; **Burned soil (hearth)** (4): In a 1.5 m area, burned soil is surrounded by bits of carbon; **Pit trap** (5): Bag-shaped pit type; **Small pit** (6): For storage? Tree hole?; **Shallow hole** (7): Use unknown. No carbon or burned soil.

though, oddly, burned earth is not usually found. Perhaps these places were used only briefly to cook something, for warmth, or for light.
- Burned soil (hearths) (Figure 13.7, specimen 4). Repeated burning in the same spot leaves burned soil and generally a large amount of charcoal. The burned area is usually 0.3–1.5 m in diameter on flat ground or in a shallow depression. While these areas are presumed to be cooking sites, it's impossible to judge whether the hearths were inside or outside a dwelling, though surely it's likely that people lived nearby.
- Pit traps (Figure 13.7, specimen 5). Presumably built to trap small- to medium-sized animals, these holes, viewed from the side, would look either straight-sided or bag-shaped. Typically they were 1–2 m long and 0.5–0.8 m across. Eighteen of these were found but only at a single site (Tachikiri). (After the Initial Period, many still larger pit traps for deer and wild boar were found. Located along game trails, they were often dug in series.)
- Small pits and shallow holes (Figure 13.7, specimens 6 and 7). Small pits 10–30 cm in diameter and 20–40 cm deep and shallow holes 0.3–1 m long and 20–30 cm deep and containing no carbon were probably originally built by different people for different purposes but are combined here for convenience. Both are too small and shallow for pit traps. We might conjecture that they were used for some kind of storage, though the small pits might have been left by the root balls of fallen trees. It has been speculated that depressions 2 m long and containing neither charcoal nor burned soil might have been used as sleeping places or possibly burial pits.

### *Definition of Artifacts (See Table 13.4)*

Artifacts are here divided into three main types, the Stone Implement Group (A), the Flaked Stone Tool Group (B), and the Stone Refuse Group (C).

The Stone Implement Group consists of natural stones that were processed into various useful items, such as:

1. Grindstones (Figure 13.8, specimen 8). Held in the hand and rubbed across a stone plate to crush something, these show polishing traces and abrasion marks. Many are spherical, fitting easily into the palm of the hand.
2. Pounding stones (Figure 13.8, specimens 9 and 10). Held in the hand and pounded against a stone anvil plate, these could have crushed things such as nuts and roots. Chips and microchips are often broken off the end. Most are cylindrical or spherical in shape.
3. Stone plates (Figure 13.8, specimen 11). Flat stones with shallow depressions, these were presumably used with grindstones and show the same polishing traces and abrasion marks. Observed carefully, some also show evidence of pounding.
4. Whetstones (Figure 13.8, specimen 12). Small enough to hold in one hand, these might have been used as a polishing or sharpening surface, perhaps to grind the edge of something like edge-ground adzes.
5. Anvil stones (Figure 13.8, specimen 13). Stones with a rough, flat surface used with pounding stones to crush food. Places where chips and microchips have broken away can be clearly seen.
6. Stone choppers (Figure 13.8, specimens 14 and 15). A round or flat pebble from which a piece has been struck away, leaving a blade-like section, is called a chopper, while one with two sides struck off is a chopping tool.

Analyzing Japanese Sites of the Upper Palaeolithic  259

**TABLE 13.4** Number of features and artifacts excavated from the Initial Period (39,000–34,000 cal BP) of the Upper Palaeolithic Age (39,000–16,000 cal BP) in Japan.

| | Site name* | Oldest cultural layer | Features | | | | | | Artifacts | | | | | | | | | | | | | | | | Stone refuse group | | | Raw ore |
|---|---|---|---|---|---|---|---|---|---|---|---|---|---|---|---|---|---|---|---|---|---|---|---|---|---|---|---|---|
| | | | | | | | | | Stone implement group | | | | | | Flaked stone tool group | | | | | | | | | | | | | |
| | | | | | | | | | | | | | | | Unworked Blades | | | Worked Blades | | | | | | | | | |
| | | | Fist-sized pebble cluster | Flake cluster | Areas of carbon concentration | Burned soil (Hearth) | Pit trap | Shallow hole, Small Pit | Grindstone | Pounding Stone | Stone Plate | Whetstone | Anvil Stone | Stone chopper | Backed point | Trapezoid | Blade | Drill | Edge-ground Adze | Chipped Adze | Scraper | Wedge-shaped Stone | Flakes and chips | Core | Natural stones | |
| 1 | Takaidohigashi | X | | | 26 | | | | | 3 | | | | 9 | 8 | 1 | | | 2 | 2 | 10 | | 153 | 14 | 9 | |
| 2 | Musashidai | Xb | | 3 | 8 | 2 | | | | 2 | | 1 | 1 | 2 | 1 | | | | 1 | 7 | 2 | | 116 | 12 | 7 | |
| 3 | Umenokizawa | Lower BB IV–Upper BBVI | 6 | 15 | 12 | | | | | 2 | | | | | | 4 | 9 | 2 | | 13 | 10 | 2 | 376 | 17 | 107 | |
| 4 | Fujiishi | BBVII (31) | | 5 | 3 | | | | | | | | | | 3 | 7 | 2 | | 1 | 2 | 1 | | 462 | 13 | 17 | |
| 5 | Nishiboru (b-1) | Surface BBVIO | | 14 | 1 | | | | | 3 | | | 1 | | 5 | 23 | | | 2 | 1 | 5 | 5 | 780 | 10 | 48 | |
| 6 | Idemaruyama | BBVII–SCIV | | 8 | 3 | | | | | | | | | | | 4 | | 2 | | | 1 | | 1304 | 18 | 23 | |
| 7 | Oiwakegun (No.1) | Layer 42 | 2 | 4 | | | | | | 6 | | | | | 2 | 26 | 3 | 2 | | | 5 | 1 | 824 | 63 | 4 | |
| 8 | Yamada | LowerXb–Upper XI | | 6 | 15 | 3 | | 2 | | | | | | 25 | | | | | 2 | | 3 | | 43 | 18 | 50 | |
| 9 | Setaikenohara | XVIc–XVIIa | 5 | 5 | 14 | | | 1 | | 3 | | | | | | 3 | 1 | | | | 4 | | 105 | 6 | 43 | |
| 10 | Ishinomotogun (Nos.8, 54, 55)** | Vg, VIa, VIb | 1 | 30 | 14 | 1 | | | 4 | 13 | | | 2 | | 1 | 11 | | 7 | 2 | | 40 | 2 | 3687 | 124 | 125 | |

(*Continued*)

**TABLE 13.4** (Continued)

| Site name* | Oldest cultural layer | Features |  |  |  |  |  | Artifacts |  |  |  |  |  | Flaked stone tool group |  |  |  |  |  |  | Stone refuse group |  | Raw ore |
|---|---|---|---|---|---|---|---|---|---|---|---|---|---|---|---|---|---|---|---|---|---|---|---|
|  |  |  |  |  |  |  |  | Stone implement group |  |  |  |  |  | Unworked Blades |  |  | Worked Blades |  |  |  |  |  |  |
|  |  | Fist-sized pebble cluster | Flake cluster | Areas of carbon concentration | Buried soil (Hearth) | Pit trap | Shallow hole, Small Pit | Grindstone | Pounding Stone | Stone Plate | Whetstone | Anvil Stone | Stone chopper | Backed point | Trapezoid | Blade | Drill | Edge-ground Adze | Chipped Adze | Scraper | Wedge-shaped Stone | Flakes and chips | Core | Natural stones |
| 11 Tachikiri | XIII | 1 | 15 | 18 | 32 | 18 | 15 | 27 |  | 5 | 4 | 1 | 9 |  | 2 |  |  | 3 | 3 | 2 |  | 27 | 3 | 5 |
| 12 Yokomine (C) | XIIIa | 3 |  | 13 |  |  |  | 3 |  |  |  |  |  |  | 1 |  |  |  | 1 | 3 |  | 114 | 1 |  |
| Sub-total |  | 18 | 105 | 127 | 38 | 18 | 18 | 34 | 55 | 5 | 5 | 5 | 45 | 20 | 82 | 15 | 13 | 13 | 29 | 86 | 10 | 7991 | 299 | 438 |
| Total |  | 324 |  |  |  |  |  | 149 |  |  |  |  |  | 268 |  |  |  |  |  |  |  | 8,290 |  | 438 |
|  |  | 3.4% |  |  |  |  |  | 1.6% |  |  |  |  |  | 2.8% |  |  |  |  |  |  |  | 87.5% |  | 4.6% |

* Reference monographs by site: 1. Takaidohigashi (1977a, 1977b); 2. Tokyoto Maizobunkazai (2004, 2010, 2014); 3. Shizuokaken Maizobunkazai (2009); 4. Shizuokaken Maizobunkazai (2010); 5. Shizuokaken Numazushi Kyoikuiinkai (1999); 6. Shizuokaken Numazushi Kyoikuiinkai (2011); 7. Naganoken Nagatomachi Kyoikuiinkai (2001); 8. Miyazakiken Maizobunkazai (2007); 9. Kumamotoken Kyoikuiinkai (2010); 10. Kumamotoken Kyoikuiinkai (1999, 2000, 2001); 11. Kagoshimaken Nakatanecho Kyoikuiinkai (1999, 2002, 20)3, 2012), Kagoshimaken Maizobunkazai (2009); 12. Kagoshimaken Minamitanecho Kyoikuiinkai (2000, 2005).

** Excavators Hirota and Ikeda of the Kumamotoken Kyoikuiinkai provided these figures but explained that the 2nd stone implement group from below the tephra in Area 55 was a mixture of ages due to erosion, so the author eliminated it from this table.

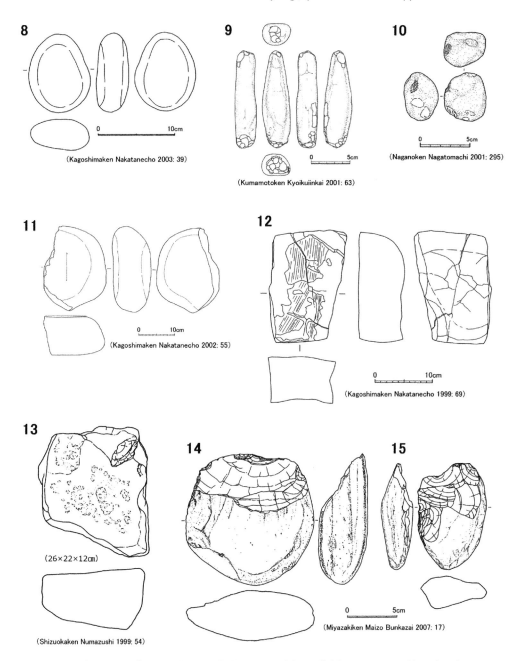

FIGURE 13.8  Stone Implement Group. **Grindstone** (8): Polishing traces and/or abrasion marks evident. Surface is smooth; **Pounding stones** (9, 10): Marks of chipping (9) and micro-chipping (10) can be seen; **Stone plate** (11): Upper surface very slightly depressed with polishing/abrasion marks; **Whetstone** (12): Polishing/abrasion marks evident. One side is smooth; **Anvil stone** (13): Working surface is pockmarked; **Stone choppers** (14, 15).

The Flaked Stone Tool Group represents flakes of stone that were struck off a piece of rock for use as tools. These can be subdivided into unworked blades (1), and worked blades (2).

Unworked blades had sharp broken edges that made it possible to use these just as is with no further processing of the blade, although other surfaces may be retouched. Examples are:

- Backed points (Figure 13.9, specimens 16 and 17). Long narrow pointed flakes, called "knives" in Japanese, sharp on one side and blunted on the other and sometimes retouched at the base. Though not found in large numbers, these are one of the representative tools of the Initial Period. They were most likely used as cutting tools, although it has been suggested that they could have been bound to pieces of wood to form spearheads. As time went on, the blades were modified in unique ways in different areas and were eventually replaced by microblades (circa 18,000 cal BP) as the end of the Upper Palaeolithic Age approached.
- Trapezoids (Figure 13.9, specimens 18–21). These were distinguished from backed points by their shorter length and characteristic shapes. Most were trapezoidal, giving the type its name, but a few were triangular or even pentagonal. Like backed points, these were retouched at the base and may have been bound to spears or used as arrowheads but could also have been used as knives (Yamaoka 2012, 2016). They, too, are representative tools of the Initial Period, but later they disappeared.
- Blades (Figure 13.9, specimens 22 and 23). Made by regular, repeated striking of a rock core, blades have long parallel left and right cutting edges. Some flakes might appear to be blades, but when made accidentally they are subtly different from tools made intentionally through repeated striking. They were used alone as tools but were also made into knives.
- Worked blades are blades on which the sharp cutting edge was modified in various ways to prepare them for different functions. Examples are:
- Drills (Figure 13.9, specimens 24 and 25). The top and sides were chipped to make a pointed tip. Except for the point, the rest of the tool was an easy-to-grip flat or rounded shape. Thinking of the tool tips in cross-section, they are mostly triangular or quadrangular. These might have been used to make holes in animal skins.
- Edge-ground adzes (Figure 13.9, specimens 26 and 27). The edge to be used, or occasionally the body of the tool, was ground or polished to make it sharp. These unique tools, often found at Initial Period sites, later disappeared entirely, only to turn up again much later at Jomon Age sites. Used by hand or bound to a wooden handle attached vertically to the blade, these could have been used for digging or to cut vines and fell small trees.
- Chipped adzes (Figure 13.9, specimens 28 and 29). Similar in shape to edge-ground adzes, some appear more axe-like. Again, they may have been used for digging or felling trees. The working edge was formed by chipping the stone, rather than grinding, though presumably the function of both types was the same. Specimen number 28, having a hilt, is very rare.
- Scrapers (Figure 13.10, specimens 30–32). The ends and sides of the flakes have been sharpened by chipping, making them suitable for cutting wood and bone, and also for scraping the meat from hides. The worked side of the tool makes some side scrapers and some end scrapers, but these are consolidated here.
- Wedge-shaped stones (Figure 13.10, specimens 33–35). These small tools have been chipped at both the top and bottom. If actually used as tools, we can imagine them being pounded to help split bones or large pieces of wood, but probably they are simply used-up cores from which flakes and blades were chipped from both ends until usable pieces could no longer be obtained.

Analyzing Japanese Sites of the Upper Palaeolithic  **263**

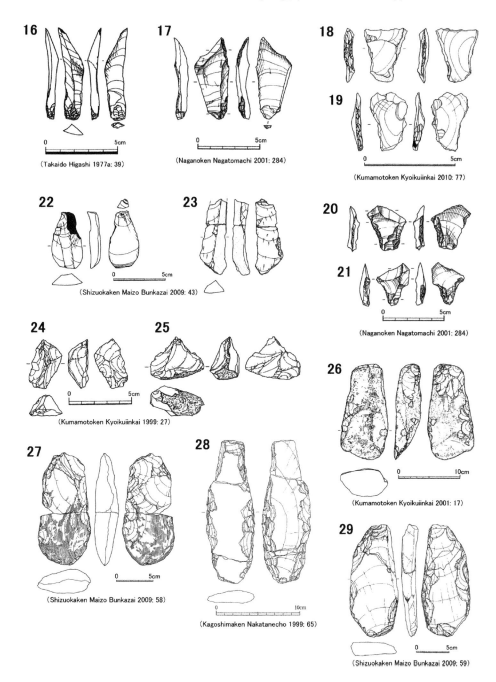

FIGURE 13.9    Flaked Stone Tool Group. **Backed points** (16, 17): Backs and bases are blunted; **Trapezoids** (18–21): Shorter backed points with sharp top and both sides of the bottom blunted; **Blades** (22, 23): Systematically flaked off a stone core; **Drills** (24, 25): Sectioned horizontally, the points are triangular or pyramidal. Used to make holes in animal skins; **Edge-ground adzes** (26, 27): First appeared in the Initial Period, then disappeared until the Jomon Age. Used in scraping and hoeing; **Chipped adzes** (28, 29): Same use as the polished type. In continuous use. 28, very rare, appears to have a hilt (for attachment?).

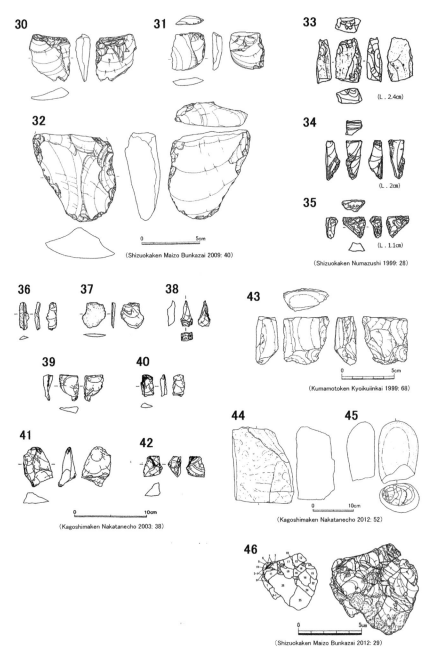

FIGURE 13.10  **Flaked** Stone Tools and Refuse Group. **Scrapers** (30–32): Ends and/or sides sharpened. Used in cleaning hides; **Wedge-shaped stones** (33–35): Possibly wedges or cores; **Flakes and chips** (36–42): Pieces struck off stone cores (flakes) or small stone bits (chips); **Core** (43): Stone in use for striking off tools or the leftover center; **Natural stones** (44, 45): Unworked stones for tool-making; **Reassembled core and its struck-off parts** (46): Carefully put together by a specialist over one month.

The Stone Refuse Group is leftover core stones and small flakes and chips broken off them. These artifacts can be described as:

- Flakes and chips (Figure 13.10, specimens 36–42). Pieces struck off a core of rock are called flakes and chips, and among these, some will be of irregular shape or overly small and of no use and become refuse.
- Cores (Figure 13.10, specimen 43). The original lump of rock from which flakes are struck off during tool-making eventually becomes too small to be of further use and is discarded.

Raw Ore is also found in sites (Table 13.4). This happened when pebbles and rocks were brought back from cliffsides and riverbanks as unworked raw materials for tool-making (Figure 13.10, specimens 44 and 45). An interesting elucidation of the tool-making process can be seen in specimen 46, which pictures a reassembled core using the flake tools that were made from it, a project that took a specialist one month.

All of the features and artifacts described here are listed by site in Table 13.4. When reading the site monographs for the 12 chosen sites, the definitions used above were generally those used by the authors.

## Stone Types

From what, exactly, did Modern Humans in Palaeolithic times in Japan make their stone tools? I investigated the types of stone identified in the Stone Implement Group, Flaked Stone Tool Group, Stone Refuse Group, and Raw Ore (Natural Stones) for all the artifacts, plus the fist-sized pebbles and flake clusters among the features, excavated from the 12 sites. The artifacts from the Stone Implement Group were scarce to start with, so when even a single item was found and identified, that was considered worth recording. Here and there in Table 13.5, stone names are enclosed in boxes or underlined. These markings signify, respectively, extremely numerous or numerous artifacts of that type of stone to distinguish them quantitatively from types of fewer numbers, which are unmarked. For comparison purposes, according to my judgment, in place of the very large actual numbers, for "extremely numerous" 3 points were assigned, for "numerous" 2 points, and for "fewer" 1 point. This merely serves to indicate relative stone types for a particular artifact within a given site, however, not a comparison with other artifacts or sites.

For example, for the flake clusters found at three sites, chert was outlined as particularly numerous at one site and hornfels at two, for 3 points each, while hornfels and obsidian were underlined as somewhat less numerous at two sites (2 points each). Following the flake cluster line to the Points column on the right, we can see the cluster point numbers: hornfels 8, obsidian 3, chert 3, and shale, siltstone, and tuff 1 each.

Adding up the Total point numbers for stone types used in all the artifacts in the table, we see that obsidian has 46 points, hornfels 39, sandstone 39, and andesite 33, making these the "top four" choices for features, implements, and tools during the Initial Period. Each type was chosen for being the best "fit" for the object being created and also for being relatively easy to obtain.

Breaking this down by group, for the three stone Features, hornfels and sandstone were the most numerous. Under Artifacts, in the Stone Implement Group sandstone, andesite, and hornfels were the most widely used. In the Flaked Tool Group obsidian came first, followed by hornfels, andesite, and tuff. Stone Refuse was chiefly composed of obsidian, hornfels, shale, and sandstone. We will come back to these overall results.

266  Takeshi Ueki

TABLE 13.5 Identifying types of Stone used by site in features and artifacts from the Initial Period of the Upper Palaeolithic Age in Japan.

| Features, artifacts | Site name | Takaido higashi | Musashidai | Umenokizawa | Fujishi | Nishiboru (b-1) | Idemaruyama | Oiwakegun (No.1) | Yamada | Setaikenohara | Ishimomotogun (Nos. 8, 54, 55) | Tachikiri | Yokomine (c) | Points* |
|---|---|---|---|---|---|---|---|---|---|---|---|---|---|---|
| Features | Fist-sized Pebble Cluster | | | | | | | | sandstone | | sandstone | Sandstone | | sandstone (5) |
| | Flake Cluster | | | chert hornfels | hornfels obsidian, siltstone | | hornfels shale, obsidian, tuff | | | | | | | hornfels (8), obsidian (3), chert (3), shale (1), siltstone (1), tuff (1) |
| | Stones Found in a Hearth | | | | | | | | | | | | | andesite (3) |
| Artifacts (1) (Stone Implements) | Grindstone | | | | | sandstone | | | | | andesite, granite | sandstone | | sandstone (3), andesite (1), granite (1) |
| | Pounding Stone | | | sandstone, andesite | | | | andesite sandstone | | | andesite, sandstone | sandstone | sandstone | sandstone (8), andesite (5) |
| | Stone Plate | | | | | | | | | | | sandstone | | sandstone (3) |
| | Whetstone | | | andesite | | | | | | | | sandstone | | sandstone (2), andesite (1) |
| | Anvil Stone | | | | | andesite | | | | | andesite | sandstone | | andesite (2), sandstone (1) |
| | Stone Chopper | andesite, sandstone, quartzite** | | | | | | | | hornfels sandstone | | sandstone | sandstone | sandstone (4), hornfels (4), andesite (1) |

(*Continued*)

## TABLE 13.5 (Continued)

| Features, artifacts | Site name | Takaido higashi | Musashidai | Umenokizawa | Fujishi | Nishiboru (b-1) | Idemaruyama | Oiwakegun (No.1) | Yamada | Setaikenohara | Ishinomotogun (Nos. 8, 54, 55) | Tachihiri | Yokomine (c) | Points* |
|---|---|---|---|---|---|---|---|---|---|---|---|---|---|---|
| Flaked Stone Tools (Artifacts (2)) | Backed Point | quartzite**, slate | chert | | obsidian | Obsidian | | Obsidian | | | | | | obsidian (3), chert (1), hornfels (1), slate (1) |
| | Trapezoid | quartzite** | | obsidian | obsidian | obsidian, shale | hornfels, obsidian | obsidian | | obsidian, tuff | andesite | | sandstone | obsidian (8), andesite (3), hornfels (2), sandstone (1), shale (1), tuff (1) |
| | Blade | | | | | | obsidian, hornfels | | | obsidian | | | | obsidian (2), hornfels (1) |
| | Drill | | | obsidian | | | obsidian | Obsidian | | | andesite | | | obsidian (3), andesite (1) |
| | Edge-ground Adze | slate, sandstone | tuff | tuff | tuff | tuff | | | | | andesite, chert | sandstone, hornfels | | tuff (6), sandstone (2), chert (1), slate (1), andesite (1), hornfels (1) |
| | Chipped Adze | sandstone | hornfels | peridotite, tuff | andesite, hornfels | | | | | | | shale | shale | hornfels (2), shale (2), tuff (1), peridotite (1), andesite (1), sandstone (1) |
| | Scraper | quartzite** | | obsidian, agate, tuff | | obsidian | hornfels | obsidian | rhyolite | | **andesite** chert | shale | sandstone | andesite (3), obsidian (3), hornfels (3), chert(1), rhyolite (1), shale (1), agate (1), tuff (1), sandstone (1) |
| | Wedge-shaped Stone | | | | | obsidian | | obsidian | | | obsidian | | | obsidian (3) |

*(Continued)*

**TABLE 13.5** (Continued)

| Features, artifacts | | Site name | Takaido higashi | Musashidai | Umenokizawa | Fujishi | Nishiboru (b-1) | Idemaruyama | Oiwakegun (No. 1) | Yamada | Setaikenohara | Ishinomotogun (Nos. 8, 54, 55) | Tachitiri | Yokomine (c) | Points* |
|---|---|---|---|---|---|---|---|---|---|---|---|---|---|---|---|
| Stone Refuse Artifacts (3) | | Flakes and Chips | sandstone, quartzite**, andesite | **chert**, hornfels, shale | hornfels, **obsidian** tuff, andesite | **obsidian hornfels** siltstone | **shale obsidian** quartzite** | obsidian, **hornfels** shale | **obsidian** | | **obsidian** | **andesite** tuff, chert, obsidian | sandstone, shale | **sandstone** | obsidian (17), hornfels (12), shale (8), sandstone (5), andesite (5), chert (4), tuff (2), siltstone (1) |
| | | Core | sandstone | | obsidian, hornfels | hornfels, obsidian | shale, obsidian, quartzite** | hornfels | | hornfels | | **andesite** chert, obsidian | sandstone, **shale** | sandstone | hornfels (5), obsidian (5), andesite (3) sandstone (3), shale (2), chert (1) |
| Raw Ore | | Natural Stones | | | | | **andesite** | beach pebble | | | | | sandstone | | andesite (3), sandstone (2), beach pebble (2) |
| | | | | | | | | | | | | | | Total | obsidian (46), sandstone (40), hornfels (39), andesite (33), etc. |

\* Numerical rating by stone type: in the table, bold (very many) = 3 points, underlining (many) = 2 points, no mark (few) = 1 point.
In the final column, Points, quartzite and hornfels are counted as hornfels.
\*\* Numerical rating by stone type: in the table, bold (very many) = 3 points, underlining (many) = 2 points, no mark (few) = 1 point.

*Cluster Analysis Based on Features and Stone Artifacts*

After reading the monographs describing the excavations of all 12 sites, I counted the total excavated features and artifacts, divided them by type, and listed them in Table 13.4. My first thought was to use this data for cluster analysis to sub-divide the sites into smaller groups based on their use (residential, tool-making, etc.), or by topography (area chosen, elevation), or by local climate (cold, warm) and create micro-models based on these distinctions. Should this prove impossible, macro-models using data from all the sites combined was my second choice, which would result in a macro-model for the Initial Period of the Upper Palaeolithic Age in Japan.

Based on the total numbers for each type of feature, artifact, and raw ore for the 12 sites, cluster analysis of this raw data was tried. Going back to Table 13.4 we can see that there are six variables under Features, six under Stone Implements, eight under Flaked Stone Tools, two under Stone Refuse, and one under Raw Ore (Natural Stones) for a total of twenty-three variables. However, the character of the refuse and natural stones is different. They are not (or not yet) implements or tools, and the flakes and chips in particular occur in exceedingly large numbers that would excessively skew the results, so, as explained below, the variables from this "leftover group" were later excluded from the analysis.

In addition, analysis following standardization of 23 and 20 data values was tried, with the results shown in Figures 13.11–13.14. Why four analyzes? I hoped to find results of significance by making increasingly smaller groups. The method used was Ward's Method based on Euclidean square distance in cluster analysis from SPSS (Statistical Package for the Social Sciences), which makes it easy to clearly discern small groups.

*Results of Cluster Analysis*

The total data values for all 23 variables for the 12 sites shown in Table 13.4 were used for cluster analysis, with the results shown in the dendrogram in Figure 13.11. A heavy vertical line was drawn by the author's judgment at two on the upper scale to create three groups where this line crossed the horizontal lines. A rather interesting geographical result is shown in this dendrogram. Group 2 sites (5, 7, 3, 4, and 6) on the lower half of the figure are all located in present-day Shizuoka or Nagano Prefectures, making a neat geographical subset (see Figure 13.6 for site location). By contrast, Group 1 sites stretch from Tokyo to Miyazaki, Kumamoto, all the way down to subtropical Tanegashima Island, showing no geographical or climatic congruence whatever (see Figure 13.4 for climate zones). In Group 3, Ishinomotogun sites in Kumamoto Prefecture (10), are far from all 11 other sites in the figure, possibly due to the very large stone refuse group found there (see Table 13.4). Overall, Figure 13.11's three groups unfortunately do not show any significant differences.

In Figure 13.12, a dendrogram minus the 3 variables from the "leftover group" (stone refuse and ore), we can see the analysis of total data values for 20 variables from Table 13.4. I considered where to draw the arbitrary line, selected distance 5, and this divided the 12 sites into 5 groups for analysis. The dendrogram shows no particular geographical or climatic grouping of sites. Similarly, sites 5–7 and 10, which appear to be toolmaking sites, did not form a group, so again, no significant groups emerged from this analysis.

In Figure 13.13 I went back to using all 23 variables, this time with standardized data values, the average set at 0 and standard deviation at 1. This helped to remove the bias created by the excessively high numbers in the refuse/ore group; however, this also created the demerit of

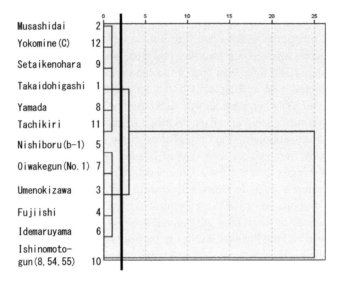

FIGURE 13.11   Dendrogram of total data values.

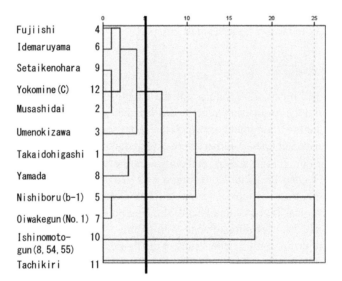

FIGURE 13.12   Dendrogram of data values for 20 variables in Table 13.4, excluding stone refuse and raw ore (Ward's Method).

canceling out the effect each variable contributes to the total data. Moving the vertical line to four resulted in the creation of six groups. No geographical or climatic confluence was seen for Groups 1, 2, and 3, and once again possible toolmaking sites 10 and 5–7 did not form a group.

Again, eliminating the three variables for refuse/ore and using standardized data values for the remaining 20, Figure 13.14 gives the dendrogram resulting. The same plus and minus effects from standardization resulted as in Figure 13.13. The vertical line was moved to five, resulting

Analyzing Japanese Sites of the Upper Palaeolithic   271

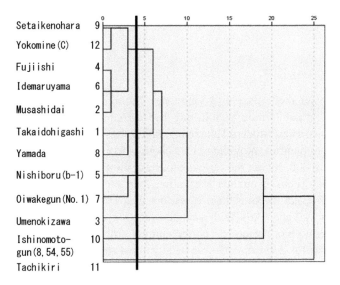

**FIGURE 13.13**   Dendrogram of standardized values for 23 variables in Table 13.4 (Ward's Method).

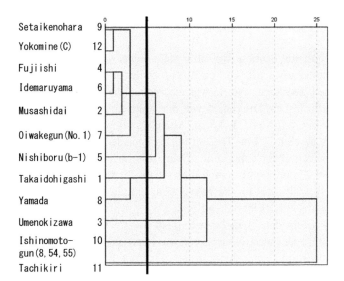

**FIGURE 13.14**   Dendrogram of standardized values for 20 variables in Table 13.4, excluding stone. Refuse and raw ore (Ward's Method).

in the creation of six groups. Disappointingly, no significant groups by location or climate topography emerged from the analysis.

I re-examined these four results, but it was clear that no meaningful small groups were revealed, not by geography, climate, or function of the sites. This meant, of course, that for this data set no group micro-models could be created. I then turned my attention to a macro approach instead. Combining the data from all 12 sites, macro-models for features and stone tools for the Japanese Archipelago during the Initial Period of the Upper Palaeolithic Age could be created.

## Macro-Model Construction

These comprehensive models serve two purposes. Naturally one is to elucidate the combined results of these 12 Initial Period sites fulfilling the four requirements for study. Second is to create a model for the earliest Modern Human habitation sites in Japan that can be compared with such sites in other countries, providing clues about where these Modern Humans came from. Starting with Table 13.6, we can see various aspects of the archaeological investigation of all the sites and the models focusing on their excavation, location, and climate/vegetation.

First, I looked at, not the sites themselves, but who excavated them, why, and how extensively (see Tables 13.2 and 13.6). With a single exception, the who were prefectural or municipal boards of education or prefectural buried cultural property investigation centers set up by them. Their reasons for excavating were typically either road construction and maintenance or the building of public facilities. Average excavated area was an extensive 4,250 m². One thing made clear is that for open land sites in Japan, particularly for residential sites, in order to grasp the whole picture, several thousand square meters or, ideally, up to 10,000 m² need to be investigated. The reason for this is the presence of multi-function sites that combine living areas with toolmaking, where, for example, stone is mined or gathered, broken into useful pieces, and also fashioned into implements. To understand the nature of such sites, large-scale excavations are needed.

Next, I looked at site location from four standpoints (see Tables 13.3 and 13.6). The first was elevation. These early settlers primarily chose sites at the base of mountains or along river terraces. Only one (Oiwakegun No. 1) was upstream at high elevation, and this pushed up the average elevation to 221 m. Digging down, the depth to the lowest, oldest cultural layer, the second factor considered, was 1.2–4.5 m. Again, the depth of the single high-elevation site raised the average depth to 2.4 m. The third thing considered was the distance from the site to the nearest fresh water, either a spring or a river. This varied widely from 15 to 1,800 m, for an average distance of 379 m. Finally, combining the results from three locales, the lowest cultural layer was at X (especially Xb) for the Tokyo area, straddled several layers (but chiefly BBVII) for Shizuoka, and was at XIII for Tanegashima.

One caution about the data on distance to fresh water is that this is the distance today. Given that the strategy of Upper Palaeolithic people was to construct their living sites in the vicinity of fresh water, we may surmise that sites currently far from this were once located near to springs, ponds, or lakes that existed at the time but have since disappeared.

For the next environmental factor, types of vegetation, I first intended to identify the genus and species of plant evidence from the lowest cultural layer and classify this as belonging to plants from subarctic coniferous, coniferous, mixed coniferous, and broad-leaved or evergreen broad-leaved forests. Plant seeds are not so easily sorted, however, so instead I listed the five climate zones for Palaeolithic Japan (Cold, Mainly Cold (–Warm), Warm–Cold, Mainly Warm (–Cold), and Warm, and the species that thrived there (Ryuji Matsuda, personal communication, 2018).

Broadly speaking, we can say that in the Warm-to-Cold Zone evergreen and deciduous broad-leaved trees flourished. In the Mainly Warm Zone deciduous broad-leaved trees predominated. From the Cold up to the Subarctic Zones there were only a very few coniferous trees.

**TABLE 13.6** Archeological investigation of Initial Period Upper Palaeolithic sites in Japan by investigating institute location, and vegetation.

| A. Investigating group | Summary of 12 chosen sites | Excavation |
|---|---|---|
| Investigating Institute | Prefectural/Municipal Board of Education or Prefectural Buried Cultural Property Investigation Center 11 cases, Private Group 1 case | Board of Education or Buried Cultural Property Investigation Center |
| Excavation Reason | Road maintenance (national roads, expressways, city streets, farm roads) 7 cases; incinerator, medical center, park, dam, National Athletic Meet site, 1 case each | Road construction and maintenance or public facility construction |
| Excavated Area | 1,000–9,000 m² | Average 4250 m² |
| *B. Site Location* | *Summary of 12 chosen sites* | *Location* |
| Elevation | Most at the base of mountains or on river terraces, one on a high mountain riverside | Average 221 m |
| Depth | Lowest (oldest) cultural layer, 1.2–4.5 m from the surface | Average 2.4 m |
| Distance to Fresh Water | 15–1,800 m to a river or spring | Average 379 m |
| Lowest Cultural Layer | All, except for Umenokizawa, which is the second lowest | Tokyo: Xb, Shizuoka Pref.: BBVII, Tanegashima I.: XIII |
| *C. Climate Zone* | *Floral Types** | *Tree Types* |
| Cold Zone | Cupressaceae hamaecyparis pisifera, Fagaceae Fagus, Ostrya japonica | In the five climate zones shown, the most types of evergreen and deciduous broad-leaved trees were found in the Warm Zone–Cold Zone. Next in types of deciduous broad-leaved trees was the Warm Zone. (Almost no coniferous trees were found in the Subarctic–Cold Zone so these are not included.) During the last glacial age, warming/cooling climate oscillations continued until the LGM, but during the Initial Period of the Upper Palaeolithic (39,000–34,000 cal BP) mainly broad-leaved species still existed. In forest floor undergrowth, in damp areas, and along rivers, sasa, bamboo, and other plants flourished. |
| Mainly Cold (~Warm) | Oleaceae Fraxinus japonica |  |
| Warm Zone~Cold Zone | Cupressaceae Taxodioideae Cryptomeria japonica, Pinaceae Pinus, Fagaceae Quercus, Cannabaceae Celtis, Ulmaceae Zelkova, Araliaceae Aralia, Araliaceae Eleutherococcus, Fabaceae Wistaria, Poaceae Bambusoideae Sasa nipponica |  |
| Mainly Warm (~Cold) | Lauraceae |  |
| Warm Zone | Hamamelidaceae Distylium, Poaceae Arundinoideae Arundineae Arundo, Poaceae Panicoideae Paniceae Panicum, Poaceae Panicoideae Andropogoneae Schizachyrium, Poaceae Pleioblastus simonii Nakai, Poaceae Bambusodae Sasa veitchii<br>Faunal Types<br>Not found (Except in Okinawa) |  |

* With the exception of Oiwakegun No. 1 and Umenokizawa sites (both no data available), all floral types are those found in the oldest cultural layer. Data on flora from pits were not used unless clearly identified as coming from the oldest cultural layer. The scientific plant names and their climate zones were provided by Ryūji Matsuda of the Paleoenvironmental Research Center.

In this age preceding the LGM, the climate fluctuated strikingly between warm and cold, yet it appears that Warm, Mainly Warm (~Cold), and Warm-to-Cold vegetation continued to grow. On the forest floor Sasa bamboo and in damp areas and along riverbanks Andropogon grasses and Pleioblastus bamboos flourished.

Looking at an overview of Features, we can see the very large numbers of flake clusters and areas of carbon concentration unearthed (see Tables 13.4, 13.5, and 13.7). Considerably fewer areas of burned soil were also found. Fist-sized pebble clusters, pit traps, shallow holes, and small pits were few. Fist-sized pebbles, the stone flakes in clusters, and some stones found in hearths were made primarily of hornfels, sandstone, andesite, and chert.

All the many Stone Artifacts were divided into two main subgroups: Stone Implements, and Flaked Stone Tools plus Refuse. Stone Implements included pounding stones and choppers that were found in moderately large numbers. Quite a few grindstones were excavated, as well. Other implements like plates, whetstones, and anvils were found only rarely (see Tables 13.4 and 13.7). These tables also showed that among Flaked Stone Tools, both worked and unworked, scrapers were found in the largest numbers, an expected result, but surprisingly trapezoids turned up in about the same numbers. Chipped adzes and edge-ground adzes have been thought to differ in function, the former possibly used in digging and the latter for cutting vines and trees or scraping wood, though this is simply conjecture. It may be best to think of these together as two versions of the same tool. Backed points, which would have served as very important tools, were found in surprisingly small numbers, and blades, drills, and wedge-shaped stones were even fewer. In the Refuse, the overwhelming number of chips and flakes is immediately apparent. Cores, too, were very numerous. As the Refuse resulted from the making of all these tools, these findings are easily predictable.

Summing up, in Model 1, Features and Artifacts for the Initial Period of the Upper Palaeolithic in Japan (see Figure 13.15 and Table 13.4), we can see diagrammed the percentages by group for all the features and artifacts plus raw ore (natural stones), based on the actual numbers found.

Finally, in Model 2, the synthesized model, the overall picture of site characteristics (elevation, depth, distance to fresh water) and the climate and vegetation of the time period in question are given, followed by the types and composition of the all-important artifacts of the time, stone tools. The raw materials used to make the artifacts of the Stone Implement Group are identified (see Table 13.8) Sandstone was by far the greatest choice, followed by andesite and hornfels. These raw stones would have been easy to find in easily transported sizes along rivers and estuaries. Slabs of sandstone and andesite with flat surfaces would also have been relatively easy to locate. By scaling cliff faces and riverbanks, chunks of hornfels could be picked out. For the raw materials for Flaked Tools and the Refuse that resulted from their manufacture, obsidian, hornfels, shale, and andesite were favorites, but a large number of other types were used on occasion, including sandstone, tuff, chert, and very occasionally slate, siltstone, agate, peridotite, and rhyolite.

In the creation of all these stone implements and tools, we can sense the basic premises of "suitable materials for suitable use" and "local production for local use." People migrating into a new area would of course be first concerned with food and firewood. Soon, however, men and women both would very likely begin an eager search for raw materials with which to make the tools that supported their lives. We can picture them locating sources of rock, splitting off movable chunks, and quickly assessing their suitability for the uses they had in mind. Obsidian and hornfels, flaked edges of which are very sharp, would certainly be seen as useful for cutting,

TABLE 13.7  Types and raw materials of features and artifacts from 12 oldest sites.

| Features and artifacts | No. found → ranking* | Features |
|---|---|---|
| D. Features |  | Areas of carbon concentration and flake clusters were very numerous, followed by burned soil, while pit traps, shallow holes, and small pits were rare. Fist-sized pebbles, flake clusters, and stone implements unearthed from hearths (burned soil) were primarily hornfels, sandstone, andesite, obsidian, and chert. |
| Fist-sized Pebble Cluster | 18 → 2 |  |
| Flake Cluster | 105 → 5 |  |
| Areas of Carbon Concentration | 127 → 5 |  |
| Burned Soil(Hearth) | 38 → 3 |  |
| Pit Trap | 18 → 2 |  |
| Shallow Hole, Small Pit | 18 → 2 |  |
| Total | 324 (3.4%) |  |
| E. Artifacts (1) |  | Stone Implements |
| Stone Implement Group |  | Pounding stones and stone choppers were the most numerous, followed by grindstones, while stone plates, whetstones, and anvil stones were rare. |
| Grindstone | 34 → 3 | Stone Implement Raw Materials |
| Pounding Stone | 55 → 5 | Sandstone, andesite, and hornfels were the most used. These probably came from riverbeds, estuaries, and cliffs. |
| Stone Plate | 5 → 1 |  |
| Whetstone | 5 → 1 |  |
| Anvil Stone | 5 → 1 |  |
| Stone Chopper | 45 → 4 |  |
| Total | 149 (1.6%) |  |

(*Continued*)

**TABLE 13.7** (*Continued*)

| Features and artifacts | No. found → ranking* | Features | |
|---|---|---|---|
| F. Artifacts (2) | | Flaked Tools and Refuse | Flaked Tool Raw Materials |
| Flaked Stone Tool Group | | For flaked stone tools, both unworked and worked, trapezoids (unworked) and scrapers (worked) were the most numerous, followed by backed points (unworked) and chipped adzes (worked). Blades (unworked) and drills, edge-ground adzes, and wedge-shaped stones (worked) were more rare. Stone refuse comprised thousands of flakes and chips and several hundred leftover cores. | Among unworked blades, worked blades, and refuse, obsidian, hornfels, andesite, sandstone, and tuff were the most common. Suitable materials/suitable tools: For example, sandstone and andesite were particularly suitable for the group of stone implements, while obsidian and hornfels, which when split have extremely sharp edges, were best for various blades. Local production/local use: Present-day Nagano and Shizuoka where obsidian was easily found had a great many implements made from that, while Tanegashima Island, where obsidian does not occur, made great use of local sandstone, while some adzes were made of shale. |
| Unworked Blades | | | |
| Backed Point | 20 → 2 | | |
| Trapezoid | 82 → 5 | | |
| Blade | 15 → 1 | | |
| Worked Blades | | | |
| Drill | 13 → 1 | | |
| Edge-ground Adze | 13 → 1 | | |
| Chipped Adze | 29 → 3 | | |
| Scraper | 86 → 5 | | |
| Wedge-shaped Stone | 10 → 1 | | |
| Total | 268 (2.8%) | | |
| G. Artifacts (3) | | | |
| Stone Refuse Group | | | |
| Flakes and Chips | 7991 → 5 | | |
| Core | 299 → 3 | | |
| Total | 8290 (87.5%) | | |
| H. Raw Ore | | Natural stones were more numerous than anticipated. | Andesite and sandstone |
| Natural Stones | 438 → 4 | | |
| Total | 438 (4.6%) | | |

* For the four groups of features and artifacts plus raw ore, the numbers of items found were ranked 5 to 1 within each group meaning very many, many, common amounts, rare, and very rare. The percentages following each total are percentages of the total items found in all five groups (9,469).

TABLE 13.8  Model 2. Synthesized model of 12 sites from the Initial Period of the Upper Palaeolithic of the Japanese Archipelago.

| Samples | Twelve upper palaeolithic sites are chosen which fulfilled our criteria for comparative analysis. These are the oldest sites in the Japanese Archipelago. |
|---|---|
| Time period | From 39,000 cal BP to 34,000 cal BP |
| Site elevation, depth, distance to fresh water | Aver. 221 m, aver. 2.4 m, aver.379 m |
| Climate zone | All sites belong to "Warm Zone–Cold Zone" and "Warm Zone." Warm Zone–Cold Zone has evergreen and deciduous broad-leaved trees and Warm Zone has deciduous broad-leaved trees. |
| Features | Flake clusters, areas of carbon concentration, burned soil(hearths), etc. |
| Artifacts (1) | |
|   stone implements | Pounding stones, choppers, grindstones, etc. |
|   stone implement materials | Sandstone, andesite, hornfels, etc. |
| Artifacts (2) | |
|   flaked stone tool group | Scrapers, trapezoids, chipped adzes, etc. |
| Artifacts (3) | |
|   stone refuse group | Flakes and chips, cores |
| Raw ore | Natural stones |

stripping, and scraping activities and in food preparation, which explains their large numbers among the flaked tools. Many types of obsidian, each mined in just a few places, crisscrossed wide areas via human hands in trade for things like salt and foods not locally available, to elicit favor, and most likely as a bride price. For stone implements like grindstones and pounding stones, the rough surface of easily obtainable sandstone and andesite saw suitable use in crushing and grinding foods.

As for local production, certain areas made good use of the types of stone available. For example, the Tokai and Chubu areas of central Honshu were fortunate to have several obsidian-producing areas, and this, as mentioned, was the first-choice material for flaked toolmaking. Hard metamorphic rock had multiple uses, and the easily obtainable hornfels was also popular. On southern islands like Tanegashima where obsidian was not found, sandstone from rivers and beaches was at hand and used not only for stone implements but also for flaked tools. Shale, harder than sandstone, was also carefully selected and worked into adzes and scrapers, further examples of finding suitable uses for local materials.

Presuming the same type of large-scale excavations continue hereafter in the archipelago, how interesting it would be to compare the similarities and differences of these Initial Period results with those from the Late and Terminal stages of the Upper Palaeolithic Age in Japan. Even more interesting would be the construction of a percentage figure comparing circa 40,000 BP findings from the Korean Peninsula, Russia, and China. The resulting analysis would help us to see ever more clearly the movements of Modern Humans into this part of the world. I hope someone will undertake this!

## Summary and Future Research

As far as we know now, Modern Humans reached Japan in about 39,000 cal BP, which marked the beginning of the Upper Palaeolithic Age in the archipelago, an era that continued for some

23,000 years until the start of the Jomon Age in about 16,000 cal BP. How they got here has been widely debated by archaeologists, but as I have mentioned, three main routes – some would say six (Nakazawa 2017) – have been put forward. The northern route from Siberia via Sakhalin Island into Hokkaido seems the least likely as no Initial Period Upper Palaeolithic sites have yet been found there. The southern route from Okinawa via the Amami Islands into southern Kyushu is so far supported by only a single Initial Period site (Yamashitacho Cave No. 1) on the main island of Okinawa, but the probable link through the Amami chain to Tanegashima and Kyushu is hard to deny. Still, with other supporting Initial Period evidence unavailable, the southern route, too, is problematical. At the present time, it's easiest to picture most of those earliest people building small canoes and coming across from the Korean Peninsula to northern Kyushu and spreading out from there south throughout Kyushu and northeast into Honshu. As for the islands south of Kyushu, it now seems reasonable to assume that Upper Palaeolithic people reached there from Taiwan, southern China, or possibly from the Philippines.

Since people of that time followed a hunter-gatherer lifestyle, they were surely directly affected by the natural conditions they encountered in their migrations. It therefore seemed logical to try to recreate something of these effects by considering the environment they faced. From the standpoint of climate, the time of their first arrival (39,000 cal BP) roughly coincided with the latter half of the Last Glacial Period (approximately 70,000–15,000 BP) when temperatures were still somewhat warm, though rising and falling toward the period of maximum coldness at the LGM between 28,000 and 24,000 cal BP, according to ice cores.

As we have noted, sea levels continued falling, reaching 100–120 m below present levels at the LGM, 6,000 years after the end of the Initial Period. At that time, standing on the southern shores of the Korean Peninsula, shadowy outlines of Kyushu in the distance would have been visible. New food sources beckoned (animals, plants, fruits, and nuts), and once again we can imagine the ever-restless *H. sapiens* setting out to find them. At that time they may also have taken advantage of the sea ice bridge connecting Siberia and Hokkaido, a supposition supported by the many Upper Palaeolithic sites that appeared in Hokkaido from then on.

In Japan today there are 111 active volcanoes. Over the long course of natural history, the effects of repeated eruptions were inescapable. Areas near and far would be showered with tephra. Since the dates of tephra have been mostly established, cultural layers excavated from above or below tephra layers can also be estimated. The widely distributed Aira Tephra (AT approximately 30,000–29,000 cal BP), found over the whole country except eastern Hokkaido and across the sea covering most of the Korean Peninsula, is particularly useful as everything excavated from below it includes the time that most concerns us, the early half of the Upper Palaeolithic Age. For archaeologists, AT provides a basic index for dividing the age, which immediately shows if the site being excavated dates from the early or the latter half.

In this chapter I attempted to construct some micro-models of the features and artifacts left behind by the earliest Modern Humans to reach this part of the world. Concentrating on the first 5,000 years after their arrival, a time I have designated the Initial Period, I selected for analysis sites from all over the country that had been dated by $^{14}$C to this time period. With a view to doing quantitative analysis of my chosen sites, I selected 12 that fulfilled four criteria that made them suitable for this approach.

Next I checked to see if there were data that suggested ways to divide the 12 sites into smaller groups. All excavated features and artifacts were listed up in Table 13.4, and using SPSS I did a cluster analysis of this data. Disappointingly, divisions by site character (living site, mining site, toolmaking site, hunting/dressing site), area, climate, and elevation were impossible to discern (see Figures 13.12–13.14). This ruled out making micro-models based on meaningful sub-groups.

With that method eliminated, I turned my sights to making macro-models for the 12 sites together. Sophisticated analysis is not particularly needed for such consolidated data, so simple addition and subtraction sufficed. I looked at the excavating groups, site elevation and distance to fresh water, climate, and vegetation of the time (Table 13.6), and the total numbers of features, stone implements, and flaked tools and refuse and their order of frequency (Table 13.7). From these I made Model 1, a pie graph showing at a glance the percentages of groups of features, artifacts, refuse, and natural stones/ore (Figure 13.15). Model 2 summarized all of the above for the 12 sites (Table 13.8).

Archaeological excavations continue apace every year in Japan. I would like to put forward several suggestions to make our picture of the Initial Period clearer. First would be to continue adding to Table 13.4 presented here as monographs for other Initial Period sites fulfilling the four conditions are published, leading to more raw data and more fruitful cluster analyzes. Second would be to create models to distinguish the functional differences of open land sites requiring large-scale excavations. It will be necessary to have more monographs in order to grasp the total picture of such sites.

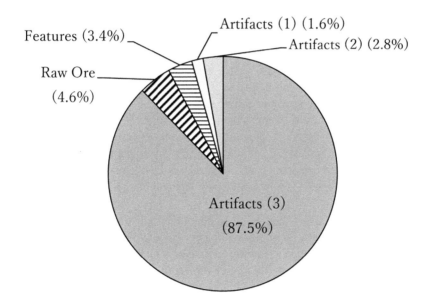

| Artifacts (1) | Stone Implement Group: Pounding Stones, Stone Choppers, Grindstones, etc. |
| Artifacts (2) | Flaked Stone Tool Group: Scrapers, Trapezoids, Chipped Adzes, Backed Points, Blades, Drills, Edge-ground Adzes, etc. |
| Artifacts (3) | Stone Refuse Group: Flakes and Chips, Cores |
| Raw Ore | Natural Stones |
| Features | Areas of Carbon Concentration, Flake Clusters, Burned Soil (Hearths), etc. |

FIGURE 13.15  Model 1. Frequency of occurrence of features and artifacts from the Initial Period of the Upper Paleolithic in Japan.

At this point, though, I would point out one stumbling block to such site differentiation, and that is the complexity of many sites. One may appear to be a stone mining site but also a rough shaping site. Another shows characteristics of a base camp or living site, yet also has evidence of large-scale toolmaking. A third appears to have been a hunting camp but also a meat butchering site. Among the 12 sites considered here, the artifacts suggested that some might have been toolmaking sites. That is particularly true of the group of sites at Ishinomotogun in central Kyushu, where a notable number of flake clusters and a huge number of scattered flakes and chips were found. Yet if the area were more extensively excavated, might we not find right next to it evidence of continued daily habitation? In the case of this study, a cluster analysis looking for clear site functions based on features and artifacts found was unsuccessful; no such groupings could be meaningfully recognized. That led to the alternate macro-models using all the site data combined, but these may well be criticized as having little meaning. One can imagine the late theory-oriented archaeologist Lewis Binford, for example, asking what is the significance of a model combining apples and oranges and bananas? And he would be correct to raise doubts. However, there are situations where such differentiation is not possible, and we are unwillingly forced to seek a broader view. This may be especially so in the case of archaeological excavations where two problems confront us. The first, as I have mentioned, is the "orange-apple," "apple-banana" mixed nature of such sites. The second related problem is our inability to judge whether the findings of a given excavation are a true sample of the whole site. Even with quantitative analysis, we may be forced to accept a degree of compromise.

And finally, another suggestion, and this is by no means limited to Japan. If archaeologists have excavated Upper Palaeolithic sites and uncovered what can be judged to be the center of life activities there, we may safely assume that they have discovered a great many artifacts and features. Put another way, they have helped to clarify the total picture of the sites. At that point I would urge them to create their own overall illustrations of the sites as I have in Models 1 and 2 (Figure 13.15 and Table 13.8). How much do these resemble the group of 12 Initial Period sites in Japan introduced here? Where do they differ? If we have for comparison a Korean Model, a Chinese Model, a Siberian Model, and others from circa 40,000 BP, eventually we can do a "site genealogy" and trace back the places our ancestors lived and worked. In Japan, too, these types of figures can help us create an overall Upper Palaeolithic Late Model and Terminal Phase Model to compare.

This chapter introduces a new method for comparative study of sites via macro-model formation through quantitative analysis of a series of Upper Palaeolithic sites considered as individual units. It is based on research papers presented at five general meetings of the Japan Association for Archaeoinformatics (Ueki 2016, 2017a, 2017b, 2018a, 2018b).

## Acknowledgments

In the course of this research, I read the site monographs for the 12 chosen sites, and wherever I came across places on which I had questions, I contacted the authors directly. All were so helpful and took great pains to clarify every point, for which I am very grateful. The authors are Hirokazu Ishido, Yuichiro Tabira, Hiroshi Akasaki, Manabu Kameda, Shizutaka Hirota, Tomoo Ikeda, Takeshi Hashiguchi, Norihiro Ito, Sachie Ootake, Noriaki Ootake, Nobuyuki Ikeya, Hideharu Maejima, and Noriyoshi Oda. Assistance with statistical analysis was given by Akira Horoiwa of the National Institute for Educational Policy Research. Akira Ono, Shizuo Oda, and

Kazutaka Shimada of Meiji University answered many technical questions. Any errors in this chapter are entirely my responsibility.

## References

Inada, Takashi and Hiroyuki Sato (eds.). 2010a *Kyusekki Jidai (Jo)* [The Palaeolithic Age, Vol. 1]. Tokyo: Aoki Shoten (in Japanese).
Inada, Takashi and Hiroyuki Sato (eds.). 2010b *Kyusekki Jidai (Ge)* [The Palaeolithic Age, Vol. 2]. Tokyo: Aoki Shoten (in Japanese).
Kagoshimaken Maizo Bunkazai Senta (Buried Cultural Property Center). 2009 *Otsubobata Kozono Iseki* [Otsubobata & Kozono Sites]. Tanegashima Maizo Bunkazai Senta Hakkutsu Chosa Hokokusho 135 (in Japanese).
Kagoshimaken Minamitanecho Kyoikuiinkai (Board of Education). 2000 *Yokomine C Iseki* [Yokomine C Site] 8 (in Japanese).
Kagoshimaken Minamitanecho Kyoikuiinkai (Board of Education). 2005 *Yokomine C Iseki* [Yokomine C Site]. Minamitanecho Maizo Bunkazai Hakkutsu Chosa Hokokusho 12 (in Japanese).
Kagoshimaken Nakatanecho Kyoikuiinkai (Board of Education). 1999 *Tachikiri Kyozuka Iseki* [Tachikiri & Kyozuka Sites]. Nakatanecho Maizo Bunkazai Hakkutsu Hokokusho 3 (in Japanese).
Kagoshimaken Nakatanecho Kyoikuiinkai (Board of Education). 2002 *Tachikiri Iseki* [Tachikiri Site]. Nakatanecho Maizo Bunkazai Hakkutsu Hokokusho 4 (in Japanese).
Kagoshimaken Nakatanecho Kyoikuiinkai (Board of Education). 2003 *Tachikiri Iseki* [Tachikiri Site]. Nakatanecho Maizo Bunkazai Hakkutsu Hokokusho 6 (in Japanese).
Kagoshimaken Nakatanecho Kyoikuiinkai (Board of Education). 2012 *Tachikiri Iseki* [Tachikiri Site]. Nakatanecho Maizo Bunkazai Hakkutsu Hokokusho 15 (in Japanese).
Kamei, Setsuo, Zenya Kawamura, and Hiroyuki Taruno. 1988 Nihon no Daiyonkei no Honyu Dobutsu Kaseki ni yoru Buntai [Distribution of Quarternary Mammalian Fossils in Japan] in *Chishitsugaku Ronshu [Memoirs of the Geological Society of Japan]* 30, 181–204 (in Japanese).
Kawamura, Zenya. 2005 Koshinsei to Kanshinsei no Honyurui [Pleistocene and Holocene Mammals], in ed Naraken Bunkazai Kenkyujo, *Doitsuten Kinen Kaisetsu, Nihon no Kokogaku (Jo) [Introduction to the German Memorial Exhibition, Japanese Archaeology*, Vol. 1]. Tokyo: Gakuseisha, 49–55 (in Japanese).
Kudo, Yuichiro. 2010 *Kyusekki Jidai ni okeru Nendai to Kokankyoron* [Research on Palaeolithic Chronology and Environment, 3], in eds. Inada, T. and Sato H. *Kyusekki Jidai (Jo)* [The Palaeolithic Age, Vol. 1], Tokyo: Aoki Shoten, 124–155 (in Japanese).
Kudo, Yuichiro. 2012 *Kyusekki Jomon Jidai no Kankyo Bunkashi* [Environment and Cultural History in the Palaeolithic and Jomon Ages]. Tokyo: Shinsensha (in Japanese).
Kumamotoken Kyoikuiinkai (Board of Education). 1999 *Ishinomoto Isekigun II* [Ishinomoto Site Group, II]. Kumamotoken Bunkazai Chosa Hokoku 178 (in Japanese).
Kumamotoken Kyoikuiinkai (Board of Education). 2000 *Ishinomoto Isekigun III* [Ishinomoto Site Group, III]. Kumamotoken Bunkazai Chosa Hokoku 194 (in Japanese).
Kumamotoken Kyoikuiinkai (Board of Education). 2001 *Ishinomoto Isekigun IV* [Ishinonoto Site Group, IV]. Kumamotoken Bunkazai Chosa Hokoku 195 (in Japanese).
Kumamotoken Kyoikuiinkai (Board of Education). 2010 *Setaichinohara Iseki* [Setaichinohara Site]. Kumamotoken Bunkazai Chosa Hokoku 252 (in Japanese).
Machida, Hiroshi. 2007 2: Nihon Retto no Keiseishi [2: History of the Formation of the Japanese Archipelago], in *Nihon no Kokogaku [Japanese Archaeology]*, eds. Inada, T., Okamura, M., Shiraishi, T., et al. Tokyo: Gakuseisha, 20–32 (in Japanese).
Machida, Hiroshi and Arai, Fusao. 2003 *Shinpen Kazanbai Atorasu [Revised Tephra Atlas]*. Tokyo: University of Tokyo Press (in Japanese).
Miyazakiken Kawaminamicho Kyoikuiinkai (Board of Education). 2002 eds Tachibana, M., Sato, H., and Yamada, T. *Ushiromuta Iseki—Miyazakiken Kawaminamicho Ushiromuta Iseki ni okeru Kyusekki Jidai no Kenkyu* [Ushiromuta Site: Palaeolithic Research on Ushiromuta Site, Kawaminamicho, Miyazaki Prefecture]. Kawaminamicho Kyoikuiinkai (in Japanese).
Miyazakiken Maizo Bunkazai Senta (Buried Cultural Property Center). 2007 *Yamada Iseki* [Yamada Site]. Miyazakiken Maizo Bunkazai Senta Hakkutsu Chosa Hokokusho 146.

Naganoken Maizo Bunkazai Senta (Buried Cultural Property Center). 2000 *Shinanochonai 1: Hinatabayashi B Hinatabayashi A Nanatsuguri Odaira B Iseki—Kyusekki Jidai Honbunron* [In Shinanocho 1: Hinatabayashi B, Hinatabayashi A, Nanatsuguri, & Odaira B Sites—Palaeolithic Age Report]. Joshinetsu Jidoshado Maizo Bunkazai Hakkutsu Chosa Hokokusho 15 and Naganoken Maizo Bunkazai Senta Hakkutsu Chosa Hokokusho 48 (in Japanese).

Naganoken Maizo Bunkazai Senta (Buried Cultural Property Center). 2004 *Shinanochonai 2: Kannoki Shogetsudai Iseki* [In Shinanocho 2: Kannoki & Shogetsudai Sites]. Ippan Kokudo 18-go Nojiri Bypass [National Highway 18, Nojiri Bypass] Maizo Bunkazai Hakkutsu Hokokusho 2 (in Japanese).

Naganoken Nagatomachi Kyoikuiinkai (Board of Education). 2001 *Kendo Omegura Nagatosen Kairyo Koji ni Tomonau Hakkutsu Chosa Hokokusho—Takayama Isekigun I Iseki oyobi Oiwake Isekigun Hakkutsu Chosa* [Excavation Carried Out at the Time of Roadwork on the Prefectural Highway Between Omegura and Nagato—Reports on Takayama Site Group I and Oiwake Site Group]. Nagatomachi Kyoikuiinkai (in Japanese).

Nakazawa, Yuichi. 2017 On the Pleistocene Population History in the Japanese Archipelago. *Current Anthropology* 58 (Suppl. 17), 539–552.

Nihon Kyusekki Gakkai (Japanese Palaeolithic Research Association). 2010 *Nihon Retto no Kyusekki Iseki—Nihon Kyusekki (Sendoki Iwajuku) Jidai no Deta Besu* [Palaeolithic Sites in the Japanese Archipelago—Japanese Palaeolithic Age Data Base (Pre-pottery Iwajuku)]. Japanese Palaeolithic Research Association (in Japanese).

Numata, Makoto and Iwase, Toru. 2002 *Zusetsu Nihon no Shokusei* [Illustrated Vegetation of Japan]. Tokyo: Kodansha (in Japanese).

Okamura, Michio, Matsufuji, K., Kimura, H., Tsuji, S. and Baba, H. 1998 *Kyusekki Jidai no Kokogaku [Archaeology of the Palaeolithic Age]*. Tokyo: Gakuseisha (in Japanese).

Shimaneken Kyoikucho Maizo Bunkazai Chosa Senta (Board of Education Buried Cultural Property Investigation Center) ed. 2008 *Harada Iseki 4, No. 1* [Harada Site 4, No. 1]. Shimaneken Kyoikuiinkai (in Japanese).

Shizuokaken Maizo Bunkazai Senta (Buried Cultural Property Center). 2012 *Nishiboru Iseki II* [*Nishiboru Site II*]. Shizuokaken Maizo Bunkazai Senta Chosa Hokokusho 2 (in Japanese).

Shizuokaken Maizo Bunkazai Chosa Kenkyujo (Buried Cultural Property Investigation Institute). 2009 *Umenokizawa Iseki II* [*Umenokizawa Site II*]. Shizuokaken Maizo Bunkazai Chosa Kenkyujo Chosa Hokoku 206 (in Japanese).

Shizuokaken Maizo Bunkazai Chosa Kenkyujo (Buried Cultural Property Investigation Institute). 2010 *Fujiishi Iseki I, Daiichi Daini Bunsatsu* [*Fujiishi Site I, Vols. 1 and 2*]. Shizuokaken Maizo Bunkazai Chosa Kenkyujo Chosa Hokoku 232 (in Japanese).

Shizuokaken Numazushi Kyoikuiinkai (Board of Education). 1999 *Nishiboru Iseki (b Ku-1) Hakkutsu Chosa Hokokusho* [*Nishiboru Site (b square 1) Investigative Excavation Report*]. Numazushi Bunkazai Chosa Hokokusho 69 (in Japanese).

Shizuokaken Numazushi Kyoikuiinkai (Board of Education). 2011 *Idemaruyama Iseki Hakkutsu Chosa Hokokusho* [*Idemaruyama Site Investigative Excavation Report*]. Numazushi Bunkazai Chosa Hokokusho 100 (in Japanese).

Sugiyama, Shinji. 2010 *4: Koshinsei no Shokusei to Kankyo* [*4: Pleistocene Vegetation and Environment*] in *Kyusekki Jidai (Jo)* [*The Palaeolithic Age*, Vol. 1], eds Inada, T. and Sato, H. Tokyo: Aoki Shoten, 156–177 (in Japanese).

Takaido Higashi Iseki Chosakai (Takaido Higashi Site Investigation Group). 1977a *Takaido Higashi Iseki, Suginamiku Seiso Kojo Kensetsu* [*Takaido Higashi Site, Suginamiku Garbage Incinerator Construction*] (in Japanese).

Takaido Higashi Iseki Chosakai (Takaido Higashi Site Investigation Group). 1977b *Takaido Higashi Iseki (Chushajo Nishi)* [*Takaido Higashi Site (West Parking Lot)*] (in Japanese).

Takeoka, Toshiki. 2019 *Kokogaku Kisoron—Shiryo no Mikata Toraekata [Archaeological Basic Theory—Considering the Data, Understanding the Data]*. Tokyo: Yuzankaku (in Japanese).

Tokyoto Maizo Bunkazai Senta (Tokyo Buried Cultural Property Center). 2004 *Fuchushi Musashi Kokubunjishi Kanren Iseki (Musashidai Nishichiku)* [*Related Sites in Fuchu & Musashi Kokubunji (Musashidai West Area)*]. Tokyoto Maizo Bunkazai Senta Chosa Hokokusho 149 (in Japanese).

Tokyoto Maizo Bunkazai Senta (Tokyo Buried Cultural Property Center). 2010 *Fuchushi Musashi Kokubunjishi Kanren Iseki Musashidai Iseki Daiichi Bunsatsu Gaiyo Kyusekki Jidai Honbunhen* [*Related Sites in Fuchu & Musashi Kokubunji and Musashidai Site No. 1 Overview—Palaeolithic Age Report*]. Tokyoto Maizo Bunkazai Senta Chosa Hokokusho 239 (in Japanese).

Tokyoto Maizo Bunkazai Senta (Tokyo Buried Cultural Property Center). 2014 *Fuchushi Musashi Kokubunjishi Kanren Iseki* [*Related Sites in Fuchu & Musashi Kokubunji*]. Tokyoto Maizo Bunkazai Senta Chosa Hokokusho 295 (in Japanese).

Ueki, Takeshi. 2016 *Kokogaku kara Mita Homo sapiens no Nihon Retto e no Torai to Kakusan* [An Archaeologist Views the Arrival and Dispersal of Homo sapiens in the Japanese Archipelago]. *Proceedings of the Japan Association for Archaeoinformatics* 17, 1–5 (in Japanese).

Ueki, Takeshi. 2017a *Kokogaku kara Mita Homo sapiens no Nihon Retto e no Torai to Kakusan, No. 2* [An Archaeologist Views the Arrival and Dispersal of Homo sapiens in the Japanese Archipelago, No. 2]. *Proceedings of the Japan Association for Archaeoinformatics* 18, 4–9 (in Japanese).

Ueki, Takeshi. 2017b *Kokogaku kara Mita Homo sapiens no Nihon Retto e no Torai to Kakusan, No. 3* [An Archaeologist Views the Arrival and Dispersal of Homo sapiens in the Japanese Archipelago, No. 3]. *Proceedings of the Japan Association for Archaeoinformatics* 19, 40–45 (in Japanese).

Ueki, Takeshi. 2018a *Kokogaku kara Mita Homo sapiens no Nihon Retto e no Torai to Kakusan, No. 4* [An Archaeologist Views the Arrival and Dispersal of Homo sapiens in the Japanese Archipelago, No. 4]. *Proceedings of the Japan Association for Archaeoinformatics* 20, 43–48 (in Japanese).

Ueki, Takeshi. 2018b *Kokogaku kara Mita Homo sapiens no Nihon Retto e no Torai to Kakusan, No. 5* [An Archaeologist Views the Arrival and Dispersal of Homo sapiens in the Japanese Archipelago, No. 5]. *Proceedings of the Japan Association for Archaeoinformatics* 21, 1–6 (in Japanese).

Yamaoka, Takuya. 2012 Use and maintenance of trapezoids in the initial Early Upper Paleolithic of the Japanese Islands. *Quaternary International* 248, 32–42.

Yamaoka, Takuya. 2016 Shooting and stabbing experiments using replicated trapezoids. *Quaternary International* XXX, 1–11.

# 14

# ARCHAEOLOGICAL MATERIALS FROM THE JAPANESE EARLY UPPER PALAEOLITHIC AND THEIR IMPLICATIONS

*Takuya Yamaoka*

## Introduction

Current studies indicate a sudden increase in archaeological sites in the Japanese Islands after 39,000 cal BP while sites older than this date are very rare or absent altogether. This is interpreted as a sign of the arrival of *Homo sapiens* to the Japanese Islands (Kudo and Kumon 2012; Izuho and Kaifu 2015; Morisaki et al. 2020). This chapter begins by introducing an outline of palaeo-environmental and Palaeolithic research from Marine Isotope Stages (MIS) 3 to 2 in the Japanese Islands. Next, it focuses on archaeological research on the Early Upper Palaeolithic (EUP, ca. 39,000–29,000 cal BP) in the Japanese Islands and reviews the chronological studies of lithic assemblages as well as research relating to the behavioural modernity of early modern humans in that time period. Finally, their implications from several perspectives are examined.

## Palaeoenvironment of the Japanese Islands During MIS 3 and 2

The Japanese Islands consist of many small islands and four main islands: Hokkaido, Honshu, Shikoku, and Kyushu (Figure 14.1). In MIS 3 and 2, Hokkaido was a part of a large peninsula formed by the development of land bridges between Hokkaido, Sakhalin, the Kurile Islands, and the Russian Far East. Honshu, Shikoku, and Kyushu were connected, forming a larger island. It is estimated that this larger island was separated from Hokkaido as well as the Korean Peninsula, even during the Last Glacial Maximum (LGM).

Takahara and Hayashi (2015) reviewed palaeovegetation research during MIS 3 on the Japanese Islands. They compiled forty-seven pollen samples from Taiwan, the Japanese Islands, Sakhalin, and the Amur River Basin, and reconstructed MIS 3 vegetation in East Asia. Figure 14.2 is a topographic and biome-level vegetation map of MIS 3 in East Asia, as presented by Takahara and Hayashi (2015). The topographic map was drawn as 60m below sea level in MIS 3, referring to Lambeck and Chappell (2001).

The MIS 3 vegetation in the Japanese Islands reconstructed in Takahara and Hayashi (2015) is summarized as follows. Hokkaido was covered by evergreen conifer forests of spruce with some larch and broadleaf trees. In northeastern Honshu, evergreen conifers such as fir, hemlock,

DOI: 10.4324/9781003427483-14

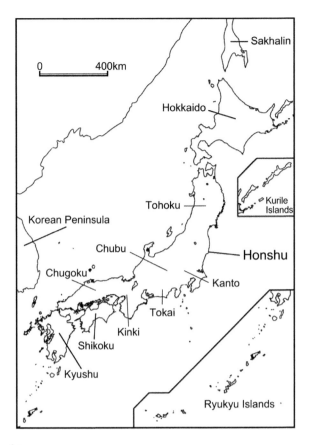

FIGURE 14.1  Map of Japan.

spruce, and pine were dominant, with some deciduous broadleaf trees such as beech, oak, and elm. On the Kanto Plain (eastern Honshu), deciduous broadleaf forests of oak, hornbeam, beech, and elm developed. The Pacific coast (Izu Peninsula) was covered by temperate conifers such as *Cryptomeria* and *Sciadopitys*, with some deciduous broadleaf trees. The broad area of western Honshu was covered by mixed forests of temperate conifers such as *Cryptomeria*, *Sciadopitys*, and *Cupressaceae* and deciduous broadleaf trees such as beech, oak, hornbeam, and elm. On the northern part of Kyushu, mixed forests of pine and beech were present. After MIS 3, deciduous broadleaf trees such as beech and oak and temperate conifers such as *Cryptomeria* were replaced by evergreen conifers (Pinaceae) on Honshu. Overall, the MIS 3 vegetation was recharacterized by relatively high amounts of deciduous broadleaf trees comprising different types of forests in each region. Distribution patterns of MIS 3 vegetation directly affected the subsequent forests of MIS 2, the LGM (Takahara and Hayashi 2015). Pinaceous conifers, which included both temperate and boreal species, prevailed on the Japanese Islands during the LGM, and temperate broadleaf trees, such as beeches and oaks, and temperate conifers, such as *Cryptomeria japonica*, existed in coastal refugia (Tsukada 1985).

Several papers introduce recent studies of Late Pleistocene fauna in the Japanese Islands (Iwase et al. 2012, 2015; Kawamura and Nakagawa 2012; Takahashi and Izuho 2012). The

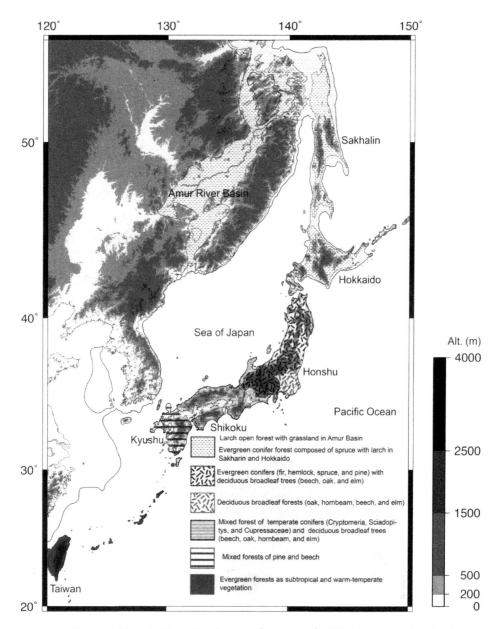

FIGURE 14.2  Topographic and biome-level vegetation map of MIS 3 in East Asia (Takahara and Hayashi (2015, fig. 22.2).

research indicates that fauna in the Japanese Islands during MIS 3 and 2 can be divided into two main groups. The first is composed of Naumann's elephants (*Palaeoloxodon naumani*), Yabe's giant deer (*Sinomegaceros yabei*), an extinct cervid (*Cervus praenipponicus*), Sika deer (*C. nippon*), brown bears (*Ursus arctos*), martens (*Martes melampus*), least weasels (*Mustela nivalis*), European badgers (*Meles meles*), raccoon dogs (*Nyctereutes procyonoides*), Japanese monkeys (*Macaca fuscata*), wolves (Canis lupus), and foxes (Vulpes vulpes). This group was called the Palaeoloxodon-Shinomegaceroides complex by Hasegawa (1972). All middle- to large-sized fossil mammals found on the Japanese Islands comprised only these species, and most of them migrated from continental Asia across the western land bridge during the mid-Middle Pleistocene (ca 0.4–0.3 Ma), or 0.13 Ma (Takahashi and Izuho 2012). The characteristics of these mammals include: (1) their principal habitat was in temperate climates, (2) the majority were forest-dwelling animals, and (3) they had a high percentage of endemic species (Kawamura 1991; Takahashi and Izuho 2012).

The second group, the mammoth fauna, mostly consisted of species that lived in grasslands. In Siberia, it included woolly mammoths, steppe bison (*Bison priscus*), European asses (*Equus hydruntinus*), red deer (*Cervus elaphus*), giant deer (*Megaloceros giganteus*), musk oxen (*Ovibos moschatus*), woolly rhinoceroses (*Coelodonta antiquitatis*), wolverines (*Gulo gulo*), arctic foxes (*Alopex lagopus*), cave hyenas (*Crocuta spelaea*), woolly weasels (*Mustela putorius*), reindeer (*Rangifer tarandus*), cave lions (*Panthera spelaea*), snowshoe rabbits (*Lepus timidus*), camargue horses (*Equus caballus*), cave bears (*Ursus spelaeus*), saiga antelope (*Saiga tatarica*), European ground squirrels (*Spermophilus citellus*), wolves (*Canis lupus*), Eurasian badgers (*Meles meles*), brown bears (*Ursus arctos*), beavers (*Castor fiber*), and moose (*Alces alces*). Sakhalin Island, comprising the large peninsula with Hokkaido, yielded species of these mammoth fauna, including mammoths, brown bears, Siberian musk deer, horses, moose, snow sheep, Panther sp., wolves, and arctic foxes. The mammoth fauna in the Japanese Islands included mammoths and bison only from localities in Hokkaido, and moose from localities on Honshu. One of the localities bearing moose has also yielded the Shino Shrew (*Sorex shinto*), Japanese shrew-mole (*Dymecodon pilirostris*), and Japanese mountain mole (*Euroscaptor mizura*). These small- to middle-sized animals in the mammoth fauna are thought to have migrated to the south according to their habitat and temperature preferences (Takahashi and Izuho 2012).

On the other hand, four samples of *P. naumanni* from Hokkaido indicate that *P. naumanni* expanded their habitats northward at around 53,000, 48,000, 42,000, and 30,000 14C BP. Kawamura and Nakagawa (2012) consider that mammoths and *P. naumanni* could have coexisted in Hokkaido during MIS 3 since it is likely that the climatic and vegetation conditions in Hokkaido were much milder and more wooded than farther north where the main distribution of the mammoth fauna existed. Iwase et al. (2012), however, indicated that mammoths and *P. naumanni* seem to have had different ecologies and preferred to inhabit different vegetation zones, implying that they could not have coexisted in the same region. Takahashi and Izuho (2012) consider that mammoths could have retreated north to the southern limit of the cool temperate forest, and *P. naumanni* could have extended north to the area where mammoths once lived during MIS 3. They also present the hypothesis that the boundary of these two faunal groups that migrated back and forth north to south could have matched the range of vegetation that shifted with climatic fluctuations.

In the Japanese Islands, mammoths, *P. naumanni*, and giant deer became extinct during the Late Pleistocene. Kawamura and Nakagawa (2012) speculated that the combination of a warming event during the MIS 2-1 transition and the cultural change from the Palaeolithic to the Jomon period correlate with the Late Pleistocene extinctions. Norton et al. (2010) proposed that the increase in human population and the expansion of human range during MIS 3-2 was possibly responsible for the extinctions of the Pleistocene large mammals. Iwase et al. (2015) have updated the extinction chronology for Japanese terrestrial Pleistocene mammals based on selected, reliable radiocarbon dates; additionally, they clarified that the woolly mammoths became extinct or migrated northward after the LGM when the climate ameliorated and the open-forest taiga and grassy plains receded in Hokkaido, and that Naumann's elephant became extinct around the onset of the LGM as a result of the shift from cool-temperate broadleaf forests to subarctic coniferous vegetation. They estimate that climate-induced vegetation change may have largely contributed to megafaunal habitat change and, ultimately, the extinction of these species (Iwase et al. 2015). They also indicated that while the primary reasons for the large mammal extinctions in the Japanese Islands might have been changes to the ecosystems driven by climatic fluctuations, it is also necessary to evaluate the causes of mammal extinction by examining the way in which humans impacted ecosystems and how their hunting pressured large mammal populations (Takahashi and Izuho 2012).

### Archaeological Materials and Chronological Studies of the Palaeolithic in the Japanese Islands

More than 10,000 Palaeolithic sites have been found in the Japanese Islands with most of them dating to MIS 2 (Figure 14.3). The dates of the oldest sites that are acceptable to most archaeologists are ca. 39,000 cal BP (Kudo and Kumon 2012; Izuho and Kaifu 2015; Morisaki et al. 2020). Many "Early Palaeolithic" records were dismissed after an Early Palaeolithic hoax was exposed. It was finally discovered that an amateur archaeologist had been forging Early and Middle Palaeolithic stone tool industries from Miyagi and other prefectures since the 1980s (Nakazawa 2010, 2017). After that, several possible sites for human occupation in the Japanese Islands before the Upper Palaeolithic (UP) were excavated, and candidate assemblages were recovered from them. However, not all Palaeolithic researchers in Japan view these assemblages as reliable records. Nakazawa (2017) reviewed the current situation and the issues with the research on lithic assemblages before the UP in the Japanese Islands.

Nakazawa (2017) also introduced the Pleistocene population history in the Japanese Islands based on research in palaeoanthropology, genetics, and archaeology. According to Nakazawa (2017), Late Pleistocene fragmentary human remains have only been obtained from Hamakita in Shizuoka Prefecture, as well as in Okinawa Prefecture. Mitochondrial DNA (mtDNA) analyses of modern Japanese people have revealed that super haplogroups M and N, which represent southern and northern routes of modern human migrations from Africa, respectively, eventually came to be found in Japanese indigenous populations. This implies that the Holocene Jomon population was founded by both northward and southward gene flows. Results of the studies of mtDNA from Jomon and Epi-Jomon skeletal remains from Hokkaido indicate that most of the Hokkaido Jomon people were direct descendants of Palaeolithic Siberians. The coalescence time (ca. 22,000 years ago) of the mtDNA haplogroup (N9b), which is predominant in the Hokkaido Jomon sample, implies that there could have been a southward migration of hunter-gatherers from northern regions to Hokkaido in the onset of the LGM (Adachi et al. 2015). However, large-scale genome studies and ancient genome studies don't find any evidence for the northern route of early modern human migrations in east Asia to the Japanese Islands so far (The HUGO Pan-Asian SNP Consortium 2009; Mccoll et al. 2018). Pleistocene human remains, ancient mtDNA studies, and ancient genome studies in the Japanese Islands are still scarce. Thus, the Pleistocene population migrations into the Japanese Islands, especially before the LGM, are estimated mainly based on archaeological records.

Most UP sites in the Japanese Islands are open-air sites. Due to the humid climate of the Japanese Islands as well as the nature of deposits that were formed from volcanic ash, aeolian dust, and so on, organic materials at open-air sites dissolve; the artefacts that remain at the sites are basically only rock materials. Aside from lithic artifacts and cobbles, charcoal has also

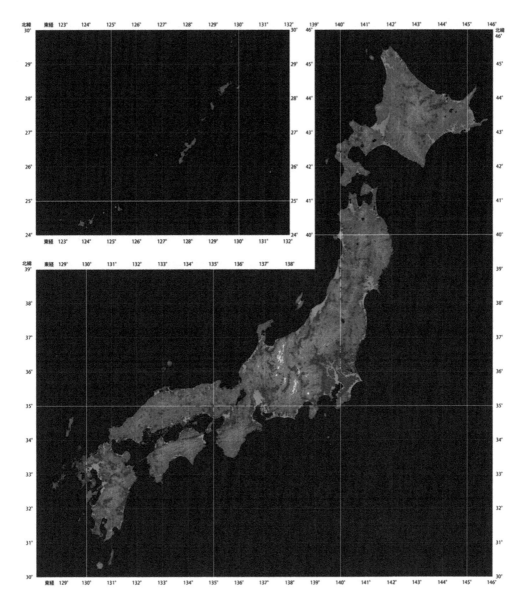

FIGURE 14.3  Distribution of archaeological sites during the Palaeolithic and the Incipient Jomon Period in the Japanese Islands (Japanese Palaeolithic Research Association 2010).

been recovered from excavations of UP sites. Most research results of the UP in the Japanese Islands are based on such archaeological excavations and the remains from these open-air sites. There are also sites where animal bones and flaked bone tools have been found, such as the Tategahana sites (Lake Nojiri) (Ono 1998), and in recent years archaeological materials from the LGM or earlier time periods have been discovered in two cave sites in Aomori and Okinawa prefectures (Nara 2015; Okinawa Prefectural Museum and Art Museum 2015). Such excavations at cave sites will continue and, hopefully, more sites bearing organic materials will be discovered.

The majority of archaeological excavations at open-air UP sites in the Japanese Islands have been salvage excavations performed to preserve a record of the site before its destruction. There have been a great number of such salvage excavations performed over large areas since the period of high economic growth in the 1970s due to the construction of roads, buildings, and facilities; as such, the distribution of archaeological features at these sites has been clarified on a large scale. Archaeological features discovered in these excavations have included lithic, cobble, and charcoal concentrations, and on rare occasions, hearth features. Although a large number of artefacts are recovered through these excavations, since they must be concluded in a limited time period, dry sieving is employed only in very rare cases. As a result, the methods of the salvage excavations may to some extent lack reliability in terms of recovering smaller materials. Under such conditions and methods, however, large archaeological materials, in particular lithic artefacts, have accumulated.

Furthermore, archaeological materials from the UP sites in several regions are buried in well-stratified, thick aeolian deposits that mainly were formed by volcanic ash. Numerous volcanic tephras in and around the Japanese Islands during the late Quaternary have been identified and catalogued. In particular, the Aira-Tn tephra, which erupted from the Aira caldera around $30,009 \pm 189$ cal BP (Smith et al. 2013; Izuho and Kaifu 2015), is distributed over a large area, covering most of the Japanese Islands, as well as the Korean Peninsula, part of eastern China, and the southern Primorye Territory in the Russian Far East (Machida and Arai 2003). It is used as an indicator to separate the EUP and the Late Upper Palaeolithic (LUP) in the Japanese Islands. Several other wide-spread tephras that fell during the Late Pleistocene have been identified, and these are also used in the chronological research along with local tephras that fell across more narrow areas.

In addition, the Mt. Ashitaka and Mt. Hakone areas in the eastern Tokai region and several areas in the southern Kyushu region have extremely favourable conditions for chronological research; there, aeolian deposits are very thick and well-stratified due to the proximity of the volcanos that are the sources of the volcanic ash in these areas (Figure 14.4). Several areas in the southern Kanto Region, such as in the Musashino and Sagamihara uplands, also have relatively thick, well-stratified aeolian deposits. In these areas in the eastern Tokai region, the southern Kyushu region, and the southern Kanto region, black bands (buried palaeosols) have also been found in addition to volcanic tephras in stratigraphy, and the changes in lithic assemblages have been studied based on those indicators. As such, chronological research has been conducted in accordance with time resolution in each region yielding detailed geochronological information.

Such chronological research across the Japanese Islands has resulted in clarification of the changes in lithic industries during the UP. The following broad change process has come to light: lithic industries mainly including pointed elongated flakes (knife-shaped tools), trapezoids, penhead- shaped points, and adzes (or axes)(with ground edges); lithic industries containing backed points (knife-shaped tools); marginal, unifacial, and bifacial points; and lithic industries including microblades. Furthermore, due to rich geochronological information, in some areas more detailed change processes in lithic industries have become clear. Also, in recent years 14 C dates have been obtained at many sites. The dates of each industry are estimated based on the 14C dates (Kudo 2012; Kudo and Kumon 2012). Basic information on the UP sites in the Japanese Islands was compiled to form a database (Japanese Palaeolithic Research Association 2010). Chronologies have been established in every region, such as Hokkaido, Tohoku, Kanto, Chubu, Tokai, Kinki, Chugoku, Shikoku, and Kyushu; in other words, over most of the Japanese Islands (Inada and Sato 2010).

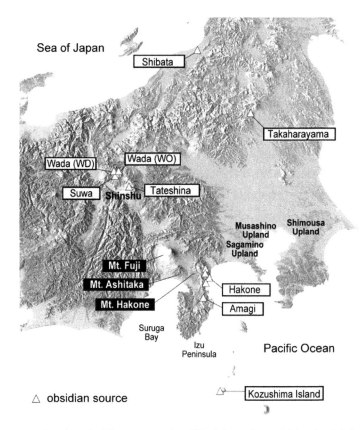

FIGURE 14.4  Map, showing obsidian sources (modified from Ikeya (2015, fig. 25.1).

## Archaeological Research of the Japanese EUP and Modern Human Behaviour Changes Seen Through Lithic Assemblages

The dates of EUP assemblages fall roughly between 39,000 cal BP and 29,000 cal BP. About 500 EUP sites have been excavated in the Japanese Islands (Izuho and Kaifu 2015). Since the 1970s, cultural chronologies have been constructed on the basis of both stratigraphy and the technological analyses of stone tools. By the 1990s, qualitative technological analyses of EUP stone tool assemblages were dominant in Japan. Studies on the processes of lithic technological changes during the EUP in the Japanese Islands (Sekki Bunka Kenkyu Kai 1991; Sato, 1992) have provided the basis of current research. Such studies revealed that flaking technology for elongated flakes and blades changed over time during the EUP. Elongated flakes and their flaking technique are found in lithic assemblages of the initial phase of the EUP, while platform and fringe trimmings and core rejuvenation are seldom found. On the other hand, blades and blade cores are frequently found in lithic assemblages of the final phase of the EUP. Platform and fringe trimmings and core rejuvenation are also found in these assemblages.

Previous studies have also clarified that the composition of formal flaked tools changed over time during the EUP. Formal tools in lithic assemblages of the initial phase of the EUP consisted of pointed flakes (knife-shaped tools), trapezoids, pen-head-shaped points, side scrapers, end scrapers, and adzes (or axes) with ground edges. Formal tools in lithic assemblages of the final phase of the EUP were composed of backed points (knife-shaped tools), side scrapers, and end scrapers. These transitions occurring in the EUP lithic assemblages were first grasped in the Musashino Upland and other regions in southern Kanto. After that, chronological studies of EUP lithic assemblages were conducted until the early 1990s all over the Japanese Islands, comparing flaking technologies and compositions of formal tools with those from the Musashino Upland. The number of 14C measurements from the EUP assemblages has also increased in recent years (Kudo and Kumon 2012; Izuho and Kaifu 2015).

The Mt. Ashitaka area has produced the most reliable data for EUP chronology since the late 1980s due to well-stratified, thick, Late Quaternary tephra sequences with detailed geochronological information. More than 90 Palaeolithic sites have been discovered at the foot of Mt. Ashitaka (Ikeya 2009b). Additionally, volcanic ash from the Palaeo-Fuji volcano and the Komitake volcano, which are located northwest of Mt. Ashitaka, has accumulated at the foot of Mt. Ashitaka (Figure 14.5). These volcanic ashes (Pleistocene tephras) created the Ashitaka Loam Formation, which is divided into three parts (Lower, Middle, and Upper Members). The lowest layer of the Upper Member of the Ashitaka Loam Formation is Layer SC IV, the fourth scoria layer, from which the oldest lithic assemblage in this area was found at the Idemaruyama site, dating back about 38,000 years ago (Takao and Harada 2011). Artefacts have never been found

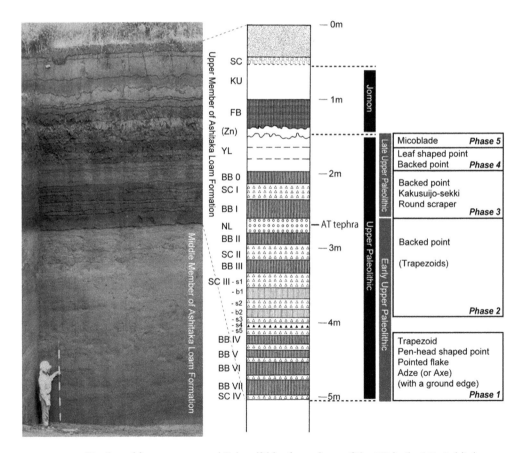

FIGURE 14.5 Stratigraphic sequences and Palaeolithic chronology of the UP in the Mt. Ashitaka area (modified from Ikeya et al. (2011, fig. 14.10).

from deposits below Layer SC IV. The Upper Members of the Ashitaka Loam Formation consist of alternate aeolian depositions of reddish brown scoria layers (Layers SC I, SC II, SC III-s1, s2, s3, s4, s5, SC IV, and so on) and ten buried palaeosol layers, called Black Bands (Layers BB 0, BB I, BB II, BB III, SC III-b1, SC III-b2, BB IV, BB V, BB VI, and BB VII). Most of the archaeological assemblages recovered were found in the Black Band layers. The middle of the Upper Member of the Ashitaka Loam Formation contains Layer NL, consisting of weathered scorias and volcanic glasses; the latter is AT tephra. These clear stratigraphic sequences provide geological contexts for establishing a detailed and reliable Upper Palaeolithic chronology in the Mt. Ashitaka area. It was reported in middle of the 1990s that changes in the lithic assemblages during the EUP in the Mt. Ashitaka area were similar to those in the Musashino Upland and in other regions in southern Kanto (Symposium Jikko Iinkai 1995) (Figure 14.6). Sites which yielded EUP assemblages have also been excavated since then; more than 95 archaeological horizons of the EUP from more than 30 sites have been excavated and reported so far.

In these previous EUP research, representative formal tools, cores, refitting specimens, and so on were analysed. However, research mainly advanced based solely on materials from the Japanese Islands, with little attempt to compare data with evidence found elsewhere; most relied on the assumption of cultural continuities during the UP in the Japanese Islands. Because of these research biases, morphological and technological changes in EUP lithic assemblages were mainly explained as the development (i.e., increasing sophistication of tool-making skills) of blade technology and methods of formal tool production (Sekki Bunka Kenkyu Kai 1991).

In this situation, the author indicated a different perspective for the study of the EUP assemblages in the Japanese Islands (Yamaoka 2006, 2011, 2012c, 2021). The author conducted quantitative comparisons of lithic raw materials, core reduction (blade technology), and formal tool production, focusing on EUP assemblages from 32 sites in the Musashino Upland where standards of EUP lithic chronology were first constructed. Formal tool production was examined through analyses of both formal flaked tools and adzes (or axes) (with a ground edge). Variability in formal flaked tools through time and across space was mainly examined through qualitative analysis. However, conventional typology of formal flaked tools was not appropriate due to their vague definitions; therefore, in that research, classes of formal flaked tools were redefined using clear criteria (Figure 14.7), and compositions of formal flaked tools and their quantities (their rates) were examined in each assemblage. For adzes (or axes), the definition as either unifacially or bifacially shaped core tools having a convex cross section, some with ground edges, was used. The provenances of all adzes (or axes) that were discovered in the EUP cultural horizons were examined.

The results of the analyses indicated transitions of the EUP lithic assemblages in three sequential phases: the initial, the middle, and the final phases (Figure 14.8). The amounts of types A–F varied across time, while types G (side scrapers) and H (end scrapers) were, by and large, evenly distributed in the assemblages of all phases. In the initial phase, types A (pointed flakes), D, E (trapezoids), and F (pen-head -shaped points) were notably found. On the other hand, in the assemblages of the final phase, types A, B, and C (backed points) were found in significant quantities. The assemblages of the middle phase had a moderate composition of formal flaked tools between the initial phase and the final phase. Adzes (or axes) were frequently included in assemblages from the initial phase, rarely included in assemblages from the middle phase, and not included in the final phase. These results confirmed and reinforced results found in previous studies.

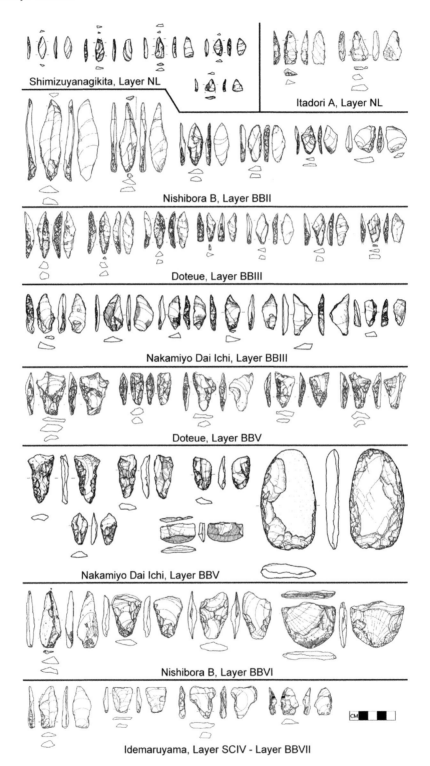

FIGURE 14.6 Representative formal stone tools during the EUP in the Mt. Ashitaka area, drawn from excavation reports of sites (Takao 1989; Numazu City Board of Education 1990; Ikeya 1998, 2004; Sasahara 1999; Mibu and Sugiyama 2009; Takao and Harada 2011).

Archaeological Materials from the Japanese Early Upper Palaeolithic  **295**

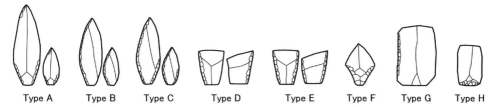

Type A: a pointed flake that was formed by secondary retouch to the tip and the base on a long axis of a blank
Type B: a pointed flake that was formed by secondary retouch to a lateral margin on a long axis of a blank
Type C: a pointed flake that was formed by secondary retouch to both lateral margins on a long axis of a blank
Type D: a flake with a flat or diagonal non-retouched edge that was formed by secondary retouch to a lateral margin on a long axis of a blank
Type E: a flake with a flat or diagonal non-retouched edge that was formed by secondary retouch to both lateral margins on a long axis of a blank
Type F: a pen-head shaped flake that was formed by secondary retouch to both sides of the base on a long axis of a blank
Type G: a flake with secondary retouche of more than 1/2 length on a long axis of a blank
Type H: a flake with abrupt secondary retouch on an extremity of a blank

**FIGURE 14.7** Definitions of formal flaked tools (modified from Yamaoka (2011, fig. 14.4).

Previous studies also focused on the changes in lithic raw material compositions and flaking technologies of blades and elongated flakes. It was confirmed that the rate of obsidian, which is an exotic raw material in the Musashino Upland, increased from the initial phase to the final phase in counts and weight. Refitting specimens relating to sophisticated blade technology were frequently found in assemblages of the final phase. It was also confirmed that the rate of

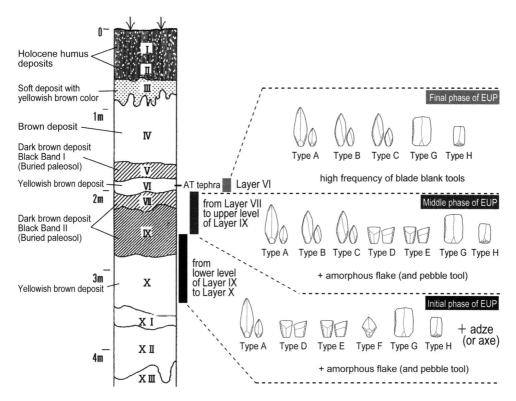

**FIGURE 14.8** Changes of lithic assemblages during the EUP in the Musashino Uplands (Yamaoka et al. 2023, fig. 5).

blade blank tools in the formal flaked tools increased from the initial phase to the final phase (Yamaoka 2006, 2011, 2012c, 2021).

The author explained these changes in EUP assemblages as reflecting changes in the purpose and the manner of lithic raw material use (Yamaoka 2004, 2006, 2011, 2012c, 2021), although they were mainly explained as the development (i.e., increasing sophistication of tool-making skills) of blade technology and methods of formal tool production in previous studies. The bases for this explanation are as follows. The results of analyses showed remarkable characteristics in all phases of the EUP with high-quality lithic raw materials (e.g., obsidian) used particularly for flaking blades and elongated flakes and making formal flaked tools. In the initial phase, however, the frequency of obsidian use and formal flaked tool production were quite low, and most of the (unmodified) flake tools and cores were made from locally available low-quality chert. This indicates that hunter-gatherers did not have a preference for "high-quality" lithic raw materials in this initial phase. Although blades, elongated flakes, and formal flaked tools were present, they were only sporadically found in assemblages. In addition, the mean weights of lithic artifacts in the assemblages were heavier than those of later phases. These patterns suggest the possibility that unmodified flakes and core tools containing adzes (or axes) were the dominant lithic tools in this phase. Hunter-gatherers in the Musashino Upland during the initial phase of the EUP preferentially employed generalized core reductions coupled with frequent use of locally available materials. On the other hand, in the final phase of the EUP, the frequency of obsidian use was highest among all phases, and most of the lithic raw materials except for obsidian were also of high quality (e.g., hard shale). These patterns indicate that high-quality lithic raw materials were commonly chosen in the final phase assemblages. Blade technology became more frequent in refitted specimens, and blade blanks were more often found in flaked tools. The frequency of formal flaked tools was also high. In addition, the mean weights of lithic artifacts in these assemblages were lighter than those in assemblages from previous phases. These characteristics of the assemblages—frequent use of high-quality materials, blades, and formal flaked tools—imply that production and use of lighter formal flaked tools came to be more critical for hunter-gatherer lifeways during the final phase compared to previous phases.

The environmental changes (previously described) roughly correlate with the transition of lithic assemblages from the initial phase to the final phase of the EUP. Consequently the changes in lithic raw material usage are thought to reflect changes of adaptational behaviour of hunter-gatherers in those time periods along with the environmental changes such as climate cooling and vegetation changes.

The changes in lithic raw material usage could be explained by transformations in the scale of foraging territories and residential mobility accompanying the environmental changes (Yamaoka 2006, 2011, 2012c, 2021). Many studies have suggested that human foraging territory expanded during the final phase of the EUP, based on the presence of relatively large amounts of obsidian from Shinshu, a few hundred kilometres away from the Musashino Upland (e.g. Kanayama 1990; Sekki Bunka Kenkyu Kai 1991; Tamura 1992) (Figure 14.2). In the UP research in the Japanese Islands, procurement strategies for lithic raw materials have been discussed by a number of researchers. Both hypotheses of direct procurement of lithic raw materials (Ono 1975) and procurement of these materials through exchange (Harunari 1976) were presented in the beginning of this discussion. Recently, most researchers seem to model procurement strategies from the assumption of an "embedded strategy" (Binford 1979). However, no data have been obtained to discuss specific foraging routes between obsidian provenance areas and sites in the Musashino Upland. At the present stage of research, we don't have any direct evidence to resolve the issue of how lithic raw materials were procured. Therefore, the author pointed out only a possibility of relative differences in the scale of foraging territories between the initial phase and the final phase (Yamaoka 2006, 2011, 2012c, 2021). In addition, the increasing reliance on obsidian for formal flaked tools between the initial phase and the final phase is clearly demonstrated in Yamaoka (2006, 2011, 2012c, 2021). Given the observations of frequent use of blade technology and lighter formal flaked tools in the assemblages of the final phase, it is estimated that the residential mobility of foraging groups increased during the final phase (Andrefsky 1998, 213–14; Yamaoka 2006, 2011, 2012c, 2021).

In addition to changes in foraging territorial scale and residential mobility, changes in lithic raw material usage could have been related to some changes in technologies associated with organic raw materials (while not archaeologically visible, presumably existing), possibly in response to changes in the environmental settings (Yamaoka 2004, 2006, 2011, 2012c, 2021). As opposed to abundant occurrences of formal flaked tools and blades during the final phase, which are ubiquitously found among Japanese later Upper Palaeolithic assemblages, unmodified flakes and core tools containing adzes (or axes) dominate the assemblages of the initial phase. These assemblages in the initial phase of the EUP appear somewhat similar to the Pleistocene assemblages of Southeast Asia, where it is thought that informal lithic tools were frequently utilized for producing perishable tools (Hutterer 1976). Use-wear analysis of adzes (or axes) have shown that they functioned to perform multiple tasks, including hide scraping and woodcutting (Tsutsumi 2006, 2012). In addition, evidence of breakage patterns suggests that large adzes (or axes) could have been used for heavy-duty tasks (Sato 2006). Thus, the most probable use for them would have been for clearing the forest and woodworking (Tsutsumi 2006, 2012).

Palaeoenvironmental data seem to support the possibility of some significant changes in organic raw material use during the EUP in this region. The pollen data show the vegetational change from MIS 3 to MIS 2 in the Japanese Islands as mentioned above. In the Kanto region where the Musashino Upland is located, analysis of the pollen spectrum and evidence of plant fossils show the occurrence of a vegetational change from broad-leaved deciduous forest to coniferous forest after the AT tephra fell (Tsuji and Kosugi 1991; Ito 1992). This shift in forest types roughly corresponds with the transition from the initial phase to the final phase. In addition, opal phytolith analysis shows that grassland vegetation was causal in creating Black Band II (Layers VII–IX: buried palaeosols) in the Tachikawa Loam (Sase et al. 2008). The expansion of grassland vegetation from Stratum X to Black Band II (Layers VII–IX) roughly corresponds with a decrease in adzes (or axes). Therefore, groups of hunter-gatherers during the initial phase of the EUP are thought to have been heavily depended on plant resources in their entire technological system.

Based on previous studies, it is thought that such a change in lithic raw material usage progressed over large areas of the Japanese Islands during the EUP. Further quantitative analyses of EUP lithic assemblages in other regions such as the Mt. Ashitaka area, which have detailed geochronological information, should be conducted. Use-wear analyses of lithic artifacts should also be conducted for clarification for organic raw material use in tool production during the Japanese EUP.

## Armatures

The stone technologies of the initial phase of the EUP may appear to be simple, but recent studies have shown that there were sophisticated and complex technologies which related to armatures during this time period. Studies on armatures from the initial phase of the EUP have continued since the 2000s. Impact fractures were found on pen-head-shaped points made from hard shale from EUP sites from the Tohoku region, and they indicate that the pen-head-shaped points were used as armatures (Kanomata 2005, 2011). Impact fractures were also found on trapezoids made from obsidian at the Doteue site in the Mt. Ashitaka area (Yamaoka 2010, 2012a) (Figure 14.6). In addition, an analysis of broken trapezoids suggests that hunting weapons equipped with trapezoids were repaired at the Doteue site; evidence of this is found in the high proportion of broken trapezoid bases left at the site (Yamaoka 2010, 2012a). Striations running parallel to the working edges were also found on some obsidian trapezoids from the Doteue site; their distributional patterns indicate that obsidian trapezoids were used for cutting or sawing soft materials (Yamaoka 2012a). Similar striations were also identified on obsidian trapezoids from sites in other regions (Tsutsumi 2012). Thus, obsidian trapezoids were used as multifunctional tools for hunting and processing.

Based on morphometric analysis, Tamura (2011) argued that some of the formal flaked tools in the EUP could have been used as darts or arrowheads. Shooting and stabbing experiments using replicated trapezoids were also conducted (Sano et al. 2012; Sano 2016; Yamaoka 2017). Sano et al. (2012) reported results of shooting and stabbing experiments using replicated trapezoids made from shale. Sano (2016) assumed that trapezoids and pen-head-shaped points made from shale from sites in the Tohoku region could have been used as arrowheads on the basis of proxies from the projectile experiments and morphometric analysis. Yamaoka (2017) reported results of shooting and stabbing experiments using replicated trapezoids made from obsidian. Based on comparisons between experimental and archaeological specimens, Yamaoka (2017) suggested that hunting weapons equipped with obsidian trapezoids had a mechanism of cushioning at their hafting parts, or the connected parts between the shafts and fore-shafts, and that several trapezoids left at the Doteue site were broken by high impact. Therefore, it is assumed that hunting weapons equipped with obsidian trapezoids used complex projectile technology (Shea 2006) such as spear-throwers and darts.

## Use of Obsidian

Studies on sources of lithic raw materials have continued since the 1970s, and obsidian sourcing studies have yielded several important results with regard to the Japanese EUP. Obsidian sourcing analysis began in the 1970s for UP sites in the Kanto region, and it has become much more common in salvage excavation reports for UP sites since the 1980s. Large-scale source analyses using X-ray fluorescence (XRF), which is a non-destructive method of measuring atomic composition, were first conducted in 1994 (Mochizuki et al.1994; Ikeya and Mochizuki 1998; Ikeya 2015). They intensively investigated sources of obsidian from UP sites in the Mt. Ashitaka area; more than 10,000 obsidian artefacts from the sites were analysed. The results of the analyses revealed that obsidian from sites in the Mt. Ashitaka area came from the Shinshu area, Hakone area, Amagi area, and Kozushima area (Figure 14.4). Temporal changes in obsidian source exploitation in the Mt. Ashitaka region and these XRF results were further supported by three Nuclear Activation Analyses (NAA) (Ikeya 2015). Kozushima is a small volcanic island located in the Pacific Ocean, currently 50 km offshore from the main Japanese island of Honshu. The two islands have never been connected, even in the LGM. The results of the analyses also revealed, however, that Kozushima obsidian was the main stone material at multiple sites during the earliest phase (Phase 1: Layer SC IV-BBIV) in the Mt. Ashitaka area. Kozushima obsidians disappeared completely from Phase II to Phase IV, but increased again in Phase V, which is characterized by microblade technology in the terminal Pleistocene. Using Kozushima obsidians in sites of the earliest phase (38,000–34,500 cal BP) suggests that active maritime transportation was performed by early modern humans (Ikeya 2015).

Recently, databases that compile all of the provenance data for more than 85,000 obsidian artefacts from Upper Palaeolithic sites in the Chubu and the Kanto regions were published (Serizawa et al. 2011; Tani et al. 2013). The databases were used by Shimada et al. (2017) to discuss human responses to climatic change on obsidian source exploitation during the Upper Palaeolithic in the Central Highlands.

## Circular Lithic Aggregations

A circular aggregation is a characteristic archaeological feature in the Japanese EUP. It is characterized by several (or many) lithic concentrations aligned in a circle. More than 100 circular aggregations were found in EUP sites throughout the Japanese Islands (Hashimoto 2006). They were left mainly in the initial phase of the EUP. Their sizes vary from about 11 m to 80 m in diameter, the average being 20 m (Hashimoto 2006). Refitting analyses indicate a high frequency of refitted lithic artefacts between those from different concentrations in most of the circular aggregations. Most researchers have assumed that a circular aggregation was formed temporarily at each site. On the other hand, several sites revealed that different groups of lithic concentrations in a circular aggregation have different compositions of lithic raw materials. For example, in a circular aggregation from the Kamibayashi site in a northern part of the Kanto region, locally available lithic raw materials such as chert were mainly left in lithic concentrations located on the west half of the circular aggregation and exotic lithic raw materials such as obsidian, aphyric andesite, rhyolite, and shale were mainly left in lithic concentrations located on the east half of the circular aggregation (Idei et al. 2004) (Figure 14.9). In circular aggregations from the Doteue site (Ikeya 1998, 2015) in the Mt. Ashitaka area and the Izumikitagawa Dai San site (Yamaoka, M. 2012) in the Shimousa Upland in the eastern part of the Kanto region, obsidian sourcing analyses show different groups of lithic concentrations (or different lithic concentrations) in a circular aggregation had different compositions of obsidian provenances. Thus, many researchers assume that the circular aggregations were formed temporarily by plural groups of hunter-gatherers who had different foraging territories.

Various interpretations of formation factors for the circular aggregations and causes of the gathering of groups of hunter-gatherers have been proposed (Tsutsumi 2012), including the exchange of lithic raw materials (Kurishima 1990), hunting large game together (Daikuhara 1991), confirming inter-group solidarity (Sato 2006), coalitions against external threats (Inada 2001), and so on. It seems difficult to judge which interpretation is more plausible than another due to the scarcity of evidence; however, the circular aggregations at least suggest that hunter-gatherers in the initial phase of the EUP in the Japanese Islands had social networks over wide geographical ranges as well as complex social organizations.

## Trap-Pits

Pitfalls of the Upper Palaeolithic have been found throughout the Japanese Islands since their initial finding in the excavations at the Hatsunegahara site (Suzuki et al. 1999) (Figure 14.10) in the Mt. Hakone area in the late 1980s. Based on both the characteristics of pitfalls and comparative

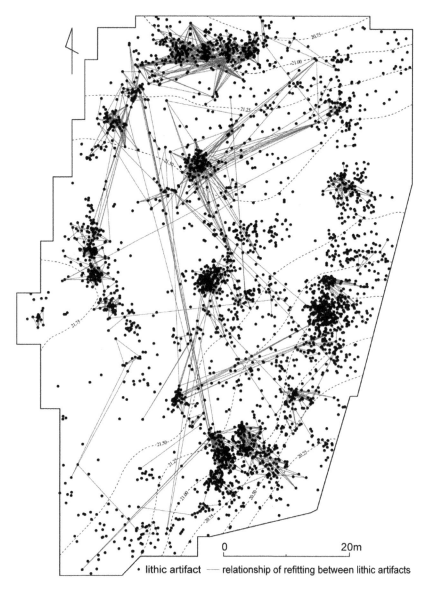

FIGURE 14.9  Circular aggregation from the Kamibayashi site (modified from Idei et al. (2004, fig. 640).

data from Jomon period sites and modern hunter-gatherers, these pitfalls are interpreted as traps (Sato 2012, 2015). A total of 376 trap-pits have been excavated from 51 Palaeolithic sites in the Japanese Islands (Sato 2012). The oldest examples were found from the Otsubobata site on Tanegashima Island located in the Pacific Ocean, currently 40 km offshore from Kyushu. They belong to the initial phase of the EUP. Trap-pits were also found at sites with microblade assemblages in the terminal Pleistocene in Kyushu (Sato 2012).

The greatest number of trap-pits, however, were found in the Mt. Ashitaka and Mt. Hakone areas; a total of more than 200 trap-pits were found from at least 15 sites in both areas. All of the trap-pits were dug from Layer BBIII, and belong to the middle phase of the EUP. Almost all

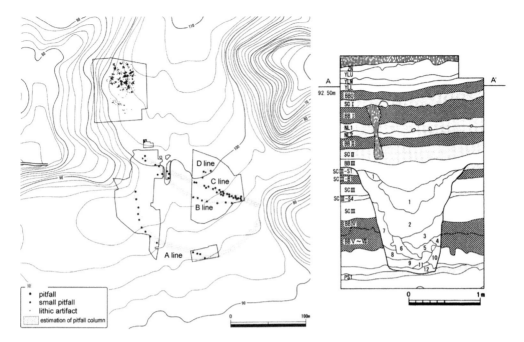

FIGURE 14.10  Pitfalls from the Hatsunegahara site (modified from Suzuki et al. (1999, figs. 175 and 245).

of them are round or nearly round in plan view. The depth is usually much more than 1m and their vertical cross sections are bucket-like shapes. There are two types of arrangement for these trap-pits, which is similar to those of the Jomon period (Sato 2012, 2015). One is that several trap-pits were set on terrace slopes or valley heads and positioned near each other, called a "set arrangement". Another is that many trap-pits were arranged in long lines on a flat terrace or a hill, called a "line arrangement". Representative examples of the line arrangements were found at the Hatsunegahara site (Figure 14.10).

Although Imamura (2004) suggested that these line arrangements crossing terraces were used for drive hunting, other researchers suggested that they were used for trap hunting because of the variety in their arrangements (Sato 2002; Inada 2001, 2004). Sato (2015) discussed it further and explained his reasons in detail. Most researchers have assumed that the main targets of trap-pits were medium-sized animals in the Palaeoloxodon-Sinomegaceroides complex such as wild boars and deer, based on the size of the trap-pits. Some researchers assume that these pitfalls must have been used in trap hunting as a part of sedentary behavioural strategy, based on data from modern hunter-gatherers and so on (Ikeya 2009a; Sato 2012, 2015). Ikeya (2009a) examined the results of obsidian sourcing analyses for obsidian artifacts from archaeological horizons in Layer BBIII and pointed out that obsidian provenances are roughly limited to near sources such as the Amagi area and the Hakone area in that time period. Sato (2012, 2015) estimated that the groups of hunter-gatherers who used trap-pits in the Mt. Ashitaka and the Mt. Hakone areas, as well as those in southern Kyushu during the EUP, also frequently exploited plant foods since floral data for the LGM in the Japanese Islands suggest a relative abundance of edible plant foods. It is also worth noting that sites where many trap-pits are found exist in the regions that have well-stratified, thick, Late Quaternary tephra sequences.

## Various Modern Behavioural Traits of People in the Japanese EUP and Their Implications

This chapter explained various modern behavioural traits recognized through artifacts and archaeological features from EUP sites in the Japanese Islands. These were selected based on previous studies from regions other than the Japanese Islands, since reliable archaeological materials older than 39,000 cal BP, which would be comparative data for materials dating to after the arrival of early modern humans, are still rare or absent in the Japanese Islands, as mentioned above. Here, their implications for understanding the behavioural modernity of early modern humans are discussed.

Lithic assemblages of the initial phase of the EUP are somewhat similar to lithic assemblages from Southeast Asia during the Pleistocene. The hunter-gatherers responsible for them in the Japanese Islands were estimated to have been heavily dependent on plant resources for tool production, based on lithic tool compositions and MIS 3 vegetation data. It is suggested that a technological system, which was very different from those in the EUP industries from other regions such as Europe, West Asia, and northern Eurasia, was present in this time period (Yamaoka 2006, 2012c). In addition, the Japanese EUP data reveals that changes in lithic technologies was possibly related to changes in resource use for tool production and residential mobility, corresponding to changes in environmental settings. Such data show changes in technological adaptation during the EUP and reflect the flexible abilities for technological adaptation of early modern humans. Recent archaeological research in Southeast Asia and Australia has also revealed adaptive behaviour in various environmental settings and demonstrated early modern humans' technological flexibility (Barker et al. 2007; O'Connor et al. 2011; Hiscock 2015; Roberts and Amano 2019). In the 1980s, Binford (1989) suggested that the techno-adaptive strategies of modern hunter-gatherers were extremely variable in planning depth, tactical depth, and curation, and that technological features reflecting differences in the components of these strategies scaled remarkably well with environmental variables in the near-modern world. He thought that such flexible abilities relating to the techno-adaptive strategies were a main aspect of modern behavioural traits (Binford 1989, 21–23). The phenomena in the Japanese EUP agree with his argument and are thought to be fine examples of the technological flexibility of early modern humans in response to environmental variables in the EUP (Yamaoka 2012c, 2014, 2021).

Recent studies of armatures such as trapezoids in the Japanese EUP lend support to arguments of complex projectile technology in Africa, west Asia, and Europe (Shea 2006; Sisk and Shea 2011). In addition, the mechanism of cushioning in hunting weapons equipped with trapezoids is thought to be a general effect of the complex structure of hunting weapons formed by connecting various raw materials for hafting. A variety of reasons for hafting have been put forth: increasing force, formation of cutting edges, conserving raw materials, and so on (Keeley 1982). The mechanism of cushioning seems to have been one of the reasons for hafting and for connecting raw materials for making tools of complex structure.

The use of exotic lithic raw materials and long-distance procurements of raw materials are regarded as examples of modern behavioural traits (McBreaty and Brooks 2000). In the Japanese EUP, obsidian sourcing studies clearly show the same behaviour in the initial phase of the EUP. Moreover, those studies indicate that active maritime transportation was performed by early modern humans. The circular aggregations suggest that hunter-gatherers in the initial phase of the EUP in the Japanese Islands had social networks over wide geographical ranges as well as complex social organizations. In Europe, hunter-gatherers in the EUP are estimated to have had larger and more complex social groups than in the previous time periods, based on the appearance of artifacts laden with symbolic meaning, such as figurines, personal ornaments, and musical instruments (Conard 2008). The Japanese EUP sites have not yielded such artefacts but provided other forms of information about social groups in the EUP. Pitfalls in the Japanese EUP, for example, provide direct evidence for trap-hunting, although trap-hunting is also presumed as one of the hunting methods used by early modern humans in Southeast Asia based on the results of analyses of faunal remains from Niah Cave (Barker et al. 2007).

Archaeological materials of the Japanese EUP support and reinforce various arguments about the behavioural modernity of early modern humans, and some findings even contribute new knowledge. Archaeological materials from the Japanese EUP are characterized as follows: substantial amounts of lithic artefacts and chronology based on rich geochronological information, significant data from obsidian sourcing analyses, and archaeological features such as trap-pits and circular aggregations which are rare or absent in other regions. These characteristic materials are significant due to geographical conditions as well as the systems and methods of excavations in the Japanese Islands. The geographic condition of the Japanese Islands as a volcanic zone has its advantages: rich geochronological information for chronological research and many obsidian sources to research. However, it also presents several disadvantages, such as the dissolving of organic materials. Many large-scale salvage excavations at open-air sites have aided in understanding the distribution of archaeological features on a larger scale than is possible with smaller, more intense excavations, although their usual excavation method brings insufficiencies in terms of recovering smaller materials (Yamaoka et al. 2023).

Human migrations, both for archaic humans and modern humans, are reflected in the archaeological materials left behind in each region. Modern human behaviour relating to adaptations to new environmental settings may also be revealed. In addition, geographical conditions and environmental settings of the sites and regions, as well as excavation systems and methods, also influence the range of archaeological artifacts and features unearthed. These are important aspects which should be considered in this research.

Finally, the implications of the Japanese EUP for studies on dispersal of early modern humans to East Eurasia are discussed. It has already been discussed that the changes of lithic assemblages during EUP in the Japanese Islands reflect changes in technological adaptations of early modern humans to different environmental settings and their flexible abilities. However, such changes in technological adaptation seem to also be due to the relationship between the process of early modern human dispersal and the geographical position of the Japanese Islands in addition to climate changes.

The Japanese Islands are located at a considerable distance from Africa from which modern humans emerged. Goebel (2007) discussed dispersals of early modern humans based on fossil, archaeological, and DNA evidence. He explained early modern human dispersal along two routes in different periods. The earlier spread of early modern humans was from an east-African source from 60,000 to 40,000 years ago. The eastward migration likely proceeded along the south-Asian coast to insular Southeast Asia, and ultimately to Australia by 50,000–45,000 years ago. On the other hand, the later spread of early modern humans was from a west-Asian source to the Mediterranean, temperate Europe, Russia, and Central Asia from 45,000 to 35,000 years ago. They reached southern Siberia by 45,000 years ago and arctic Siberia by 30,000 years ago. Based on this explanation, the Japanese Islands are situated in the middle of both routes, and could have been reached by early modern humans from both routes.

Furthermore, Kaifu et al. (2015) compiled palaeoanthropological and archaeological data relating to the dispersals of early modern humans in east Eurasia. They suggested that the new data set supports simultaneous, explosive patterns of the initial dispersal of modern humans across almost all of Eurasia after 50,000 years ago. However, Clarkson et al. (2017) suggested that human occupation began around 65,000 years ago in northern Australia. Bae et al. (2017) estimated that the initial dispersal of modern humans across Asia goes back to before 60,000 years ago, mainly based on fossil, and archaeological evidence. Discussions of the dispersal dates of early modern humans in the east Eurasia seem to continue; however, it is worth noting that the technological features of lithic assemblages from the initial phase of the Japanese EUP are similar to those of Pleistocene lithic assemblages in Southeast Asia and Australia on the southern route, while technological features of lithic assemblages from later phases (especially the final phase) of the Japanese EUP are similar to those of lithic assemblages of the EUP in Northern Asia on the northern route (Yamaoka 2012b; 2014, 2021).

Late Pleistocene lithic assemblages in Southeast Asia, Australia, and so on are mainly composed of amorphous flakes and core tools (pebble tools); they also contain axes or adzes. Core-axes/adzes are found in Late Pleistocene Hoabinhian lithic assemblages from Vietnam (Nguyen 2015; Yi et al. 2008; Nguyen 2005) and southern China (Ji et al. 2016), with the oldest dating to 43,500 years ago (Ji et al. 2016). Edge-ground and/or waisted adzes/hatchets are contained in late Pleistocene lithic assemblages in Australia and New Guinea (Habgood and Franklin 2008), with the oldest dating to 65,000 years ago (Clarkson et al. 2017).

In contrast, lithic assemblages of the EUP in northern Asia have blade-based lithic technologies with sophisticated blade flaking technology. Recently, dates marking the appearance of blade technology in regions in East Asia have been clarified, and the reason it appeared has been argued in each region. The Levallois and prismatic blade method combined to form the characteristics of the early stage of the UP in China. Artefacts bearing such characteristics are distributed in northern China dating to 30,000–40,000 years ago (Li et al. 2016). Based on similarities in technological organization and geographical connections with those discovered in Siberia and Mongolia, their emergence is interpreted as a reflection of population migrations (Li et al. 2016). Reliable dates for blades and the tanged point industry in the Korean peninsula are set at around 36,000 years ago (Seong 2011). Some researchers think of this emergence and establishment as results of direct occasional migrations from northern regions or some type of trade interactions (Bae and Bae 2012). On the other hand, many Japanese researchers have estimated that blade technology was independently developed in the Japanese Islands (e.g. Anzai 2003; Suto 2017), although other researchers explain the appearance of blade technology and changes in it by technological diffusion or population migrations (Inada 2001; Takeoka 2011; Tamura 2015). Recently, Morisaki et al. (2019) evaluated Accelerator Mass Spectrometry (AMS) radiocarbon dates from Japanese EUP assemblages and roughly compared Japanese EUP blade technology with that from the Initial Upper Palaeolithic (IUP) industry of west Eurasia, IUP-like assemblages in China, and EUP assemblages in Korea. Based on this comparison, they estimated multiple technological diffusions or population migrations among the Japanese Islands and the Korean Peninsula, while they also suggested that direct influence from China or western Eurasia was improbable. However, Kunitake et al. (2022) estimated the direct influence from the IUP industry of Eurasia, based on technological similarities between the IUP industry there and a lithic assemblage from the Kosakayama site in Chubu region. Discussions concerning the reasons for the appearance of blade technology in the Japanese Islands seem likely to continue for the time being.

Pleistocene lithic assemblages from Australia contain important comparative data in terms of the meaning of the changes in technological adaptation and the appearance of sophisticated blade technology in the Japanese EUP. Amorphous flake assemblages with little blade technology continued during the Pleistocene in Australia (Habgood and Franklin 2008), despite various environmental settings and large climatic changes during this time (Davidson 2010). This indicates that modern humans would not necessarily or consistently invent a new technological system, including blade technology, according to environmental conditions. Like the Japanese Islands, Australia is also situated a considerable distance from Africa, but it is located in the southern hemisphere, farthest away from the northern route. This suggests that the changes in technological adaptations identified during the Japanese EUP may not have arisen only from the technological flexibility of hunter-gatherers, but that the technological system, including blade technology, could have been transmitted or brought by another human group onto the Japanese Islands. Based on this hypothesis, it is thought that early modern humans from both the southern and northern routes could have reached the Japanese Islands, and lithic assemblages of the Japanese EUP as well as their changes during the EUP could also reflect early modern human migrations into the Japanese Islands. Furthermore, it suggests that there could have already been several migrations of early modern humans into the Japanese Islands during the EUP (Yamaoka 2012b, 2014, 2021). This argument is added to previous discussions concerning technological flexibility, suggesting that early modern humans as a species demonstrated appreciable flexibility.

## Conclusion

As a result of intensive excavations, more than 10,000 Upper Palaeolithic sites have been discovered and reported all over the Japanese Islands. Recent studies indicate that the arrival of *H. sapiens* to the Japanese Islands dates to 39,000 years ago. In the beginning of this chapter, outlines of palaeo-environmental studies, such as flora and fauna, as well as archaeological studies from MIS 3 to 2 in the Japanese Islands were introduced. Based on these studies, archaeological research of the EUP on the Japanese Islands was examined. To date, about 500 EUP sites have been reported across the Islands. The author indicates modern behavioural traits recognized in the lithic artefacts in the Japanese EUP, including lithic technologies relating to resource use and mobility, standardized armatures such as trapezoids and hunting technology, and the use of high quality lithic raw material such as obsidian. In addition, the author also indicates unique archaeological features in the Japanese EUP reflecting behavioural modernity, such as circular lithic aggregations and trap-pits, which have been discovered only in the Japanese Islands as archaeological features belonging to the UP. Such archaeological materials reveal complex technology and flexible abilities, as well as a wide social network among early modern humans in the Japanese Islands. These characteristic materials reflect the geographical conditions and environmental settings of sites and regions, as well as systems and methods of excavation in the Japanese Islands. Moreover, changes in the lithic assemblages in the Japanese EUP also suggest the possibility that early modern humans from both the southern and northern routes could have reached the Japanese Islands, and there could have already been several migrations of early modern humans there during the EUP.

## References

Adachi, Noboru, Shinoda, Kenichi, and Izuho, Masami. 2015 Further Analyses of Hokkaido Jomon Mitochondrial DNA, in *Emergence and Diversity of Modern Human Behavior in Palaeolithic Asia*, Kaifu, Yousuke, Izuho, Masami, Goebel, Ted, Sato Hiroyuki, and Ono, Akira eds. College Station: Texas A & M University Press, 406–17.

Andrefsky, William Jr. 1998 *Lithics: Macroscopic Approaches to Analysis*. Cambridge: Cambridge University Press.

Anzai, Masahito. 2003 *Kyusekki Shakai no Kozo Hendo [Structural Changes of Palaeolithic Society]*. Tokyo: Doseisha. (In Japanese)

Bae, Christopher. And Bae, Kidong. 2012 The nature of the early to late Palaeolithic transition in Korea: Current perspectives. *Quaternary International* 281, 26–35.

Bae, Christopher, Douka, Katerina, and Petraglia, Michael. 2017 On the origin of modern humans: Asian perspectives, *Science* 358: DOI: 10.1126/science.aai9067.

Barker, Graeme, Barton, Huw, Bird, Michael, Daly, Patrick, Datan, Ipoi, Dykes, Alan, Farr, Lucy, Gilbertson, David, Harrisson, Barbara, Hunt, Chris, Higham, Tom, Kealhofer, Lisa, Krigbaum, John, Lewis, Helen, McLaren, Sue, Paz, Victor, Pike Alistair, Piper, Phil, Pyatt, Brian, Rabett, Ryan, Reynolds, Tim, Rose, Jim, Rushworth, Garry, Stephens, Mark, Stringer, Chris, Thompson, Jill, and Turney, Chris. 2007 "The 'Human Revolution' in Lowland Tropical Southeast Asia: the Antiquity and Behavior of Anatomically Modern Humans at Niah Cave (Sarawak, Borneo)." *Journal of Human Evolution* 52: 243–61.

Binford, Lewis R. 1979 "Organization and formation processes: Looking at curated technologies." *Journal of Anthropological Research* 25: 255–73.

Binford, Lewis R. 1989 "Isolating the transition to cultural adaptations: An organizational approach," in *The Emergence of Modern Humans: Biocultural Adaptations in the Later Pleistocene*, ed. Trinkaus, Erik. Cambridge: Cambridge University Press, 18–41

Clarkson, Chris, Jacobs, Zenobia, Marwick, Ben, Fullagar, Richard, Wallis, Lynley, Smith, Mike, Roberts, Richard, Hayes, Elspeth, Lowe, Kelsey, Carah, Xavier, Florin, Anna, McNeil, Jessica, Cox, Delyth, Arnold, Lee, Hua, Quan, Huntley, Jillian, Brand, Helen, Manne, Tiina, Fairbairn, Andrew, Shulmeister, James, Lyle, Lindsey, Salinas, Makiah, Page, Mara, Connell, Kate, Park, Gayoung, Norman, Kasih, Murphy, Tessa, and Pardoe, Colin. 2017 Human occupation of northern Australia by 65,000 years ago. *Nature* 547, 306–10.

Conard, Nicholas. 2008 A critical view of the evidence for a Southern African origin of behavioural modernity. *South African Archaeological Society Goodwin Series* 10, 175–79.

Daikuhara, Yutaka. 1991 AT Kai Sekkigun no Iseki Kozo Bunseki nikansuru Ichi Shiron [An Essay on Structural Analysis of Sites in the Palaeolithic Stone Industries under the Aira Tanzawa Volcanic Ash: Part 2] *Kyusekki Kokogaku* 42, 33–40. (In Japanese)

Davidson, Iain. 2010 The colonization of Australia and its adjacent islands and the evolution of modern cognition. *Current Anthropology* 51, S177–89.

Goebel, Ted. 2007 The missing years for modern humans. *Science* 315, 194–96.

Habgood, Phillip. And Franklin, Natalie. 2008 The revolution that didn't Arrive: A review of Pleistocene Sahul. *Journal of Human Evolution* 55, 187–222.

Harunari, Hideji 1976 Sendoki Jomon Jidai no Kakki nitsuite (1) [Innovative changes between the Palaeolithic and the Jomon period (1)]. *Kokogaku Kenkyu* 22, 68–92. (in Japanese)

Hasegawa, Yoshikazu. 1972 Naumann's Elephant, Palaeoloxodon naumanni (Makiyama) from the Late Pleistocene off Shakagahana, Shoshima Is. In Inland Sea, Japan. *Bulletin of the National Science Museum* 15, 513–91.

Hashimoto, Katsuo. 2006 Kanjyo Yunitto to Sekifu no Kakawari [The relationship of Circular Unit and Axe]. *Kyusekki Kenkyu* 2: 35–46. (In Japanese with English abstract)

Hiscock, Peter. 2015 Cultural Diversification and the Global Dispersion of the Homo sapiens: Lessons from Australia, in *Emergence and Diversity of Modern Human Behavior in Palaeolithic Asia*, Kaifu, Yousuke, Izuho, Masami, Goebel, Ted, Sato Hiroyuki, and Ono, Akira. eds. College Station: Texas A and M University Press, 225–36.

Hutterer, Karl. 1976 An evolutionary approach to the Southeast Asia cultural sequence. *Current Anthropology* 17, 221–42.

Idei, Hiroshi, Matsuura, Mayumi, Kurihara, Yumi, and Paleoenvironment Research Institute Co., Ltd. 2004 *Kamibayashi Iseki [The Kamibayashi site]*. Sano: Sano City Board of Education. (In Japanese)

Ikeya, Nobuyuki. 1998 *Doteue Iseki (d, e Ku-2) Hakkutsutyousa Hokokusyo [Excavation Report of the Doteue site, Loc. d,e - 2]*. Numazu: Numazu City Board of Education. (In Japanese)

Ikeya, Nobuyuki. 2004 *Maizou Bunkazai Hakkutsutyousa Hokokusyo 4 Doteue Iseki (d, e Ku-3) Maruyama Iseki [Excavation Report of Buried Cultural Properties 4 the Doteue site, Loc. d, e – 3 and the Maruyama site]*. Numazu: Numazu City Board of Education. (In Japanese)

Ikeya, Nobuyuki. 2009a Kyusekki Jidai niokeru Otoshiana Ryo to Sekizai Kakutoku Sekki Seisaku Kodo [Pit-fall Hunting and Palaeolithic Human Behavior for Raw Material Acquisiotion and Stone Tool

Production: Focused on Cultural Phase BBIII at the Foot of Mt. Ashitaka-hakone]. *Sundai Shigaku* 135, 71–90. (In Japanese with English abstract)

Ikeya, Nobuyuki 2009b *Kokuyoseki Koukogaku [Obsidian Archaeology: Social Structure and its Changes as viewed from Obsidian Source Analyses]*. Tokyo, Shinsensha. (In Japanese)

Ikeya, Nobuyuki, Maejima, Hideharu, Yamaoka, Takuya, Kadowaki, Seiji, and Suwama, Jun. 2011 A guide for the excursion to upper Palaeolithic sites in the Mt. Ashitaka Area in Numazu City, in *Program of the Dual Symposia: The Emergence and Diversity of Modern Human Behavior in Palaeolithic Asia & The 4th Annual Meeting of the Asian Palaeolithic Association*, Izuho, Masami, et al.eds. Tokyo: National Museum of Nature and Science, Tokyo & Japanese Palaeolithic Research Association, 137–55.

Ikeya, Nobuyuki. 2015 Maritime Transport of Obsidian in Japan during the Upper Palaeolithic, in *Emergence and Diversity of Modern Human Behavior in Palaeolithic Asia*, Kaifu, Yousuke, Izuho, Masami, Goebel, Ted, Sato Hiroyuki, and Ono, Akira. eds. College Station: Texas A & M University Press, 362–75.

Ikeya, Nobuyuki, and Akihiko Mochizuki. 1998 Ashitaka Sanroku niokeru Sekizai Sosei no Hensen [Composition and changes in lithic raw materials at the Mt. Ashitaka area during the upper Palaeolithic]. *Shizuoka Ken Kokogaku Kenkyu* 30, 21–44. (In Japanese)

Imamura, Keiji. 2004 Hakone Nansei Sanroku Sendoki Jidai Otoshiana no Shiyo Hoho. [Using Way of Pre-ceramic Pitfalls on the Southwestern Foot of Mt. Hakone]. *Kokogaku Kenkyu* 51, 18–33. (In Japanese with English abstract)

Inada, Takashi. 2001 *Yudo Suru Kyusekki Jin [Palaeolithic Foragers]*. Tokyo: Iwanami Shoten. (In Japanese)

Inada, Takashi 2004 Koki Kyusekki Jidai no Syuryo to Doubutsu Gun [Hunting and Fauna during the Upper Palaeolithic Period], in *Bunka no Tayousei to Hikaku Kokogaku [Cultural Diversity and Comparative Archaeology]*, Kokogaku Kenkyu Kai ed. Okayama: Kokogaku Kenkyu Kai, 85–101. (In Japanese with English abstract)

Inada, Takashi and Hiroyuki Sato (eds). 2010 *Koza Nihon no Kokogaku 1 Kyusekki Jidai Jyo [Course of Japanese Archaeology 1 the Palaeolithic the first volume]*. Tokyo: Aoki Shoten. (in Japanese)

Ito, Fujio. 1992 Musashino Daichi Niokeru Tachikawa Ki no Kankyo Hensen to Sekki Bunka [Environmental changes and lithic industries in Tachikawa Loam on Musashino upland], *Musashino no Kokogaku [Archaeology in Musashino]*. Tokyo: Yoshida Itaru Sensei Koki Kinen Ronbun Shu Kanko Kai, 31–44. (in Japanese)

Iwase, Akira, Hashizume, Jun, Izuho Masami, Takahashi Keiichi, Sato, Hiroyuki. 2012 Timing of megafaunal extinction in the late Pleistocene on the Japanese Archipelago. *Quaternary International* 255, 114–24.

Iwase, Akira, Keiichi Takahashi and Masami Izuho. 2015 Further study on the Late Pleistocene megafaunal extinction in the Japanese Archipelago, in *Emergence and Diversity of Modern Human Behavior in Palaeolithic Asia*, Kaifu, Yousuke, Izuho, Masami, Goebel, Ted, Sato Hiroyuki, and Ono, Akira. eds.College Station: Texas A & M University Press, 325–44.

Izuho, Masami, and Kaifu, Yousuke. 2015 The appearance and characteristics of the early upper Palaeolithic in the Japanese Archpelago, in *Emergence and Diversity of Modern Human Behavior in Palaeolithic Asia*, Kaifu, Yousuke, Izuho, Masami, Goebel, Ted, Sato Hiroyuki, and Ono, Akira. eds. College Station: Texas A & M University Press, 289–313.

Japanese Palaeolithic Research Association 2010 *Nihon Retto no Kyusekki Jidai Iseki: Nihon Kyusekki (Sendoki, Iwajyuku) Jidai Iseki no Database [Palaeolithic Sites in the Japanese Islands: A Database]*, Tokyo: Japanese Palaeolithic Research Association. (In Japanese)

Ji, Xueping, Kuman, Kathleen, Clarke, R., Forestier, Hubert, Li, Yinghua, Ma, Juan, Qiu, Kaiwei, Li, Hao, and Wu, Yun. 2016 The Oldest Hoabinhian Technocomplex in Asia (43.5 ka) at Xiaodong Rockshelter, Yunnan Province, Southwest China, *Quaternary International* 400, 166–74.

Kaifu, Yousuke, Izuho, Masami, Goebel, Ted, Sato Hiroyuki, and Ono, Akira. 2015 *Emergence and Diversity of Modern Human Behavior in Palaeolithic Asia*, College Station: Texas A & M University Press.

Kanomata, Yoshitaka. 2005 Tohoku Chiho no Koki Kyusekki Jidai Shoto no Sekki Seisaku Gijyutsu to Kino no Kenkyu [A Technological and Functional Study on Early Upper Palaeolithic Assemblages from II b Archaeological Horizon of the Kamihagimori site in the Tohoku Region], *Miyagi Kokogaku* 7, 1–26. (In Japanese)

Kanomata, Yoshitaka. 2011 Jizoden Iseki Syutsudo Sekki no Kino Kenkyu to Kanjyo Burokku Gun Keisei no Kaisyaku, [Functional Analysis of Stone Tools Excavated from the Jizoden Site and Interpretation of the Formation Process of the Circular Shaped Lithic Distribution], in *Jizoden Iseki: Kyusekki Jidai Hen*. Yasuda, Tadaichi, and Kanda, Kazuhiko. eds. Akita: Akita City Board of Education, 182–92. (In Japanese with English abstract)

Kanayama, Yoshiaki. 1990 Aira Tn Kazanbai Kouhai Ki niokeru Kokuyouseki Sekkigun [The Obsidian Stone Tool Assemblage in the Period of Aira Tanzawa Pumice]. *Kouko Siryoukan Kiyo* 6, 1–15. (In Japanese)

Kawamura, Yoshinari. 1991 Quaternary mammalian Faunas in the Japanese Islands. *Quaternary Research* 30, 213–220.

Kawamura, Yoshinari, and Nakagawa, Ryohei. 2012 Terrestrial Mammal Faunas in the Japanese Islands during OIS 3 and OIS 2, in *Environmental Changes and Human Occupation in East Asia during OIS 3 and OIS 2*, Ono, Akira and Izuho, Masami. eds. Oxford: Archaeopress, 33–54.

Keeley, Lawrence. 1982 Hafting and retooling: effects on the archaeological Record, *American Antiquity* 47, 798–809.

Kudo, Yuichiro. 2012 Absolute Chronology of Archaeological and Paleoenvironmental Records from the Japanese Islands, 40–15 ka BP, in *Environmental Changes and Human Occupation in East Asia during OIS 3 and OIS 2*. Ono, Akira and Masami Izuho. eds. Oxford: Archaeopress, 13–32.

Kudo, Yuichiro and Fujio Kumon. 2012 Palaeolithic cultures of MIS 3 to MIS 1 in relation to climate changes in the central Japanese islands. *Quaternary International* 248, 22–31.

Kunitake, Sadakatsu, Kunikita Dai, and Sato Hiroyuki. 2022 Sekijin Sekkigun karamita Nihon Retto niokeru Kokikyusekki Jidai Bunka no Seiritsu [The formative process of the Upper Palaeolithic culture in the Japanese archipelago in terms of the origin of the blade industry]. *Kokogaku Kenkyu* 69, 56–73. (In Japanese with English abstract)

Kurishima, Yoshiaki. 1990 Ibutsu Bunpu kara Miru Iseki no Kousei [The structure of sites based on the distribution of artifacts]. *Sekki Bunka Kenkyu 2*, Hiratsuka: Sekki Bunka Kenkyu Kai. (In Japanese)

Lambeck, Kurt and Chappell, John. 2001 Sea level change through the last glacial cycle. *Science* 292, 679–86.

Li, Feng, Chen, FuYou, Wang, YingHua, and Gao, Xing. 2016 Technology diffusion and population migration reflected in blade technologies in northern China in the Late Pleistocene. *Science China Earth Science* 59, 1540–53.

Machida, Hiroshi and Arai, Fusao. 2003 *Shinpen Kazanbai Atlas: Nihon Retto to Sono Shuhen [Atlas of Tephra in and around Japan]*. Tokyo: University of Tokyo Press. (In Japanese)

McBreaty, Sally and Brooks, Alison. 2000 The Revolution that Wasn't: New Interpretation of the Origin of Modern Human Behavior. *Journal of Human Evolution* 39, 453–563.

McColl, Hugh, Racimo, Fernando, Vinner, Lasse, Demeter, Fabrice, Gakuhari, Takashi, Moreno-Mayar, Victor, van Driem, George, Wilken, Uffe, Seguin-Orlando Andaine, de la Fuente Castro, Constanza, Wasef, Sally, Shoocongdej, Rasmi, Souksavatdy, Viengkeo, Sayavongkhamdy, Thongsa, Saidin, Mohd, Allentoft, Morten, Sato, Takehiro, Malaspinas, Anna-Sapfo, Aghakhanian, Farhang, Korneliussen, Thorfinn, Margaryan, Ana, de Barros Damgaard, Peter, Kaewsutthi, Supannee, Lertrit, Patcharee, Nguyen, Thi, Hung, Hsiao-Chun, Tran, Thi, Truong, Huu, Nguyen, Giang, Shahidan, Shaiful, Wiradnyana, Ketut, Matsumae, Hiromi, Shigehara, Nobuo, Yoneda, Minoru, Ishida, Hajime, Masuyama, Tadayuki, Yamada, Yasuhiro, Tajima, Atsushi, Shibata, Hiroki, Toyoda, Atsushi, Hanihara, Tsunehiko, Nakagome, Shigeki, Deviese, Thibaut, Bacon, Anne-Marie, Duringer, Philippe, Ponche, Jean-Luc, Shackelford, Laura, Patole-Edoumba, Elise, Nguyen, Anh, Bellina-Pryce, Bérénice, Galipaud, Jean-Christophe, Kinaston, Rebecca, Buckley, Hallie, Pottier, Christophe, Rasmussen, Simon, Higham, Tom, Foley, Robert, Lahr, Marta, Orlando, Ludovic, Sikora, Martin, Phipps Maude, Oota, Hiroki, Higham, Charles, Lambert David, and Willerslev, Eske. 2018 The prehistoric peopling of Southeast Asia. *Science* 361, 88–92.

Mibu, Ryousuke and Kazunori Sugiyama. 2009 *Itadori A Iseki, Itadori B Iseki, Itadori C Iseki [The Itadori A site, the Itadori B site, and Itadori C site]*. Shizuoka: Shizuoka Prefecture Institute for Buried Cultural Property. (In Japanese)

Mochizuki, Akihiko, Ikeya, Nobuyuki, Kobayashi, Ktsuji, and Mutou, Yuri. 1994 Iseki Nai niokeru Kokuyoseki Sei Sekki no Gensanchi Betsu Bunpu nitsuite: Numazu Shi Doteue Iseki BBV Sou no Gensanchi Suitei kara [Source analysis for the Obsidian from Layer BBV, the Doteue Site, Numazu City], *Shizuoka Ken Kokogaku Kenkyu* 26, 1–24. (In Japanese)

Morisaki, Kazuki, Sano, Katsuhiro, and Izuho, Masami. 2019 Early upper Palaeolithic blade technology in the Japanese Archipelago. *Archaeological Research in Asia* 17, 79–97.

Morisaki, Kazuki, Kunikita, Dai, Ikeda, Tomoo, Hasebe, Yoshikazu, and Murasaki, Takahiro. 2020 Ishinomoto Saihou: Nihonrettou Kouki Kyusekki Jidai no Kaishi nikansuru Kenkyu [Ishinomoto revisited: A chronological study on the beginning of the upper Palaeolithic period in the Japanese Archipelago]. *Kyusekki Kenkyu* 16, 43–58. (In Japanese with English abstract)

Nakazawa, Yuichi. 2010 Dual nature in the creation of disciplinary identity: A socio-historical review of Palaeolithic archaeology in Japan. *Asian Perspectives* 49, 231–50.

Nakazawa, Yuichi. 2017 On the Pleistocene population history in the Japanese Archipelago. *Current Anthropology* 58, S539–52.

Nara, Takashi, Watanabe, Takehiko, Sawada, Junmei, Sawaura, Ryohei, and Sato, Takao (eds). 2015 *Shitsukari Abe Dokutsu I [Shitsukari-Abe Cave Vol. 1]*. Tokyo: Rokuichi Shobo. (In Japanese with English summery)

Nguyen, Gia, Doi. 2005 Results of recent research into the Lithic Industries from Late Pleistocene/Early Holocene Sites in Northern Vietnam. *Bulletin of the Indo-pacific Prehistory Association* 25, 95–97.

Nguyen, Viet. 2015 First Archeological Evidence of Symbolic Activities from the Pleistocene of Vietnam, in *Emergence and Diversity of Modern Human Behavior in Palaeolithic Asia*, Kaifu, Yousuke, Izuho, Masami, Goebel, Ted, Sato Hiroyuki, and Ono, Akira. eds. College Station: Texas A & M University Press, 133–39.

Norton, Christopher, Kondo, Youichi, Ono, Akira, Zhang, Yingqi, and Diab, Mark. 2010 The nature of megafaunal extinctions during the MIS 3–2 transition in Japan. *Quaternary International* 211, 113–22.

Numazu City Board of Education. (ed). 1990 *Shimizuyanagikita Iseki Hakkutuyousa Hokokusyo Sono 2 [Excavation Report of the Shimizuyanagikita site (Part 2)]*. Numazu: Numazu City Board of Education. (In Japanese)

O'Connor, Sue, Ono, Rintaro, and Clarkson, Chris. 2011 Pelagic fishing at 42,000 years before the present and the maritime skills of modern humans. *Science* 334, 1117–21.

Okinawa Prefectural Museum and Art Mseum (ed). 2015 *Sakitari Do Iseki Hakkutsu Tyosa Gaiyo Houkokusyo [Excavation Report of the Sakitari-do Cave site, Okinawa]*. Naha: Okinawa Prefectural Museum and Art Museum. (In Japanese)

Ono, Akira. 1975 Sendoki Jidai Sekizai Unpan Ron Noto [Transportation of lithic raw material in Palaeolithic]. *Kokogaku Kenkyu* 21, 17–19. (in Japanese)

Ono, Akira (ed). 1998 *Flaked Bone Tools in the Palaeolithic*. Tokyo: Tokyo Metropolitan University Archaeology Laboratory.

Roberts, Patrick and Amano, Noel. 2019 Plastic pioneers: Hominin biogeography east of the Movius Line during the Pleistocene. *Archaeological Research in Asia* 17, 181–92.

Sano, Katsuhiro, Yoshitaka Denda, and Masayoshi Oba. 2012 Syuryo Ho Doutei notameno Tosha Jikken Kenkyu (1): Daikeiyo Sekki [Projectile experimentation for identifying hunting methods (1): Trapezoids]. *Kyusekki Kenkyu* 8, 45–63. (In Japanese with English abstract)

Sano, Katsuhiro. 2016 Evidence for the use of the bow-and-arrow technology by the first modern humans in the Japanese islands. *Journal of Archaeological Science: Reports* 10, 130–41.

Sasahara, Yoshiro. 1999 *Nishibora Iseki (b Ku-1) Hakkutuyousa Hokokusyo [Excavation Report of the Nishibora site, Loc. b -1]*. Numazu: Numazu City Board of Education. (In Japanese)

Sase, Takashi., Machida, Hiroshi., and Hosono, Mamoru. 2008 Sagamino Daichi, Oiso Kyuryo, Fujisan Toroku no Tachikawa-Musashino Loam So ni Kiroku Sareta Syokubutsu Keisantai Gunshu Hendo [Fluctuations of Opal Phytolith Assemblage in the Tachikawa and Musashino Loam Formations in Southwest Kanto, Central Japan: Changes in Vegetation, Climate, Terrace, and Soil-facies since Marine Isotope Stage 5.1.]. *Dai Yon Ki Keikyu* 47, 1–14. (In Japanese with English abstract)

Sato, Hiroyuki. 1992 *Nihon Kyusekki Bunka no Kozo to Shinka. [Evolution and Structure of Palaeolithic Culture in Japan]*. Tokyo: Kashiwashobo. (In Japanese)

Sato, Hiroyuki. 2002 Nihon Retto Kyusekki Jidai no Otoshiana Ryo [Trap-pit Hunting in the Japanese Palaeolithic Period]. *Senri Ethnological Reports* 33, 83–108.

Sato, Hiroyuki. 2006 Kanjyo Syuraku no Syakai Seitaiga Gaku [Socio-ecological research of the circular settlements in the Japanese early upper Palaeolithic]. *Kyusekki Kenkyu* 2, 47–54. (In Japanese with English abstract)

Sato, Hiroyuki. 2012 Late Pleistocene trap-pit hunting in the Japanese Archipelago. *Quaternary International* 248, 43–55.

Sato, H. 2015 Trap-Pit Hunting in Late Pleistocene Japan, in *Emergence and Diversity of Modern Human Behavior in Palaeolithic Asia*, Kaifu, Yousuke, Izuho, Masami, Goebel, Ted, Sato Hiroyuki, and Ono, Akira, eds. College Station: Texas A & M University Press, 389–405.

Sekki Bunka Kenkyu Kai (ed). 1991 *Symposium AT Kohai Izen no Sekki Bunka: Retto Nai no Yoso to Taihi. [Symposium Lithic Culture before the Deposition of AT Tephra: Regional Differences and its Correlation]*. Sekki Bunka Kenkyu 3. Tokyo: Sekki Bunka Kenkyu Kai. (In Japanese)

Seong, Chuntaek. 2011 Evaluating radiocarbon dates and late Palaeolithic chronology in Korea. *Arctic Anthropology* 48, 93–112.
Serizawa, Seihachi, Goto, Shinsuke, Tsukamoto, Moroya, Taninaka, Takashi, Ehara, Ei, Kameda, Yukihisa, Katane, Yoshiyuki. Aida, Emiko, Takekawa, Natsuki, Nakamura, Nobuhiro, and Tsunoda, Yosuke. 2011 Sekki Jidai niokeru Sekizai Riyo no Chiiki So (Siryo) [Regionality of Lithic Raw Material Exploitation in the Atone Age (Database)], In *Nihon Kokogaku Kyokai 2011 Nendo Tochigi Taikai Kenkyu Happyo Siryoshu [Abstracts and Database]*, Nihon Kokogaku Kyokai 2011 Nendo Tochigi Taikai Jikko Iinkai ed. Tochigi: Nihon Kokogaku Kyokai 2011 Nendo Tochigi Taikai Jikko Iinkai, 61–306. (in Japanese).
Shea, John. 2006 The origins of lithic projectile point technology: Evidence from Africa, the Levant, and Europe. *Journal of Archaeological Science* 33, 823–46.
Shimada Kazutaka, Yoshida Akihiro, Hashizume Jun, Ono, Akira. 2017 Human responses to climate change on obsidian source exploitation during the upper Palaeolithic in the central highlands, Central Japan. *Quaternary International* 442, 12–22.
Sisk, Matthew, and Shea, John. 2011 The African origin of complex projectile technology: An analysis using tip cross-sectional area and perimeter. *International Journal of Evolutionary Biology*. doi: 10.4061/2011/968012.
Smith Victoria, Staff, Richard, Blockley, Simon, Ramsey Christopher, Nakagawa Takeshi, Mark Darren, Takemura Keiji, Danhara Toru, and Suigetsu 2006 Project Members. 2013 Identification and correlation of visible Tephras in the Lake Suigetsu SG06 sedimentary archive, Japan: Chronostratigraphic markers for synchronizing of east Asian/west Pacific Palaeoclimatic records across the last 150 ka. *Quaternary Science Reviews* 67, 121–37.
Suto, Takashi. 2017 Sekijin Gijyutsu Kakushin [An Innovation of Blade technology], in *Riron Kokogaku no Jissen II [Practice of Theoretical Archaeology II]*, Anzai, Masahito, ed. Tokyo: Doseisha, 91–113. (In Japanese)
Suzuki, Toshinaka, Tsunehiko Ito, and Hideharu Maeshima. 1999 *Hatsunegahara Iseki [The Hatsunegahara site]*. Mishima: Mishima City Board of Education. (In Japanese)
Symposium Jikko Iinkai. (ed.) 1995 *Ashitaka Hakone Sanroku no Kyusekki Jidai Hennen. [Palaeolithic Chronology at the Mt. Ashitaka and Mt. Hakone areas]*. Numazu: Shizuoka Ken Koko Gakkai. (In Japanese)
Takahara, Hikaru and Hayashi, Ryoma. 2015 Paleovegetation during marine isotope stage 3 in East Asia. in *Emergence and Diversity of Modern Human Behavior in Palaeolithic Asia*, eds Kaifu, Yousuke, Izuho, Masami, Goebel, Ted, Sato Hiroyuki, and Ono, Akira. eds. College Station: Texas A & M University Press, 314–24.
Takahashi, Keiichi, and Izuho, Masami. 2012 Formative History of Terrestrial Fauna of the Japanese Islands during the Plio-Pleistocene, in *Environmental Changes and Human Occupation in East Asia during OIS 3 and OIS 2*, Ono, Akira and Izuho, Masami. Eds. Oxford: Archaeopress, 73–86.
Takao, Yoshiyuki. 1989 *Nakamiyo Dai Ichi Iseki Hakkututyousa Hokokusyo [Excavation Report of the Nakamiyo Dai Ichi site]*. Numazu: Numazu City Board of Education. (In Japanese)
Takao, Yoshiyuki and Harada, Yuki. 2011 *Idemaruyama Iseki Hakkututyousa Hokokusyo [Excavation Report of the Idemaruyama site]*. Numazu: Numazu City Board of Education. (In Japanese)
Takeoka, Toshiki. 2011 *Kyusekki Jidai Jin no Rekishi: Africa kara Nihon Retto e [History of Mankind: from Africa to the Japanese Islands]*. Tokyo: Kodansha. (In Japanese)
Tamura, Takashi. 1992 Toiyama Kuroi Ishi: Musashino 2 Ki Sekkigun no Shakai Seitaigakuteki Ichi Kosatsu [A Socio-Ecological Study on the Lithic Assemblages of 'Musashino 2nd Stage']. *Senshi Koukogaku Ronshu* 2, 1–46.
Tamura, Takashi. 2011 Kyusekki Jidai kara Jomon Jidai no Kari no Dougu [Transiotion of Hunting tools from the Old Stone Age to the Jomon Period]. *Kaizuka* 67, 1–31. (In Japanese)
Tamura, Takashi. 2015 Marebito no Otonai [Neighbors, not auslanders: Some thoughts on the appearance of laminar technologies in the Japanese archipelago]. *Kokogaku Kenkyu* 61, 24–44. (In Japanese with English abstract)
Tanaka, Masashi, Cabrera, Vicente, González, Ana, Larruga, José, Takeyasu1, Takeshi, Fuku1, Noriyuki, Guo1, Li-Jun, Hirose, Raita, Fujita, Yasunori, Kurata, Miyuki, Shinoda, Ken-ichi, Umetsu, Kazuo, Yamada, Yoshiji, Oshida, Yoshiharu, Sato, Yuzo, Hattori, Nobutaka, Mizuno Yoshikuni, Arai, Hirose, Yasumichi, Nobuyoshi, Ohta, Shigeo, Ogawa, Osamu, Tanaka, Yasushi, Kawamori, Ryuzo, Shamoto-Nagai1, Masayo, Maruyama, Wakako, Shimokata, Hiroshi, Suzuki, Ryota, and Shimodaira, Hidetoshi. 2004 Mitochondorial genome variation in Eastern Asia and the peopling of Japan. *Genome Research* 14, 1832–50.

Tani, Kazutaka, Tsukahara, Hideyuki, Tsuruta, Noriaki, Nakajima, Toru, Hashizume, Jun, Habu, Toshiro, Maeda, Kazuya, Murata, Hiroyuki, and Yamashina, Akira. 2013 Chubu Kochi no Kokuyoseki Gensanchi Bunseki Siryo [Database of Obsidian Provenance Analysis in the Chubu Region], In *Nihon Kokogaku Kyokai 2013 Nendo Nagano Taikai Kenkyu Happyo Siryoshu [Abstracts and Database]*, Nihon Kokogaku Kyokai 2013 Nendo Nagano Taikai Jikko Iinkai ed. Nagano: Nihon Kokogaku Kyokai 2013 Nendo Nagano Taikai Jikko Iinkai, 63–174. (in Japanese).

The HUGO Pan-Asian SNP Consortium. 2009 Mapping human genetic diversity in Asia. *Science* 326, 1541–45.

Tsuji, Seiichiro, and Kosugi, Masato. 1991 Aira Tn Kazanbai (AT) Funka ga Seitaikei ni Oyoboshita Eikyo [Influence of Aira-Tn Ash (AT) Eruption on Ecosystem]. *Dai Yon Ki Kenkyu* 30, 419–26 (In Japanese with English abstract)

Tsukada, Matsuo. 1985 Map of vegetation during the last glacial maximum in Japan. *Quaternary Research* 23, 369–81.

Tsutsumi, Takashi. 2006 Kouki Kyusekki Jidai Syoto no Sekifu no Kino wo Kangaeru [The function of Upper Palaeolithic axes: Use-wear analyses of Lithic Artifacts from the Hinatabayashi B site]. *Naganoken Koko Gakkai Shi* 118, 1–12. (in Japanese)

Tsutsumi, Takashi. 2012 MIS3 edge-ground axes and the arrival of the first Homo sapiens in the Japanese archipelago. *Quaternary International* 248, 70–78.

Yamaoka, Mayuko. 2012 Izumikitagawa Dai 3 Iseki Kanjyo Burokku Gun no Ba [Place of Circular aggregation at the Izumikitagawa 3 site]. *Kenkyu Renraku Shi* 73, 1–15.

Yamaoka, Takuya. 2004 Kouki Kyusekki Jidai niokeru Sekki Sozai Riyou Keitai no Ichi Kakki [Innovatin of lithic raw material utilization during the upper Palaeolithic]. *Kokogaku Kenkyu* 51, 12–31. (In Japanese with English abstract)

Yamaoka, Takuya. 2006 Musashino Daichi niokeru Kouki Kyusekki Jidai Zenhanki Sekkigun no Hensen Katei [An innovative process of lithic raw material utilization during the Early Upper Palaeolithic on the Musashino Upland]. *Kodai Bunka* 58, 107–25. (In Japanese with English abstract)

Yamaoka, Takuya. 2010 'Daikeiyousekki' no Kesson Shiryo [Broken Trapezoids: Evidence of modern human behavior from stone artifacts during the Early Upper Palaeolithic on the Japanese Islands]. *Kyusekki Kenkyu* 6, 17–32. (In Japanese with English abstract)

Yamaoka, Takuya. 2011 Transitions in the Early Upper Palaeolithic: An examination of Lithic assemblages on the Musashino Upland, Tokyo, Japan. *Asian Perspectives* 49, 251–78.

Yamaoka, Takuya. 2012a Use and maintenance of trapezoids in the initial early upper Palaeolithic of the Japanese Islands. *Quaternary International* 248, 32–42.

Yamaoka, Takuya. 2012b Dougu Shigen Riyou nikansuru Jinrui no Koudoutekigendaisei [Behavioral modernity in raw material use: Implications of early upper Palaeolithic Assemblages on the Musashino Upland]. *Kyusekki Kenkyu* 8, 91–104. (In Japanese with English abstract)

Yamaoka, Takuya. 2012c *Kouki Kyusekki Jidai Zenhanki Sekkigun no Kenkyu: Minami Kanto Musashino Daichi karano Tenbo. [Study on Early Upper Palaeolithic Assemblages: A Perspective from the Musashino Upland in southern part of the Kanto region]*. Tokyo: Rokuichi Shobo. (In Japanese)

Yamaoka, Takuya. 2014 Early upper Palaeolithic assemblages from the Japanese Islands: A case study from the Musashino upland around Tokyo. *Archaeology Ethnology & Anthropology of Eurasia* 42/2, 18–30.

Yamaoka, Takuya. 2017 Shooting and stabbing experiments using replicated trapezoids. *Quaternary International* 442, 55–65.

Yamaoka, Takuya. 2021 Technology and resource use during the early upper Palaeolithic on the Japanese islands. *Senri Ethnological Studies* 106, 29–60.

Yamaoka, Takuya., Ikeya, Nobuyuki., Miyoshi, Motoki., and Takakura, Jun. 2023 New Perspectives on the Behavioral Patterns of Early Modern Humans from the Japanese Islands. *MGfU* 31, 41–70.

Yi, Seonbok, Lee, June-Jeong, Ki, Seongnam. 2008 New date on the Hoabinhian: Investigations at Hang Cho Cave, Northern Vietnam. *Bulletin of the Indo-pacific Prehistory Association* 28, 73–79.

# 15

## PLEISTOCENE OKINAWA

Unique Culture and Lifeway in the Oceanic Islands of the Western Pacific

*Masaki Fujita*

### Introduction

Early modern human first migrated to oceanic islands in the Late Pleistocene in the continuing dispersal beyond Africa. They would have faced many difficulties both in crossing the ocean and in sustaining their lives on relatively small islands with unique and limited natural resources. The oldest evidence of seafaring and island adaptation by early modern human was reported from Island Southeast Asia (ISEA), midway in the course of their migrations from Eurasia to Australia and New Guinea (e.g. O'Connor et al. 2011). The second oldest evidence for these ocean voyages is found in Japan, including the Ryukyu archipelago (Kaifu et al. 2015; Fujita et al. 2016). Early modern humans inhabited the Ryukyus no later than 30,000 years BP and probably earlier than 36,500 years BP (Kaifu and Fujita 2012; Kaifu et al. 2015). Their Palaeolithic sites are spread along most of the relatively large islands of this archipelago, suggesting intentional voyaging there. However, knowledge of these early people's culture and lifeway has been poor due to the relative paucity of cultural Palaeolithic items and organic materials except for a few human bones unearthed from archaeological sites in the Ryukyus.

The key site in understanding past occupation is Sakitari Cave, located on Okinawa Island, where evidence was found of continuous or successive occupation for early modern humans after 35,000–30,000 years cal BP. This has now been joined by another recently found site at Shiraho-Saonetabaru Cave on Ishigaki Island where well-preserved Late Pleistocene human fossils were found. These are expected to shed light on the burial practices, morphological variability, and/or genetic information about these Palaeolithic Ryukyu islanders. This chapter will review these Palaeolithic materials and discuss how they have contributed to our understanding of early humans' unique adaptations to life on these oceanic islands.

### Geographic Setting and Palaeofauna of the Ryukyu Islands

The Ryukyu archipelago is spread over ca. 1,200 kms between mainland Japan and Taiwan in the western Pacific Ocean. It consists of more than 150 relatively small islands distributed along a northeast-southwest direction at about 27 degrees north in latitude (Figure 15.1). Although dry

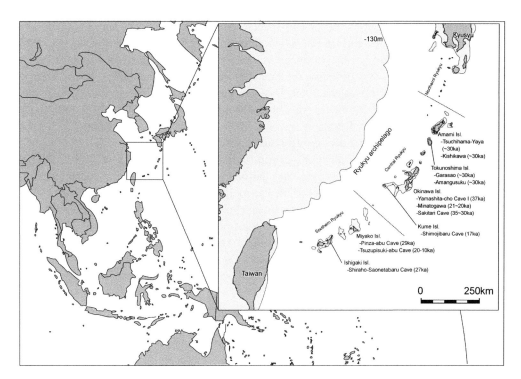

FIGURE 15.1  Palaeolithic sites and the ages of the oldest layer in the Ryukyu archipelago. The light gray area shows the estimated coastline at the Last Glacial Maximum (LGM) period.

and sandy climatic conditions generally stretch around the world at this latitude, the Ryukyus are covered with subtropical forests nourished by the hot and humid atmosphere resulting from the nearby Kuroshio ocean current.

The Ryukyus were previously part of the eastern end of the Eurasian continent. Tectonic movements of the Eurasian and Philippine plates ultimately formed the deep ocean basin named the "Okinawa trough" located west of the Ryukyus, and separated the islands from the continent. This geological event probably culminated no later than the Early Pleistocene, while the basis of the terrestrial fauna probably formed before this (e.g. Ota 2003; Takahashi et al. 2008; Kawamura et al. 2016). Although some islands were connected with each other because of sea-level changes and crustal movements, they became isolated from the continent during the Pleistocene. Furthermore, two deep-sea troughs/channels (>−1000 m), the Tokara and Kerama Gaps, divide the archipelago into three parts, the northern, central, and southern Ryukyus. The islands are located at the margin of two biogeographic regions, the Oriental and Sino-Japanese Regions (Holt et al. 2012). Going from north to south, the fauna, and flora gradually shifted from Sino-Japanese species to Oriental species.

Over several million years, isolation from the Asian continent promoted unique terrestrial fauna which came to consist of many endemic species which mostly lack middle- and large-sized animals except for the wild pig *Sus scrofa riukiuanus*. The Late Pleistocene fauna from these islands have not been extensively studied, although reviews have been made by several authors (Oshiro and Nohara 2000; Kawamura et al. 2016). The consensus from these studies is that the Pleistocene fauna were similar to the extant fauna in each island. There were a few middle-sized animals such as one or two species of medium-sized deer and a medium-sized tortoise, but these became extinct almost simultaneously at the end of the Pleistocene. While the precise timing of their extinction is not yet known, they were considered to have become extinct around 20,000 years BP based on the chronology of the Minatogawa Site on Okinawa Island (Watanabe 1973; Hasegawa 1980; Hasegawa et al. 2017). However recent excavations have revealed that the extinction was probably much older, between 35,000 and 30,000 years BP (Fujita et al. 2014, 2016), with Minatogawa faunal remains consisting of not only 20,000-year-old fauna but also much older deer fossils (Hasegawa et al. 2017).

This proposed timing of extinction occurred at almost the same time or shortly after the arrival of humans ca. 36,500 years ago. The charred lumber vertebra of *C. astylodon*, unearthed from the 35,000- to 30,000-year-old sediments from Sakitari Cave, suggests that Late Pleistocene people possibly hunted the Pleistocene deer (Fujita et al. 2016). Although the evidence is still scanty, this might be the first evidence that Pleistocene humans consumed the endemic deer of Okinawa Island. Palaeolithic-ecological studies of these extinct deer indicate that they probably were a K-strategist species as a result of island adaptation (Kubo et al 2011, 2015). If so, it is easy to imagine that they were strongly impacted by human hunting pressure because of their low reproductive rate.

In contrast to this hunting pressure hypothesis, Kuroda and Ozawa (1996) suggested a natural environmental cause for deer extinction. They studied the pollen sample in a boring core taken from Izena Island, which is located north-west of Okinawa Island, and this suggested a reduction in the evergreen broad-leaf forests as pine trees became dominant around the LGM. Based on this result, they argued that Pleistocene deer could have become extinct because of the reduction of food plants related to environmental changes at that time period (Kuroda & Ozawa 1996). Since isotope studies of molar enamel of extinct deer suggested that their major food plants were broad-leaf plants (Kubo et al. 2011, 2015), the decrease of the broad-leaf forests could have brought about serious food shortages. However, the compositions of terminal Pleistocene fossil amphibian species from two southern localities were similar to the modern fauna in the northern forested area of Okinawa Island (Nakamura and Ota 2015). The dominance of forest species is also reported in studies of avifauna (Matsuoka 2000; Matsuoka and Hasegawa 2018), reptiles, and mice (Nohara and Irei 2002; Hasegawa et al. 2018; Takahashi et al. 2018) from the Minatogawa Site, a terminal Pleistocene (ca. 20,000 years BP) fossil locality in the southern part of Okinawa. Considering these fossil species' composition, a large area of Okinawa Island was probably covered with broad-leaf evergreen forests in the Late Pleistocene, perhaps even during the LGM. Thus, extinction attributed to environmental changes is still controversial. Though we do not conclusively know the cause of the deer extinction, the recent studies are steadily shedding light on this problem at least in the central Ryukyus. Further studies should resolve the problem in the near future.

**First Migration to the Ryukyu Islands**

Hominids first migrated to the Ryukyus during the Late Pleistocene. The oldest evidence of early modern humans from this area is the 36,500-year-old partial human skeleton, stone tools, and possible food refuse found at Yamashita-cho Cave I, on Okinawa Island (Takamiya et al. 1975a; Oda 2003; Kaifu and Fujita 2012). The second oldest evidence consists of charred animal remains, which were certainly food remains, unearthed from 35,000- to 30,000-year-old sediments at Sakitari Cave, Okinawa Island (Fujita et al. 2016). There are several more Palaeolithic sites as old as 30,000 years in the Amami, Tokunoshima, and Miyako islands (e.g. Kaifu et al. 2015; Figure 15.1). These earliest inhabitants certainly came to the Ryukyus much earlier than 30,000 years ago and probably around 36,000–37,000 years ago.

It is notable that most of the relatively large islands of the Ryukyus were occupied in the Late Pleistocene. Because these islands are distant from each other and from larger landmasses including mainland Japan and Taiwan, the early populations would have crossed the open ocean in their colonization. Previously, some researchers proposed the land-bridge hypothesis from Taiwan to Okinawa during the Last Glacial Maximum (Suzuki 1982; Kimura 1996), while others doubted it (Kawana 1980; Oshima 1980). The major opinion today is that the islands were isolated from each other during the late Pleistocene, including the LGM, both from the viewpoint of geography (e.g. Ota et al. 2001) and from biogeography (e.g. Ota 2003; Kawamura et al. 2016). Therefore, late Pleistocene people must have crossed the sea in migrating to the Ryukyus, as mentioned above.

We need to consider the possibility that such crossings were a result of accidental drifting. However, there is difficulty in accepting drifting dispersal not only because these early inhabitants occupied such a wide area of the Ryukyus, but also because Palaeolithic human remains so far discovered have consisted not only of adult males but also of females (Minatogawa, Pinza-abu, Shiraho-Saonetabaru) and infants (Yamashita-cho Cave 1, Sakitari Cave, and Shimoji-baru Cave). It is argued here that these early colonizers made deliberate crossings of the open ocean, voyaging to arrive at these islands (Kaifu et al. 2015).

The world's oldest seafaring was carried out ca. 45,000–63,000 years ago from Sundaland to Australia (e.g. Clarkson et al. 2017). Pelagic fishing might have been an important trigger for developing seafaring techniques. From islands located along the southern route of migration to Australia, O'Connor et al. (2011) found evidence of pelagic fishing dating back to 42,000 years ago and also a Late Pleistocene fishhook (16,000–23,000 years BP) from Jerimalai Rockshelter in East Timor. Of importance here is that the colonisation of the Ryukyus and the Japanese archipelago is evidence for the second oldest recorded open ocean voyaging in the world, accompanied by the oldest fishhook yet found along with evidence of aquatic resource consumption dated to 35,000 year ago (Fujita et al. 2016).

The exploitation of marine products is one of the innovations of modern human behaviour which enabled worldwide human dispersals (Erlandson 2001). The 36,500-years-old fish bones and shells from the Yamashita-cho Cave I in Okinawa (Takamiya et al. 1975a) demonstrate the adaptation to coastal/aquatic resources by these earliest inhabitants of Okinawa, although a detailed taxonomical analysis has not yet been made available. Another demonstration of the seafaring abilities of these Palaeolithic inhabitants in Japan is the transportation of obsidian from Kozu Island to Honshu by 38,000 years ago (Ikeya, 2015). All this evidence indicates that Palaeolithic people in the Japanese archipelago, including the Ryukyus, exploited marine resources and were technologically competent ocean voyagers.

**Sustainable Life of Palaeolithic Populations in the Island**

After their arrival in the Ryukyus, the earliest colonists had to adapted to living in the relatively small island areas, with their limited terrestrial resources compared to large-sized landmasses including continents. In adapting to these limitations, terrestrial animals generally modified their size, body proportions, and many physical traits in their evolution (e.g., Van der Geer et al. 2011). This is also seen in the case of hominins with *Homo floresiensis* as an example of an island-adapted hominin (Brown et al. 2004).

In contrast to the pre-sapiens hominins, *Homo sapiens* have shown the ability to achieve an adaptive lifestyle in variable environments by developing their culture. Cultural adaptation surely played an important role, especially in severe environments such as those of the arctic, high altitude mountains, and oceanic islands. The exploitation of aquatic resources is one important cultural behaviour adaptive to the island environment. Although the use of marine shell tools is known in *Homo neanderthalensis* (Douka and Spinapolice 2012; Romagnoli et al. 2015), the maritime adaptation of *H. sapiens* is much more drastic, involving specialised shell-fishing, pelagic fishing, long-distance seagoing, and migration to oceanic islands. The oldest cases of island adaptation of *H. sapiens* are reported from ISEA where the voyagers consumed rich marine resources such as shellfish and both inshore and pelagic fish (Tanudirjo 2007; Ono et al. 2009; O'Connor et al. 2011).

In the Ryukyus there has been the problem is assessing the sustainability of these colonising populations as there had been a gap in the archaeological record of some 10,000 years between the latest Palaeolithic and the oldest Holocene archaeological sites. Such a paucity of cultural materials, such as lithic tools and midden material, led some archaeologists to believe that early colonisers might have arrived by accident to the islands and were not able to sustain their population (Takamiya 1996; Bellwood, 2015).

Studies in physical anthropology did not help as they provided supportive data for the discontinuity between Pleistocene and Holocene populations. Morphological analyses of human skeletons exhibited many differences between Jomon/modern-Japanese populations and Pleistocene Okinawan remains, named "Minatogawa" (Kaifu et al. 2011; Suwa et al. 2011; Kubo et al. 2011; Saso et al. 2011). The genetic study of modern Okinawans also indicated that they separated from continental Asia (e.g. Han Chinese) no earlier than 15,000 years ago, suggesting a genetic discontinuity between late Pleistocene people and modern Okinawans (Sato et al. 2014).

There were thus many difficulties in assessing the discontinuity of Pleistocene and Holocene populations in the Ryukyus. However, this gap in the archaeological record and the relative paucity of cultural materials could be seen to illustrate the saying that "the absence of evidence is not evidence of absence." Indeed the situation is changing now, and recent fieldwork is filling some of that gap with excavations showing nearly continuous or successive evidence of human occupation for over 20,000 years after 35 ka as a result of the development of unique lifeways adaptive to island conditions (see below) (Fujita et al. 2016). As for the morphological and genetic studies, we need to carefully consider and assess that we do not yet have good data on morphological variability nor genetic information for Pleistocene Ryukyu islanders. These problems can be expected to be solved by ongoing research projects including the morphological and genetic studies on the Shiraho-Saonetabaru Pleistocene human remains from Ishigaki Island. Such recent and ongoing works will be covered in the following sections.

## Palaeolithic Culture of the Ryukyus

The Palaeolithic culture of the Ryukyus had been relatively unknown for a long time, mainly due to so few discoveries of Palaeolithic artefacts. In contrast to the good preservation of some human fossils, Palaeolithic artefacts had rarely been found there. The exception was Tanegashima

Island, which was connected to mainland Japan (Kyushu Island) during the LGM (Figure 15.1). A variety of Palaeolithic stone tools and the world's oldest pitfalls (30ka) for catching wild pig, deer, and other animals were found on Tanegashima (Sato et al., 2014).

However, lithic items and other cultural remains found on the rest of the Ryukyus were very few, consisting of small amounts of amorphous flakes and hammer and grinding stones. Specifically, shale flakes were found from the sediments underneath the AT tephra, which dated to about 30 kya cal BP, at Tsuchihama-Yaya Site, Amami Island, small-sized chert flakes were uncovered from the layer older than the AT tephra at the Kishikawa Site, Amami Island, and chert flakes and limestone cobbles were reported from the Amangusuku and Garazao sites on Tokunoshima Island, respectively. Unfortunately, no midden materials nor human remains or other materials had been found from these sites, and the lifeway of their inhabitants is still conjectural.

From Yamashita-cho Cave I site on Okinawa Island, three sandstone cobbles were excavated from a 36,500-year-old charcoal-rich layer, along with many animal bones and a partial infant human skeleton (Takamiya et al. 1975a; Suzuki 1982; Kaifu and Fujita 2012). These sandstone cobbles were first reported as throwing ballstones by Takamiya et al. (1975b), but recently they have been reevaluated as hammer stones and/or grinding stones based on their appropriate size for handling, rounded shape, and microfractures observed on one side of the stones (Oda 2003).

Although there are some Palaeolithic artefacts in the Ryukyus, as briefly mentioned above, it has been difficult to know how to evaluate these small amorphous flakes and grinding stones based on their morphology. It has also been difficult to consider their cultural relationship to the stone-tool assemblages of surrounding areas just by analysing their typology. With such a background in mind, the recent findings at Sakitari Cave, Okinawa, provided unexpected but welcome cultural materials with rich evidence of island adaptation (Yamasaki et al. 2012, 2014; Fujita et al. 2016).

## Shell Artifacts of Palaeolithic Okinawa

Sakitari Cave has a relatively large hall (c. 620 m$^2$) having two entrances toward the east and west, the latter facing the Yuhi river (Figure 15.2). The Minatogawa site is 1.5 km downstream from Sakitari along this river. Palaeolithic sediments dating back to 30,000–35,000 years ago which contain evidence of human occupation had accumulated around the west entrance.

Most of the Palaeolithic artefacts from Sakitari cave were made from marine shells (Figure 15.2). The world's oldest shell fishhooks (23 ka), several types of shell scrapers, and several types of shell beads were unearthed from the 20,000- to 23,000-year-old layer containing abundant charcoal and food refuse. Although Palaeolithic shell artefacts have been reported from all over the world, including ISEA (Szabo and Koppel 2015; Langley et al. 2016), they are usually found with many more stone artefacts. In contrast, most of the Sakitari artifacts were shell items with stone artifacts being rare. The lithic artefacts from Sakitari consisted only of a possible whetstone from 23,000-years-old sediments and three quartz flakes from the 14,000-year-old layer. Such a paucity of stone artefacts is probably related to the limited distribution of stone materials on Okinawa Island; for example, there is quartz and chert in the northern area of the island, but this is more than 30 km distant from Sakitari Cave (Yamasaki et al. 2012).

The artefacts from Sakitari show us that there was not only the occasional transfer of stone from this distance away, but that this was probably part of their home foraging range within

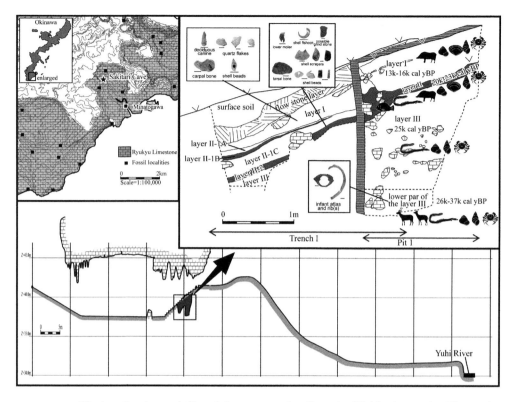

**FIGURE 15.2** The location (upper left) and the cross section (lower) of Sakitari cave site. The section and the major remains of Trench I and Pit I (upper right).

Okinawa. We do not know how and when they developed this kind of life adaptation, but it suggests *H. sapiens*' behavioral plasticity for adapting to life on an island with both limited area and limited natural resources.

### Behavioral Plasticity of Palaeolithic Ryukyu Islanders

Behavioral plasticity of Palaeolithic inhabitants is observed not only by their material culture but also in their hunting-gathering behaviour. The abundant freshwater crabs (Japanese mitten crab - Eriocheir japonica) and freshwater snails unearthed from the Pleistocene layers (35,000–14,000 years BP) of Sakitari Cave were the major animal resources consumed as food. Three to five percent of these crabs and snails were charred, indicating that they were clearly part of the diet. Small-sized vertebrates such as mice, birds, lizards, snakes, frogs, and fish (freshwater and marine) also were eaten.

Taking a brief look at diet at Sakitari, freshwater small-sized animals were dominant. This subsistence pattern was able to sustain populations for more than 20,000 years from 35,000 to 30,000 years ago. If we focus only on large-sized terrestrial mammals as prey animals, island fauna would have been insufficient as a food supply. However, looking at the small-sized and/ or aquatic animals, there is a variety of common and highly reproductive animals even on small oceanic islands such as Okinawa.

When humans first arrived in Okinawa, there were two species of endemic deer, as described above. At the bottom of the excavation trench at Sakitari Cave, 30,000- to 35,000-year-old levels were reached, where fragmented bones of deer were found, including one charred lumber vertebra (Fujita et al. 2016). The presence of deer may indicate that the inhabitants hunted these middle-sized deer during the first stage of island occupation. After the deer became extinct prior to 30,000 years ago, people started to concentrate on smaller land and freshwater animals for subsistence. This major change in food selection is an important aspect of the behavioural plasticity of the Palaeolithic islanders.

Another important behaviour seen in the archaeological record is the obvious seasonality of food consumption as evident from both the morphological analysis of freshwater crabs, and the oxygen isotope analysis of freshwater snails (Fujita et al. 2016). First, it was noticed that large-sized Japanese mitten crabs (Eriocheir japonica) were dominant in the cave deposits. This suggests that these crabs were collected during autumn which is their optimum season. Japanese mitten crabs grow in rivers and migrate downstream for reproduction during autumn nights (Kobayashi and Matsuura 1995). This is the optimum time to catch these large-sized nutritious adult crabs. Second, oxygen isotope analysis was conducted on 35 snails in order to estimate the season of their death. Twenty-seven snails were successfully analysed, demonstrating that up to 70% died in autumn and 30% in summer. Only one in the sample (0.8%) died in winter. These results clearly show that these Palaeolithic people seasonally visited the cave in autumn to target and collect the delicious crabs when they were at their optimum availability. Although we do not know how and where the inhabitants spent the other seasons, the excavations and research at Sakitari Cave have shown that Palaeolithic hunter-gatherer-fishers were able to maintain and sustain their populations by seasonally exploiting freshwater products.

Another important behaviour of these oceanic islanders is the possible translocation of food animals. After the extinction of endemic deer by 35,000–30,000 years ago, the number of wild pigs suddenly increased around 23,000–20,000 years ago (Hasegawa 1980; Fujita et al. 2014; Kawamura et al. 2016; Hasegawa et al. 2018). As Okinawa Island was isolated in the Pleistocene from the Eurasian continent and mainland Japan, not to mention the other islands of the Ryukyus, the increase in the number of wild pigs during the Late Pleistocene suggests their purposeful translocation by people into this island chain from outside. (Harunari 2001; Fujita et al. 2014; Kawamura et al. 2016). However, the recent analysis of mtDNA of extant wild pigs (*Sus scrofa riukiuanus*) demonstrates that it was a unique endemic species of the Ryukyus that separated out from the Eurasian populations much earlier than the arrival or humans, probably during the Middle Pleistocene (Yoshikawa et al. 2016).

One possible hypothesis that explains this contradiction is that the isolated unique wild pig population was originally found on some limited islands of the Ryukyus, with their translocation to the other islands by people around 20,000 years ago. If this scenario is true, it might be one of the world's oldest cases of animal transport by island immigrants. In any case, we need to consider this problem carefully, as the ancient DNA study of wild pigs from Holocene archaeological sites does suggest their possible translocation by Holocene prehistoric peoples (e.g. Takahashi et al. 2017). The impact of the translocation of pigs during the Holocene on the genetic traits of modern populations of Ryukyu wild pigs in unknown in any detail. Therefore, how and when the endemic Ryukyu wild pigs distributed throughout the Ryukyus is still a controversial topic.

## Burial Culture in the Palaeolithic Ryukyus

Although there are more than 10,000 Palaeolithic sites in the Japanese Archipelago, the discovery of human remains has been limited only to karstic caves and fissures. These locations with weak alkaline sediments are good for the preservation of bone. Another possible reason is that Late Pleistocene humans used the caves and rock shelters as burial places. The dominance of adult human remains supports this idea. More than five individuals, including four well-preserved adults, were found from the Minatogawa Site (Suzuki and Hanihara 1982), and more than 14 adults, including four well-preserved skulls, were excavated from Shiraho-Saonetabaru Cave (Okinawa Prefectural Archaeology Research Center (OPARC, 2017). The only exception from Shiraho-Saonetabaru Cave was a deciduous molar tooth which belonged to a young individual estimated to be aged from 10 to 13 years old (OPARC 2017). Although we do not know the life history of Palaeolithic people of the Ryukyus, the 10- to 13-year-old person might be treated as an adult. In contrast, infant partial human remains were found from Yamashita-cho Cave I (Takamiya et al., 1975a,b) and Sakitari Cave (Yamasaki et al. 2012; Fujita et al. 2016) in Okinawa, and Shimojibaru Cave in Kumejima Island (Oshiro 2001). If we can generalize from the finds found in these cases, Late Pleistocene humans may have buried infants and adults separately, even though we need much more evidence in assessing the burial culture of the Palaeolithic Ryukyu islanders.

In one case, however, the burial style of Late Pleistocene Ryukyu islanders is discussed in the report of Shiraho-Saonetabaru Cave (OPARC, 2017). The human remains from this site were fragmented into small pieces, and their surfaces were damaged by weathering and animal gnawing. The concentration of relatively large bone pieces with small fragments distributed round them, both coming from the same individuals, suggests that the dead were placed on the cave floor without earth covering. A similar style of burial was known in the Ryukyu Islands from the Late Jomon (about 3,000 years ago) to the present (OPARC, 2017).

In contrast to Shiraho-Saonetabaru human remains, the Minatogawa fossils were well preserved and had kept parts of their anatomical positions (Watanabe 1973; Suzuki 1982). That is, the Minatogawa humans were brought into the fissure before they had decomposed and covered with soil. Thus, the human remains from both Shiraho-Saonetabaru and Minatogawa sites showed different burial behaviour. We now have only these two cases of probable Palaeolithic burial, but they still provide some important information for considering the burial culture of Late Pleistocene humans in East Asia.

## Preliminary Discussion About Migration Route(s) to the Japanese Archipelago

Although there are many difficulties when modelling the route(s) of migration to the Ryukyus by Late Pleistocene humans, Kato (1996) suggested possible connections with Taiwan and Thailand based on similarities between stone assemblages (amorphous flakes and cobble tools) from the Ryukyus and those from Baxian Cave (Taiwan) and the Lang Rongrien Rockshelter (Thailand). Oda (2003) supports this model and argued that the dominance of cobble tools is a notable characteristic of assemblages observed in both the Ryukyus and in Southeast Asia. Recently excavated shell fish hooks (Fujita et al. 2016) also suggests a cultural affinity to Palaeolithic sites in Timor (O'Connor et al. 2011) and New Ireland (Smith and Allen, 1999).

Human remains also provide some information about their southern origin. Suzuki (1982) indicated craniometric similarities between those from Minatogawa and Liujiang (Tongtianyan Cave in Liujiang, Guangxi, China) as well as to some of the Neolithic populations from Indochina. Wu (1991) also supported this possible connection between Minatogawa and Liujiang. However, Yamaguchi (1991) suggested, based on his craniometric analyzes, that Minatogawa is similar not only to Liujiang but also to Wajak (Indonesia). (Baba and Narasaki 1991, Baba et al. 1998) put forward another contrasting view in which their non-metric cranial morphological comparisons led these authors to suggest Minatogawa was more similar to Wajak than to Liujiang. In a recent study of the mandibles belonging to two males (Minatogawa I and B) and two females (Minatogawa A and C), Kaifu et al. (2011) suggested Australo-Melanesian affinities. This is consistent with a view that populations with Australo-Melanesian affinities were once distributed over a wide area of Southeast Asia until the mid-Holocene (Matsumura and Hudson 2005; Matsumura et al. 2008a,b), and deserves further examination.

As reviewed above, the previous studies of physical anthropology achieved broad consensus that late Pleistocene people in the Ryukyu Islands probably came from Southeast Asia or surrounding areas. In contrast, the relationship between the Palaeolithic Ryukyus and mainland Japan is not clear, mainly because of the limited human remains from mainland Japan. Earlier studies (Suzuki 1966) argued for morphological similarity between Palaeolithic humans from the Hamakita-Negata Site in central Honshu and Holocene human remains of the Jomon era. Yet recent studies demonstrate that the Minatogawa remains were different from Jomon people and/or modern Japanese in the morphological traits of the mandible (Kaifu et al. 2011), tooth root (Suwa et al. 2011), glabella region (Saso et al. 2011), and endocast (Kubo et al. 2011). From the above we can argue that Palaeolithic Ryukyu Islanders (Minatogawa) were different from Palaeolithic peoples of mainland Japan (Hamakita-Negata). Again, we should note that these models are based on limited data and we look forward to further research on the Palaeolithic human fossils from Shiraho-Saonetabaru Cave which we hope will shed light on this problem.

## Conclusion

Palaeolithic sites are distributed throughout the Ryukyu Islands with the initial colonisation by purposeful open-ocean voyages. These populations developed subsistence strategies which kept the population sustainable. Their unique lifeway with the seasonal consumption of freshwater animals and their unique culture with its variety of shell artifacts enabled the Palaeolithic islanders to adapt to the limited resources of these small islands. We do not know how these people came across the ocean to the Ryukyus, but the morphological studies of these early modern humans indicate an origin to the south of the Ryukyus. Recently discovered well-preserved Late Pleistocene human fossils from Ishigaki are expected to shed more light on these issues.

## References

Baba, H., and Endo, B. 1982 Postcranial skeleton of the Minatogawa Man, in *The Minatogawa Man*, eds Suzuki, H., and Hanihara, K.. Tokyo: University Museum of the University of Tokyo, 61–159.

Baba, H., and Narasaki, S. 1991 Minatogawa man, the oldest type of modern *Homo sapiens* in East Asia. *Quaternary Research* 30, 221–230.Ba

Baba, H., Narasaki, S., and Ohyama, S. 1998 Minatogawa hominid fossils and evolution of late Pleistocene humans in East Asia. *Anthropological Science* 106, 27–45.

Bellwood, Peter. 2015 Migration and the origins of *Homo sapiens*, in *Emergence and Diversity of Modern Human Behavior in Palaeolithic Asia*, eds Kaifu, Yousuke, Izuho, Masami, Goebel, Ted, Sato, Hiroyuki, and Ono, Akira. College Station: Texas A&M University Press, 51–58.

Brown, Peter, Sutikna, T., Morwood, M., Soejono, R., Saptomo, E., and Due, R. 2004 A new small-bodied hominin from the Late Pleistocene of Flores, Indonesia. *Nature* 431, 1055–1061.

Clarkson, Chris, Jacobs, Zenobia, Marwick, Ben, Fullagar, Richard, Wallis, Lynley, Smith, Mike, Roberts, Richard, Hayes, Elspeth, Lowe, Kelsey, Carah, Xavier, Florin, Anna, McNeil, Jessica, Cox, Delyth, Arnold, Lee, Hua, Quan, Huntley, Jillian, Brand, Helen, Manne, Tiina, Fairbairn, Andrew, Shulmeister, James, Lyle, Lindsey, Salinas, Makiah, Page, Mara, Connell, Kate, Park, Gayoung, Norman, Kasih, Murphy, Tessa, and Pardoe, Colin. 2017 Human occupation of northern Australia by 65,000 years ago. *Nature* 547, 306–310.

Douka, Katerina, and Spinapolice, Enza. 2012 Neanderthal shell tool production: Evidence from Middle Palaeolithic Italy and Greece. *Journal of World Prehistory* 25, 45–79.

Erlandson, Jon. 2001 The archaeology of aquatic adaptations: Paradigms for a new millennium. *Journal of Archaeological Research* 9, 287–350.

Fujita, Masaki, Yamasaki, Shinji, Sugawara, Hiroshi, and Eda, Masaki. 2014 Body size reduction in wild boar (*Sus scrofa*) from the late Pleistocene Maehira Fissure Site in Okinawa-jima Island, Japan, with relevance to human arrival. *Quaternary International* 339, 289–299.

Fujita, Masaki, Yamasaki, Shinji, Katagiri, Chiaki, Oshiro, Itsuro, Sano, Katsuhiro, Kurozumi, Taiji, Sugawara, Hiroshi, Kunikita, Dai, Matsuzaki, Hiroyuki, Kano, Akihiro, Okumura, Tomoyo, Sone, Tomomi, Fujita, Hikaru, Kobayashi, Satoshi, Naruse, Toru, Kondo, Megumi, Matsu'ura, Shuji, Suwa, Gen, and Kaifu, Yousuke. 2016 Advanced maritime adaptation in the western Pacific coastal region extends back to 35,000–30,000 years before present. *Proceedings of the National Academy of Sciences* 113, 11184–11189.

Harunari, H. 2001 Relationship between the extinction of the big mammals and the human activities at the late Pleistocene in Japan. *Bulletin of the Natural Museum of Japanese History* 90, 1–52. (In Japanese with English abstract)

Hasegawa, Y. 1980 Notes on vertebrate fossils from late Pleistocene to Holocene of Ryukyu islands, Japan. *Quaternary Research* 18, 263–267. (In Japanese with English summary).

Hasegawa, Y., Chinzei, K., Nohara, T., Ikeya, N., Wada, H., and Oyama, S. 2017 Topography and deposits of Late Pleistocene Minatogawa man site, Okinawa, Ryukyu Islands. *Bulletin of the Gunma Museum of Natural History* 21, 7–18.

Hasegawa, Y., Anezaki, T., Oyama, S., Matsuoka, H., and Chinen, S. 2018 Late Pleistocene mammals from Minatogawa man site, southern Okinawa Island and on the morphological changes of the largest wild boar specimens. *Bulletin of the Natural Museum of Japanese History* 22, 23–49.

Holt, Ben, Lessard, Jean-Philippe, Borregaard, Michael, Fritz, Susan, Araújo, Miguel, Dimitrov, Dimitar, Fabre, Pierre-Henri, Graham, Catherine, Graves, Gary, Jønsson, Knud, Nogués-Bravo, David, Wang, Zhiheng, Whittaker, Robert, Fjeldså, Jon, and Rahbek, Carsten. 2012 An update of Wallace's zoogeographic regions of the world. *Science* 339, 74–78. DOI: 10.1126/science.1228282.

Ikeya, N. 2015 Maritime transport of obsidian in Japan during the Upper Palaeolithic, in *Emergence and Diversity of Modern Human Behavior in Palaeolithic Asia*, eds Kaifu, Yousuke., Izuho, Masami., Goebel, Ted., Sato, Hiroyuki., and Ono, Akira. Texas A&M University Press, 362–375.

Kaifu, Yousuke, Fujita, M., Kono, R.T., and Baba, H. 2011 Late Pleistocene modern human mandibles from the Minatogawa Fissure site, Okinawa, Japan: Morphological affinities and implications for modern human dispersals in East Asia. *Anthropological Science* 119, 137–157.

Kaifu, Yousuke, and Fujita, M. 2012 Fossil record of early modern humans in East Asia. *Quaternary International* 248, 2–11.

Kaifu, Y., Fujita, M., Yoneda, M., and Yamasaki, S. 2015 Pleistocene seafaring and colonization of the Ryukyu Islands, southwestern Japan, in *Emergence and Diversity of Modern Human Behavior in Palaeolithic Asia*, eds Kaifu, Yousuke., Izuho, Masami., Goebel, Ted., Sato, Hiroyuki., and Ono, Akira.. Texas A&M University Press, 345–361.

Kato, S. 1996 On the dispersion of Palaeolithic culture to the Nansei Islands. *Journal of Geography (Chigaku Zasshi)* 105, 372–383.

Kawamura, A., Chang, C. H., and Kawamura, Y. 2016 Middle Pleistocene to Holocene mammal faunas of the Ryukyu Islands and Taiwan: An updated review incorporating results of recent research. *Quaternary International* 397, 117–135.

Kawana, T. 1980 Primary objectives of the interdisciplinary discussion on the problems of the late Pleistocene-Holocene periods in the Ryukyu Islands. *The Quaternary Research* 18, 181–188. (In Japanese with English abstract)

Kimura, M. 1996 Quaternary paleogeography of the Ryukyu Arc. *Journal of Geography* 105, 259–285. (In Japanese with English abstract)

Kobayashi, S., and Matsuura, S. 1995 Reproductive ecology of the Japanese mitten crab *Eriocheir japonicus* (De Haan) in its marine phase. *Benthos Research* 1995, 15–28.

Kubo, M.O., Fujita, M., Matsu'ura, S., Kondo, M., and Suwa, G. 2011 Mortality profiles of Late Pleistocene deer remains of Okinawa Island; evidence from the Hananda-Gama Cave and Yamashita-cho Cave I sites. *Anthropological Science* 139, 137–157.

Kubo, M. O., Yamada, E., Fujita, M., and Oshiro, I. 2015 Paleoecological reconstruction of Late Pleistocene deer from the Ryukyu Islands, Japan: Combined evidence of mesowear and stable isotope analyses. *Palaeogeography, Palaeoclimatology, Palaeoecology* 435, 159–166.

Kuroda, T., and Ozawa, T. 1996 Paleoclimatic and vegetational changes during the Pleistocene and Holocene in the Ryukyu Islands inferred from pollen assemblages. *Journal of Geography* (Chigaku Zasshi) 105, 328–342.

Langley, Michelle, O'Connor, Sue, and Piotto, E. 2016 42,000-year-old worked and pigment-stained *Nautilus* shell from Jerimalai (Timor-Leste): Evidence for an early coastal adaptation in ISEA. *Journal of Human Evolution* 97, 1–16.

Matsumura, H., and Hudson, M. J. 2005 Dental perspectives on the population history of Southeast Asia. *American Journal of Physical Anthropology* 127, 182–209.

Matsumura, H., Yoneda, M., Dodo, Y., Oxenham, M.F., Cuong, N.L., Thuy, N.K., Dung, L.M., Long, V.T., Yamagata, M., Sawada, J., Shinoda, K., and Takigawa, W. 2008a Terminal Pleistocene human skeleton from Hang Cho Cave, northern Vietnam: Implications for the biological affinities of Hoabinian people. *Anthropological Science* 116, 201–217.

Matsumura, H., Oxenham, M. F., Dodo, Y., Domett, K., Thuy, N. K., Cuong, N. L., Dung, N. K., Huffer, D., and Yamagata, M. 2008b Morphometric affinity of the late Neolithic human remains from Man Bac, Ninh Binh Province, Vietnam: Key skeletons with which to debate the 'two layer' hypothesis. *Anthropological Science* 116, 135–148.

Matsuoka, H. 2000 The late Pleistocene fossil birds of the Central and Southern Ryukyu Islands, and their zoogeographical implications for the recent avifauna of the archipelago. *Tropics* 10, 165–188.

Matsuoka, H., and Hasegawa, Y. 2018 Birds around the Minatogawa Man: The late Pleistocene avian fossil assemblage of the Minatogawa Fissure, southern part of Okinawa Island, Central Ryukyu Islands, Japan. *Bulletin of Gunma Museum of Natural History* 22, 1–21.

Nakamura, Y., and Ota, H. 2015 Late Pleistocene-Holocene amphibians from Okinawajima Island in the Ryukyu Archipelago, Japan: Reconfirmed faunal endemicity and the Holocene range collapse of forest-dwelling species. *Palaeontologia Electronica* 18, 1–26.

Nohara, T., and Irei, S. 2002 Animal remains of the Minatogawa fissure site, in *Minatogawa fissure site*. Board of Education, Gushikami Village, Okinawa, 29–87. (In Japanese)

Oda, S. 2003 Stone Tools found from Yamashita-cho Cave I. *Nanto-Koko* 22, 1–19. (in Japanese)

Okinawa Prefectural Archaeology Research Center (OPARC). 2017 *Report on survey excavation of the Shiraho-Saonetabaru Cave Site 2*. (In Japanese)

O'Connor, Sue, Ono, Rintaro, and Clarkson, Chris. 2011 Pelagic fishing at 42,000 years before the present and the maritime skills of modern humans. *Science* 334, 1117–1121.

Ono, Rintaro, Soegondho, S., and Yoneda, M. 2009 Changing marine exploitation during late Pleistocene in northern Wallacea: Shell remains from Leang Sarru Rockshelter in Talaud Islands. *Asian Perspectives* 48, 318–341.

Oshima, K. 1980 Late Quaternary sea-level change recorded on the topographic features of several straits around the Okinawa Islands. *The Quaternary Research* 18, 251–257. (In Japanese with English abstract)

Oshiro, I., and Nohara, T. 2000 Distribution of Pleistocene terrestrial vertebrates and their migration to the Ryukyus. *Tropics* 10, 41–50.

Oshiro, I. 2001 Geological study of quaternary terrestrial vertebrate remains from the Ryukyu Islands. *Nohara Tomohide Kyojyu Taikan Kinen Ronbunshu*, 37–136. (In Japanese)

Ota, Y., Ohmura, A., and Machida, H. 2001 Nansei-Shoto no chikei hattatsu-shi, in *Nihon no Chikei vol. 7: Kyushu-Nansei Shoto*, eds Machida, H., Ota, Y., Kawana, T., Moriwaki, H., and Nagaokapp, S.. Tokyo: University of Tokyo Press, 301–311. (In Japanese)

Ota, H. 2003 Toward a synthesis of paleontological and neontological information on the terrestrial vertebrates of the Ryukyu Archipelago. I. Systematic and biogeographic review. *Journal of Fossil Research* 36, 43–59.

Romagnoli, Francesca, Baena, Javier, and Sarti, Lucia. 2015 Neanderthal retouched shell tools and Quina economic and technical strategies: An integrated behavior. *Quaternary International* 407, 29–44.

Saso, A., Matsukawa, S., and Suwa, G. 2011 Comparative analysis of the glabellar region morphology of the late Pleistocene Minatogawa crania: A three-dimensional approach. *Anthropological Science* 119, 113–121.

Sato, H. 2015 Trap-Pit Hunting in Late Pleistocene Japan, in *Emergence and Diversity of Modern Human Behavior in Palaeolithic Asia*, eds Kaifu, Yousuke., Izuho, Masami., Goebel, Ted., Sato, Hiroyuki., and Ono, Akira. College Station: Texas A&M University Press, 389–405.

Sato, T., Nakagome, S., Watanabe, C., Yamaguchi, K., Kawaguchi, A., Koganebuchi, K., Haneji, K., Yamaguchi, T., Hanihara, T., Yamamoto, K., Ishida, H., Mano, S., Kimura, R., and Oota, H. 2014 Genome-wide SNP analysis reveals population structure and demographic history of the Ryukyu islanders in the southern part of the Japanese archipelago. *Molecular Biology and Evolution* 31, 2929–2940.

Smith, A. and Allen, J. (1999) Pleistocene shell technologies: Evidence from Island Melanesia. *Australian Coastal Archaeology*, (eds) Hall, J., McNiven (ANU, Canberra) pp. 291–297.

Suwa, G., Fukase, H., Kono, R.T., Kubo, D., and Fujita, M. 2011 Mandibular tooth root size in modern Japanese, prehistoric Jomon, and Late Pleistocene Minatogawa human fossils. *Anthropological Science* 119, 159–171.

Suzuki, H. 1966 Hamakita man and the site of Nekata limestone quarry at Hamakita. *Journal of the Anthropological Society of Nippon* 74, 119–136. (In Japanese)

Suzuki, H., and Hanihara, K. (Eds.). 1982 *The Minatogawa man: the Upper Pleistocene man from the island of Okinawa*. University Museum of the University of Tokyo, University of Tokyo Press.

Suzuki, H. 1982 Pleistocene man in Japan. *Journal of the Anthropological Society of Nippon* 90, 11–26.

Szabo, Katherine, and Koppel, B. 2015 Limpet shells as unmodified tools in Pleistocene Southeast Asia: An experimental approach to assessing fracture and modification. *Journal of Archaeological Science* 54, 64–76.

Takahashi, A., Otsuka, H., and Ota, H. 2008 Systematic review of late Pleistocene turtles (Reptilia: Chelonii) from the Ryukyu Archipelago, Japan, with special reference to Paleogeographical implications. *Pacific Science* 62, 395–402.

Takahashi, A., Ikeda, T., Manabe, M., and Hasegawa, Y. 2018 Freshwater and terrestrial turtle fossils discovered from the Minatogawa man site, southern part of Okinawajima Island, Ryukyu Archipelago, southwestern Japan. *Bulletin Gunma Natural History* 22, 51–58.

Takahashi, R., Kurosawa, Y., Adachi, N., and Hongo, H. 2017 DNA analysis of modern Ryukyu wild boar: As a basic data for interpretation of results of ancient DNA analyses of archaeological samples. *Zooarchaeology* 33, 63–77. (In Japanese with English abstract)

Takamiya, H., Kin, M., and Suzuki, M. 1975a Excavation report of the Yamashita-cho Cave site, Naha-shi, Okinawa. *Journal of the Anthropological Society of Nippon* 83, 125–130.

Takamiya, H., Tamaki, M., and Kin, M. 1975b Artefacts of the Yamashita-cho cave site. *Journal of the Anthropological Society of Nippon* 83, 137–150.

Takamiya, H. 1996 Initial colonization, and subsistence adaptation processes in the late prehistory of the Island of Okinawa. *Indo-Pacific Prehistory Association Bulletin* 15, 143–150.

Tanudirjo, Daud. 2007 Long and continuous or short term and occasional occupation? The human use of Leang Sarru rock shelter in the Talaud Islands, northeastern Indonesia. *Bulletin of the Indo-Pacific Prehistory Association* 25, 15–20.

Van der Geer, Alexandra, Lyras, George, De Vos, John, and Dermitzakis, Michael. 2011 *Evolution of Island Mammals: Adaptation and Extinction of Placental Mammals on Islands*. John Wiley & Sons, Hoboken, New Jersey.

Watanabe, N. 1973 Research for the Pleistocene man of Okinawa. Nanto-Koko. the *Journal of the Okinawa Archaeological Society* 3, 1–4. (In Japanese)

Wu, X. 1991 Origins and affinities of the stone age inhabitants of Japan, in *Japanese as a Member of the Asian and Pacific Populations*, ed Hanihara, K.. Kyoto: International Research Center for Japanese Studies, 1–8.

Yamaguchi, B. 1991 Skeletal morphology of the jomon people, in *Japanese as a Member of the Asian and Pacific Populations*, ed Hanihara, K.. Kyoto: International Research Center for Japanese Studies, 53–63.

Yamasaki, S., Fujita, M., Katagiri, C., Kunikita, D., Matsu'ura, S., Suwa, G., and Oshiro, I. 2012 Excavations (2009–2011) at Sakitari-do cave site, Nanjo city, Okinawa prefecture — A new Late Pleistocene paleoanthropological site. *Anthropological Science* 120, 121–134. (In Japanese with English abstract)

Yamasaki, S., Fujita, M., Katagiri, C., Kurozumi, T., and Kaifu, Y. 2014 Human use of marine shells from Late Pleistocene layers of Sakitari-do cave site, Nanjo city, Okinawa prefecture. *Anthropological Science* 122, 9–27. (In Japanese with English abstract)

Yoshikawa, Saka, Miura, Makiko, Watanabe, Shin, Lin, Liang-Kong, Ota, Hidetoshi, and Mizoguchi, Yasushi. 2016 Historical relationships among wild boar populations of the Ryukyu Archipelago and other Eurasian regions, as inferred from mitochondrial cytochrome b gene sequences. *Zoological Science* 33, 520–526.

# APPENDIX A
## Comparison of Radiocarbon and Calibrated Dates

*Yuichiro Kudo*

### The Principles of Radiocarbon ($^{14}$C) Dating

There exist three isotopes of carbon, each with a different mass: carbon-12 ($^{12}$C), carbon-13 ($^{13}$C), and carbon-14 ($^{14}$C). The third of these isotopes, $^{14}$C, exists at an almost constant level in the atmosphere, with scarcely any regional variation. The abundance ratios are $^{12}$C: $^{13}$C: $^{14}$C = 0.989: 0.011: $1.2 \times 10^{-12}$. $^{14}$C dating (radiocarbon dating) is a dating method (a method of age determination) that exploits the fact that the radionuclide $^{14}$C has a half-life of $5,730 \pm 40$ years (usually, the figure adopted in calculations is 5,568, as determined by Willard Libby), over which time the nuclide will have transformed (Figure A.1). Radiocarbon dating uses the half-life of $^{14}$C to determine the age of something. It relies on the premise that the $^{14}$C generated by cosmic rays remain at a nearly constant level, regardless of region or time period.

Carbon-containing organic materials can be used as samples for radiocarbon dating. As such, there is a wide range of archaeological materials to which radiocarbon dating can be applied, examples being carbonised materials, carbonised and non-carbonised plant remains, human or non-human animal bones, and carbides attached to pottery. For this reason, radiocarbon dating is currently the most widely used method for dating archaeological ruins and artefacts.

Radiocarbon dating comprises two techniques. The first is the beta-counting method, which involves counting the beta rays emitted during the radioactive decay. The second is accelerator mass spectrometry (AMS), which was developed in the late 1970s. For every 1 mg sample of carbon, only 0.8 individual atoms will decay every hour. Accordingly, the sample used in beta-counting must contain several grams of carbon. In AMS, the material is radiocarbon dated by directly measuring the concentrations of $^{12}$C, $^{13}$C, and $^{14}$C in the sample. Unlike in beta-counting, AMS can be conducted even with only 1 mg of carbon in the sample, which allows the measurement to be performed in a short time. With beta-counting, it is difficult to date material back to 30,000 years. This is because the emitted beta rays are extremely weak, meaning that the beta rays emitted from the sample itself may be hidden by the background radiation (radiation in natural world). Beta-counting is accurate up to 40,000–30,000 $^{14}$C BP. Therefore, when discussing the proliferation of *Homo sapiens* in East Asia, one should not use radiocarbon dates that were determined by the beta-counting before AMS was developed. With AMS, on the other hand, radiocarbon dates as far back as 40,000–45,000 $^{14}$C BP can be used (Figure A.2).

Appendix A: Comparison of Radiocarbon and Calibrated Dates **327**

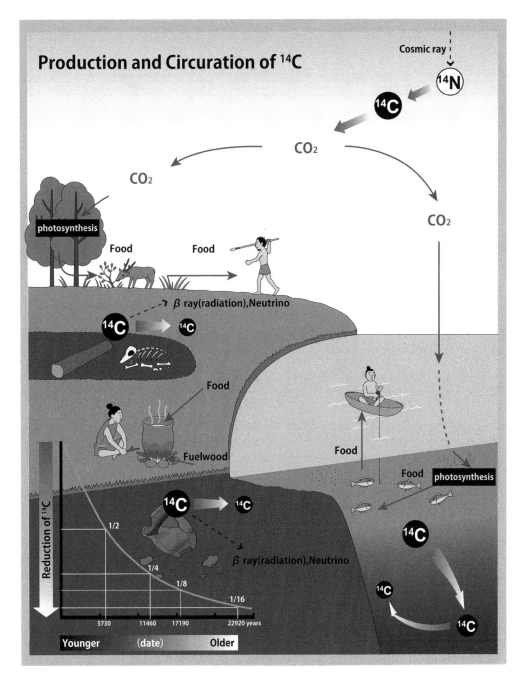

**FIGURE A.1** The Principles of Radiocarbon Dating. Once an organism has died and ceased its carbon exchange with the environment, the $^{14}C$ in the organism will have been reduced to half its original amount in 5,730 years, a quarter of its original amount in 11,460 years, and an eighth of its original amount in 17,190 years.

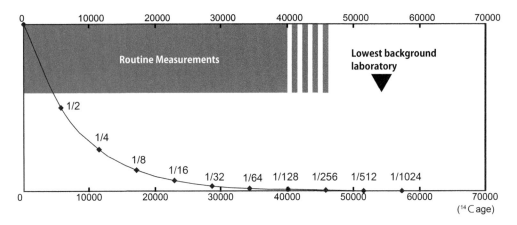

FIGURE A.2  The Relationship between $^{14}$C Reduction and Chronology (Kudo 2012). In regular accelerator-based dating, the accelerator and vacuum-refining equipment yield a background of around 40,000–45,000 $^{14}$C BP. Accordingly, the routine measurements typically go back no further than 45,000 $^{14}$C BP.

## Calibrating Radiocarbon Dates

Radiocarbon dating was first developed by Willard Libby in 1949. Initially, people believed that the amount of atmospheric $^{14}$C generated by cosmic rays approximately equals the amount of $^{14}$C that has been reduced as a result of radioactive decay. However, as $^{14}$C measurements became more precise, it became clear that atmospheric $^{14}$C had varied over different time periods rather than remaining at a constant level (Libby 1963). Radiocarbon dates are hypothetical dates; they are not directly linked with calendar dates. One way of calibrating radiocarbon dates is found in dendrochronology (tree ring dating), which determines age based on tree rings.

A tree develops a new outer layer of cells (cambium) each year. During the time the tree is developing these rings, it is absorbing $^{14}$C in the form of carbon dioxide through photosynthesis. Consequently, the cells in the cambium bear witness to the level of atmospheric $^{14}$C at the time of their formation. When the tree gets a new tree ring with each successive year, the cells in the completed ring no longer absorb atmospheric $^{14}$C; therefore, during the tree's lifetime, the amounts of $^{14}$C become progressively smaller the closer you get to the core. By taking dendrochronologically dated timber core specimens and then dating the $^{14}$C in the specimens, researchers can identify the gap between the dendrochronological age and the radiocarbon age.

By systematically implementing this measurement approach, the international working group International Calibration (IntCal) has accumulated data and developed an internationally standardised calibration curve. To date, IntCal has used dendrochronology to amass a database spanning 13,910 years into the past/back in time.

The spread of *H. sapiens* in Asia took place, for the most part, prior to the approximately 13,910-year period covered by the above-mentioned dendrochronological database. Thus, to calibrate radiocarbon dates in this region of time, one must rely on data outside dendrochronology. The data used to calibrate radiocarbon dates earlier than 13,910 BP include a set of coral carbon dating and uranium-thorium dating data, benthic foraminifera carbon dating data, and the radiocarbon dating data of specimens from lacustrine varved sediments. The latest IntCal calibration curve, which was released in 2020, is IntCal20 (Reimer et al. 2020) (Figure A.3).

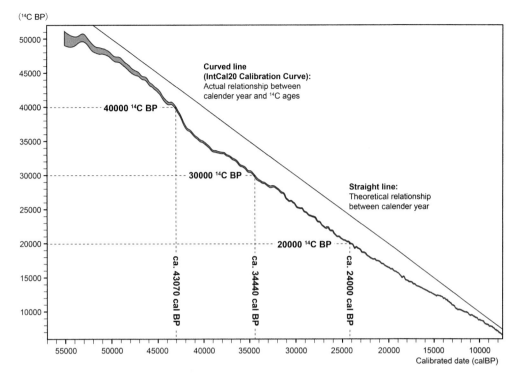

FIGURE A.3  IntCal20 Calibration Curve. The IntCal20 calibration curve presents a theoretical straight line that assumes a one-to-one relationship between radiocarbon dates and calibrated dates. Divergence from this line indicates a gap between calendar years and radiocarbon years. For example, if something is radiocarbon dated to around 30,000 years in the past (30,000 $^{14}$C BP), the calibrated date will be around 34,440 cal BP, a gap of around 4,400 years.

Radiocarbon measurements will be closer to calendar dates when one calibrates them using software such as OxCal (https://c14.arch.ox.ac.uk/), which are available online (Figure A.4).

However, although the calibration curve covers a timespan going back to 50,000 cal BP, or in radiocarbon dating terms, back to around 46,000 $^{14}$C BP, one should bear in mind that 40,000 $^{14}$C BP is very close to the point where measurement accuracy starts to fall. Specimens that are radiocarbon dated to around 40,000 $^{14}$C BP contain only trace amounts of $^{14}$C—less than one hundredth the amount found in specimens from 1950 (see Figure A.1). When using radiocarbon dates with materials left in the spread of H. sapiens in East Asia, one should always bear in mind that this is such a period.

For example, the earliest radiocarbon dates for the H. sapiens in east Asia were dated at Tianyuan Cave (Tianyuandong) in China (Table A.1). A sample from one of the human femora provided an age of 34,430 ± 510 $^{14}$C BP(BA-03222) (Shang et al. 2007), but also placing the human partial skeleton at 40,850–38,070 by cal BP (2σ, using IntCal20). In the case of Southeast Asia, the earliest secure evidence of an anatomically modern human (the Deep Skull) at the Niah Cave, Borneo Island, East Malaysia, has been placed at 44,000–40,000 cal BP (Baker et al., 2007). Charcoal samples that seemed to lay directly on the anatomically modern "Deep Skull", were dated to 35,690 ± 280 $^{14}$C BP(OxA-V-2016-16) and 35,000 ± 400 $^{14}$C BP(OxA-15126) (Barker et al., 2007). Calibrated dates using IntCal13 are 41,330–40,220 cal BP and 40,970–39,410 cal BP respectively.

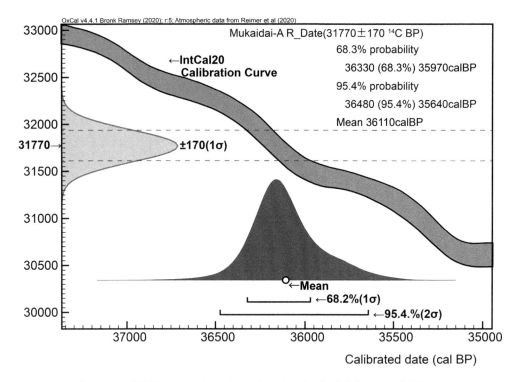

FIGURE A.4  Example of Calibration of a radiocarbon date by OxCal (Ramsey 2009).

In addition, early human occupation at the Niah Cave is estimated to be earlier than 46,000 cal BP, though this time range is close to the measurement limitation of radiocarbon dating and its calibration (see Figure A.3).

Recently, people have started using ultrafiltration when measuring gelatin collagen from human or non-human animal bones. Ultrafiltration allows researchers to filter out organic matter with low molecular mass. Higham et al. compared Neanderthal bone dates determined using ultrafiltration with existing bone dates determined without using ultrafiltration. They concluded that gelatin collagen samples that had been dated (without ultrafiltration) back to 30,000 $^{14}$C BP should in some cases be dated to some several thousand years later (Higham et al. 2006).

## Dating Notation

Recently, researchers have started using other dating methods in addition to radiocarbon dating, and they have also started routinely using calibrated radiocarbon dates (Kudo 2012). This situation can lead to date notations being confused with each other. When reporting dates, I try as much as possible to state the measurement method underlying the date, except when I use the general notation (as in # years ago). Take, for example, the notation in Table A.2. In order to avoid the reader mixing up dates, it is essential to clarify the measurement method underlying each date.

As for "# years ago" type dates, in which the above notation is not used, such dates should not be based on the radiocarbon dates used in the past. Rather, they should be based on calibrated radiocarbon dates. Calibrated and uncalibrated radiocarbon dates can diverge by as much as 2,000–3,000 years in the Late Glacial Period, and by as much as 4,000–5,000 in the

TABLE A.1 Radiocarbon dates related to the early evidence of *Homo sapiens* in the East and South East Asia: example of the Tianyuan Cave and Niah Cave (Shang et al., 2007; Barker et al. 2007).

| Site name | Context | Sample | Labo-code | $^{14}C$ BP (un calibrated) | Intcal 20 Calibrated date (cal BP, 2 σ) | µ (cal BP) | References |
|---|---|---|---|---|---|---|---|
| Tianyuan Cave, China | III | Animal bone | BA-03226 | 30500 ± 370 | 35670–34270 | 34950 | Shang et al. (2007) |
| Tianyuan Cave, China | III | Bone flake | BA-04247 | 31115 ± 190 | 36090–34950 | 35530 | Shang et al. (2007) |
| Tianyuan Cave, China | III | Animal bone | BA-03225 | 33970 ± 540 | 40370–37370 | 38860 | Shang et al. (2007) |
| Tianyuan Cave, China | III | Animal bone | BA-03227 | 34990 ± 400 | 40960–39400 | 40170 | Shang et al. (2007) |
| Tianyuan Cave, China | III | Animal bone | BA-03224 | 39430 ± 680 | 44140–42320 | 43080 | Shang et al. (2007) |
| Tianyuan Cave, China | III | Human femur | BA-03222 | 34430 ± 510 | 40850–38070 | 39570 | Shang et al. (2007) |
| Tianyuan Cave, China | IV | Bone flake | BA-03248 | 37785 ± 250 | 42410–41970 | 42190 | Shang et al. (2007) |
| Niah Cave, Malaysia | 3121 | Charcoal | Niah-312 | 40100 ± 550 | 44310–42670 | 43440 | Barker et al. (2007) |
| Niah Cave, Malaysia | 3131 | Charcoal | OxA-V-2057-27 | 44250 ± 650 | 48100–45430 | 46700 | Barker et al. (2007) |
| Niah Cave, Malaysia | 3134(1) | Charcoal | OxA-V-2059-11 | 34880 ± 390 | 40860–39330 | 40080 | Barker et al. (2007) |
| Niah Cave, Malaysia | 3134(2) | Charcoal | OxA-V-2057-28 | 34000 ± 270 | 39800–38010 | 39050 | Barker et al. (2007) |
| Niah Cave, Malaysia | 3140 | Charcoal | OxA-V-2057-29 | 44100 ± 700 | 48080–45230 | 46580 | Barker et al. (2007) |
| Niah Cave, Malaysia | 3143 | Charcoal | OxA-V-2057-30 | 44100 ± 700 | 48080–45230 | 46580 | Barker et al. (2007) |
| Niah Cave, Malaysia | 3158 | Charcoal | OxA-V-2057-31 | 45900 ± 800 | 50620–46250 | 48460 | Barker et al. (2007) |
| Niah Cave, Malaysia | Litho-facies 2'hearth' | Charcoal | Niah-310 | 42490 ± 600 | 46110–44320 | 45180 | Barker et al. (2007) |
| Niah Cave, Malaysia | Litho-facies 2'hearth' | Charcoal | Niah-311 | 41690 ± 600 | 45530–43330 | 44540 | Barker et al. (2007) |
| Niah Cave, Malaysia | 96–99" | Charcoal | OxA-15621 | 42550 ± 500 | 45960–44480 | 45180 | Barker et al. (2007) |
| Niah Cave, Malaysia | 99–102" | Charcoal | OxA-15622 | 34180 ± 230 | 39910–38720 | 39360 | Barker et al. (2007) |
| Niah Cave, Malaysia | 105–108" | Charcoal | OxA-15623 | 39750 ± 450 | 44020–42550 | 43160 | Barker et al. (2007) |
| Niah Cave, Malaysia | 108–111" | Charcoal | OxA-15624 | 33940 ± 230 | 39680–38080 | 38990 | Barker et al. (2007) |
| Niah Cave, Malaysia | 111–114" | Charcoal | OxA-15625 | 42650 ± 500 | 46010–44510 | 45240 | Barker et al. (2007) |
| Niah Cave, Malaysia | 114–117" | Charcoal | OxA-15626 | 42850 ± 500 | 46170–44570 | 45380 | Barker et al. (2007) |
| Niah Cave, Malaysia | 111–114" | Charcoal | OxA-15126 | 35000 ± 400 | 40970–39410 | 40180 | Barker et al. (2007) |
| Niah Cave, Malaysia | 48–60" | Charcoal | OxA-15627 | 15365 ± 60 | 18830–18330 | 18660 | Barker et al. (2007) |

(*Continued*)

TABLE A.1 (Continued)

| Site name | Context | Sample | Labo-code | ¹⁴C BP (un calibrated) | Intcal 20 Calibrated date (cal BP, 2 σ) | μ (cal BP) | References |
|---|---|---|---|---|---|---|---|
| Niah Cave, Malaysia | 48–60" | Charcoal | OxA-15628 | 15485 ± 65 | 18890–18680 | 18790 | Barker et al. (2007) |
| Niah Cave, Malaysia | 72–96" | Charcoal | OxA-15629 | 43400 ± 700 | 47420–44680 | 45940 | Barker et al. (2007) |
| Niah Cave, Malaysia | 120–123" | Charcoal | OxA-15630 | 41200 ± 400 | 44740–43260 | 44100 | Barker et al. (2007) |
| Niah Cave, Malaysia | 1066 | Charcoal | OxA-V-2076-13 | 37800 ± 230 | 42400–41990 | 42200 | Barker et al. (2007) |
| Niah Cave, Malaysia | 1067 | Charcoal | OxA-V-2076-14 | 36960 ± 300 | 42150–41320 | 41760 | Barker et al. (2007) |
| Niah Cave, Malaysia | 1057 | Charcoal | OxA-V-2076-15 | 44750 ± 650 | 48540–45850 | 47130 | Barker et al. (2007) |
| Niah Cave, Malaysia | 72–78" | Charcoal | OxA-15164 | 36470 ± 250 | 41910–41070 | 41480 | Barker et al. (2007) |
| Niah Cave, Malaysia | 2096 | Charcoal | OxA-11302 | 33790 ± 330 | 39580–37600 | 38670 | Barker et al. (2007) |
| Niah Cave, Malaysia | 2085 | Charcoal | OxA-11303 | 29070 ± 220 | 34220–33010 | 33590 | Barker et al. (2007) |
| Niah Cave, Malaysia | 2075 | Charcoal | OxA-V-2077-7 | 17770 ± 65 | 21870–21350 | 21590 | Barker et al. (2007) |
| Niah Cave, Malaysia | 2078 | Charcoal | OxA-V-2077-8 | 21360 ± 90 | 25930–25350 | 25730 | Barker et al. (2007) |
| Niah Cave, Malaysia | 2079 | Charcoal | OxA-V-2077-9 | 20480 ± 90 | 24960–24280 | 24630 | Barker et al. (2007) |
| Niah Cave, Malaysia | 1015 | Charcoal | OxA-111549 | 8630 ± 45 | 9700–9530 | 9600 | Barker et al. (2007) |
| Niah Cave, Malaysia | 1020 | Charcoal | OxA-111550 | 19650 ± 90 | 23860–23340 | 23600 | Barker et al. (2007) |
| Niah Cave, Malaysia | 1027 | Charcoal | OxA-11034 | 27960 ± 200 | 32860–31400 | 31990 | Barker et al. (2007) |
| Niah Cave, Malaysia | 106" | Charcoal | OxA-V-2076-16 | 35690 ± 280 | 41330–40220 | 40820 | Barker et al. (2007) |

**TABLE A.2** Examples of date notation.

| Kind of age | Example of description | Example of description | (in millennia)[*2] |
|---|---|---|---|
| $^{14}$C age | 20,000 $^{14}$C BP | 20 ka $^{14}$C BP | 20 $^{14}$C kyr BP, |
| Calibrated date $^{14}$C age[*1] | 20,000 cal BP | 20 ka cal BP | 20 cal kyr BP |
| U/Th age (in case of $^{230}$Th) | 20,000 $^{230}$Th BP | 20 ka $^{230}$Th BP | 20 $^{230}$Th kyr BP |
| Varve counting age | 20,000 varve BP | 20 ka varve BP | 20 varve kyr BP |
| Ice core counting age | 20,000 ice-core BP | 20 ka ice-core BP | 20 ice-core kyr BP |
| Ice core counting age (NGRIP)[*3] | 20,000 ice-core $BP_{NGRIP}$ | 20 ka ice-core $BP_{NGRIP}$ | 20 ice-core kyr $BP_{NGRIP}$ |

It is important to clarify the measurement method on which the date is based. *1: "cal" means calibrated radiocarbon age; it does not mean calendar age. "BP" indicates years before 1950 A.D. *2: "ka" means *kilo annum* (1,000 year-period). Oftentimes, "20 ka" is intended to mean 20,000 BP even without the "BP", but it is important to add the "BP" notation to avoid the confusion between this (BP) and BC or AD. *3: When it is particularly important to differentiate from other ice core age models.

40,000–20,000 radiocarbon BP range. Uncalibrated radiocarbon dates also differ from uranium-thorium dates, varved sediment counting dates of lacustrine sediments, and ice core counting dates. These dates are similar in timescale to calibrated radiocarbon dates. It is preferable to use notations like "$^{14}$C BP" or "uncal BP" (for dates based on uncalibrated radiocarbon dates) or "cal BP" (for dates based on calibrated radiocarbon dates).

## Case Study of the Spread of *Homo sapiens* to the Japanese Archipelago: Key Dates

The arrival of *H. sapiens* to the Japanese archipelago coincided with the beginnings of human settlement on these places. In terms of archaeological chronology, this development marked the start of the Upper Palaeolithic period. Early Upper Palaeolithic stone tools are co-present with polished stone axes. Accordingly, such stone tools are characterised for their blade techniques, trapezoids, and knife-shaped stone tools, and in many cases, there is a circular distribution of stone artifacts (circular camp sites). Stone assemblages discovered in Tachikawa loam layer X correspond to stone assemblages of the earliest stage of the Upper Palaeolithic (see Figure A.5) on Palaeo-Honshu Island. According to Ono (2011), "Tachikawa loam layer X marks the earliest stage of human settlement in the Japanese archipelago." In recent surveys of sites in the areas of Ashitaka and Hakone, researchers have systematically conducted radiocarbon dating of Upper Palaeolithic stone assemblages. At the Fujiishi site, for instance, researchers have pinpointed with considerable precision the stratigraphic changes with respect to the stone assemblages and dates of each cultural stratum (see Figure A.6) (Shizuoka Archaeological Research Institute, 2010).

A huge volcanic eruption occurred from the Aira caldera, south Kyushu, and volcanic ash spread over most of the Japanese islands as well as the Korean peninsula, a part of east China, and southern Primorye in the Russian Far East. This key tephra is called Aira-Tn tephra (AT), and is critically important for the Upper Palaeolithic chronology. This is the most important marker that divides Early Upper Palaeolithic and Late Upper Palaeolithic in Japan. Recently, its dates have been estimated 30,009 ± 189 varve BP by the lake Suigetsu varved sediment (Smith et al. 2013).

Table A.3 and Figure A.6 show cases of archaeological sites in the Japanese archipelago that were radiocarbon dated to before 34,000 cal BP. Many of the sites from the earliest stage of the

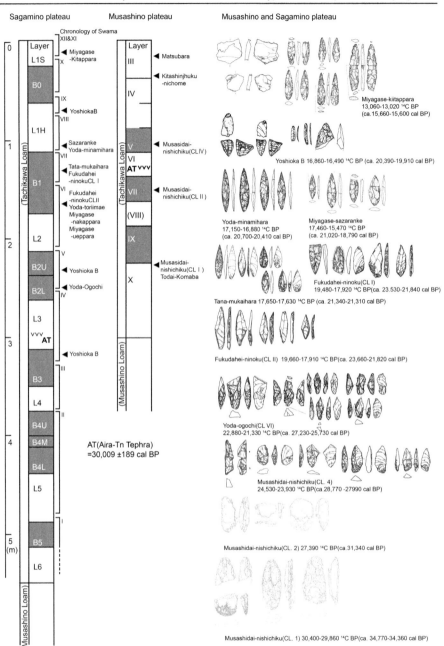

**FIGURE A.5** Musashino Plateau and Sagami Plateau Stratotypes and the Radiocarbon Ages of Key Stone tools (Kudo 2012).

Appendix A: Comparison of Radiocarbon and Calibrated Dates **335**

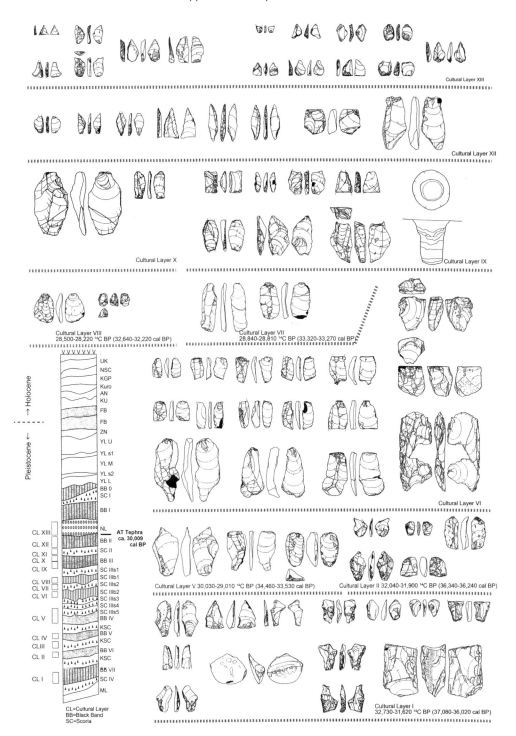

**FIGURE A.6** Stratigraphy of the Fujiishi site and radiocarbon dates to Each Cultural Stratum excavated under the AT Tephra (ca. 30,009 varve BP) (modified after Shizuoka Archaeological Research Institute, 2010).

TABLE A.3  List of radiocarbon dates of the representative Early Upper Palaeolithic sites dated to as far back as 34,000 cal BP.

| No. | Site name | Pref. | Sample position | Sample | Labo-code | ¹⁴C age (BP; ± 1 σ) | IntCal20 2 σ (whole range) (cal BP) | Mean (cal Bp) | δ ¹³C | Method | Characteristic artifacts |
|---|---|---|---|---|---|---|---|---|---|---|---|
| 1 | Okubo | Miyagi | Layer IV | Charcoal | IAAA-82998 | 30760 ± 160 | 35460–34680 | 35080 | (−24.0) | AMS | Retouched flakes |
|  |  |  | Layer IV | Charcoal | IAAA-82999 | 30480 ± 150 | 35270–34530 | 34890 | (−22.7) | AMS | Retouched flakes |
|  |  |  | Layer IV | Charcoal | IAAA-83000 | 30620 ± 180 | 35370–34590 | 34980 | (−24.3) | AMS | Retouched flakes |
| 2 | Happusan-II | Nagano | HPV F76·Xb | Charcoal | Beta-86229 | 31860 ± 250 | 36810–35600 | 36210 | −23.7 | AMS | Backed blades, blades |
|  |  |  | HPV F76·Xb | Charcoal | Beta-86230 | 32240 ± 260 | 37160–36090 | 36600 | −24.2 | AMS | Backed blades, blades |
|  |  |  | HPV F76·Xb | Charcoal | Beta-86231 | 31360 ± 230 | 36200–35290 | 35740 | −26.4 | AMS | Backed blades, blades |
|  |  |  | HPV F76·Xb | Charcoal | Beta-86232 | 32190 ± 260 | 37110–36050 | 36560 | −25.6 | AMS | Backed blades, blades |
|  |  |  | HPV F76·Xb | Charcoal | Beta-86233 | 32180 ± 260 | 37110–36050 | 36550 | −25.1 | AMS | Backed blades, blades |
| 3 | Kanmoki | Nagano | Layer Vb | Charcoal | Beta-82577 | 33070 ± 540 | 39270–36420 | 37860 | −25.5 | AMS | Polished axes, Trapezoids |
|  |  |  | Layer Vc | Charcoal | Beta-82580 | 33040 ± 530 | 39240–36410 | 37820 | −26.1 | AMS | Polished axes, Trapezoids |
|  |  |  | Layer V? | Charcoal | Beta-109414 | 32260 ± 590 | 38710–35420 | 36880 | — | AMS | Polished axes, Trapezoids |
|  |  |  | Layer V? | Charcoal | Beta-109416 | 32110 ± 610 | 38590–35280 | 36700 | — | AMS | Polished axes, Trapezoids |
|  |  |  | Layer Vb | Charcoal | Beta-109417 | 30510 ± 510 | 36060–34160 | 35010 | — | AMS | Polished axes, Trapezoids |
|  |  |  | Layer Vb | Charcoal | Beta-109419 | 32410 ± 340 | 37670–36060 | 36820 | — | AMS | Polished axes, Trapezoids |
| 4 | Oiwake-1 | Nagano | IW Cultural layer 5 block-2 | Charcoal | TERRA-b033051cl9 | 31040 ± 300 | 36090–34730 | 35430 | — | AMS | Trapezoids, Backed blades |
|  |  |  | IW Cultural layer 5 block-5 | Charcoal | TERRA-b033051c20 | 29310+ 250 | 34370–33230 | 33840 | — | AMS | Trapezoids, Backed blades |
|  |  |  | IW Cultural layer 5 block-5 | Charcoal | TERRA-b033051c23 | 30640 ± 300 | 35640–34440 | 35020 | — | AMS | Trapezoids, Backed blades |
| 5 | Yamakawa-kofungun | Ibaraki | Fire place | Charcoal | IAAA-31419 | 31640 ± 200 | 36370–35480 | 35960 | (−24.5) | AMS | Trapezoids |
|  |  |  | Fire place | Charcoal | IAAA-31420 | 31490 ± 190 | 36230–35410 | 35840 | (−25.8) | AMS | Trapezoids |
| 6 | Tokyo Univ. Komaba | Tokyo | Layer X | Charcoal | MTC-03710 | 30800 ± 200 | 35580–34640 | 35120 | — | AMS | Trapezoids |

*(Continued)*

TABLE A.3 (Continued)

| No. | Site name | Pref. | Sample position | Sample | Labo-code | $^{14}C$ age (BP; ± 1 σ) | IntCal20 2 σ (whole range) (cal BP) | Mean (cal Bp) | $δ^{13}C$ | Method | Characteristic artifacts |
|---|---|---|---|---|---|---|---|---|---|---|---|
| 7 | Takaido-higashi | Tokyo | Charcoal concentration 4 | Charcoal | IAAA-51557 | 32000 ± 170 | 36800–36020 | 36360 | — | AMS | Polished axes |
|  |  |  | Charcoal concentration 4 | Charcoal | IAAA-51558 | 31790 ± 160 | 36480–35690 | 36130 | — | AMS | Polished axes |
|  |  |  | Charcoal concentration 6 | Charcoal | IAAA-51559 | 31780 ± 200 | 36560–35580 | 36110 | — | AMS | Polished axes |
| 8 | Donoshita | Tokyo | Layer X, Charcoal concentration 2 | Charred material | IAAA-70603 | 31350 ± 210 | 36170–35310 | 35740 | (−24.6) | AMS | Polished axes, Trapezoids |
|  |  |  | Layer X, Charcoal concentration 3 | Charred material | IAAA-70604 | 30310 ± 190 | 35220–34370 | 34750 | (−26.3) | AMS | Polished axes, Trapezoids |
|  |  |  | Layer X, Charcoal concentration 1 | Charred material | IAAA-70606 | 31200 ± 200 | 36120–35200 | 35620 | (−22.6) | AMS | Polished axes, Trapezoids |
|  |  |  | Layer X, Charcoal concentration 1 | Charred material | IAAA-70607 | 30960 ± 200 | 35880–34740 | 35320 | (−23.9) | AMS | Polished axes, Trapezoids |
| 9 | Musashidai-west | Tokyo | Cultural layer 1, Fire place SX-47 | Charcoal | Beta-156135 | 30400 ± 400 | 35650–34170 | 34880 | −23.8 | AMS | Polished axes |
|  |  |  | Cultural layer 1, Fire place SX-104 | Charcoal | Beta-182638 | 29860 ± 150 | 34620–34100 | 34360 | −24.7 | AMS | Polished axes |
| 10 | Yoshioka B | Kanagawa | Layer B5 Layer, Charcoal concentration | Chaired material | Beta-142921 | 30550 ± 290 | 35500–34410 | 34950 | −27.9 | AMS | Trapezoids |
| 11 | Mukaida-A | Shizuoka | Layer BB7–BB6, Charcoal concentration | Charcoal | IAAA-10619 | 31770 ± 170 | 36480–35640 | 36110 | (−30.7) | AMS | Backed blades |
| 12 | Nishibora-b | Shizuoka | Layer BB6, Charcoal concentration | Charcoal | Beta-122043 | 30200 ± 360 | 35380–34080 | 34710 | −24.9 | AMS | Polished axes, Trapezoids |
|  |  |  | Layer BB6, Charcoal concentration | Charcoal | Beta-122044 | 29690 ± 210 | 34580–33800 | 34220 | −25.6 | AMS | Polished axes, Trapezoids |
|  |  |  | Layer BB6, Charcoal concentration | Charcoal | Beta-122045 | 30390 ± 230 | 35290–34390 | 34830 | −25.6 | AMS | Polished axes, Trapezoids |

(Continued)

TABLE A.3 (Continued)

| No. | Site name | Pref. | Sample position | Sample | Labo-code | ¹⁴C age (BP, ± 1 σ) | IntCal20 2 σ (whole range) (cal BP) | Mean (cal Bp) | δ ¹³C | Method | Characteristic artifacts |
|---|---|---|---|---|---|---|---|---|---|---|---|
| 13 | Idemaruyama | Shizuoka | Layer SCIV–BBVII | Charcoal | IAAA-63169 | 32720 ± 190 | 37600–36520 | 37090 | (−23.7) | AMS | Trapezoids |
|  |  |  | Layer SCIV–BBVII | Charcoal | IAAA-63170 | 32920 ± 200 | 38320–36740 | 37400 | (−25.6) | AMS | Trapezoids |
|  |  |  | Layer SCIV–BBVII | Charcoal | IAAA-63171 | 33040 ± 190 | 38850–36930 | 37610 | (−22.7) | AMS | Trapezoids |
|  |  |  | Layer SCIV–BBVII | Charcoal | IAAA-63172 | 33180 ± 180 | 38810–37100 | 37880 | (−26.0) | AMS | Trapezoids |
|  |  |  | Layer SCIV–BBVII | Charcoal | IAAA-63173 | 32230 ± 190 | 36980–36180 | 36570 | (−25.7) | AMS | Trapezoids |
|  |  |  | Layer SCIV–BBVII | Charcoal | IAAA-63174 | 32770 ± 170 | 37620–36620 | 37150 | (−23.1) | AMS | Trapezoids, Polished axes |
| 14 | Fujiishi | Shizuoka | Layer BBVI cultural layer I | Charcoal | IAAA-60628 | 32620 ± 190 | 37500–36440 | 36960 | (−27.2) | AMS | Trapezoids, Polished axes |
|  |  |  | Layer BBVI cultural layer I | Charcoal | IAAA-60629 | 32580 ± 190 | 37460–36400 | 36910 | (−27.0) | AMS | Trapezoids, Polished axes |
|  |  |  | Layer BBVII cultural layer I | Charcoal | IAAA-60632 | 32730 ± 190 | 37610–36520 | 37110 | (−26.4) | AMS | Trapezoids, Polished axes |
|  |  |  | Layer BBVII cultural layer I | Charcoal | IAAA-60633 | 32110 ± 190 | 36910–36100 | 36470 | (−27.4) | AMS | Trapezoids, Polished axes |
|  |  |  | Layer BBVII cultural layer I | Charcoal | IAAA-60634 | 31620 ± 190 | 36330–35480 | 35950 | (−27.0) | AMS | Trapezoids, Polished axes |
|  |  |  | Layer BBVII cultural layer I | Charcoal | IAAA-60635 | 32500 ± 180 | 37300–36330 | 36810 | (−27.3) | AMS | Trapezoids, Polished axes |
|  |  |  | Layer BBVII cultural layer I | Charcoal | IAAA-60636 | 32550 ± 190 | 37410–36370 | 36870 | (−25.7) | AMS | Trapezoids, Polished axes |
|  |  |  | Layer BBVII cultural layer I | Charcoal | IAAA-60637 | 31840 ± 180 | 36610–35700 | 36190 | (−26.9) | AMS | Trapezoids, Polished axes |
|  |  |  | Layer BBVII cultural layer I | Charcoal | IAAA-60638 | 31930 ± 180 | 36760–35890 | 36290 | (−29.3) | AMS | Trapezoids, Polished axes |
|  |  |  | Layer BBVI cultural layer II | Charcoal | IAAA-60630 | 31900 ± 190 | 36740–35790 | 36250 | (−29.6) | AMS | Trapezoids, Polished axes |
|  |  |  | Layer BBVI cultural layer II | Charcoal | IAAA-60631 | 32040 ± 200 | 36890–36030 | 36410 | (−26.1) | AMS | Trapezoids, Polished axes |
| 15 | Seta-ikenohara | Kumamoto | Cultural layer I, Layer 16c | Charcoal | Beta-227794 | 30300 ± 250 | 35270–34320 | 34760 | −25.7 | AMS | Trapezoids |
|  |  |  | Cultural layer I, Layer 16c | Charcoal | Beta-227795 | 28440 ± 210 | 33290–31880 | 32600 | −26.1 | AMS | Trapezoids |
|  |  |  | Cultural layer I, Layer 17a | Charcoal | IAAA-72245 | 30260 ± 170 | 35170–34350 | 34690 | (−10.3) | AMS | Trapezoids |
|  |  |  | Cultural layer I, Layer 17a | Charcoal | IAAA-72246 | 30340 ± 170 | 35210–34410 | 34770 | (−28.0) | AMS | Trapezoids |
|  |  |  | Cultural layer I, Layer 17a | Charcoal | IAAA-72247 | 31830 ± 170 | 36570–35710 | 36180 | (−28.9) | AMS | Trapezoids |
|  |  |  | Cultural layer I, Layer 17a | Charcoal | IAAA-72248 | 32210 ± 180 | 36950–36180 | 36550 | (−22.1) | AMS | Trapezoids |

(Continued)

TABLE A.3 (Continued)

| No. | Site name | Pref. | Sample position | Sample | Labo-code | $^{14}C$ age (BP, ± 1 σ) | IntCal20 2 σ (whole range) (cal BP) | Mean (cal Bp) | $δ^{13}C$ | Method | Characteristic artifacts |
|---|---|---|---|---|---|---|---|---|---|---|---|
| 16 | Ishinomoto | Kumamoto | Layer VIb | Charcoal | Beta-84289 | 32740 ± 1060 | 40280–35310 | 37690 | −25.8 | β | Polished axes, Trapezoids |
|  |  |  | Layer VIb | Charcoal | Beta-84290 | 33720 ± 430 | 39710–37290 | 38560 | −24.3 | β | Polished axes, Trapezoids |
|  |  |  | Layer VIb | Charcoal | Beta-84291 | 33140 ± 550 | 39340–36460 | 37940 | −27.8 | β | Polished axes, Trapezoids |
|  |  |  | Layer VIb | Charcoal | Beta-84292 | 31460 ± 270 | 36310–35300 | 35820 | −27.3 | β | Polished axes, Trapezoids |
|  |  |  | Charcoal concentration, No.5 | Charcoal | Beta-117661 | 32750 ± 430 | 38870–36260 | 37390 | — | AMS | Polished axes, Trapezoids |
|  |  |  | Charcoal concentration, No.6 | Charcoal | Beta-117662 | 31790 ± 270 | 36740–35480 | 36120 | — | AMS | Polished axes, Trapezoids |
| 17 | Yamada | Miyazaki | Layer IX, Charcoal concentration C1 | Charcoal | Beta-184680 | 30550 ± 220 | 35370–34500 | 34940 | −28.5 | AMS | Polished axes |
|  |  |  | Layer IX, Charcoal concentration C1 | Charcoal | Beta-184669 | 30630 ± 230 | 35450–34530 | 34990 | −26.3 | AMS | Polished axes |
| 18 | Tachikiri | Kagoshima | Fire place 1 | Charcoal | Beta-114267 | 30480 ± 210 | 35320–34470 | 34890 | −26.3 | AMS | Polished axes, Grinding stones |
|  |  |  | Pit2 | Charcoal | Beta-169707 | 30400 ± 600 | 36160–33840 | 34930 | −24.3 | AMS | Polished axes, Grinding stones |
|  |  |  | Fire place G | Charcoal | Beta-169708 | 28480 ± 500 | 34100–31580 | 32760 | −26.4 | AMS | Polished axes, Grinding stones |
| 19 | Yokomine-C | Kagoshima | Pebble concentration 1 | Charcoal | Beta-102399 | 31280 ± 690 | 37300–34380 | 35780 | −25.8 | AMS | Pebble tools |
|  |  |  | Pebble concentration 1 | Charcoal | Beta-102400 | 29670 ± 540 | 35400–32890 | 34110 | −24.6 | AMS | Pebble tools |
|  |  |  | Around grinding stones | Charcoal | Beta-102401 | 30490 ± 590 | 36200–33980 | 35010 | −24.3 | AMS | Pebble tools |
|  |  |  | Pebble concentration | Charcoal | Beta-102402 | 29300 ± 520 | 34740–32140 | 33660 | −25.2 | AMS | Pebble tools |

Early Upper Palaeolithic are almost entirely confirmed to be younger than the earliest estimated date of 38,000 cal BP. Early Upper Palaeolithic sites increased in quantity rapidly on the entire Palaeo-Honshu Island from around 38,000 cal BP onward. The number of cases enters a definite increasing trend at a time later than 36,000 cal BP.

From these data, we can draw the following conclusion: Upper Palaeolithic sites began to emerge in the Japanese archipelago later than around 38,000 cal BP, and most of the sites emerge after around 37,000 cal BP. Additionally, while the route by which *H. sapiens* migrated into the Japanese archipelago remains unclear, given that sites from the earliest stage of the Upper Palaeolithic period proliferated broadly in the Palaeo-Honshu island no later than around 36,000 cal BP, it is reasonable to assume that *H. sapiens* proliferated on the Palaeo-Honshu island in a short space of time (see Figure A.7).

The following correspondence table of radiocarbon dates and calibrated dates using IntCal20 could help researchers determine more accurately the age of previously dated sites (See Table A.4)

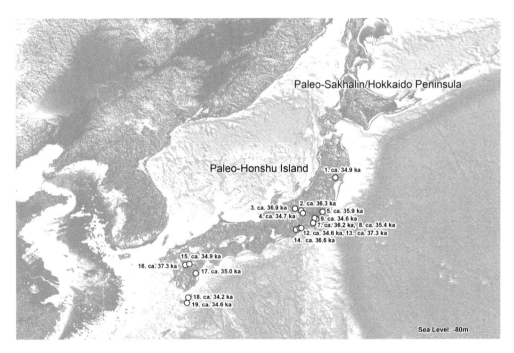

FIGURE A.7  The distribution of Early Upper Palaeolithic sites dated to as far back as 34,000 cal BP.

TABLE A.4  Correspondence table of radiocarbon dates and calibrated dates using IntCal20.

| $^{14}C$ BP ±1 | cal BP 2σ (95.4%) | | Mean | cal BC/AD 2σ (95.4%) | | Mean |
|---|---|---|---|---|---|---|
| 300 | 430 | 300 | 390 | 1520 | 1650 | 1560 |
| 400 | 500 | 470 | 490 | 1450 | 1480 | 1460 |
| 500 | 540 | 510 | 520 | 1410 | 1440 | 1430 |
| 600 | 640 | 550 | 600 | 1310 | 1400 | 1350 |
| 700 | 680 | 650 | 660 | 1270 | 1300 | 1290 |
| 800 | 730 | 680 | 710 | 1220 | 1270 | 1240 |
| 900 | 900 | 740 | 810 | 1050 | 1210 | 1140 |
| 1000 | 930 | 910 | 920 | 1020 | 1040 | 1030 |
| 1100 | 1060 | 950 | 1000 | 890 | 1000 | 950 |
| 1200 | 1170 | 1060 | 1110 | 780 | 890 | 840 |
| 1300 | 1290 | 1170 | 1220 | 660 | 780 | 730 |
| 1400 | 1340 | 1290 | 1300 | 610 | 660 | 650 |
| 1500 | 1390 | 1350 | 1370 | 560 | 600 | 580 |
| 1600 | 1530 | 1410 | 1470 | 420 | 540 | 480 |
| 1700 | 1690 | 1540 | 1590 | 260 | 410 | 360 |
| 1800 | 1730 | 1630 | 1690 | 220 | 320 | 260 |
| 1900 | 1870 | 1740 | 1800 | 80 | 210 | 150 |
| 2000 | 1990 | 1890 | 1950 | −50 | 60 | 1 |
| 2100 | 2120 | 2000 | 2060 | −170 | −50 | −110 |
| 2200 | 2310 | 2140 | 2230 | −360 | −190 | −280 |
| 2300 | 2350 | 2330 | 2340 | −400 | −380 | −390 |
| 2400 | 2470 | 2350 | 2400 | −520 | 400 | −450 |
| 2500 | 2720 | 2490 | 2590 | −770 | −550 | −640 |
| 2600 | 2760 | 2730 | 2740 | −810 | −780 | −790 |
| 2700 | 2850 | 2760 | 2800 | −900 | −810 | −850 |
| 2800 | 2950 | 2860 | 2900 | −1000 | −910 | −950 |
| 2900 | 3080 | 2960 | 3030 | −1130 | −1010 | −1080 |
| 3000 | 3230 | 3140 | 3190 | −1280 | −1200 | −1240 |
| 3100 | 3370 | 3250 | 3310 | −1420 | −1300 | −1360 |
| 3200 | 3450 | 3380 | 3420 | −1500 | −1430 | −1470 |
| 3300 | 3570 | 3460 | 3520 | −1620 | −1510 | −1570 |
| 3400 | 3700 | 3580 | 3640 | −1750 | −1630 | −1690 |
| 3500 | 3840 | 3700 | 3770 | −1890 | −1750 | −1820 |
| 3600 | 3970 | 3840 | 3910 | −2020 | −1890 | −1960 |
| 3700 | 4090 | 3980 | 4030 | −2140 | −2030 | −2080 |
| 3800 | 4240 | 4100 | 4190 | −2290 | −2150 | −2240 |
| 3900 | 4420 | 4290 | 4350 | −2470 | −2340 | −2400 |
| 4000 | 4520 | 4420 | 4470 | −2570 | −2470 | −2520 |
| 4100 | 4800 | 4520 | 4620 | −2850 | −2570 | −2670 |
| 4200 | 4840 | 4650 | 4760 | −2890 | −2700 | −2810 |
| 4300 | 4870 | 4840 | 4850 | −2920 | −2890 | −2900 |
| 4400 | 5040 | 4870 | 4960 | −3090 | −2920 | −3010 |
| 4500 | 5290 | 5050 | 5150 | −3340 | −3100 | −3210 |
| 4600 | 5440 | 5300 | 5340 | −3490 | −3350 | −3390 |
| 4700 | 5480 | 5320 | 5380 | −3530 | −3370 | −3430 |

(Continued)

**TABLE A.4** (*Continued*)

| $^{14}C$ BP $\pm 1$ | cal BP 2σ (95.4%) | | Mean | cal BC/AD 2σ (95.4%) | | Mean |
|---|---|---|---|---|---|---|
| 4800 | 5590 | 5480 | 5520 | −3640 | −3530 | −3570 |
| 4900 | 5660 | 5590 | 5620 | −3710 | −3640 | −3670 |
| 5000 | 5850 | 5650 | 5720 | −3900 | −3710 | −3770 |
| 5100 | 5910 | 5750 | 5820 | −3970 | −3800 | −3870 |
| 5200 | 6000 | 5920 | 5960 | −4050 | −3970 | −4010 |
| 5300 | 6180 | 5990 | 6090 | −4240 | −4050 | −4140 |
| 5400 | 6280 | 6190 | 6240 | −4340 | −4240 | −4290 |
| 5500 | 6310 | 6280 | 6300 | −4360 | −4330 | −4350 |
| 5600 | 6410 | 6310 | 6360 | −4460 | −4360 | −4410 |
| 5700 | 6540 | 6400 | 6470 | −4590 | −4450 | −4520 |
| 5800 | 6660 | 6550 | 6610 | −4720 | −4600 | −4660 |
| 5900 | 6750 | 6660 | 6710 | −4800 | −4710 | −4760 |
| 6000 | 6890 | 6790 | 6830 | −4940 | −4840 | −4890 |
| 6100 | 7150 | 6900 | 6970 | −5210 | −4950 | −5020 |
| 6200 | 7170 | 7010 | 7080 | −5220 | −5060 | −5130 |
| 6300 | 7270 | 7160 | 7210 | −5320 | −5210 | −5260 |
| 6400 | 7420 | 7270 | 7330 | −5470 | −5320 | −5380 |
| 6500 | 7430 | 7330 | 7400 | −5490 | −5380 | −5460 |
| 6600 | 7570 | 7430 | 7490 | −5620 | −5480 | −5540 |
| 6700 | 7590 | 7510 | 7550 | −5650 | −5560 | −5610 |
| 6800 | 7680 | 7600 | 7640 | −5730 | −5650 | −5690 |
| 6900 | 7780 | 7670 | 7720 | −5830 | −5720 | −5770 |
| 7000 | 7930 | 7790 | 7850 | −5980 | −5840 | −5900 |
| 7100 | 7970 | 7870 | 7920 | −6020 | −5920 | −5970 |
| 7200 | 8030 | 7970 | 8000 | −6080 | −6020 | −6050 |
| 7300 | 8180 | 8030 | 8110 | −6230 | −6080 | −6160 |
| 7400 | 8320 | 8170 | 8240 | −6370 | −6220 | −6290 |
| 7500 | 8380 | 8210 | 8330 | −6430 | −6260 | −6380 |
| 7600 | 8420 | 8370 | 8400 | −6470 | −6420 | −6450 |
| 7700 | 8540 | 8420 | 8480 | −6590 | −6470 | −6530 |
| 7800 | 8600 | 8540 | 8570 | −6650 | −6590 | −6620 |
| 7900 | 8780 | 8600 | 8690 | −6830 | −6650 | −6740 |
| 8000 | 9000 | 8770 | 8880 | −7050 | −6820 | −6930 |
| 8100 | 9090 | 8990 | 9020 | −7140 | −7040 | −7070 |
| 8200 | 9270 | 9020 | 9150 | −7330 | −7070 | −7200 |
| 8300 | 9420 | 9140 | 9330 | −7470 | −7200 | −7380 |
| 8400 | 9480 | 9320 | 9440 | −7540 | −7380 | −7490 |
| 8500 | 9540 | 9480 | 9510 | −7590 | −7530 | −7560 |
| 8600 | 9550 | 9530 | 9540 | −7610 | −7580 | −7590 |
| 8700 | 9690 | 9550 | 9620 | −7740 | −7600 | −7670 |
| 8800 | 9900 | 9710 | 9820 | −7960 | −7760 | −7870 |
| 8900 | 10180 | 9900 | 10040 | −8230 | −7960 | −8090 |
| 9000 | 10230 | 10180 | 10200 | −8280 | −8230 | −8250 |
| 9100 | 10250 | 10220 | 10240 | −8310 | −8270 | −8290 |
| 9200 | 10490 | 10250 | 10350 | −8540 | −8300 | −8400 |

(*Continued*)

**TABLE A.4** (*Continued*)

| ¹⁴C BP ±1 | cal BP 2σ (95.4%) | | Mean | cal BC/AD 2σ (95.4%) | | Mean |
|---|---|---|---|---|---|---|
| 9300 | 10570 | 10430 | 10510 | −8620 | −8480 | −8560 |
| 9400 | 10690 | 10570 | 10630 | −8740 | −8620 | −8680 |
| 9500 | 11060 | 10690 | 10790 | −9120 | −8740 | −8840 |
| 9600 | 11110 | 10780 | 10920 | −9160 | −8830 | −8970 |
| 9700 | 11200 | 11110 | 11160 | −9250 | −9160 | −9210 |
| 9800 | 11250 | 11200 | 11220 | −9300 | −9250 | −9270 |
| 9900 | 11390 | 11240 | 11280 | −9440 | −9290 | −9330 |
| 10000 | 11620 | 11320 | 11480 | −9670 | −9370 | −9530 |
| 10100 | 11820 | 11510 | 11710 | −9870 | −9560 | −9760 |
| 10200 | 11940 | 11820 | 11880 | −9990 | −9870 | −9930 |
| 10300 | 12430 | 11940 | 12020 | −10480 | −9990 | −10070 |
| 10400 | 12480 | 12100 | 12300 | −10530 | −10150 | −10350 |
| 10500 | 12620 | 12470 | 12560 | −10670 | −10520 | −10610 |
| 10600 | 12690 | 12610 | 12650 | −10740 | −10660 | −10700 |
| 10700 | 12740 | 12700 | 12720 | −10790 | −10750 | −10770 |
| 10800 | 12760 | 12730 | 12740 | −10810 | −10780 | −10800 |
| 10900 | 12830 | 12750 | 12800 | −10890 | −10810 | −10850 |
| 11000 | 12990 | 12830 | 12900 | −11040 | −10880 | −10950 |
| 11100 | 13100 | 12930 | 13050 | −11150 | −10980 | −11110 |
| 11200 | 13170 | 13090 | 13120 | −11220 | −11140 | −11170 |
| 11300 | 13240 | 13120 | 13190 | −11290 | −11170 | −11240 |
| 11400 | 13320 | 13180 | 13270 | −11370 | −11230 | −11320 |
| 11500 | 13440 | 13310 | 13370 | −11490 | −11360 | −11420 |
| 11600 | 13570 | 13410 | 13470 | −11630 | −11460 | −11520 |
| 11700 | 13600 | 13490 | 13550 | −11650 | −11540 | −11600 |
| 11800 | 13760 | 13590 | 13670 | −11810 | −11640 | −11720 |
| 11900 | 13800 | 13610 | 13760 | −11850 | −11660 | −11810 |
| 12000 | 14020 | 13790 | 13900 | −12070 | −11840 | −11950 |
| 12100 | 14070 | 13860 | 13980 | −12120 | −11910 | −12030 |
| 12200 | 14140 | 14050 | 14090 | −12190 | −12100 | −12140 |
| 12300 | 14780 | 14130 | 14260 | −12830 | −12180 | −12310 |
| 12400 | 14830 | 14280 | 14500 | −12890 | −12330 | −12560 |
| 12500 | 14980 | 14540 | 14780 | −13030 | −12590 | −12830 |
| 12600 | 15120 | 14930 | 15020 | −13170 | −12980 | −13070 |
| 12700 | 15250 | 15040 | 15150 | −13310 | −13090 | −13200 |
| 12800 | 15380 | 15150 | 15270 | −13430 | −13200 | −13320 |
| 12900 | 15560 | 15290 | 15420 | −13610 | −13340 | −13470 |
| 13000 | 15690 | 15420 | 15570 | −13740 | −13470 | −13620 |
| 13100 | 15810 | 15610 | 15710 | −13860 | −13660 | −13760 |
| 13200 | 15960 | 15730 | 15840 | −14010 | −13780 | −13890 |
| 13300 | 16090 | 15850 | 15980 | −14140 | −13900 | −14030 |
| 13400 | 16240 | 16020 | 16130 | −14290 | −14070 | −14190 |
| 13500 | 16370 | 16180 | 16280 | −14420 | −14230 | −14330 |
| 13600 | 16540 | 16310 | 16420 | −14590 | −14360 | −14470 |
| 13700 | 16690 | 16430 | 16560 | −14740 | −14480 | −14620 |

(*Continued*)

**TABLE A.4** (*Continued*)

| $^{14}C$ BP $\pm 1$ | cal BP 2σ (95.4%) | | Mean | cal BC/AD 2σ (95.4%) | | Mean |
|---|---|---|---|---|---|---|
| 13800 | 16900 | 16590 | 16750 | −14950 | −14650 | −14800 |
| 13900 | 17030 | 16770 | 16920 | −15080 | −14820 | −14970 |
| 14000 | 17100 | 16960 | 17040 | −15150 | −15010 | −15090 |
| 14100 | 17330 | 17050 | 17180 | −15380 | −15100 | −15230 |
| 14200 | 17380 | 17100 | 17240 | −15430 | −15150 | −15290 |
| 14300 | 17460 | 17290 | 17380 | −15510 | −15340 | −15430 |
| 14400 | 17790 | 17370 | 17550 | −15840 | −15420 | −15600 |
| 14500 | 17870 | 17470 | 17670 | −15930 | −15520 | −15730 |
| 14600 | 18020 | 17760 | 17890 | −16070 | −15820 | −15940 |
| 14700 | 18180 | 17890 | 18040 | −16230 | −15940 | −16090 |
| 14800 | 18240 | 18050 | 18160 | −16300 | −16100 | −16210 |
| 14900 | 18270 | 18180 | 18220 | −16320 | −16230 | −16270 |
| 15000 | 18590 | 18200 | 18300 | −16650 | −16250 | −16350 |
| 15100 | 18630 | 18250 | 18480 | −16680 | −16300 | −16530 |
| 15200 | 18670 | 18280 | 18450 | −16720 | −16330 | −16500 |
| 15300 | 18730 | 18320 | 18560 | −16780 | −16370 | −16610 |
| 15400 | 18800 | 18670 | 18740 | −16850 | −16720 | −16790 |
| 15500 | 18860 | 18760 | 18810 | −16910 | −16810 | −16860 |
| 15600 | 18920 | 18820 | 18870 | −16970 | −16870 | −16920 |
| 15700 | 19020 | 18880 | 18950 | −17080 | −16930 | −17000 |
| 15800 | 19140 | 18960 | 19050 | −17190 | −17010 | −17100 |
| 15900 | 19300 | 19080 | 19170 | −17350 | −17130 | −17220 |
| 16000 | 19440 | 19190 | 19320 | −17490 | −17240 | −17370 |
| 16100 | 19540 | 19380 | 19460 | −17600 | −17430 | −17510 |
| 16200 | 19600 | 19480 | 19540 | −17650 | −17530 | −17590 |
| 16300 | 19830 | 19550 | 19680 | −17880 | −17600 | −17730 |
| 16400 | 19890 | 19610 | 19750 | −17940 | −17660 | −17800 |
| 16500 | 20080 | 19840 | 19930 | −18130 | −17890 | −17980 |
| 16600 | 20170 | 19920 | 20050 | −18230 | −17970 | −18100 |
| 16700 | 20310 | 20080 | 20200 | −18360 | −18130 | −18250 |
| 16800 | 20430 | 20220 | 20330 | −18490 | −18280 | −18380 |
| 16900 | 20510 | 20340 | 20430 | −18570 | −18390 | −18480 |
| 17000 | 20590 | 20440 | 20520 | −18650 | −18500 | −18570 |
| 17100 | 20790 | 20530 | 20650 | −18840 | −18580 | −18700 |
| 17200 | 20880 | 20610 | 20770 | −18940 | −18660 | −18820 |
| 17300 | 20950 | 20810 | 20880 | −19000 | −18860 | −18930 |
| 17400 | 21050 | 20870 | 20960 | −19100 | −18920 | −19010 |
| 17500 | 21310 | 20950 | 21100 | −19360 | −19000 | −19150 |
| 17600 | 21410 | 21070 | 21260 | −19460 | −19120 | −19310 |
| 17700 | 21720 | 21330 | 21460 | −19770 | −19380 | −19510 |
| 17800 | 21790 | 21420 | 21610 | −19840 | −19470 | −19660 |
| 17900 | 21980 | 21450 | 21790 | −20030 | −19500 | −19840 |
| 18000 | 22050 | 21840 | 21950 | −20100 | −19890 | −20000 |
| 18100 | 22150 | 21960 | 22050 | −20200 | −20010 | −20110 |
| 18200 | 22260 | 22060 | 22160 | −20310 | −20110 | −20210 |

(*Continued*)

**TABLE A.4** (*Continued*)

| $^{14}C$ BP $\pm 1$ | cal BP 2σ (95.4%) | | Mean | cal BC/AD 2σ (95.4%) | | Mean |
|---|---|---|---|---|---|---|
| 18300 | 22360 | 22160 | 22260 | −20420 | −20210 | −20320 |
| 18400 | 22440 | 22270 | 22350 | −20490 | −20320 | −20400 |
| 18500 | 22480 | 22340 | 22410 | −20540 | −20390 | −20460 |
| 18600 | 22570 | 22370 | 22470 | −20620 | −20420 | −20520 |
| 18700 | 22850 | 22430 | 22600 | −20900 | −20480 | −20650 |
| 18800 | 22920 | 22550 | 22740 | −20980 | −20600 | −20790 |
| 18900 | 22990 | 22610 | 22860 | −21040 | −20660 | −20910 |
| 19000 | 23020 | 22890 | 22960 | −21070 | −20940 | −21010 |
| 19100 | 23060 | 22930 | 23000 | −21120 | −20980 | −21050 |
| 19200 | 23170 | 22970 | 23070 | −21220 | −21020 | −21120 |
| 19300 | 23680 | 23030 | 23210 | −21730 | −21080 | −21260 |
| 19400 | 23730 | 23170 | 23430 | −21780 | −21220 | −21480 |
| 19500 | 23760 | 23330 | 23530 | −21810 | −21380 | −21580 |
| 19600 | 23800 | 23390 | 23560 | −21850 | −21440 | −21610 |
| 19700 | 23840 | 23440 | 23750 | −21890 | −21490 | −21800 |
| 19800 | 23870 | 23760 | 23820 | −21920 | −21810 | −21870 |
| 19900 | 24010 | 23790 | 23880 | −22060 | −21840 | −21930 |
| 20000 | 24170 | 23850 | 24000 | −22220 | −21910 | −22050 |
| 20100 | 24260 | 23960 | 24110 | −22310 | −22010 | −22160 |
| 20200 | 24450 | 24120 | 24240 | −22500 | −22170 | −22290 |
| 20300 | 24560 | 24200 | 24380 | −22610 | −22250 | −22430 |
| 20400 | 24660 | 24270 | 24480 | −22710 | −22320 | −22530 |
| 20500 | 24900 | 24370 | 24670 | −22950 | −22420 | −22720 |
| 20600 | 24980 | 24650 | 24830 | −23030 | −22700 | −22880 |
| 20700 | 25140 | 24850 | 24990 | −23190 | −22900 | −23040 |
| 20800 | 25210 | 24990 | 25100 | −23260 | −23050 | −23160 |
| 20900 | 25290 | 25100 | 25200 | −23350 | −23160 | −23250 |
| 21000 | 25550 | 25170 | 25310 | −23600 | −23220 | −23360 |
| 21100 | 25630 | 25270 | 25450 | −23680 | −23320 | −23500 |
| 21200 | 25710 | 25320 | 25550 | −23760 | −23380 | −23600 |
| 21300 | 25790 | 25620 | 25700 | −23850 | −23670 | −23750 |
| 21400 | 25880 | 25690 | 25780 | −23930 | −23740 | −23830 |
| 21500 | 25940 | 25760 | 25840 | −23990 | −23810 | −23890 |
| 21600 | 25980 | 25820 | 25900 | −24030 | −23870 | −23950 |
| 21700 | 26020 | 25860 | 25940 | −24070 | −23910 | −23990 |
| 21800 | 26240 | 25890 | 26000 | −24300 | −23940 | −24050 |
| 21900 | 26320 | 25940 | 26130 | −24370 | −23990 | −24180 |
| 22000 | 26390 | 25990 | 26200 | −24440 | −24050 | −24250 |
| 22100 | 26480 | 26000 | 26310 | −24530 | −24050 | −24360 |
| 22200 | 26800 | 26320 | 26490 | −24850 | −24370 | −24540 |
| 22300 | 26890 | 26370 | 26650 | −24940 | −24420 | −24710 |
| 22400 | 26950 | 26430 | 26710 | −25000 | −24480 | −24760 |
| 22500 | 27050 | 26440 | 26760 | −25110 | −24490 | −24810 |
| 22600 | 27170 | 26460 | 26960 | −25220 | −24520 | −25010 |
| 22700 | 27240 | 26650 | 27100 | −25290 | −24700 | −25150 |

(*Continued*)

**TABLE A.4** (*Continued*)

| ¹⁴C BP ±1 | cal BP 2σ (95.4%) | | Mean | cal BC/AD 2σ (95.4%) | | Mean |
|---|---|---|---|---|---|---|
| 22800 | 27270 | 27110 | 27190 | −25320 | −25160 | −25240 |
| 22900 | 27300 | 27170 | 27240 | −25360 | −25220 | −25290 |
| 23000 | 27340 | 27210 | 27280 | −25400 | −25260 | −25330 |
| 23100 | 27550 | 27230 | 27340 | −25610 | −25290 | −25390 |
| 23200 | 27640 | 27300 | 27450 | −25690 | −25350 | −25500 |
| 23300 | 27700 | 27360 | 27530 | −25750 | −25410 | −25580 |
| 23400 | 27770 | 27430 | 27620 | −25820 | −25480 | −25670 |
| 23500 | 27830 | 27620 | 27720 | −25880 | −25670 | −25770 |
| 23600 | 27850 | 27680 | 27760 | −25900 | −25730 | −25820 |
| 23700 | 27890 | 27710 | 27800 | −25940 | −25770 | −25860 |
| 23800 | 27980 | 27750 | 27860 | −26030 | −25800 | −25910 |
| 23900 | 28140 | 27790 | 27950 | −26190 | −25840 | −26000 |
| 24000 | 28310 | 27850 | 28080 | −26360 | −25900 | −26130 |
| 24100 | 28530 | 27980 | 28250 | −26590 | −26030 | −26300 |
| 24200 | 28660 | 28230 | 28440 | −26710 | −26280 | −26490 |
| 24300 | 28710 | 28380 | 28570 | −26770 | −26430 | −26620 |
| 24400 | 28780 | 28570 | 28670 | −26830 | −26620 | −26730 |
| 24500 | 28860 | 28640 | 28750 | −26910 | −26690 | −26800 |
| 24600 | 29020 | 28710 | 28850 | −27070 | −26760 | −26900 |
| 24700 | 29110 | 28800 | 28950 | −27160 | −26850 | −27010 |
| 24800 | 29180 | 28890 | 29050 | −27230 | −26940 | −27100 |
| 24900 | 29220 | 29040 | 29140 | −27280 | −27090 | −27190 |
| 25000 | 29250 | 29120 | 29190 | −27310 | −27170 | −27240 |
| 25100 | 29490 | 29140 | 29250 | −27540 | −27190 | −27300 |
| 25200 | 29700 | 29200 | 29430 | −27750 | −27250 | −27480 |
| 25300 | 29850 | 29270 | 29570 | −27900 | −27320 | −27620 |
| 25400 | 29970 | 29340 | 29770 | −28020 | −27390 | −27820 |
| 25500 | 30020 | 29790 | 29910 | −28070 | −27840 | −27960 |
| 25600 | 30050 | 29880 | 29970 | −28100 | −27930 | −28020 |
| 25700 | 30090 | 29930 | 30010 | −28140 | −27980 | −28060 |
| 25800 | 30140 | 29970 | 30060 | −28190 | −28030 | −28110 |
| 25900 | 30230 | 30010 | 30120 | −28280 | −28060 | −28170 |
| 26000 | 30320 | 30070 | 30190 | −28370 | −28120 | −28240 |
| 26100 | 30390 | 30120 | 30270 | −28440 | −28170 | −28320 |
| 26200 | 30750 | 30230 | 30450 | −28800 | −28280 | −28500 |
| 26300 | 30800 | 30350 | 30580 | −28850 | −28400 | −28630 |
| 26400 | 30890 | 30400 | 30660 | −28940 | −28460 | −28710 |
| 26500 | 31040 | 30470 | 30860 | −29090 | −28530 | −28910 |
| 26600 | 31060 | 30820 | 30940 | −29110 | −28880 | −28990 |
| 26700 | 31110 | 30900 | 31010 | −29160 | −28950 | −29060 |
| 26800 | 31140 | 30970 | 31060 | −29190 | −29030 | −29110 |
| 26900 | 31170 | 31020 | 31090 | −29220 | −29070 | −29140 |
| 27000 | 31190 | 31050 | 31120 | −29250 | −29100 | −29170 |
| 27100 | 31230 | 31080 | 31150 | −29280 | −29130 | −29200 |
| 27200 | 31270 | 31100 | 31190 | −29320 | −29150 | −29240 |

(*Continued*)

**TABLE A.4** (*Continued*)

| $^{14}C$ BP ±1 | cal BP 2σ (95.4%) | | Mean | cal BC/AD 2σ (95.4%) | | Mean |
|---|---|---|---|---|---|---|
| 27300 | 31550 | 31110 | 31250 | −29600 | −29160 | −29300 |
| 27400 | 31580 | 31170 | 31350 | −29630 | −29230 | −29400 |
| 27500 | 31640 | 31240 | 31430 | −29690 | −29290 | −29480 |
| 27600 | 31720 | 31300 | 31520 | −29770 | −29360 | −29570 |
| 27700 | 31800 | 31420 | 31630 | −29850 | −29480 | −29680 |
| 27800 | 31870 | 31540 | 31710 | −29920 | −29590 | −29760 |
| 27900 | 31960 | 31620 | 31790 | −30010 | −29670 | −29840 |
| 28000 | 32080 | 31690 | 31880 | −30130 | −29740 | −29930 |
| 28100 | 32740 | 31740 | 32010 | −30790 | −29790 | −30060 |
| 28200 | 32850 | 31840 | 32220 | −30900 | −29890 | −30270 |
| 28300 | 32890 | 32000 | 32420 | −30940 | −30050 | −30470 |
| 28400 | 32970 | 32110 | 32530 | −31030 | −30160 | −30580 |
| 28500 | 33080 | 32210 | 32640 | −31130 | −30260 | −30700 |
| 28600 | 33200 | 32290 | 32840 | −31250 | −30340 | −30890 |
| 28700 | 33370 | 32360 | 33070 | −31420 | −30410 | −31120 |
| 28800 | 33610 | 33010 | 33260 | −31660 | −31070 | −31310 |
| 28900 | 33690 | 33150 | 33400 | −31740 | −31200 | −31450 |
| 29000 | 33790 | 33230 | 33520 | −31840 | −31290 | −31570 |
| 29100 | 33960 | 33330 | 33650 | −32010 | −31380 | −31710 |
| 29200 | 34110 | 33480 | 33810 | −32160 | −31530 | −31860 |
| 29300 | 34190 | 33690 | 33930 | −32240 | −31740 | −31980 |
| 29400 | 34260 | 33790 | 34030 | −32310 | −31840 | −32080 |
| 29500 | 34330 | 33890 | 34120 | −32380 | −31950 | −32170 |
| 29600 | 34390 | 33990 | 34200 | −32440 | −32040 | −32250 |
| 29700 | 34440 | 34090 | 34270 | −32490 | −32140 | −32320 |
| 29800 | 34490 | 34150 | 34330 | −32540 | −32200 | −32380 |
| 29900 | 34550 | 34210 | 34380 | −32600 | −32260 | −32440 |
| 30000 | 34610 | 34270 | 34440 | −32660 | −32320 | −32490 |

| $^{14}C$ BP ±30 | cal BP 2σ (95.4%) | | Mean | cal BC/AD 2σ (95.4%) | | Mean |
|---|---|---|---|---|---|---|
| 30100 | 34660 | 34330 | 34500 | −32710 | −32380 | −32550 |
| 30200 | 34730 | 34380 | 34560 | −32780 | −32430 | −32620 |
| 30300 | 35000 | 34410 | 34650 | −33050 | −32460 | −32700 |
| 30400 | 35130 | 34530 | 34770 | −33180 | −32580 | −32820 |
| 30500 | 35200 | 34610 | 34890 | −33250 | −32660 | −32940 |
| 30600 | 35250 | 34690 | 34970 | −33300 | −32740 | −33020 |
| 30700 | 35320 | 34750 | 35040 | −33370 | −32800 | −33100 |
| 30800 | 35400 | 34810 | 35150 | −33450 | −32860 | −33200 |
| 30900 | 35500 | 34900 | 35270 | −33550 | −32950 | −33320 |
| 31000 | 35560 | 35190 | 35360 | −33610 | −33240 | −33420 |
| 31100 | 35650 | 35250 | 35440 | −33700 | −33300 | −33500 |
| 31200 | 35850 | 35290 | 35550 | −33900 | −33340 | −33600 |
| 31300 | 35990 | 35390 | 35670 | −34040 | −33440 | −33720 |

(*Continued*)

**TABLE A.4** (*Continued*)

| ¹⁴C BP ±30 | cal BP 2σ (95.4%) | | Mean | cal BC/AD 2σ (95.4%) | | Mean |
|---|---|---|---|---|---|---|
| 31400 | 36070 | 35480 | 35780 | −34120 | −33530 | −33830 |
| 31500 | 36150 | 35580 | 35880 | −34200 | −33630 | −33930 |
| 31600 | 36220 | 35720 | 36000 | −34270 | −33770 | −34050 |
| 31700 | 36280 | 35890 | 36100 | −34330 | −33940 | −34150 |
| 31800 | 36330 | 36010 | 36170 | −34380 | −34060 | −34220 |
| 31900 | 36390 | 36080 | 36240 | −34440 | −34130 | −34290 |
| 32000 | 36480 | 36130 | 36300 | −34530 | −34180 | −34360 |
| 32100 | 36610 | 36190 | 36390 | −34660 | −34240 | −34440 |
| 32200 | 36750 | 36250 | 36480 | −34800 | −34300 | −34530 |
| 32300 | 36860 | 36340 | 36590 | −34910 | −34390 | −34640 |
| 32400 | 36950 | 36430 | 36690 | −35000 | −34480 | −34740 |
| 32500 | 37020 | 36530 | 36800 | −35080 | −34580 | −34850 |
| 32600 | 37130 | 36630 | 36910 | −35180 | −34690 | −34960 |
| 32700 | 37300 | 36770 | 37030 | −35350 | −34820 | −35090 |
| 32800 | 37460 | 36940 | 37170 | −35510 | −34990 | −35220 |
| 32900 | 37530 | 37040 | 37280 | −35580 | −35090 | −35330 |
| 33000 | 37610 | 37120 | 37380 | −35670 | −35170 | −35430 |
| 33100 | 38110 | 37160 | 37530 | −36160 | −35210 | −35580 |
| 33200 | 38320 | 37370 | 37780 | −36370 | −35420 | −35840 |
| 33300 | 38540 | 37540 | 37980 | −36590 | −35590 | −36040 |
| 33400 | 38820 | 37630 | 38170 | −36870 | −35680 | −36220 |
| 33500 | 39020 | 37770 | 38440 | −37070 | −35820 | −36490 |
| 33600 | 39150 | 38140 | 38690 | −37200 | −36190 | −36740 |
| 33700 | 39210 | 38440 | 38850 | −37260 | −36490 | −36910 |
| 33800 | 39280 | 38570 | 39000 | −37330 | −36620 | −37050 |
| 33900 | 39380 | 38830 | 39140 | −37430 | −36880 | −37190 |
| 34000 | 39420 | 39070 | 39240 | −37470 | −37120 | −37290 |
| 34100 | 39490 | 39140 | 39310 | −37540 | −37190 | −37360 |
| 34200 | 39570 | 39190 | 39380 | −37620 | −37250 | −37430 |
| 34300 | 39660 | 39250 | 39450 | −37710 | −37310 | −37510 |
| 34400 | 39750 | 39320 | 39530 | −37810 | −37370 | −37580 |
| 34500 | 39840 | 39390 | 39620 | −37900 | −37440 | −37670 |
| 34600 | 39940 | 39470 | 39710 | −37990 | −37520 | −37760 |
| 34700 | 40060 | 39550 | 39800 | −38110 | −37600 | −37860 |
| 34800 | 40280 | 39640 | 39920 | −38330 | −37690 | −37970 |
| 34900 | 40390 | 39750 | 40050 | −38450 | −37800 | −38100 |
| 35000 | 40480 | 39850 | 40160 | −38530 | −37900 | −38210 |
| 35250 | 40690 | 40080 | 40420 | −38740 | −38140 | −38470 |
| 35500 | 40930 | 40470 | 40700 | −38990 | −38520 | −38750 |
| 35750 | 41110 | 40680 | 40900 | −39160 | −38730 | −38950 |
| 36000 | 41270 | 40920 | 41100 | −39320 | −38970 | −39150 |
| 36250 | 41430 | 41090 | 41260 | −39480 | −39140 | −39310 |
| 36500 | 41740 | 41250 | 41470 | −39790 | −39300 | −39520 |
| 36750 | 41900 | 41420 | 41670 | −39960 | −39470 | −39720 |
| 37000 | 42060 | 41660 | 41870 | 40110 | −39710 | −39920 |

(*Continued*)

**TABLE A.4** (*Continued*)

| ¹⁴C BP ±30 | cal BP | | | cal BC/AD | | |
|---|---|---|---|---|---|---|
| | 2σ (95.4%) | | Mean | 2σ (95.4%) | | Mean |
| 37250 | 42150 | 41850 | 42000 | −40200 | −39900 | −40050 |
| 37500 | 42230 | 41960 | 42100 | −40280 | −40010 | −40150 |
| 37750 | 42310 | 42060 | 42190 | −40360 | −40110 | −40240 |
| 38000 | 42380 | 42150 | 42270 | −40440 | −40200 | −40320 |
| 38250 | 42460 | 42230 | 42350 | −40510 | −40280 | −40400 |
| 38500 | 42550 | 42310 | 42430 | −40600 | −40360 | −40480 |
| 38750 | 42650 | 42390 | 42520 | −40700 | −40450 | −40570 |
| 39000 | 42760 | 42480 | 42620 | −40810 | −40530 | −40670 |
| 39250 | 42870 | 42580 | 42730 | −40920 | −40630 | −40780 |
| 39500 | 42980 | 42690 | 42830 | −41030 | −40740 | −40890 |
| 39750 | 43110 | 42790 | 42950 | −41160 | −40840 | −41000 |
| 40000 | 43260 | 42890 | 43070 | −41310 | −40940 | −41120 |
| 40250 | 43940 | 42980 | 43330 | −41990 | −41030 | −41380 |
| 40500 | 44060 | 43160 | 43600 | −42110 | −41210 | −41650 |
| 40750 | 44240 | 43310 | 43780 | −42300 | −41360 | −41840 |
| 41000 | 44440 | 43450 | 44110 | −42490 | −41500 | −42160 |
| 41250 | 44530 | 44040 | 44300 | −42580 | −42090 | −42350 |
| 41500 | 44650 | 44200 | 44430 | −42700 | −42250 | −42490 |
| 41750 | 44800 | 44350 | 44570 | −42850 | −42400 | −42620 |
| 42000 | 44960 | 44480 | 44710 | −43010 | −42530 | −42760 |
| 42250 | 45150 | 44590 | 44860 | −43200 | −42640 | −42910 |
| 42500 | 45370 | 44710 | 45030 | −43420 | −42770 | −43080 |
| 42750 | 45570 | 44850 | 45220 | −43620 | −42900 | −43270 |
| 43000 | 45840 | 45050 | 45440 | −43890 | −43110 | −43490 |
| 43250 | 45980 | 45300 | 45640 | −44030 | −43350 | −43690 |
| 43500 | 46120 | 45470 | 45810 | −44170 | −43520 | −43860 |
| 43750 | 46440 | 45590 | 46020 | −44490 | −43640 | −44070 |
| 44000 | 46750 | 45890 | 46280 | −44800 | −43940 | −44330 |
| 44250 | 46970 | 46000 | 46490 | −45030 | −44050 | −44540 |
| 44500 | 47470 | 46120 | 46750 | −45520 | −44170 | −44800 |
| 44750 | 47830 | 46380 | 47100 | −45880 | −44430 | −45150 |
| 45000 | 47990 | 46790 | 47350 | −46040 | −44840 | −45400 |
| 45250 | 48170 | 46940 | 47560 | −46220 | −44990 | −45610 |
| 45500 | 48400 | 47090 | 47790 | −46450 | −45140 | −45850 |
| 45750 | 48700 | 47360 | 48050 | −46750 | −45410 | −46110 |
| 46000 | 48940 | 47630 | 48300 | −46990 | −45680 | −46350 |
| 46250 | 49440 | 47860 | 48540 | −47490 | −45910 | −46590 |
| 46500 | 49700 | 48080 | 48830 | −47750 | −46140 | −46880 |
| 46750 | 49910 | 48350 | 49120 | −47970 | −46400 | −47170 |
| 47000 | 50120 | 48570 | 49370 | −48170 | −46620 | −47420 |
| 47250 | 50730 | 48620 | 49650 | −48780 | −46670 | −47700 |
| 47500 | 51530 | 48870 | 50090 | −49580 | −46920 | −48140 |

With an error range of 1 year for each radiocarbon dates, the probability distribution of calibrated dates within the 2σ confidence range and average values are represented as cal BP, cal BC/AD.

## References

Barker, Graeme, Barton, Huw, Bird, Michael, Daly, Patrick, Datan, Ipoi, Dykes, Alan, Farr, Lucy, Gilbertson, David, Harrisson, Barbara, Hunt, Chris, Higham, Tom, Kealhofer, Lisa, Krigbaum, John, Lewis, Helen, McLaren, Sue, Paz, Victor, Pike, Alistair, Piper, Phil, Pyatt, Brian, Rabett, Ryan, Reynolds, Tim, Rose, Jim, Rushworth, Garry, Stephens, Mark, Stringer, Chris, Thompson, Jill, and Turney, Chris. 2007 The "human revolution" in lowland tropical Southeast Asia: The antiquity and behaviour of anatomically modern humans at Niah Cave (Sarawak, Borneo). *Journal of Human Evolution 52*, 243–261.

Higham, Tom, Ramsey, Christopher, Karavanić, Ivor, Smith, Fred, and Trinkaus, Erik. 2006 Revised direct radiocarbon dating of the Vindija G1 Upper Palaeolithic Neandertals. *Proceedings of the National Academy of Sciences 10*, 1–5.

Kudo, Y. 2012 *Environmental and Culture History of the Upper Palaeolithic and the Jomon Period: High-Precision Radiocarbon Dating and Archaeology*. Tokyo: Shinsensha. (in Japanese)

Libby, Willard. 1963 Accuracy of radiocarbon dates. *Science 140*, 278–280.

Ono, A. 2011 Frameworks and the present state of Palaeolithic studies in Japan. *Anthropological Science (Japanese Series) 119*, 1–8 (in Japanese with English abstract).

Ramsey, Christopher. 2009. Bayesian analysis of radiocarbon dates. *Radiocarbon 51 (1)*, 337–360.

Reimer, Paula, Austin, William, Bard, Edouard, Bayliss, Alex, Black-well, Paul, Ramsey, Christopher, Butzin, Martin, Edwards, Lawrence, Friedrich, Michael, Grootes, Pieter, Guilderson, Thomas, Hajdas, Irka, Heaton, Timothy, Hogg, Alan, Hughen, Konrad, Kromer, Bernd, Manning, Sturt, Muscheler, Raimund, Palmer, Jonathan, Pearson, Charlotte, van der Plicht, Johannes, Reimer, Ron, Richards, David, Scott, Marian, Southon, John, Turney, Christian, Wacker, Lukas, Adolphi, Florian, Büntgen, Ulf, Fahrni, S, Capano, Manuela, Fahrni, Simon, Fogtmann-Schulz, Alexandra, Friedrich, Ronny, Köhler, Peter, Kudsk, Sabrina, Miyake, Fusa, Olsen, Jesper, Reinig, Frederick, Sakamoto, Minoru, Sookdeo, Adam, and Talamo, Sahra. 2020 The IntCal20 Northern Hemisphere radiocarbon age calibration curve (0–55 cal kBP). *Radiocarbon 62*, 725–757.

Shang, Hong, Tong, Haowen, Zhang, Shuangquan, Chen, Fuyou, and Trinkaus, Erik. 2007 An early modern human from Tianyuan Cave, Zhoukoudian, China. *Proceedings of the National Academy of Sciences 104*, 6573–6578.

Shizuoka Archaeological Research Institute 2010. *Fujiishi site I*. Shizuoka archaeological research institute research report vo. 232. Shizuoka. (in Japanese)

Smith, Victoria, Staff, Richard, Blockley, Simon, Ramsey, Christopher, Nakagawa, Takeshi, Mark, Darren, Takemura, Keiji, Danhara, Toru, and Suigetsu Project Members. 2013 Identification and correlation of visible tephras in the Lake Suigetsu SG06 sedimentary archive, Japan: chronostratigraphic markers for synchronising of east Asian/west Pacific palaeoclimatic records across the last 150 ka. *Quaternary Science Reviews 67*, 121–137.

# APPENDIX B

## Analysing the Age and Heating History of Archaeological Materials Using Remanent Magnetization

*Hideo Sakai*

### Introduction – Magnetic Materials and Remanent Magnetization

Generally, archaeological materials such as soil and stone tools contain ferromagnetic particles having remanent magnetization, which is a record of the Earth's geomagnetic field. Remanent magnetization can also memorize the heating temperature when such materials were heated. Thus, by the study of their remanent magnetization, we have a means to analyse the age and heating history of archaeological materials

### Study of the Heating of Archaeological Materials by Their Magnetism

Remanent magnetization is useful to determine the signature of a heating event, as well as the absolute temperature to which the archaeological materials were heated. Such data are valuable in archaeology; for example, the discovery of the baked clay of a hearth, i.e., the artificial burning of earth, is evidence of human residence.

A study was undertaken of the heated remains of a Neanderthal Middle Palaeolithic hearth from Douara Cave in Syria (Akazawa and Sakaguchi 1987; Sakai et al. 2017). Oriented baked earth samples (cubes of 4 cm side length) were collected from a hearth of 2 m x 3 m horizontally, with a depth of 2 m. The temperature to which the baked soil had been heated was examined by Thelliers' method (Thellier and Thellier 1959). Figure B.1 shows that data fall on the straight line, and we know that the sample has been heated to the temperature at the end of the straight line. The result shown in Figure B.1 indicates that this sample had acquired its thermo-remanent magnetization by heating to 320°C in the hearth.

Thelliers' experiment was conducted on eight samples collected from several areas of the hearth. In Figure B.2, the estimated heating temperature of each sample is shown. We understand that the central part of the hearth had been heated to a temperature of over 430°C. The samples showing the lowest temperature (150°C) correspond to the bottom of the hearth. These results indicate the usefulness of a magnetic study as a source of evidence for the existence of the hearth and the distribution of maximum temperature within it.

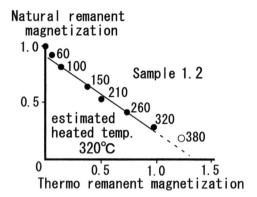

FIGURE B.1  Result of Thelliers' method.

## Dating by Remanent Magnetization

The earth's geomagnetic field changes with time. Therefore, if we know these changes in the geomagnetic field, by comparing them with the remanent magnetization of archaeological materials, we can estimate their age. In Japan, detailed changes in the geomagnetic field during the past 2000 years have been described (Figure B.3; Hirooka 1971; Sakai and Hirooka 1986), and the dating of remains whose age is unknown can be done with a precision of a few tens of years.

There is little archaeological material whose age is well known with which to study geomagnetic field measurements older than ten thousand years. Since changes in the geomagnetic field in this time period have not been studied in detail, the dating of remains of this age is difficult. On the other hand, the changes in the geomagnetic field with time have also been studied by the remanent magnetization of sediments deposited in lakes or the sea bottom, which can be used

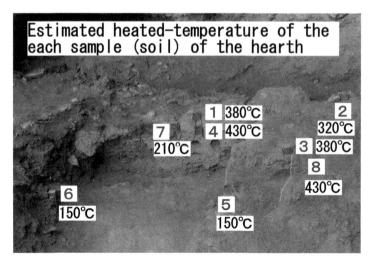

FIGURE B.2  The heated temperature distribution obtained by magnetic study of the hearth in the Neanderthal Douara Cave.

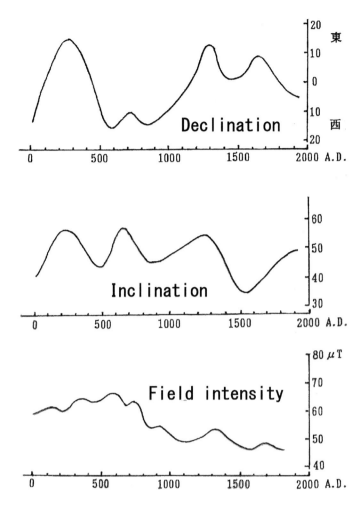

FIGURE B.3   Changes in the geomagnetic field during the past 2000 years (Hirooka 1971; Sakai and Hirooka 1986).

to date geological materials. This dating method is not yet generally used in archaeology, for example on Palaeolithic remains; however, it may become useful in the future.

Figure B.4 shows the main polarity events of the geomagnetic field during the last few hundreds of thousands of years (referred from Channell 2006). These geomagnetic events are also useful for dating the strata of a Palaeolithic site.

## Study of the Intensity of the Geomagnetic Field and the Dating of 14C and 10Be

When dating materials using the radioisotopes of carbon-14 (14C; a half-life of 5730 years) and beryllium-10 (10Be; a half-life of 1,000,000 years), it is important to note that these radioisotopes are produced in the Earth's stratosphere (a height of a few km to a few tens of km from the ground) by the intrusion of cosmic rays. This incursion of cosmic rays, and therefore

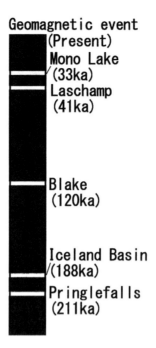

FIGURE B.4    Timetable of the polarity events of the geomagnetic field during the last few tens of thousands of years (referred from Channell 2006).

the formation of radioisotopes, is controlled by the strength of the geomagnetic field (i.e., the size of the magnetosphere). Therefore, a change in the amount of radioisotopes being produced is caused by a change of geomagnetic field intensity, which causes a deviation between the 14C (10Be) age and the real age.

Barbetti and Flude (1979) showed that the geomagnetic field intensity had been generally weak during the period from 10,000 to 50,000 years before the present (BP) (Figure B.5). Also, they showed that 14C ages for this period are apt to be younger than the age estimated by other methods such as fission track or thermoluminescence (TL) dating.

Modern 14C dating uses a calibrated 14C age, considering the variation of the production rate of 14C in the stratosphere. Sakai et al. (2017) showed that the geomagnetic field intensity at the age of 60,000–75,000 years BP was 60–70% of the present intensity (Figure B.5). The data were obtained from the magnetic study (Thelliers' method in Figure B.1) on the baked soil of the aforementioned hearth of Douara Cave, whose age was determined from the fission track dating of a baked stone tool. The weak geomagnetic field means that the magnetosphere was smaller in some way and the incursion of cosmic rays into the stratosphere increased at that time.

For the period before 50,000 years, the use of the 14C dating method is difficult because the objective age exceeds the resolving limit of the 14C method. On the other hand, the 10Be dating method could be applicable. When the 10Be dating method is used on archaeological materials of this period, the estimated 10Be age will be younger than the real age, by several thousand years. Thus, creation of a calibrated 10Be age will be necessary in order to be able to use 10Be dating in the future.

Appendix B: Analysing the Age and Heating History of Archaeological Materials    355

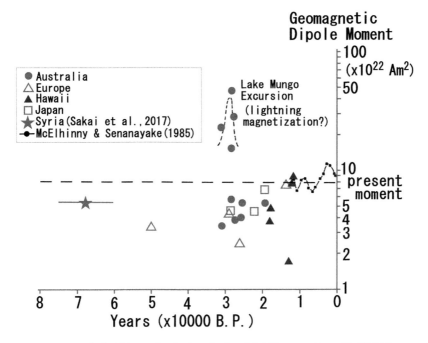

**FIGURE B.5**  Geomagnetic field intensity during the last 80,000 years. Data (0–50,000 years) is from the summary by Barbetti and Flude (1979); Data (1–10,000 years) is from the summary by McElhinny and Senanayake (1985).

## Signature of a Lightning Strike at a Palaeolithic Ruin in Japan

Figure B.6 shows the distribution of remanent magnetization studied at a Palaeolithic ruin in Japan (Sakai and Yonezawa 2002). Each arrow in the figure shows the direction of remanent magnetization of the soil sample collected at that point. The rotational distribution (the

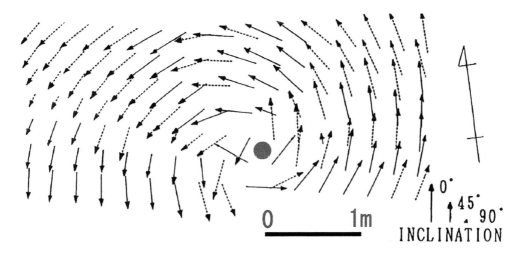

**FIGURE B.6**  Directional distribution of the remanent magnetization.

FIGURE B.7   The site of the Palaeolithic ruin.

concentric circle) shows the direction of magnetization, indicating that the lightning current flew into the centre of the concentric circle. That is, the soil of the ruin acquired remanent magnetization caused by the magnetic field of the lightning strike (Figure B.7). Taking the age of the studied strata of the ruin into consideration, the lightning might have struck there at about 13,000 years BP. From the study of the remanent magnetization, we also could investigate the lightning itself (and thus the climate) of the Palaeolithic age. Magnetic study could contribute significantly to the dating of archaeological materials, detecting of heated remains, and research on palaeo-lightning (climate).

## References

Akazawa, T., and Sakaguchi, Y. (eds.) 1987 *Palaeolithic Site of Douara cave and Palaeogeography of Palmyra Basin in Syria. Part IV: 1984 Excavations*. University Museum, University of Tokyo, Bulletin 29.
Barbetti, M., and Flude, K. 1979 Palaeomagnetic field strengths from sediments baked by lava flows of the chaine des Puys, France. *Nature* 278, 153–156.
Channell, J. 2006 Late Brunhes polarity excursions (Mono Lake, Laschamp, Iceland Basin and Pringle Falls) recorded at ODP Site 919 (Irminger Basin). *Earth and Planetary Science Letters* 244, 378–393.
Hirooka, K. 1971 Archaeomagnetic study for the past 2,000 years in Southwest Japan. *Memoir of the Faculty of Science, Kyoto University, Series Geology and Mineralogy* 38, 167–207.
McElhinny, M., and Senanayake, W. 1985 Variations in the palaeomagnetic dipole 1: The past 50000 years. *Journal of Geomagnetism and Geoelectrics* 34, 39–52.
Sakai, H., and Hirooka, K. 1986 Archaeointensity Determinations from Western Japan. *Journal of Geomagnetism and Geoelectrics* 38, 1323–1329.
Sakai, H., Kimura, T., and Akazawa, T. 2017 Palaeomagnetic study on the middle Paleolithic hearth of Douara Cave and the survey of the heated temperature distribution. *Papers and Proceedings of the Japan Society for the Archaeological Information* 19, 50–55. (in Japanese)
Sakai, H., and Yonezawa, K. 2002 Remanent magnetization as a fossil of lightning current. *Proceedings of Japan Academy* 78, 1–5.
Thellier, E., and Thellier, O. 1959 Sur l'intensite du Champ magnetique terrestre dans le passe historique et geologique. *Annals of Geophysics* 15, 285–376.

# INDEX

**Note:** *Italicized* and **bold** page numbers refer to figures and tables respectively, and page numbers followed by "n" refer to notes.

Accelerator Mass Spectroscopy (AMS) dating 102
adaptations, late Pleistocene, changes in 119–120
adze-like tools 73
Africa: archaeological evidence of early exit of *Homo sapiens* from 9–11; biological origin of *Homo sapiens* in 1; genetic evidence of early exit of *Homo sapiens* from 6–9; hominin dispersals out of 1; late exit of *Homo sapiens* from 11–12; mutation rates 12
African Eve model 45
African fauna 3
African haplotypes 7
African Middle Stone Age 13
age of non-African MRCA 11–12
agile wallaby *(Macropus agilis)* 93
Alor Island 214
Altai Neanderthal 7
*Amnok* (*Yalu* in Chinese) 229
AMS $^{14}$C dates 211
anatomically modern humans (AMHs) 38, 201; arrival in Southern China 46–47; as beachcombers 41; expansion after Toba eruption 44–45; expansion out of Africa 43; Irhoud and 42–43; in Korean Peninsula 226–243; origins of 42
ancestral allele frequencies (AAFs) 4
Anonymous Cave 11 (LH-27) 166
Anonymous Cave 11 (LH-30) 163–165, *164*
Anonymous Caves 4 (LH-24) 165
Anonymous Caves 10 (LH-29) *165*, 165–166, *166*
archaeological chronologies 13–14
archaeology, evidence of 45–49, *47*
archaic admixture 5

argon-argon (Ar/Ar) 2, 204
armatures, Japanese Islands 297–298
artefact, upper Palaeolithic age of Japanese site 258–265, **259–260**, *261*, *263–264*
Aru Islands 216
Asitau Kuru 112
Astrakhanka site 146
Attirampakkam 24–25
Australasian marsupial fauna 87
Australia, Pleistocene lithic assemblages from 304–305
Australo-Denisovan genetics 96
Australo-Melanesian affinities 321
Australo-Papuan affinity 96
Australopiths 1
axe-like tools 73
*Axis calamianensis* 208

babirusa *(Babyrousa* sp.) 92
Bae, C. 304
*Baekdu* (*Changbai* in Chinese) 229
Baishiya Karst Cave 153
Balabac Strait 202
bamboo 50
bandicoot *(Echymipera kalubu)* 120
Bang Pakong River 62
Ban Rai 55–56, *56*
Banyan Valley Cave 56
Barbetti, M. 354
Bau Du 62
Baxian Caves 150, 160–166, 173n2
behavioral plasticity of Palaeolithic Ryukyu Islands 318–319

## Index

Belmaker, M. 2
betel nuts 56
Bilat Cave 209
Binford, Lewis R. 302
Birdsell, J. 96, 99
Bismarck archipelago 115, 119
blade industry 140, *141*
bladelets, elongated 77
blade tools, Sonvian culture and 79
Blinkhorn, J. 23
Boodie Cave 127–128
brown bear *(Ursus arctos)* 140
Buang Merabak 117, 119
*Bubalus mindorensis* (Tamaraw) 206, 208
Bubog I and II, Ilin Island 210–211, *211*
Buchanan, B. 30
Bulu Buttue cave 99
burial culture, in Palaeolithic Ryukyu
 Islands 320

*Cabalwanian* 204
Cabrera, V. 8
Cagayan Valley 204, 206
Callao Cave 89, 95, 206
Callao fossils 214
*Camaena vayssierei* 78
*Canarium indicum* nuts 120
*Canarium* seeds 55
C and D lineages 5–6
cassowary (*Casuarius* sp.) 93
cave lion *(Panthera leo spelaea)* 140
cave painting: types of 97; warty pig in Maros
 Cave 98, *99*
Cebu Island 211
*Cervus unicolor* 54
Changbin cobble-tool Industry 160–166
*Changbinian [Changpinian]* culture 161
Chaochen Cave (LH-6) 165, 166
Chaoyin Cave 160, 161–162, *162, 163*
Chappell, J. 284
Charcoal 48
Chen, K. 155, 159
China: *H. sapiens* fossils in 10; Loess Plateau 3
chisel-like (adze-like) tools 73
*Chitons* 119
Chongpadae Cave 231
choppers 73, 77
chronometric hygiene 129
circular lithic aggregations 299; from Kamibayashi
 site *300*
'citrus slice' reduction technique 81
Cladistic analysis 27–32; by region and
 period **29**
cladogram 27
Clark, G. 242
Clarkson, C. 23, 304
coastal-first dispersion model 131

Coastal Zone of Maritime Region: blade industry
 140–142, *141*; microblade industry 142–144,
 *143*
cobble-chopping tool from Longxia Cave 171, *171*
cobble cores 79
Collard, M. 30
Con Co Ngua 61–62
Con Moong Cave 75, 78–79, 83
Conrad, C. 54, 55
*Conus* and *Strombus* shells 212
crude flake tools 92
cuscus *(Spilocuscus kraemeri)* 120
cuscuses (*Spilocuscus maculatus,
 Phalanger* spp.) 93
*Cyclophorus* 53
*Cyclophorus fulguratus* 78

Dali site in Shaanxi 179, 181
Darwin, C. 1, 88
Dedan 52
deer *(Rusa marianna)* 206
DeGiorgio, M. 4–5
Denisovan genetic markers 104
Denisovan-like mtDNA 7
Denisovans 7, 98; in Siberian Altai 189
denticulate tools 73
Dhaba, Middle Son River Valley 26
*Dicerorhinus mercki* 182
Diem Cave 80, 83
Diprotodontids 115
disjunctions 14
Dmanisi: carcases at 3
DNA xix
DNA haplogroups 45
Doi Pha Kan 58
Dongshan Island, human remains from 153–154
Douara Cave 354
Dubois, E. 88–89
Durbin, R. 11–12
Du Sang 58
dwarf stegodon *(Stegodon florensis insularis)* 93

early exit of *H. sapiens* from Africa:
 archaeological evidence 9–11; genetic evidence
 6–9
early hominin colonization of Philippines
 202–207
Early out of Africa with hybrid MSA technology
 30, *31*, 32, **32**
East Asia, peopling of 138–148
echidna *(Tachyglossus aculeatus)* 93
elk *(Alces alces)* 140
Eluanbi II: rock shelter 170, *170*; tools from 171,
 *171*
emergence of modern humans xix
endemic bovid Anoa (*Bubalus* sp.) 92
endemic pig *(Sus oliveri)* 208

Eurasia, *H. sapiens* reaching eastern 10
Eurasian fauna 2–3
extinct giant rat *(Crateromys paulus)* 208

fish bones 101
Flaked Stone Tool Group 262, *263–264*; backed points 262, *263*; blades 262, *263*; chipped adzes 262, *263*; drills 262, *263*; edge-ground adzes 262, *263*; scrapers 262, *264*; trapezoids 262, *263*; wedge-shaped stones 262, *264*
Flaked Stone Tools plus Refuse 274
flakes 77
flake tools 72–73, 74, 76
Flora 247–249
Flores Island 213–214
Flude, K. 354
forest wallaby *(Dorcopsis* sp.) 93
Fox, R. 204
Fromaget, F. 81
Fu, Q. 12
Fuyan Cave in Hunan Province 46, 188

Gebe Island 100
*Geloina* shell tools 212
genetic OOA model 12–13
genetics: late exit of *H. sapiens* from Africa 11–12; mixed migration models 12–13
Geographical Society Cave 140
geomagnetic field, intensity of, radiocarbon dating and 353–355, *354–355*
Geomeunmoru 235–237
Geumcheon Cave 231
giant pangolin *(Manis javanica)* 97
giant pigs *(Celebochoerus heekereni)* 92
giant tortoise *(Testudo margae)* 92
Goebel, T. 303
Golo Cave 95, 100, 215
goral *(Naemorhedus goral)* 140
Gorbatka 3 146
Gorman, C. 55
Goryeri site 241
Ground-Edge Artefacts (GEA) 132
Gua Cha 59
Gua Gunung Runtuh Cave 57–58
Gulpori 234–235
Gunang Cave 231

Hailei Cave (LH-4) 160, 166
Hallam Movius's chopper chopping tools 89
Hamakita in Shizuoka Prefecture 288
Hang Boi Cave 53
Hang Cho, excavations at 53
Hang Hum Cave 83
Hang Lang Gao Cave 58
Hang Pong Cave 79
Hanoi depression 79
Hasegawa, Y. 287

Hayashi, R., 284
heterozygosity 4, 5
Heungsu Cave of Durubong site 231
Hoabinhian 51–53, *52*; culture 76; lithic industries 80–82, *81*
Hohlenstein–Stadel Cave 7
Hokkaido 284
Holocene GEA 133
hominids 123
hominin fossils exhibiting mosaic anatomical morphology in North China 180–183, **181**
*Homo erectus* 2, 89, 98; fossils 94
*Homo erectus Mojokertensis* 94
*Homo erectus sensu lato* 82
*Homo erectus soloensis* 94
*Homo floresiensis* 2, 42, 89, 98, 316; at Leang Bua cave 95; in Liang Bua cave *104*
*Homo habilis* 1, 2
*Homo heidelbergensis* 2, 31
homologies 27
*Homo luzonensis* 42, 95, 214; at Leang Bua cave 95; origins of 206
*Homo neanderthalensis* 82–83, 316
homoplasies 27
*Homo sapiens*: archaeological evidence of early exit of 9–11; colonisation of South Asia by 22–32; fossils in China 10; genetic evidence of early exit of 6–9; genomic and archaeological evidence 13–14; introgression with 8; in island Southeast Asia 94–95; presumptive markers for the arrival of 10; reaching eastern Eurasia 10; in Southern Asia 10; unidirectional expansion of 5–6
*Homo sapiens africanensis* 84–85
*Homo sapiens altaiensis* 83
*Homo sapiens orientalensis* 84
Hopyeongdong site 238, *239*
horse *(Equus* sp.) 140
horse-hoof core 204
Huai River 179
Hualongdong Cave: in Anhui 179
Huanglong Cave 188; in Hubei 179
Huang, S. 162, 167
human arrival: in North China 178–192; in Philippines 207–209; in Sahul 126–127
human burials from Liang Island (Liangdao), Matsu Archipelago 156
human dispersals: across southern and central Sahul 125–134; in North China 188 190; in North China, future directions 190–192, *191*; to northern Sahul *112*, 112–113
human/faunal remains: from Taiwan Strait *154*, 154–155, *155*; from Zuozhen 156–160, **157–158**, *159*
human genetics, analysis of 45
human remains from Dongshan Island 153–154
hunting pressure hypothesis 314

Huxley, T. 87; modification of Wallace's Line 214
*Hybocystis srossei* 78

Ikeya, N. 301
Ilin Island 210, 214, 215
Ilistaya 1 146
Imamura, K. 301
Indian Stone Age 44
Indonesian Papua island 102
Initial Upper Palaeolithic (IUP) industries 189
International Calibration (IntCal) 328–330
Island Southeast Asia: arrival and dispersal of early modern humans in 94–96; Australo-Papuan phenotype 94–95; cave paintings 103; cultural aspects of EMH in 96–102; early modern humans in 87–104, *88*; emergence of personal or social identity 103; *H. sapiens* in 94–95; late Pleistocene settings 89–94, *91*; migration routes from Sundaland to Sahulland 96; Nusa Tenggara island 93; Philippines in Archaeology of 213–216; simple stone tool assemblages in 103; southern migration routes of Nusa Tenggara 100; "three layers" migration hypothesis 96
Ivane Valley: archaeological sites in *115*; late Pleistocene stone tools *116*, *117*
Iwase, A. 287
Izena Island 314
Izumikitagawa Dai San site 299

Japanese archipelago: case study of arrival of *H. sapiens* to, radiocarbon dating and 333–349, *334–335*, **336–339**, *340*, **341–349**; migration route(s) to 320–321
Japanese Islands: archaeological materials and chronological studies of Palaeolithic in 288–291, *289*, *291*; archaeological research of 291–297; archaeological sites during Palaeolithic and Incipient Jomon period in *289*; archaeological sites in 284–305; armatures 297–298, 302; changes in lithic raw material usage during EUP 296–297; circular lithic aggregations 299; EUP lithic assemblages in 291–297, *292*, *294–295*; formal flaked tools, definitions of *295*; formal flaked tools in EUP 298; human behaviour changes through lithic assemblages 291–297, *294–295*; human migrations 303; implications of EUP 303; Late Pleistocene fauna in 285–287; lithic assemblages during EUP in Musashino Uplands *295*; mammoth fauna in 287; Marine Isotope Stage (MIS) 3 to 2 in 284–288, *285*, *286*; modern behavioural traits of people in EUP 302–305; pitfalls of 299–301, *301*, 303; Pleistocene population history in 288; *P. naumanni* from Hokkaido 287–288; use of obsidian in 298–299

Japanese site, Upper Palaeolithic age of 245–280; cluster analysis based on features and stone artefacts 269, *270*, *271*; frequency of occurrence of features and artefacts *279*; macro-model construction 272–277, *273*, **275–277**; results of cluster analysis 269–272; stone types 265, **266–268**; types and raw materials of features and artefacts from **275–276**
Jebel Irhoud in Morocco 42–43, *43*, 179
Jeommal Cave 231
Jeongokri and the IHRA handaxe sites *236*, 236–237
Jingeuneul site 239–240, *240*
Jinniushan site 182
Jinsitai Cave 189
Ji, Xueping 52
Jordan, P. 30
Jwalapuram 3 and 22, Jwalapuram River Valley 26
Jwalapuram 9 26

Kaifu, Y. 303–304
Kain Hitam Cave 97
Kana, Bengal 26
Kanto region 289
Karakelong 99
Karimata Strait 90
karst limestone landmasses 202
Katoati, Thar Desert, Rajasthan 25
Kato, S. 320
Kawamura, Y. 287
Khlong Yai Stream 50
Khwae Noi Valley 56–57
Kilu Cave 116–117
Kishino-Hasegawa (K-H) test 30, **32**
Kitulgala Beli-lena and Fa Hien Lena Caves, Sri Lanka 27
knapping strategy 204
Koenigswald, G. 204
Komodo dragons *(Varanus komodoensis)* 93
Korean palaeolithic research 226
Korean Peninsula: AMH's lifeways in 241–243; anatomically modern humans (AMH) in 226–243; archaeological evidence before Pleistocene modernity 234–237, *235*, *236*; archaeological/palaeoanthropological data from 227–228; emergence of Pleistocene modernity in 227; feological zones of *229*; Geomeunmoru 235–237; Gulpori 234–235; hominin fossils in **232**; Hopyeongdong site 238, *239*; issue of emergence of AMH in 237–241, *238–240*; Jeongokri and the IHRA handaxe sites *236*, 236–237; *Mandalri* site *233*; mountain ranges and major river channel systems of *230*; Palaeolithic assemblages and its periodization 231–234, *233*; Pleistocene environmental background 227–228; Pleistocene hominin

occupation in 230–231; Seungnisan site 231, 238, *238*; topography and fluvial system of 228–230, *229*, *230*; Yonggok Cave 237; Yongsandong site 239, *240*
Krabi River 50
Kumejima Island 320
Kunlun Cave (LH-7) 160, 165
Kun-yu Tsai 153
Kupona na Dari 119
Kuroda, T. 314
Kyushu region 289

Laili Cave 102
Lambeck, K. 284
Langjong Cave 231
Lang Kamnan 57
Lang Rongrien Cave 50–51, *51*
Lang Vanh Cave 53
laser ablation U-series analysis of human teeth 206
Last Glacial Maximum (LGM) 97, 202, 230
late Acheulian sites 24–25, *25*
'Late Exit' (LE) model 6
Late out of Africa: with microlithic technology 23–24, 30, *31*, 32, **32**; MSA technology 24, 30, *31*, 32, **32**
late Pleistocene: changes in adaptations 119–120; life in, New Guinea 118, *118*; lithic technologies 209–213, *211*, *212*; stone tools, Ivane Valley *116*, *117*
Leang Bua cave: *H. floresiensis* at 95; *Homo luzonensis* at 95
Leang Sarru on Sulawesi 214
Lene Hara Cave 102
Lenggong Valley (Malaysia) 51
Levallois core technology 25
Levallois-like points 98
Liang Bua cave 89; fossils of *Homo floresiensis* excavated in *104*
Liang Bua flaked tool technology 100, *101*
Liang Island (Liangdao) 156
Liang Lemdubu in Aru Islands 216
Libby, W. 328
Licent, E. 185
Lida Ajer Cave 48, 88, 96
Li, F. 182–183, 185, 189
Li, K. 170
limestone 53
limestone flake tools 92
Lin, C. 160
line arrangement 301
Lingjing site in Henan 179, 183
linkage disequilibrium 4
lithic artefacts 72–73; from Arubo, Nueva Ecjia 204–205, *205*
lithic industry 75
long-nosed spiny bandicoot *(Echymipera rufescens)* 93

Longtanshan Cave 46
Luna Cave 188; in Guangxi 46
Luzon island 203–204, 209

*Macaca robustus* 182
macaque *(Macaca fascicularis philippinensis)* 208
macro-model construction of upper Palaeolithic age of Japanese site 272–277, **273**, **275**–**277**
Madjedbebe 49; age of artefacts in Phase 2 at 129
magnetism, heating of archaeological materials by 351, *352*
Maluku Islands 215
mammoth *(Mammuthus primigenius)* 140
*Mandalri* site 231–234, *233*
mangrove shell *(Geloina coaxans)* 215
Marine Isotope Stages (MIS) 38; changes in sea level during *40*; vegetation at the onset of *41*; Vostok ice core in Antarctica 39, *39*
Maritime Region: early upper Palaeolithic sites in 138–140, *139*; final Palaeolithic sites in inland part of 144–146, *145*, *147*; human occupation of 138; Russian Far East (Primorye) 138–148; and Sakhalin Islands, territories of *139*
Maros Caves 95, 98
Maros points 98
marsupial cuscus *(Ailurops* sp.) 92
Marwick, B. 57
Matenbek 119
material culture 6
Matja Kuru Cave 2 102
Matsu Archipelago 156
Matsumura, H. 59, 169
*Megaloceros pachyosteus* 182
*Megantereon* sp. 3
Mehtakheri, Narmada River Valley 26
*Melanoides tuberculata* 53
Mellars, P. 23–24; model 45
*Meretrix lusoria* 62
Microlithic Sites 26–27; Jwalapuram 9 26; Kana, Bengal 26; Kitulgala Beli-lena and Fa Hien Lena Caves, Sri Lanka 27; Mehtakheri, Narmada River Valley 26
*Microtus brandtioides* 182
Middle Palaeolithic model 44–45
Middle Palaeolithic sites 25–26; Dhaba, Middle Son River Valley 26; Jwalapuram 3 and 22, Jwalapuram River Valley 26; Katoati, Thar Desert, Rajasthan 25; Patne, Maharashtra 26; Site 70, Bundala, Sri Lanka 26
Minatogawa. *see* Pleistocene Okinawa
Mindoro Island 202, 208; excavations on 201
Mishra, S. 10
mitochondrial (mtDNA) 7
mixed migration models, genetics 12–13
modern biological diversity 4, 4–6
Modern Humans migration xix
Mojokerto (1936) 89

molecular anthropology xx
molecular clock 45
molecular haematology xix
Morisaki, K. 304
"Moro-type" tools of Japan 142
Movius, Halam Jr. 234
MSMC (multiple sequential Markovian coalescent) 12
Mt. Ashitaka 289; representative formal stone tools during EUP in *294*; stratigraphic sequences and Palaeolithic chronology of UP in *292*
mtDNA 38; and nDNA, discordance between 7
Mt. Hakone 289
"Multiregional Evolution" paradigm 178
Mu Us (Maowusu) desert. 185

Nakagawa, R. 287, 288
Nam Tun Cave 73, 79
National Taiwan University 160, 167
Neanderthal mtDNAs 7–8
New Guinea: animals and nut trees 120; archaeological sites 120; life in late Pleistocene of *118*, 118–119; waisted tools in 118, *118*
Ngandong (1931–1933) 89
Nguomian industry 70–76, *71, 72*
Nguom rock shelter 74; age of 75
Niah Cave *49*, 49–50, 95, 96, 97, 213, 214
Nombe Cave 115
non-African MRCA, age of 11–12
non-Pama–Nyungan languages 133
North China: discovered sites in 179, *180*; early modern human fossils or early Upper Palaeolithic artefacts in 184–187; future directions in exploring modern human origins and dispersals in 190–192, *191*; hominin fossils exhibiting mosaic anatomical morphology in 180–183, **181**; hominin fossils in 187–188; human arrivals in 178–192; human dispersals in 188–190; implications of discoveries of late middle and early late Pleistocene fossils in 187–188; key late middle Pleistocene and early late Pleistocene fossils and lithic assemblages, discoveries of 179–180; material culture 188
northern Asia, lithic assemblages of EUP in 304
northern brown bandicoot *(Isoodon macrourus)* 93
northern Sahul and Bismark archipelago 111–120; advances in DNA research 111, 113; first inhabitants *113*, 113–117, **114**, *115–117*; migrations of people to Sahul *112*
northern Vietnam 58–59, *59*; Hoabinhian lithic industries in 80–82, *81*; Nguomian industry 70–76, *71, 72*; pebble-flake industry in 70; research work (2010-2014) 78; Sonvian industries 76–80, *77*
northwestern Thailand 53–56, *54, 55*
Norton, C. 287

notched tools 73
Nui Mot Cave, excavations at 79–80
Nui Nuong 73–74
Nusa Tenggara 100
Nwya Devu (ND) site 186–187

obsidian débitage 211
obsidian industry. 144–146, *145*
obsidian, use of, in Japanese Islands 298–299
O'Connell, J. 49, 128
Oda, S. 320
Okinawa Island 314
Okladnikov, A. P. 139
Oppenheimer, S. 41, 82
optically stimulated luminescence (OSL) dating 38
orangutan *(Pongo pygmaeus)* 90
Oriental mammalian fauna 87
Osinovka 139–140
otassium-argon technique 2
Out of Africa (OOA) dispersion 2; fossil evidence for 2–4; genetic evidence for 7; modern biological diversity as signals of *4*, 4–6
Ozawa, T. 314

palaeo-anthropologists xix
Palaeolithic assemblages in Korean Peninsula 231–234, *233*
Palaeoloxodon-Shinomegaceroides complex 287
Palawan Island 202, 207–208
Palawan pangolin *(Manis culionensis)* 208
Palawan porcupine *(Hystrix pumila)* 208
Paleo-SHK 148
Pama–Nyungan languages 133
Panxian Dadong site in Guizhou 179
Papua New Guinea, Pleistocene sites of *113*
Patne, Maharashtra 26
PAUP* 4.0 28
pebble-flake industry 70, 81–82
pebble tools 75–76
Pei, W. 184
Penghu 1 hominin 153
Penghu 1 mandible 151, *152*
Penghu Channel Fauna 155
Penghu fauna 153
Penghu-Tainan Fauna 155
peopling of East Asia 138–148
*Phalanger orientalis* 119
Philippine archipelago 201–217; absence of 'modern' tool types and formal tools in industries 209–210; bone and shell tools 210, *212*; Denisovan genomic content in 206; early hominin colonization of 202–207; geographical location of *203*; late Pleistocene lithic technologies 209–213, *211, 212*; Luzon island 203–204; potential migration routes and 202–203; *see also* Philippines

Philippines: AMH fossils in 207–209; in archaeology of island Southeast Asia 213–216; chrono-stratigraphic sequence of stone artefacts in 210; hominin inhabitants of 213; lithic and shell technologies in 212
pig *(Sus philippensis)* 206
Pilanduk Cave 208
Piper, P. 50
*Pithecanthropus erectus* (walking ape-man) 88–89
Pleistocene–Holocene transition 80
Pleistocene hominin occupation in Korean Peninsula 230–231
Pleistocene landmasses of Luzon 213
Pleistocene Okinawa 312–321; shell artefacts of 317–318, *318*
Posth, C. 7
Preceramic Culture 161–162
progressive MIS3 regional diversification 133
Protemnodon 115
Punung (1935–1936) 89, 96
Punung fauna 40, 90–91
Punung faunal assemblage 48
pygmy elephants *(Archidiskodon celebensis)* 92

Qianyuan Cave 160, 162
Qinling Mountains 179
Q-mode correlation coefficients *169*
quartzite pebbles 75, 78
Quynh Van 62

Rabett, R. 50
radiocarbon dating: arrival of *H. sapiens* to Japanese archipelago case study 333–349, *334–335*, **336–339**, *340*, **341–349**; calibrating 328–330, *329–330*; intensity of geomagnetic field and 353–355, *354–355*; notations of 330–333, **331–333**; principles of 326–328, *327–328*; by remanent magnetization 352–353, *352–353*; stratigraphy of Fujiishi site and *335*
rat species *(Rattus sordidus)* 93
"Recent Out-of-Africa" model 178
reconciling genetic 13–14
remanent magnetization: dating by 352–353, *352–353*; directional distribution of *355*; magnetic materials and 351; studied at Palaeolithic ruin in Japan 355–356, *355–356*
Retention Index (RI) 28, 30
retouched flakes 77
rhinoceros *(Coelodonta antiquitatis)* 140
river cobbles 80
Rizal artefacts 204–205
roe deer *(Capreolus capreolus)* 140
Ru Diep 62
Russian Far East (Primorye) 138–148
Ryonggok Cave 231
Ryukyu Islands: archipelago of 312–314, *313*; behavioral plasticity of Palaeolithic 318–319;
burial culture in Palaeolithic 320; first migration to 314–315; Late Pleistocene fauna from 312–314, *313*; migration route(s) to Japanese archipelago 320–321; Palaeolithic culture of 316–317; sustainable life of Palaeolithic populations in 315–316

Sahul: human arrival in 126–127; northern, and Bismark archipelago 111–120; southern and central, human dispersal across 125–134
Sakai Cave 57
Sakhalin Island, Palaeolithic sites on 146–147
Sakitari Cave 315, 317–318, *318*
Saleh, R. 88
Sangiran (1936–1941) 89
Sangiran Flake Industry 89
Sangkulirang Cave 95
Sano, K. 298
Sanyou Cave 46
Sapiens-Neanderthal genetic exchange 7–8
Sato Hiroyuki 301
Saurin, E. 81
Scally, A. 11–12
scoria 247
scrapers 73, 77
seafaring 315
Selenka, M. E. 89
set arrangement 301
Seungnisan site 231, 238, *238*
shell artefacts, of Pleistocene Okinawa 317–318, *318*
shellfish 50, 53, 54, 119
shell midden deposits of Bubog I 210
Shennan, S. 30
Shikama, T. 160
Shimoji-baru Cave 315
Shipton, C. 112
Shiraho-Saonetabaru Cave 320
Shoocondej, R. 54, 57
Shuidonggou (SDG) site complex 185–186
siamang gibbons *(Hylobates syndactylus)* 90
Sima de los Huesos hominin 7
Site 70, Bundala, Sri Lanka 26
smaller monitor lizards *(Varanus hooijeri)* 93
Sobaek Mts 241
Sonvian industries 76–80, *77*
Sonvian reduction strategy 76
South Asia: Attirampakkam 24–25; colonisation of, by *H. sapiens* 22–32; early out of Africa with hybrid MSA technology model 23; entry into, hypotheses 23–24; key sites in, dating 100–40 ka 24–32; late Acheulian sites 24–25, *25*; late out of Africa with microlithic technology model 23–24; Microlithic Sites 26–27; Middle Palaeolithic sites 25–26; Middle Son River Valley 25

Southeast Asia: anatomically modern humans in mainland 49–51; arrival of AMHs into 48–49; Ban Rai 55–56, *56*; canopied rainforests of 42; climate of mainland 40; continental glaciers of 39–40; expansion of AMHs into 39; *Homo erectus* AMHs in 42; hunter gatherers 41; Khwae Noi Valley, Central Thailand 56–57; lakes and rivers of 42; Lang Rongrien cave 50–51, *51*; Marine Isotope Stages in 38–39, *39*; mortuary remains of early hunter gatherers 58–59, *59*; Niah cave on the northern coast of Borneo *49*, 49–50; northwestern Thailand 53–56, *54*, *55*; origin of anatomically modern humans in east and 82–85, *84*; peninsular Thailand 57–58; pre and post Toba models for human expansion into 45–46

southern and central Sahul, human dispersal across 125–134; age of artefacts in Phase 2 at Madjedbebe 129; cautious estimate 127–128; coastal first model hypothesis 131; daring estimate 128–129; GEA in 132–133; ground edged artefacts during MIS3 133; human arrival in *126*, 126–127; location of *126*; molecular dating sets an upper limit of human arrival in 129–130; progressive MIS3 regional diversification 133; regional differentiation 133–134; sandy deposits of Nauwalabila and Madjedbebe 128; 'waterway' model hypothesis 131; 'woodland first' model hypothesis 131

Southern China, arrival of AMHs in 46–47
Spirit Cave research 55–56
Stone Implement Group 258, *261*, 274
Stone Refuse Group 265
Strait of Makassar 87
Sulawesi 92–93
Sulu Archipelago 215
sumatraliths 51–52, *52*
sun bear *(Helarctos malayanus)* 90
Sundaic biogeographic zone 208
Sundaland 39
Su, Nguyen Khac 76
Sung, W. 160, 161
Sun, Xue-feng 46
supraorbital torus 48
Suvorovo 3 site 142–144
Suvorovo 4 site 144
Suvorovo 6 site 144
Suyanggae 238–239
Suzuki, H. 321

Tabon Cave 95, 96, 207–208, 210
Taiwan: chronology, stratigraphy, and distribution 161–166, *162–166*; coastal zones of 150–151, *151*; Dongshan Island, human remains from 153–154; early peopling in and around 150–173; East Coast Mountain Range in 150; Eluanbi II, Longkeng, and Longxia Cave *170–171*, 170–172; evolution of coastline since LGM *151*; Palaeolithic and preceramic lithic assemblages 166–167; Palaeolithic and preceramic sites in **157–158**; "Preceramic Culture" in eastern 161–166, *162–166*; two human burials from Liang Island (Liangdao), Matsu Archipelago 156; Xiaoma Caves *167–169*, 167–170

Taiwan Land Bridge Fauna 155
Taiwan Neolithic (ca. 5000–4800 BP) 150
Taiwan Strait 150; human remains and related fauna from 151–153, *152–153*; human remains from *154*, 154–155, *155*; Penghu 1 mandible 151, *152*
Takahara, H. 284
Takahashi, K. 287
Talaud island 214
Tam Hang Cave 216
Tam Pa Ling Cave 48, 84
Tamura, T. 298
Tan, Ha Van 76
Tasmania 132
taxa 27–28, *28*
*Tectus niloticus* 112
Teilhard de Chardin, P. 185
tephra 247, *248*
*terminus ante quem* 140
Tham Khuyen Cave 75
Tham Om cave 83
Thar Desert 44
Thelliers' method.results *352*
Tianyuan Cave 179, 184, 188
tiger *(Panthera tigris)* 140
Timorese caves 102
Timor Island 100–102; Pleistocene paintings at 102
Timor Leste island 214
Toala hunter-gatherers 98
Toalian culture 98
Toe Cave 116
Tohoku region 298
Tokai region 289
Tokara and Kerama Gaps 313
Tongtian Cave 189
trap-pits 299–301, *301*, 303; pitfalls from the Hatsunegahara site *301*
tree mouse *(Pogonomys* sp.) 93
*Tridacna/Hippopus* valves 215
*Trochus* fishhooks 215
*Trogontherium* sp. 182
Tsang, C. 160, 162
*Turbo argyrostema* 119

Ubeidiya 3
unifacial tools 73
Upper Palaeolithic age of Japanese site 245–280; artefacts 258–265, **259–260**, *261*, *263–264*;

climate and sea level *246*, 246–251; excavation sites fulfilling four conditions of *254*; features 256–258, *257*; human arrival in 251–254, **252**; late Pleistocene mammals of *251*; locations and conditions of 253–254, *254*, **255**; Palaeovegetation in Japan during LGM *250*; tephra 247, *248*; vegetation zones in East Asia during LGM *249*; *see also* Upper Palaeolithic sites
Upper Palaeolithic sites: in Coastal Zone of Maritime Region 140–144, *141*, *143*; in Maritime Region 138–140, *139*; Sakhalin Island 146–147
Upper Pleistocene, Zhiren Cave in Guangxi 179
uranium 48
Ustinovka 1, 4, 6 site 140–142, *141*

van Rietschoten, B.D. 88
Vinh Phuc Province 76
Visayan Islands 202
von Koenigswald, G.H.R. 89
Vostok ice core in Antarctica 39, *39*

Wadjak Cave 96
waisted tools 118, *118*
Walenae depression 98
Wallacea 90
Wallacean archipelago 112
Wallace, A.R. 87–88
Wallace's Line 87, 103, 201, 206
Wang, F. 182
warty pig *(Sus celebensis)* 92
wild boar *(Sus ahoenobarbus)* 208
wild pig *(Sus scrofa riukiuanus)* 313
Willandra Lakes 134

Wu, D. 167
Wu, X. 187, 321

Xiaodong 52
Xiaoma Caves 162, *167–169*, 167–170; preceramic stone tools from *168*; squatting burial of Xiaoma Woman in *168*
Xiaomalong Cave 170
Xing, S. 183
Xujiayao-Houjiayao site 182–183

Yamaguchi, B. 321
Yamaoka, T. 298
Yamashita-cho Cave I 314
Yangjiapao Cave in Hubei 46
Y chromosomes: diversification 6; implication of 5–6; pattern 6
Yeokpori Cave 231
Y haplogroups 5
Yombon 119
Yonggok Cave 237
Yongsandong site 239, *240*
Younger Toba eruption 44
You, Y. 154
Y-phylogeny 5

Zanolli, C. 206
Zerkalnaya River valley 140
Zhiren Cave 46, 179, 188
Zhishanyan 172
Zhoukoudian Upper Cave (ZKD UC), 179, 184–185, 188
Zuozhen: human/faunal remains from 156–160, **157–158**, *159*; mammalian fauna 156
Zuraina, M. 59

9781032547824